Arthurian Legends
on Film and Television

ARTHURIAN LEGENDS
ON FILM
AND TELEVISION

Bert Olton

McFarland & Company, Inc., Publishers
OCM 43036809
Jefferson, North Carolina, and London

Library of Congress Cataloguing-in-Publication Data

Olton, Bert.
    Arthurian legends on film and television / Bert Olton.
       p.   cm.
    Includes bibliographical references and index.
    ISBN 0-7864-0718-2 (illustrated case binding : 50# alkaline paper)
    1. Arthurian romances in motion pictures.   2. Arthurian romances
on television.   I. Title.
PN1995.9.A75O48   2000
791.43'6352 — dc21   99-59789

British Library cataloguing data are available

Manufactured in the United States of America

*McFarland & Company, Inc., Publishers
  Box 611, Jefferson, North Carolina 28640
   www.mcfarlandpub.com*

To my parents with thanks for their persistently fine example and unfailingly good advice on life and everything in it. I thank God for allowing me to wake up in time for them to see this.

ACKNOWLEDGMENTS

First, I must thank my wife, Bonnie, for her steadfast willingness to assist in any way possible, for her fending off of our six children while I tried to concentrate and for her love of in-depth discussions of sources, stages of involvement and any other minutiae that I might have been in the middle of. She is always there with intelligence, objectivity and practicality.

Thanks to Professor Alan J. Lupack, curator of the Robbins Collection, University of Rochester, for his interest, encouragement and kind assistance.

Thank you, Joan Thiry, for a great film on Percival.

Scott Madden, thank you for the kind donation of the tape of a terrific television production.

Thanks to Peter Vernon for his speedy conversion of PAL tapes to NTSC and his terrific stories and help.

To Anna-Lisa Janaer and the folks at S4C, my gratitude for two fine films and your help in getting them to me.

To Ms. Pamela J. Richardson, thank you for your help with the *MacGyver* episodes.

Thanks, too, to Don and Patti Peterson, my computer gurus (who would believe a den leader would demand this kind of retribution?). They saw me through many a self-inflicted crisis as I came out of the Stone Age of my old Royal mechanical typewriter into the new technology of on-screen word processing.

This book could not have been completed without the enormous help of the staffs of the Fairport Public Library, Fairport, New York, and the Palmyra Kings Daughters Library, Palmyra, New York.

TABLE OF CONTENTS

PREFACE

The main goal of this book is to gather into one volume as many of the film titles having to do with the legends of King Arthur as possible. The hope is that it will serve as a useful supplement to the scholarly works which are available on Arthurian film and perhaps provide a starting point for others interested in the subject.

This is not a scholarly work. Kevin J. Harty's *Cinema Arthuriana*, with its many excellent articles; *The Use of Arthurian Legend in Hollywood Film* by Rebecca and Samuel Umland; the commentaries of Norris J. Lacy, Geoffrey Ashe, Alan J. Lupack; and a number of others really lead the field.

When I blithely proposed the idea for this book I was under the impression that there were perhaps 30 or 40 films, videos and filmstrips dealing with the legends of King Arthur. That uninformed estimate was obviously inaccurate. More than two years later I was still discovering productions buried in remote archives, libraries and collections, and new ones appear all the time. For those reasons, I must apologize for the incompleteness of this book. The search will continue.

The criteria for including films are fairly loose, but ultimately the test has been that the production must contain Arthurian references more substantial than a comment like that from the movie *Beetlejuice,* "She's sleeping with Prince Valium tonight."

In researching this book I viewed as many of the films and television shows as possible. Those I was not able to view are identified as "not viewed." All other titles, incidentally, may be assumed to be available on video, as it was in that format that I saw them.

All film genres but one (pornography, which does address the subject in its own unique fashion) are included. Except for a couple of examples of singular compact discs, I have not attempted to keep up with what is being made available on CD versus video tape versus DVD. Video tape is the primary medium commercially available and what is available even there changes from day to day. Video and computer games are not included here.

Since the release of *First Knight,* the number of productions in this field have been increasing almost every month. Whereas, previously, Arthurian movies and episodes of television shows were an occasional, infrequent occurrence, suddenly, top-rated cartoons (e.g., *Gargoyles*) and live-action shows (e.g. *Hercules* and *Xena*) are weighing in with Arthurian episodes. The Matter of Britain is subtly or blatantly incorporated into the plot lines of long-running shows like *Babylon 5* and *Northern Exposure.* The recently released Warner Bros. full-length feature cartoon *Quest for Camelot* joins the fray, and new television shows and movies are being proposed or launched. Films like *Dragonheart* and *The Mighty* take an indirect look at Arthur and his influence on our culture.

No discernible trend seems to be common to any of the movies and shows, except perhaps the one toward longer and longer credits. *Dragonheart* seemed to have won the prize for the most names cited until *Quest for Camelot* came out. From *Dragonheart,* a family joke evolved about the credited position of "Shoe Master," but that was nothing compared to the reaction that *Quest for Camelot*'s "Pencil Tester" credit received.

On a more serious note, overall quality does not seem to be on the upswing in Arthurian films. One program may be excellent, the next ridiculous. The film productions based on Arthurian legends are just as varied in quality and content as the vast body of literature that addresses King Arthur and his knights. Film evaluation is such a subjective thing that one simply has to judge for oneself. I tried to remain as objective as possible in describing each of the works included here but did not always succeed.

All mistakes, inaccuracies and inconsistencies are mine alone.

THE FILMS AND TELEVISION PROGRAMS

The Adventures of Sir Galahad (1919)

Not viewed; Black and White; Copyright 1919

The Adventures of Sir Galahad (1949)

15-episode serial, 252 minutes total; Black and White; Live Action; Copyright 1949, 1950, Columbia Pictures Corporation

CAST: George Reeves (Sir Galahad); Charles King (Bors); William Fawcett (Merlin); Pat Barton (Morgan Le Fay); Hugh Prosser (Sir Lancelot); Lois Hall (Lady of the Lake); Nelson Leigh (King Arthur); Jim Diehl (Kay); Don Harvey (Bartog); Marjorie Stapp (Queen Guinevere); John Merton (Ulric); Pierre Lyden (Cawker)

CREDITS: Director — Spencer Bennet; Producer — Sam Katzman; Writers — George H. Plympton, Lewis Clay, David Mathews; Director of Photography — Ira H. Morgan; Art Director — Paul Palmentola; Film Editors — Earl Turner, Dwight Caldwell; Set Decorator — Sidney Clifford; Set Continuity — Robert Walker; Musical Director — Mischa Bakaleinikoff; Production Manager — Herbert Leonard

SYNOPSIS: *The Adventures of Sir Galahad* was a 15-part serial presented in movie theaters. Each episode ran approximately 15 minutes, including a review of the previous "chapter" and a trailer for the next. Cast and credit listings remained the same for each episode, so they have only been listed once here.

The series has the look and feel of an old Western. Cowboys and Indians are replaced by Arthur's knights and their enemies, respectively. There are lots of horse-mounted chase scenes through a dusty southern California landscape that does not look much like Britain. The great courtyard of Camelot from which the knights sally forth is a Spanish-style hacienda. One almost expects John Wayne to swagger into view. The armor and other costumes are fully medieval rather than Dark Ages, as is traditional with Hollywood productions.

The Adventures of Sir Galahad was among the last of the serials produced for movie theater distribution in the era of the introduction of television. Galahad, incidentally, is played by the same George Reeves who, several years after this series, became television's *Superman* in the early 1950s.

Put in a nutshell, the story revolves around Galahad trying to regain his honor. While in training to become a knight of the Round Table, Excalibur is put into Galahad's care. It is stolen and all 15 episodes deal with the plots and adventures that develop from the theft. In the last episode Excalibur is finally recovered and Galahad becomes a member of the Round Table fraternity. There are no references made to any associations between Galahad and the Holy Grail nor for that matter to much else from the legendary literature.

CHAPTER 1: "THE STOLEN SWORD"

This introductory episode contains more narration than the rest. The opening scene is a large tournament put on by Arthur to keep

UNKNOWN
BETRAYER
CHAPTER 7
THE
ADVENTURES OF SIR GALAHAD
BOLDEST KNIGHT OF THE ROUND TABLE
A COLUMBIA
SERIAL

Sir Galahad (George Reeves) battles the "Unknown Betrayer" in *The Adventures of Sir Galahad.*

his knights in fighting shape. We meet the main characters, King Arthur, Queen Guinevere, Lancelot, Merlin and Morgan Le Fay, who are all stiffly observing the festivities from a reviewing stand.

Guinevere is a dark-haired beauty, Merlin is typically Druidical and King Arthur's wavy, square-cut goatee looks positively Babylonian. A Robin Hood–esque herald announces the main event: a joust pitting Sirs Bors and Mordred, representing Arthur and Camelot, versus Sirs Roderick and Meritor, from the court of the "friendly king of Cornwall."

Bors and Mordred win and offer the opportunity for anyone to take them on. Just when it appears their victory will go unchallenged a young fellow rides up demanding to fight them both by himself. Interestingly, half of the knights, Galahad among them, joust in

a fashion not seen in any other film. Holding their lances in their right hands, they charge their opponents from the left side. In other words, the lance points off to the right, making their shields all but useless.

Galahad defeats both men and is offered the tournament's prize. He declines it, requesting instead to be made a knight of the Round Table. A formal ceremony is arranged for that evening.

After the celebratory feast Arthur and the knights retire from the hall and instruct Galahad "in the solemn mysteries of the Round Table." In the sword room, Sir Kay takes Excalibur from its display spot on the wall and recounts the history of the blade. In flashback we see Merlin rowing a small Viking-style boat into a lake and Arthur prayerfully taking Excalibur from a hand emerging from the water.

Galahad's last task before being knighted is to stand guard over Excalibur through the night. While on duty, he is to be provided with a traditional goblet of wine. Bors brings the goblet but is distracted by a chambermaid before entering the sword room. He puts the goblet down and, while he is frisking with the maid, a chainmail-clad hand emerges from behind a curtain. The hand takes the goblet, disappears behind the curtain for a moment, then replaces the goblet. Finally getting about his business, Bors brings the wine to Galahad.

Late in the night Galahad sips the wine. He starts to feel drowsy. As he succumbs to the drugged beverage a suit of displayed armor seems to come to life. It moves toward the sword as Galahad collapses. Galahad tries to stop the theft, but the drug knocks him out and Excalibur is stolen.

The next day, as Galahad is being rebuked for his negligence, a messenger arrives stating that the Saxon leader, Ulric, is attacking once again. Of course Galahad's knighthood is on hold until he can prove he had no part in the plot to steal the sword and he vows he won't rest until it is recovered. As everyone saddles up to strike at Ulric, Morgan Le Fay informs Galahad that the way to the sword is through the Enchanted Forest.

Ulric is holed up on Thunder Mountain. On the way there Galahad detours away from Arthur's army and rides into the Enchanted Forest. Bors, the jovial sidekick-to-be, is sent by Lancelot to follow Galahad in case help is needed.

In the forest, Galahad is waylaid by none other than Merlin. The ancient wizard puts a spell on the youth and Galahad's arms fall lifeless to his side. The limbs of a tree come to life and encircle Galahad while Merlin calls up unearthly flames to kill him.

As the episode ends, the narrator's voice asks, "What is to become of the great sword Excalibur? Will King Arthur fall before the Saxon attack? Don't miss 'Galahad's Daring,' the second exciting episode."

CHAPTER 2: "GALAHAD'S DARING"

After a quick review of the essentials of the last episode, we rejoin Galahad, who is trapped by Merlin's magic, about to die in flames. Merlin is furious that Galahad has trespassed in the Enchanted Forest and has accused the old wizard of blocking the way to the sword. In the nick of time, however, a woman's voice warns Merlin off. Merlin's magic becomes ineffective before the powers of the Lady of the Lake and he is driven away. She advises Galahad to rejoin Arthur rather than try to find the sword.

Bors finally catches up with Galahad. Debating what to do next, Galahad suddenly realizes that Camelot has been left undefended. The two mount their horses and head in that direction. Meanwhile, back at the castle, a Saxon sneaks into a secret entrance. An armored figure hands Excalibur over to the invader. As the Saxon departs he passes Galahad and Bors on the road. Bors recognizes the fellow as Bartog, lord chamberlain to Ulric. And could that be Excalibur strapped to his back? The duo give chase.

Bartog makes it to Ulric's base and Galahad sneaks into the camp. Spying on Ulric, Galahad overhears the attack plan. He rushes to his horse to warn King Arthur, the Saxon force hard on his heels. Unfortunately he rides too fast under the limb of a tree and is knocked off his horse. The episode ends with Galahad on the verge of being trampled to death by Ulric's hard-riding army.

CHAPTER 3: "PRISONERS OF ULRIC"

Galahad manages to save himself from being crushed but he is unable to warn Arthur of Ulric's attack. In the pitched battle that ensues, so many of Arthur's men are lost that he is forced to call a retreat. While the king's army returns to Camelot, Galahad and Bors head back to Ulric's camp.

On the way they come across a peddler, who is bringing clothes and other goods to Ulric. They tie the man up, dress Bors up as a lady and Galahad hides in the peddler's cart.

Lois Hall as the Lady of the Lake and George Reeves as Sir Galahad in a lobby card for the Columbia serial *The Adventures of Sir Galahad*.

The plan is to use this ploy to get into Ulric's camp.

In the Saxon camp preparations are being made for a siege of Camelot. Ulric has a secret weapon, a gigantic crossbow which shoots spears instead of bolts. The disguised Bors pulls up in the cart and manages to briefly fool the guards. Though the ploy soon fails and Bors is quickly captured, it does give Galahad enough time to creep out of the cart and spy on Ulric's tent once more.

This time, Merlin is there, giving Ulric advice on which wall of Camelot would be best to attack. He convinces Ulric to attack from the south. As the commotion of Bors's capture distracts Ulric, Merlin tells him to leave Excalibur on the table, that it will be there when he needs it. Ulric leaves the tent to see what's going on and Galahad takes the opportunity to slice his way into the back of the tent. He tries to take Excalibur, but the sword seems riveted to the table.

Galahad gives up and escapes the tent before the Saxon returns. He saves Bors and tells him to go to King Arthur, but then Galahad is captured. Galahad is tied to a post in front of the loaded crossbow. As Bors struggles with the Saxons to try to free Galahad, someone accidentally pulls the release rope on the crossbow. The spear flies straight for Galahad — and the episode ends.

CHAPTER 4: "ATTACK ON CAMELOT!"

Just in the nick of time, Galahad is able to dive out of the path of the spear. He and Bors battle their way out of the Saxon camp and head for Camelot. In the castle Merlin is in conference with King Arthur. He tells Arthur that the Saxons will concentrate their attack on the east wall. Will his duplicity never end? While this is going on, Galahad and Bors approach Camelot under a flag of truce. They are brought before the king, and Galahad accuses Merlin of plotting against Arthur. He and Bors are both put in the dungeon.

Morgan Le Fay appears in Galahad's cell and offers to help. Galahad asks for a quill, ink, parchment and "a talisman of Merlin." The sorceress brings all these things to our hero, the talisman being one of Merlin's rings. Galahad makes a false map, then Morgan helps the pair escape the castle.

Galahad takes the map straight to Ulric, trying to convince the Saxon king to attack the east wall of Camelot. Only partially trusting that Galahad is on his side, Ulric puts the youth at the head of a sort of pre-siege battle. Galahad is sent up a siege ladder to fight off Arthur's attacking men, while both Ulric and King Arthur watch his actions with interest. Arthur's men tip the ladder off the rock and Galahad goes crashing to the ground.

CHAPTER 5: "GALAHAD TO THE RESCUE"

Despite the horrendous fall from the siege ladder, Galahad jumps to his feet as if nothing happened. He immediately begins fighting Ulric's men. Sir Bors too starts battling the Saxons and soon the two have turned the tide of the fight. Looking on, Lancelot comments to Arthur that Galahad seems surely to be on their side. Arthur, however, seems to reserve judgment.

Galahad attacks Ulric himself and manages to win Excalibur from the Saxon. With the invincible sword in Galahad's hands, the Saxons decide to withdraw. They divide into two groups on their way back to camp. Chasing them, Galahad and Bors follow one trail, Lancelot, Gawain and Bedevere the other. These last three are captured when Saxon ambushers throw bolas around their necks.

Once again Galahad dresses Bors in a disguise, this time as a traveling armorer. While Bors distracts Ulric and his men, Galahad sneaks into their camp again. He goes straight to the cave where the three Round Table knights are being held and releases them. Bors's disguise fails again, of course, but all of the Camelot crew manage to get out of the Saxon camp without further incident.

Galahad brings Excalibur to Camelot but is stopped by Sir Kay, Sir Mordred, Merlin and some others before getting to Arthur. Merlin states that this is not Excalibur but an imitation. Mordred decides to execute Galahad on the spot, and the episode ends as Mordred's sword falls toward Galahad's neck.

CHAPTER 6: "PASSAGE OF PERIL"

Luckily, just as Mordred's sword is falling, King Arthur walks into the room. Thinking fast, Bors pulls his own sword and parries Mordred's blow. Before the king, Galahad is accused of "consorting with the enemy with traitorous intent" and Arthur is shown the false Excalibur.

Galahad's defense is that Ulric must never have had Excalibur at all since neither he nor King Arthur are dead. Surely neither of them would have survived facing the invincible sword. Galahad posits that Bartog must have kept Excalibur for himself and given Ulric the copy. Arthur allows Bors and Galahad to hunt for Bartog.

Returning once more to Ulric's hideout, Galahad sneaks into the cave and overhears Bartog speaking with the Saxon king. Bartog accuses their ally inside Camelot, the mysterious Black Knight, of having Excalibur and talks Ulric into letting him return to Camelot to find out. Donning the Robin Hood outfit that must have passed for civilian clothes, Bartog goes to the castle with Galahad snooping along behind him. The Saxon enters Camelot through a secret entrance and disappears into the tunnels of the castle. Galahad follows Bartog into the entrance but in one of the narrow passages, sword blades emerge from the wall, trapping him. As the other wall begins to slide sideways to crush Galahad, the episode ends.

CHAPTER 7: "UNKNOWN BETRAYER"

With quick ingenuity, Galahad wedges his sword between the walls, preventing himself from being impaled. He stumbles back out of the passage to get Bors, and the two of them return to the bowels of the castle.

This time, it is Bartog who gets captured by Arthur's guards. Arthur has Bartog thrown into the dungeon before being executed but Galahad has a plan. He suggests delaying the execution and leaking a false rumor that Bartog is to be tortured until he reveals who the traitor inside Camelot might be. Thus, using Bartog as bait, they should be able to draw the Black Knight out.

The Black Knight does indeed appear in the dungeon to free Bartog, but he also manages to lock Galahad in a cell and chain Bors to a wall. The Black Knight and Bartog make their escape from Camelot as Sir Kay comes to the dungeon and accuses Galahad again of treachery. Galahad locks Kay in a cell and he and Bors begin their pursuit of the real traitors.

In the meantime, the Black Knight talks Bartog into leaving Ulric's service and joining him in turning the people against King Arthur. He gives Bartog a monk's outfit to wear and tells him to meet a man named Cawker at the Inn of the Ram's Head.

Bors learns of the meeting of the dissidents at the inn. Galahad dons a disguise and enters the place to spy on the goings-on. When Sir Kay and his men come in to break the meeting up, he spots Galahad and a fight erupts. As Galahad stands beneath a huge chandelier, fighting for his life, the Black Knight emerges from an upstairs room. Seeing Galahad's position, the Black Knight cuts the rope holding the chandelier.

CHAPTER 8: "PERILOUS ADVENTURE"

Agile as ever, Galahad manages to dive out of the way of the falling chandelier. At first, Kay fights with the Black Knight, then he battles with Galahad. Finally Galahad and Bors make their escape and go looking for the Black Knight's camp.

The next day, Lancelot is the only knight of the Round Table to show up late for roll call. Could he be the Black Knight? Back on the trail, someone in a hurry rides past Galahad and Bors. Curious, they follow the man, who turns out to be a messenger sent to the Black Knight's camp.

As Galahad listens (having sneaked up to the back of the tent, as always), he hears the man say that he was sent by the Black Knight in Camelot to order Bartog to send out a force of men. King Arthur is going to send out some knights to pick up the arms and supplies left behind by Ulric in the last battle. Bartog is to lead an attack on Arthur's men and get the weapons for the Black Knight and his personal army.

Galahad and Bors try to warn Sir Kay of the imminent attack on his column, but Kay attacks Galahad. Bartog's raiders attack and one of them makes off with the wagonload of materiel. Galahad chases after it, jumps aboard and fights with the driver. Out of control, the horses and wagon approach a cliff. Turning, the horses run on, but the wagon breaks loose and goes over the cliff.

CHAPTER 9: "TREACHEROUS MAGIC"

With incredible good fortune, the two men roll out of the wagon just in time. Galahad and Bors go back to the Inn of the Ram's Head to spy on the insurrectionists again. With the help of a pretty barmaid, they eavesdrop on Bartog and learn that the Black Knight, with Excalibur, will appear to speak to the men at noon. The duo are discovered. Galahad manages to fight his way out of the inn but Bors is captured.

At Camelot, Galahad runs into Lancelot and tells him what's going on. They go to Morgan Le Fay for help and she gives Galahad a magic ring which will make him invisible—but only once. Galahad returns to the inn and frees Bors. The Black Knight shows up and Galahad attacks him. Wielding Excalibur, the Black Knight merely holds the invincible blade before him. The sword begins to glow and emit a weird noise. Galahad seems stunned. Swinging the mighty sword in slow motion, the Black Knight does not even have to touch Galahad with it to make the hero fall right over the edge of the balcony.

CHAPTER 10: "THE SORCERER'S SPELL"

Galahad's fall from the balcony is broken by the band of men listening to the Black Knight. He and Bors get away and Galahad decides to inform Ulric that Bartog and the Black Knight have Excalibur. Galahad hopes that this will turn the Saxon forces against the Black Knight's troops, thus eliminating both of King Arthur's enemies in one stroke.

Galahad writes a note to Ulric, signs it and, wrapping it around an arrow, shoots it into Ulric's camp. The note invites Ulric to meet him in Echo Canyon; Galahad figures that there he can be heard by Ulric without being seen. Ulric, of course, does not go to the meeting with only one retainer, as Galahad asks, but with a force.

The Saxons chase Galahad and Bors. The pair nearly escape but Merlin appears in a big puff of smoke. He casts a spell which causes the two to fall from their horses. Galahad and Bors are tied to a tree. Ulric's archers are about to execute them when Merlin makes another smoky entrance and tells Ulric that Galahad spoke the truth about Bartog and the Black Knight.

Ulric forces Bors and Galahad to lead the attack on the men at the inn. The Black Knight is about to do Ulric in when Merlin shows up again, magically causing Excalibur to fly from the Black Knight's hand into the sky. Now, with everyone after them, Galahad and Bors run away again. Cornered, Galahad uses a vine to try to swing over a pool of quicksand, but an arrow cuts the vine and he falls in.

CHAPTER 11: "VALLEY OF NO RETURN"

Bors shows up to pull Galahad from the quicksand and the two men start tracking the Black Knight. Along the way, they discover that the Black Knight's horse has thrown a shoe. Knowing he must now be on foot, they make their search more carefully. Oddly, they run across a horseless Sir Mordred. Nearby, they discover a cave inside of which is a large chest. In the chest is the armor of the Black Knight.

There is another big puff of smoke and when it clears, Excalibur is sticking out of the wall of the cave. None of them are able to pull the sword free. Merlin shows up, pulls the sword out of the cave wall and disappears with it. Mordred and Galahad fight, then Galahad and Bors leave to chase Merlin. They head right for the Enchanted Forest.

They become separated in that stronghold of illusion. Bors is distracted by a table full of food, then he has a sword fight with a tree. He finally finds Galahad again and the two make their way to the most magical part of the Enchanted Forest, the Valley of No Return.

There, Merlin causes Excalibur to appear this time sticking out of a stone. Both Bors and Galahad grasp the sword, but Merlin's magic glues their hands to it. He tells them their bones will be found there, clinging to the blade. Just then the Lady of the Lake comes along and shoos Merlin away. She gives Galahad the sword, tells him to take it to Arthur and then she wanders off.

Not to be so belittled, Merlin calls up three warriors, who stop Bors and Galahad's progress out of the forest. Standing his ground, Galahad faces them. They charge and are about to trample Galahad under their horses' hooves when the episode ends.

CHAPTER 12: "CASTLE PERILOUS"

Just as the riders are about to trample Galahad, he disappears, then reappears at Bors's feet. Excalibur, of course, is missing again. Deducing that the Black Knight must be at the outlaws' camp, Galahad and Bors go there and promptly get captured. Even with his hands tied, Galahad is able to sneak behind the villain's tent and listen to the latest plotting.

The Black Knight has learned that Queen

Guinevere will be traveling to visit her sister. His plan is to have Bartog kidnap the queen. Arthur will send most of his forces out to save her and the Black Knight will take over Camelot. Galahad and Bors escape the outlaws' camp and try to save the queen but they are seconds late. Morgan Le Fay is there to cover the departure of the kidnappers with a cloud of smoke.

Mordred shows up, arrests Galahad and Bors and takes them to Camelot. King Arthur leaves Mordred and a skeleton crew of fighters to defend the castle as he and the Knights of the Round Table go to find Guinevere. Mordred has Galahad tied to a table beneath a gigantic iron spiked ball pendulum. As it swings, it drops lower and lower. Suddenly, it falls.

CHAPTER 13: "THE WIZARD'S VENGEANCE"

Happily, the deadly pendulum was cut loose on purpose by Bors so that it fell clear of the table. Bors and Galahad fight their way out of the dungeon. Meanwhile, the Black Knight makes an appearance at Camelot. Bartog shows up and the two villains have a meeting. In exchange for all of Lancelot's lands and some other rewards, Bartog agrees to kill King Arthur. Bartog escapes Galahad's attempt to stop him and makes his way to the outlaw camp. There he has his men prepare a trap for King Arthur. He next meets with Arthur and gets Arthur to come with him, claiming he can lead the king to Guinevere.

Merlin informs Galahad and Bors that Arthur is in trouble. Wondering at this seeming change in loyalty, they nonetheless take his word for it. They try to get Kay to help them, but the knight still thinks Galahad is to blame for all of this. Galahad and Bors go alone to help Arthur. The outlaws' trap is sprung. In the fight, Galahad is hit in the side by an arrow and falls off a cliff.

CHAPTER 14: "QUEST FOR THE QUEEN"

Our eyes must have deceived us at the end of the last episode, because at the beginning of this one the arrow actually hits the out-

law. Galahad speaks with King Arthur and comes up with a counterplot to get Guinevere back. He puts on the Black Knight's spare armor and rides off with Bartog to move Guinevere to a different location. When they arrive at the outlaw camp, however, the guards there say that the Black Knight already moved the queen. Galahad is knocked out by the outlaws and he is left as Bartog and his men depart.

Arthur and Bors find Galahad unconscious and take him to the inn. None of Arthur's men can find the queen. Galahad suggests that perhaps she's right under everyone's noses, namely, being held by Mordred in Camelot. Arthur becomes furious at the idea and banishes Galahad from the kingdom. Even Bors finds this to be too much and he too abandons Galahad.

Galahad sneaks into the dungeons of Camelot and finds Lancelot chained in a cell. He frees the knight, then makes his way upstairs. Hiding behind a curtain he spies on Mordred and Bartog. He overhears them planning to unite the outlaw forces with the Saxon army in order to end Arthur's reign once and for all. They see Galahad's feet sticking out from under the tapestry though and, just as they jab their swords through it, the episode ends.

CHAPTER 15: "GALAHAD'S TRIUMPH"

As Mordred and Bartog stab at him with their swords, Galahad pulls the heavy wall hangings down on them. He and Lancelot head to find King Arthur. Merlin decides it is time to set things right finally. He first appears to Arthur, telling the king to return to Camelot. Next he interrupts Galahad and Lancelot, telling Galahad to go to the Lady of the Lake for Excalibur and sending Lancelot to join King Arthur at Camelot.

Bartog brings Ulric and his men to Camelot. They meet with the Black Knight and lay their plans. When Arthur returns they will let him and his knights ride into the courtyard. Then the combined force of outlaws and Saxons will fall on Arthur and destroy him.

Galahad, meanwhile, has found the Lady

of the Lake. He receives from her Excalibur and a fresh charger. He mounts the great war-horse and speeds to Camelot. The fight there has already begun and in the heat of it Galahad arrives with Excalibur.

Galahad kills Ulric, then tosses Excalibur to King Arthur. The sword sings again as Arthur very gently touches the Black Knight's helmet with it. The Black Knight is hurled to the ground as if smashed by a club. His helmet falls off, revealing none other than Mordred. Mordred jumps up and attacks the king, but Arthur is invincible with Excalibur and Mordred is killed.

With the Saxons and the outlaws both crushed, Excalibur and the queen recovered and his name cleared, Galahad can finally be knighted. The formal ceremony takes place with great pomp. Bors expresses his pleasure that his friend Galahad is finally vindicated. Merlin explains that all his apparent nefarious actions were merely means to prove Galahad worthy. Bors gets a promise out of Merlin to use no more magic. As Galahad and Bors head for the door, a huge puff of smoke explodes and the series ends with Bors floating in the air, Morgan Le Fay smiling knowingly and the entire court laughing happily.

The Adventures of Sir Lancelot (1951)

Alternate Title: The Adventures of Sir Lancelot with William Russell; 10 Episodes, 53 minutes each; Black and White; Television series; Copyrights 1951, 1952, Sapphire Films Limited; A Weinstein Production for Sapphire Films Limited; Made at Nettlefold Studios and Walton Studios, Walton-on-Thames, England; An Official Films, Inc., Presentation for NBC Television; Castle Reproductions are British Crown copyright

The 10 episodes of *The Adventures of Sir Lancelot* which are available on video tape are a random selection from the original television series. Viewed in the sequence presented on the five tapes, they are also completely out of order. Below is a chronological list of the original shows, including the 20 that are not available commercially. A **V** appears after each epi-

sode below which is on video tape. Where known, the U.S. broadcast date is given: 1. "The Knight with the Red Plume," **V**, 2. "The Ferocious Fathers," **V**, 3. "Queen's Knight," 4. "Winged Victory," 10-22-57, 5. "Sir Bliant," 10-29-57, 6. "The Magic Sword," 11-5-57, 7. "Lancelot's Banishment," 11-12-57, 8. "Caledon," 11-19-57, 9. "Pirates," 11-26-57, 10. "The Black Castle," 12-3-57, 11. "Theft of Excalibur," 12-10-57, **V**, 12. "Magic Book," 12-17-57, 13. "Knight Errant," 12-24-57, 14. "The Lesser Breed," 12-31-57, **V**, 15. "Sir Crustabread," 1-7-58, 16. "Lady Lilith," 1-14-58, **V**, 17. "The Mortaise Fair," 1-21-58, **V**, 18. "The Missing Princess," 1-28-58, 19. "Outcast," 2-4-58, 20. "The Ruby of Radnor," 2-11-58, **V**, 21. "Witches' Brew," 2-18-58, **V**, 22. "The Maid of Somerset," 2-25-58, 23. "Double Identity," 3-4-58, 24. "Bridge," 3-11-58, 25. "The Ugly Duckling," 3-18-58, **V**, 26. "Knight's Choice," 3-25-58, 27. "Thieves," 4-1-58, 28. "Roman Wall," 4-8-58, 29. "Shepherd's War," 4-15-58, 30. "The Prince of Limerick," 4-22-58, **V**.

The write-ups on the 10 videotaped episodes are presented here in the order in which they appear on the tapes. Within each volume and episode heading, however, the show number in parentheses identifies the original broadcast sequence for each episode.

VOLUME 1, EPISODE 1 (SHOW #11): "THEFT OF EXCALIBUR"

CAST: William Russell (Sir Lancelot); Alfie Bass (Barney Brandygore); Ronald Leigh-Hunt (King Arthur); Jane Hylton (Queen Guinevere); Robert Scroggins (Brian); Cyril Smith (Merlin); David Bough (Michael); John Charlesworth (Robert); David Morrell (Sir Kay); Derry Nesbitt (Tristram); Frederick Treves (1st Thief); Nigel Green (2nd Thief); Garry Thorne (Squire)

CREDITS: Producer — Dallas Bower; Director — Bernard Knowles; Screenplay — Hamish Hamilton Burns, Peggy Phillips; Script Supervision — Albert G. Ruben; Music — Albert Elms; Director of Photography — Ernest Palmer; Production Designer — William Kellner; Supervising Editor — Thelma Connell; Production Manager — E. S. Laurie; Sound — Fred Ryan; Editor — David Hawkins; Dubbing Editor — Michael Deeley; Assistant Editor—Peter Weingreen; Camera Operator—Anthony Heller; Continuity—Doris Martin; Makeup Supervisor—Walter Schneiderman; Hairdresser—Betty Sherriff; Wardrobe Supervisor—Brenda Gardner; Master at Arms—Charles Alexis; Made at Nettlefold Studios, Walton-on-Thames, England

SYNOPSIS: It is St. Steven's Day in Britain, a day when knights do humble tasks and pages get to act like knights. The episode opens in the kitchen of Camelot: King Arthur is making breakfast and Lancelot is washing pots and pans. The squires and pages are guarding Excalibur.

Squire Robert inexplicably rides off with the king's sword. It turns out that three thieves have kidnapped Robert's father in order to get Excalibur. Lancelot and some squires ride out to find Robert and the squires are promptly captured by Barney Brandygore, the leader of the blackmailers.

Trapped by his St. Steven's Day oath, Lancelot is unable to do anything. One of the boys, Brian, tricks Lancelot into thinking the day is over by rotating the sundial. Lancelot beats Barney, the sword is recovered and Robert's father is freed.

VOLUME 1, EPISODE 2 (SHOW #16):
    "LADY LILITH"

CAST: William Russell (Sir Lancelot); Ronald Leigh-Hunt (King Arthur); Cyril Smith (Merlin); Robert Scroggins (Brian); Shirley Cooklin (Lady Lilith); Richard Leech (Sir Liones); Edward Judd (Abel); David Morrell (Sir Kay); Eric Corrie (Seneschal); Reginald Hearne (Blacksmith)
CREDITS: Producer—Bernard Knowles; Director—Lawrence Huntington; Screenplay—Leslie Poynton; Script Supervision—Albert G. Ruben; Music—Albert Elms; Director of Photography—Ernest Palmer; Art Director—Bill Bennison; Supervising Editor—Maurice Rootes; Sound—W. Lindop; Made at Walton Studios, Walton-on-Thames, England

Sir William Goodhugh left his estate to his daughter, Lilith, but Sir Liones claims it by the right of primogeniture. By a twist of descent, Liones is not Lilith's brother. King Arthur is forced to grant Liones's inheritance and he sends Lancelot to evict Lilith in as gentle a manner as possible.

The beautiful Lilith, it turns out, has become very competent at running the castle and lands. In a sort of love quadrangle, Liones and Lancelot's squire, Brian, both become infatuated with Lilith while Lilith has stars in her eyes for Lancelot. The wise and experienced knight of the Round Table sees a way out of the dilemma.

Suddenly taking on boorish, uncourtly manners, Lancelot manages to make Liones look good to Lilith. The shift in romantic interest solves the problem of who shall own the estate.

VOLUME 2, EPISODE 1 (SHOW #2):
    "THE FEROCIOUS FATHERS"

CAST: William Russell (Sir Lancelot); Robert Scroggins (Brian); George Woodbridge (Sir Melias); Ballard Berkeley (Sir Urgan); Norah Gorsen (Helen); Pauline Olsen (Enid); David Morrell (Clodion); Derry Nesbitt (Andred); Frederick Treves (Rolf)
CREDITS: Producer—Sidney Cole; Director—Ralph Smart; Screenplay—Leighton Reynolds; Production Supervisor—George Mills; Script Supervision—Albert G. Ruben; Music—Albert Elms; Director of Photography—Ken Hodges; Art Director—Peter Proud; Supervising Editor—Thelma Connell; Production Manager—Harold Buck; Sound—H. C. Pearson; Editor—David Hawkins; Dubbing Editor—Michael Deeley; Assistant Editor—Christopher Noble; Camera Operator—Noel Rowland; Continuity—Angela Martelli; Makeup Supervisor—Walter Schneiderman; Hairdresser—Pearl Tipaldi; Wardrobe Supervisor—Brenda Gardner; Made at Nettlefold Studios, Walton-on-Thames, England

SYNOPSIS: Lancelot is new to the Round Table. A kitchen boy arrives as a messenger from the besieged castle of Sir Urgan, who seeks Arthur's assistance. Arthur sends Lancelot to quell the dispute as his first mission.

With Brian, the kitchen boy, acting as Lancelot's squire, the two defeat the three-man siege of the castle. As reward, Urgan offers Lancelot 100 pieces of gold and the hand of his daughter, Helen. Helen's heart belongs to another, so to avoid further argument, Lancelot leaves unannounced. Brian runs away to follow Lancelot.

Urgan and Helen's lover's father are constantly feuding. Lancelot intercedes once more and takes Brian to be his official squire as "boon" for his good deeds.

VOLUME 2, EPISODE 2 (SHOW #17):
 "THE MORTAISE FAIR"

CAST: William Russell (Sir Lancelot); Robert Scroggins (Brian); Martin Benson (Hassim); Chin Yu (Zuleika); William Franklyn (Baron Mortaise); Eric Corrie (Osbert); Edward Judd (Ronk); Terence Yorke (Man-at-Arms); Robert Robinson (Merchant); Reginald Hearne (Rajah); Paul Way (Chinese Dice Player); missing from credits on tape: Jane Hylton (Guinevere)

CREDITS: Producer — Bernard Knowles; Director — Lawrence Huntington; Screenplay — Leslie Poynton; Script Supervision — Albert G. Ruben; Music — Albert Elms; Director of Photography — Ernest Palmer; Production Manager — E. S. Laurie; Production Designer — Peter Proud; Supervising Editor — Maurice Rootes; Sound — W. Lindop; Made at Walton Studios, Walton-on-Thames, England

SYNOPSIS: Though Arthur can't make it, Guinevere and Lancelot go to a fair put on by Baron Mortaise. Since people from all over the world will be there, it is Arthur's hope to establish trade relations with nations of the East. There are representatives from Baghdad, Rome and many other places.

As a token of good will, the Rajah gives Guinevere a huge emerald. In the confusion of a fire, the gem is stolen. Guinevere has the fair postponed until the jewel can be recovered lest diplomatic relations fail. A whole cast of suspects are present, including robbers and the many foreigners visiting the land. Even Hassim is suspected and arrested. Through Lancelot's detective work, however, the true culprit is found: Baron Mortaise's former seneschal, a man with gambling debts.

VOLUME 3, EPISODE 1 (SHOW #25):
 "THE UGLY DUCKLING"

CAST: William Russell (Sir Lancelot); Ronald Leigh-Hunt (King Arthur); Cyril Smith (Merlin);

Carol Marsh (Sybil); Jeanette Hutchinson (Amora); Hector Ross (Sir Egbert); Avice Landone (Lady Lamorak); Ian Wittaker (Gault); David Morrell (Sir Kay); Edward Judd (Sir Christopher)

CREDITS: Producer — Bernard Knowles; Director — George More O'Ferrall; Screenplay — Leslie Poynton; Script Supervision — Albert G. Ruben; Music — Albert Elms; Director of Photography — Ernest Palmer; Production Manager — E. S. Laurie; Art Director — Bill Bennison; Supervising Editor — Maurice Rootes; Sound — W. Lindop; Made at Walton Studios, Walton-on-Thames, England

SYNOPSIS: King Arthur takes Lancelot with him to a Middlemass gala thrown by Sir Egbert of Lamorak. Lancelot is disappointed to miss the tournament at Sussex, especially when it becomes obvious that Sir Egbert's real purpose for the get-together is to marry off his spoiled daughter, Amora.

Just as the Lamorak clan is showing off their new window to Arthur, Merlin and Lancelot, a rock with a message tied to it crashes through the glass. It is a threat to kill Sybil if a large sum of gold is not paid. The group goes falconing anyway, leaving Lancelot to protect the girl just in case. While they are gone another note, this time a ransom letter, is found in Sybil's room. However, Merlin and Lancelot notice that the broken glass is on the outside of the window and that the handwriting matches Sybil's. The embarrassed girl runs off.

Lancelot figures out that Sybil is jealous of her big sister and pining for some attention. A third ransom note arrives, but this time it's for real. Arthur and Lancelot capture the culprit (Sir Egbert's slimy nephew, Gault), Sybil dresses up for the dance and all is well.

VOLUME 3, EPISODE 2 (SHOW #1):
 "THE KNIGHT WITH THE RED PLUME"

CAST: Jane Hylton (Queen Guinevere); Bruce Seton (King Arthur); Cyril Smith (Merlin); Andrew Crawford (Sir Gawaine); Peter Bennett (Leonides); Brian Worth (Sir Kay); Paul Hansard (Sir Lionel); Edwin Richfield (Sir Christopher); William Russell (Sir Lancelot)

CREDITS: Executive Producer — Hannah Weinstein; Producer — Sidney Cole; Director — Ralph

Smart; Screenplay — Leighton Reynolds; Production Supervisor — George Mills; Script Supervision — Albert G. Ruben; Music — Edwin Astley; Director of Photography — Ken Hodges; Art Director — Peter Proud; Supervising Editor — Thelma Connell; Production Manager — Harold Buck; Sound — H. C. Pearson; Dubbing Editor — Michael Deeley; Assistant Director — Christopher Noble; Camera Operator — Noel Rowland; Continuity — Angela Martelli; Makeup Supervisor — Walter Schneiderman; Hairdresser — Pearl Tipaldi; Wardrobe — Brenda Gardner; Made at Nettlefold Studios, Walton-on-Thames, England

SYNOPSIS: This was the first episode of the series. Sir Lancelot approaches Camelot to join the Round Table and stops to chat with the hermit Leonides. Three knights come along, words are exchanged and Lancelot winds up defeating all of them. As he continues on his way with the three prisoners, Leonides sends light signals to Merlin, using a mirror.

In the meantime, King Arthur, Gawaine and the few remaining Knights of the Round Table are recovering from a fierce battle they had fought the previous week. Gawaine's brother lies mortally wounded and soon dies. Gawaine has a piece from the sword of the man who killed Gareth, the knight with the red plume (shades of the Tristan legend).

Lancelot arrives with his three prisoners, who turn out to be Knights of the Round Table. Gawaine spots Lancelot's sword, which has a chink that matches the incriminating piece. Gawaine challenges Lancelot to a duel of honor. Lancelot wins but spares the good knight's life, explaining to Arthur that he indeed had fought against the Knights of the Round Table but only because of an oath he had sworn to his father. Now free from that oath, he can, without guilt, join Arthur's court. Lancelot is knighted and becomes a member of the Round Table fraternity.

VOLUME 4, EPISODE 1 (SHOW #14): "THE LESSER BREED"

CAST: William Russell (Sir Lancelot); Ronald Leigh-Hunt (King Arthur); Cyril Smith (Merlin);

Robert Scroggins (Brian); Ann Stephens (Sella); Gerard Heinz (Eck); Fred Goddard (Horg); David Morrell (Sir Kay); Wilfred Brambell (Fisherman); Eric Corrie (Overseer); Brian Moorehead (Guard); Edward Judd (Auctioneer)

CREDITS: Producer — Bernard Knowles; Director — Terry Bishop; Screenplay — Peggy Phillips; Script Supervision — Albert G. Ruben; Music — Albert Elms; Director of Photography — Ken Hodges; Production Manager — E. S. Laurie; Art Director — David Rawnsley; Supervising Editor — Thelma Connell; Sound — Fred Ryan; Made at Nettlefold Studios, Walton-on-Thames, England

SYNOPSIS: A fisherman comes to Arthur's court with a story of a sea monster carrying off the village men. Arthur sends Lancelot to investigate. Lancelot and Brian find a Viking ship but before they can search for the pillagers they are captured by Horg and his men.

Taken as slaves back to Horg's land, the journey is so long that Lancelot has a beard by the time they arrive. As Lancelot stands on the auction block, Horg learns that the father of the beautiful Sella has fallen on hard times. Horg makes a deal with Sella's dad. He buys all the British slaves and gives them to Sella's father in exchange for Sella's hand in marriage.

Sella, however, loves someone else: Prince Lief of the Northlands. As luck would have it, Lancelot resembles Lief strongly enough that, even if anyone in the village besides Sella and her handmaid had ever seen Lief before (which they haven't), they'd think he was the genuine article. So Sella and Lancelot hatch a plot. She helps Lancelot escape and disguises him as Lief. Then "Lief" shows up to claim his princely right of taking her as his wife despite Horg's objections.

Unfortunately, Lancelot is unmasked and has to fight his way out. Brian manages to get the other slaves loose to help and they make their way to a boat. Lancelot and Sella bid each other a sad adieu and then part.

VOLUME 4, EPISODE 2 (SHOW #20): "THE RUBY OF RADNOR"

CAST: William Russell (Sir Lancelot); Ronald Leigh-Hunt (King Arthur); Jane Hylton (Queen

Guinevere); Cyril Smith (Merlin); Robert Scroggins (Brian); David Morrell (Sir Kay); Colin Tapley (Everard); Edward Judd (Garth); Eric Corrie (Robert); Reginald Hearne (Hugo); Harold Goodwin (Peasant); Desmond Raynor (Jailer)

CREDITS: Producer — Bernard Knowles; Director — Lawrence Huntington; Screenplay — Hamish Hamilton Burns; Script Supervision — Albert G. Ruben; Music — Edwin Astley; Director of Photography — Ken Hodges; Production Manager — E. S. Laurie; Art Director — David Rawnsley; Supervising Editor — Thelma Connell; Sound — Fred Ryan; Made at Nettlefold Studios, Walton-on-Thames, England

SYNOPSIS: The crown jewels are to be displayed at Radnor Abbey for three days. Lord Everard, King Arthur's cousin, is to supply guards for the duration but the king's relative has plans of his own. With his men he snatches the whole collection but the disappearance of the Ruby of Radnor, a particularly important stone, causes the most consternation. For some reason, he who possesses that jewel possesses power — enough power to threaten even King Arthur.

While this is occurring, Merlin is being driven to distraction by the pranks of Lancelot's squire, Brian. The old magician promised Lancelot that he would tutor Brian, but goldfish in the washbasin is too much. To get some relief from the boy, Merlin sends Brian on an errand. Brian is to take two homing pigeons to Sir Giles of Coventry, one point in the network of Merlin's messaging system.

On the way to Coventry, Brian stumbles upon the robbers making away with the crown jewels and is himself captured. He is imprisoned by Everard but is cleverly able to get a message to Merlin via the homing pigeons. Lancelot shows up and saves not only the day but Brian and the jewels as well.

VOLUME 5, EPISODE 1 (SHOW #30): "THE PRINCE OF LIMERICK"

CAST: William Russell (Sir Lancelot); Robert Scroggins (Brian); Jerome Willis (Prince of Limerick); Thomas R. Duggan (Baron Wicklaw); Lynne Furlong (Princess Kathleen); Tony Quinn (King Anguish)

CREDITS: Producer — Bernard Knowles; Director — Lawrence Huntington; Screenplay — Leslie Poynton; Script Supervision — Albert G. Ruben; Music — Albert Elms; Director of Photography — Ernest Palmer; Production Manager — E. S. Laurie; Art Director — Bill Bennison; Supervising Editor — Maurice Rootes; Sound — W. Lindop

SYNOPSIS: King Anguish of Ireland has invited King Arthur to attend a tournament but Arthur sends Lancelot in his place. On their way, Lancelot and Brian run across the prince of Limerick, a peaceful poet who has been exiled by King Anguish, who is a comically browbeaten father who wants nothing more than to get his fiery daughter out from under his roof. Limerick and Anguish's daughter, Kathleen, are in love and it turns out the real purpose of the tournament is to select a husband for Kathleen.

Lancelot carries a love poem to Kathleen for Limerick and, seeing how much the two love each other, he decides to help them. First, Lancelot delivers an insulting limerick to Baron Wicklaw, the prime contender for the hand of Kathleen. This has the expected effect of making the baron angry, the theory being that he won't be able to fight as well. Next, Lancelot tries to teach Limerick to fight but to no avail.

As might be expected, Lancelot fights in Limerick's place and wins, but Wicklaw demands a rematch using shillelaghs. This time Limerick steps into the lists with Lancelot and Brian and the three hearties soundly beat Wicklaw and his men. Limerick and Kathleen are happily reunited.

VOLUME 5, EPISODE 2 (SHOW #21): "WITCHES BREW"

CAST: William Russell (Sir Lancelot); Cyril Smith (Merlin); Ronald Leigh-Hunt (King Arthur); Robert Scroggins (Brian); Maxine Audley (Eunice); Leonard Sachs (King Rolf); Graham Stewart (Damien); Reginald Hearne (Hedrick); Brian Roper (Alan); Edward Judd (Soldier); Eric Corrie (Jailer)

CREDITS: Producer — Bernard Knowles; Director — Terry Bishop; Screenplay — Peggy Phillips;

Script Supervision — Albert G. Ruben; Music — Albert Elms; Director of Photography — Ernest Palmer; Production Manager — E. S. Laurie; Art Director — Bill Bennison; Supervising Editor — Thelma Connell; Sound — Fred Ryan; Made at Nettlefold Studios, Walton-on-Thames, England

SYNOPSIS: The squire of Prince Damien has come to Camelot with the news that King Rolf has inexplicably imprisoned his son, Damien, for treason. King Arthur sends Sir Lancelot to investigate.

Lancelot finds Rolf's castle preparing for battle, though peace reigns throughout the land. He also finds King Rolf strangely distant and vague. The cause soon becomes apparent as the ever-present court magician and counselor, Eunice of Ethelstone, gradually exposes her hand.

Not only is Damien in prison but he is to be executed. While Lancelot goes to talk to Damien, Eunice entices Brian up to her laboratory and hypnotizes him. She learns all she can about Lancelot then causes Brian to forget everything that he said to her. Lancelot is convinced of Damien's innocence and he goes to Rolf to try to talk sense to the man. Rolf is bewitched though and calls on Eunice to advise him. To prove her loyalty, Eunice pretends to go into a trance and "in voices" tells the things she knows of Lancelot. Rolf is convinced but not Lancelot.

To avoid immediate disaster, Lancelot sneaks Damien away to Camelot by hiding him inside a suit of armor that he purchased from Rolf's armorer. King Arthur then invites Rolf to Camelot to discuss matters. Merlin squires Eunice to his chambers and there tricks her into confessing her plot to control Rolf's kingdom. Her henchman, Hedrick, nearly escapes but Damien stops him and defeats him in a sword fight.

The Adventures of Timmy the Tooth: The Brush in the Stone (1994)

34 minutes; Color; Puppets (for ages 2–7); Copyright 1994, MCA Home Video, Inc.; MCA/Universal Home Video; MCA Home Entertainment; BOMP Products

CREDITS: Created by — James Murray, Kevin Carlson, Dina Fraboni; Written by — James Murray, Kevin Carlson, Phil Baron; Directed by — Rick Locke; Producer — Dina Fraboni; Executive Producer — Jillian Sosin; Co-Executive Producers — James Murray; Line Producer — Gary L. Stephenson; Puppet Performers — Kevin Carlson, Todd Mattox, Michael Earl, Cheryl Blaylock, Phil Baron, Bruce Lanoil, Alan Trautman, Christine Papalexis, Greg Gallora, Dina Fraboni, James Murray; Character Design by — Drew Massey, Bob Fappiano; Puppets Designed and Built by — Bob Fappiano; Puppet Mechanical Animation by — Randy Simper; Story Editor — Phil Baron; Music by — Joyce Imbesi; Production Designer — Naomi Slodki; Edited by — Dave Moorman, Eytan Sternberg; Associate Director — Syngehilde Schweikart; Stage Manager — Scott Schwartz; Lighting Designed by — Richard Ocean, Lee Rose; Costumes Designed by — Jason Cort; More Puppets and Marionettes by — Christine Papalexis; Puppet Rigger/Wrangler — Pat Brymer; Associate Producer — Greg Hampson; Script Supervisor — Michael Dempsey; Script Coordinator — Diana M. Kuhns; Assistant to the Producers — Leaf Fisher; Production Coordinators — Robert C. Mora, David Naves; Production Associate — Paul Jensen; Production Intern — Rick Locke, Jr.; Art Directors — Tim Papie, Raymond Naylor; Prop Master — Beth Horbury; Illustrator — Sarah Halpern; Scenic — Lynn Pollard, Kelly Van Patter, Robin Jacobsen; Assistant Puppet Wrangler — Alissa Levisohn; Puppeteer Coordinator — Allan Trautman; Music and Songs Produced by — Joyce Imbesi ("I Love Adventure" — Music and Lyrics by Joyce Imbesi and Kevin Quinn; "To the Fair We Go" — Music and Lyrics by Craig Thomas; "Itchy Polka Dot Blues" — Lyrics by Willow Wray, Music by Joyce Imbesi; "Not So Sure It's a Forest" — Music and Lyrics by Tina Mitchell and Jonathan Raines); Choreography Consultant — Michael Earl; Sound Designer/Mixer — Thomas Orsi; Music Engineer — Rob Hart; Music Editor — Allen Rosen; Video — Ron Stutzman; Camera Operators — Mare Hunter, Dean Hall, Parker Bartlett, Danny Webb, David Irete; Utilities — Robert Lorenz, Jeff Rosa; Audio Mixer — Ish Garcia; Audio Assistant — Tom Holmes; Gaffer — Jack Rappaport; Lighting Crew — Christopher Dale, Michael Fink, Bill Lehm Kuhl, Brett Santucci; Post Production Coordinator — Dave Moorman; Composium Effects — Jonathan Curtis; Colorist — Claudius Neal; Business Manager/Production Consultant — Merlis Green and Associates; Post Production Facilities — Beverly Hills Video Group; Video Facilities — Starfax, Inc.; Video Taped at — Hollywood Center Studios

SYNOPSIS: This episode from a series of children's films is one of the more superficial and least edifying uses of Arthurian legend. The only similarities to the original are a magician (though his name in this is Merlys) and the fact that the main character must pull an object from a stone to become a knight. In this case the object is a toothbrush.

Alakazam the Great (1961)

84 minutes; Color; Cartoon; Copyright 1961, Alta Vista Productions; Copyright 1989, Orion Pictures Corp.; Copyright 1995, Orion Home Video; Orion Home Video; American International; An American International Picture, successor to Alta Vista

STARRING THE VOICES OF: Frankie Avalon; Dodie Stevens; Jonathan Winters; Arnold Stang; Sterling Holloway

CREDITS: James H. Nicholson and Samuel Z. Arkoff present A TOEI Production; Produced by — Hiroshi Okawa; American Version Produced by — Lou Rusoff; Original Adaptation — Hideyuki Takahashi, Goro Kontaibo; Screenplay by — Osamu Tezuka, Lou Rusoff, Lee Kressel; Scenario — Keinosuke Uegusa; Co-Directors — Taiji Yabushita, Osamu Tezuka, Daisaku Shirakawa; Music by — Les Baxter; Music Coordinator — Al Simms; Orchestrations by — Albery Harris; Music Editors — Bye Newman, George Brand; Songs — "Ali the Great;" "Bluebird in the Cherry Tree;" "Under the Waterfall;" "Aliki Aliko Alakazam;" Music and Lyrics by — Les Baxter;Animation by Koichi Mori, Masao Kumakawa,Yasuo Oysuka, Akira Daikuhara, Hideo Furuzawa; Artwork and Color by — Masaaki Yano, Hajima Numa, Koichi Maeba; Backgrounds by — Eiko Sugimoto, Kazuko Ozawa, Kimiko Saito, Mataji Urata, Saburo Yokoi; American Version Directed by — Lee Kesel at Titra Sound Studios, New York; Edited by — Salvatore Billiteri, Laurette Odney; Sound Editor — Kay Rose; Photographed by — Harusato Otsuka, Komei Ishikawa, Kenji Sugiyama; Color by PATHE

SYNOPSIS: Another children's film in which the irrelevant use of Merlin is the only significant connection to Arthurian legend.

Mijutso Land is an island that floats in the sky off the coast of Japan. It is ruled by a father, wife and son team of godlike beings named Amo, Amas and Amat, respectively. Mijutso Land also happens to be the home of all the wizards who ever lived.

Looking down from their domain, the three rulers notice a new genus of monkey evolving. One of the little talking monkeys, Alakazam (called Ali for short), becomes the king by finding a magical land under a waterfall. Ali becomes corrupted by his new powers and wants more. Knowing that Merlin is the wisest and most powerful of all the wizards, Ali goes to Merlin to learn. Done with that, Ali challenges Amo himself, eats forbidden fruit and battles with the heavenly police and with Hercules.

Finally, Amo imprisons Ali, then commands him to go on a pilgrimage (quest?) with Amat, during which they have many adventures. Ali learns humility and goes home to rule happily.

Alchemy see under *Deepak Chopra: Alchemy and the Crystal Cave*

All the Great Operas in 10 Minutes (1992)

10 minutes; Color; Animated stills; Copyright 1992, Kim Thompson; Copyright 1996, Design and release by Picture Start and Videos.com, Inc.

CREDITS: Written by — Kim Thompson; Photographed by — Kim Thompson; Edited by — Kim Thompson; Narrated by — Kim Thompson; Just Generally Created by — Kim Thompson; Sound Recorded and Mixed by — Darcy Kite; With the Assistance of — Ryerson Polytechnical Institute, Film House, Roland W. Schlimme, Canada, and Saskatchewan Student Loans

SYNOPSIS: This video delivers exactly what it claims in less than the time it claims. Eleven of the greatest operas are comically and very briefly described by the filmmaker in 9 minutes and 30 seconds flat.

The clever presentation includes Monty Python-esque still photo cutouts animated on a curtained stage set, acting out the rapid-fire synopses narrated by Thompson. The eleven operas reviewed are *La Traviata, Carmen, Don Giovanni, Aida, Tosca, Tristan and Isolde, Madama Butterfly* and the four operas of the *Ring of the Nibelung*.

Of interest for this book is the presentation of *Tristan and Isolde*. Rather than trying to describe the terrific job done by Thompson, the following is her narration verbatim:

> *Tristan and Isolde* is cool because it has knights in armor and magic and stuff. Isolde is going to become King Mark's wife against her will. She hates Tristan but of course she loves him too. She plots for them both to drink poison but they get a love potion instead, so they just sit staring at each other like idiots. Even though they are warned in time they can't bear to leave each other and King Mark finds them. Tristan is wounded and when Isolde shows up to cure him he gets so excited he rips off his bandages and dies in her arms. These two other guys kill each other and then Isolde just falls over Tristan's body and dies right there of love or something. [quoted with permission]

All These Women (1964) (För att Inte Tala om Alla Dessa Kvinnor)

85 minutes; Black and White, Color; Comedy; Swedish with English subtitles; Copyright 1964, AB Svensk Filmindustri; Copyright 1997, MDM Productions

CAST: Bibi Andersson (Humlan); Harriet Andersson (Isolde); Eva Dahlbeck (Adelaide); Karin Kavli (Madame Tussaud); Gertrud Fridh (Traviata); Mona Malm (Cecilia); Barbra Hiortaf Ornäs (Beatrice); Allan Edwall (Jillker); Georg Funkquist (Tristan); Carl Billquist (Young Cellist); Jarl Kulle (Cornelius); Jan Blomberg (English Radio Reporter); Göran Graffman (French Radio Reporter); Gösta Prüzelius (Swedish Radio Reporter); Jan-Olaf Strandberg (German Radio Reporter); Axel Düberg (Man in Black); Ulf Johansson (Man in Black); Doris Funcke (Waitress); Yvonne Igell (Waitress)

CREDITS: Director — Ingmar Bergman; Writers — Erland Josephson, Ingmar Bergman; Producer — Allan Ekelund; Film Editor — Ulla Ryghe; Production Designer — P. A. Lundgren; Camera — Sven Nykvist; Sound — P. A. Lundgren; Music — Diverse, Erik Nordgren; Color by — Eastman Color, AGA

SYNOPSIS: This is one of only a couple of comedies produced by the famous Swedish director Ingmar Bergman. Even with the comic elements, however, the story retains some of the sadness of the Tristan and Isolde legend. Bergman's signature surrealistic style accentuates both the comedy and the pathos of the odd characters involved in this peculiar tale.

A famous music critic named Cornelius has decided to write the biography of a virtuoso cellist, Felix. Attempting to interview Felix, Cornelius makes an extended visit to the musician's summer home.

The film actually opens (in black and white) at the funeral of Felix. Cornelius more or less presides over the ceremony as a parade of no fewer than seven "widows" pay their respects at the bier. Their names, in order of appearance at the coffin, are Tussaud, Beatrice, Traviata, Cecilia, Isolde, Bumble Bee and finally Adelaide. The rest of the movie unfolds as a flashback, recounting the events that led to the master's death.

Though Cornelius is a studied fop who sports dandified clothing and an enormous quill pen, the master's women soon have him romping around the bedrooms and grounds of the residence. Bumble Bee is the first of the master's mistresses to seduce the would-be biographer.

In spite of many slapstick mishaps, Cornelius gradually manages to put together a picture of Felix, though not through any significant contact with the cellist himself. The reclusive musician is never in fact seen by the audience except in silhouette or from behind. Cornelius never really manages to get an interview with the man but gathers his information from all the women who inhabit the master's life.

The domineering and demanding Felix has gathered these people around him like a collection. He has also renamed each of them. Madame Tussaud, the oldest of the women, financed Felix's early career. Her real name is Jeanette. Isolde is the maid in the household and her real name is Lisa. Felix's chauffeur is called Tristan, but we never learn his real name. Only Adelaide, apparently Felix's true wife, seems not to have an alter ego.

Cornelius learns that 32 years ago Felix beat Tristan in a cello competition. Felix then seduced Tristan's wife and hired Tristan to drive his cars. With all these sordid details coming to light, Cornelius hatches a plot.

Craving the kind of real fame that Felix has instead of the notoriety of a leechlike critic, Cornelius has written a musical composition. Of course, it is terrible but Cornelius isn't musically inclined enough to know that. He blackmails Felix by telling him he will write a complimentary biography if Felix will play his composition on a nationally broadcast radio concert. Felix agrees, but, sitting at the microphone in the studio, he dies before he plays even one note of Cornelius's music.

After the master's death, Tristan departs with Adelaide. A new young cellist arrives at the house and, with knowing looks at each other, the remaining women and Cornelius start the whole process over again.

The quality of the tape this film was viewed from was poor and many of the subtitles were nearly illegible. A certain amount of detail from the story therefore is incomplete in this writing. Nonetheless, the bare bones of the Tristan and Isolde legend can be deciphered.

Tristan, the chauffeur, is like the legendary Tristan in that he loves someone who is attached to another. Felix fits the bill of King Mark since he is, at least for a time, the regent of this strange kingdom. The rest of any connections, if any, to the legend are something of a jumble. That Tristan is a contemporary of Felix is a departure although Cecilia is some sort of relative. Isolde/Lisa seems a gratuitous throw-in but this is, after all, a comedy.

Alley Oops see The Angry Beavers: "Alley Oops"

The Angry Beavers: "Alley Oops" (1998)

Approximately 22 minutes; Color; Cartoon; Copyright 1998, Viacom International, Inc.; Gunther Wahl Productions, Inc.; Nicktoons

STARRING THE VOICES OF: Nick Bakay (Norbert); Richard Horvitz (Daggett); Stacy Schauer (Stacy); Chelsea Schauer (Chelsea); Marcia Wallace (Mom); Lorin Dreyfuss (Dad); Tom Wilson (Otis Otto; Bowling Patron #2); William Sanderson (Ditto Otto; Clerk); Kate Donahue (Laverta Lutz)

CREDITS: Executive Producer—Mitchell Schauer; Creative Supervising Producer/Director—Michael R. Gerard; Executive Story Editor—Keith Kaczorek; Series Developed by—Keith Kaczorek, Mitchell Schauer; Production Manager—Suzanne Benton; Assistant Production Manager—Anne Michaud; Music—Charlie Brissette; Writer—John Derevlany; Animation Director—Swinton O. Scott III; Storyboard—Joel Seibe; Mr. Brissette's Transportation Furnished by—Crash Test Imports; Animation Timers—Tom Yasumi, Tammy Slusser, Nancy Avery, Andrew Overtoom; Checker—Gary C. Hall; Animation Coordinator—Tony Ostyn; Animation Assistant—Brian Robitaille; Main Character Design—Mitchell Schauer; Character Design Supervisor—Michael Q. Ceballos; Character Design—John R. Statema; Prop Design—Jerry Royal, John Seymore; Character Clean-up—Shoshanna Stolove, Jin Sur; Layout Supervisor—Maurice F. Morgan II; Layout Design—Spenser Davis; Production Coordinators—Scott Ninneman, Vito Curcuru; Production Assistants—Justin Brinsfield, Angela Guajardo; Executive Assistants—Rosanna DiLoreto, Dina Butyn; Script Supervisor—Micah Wright; Art Director—Dan Chessher; Background Stylists—Craig Gardener; Andy Clark, Pablito Paguio, Eric Mahady; Background Assistant—Walter Hong; Color Key Supervisor—Geri Rochon; Color Keyist—Carie Herman; Assistant Color Keyist—Jackie Stewart; Storyboard Clean-up—Louis C. Gallegos, Arpi Krikorian, Arnie C. Miclat; Post Production Director—Heather Adams; Editor—Brad Carow; EMR Editor—Matt Corey; Post Production Coordinator—Jessica Dorff; Post Production Assistants—Kimberly Goosen, Shawn Trask; Voice Casting—Donna Grillo; Recording Studio—Score One; Engineer—Al Johnson; Track Reading—Glenwood Editorial, Inc.; Sound Supervisor and Mixer—Timothy J. Borquez; Supervising Sound FX Editor—Tom Syslo; Sound Editors—Rick Hinson, Eric Freeman, Les Wolf, Marc Mailand; Foley Mixer—Brad Brock; Foley Artist—Dianne Greco; Re-recording Mixers—Timothy J. Borquez, Timothy J. Garrity; Post Production Sound Services provided by—Horta Editorial & Sound, Inc.; On-Line Editors—Barry Cohen, Dan Aguilar; DaVinci Colorist—Dexter P.; Post Production Services—Hollywood Digital, Anderson Video, Encore Video; Animation Services — Rough Draft Studios, Inc.; Overseas Supervising Director — Scott Mansz; Overseas Layout Supervisor — Carl Linton; Main Title Design — Mitchell Schauer; Main Title Supervisors — Michael R. Gerard, Mitchell Schauer, Michael Lessa, Geri Rochon, Mario D'Anna; Main Title Coordinators — Jerry Royal, Suzanne Benton; Digital Ink and Paint — Class 6; Executive Producers — Lee Gunther, Michael Wahl; Special thanks to Andra Shapiro; A very special thanks to Herb Scannell for the fishnet hankies; For Nicktoons: Executive Producer — Mary Harrington; Senior Producer — Michael Lessa; Story Editor — Merriwether Williams; General Manager for Nicktoons — Mark Taylor; Production Executive — Richard Mair; *The Angry Beavers* is a trademark of Viacom International, Inc.

SYNOPSIS: *The Angry Beavers* is a cartoon series on the cable television network Nickelodeon. It is about two beavers, Norbert and Daggett, brothers who were thrown out of their mother's dam when she had more kids. On their own now, they get into all kinds of trouble.

The series premiered in 1997. Episode 24 of the second season included "If You In-Sisters" and "Alley Oops." In "Alley Oops" the boys go to Camelot Lanes, a bowling alley that is constructed on the outside to look like a medieval castle. When Daggett accidentally knocks all the pins down in every lane, he wins Excaliball, delivered to him by a sort of Lady of the Lanes. Before going home, however, he has to return it.

Animaniacs Stew (1994)

50 minutes; Color; Cartoon; Copyright 1994, Warner Bros.; A Time-Warner Entertainment Company; Amblin Entertainment; Warner Bros. Television Distribution, Warner Home Video; A Steven Spielberg Presentation

STARRING THE VOICES OF: Rob Paulsen (Yakko); Jess Harnell (Wakko); Tress MacNeille (Dot); Sherri Stoner (Slappy); Nathan Ruegger (Skippy); Nancy Cartwright (Mindy); Frank Welker (Buttons); Colin Wells (Randy Beaman's Pal); Maurice LaMarche (The Brain); Dave Thomas (King Arthur); Tanner King (Bumbie); Tom Bodett (The Announcer); Jon Bauman (Singer); Edie Lehmann (Singer); Myrna Mathews (Singer); Randy Crenshaw (Singer); Jon Joyce (Singer)

CREDITS: Senior Producer — Tom Ruegger; Producers — Rich Arons; Sherri Stoner; Music by — Richard Stone; Steve Bernstein; Carl Johnson; Orchestration by — Julie Bernstein; Casting and Voice Direction — Andrea Romano; Compilation Produced by — Kevin Miller for Toon Tunes Productions; *Slugging:* Rich Arons, Jeff Hall, Bill Knoll, Greg Reyna; *Sheet Timing:* Rich Arons, Vincent Bassois, Richard Calado, Jeff Hall; *Story Boards:* Rich Arons, Barry Caldwell, Chris Otsuki, John Over, Audu Paden, Ryan Roberts, Lenard Robinson, Larry Scholl, Al Zegler; *Model Design:* Arland Barran, Frederick Gardner, Dave Kuhn, Eric Mahady, Rogerio Nogueira, Cynthia Petrovic, Bonnie Robinson, Robert Sledge, Maureen Trueblood, Mark Zoeller; *Layout Supervisor:* Perry Kiefer; *B.G. Key Design:* Grigor Bay, Nick Dubois, Frank Frezzo, Robert Haverland, Dan McHugh, Thomas Warkentin, Keith Weesner; *Character Layout:* Chris Aguirre, Ed Baker, Bob Doucette, Paul Fisher, Tim George, Phil Mosness, Cynthia Petrovic, Ryan Roberts, Joe Sibilski; *Ink and Paint Supervisor:* Bunny Munns; *B.G. Layout* Jim Fletcher, Ernie Guanlao, Ed Haney, Terry Hennson, David West; *B.G. Paint:* Hye Coh, Ann Guenther, Michael Lowery, Rolando Oliva, Jeff Richards, Kathryn Yelsa; *B.G. Color Key:* Carolyn Guske; *Color Key:* Richard Daskas, Robin Kane, Bunny Munns, Chris Naylor; *Mark Up:* Jean DuBois, Valerie Walker; *Painter:* Eric Nordberg; Retake Coordinator — Howard Schwartz; Animation Checking — Jan Browning, Brenda Brummet, Jennifer Damiani, Bunty Dranko, Karl Jacobs Howard Schwartz; Production Coordinator — Ken Fredrich Boyer; Copying and Shipping — Carlton Battea, Ana Durand; Digital Production — Alan G. Brown for Animated F/X, Inc.; Post Production Supervisor — Joe Sandusky; Supervising Film Editor — Joe Gail; ADR Coordinator — Kelly Ann Foley; Film Editors — Al Breitenback, Kelly Ann Foley, Theresa Gilroy-Nielsen; Sound Reading — Bradley Carow, Steve Siracusa, Denise Whitfield; Re-recording Mixers — Thomas J. Maydeck, C.A.S., Pat Rodman, 2nd Eng.; Dialogue Editors — Mark Keatts, Aaron L. King, Mick Broolin, Andrew I. King, Bob Lacivita; Music Editor — Tom Lavin for Triad Music; Sound Effects — Russell Brower, Robert Hargreaves, Matt Thorne; ADR Recording — Mark Keatts; Voice Recording Studio — Soundcastle/Postmodern, Harry Andronis, Engr., Gregory Catheart, 2nd Engr.; Sound Services Provided by — Monterey Post Production; Post Production Facilities — The Post Group, Varitel Video; Recording Administrator — Leslie Lamers; Production Administrator — Alyson Brown; Videotape Supervision — Jay Weinman, Scott

Williams; Amblin Story Consultant—Douglas Wood; Assistants to the Producer—Kathryn Page, Richard Freeman; Mix Coordinator—Richard Freeman; Voice Over Assistant—Erin Keeler; Production Assistants—Barry Blalock, Bill Devine, Geno DuBois, Dustin Foster, John Morris, Bobbie Page, Marcus Williams; Animation Services—Akom Production Company (President: Nelson Shin; Supervisor: Dev Ramsaran; Tokyo Movie Shinsha Co., Ltd.; Directors: Takash Kawaguchi, Toshihiko Masuda, Hiroaki Noguchi, Keiko Oyamada); Wang Film Productions Co., Ltd. (President: James Wang; Layout Supervisor: Peter Ferk); Startoons: Tony Cervone, Chris McClenahan, Ron Fleischer, Jon McClenahan, Stan Fukuoka, Jeff Siergey, Marty Lenno, Neal Stervecky; Production Manager—Barbra J. Gerard; Production Supervisor—Ken Duer, Barbara Simon Dierks, Liza-Ann Warren; Production Management—Tim Sarnoff; Executive in Charge of Production—Jean McCurdy; Executive Producer—Steven Spielberg

SYNOPSIS: In the segment "Sir Yaksalot" (written by Paul Rugg, directed by Barry Caldwell), a dragon attacks Camelot. King Arthur has Merlin summon help and the characters Yakko, Wakko and Dot show up.

A caricature of Raymond Burr appears in a science fiction–style war room. The dragon is blown up with dynamite and turns out to be a mechanical creation of two other *Animaniacs* regulars, Pinky and the Brain.

Army of Darkness (1992)

81 minutes; Color; Horror/Comedy; Copyright 1992, Dino De Laurentiis Communication; Copyright 1993, MCA Universal Home Video, #81288; A Renaissance Pictures Production

CAST: Bruce Campbell (Ash); Embeth Davidtz (Sheila); Marcus Gilbert (Arthur); Ian Abercrombie (Wiseman); Richard Grove (Duke Henry); Michael Earl Reid (Gold Tooth); Timothy Patrick Quill (Blacksmith); Bridget Fonda (Linda); Patricia Tallman (Possessed Witch); Theodore Raimi (Cowardly Warrior); Deke Anderson (Tiny Ash #1); Bruce Thomas (Tiny Ash #2); Sarah Shearer (Old Woman); Shiva Gordon (Pit Deadite #1); Billy Bryan (Pit Deadite #2); Nadine Grycan (Winged Deadite); Bill Moseley (Deadite Captain); Micheal Kenney (Henry's Man); Andy Baile (Lieutenant #1); Rad Milo (Tower Guard); Brad Bradbury (Chief Archer); Sol Abrams, Lorraine Axeman, Josh

Becker, Sheri Burke, Don Campbell, Charlie Campbell, Harley Cokeliss, Ken Jepson, William Lustig, David O'Malley, David Pollison, Ivan Raimi, Bernard Rose, Bill Vincent, Chris Webster, Ron Zwang

CREDITS: Writers—Sam Raimi, Ivan Raimi; Director—Sam Raimi; Producer—Robert Tapert; Co-Producer—Bruce Campbell; Co-Producer—Introvision International, Inc.; Director of Photography—Bill Pope; Music—Joseph LoDuca; "March of the Dead" Theme—Danny Elfman; Visual Effects—Introvision International, Inc.; Director of Visual Effects—William Mesa; Special Makeup Effects—Kurtzman, Nicotero & Berger EFX Group; Ash and Sheila Makeup Effects—Tony Gardner; Alterian Studios, Inc.; Production Design—Tony Tremblay; Editors—Bob Murawski, R.O.C. Sandstorm; Casting Director—Ira Belgrade; Unit Production Manager—Eric Gruendemann; Unit Assistant Director—John Cameron; 2nd Assistant Director—Sarah Addington; Stunt Coordinator—Chris Doyle; Stunt Players: Sandy Berumen, Chuck Borden, George B. Colucci, Jr., Yannick Derrien, Bill Hart, Maria Kelly, Ken Lesco, Dennis Madalone, Tom Morga, Gary Morgan, John Nowak, Christian Page, Tim Trella, Jack Verbois, Richard Blackwell, Eddie Braun, B. J. Davis, Dick Hancock, Donna Keegan, Steven Hall Lambert, Jack Lilley, "Wild Bill" Mock, Bruce Morgan, Keith Morrison, Janet Lee Orcutt, John Sistrunk, Christopher J. Tuck, Brian John Williams; Swordmaster—Dan Speaker; Assistant Swordplay Choreographer—Jan Bryant; Swordfighters—Dana Fredsti, Bridget Hoffman, Julianne Mazziotti, Vaughn Roberts, David C. Speaker, Geoffrey Donne; 2nd Second Assistant Director—Steve Coatney; Script Supervisor—Steve Gehreke; 2nd Unit Director—Doug Leffler; 2nd Unit Assistant Director—Robert Hume; Production Coordinator—Anna Lisa Nilsson; Assistant to the Production Manager—Mary Carol Bulger; Production Secretary—Sue Binder; Assistant to Robert Tapert—Ruth Jessup; Assistant to Bruce Campbell—Jim Auker; Assistant to Sam Raimi—David Pollison; Bruce Campbell's Weight Trainer—Wogbe Ofori of Dynatechnics; Unit Publicist—Patti Hawn; Publicist—Dennis Davidson Associates; Production Auditor—Jeff McCraig; Assistant Auditor—Jasmine McCraig; Post Production Auditor—Beverly Cusack; Set Production Assistants: Kevin Brown, Lauri Mullens, Keith Peltz, Jean Veber, Bill Cubey, Tony Patterson, Kyle Silverman; Office Production Assistants—Cheryl Cain, Dan DaSilva, Chris Grant, Liz Friedman; Extra Casting—Genex Casting: Diana Carroll, Julie Calman;

Bruce Campbell brandishing weapons in Sam Raimi's *Army of Darkness* (1992).

1st Assistant Camera — Gregor Tavenner, Carolyn Chen; 2nd Assistant Camera — James Fitzgerald; Loader — David Garcia; Still Photographer — Melissa Mosely; Video Playback Operator — Troy Stauffer; 2nd Unit Director of Photography — Ken Arlidge; 2nd Unit 1st Assistant Camera — Ron Turowski; 2nd Unit Photography — Andrea Dietrich, William Mesa; Sound Mixer — Al Rizzo; Boom Operator — Brad Knopf; Art Director/Construction Coordinator — Aram Allan; Construction Foreman — Marc Alexandre; Lead Scenic — John Snow; Scenics — David Snow, Robert Campbell, Simon Addyman, Mark Donoghue, Thomas Bell; Stand-by Scenic — Ernest "Spike" Trevino; Carpenters: Adrian Saxton, Mark Shouten, Richard Weavers, Robert Strahan, Daniel Espinoza, Silvano Rusata, Patric Murrough, Rocky Grisez, Richard Berry; Stand-by Carpenters — H. Christopher Roy, Mark Tremblay; Set Decorator — Michele Poulik; Leadman — Peter Gurski; On-Set Dressers — Jonathan Bruce, Julie Hermelin; Swing Gang — Carlton Rude, Michael Franco, Greg Bartkus, David Marinaccio, David Sette; Property Master — Michael Courville; Assistant Property Master — Charlotte Garnell; Assistant Props — Michael Goyak, John Diaz; On-Set Armorer — Brian Thomas; Assistant Armorers — Dana Fredsti, Paul Best; Special armor and weapons designed and constructed by Jeff Hedgecock and Vorhut Fahlein Arms, San Diego, California: Dave Hammon, John Hart, Jim Hedgecock, John Knightsbury, Cat Lamson, Nick Petrosino, Eric Ray; Boss Wrangler — Davey Rogers; Horses and Riders Provided by — Deanna Esmaeel; Wranglers — Carol Sonheim, Donald D. York; Horseback Riding Lessons — The Riding Coach; Location Manager — Steve Garrett; Location Assistants: Ken Harback, Eddie Stalter, Scott Buzz, Nelson Drake, Nick Styne, Kevin Cortez; Caterer — Michelson's Catering; Chef — Schuyler Collins; First Aid — Sandy Ohlfest; Craft Service — Stephen Gates; Craft Service Assistants — Jason Ryan, Kevin O'Hara, John Lant; Security — Harry Stanback; Makeup Supervisor — Camille Calvet; Key Makeup Artist — Anne Hieronymus; Assistant Makeup — Karen Keener; Key Hairstylist — Jeri Baker; 2nd Hairstylist — Julie Woods; Assistant Hairstylist — Rebecca Alling; Costume Designer — Ida Gearon; Costume Supervisor — Karyn Wagner; Key Costumer — Marisa Aboitiz; Assistant Costume Design — Leslie Daniel Rainer; Costumers — Karen Hare, Nicky Bradshaw; Textile Artist — Victoria Wendell; Additional Assistants — Deva Stevens, Maria Cittadini; Horse Dresser — Dena Matranga; Assistant Horse

Dresser—Bo Boreanoz; Horse Armor—Clark Acton, Bill Murphree, Ken Cornett; Gaffers—Jim Gilson, Joel Unangst; Best Boy Electric—John Martens; Electricians: Joe Martens, Eric Von Neumann, Tony Pica, Ray Gonzales, Ross Warren, William Koski; 2nd Unit Gaffer—Dante Cardone; Husco Lighting Technicians—Tom Webb, Todd Braden; Key Grip—Tony Mazzucchi; Best Boy Grip—Kurt Grossi; Dolly Grip—Jamie Young, Billy Pearson; Grips—Walt Royle, Louis Cicero, Mike Landsburg, Randy Verdugo, Ken King; 2nd Unit Key Grip—Mark Gambino; Transportation Coordinator—Mike McDuffer; Transportation Captain—Gerald Henry; Transportation Co-Captain—Eddie Demerst; Drivers—Sam Papailo, Tommy "Bluto" Smith; Editorial Supervisor—Doug Haines; 1st Assistant Editor—Jody Fidele; 2nd Assistant Editor—Debbie Ross; Assistant Editors—Gus Medina, Caoilfhionn Sweeney; Editorial Production Assistant—Rob Anderson; Editorial Computer System—Riggs Eckelberry; EMC2 Systems Provided by—Preferred Video Products; EMC2 Assistants—Jon Miles, Alan Ravick; Post Production Supervisor—Gary Chandler; Post Production Sound—Skywalker Sound; Re-recording Mixers—Mathew Iadarola, Gary Gegan; Recordists—Rich Gooch, Robert Jansen; Stage Engineer—John Rotondi; ADR Mixer—Bob Deschaine; ADR Recordists—Ellen Heuer, Joan Rowe; Sound Transfers—Post Master; Orchestration—Tim Simonec; Additional Orchestration—Larry Kenton; Music Preparation—Gregg Nestor; Conductor—Tim Simonec; Choral Conductor—Dennis J. Tini; Music Editor—Doug Lackey; Music Scoring Mixer—Dennis Sands; Assistant to Mr. Loduca—Trisha Hagan; Digital Audio Editorial—Electric Melody Studios, Inc.; Sound Designer—Alan Howarth; Sound Supervisors—Steve Williams, M.P.S.E., Alan Howarth; ADR Supervisor—Craig Clark; ADR—Brian Risner, M.P.S.E., Miguel Rivera, M.P.S.E., Ken Burton; Dialogue—Rick Freeman, Jim Brookshire; Sound Effects—Lance Brown, Lewis Goldstein, Larry Goodwin, Jack Levy, Paul Menichini, George Nemzer, Jason King; Foley Programming—Jackson Schwartz; Assistants—Gayle Wesley, John Chalfant; Apprentices—Martin Vites, Anne Laing; Technical Support—Malcolm Cecil, Randy Honaker, Burke Greer; Spatial Audio Processing—B.A.S.E.; Mechanical Effects Supervisor—Vern Hyde; Mechanical Effects Foreman—Gary Jones; Effects Technicians: Andrew Hyde, David Wogh, Brian Rae, Michael Faba, Jeff Hyde, Richard Jacobson, Mary Nelson; Pyrotechnicians—Gary Bentley, Dan Cangemi; Special Makeup Effects—Kurtzman,

Nicotero & Berger EFX Group; Special Makeup Effects Supervisors—Robert Kurtzman, Gregory Nicotero, Howard Berger; Mechanical Department—Mark Goldberg, Jeff Edwards, Wayne Toth, Mark Rappaport; Sculptors/Modelmakers—Brent Armstrong, John Bisson, David Smith, Andy Clement, Paul Sciacca; Lab Technicians: Hank Carlson, Melanie Tooker, Christopher Robbins, Mark Hofeling, Terry Prince, David Haft; Coordinator—Susan Mallon; Form Fabricator—William Bryan; Seamstress—Karen Mason; Ash and Sheila Makeup Effects—Alterian Studios, Inc.; Project Supervisor—Tony Gardner; Evil Ash Skeleton Project Foreman—Bill Sturgeon; Shop Coordinator—John Henny, Jr.; Evil Ash Sculpture and Application—Bruce Spaulding Fuller; Evil Sheila Sculpture—Roger Borelli; Likeness Sculpture—James McPherson; Prosthetic Makeup Application—Garrett Immel; Foam Technician—Greg Solomon; Mechanical Design—David Penikas, Mark Goldberg; Hair Technicians—Max Alvarez, Becky Ochoa; Skeletal Assistance—Vance Hartwell; Fiberglass Fabrication—John Calpin; Molds—Scary Gary Pawlowski, James Roland; Foam Cosmetics—Carolyn Oros; Production Assistants—Tim Turner, Robert Meyer Burnett, Scott Malchus; Opticals Compositing—24 Hour Post, Huck Penzell; Negative Cutter—Dave Parmenter & Associates; Color Timer—Phil Hetos; Titles Design—Jennifer Berkowitz; Title Animation and Montage Compositing—Perpetual Motion Pictures; Visual Effects Supervisor—Richard Malzahn; Optical Supervisor—Robert Habros; Animator—Sallie McHenry; Ink and Paint—Heather Davis, Judith Bell, Liz Lord; "Book of the Dead" Animation and Design—Tom Sullivan; Special Visual Effects—Introvision International, Inc.; Producers—Andy Naud, Linda Landry-Nelson, Nick Davis; Camera Technicians—David Stump, John Mesa, Mike Rall, Dave Zanzinger, Dave Parks; Assistants—Chris Briles, Evan Taylor; Stop Motion Supervisor—Peter Kleinow; Puppet Creator—Mike Joyce; Sculptor—Dan Platt; Assistant Art Director—Charles Wood; Draftsman—Dan Ross; Story Board Artists—Matsume Suzuki, James Mayeda, Dough Leffler; Model Shop Supervisor—Gene Rizzardi; Model Shop Coordinator—Laura Cram; Modelmakers: Glen Harrison, Carl Bostrom, Adam Hill, Gary Young, Omei Eaglerider, Olivia Rameriz, Ana Ellis, Zuzana Swansen, Bruce Macray; Painters—Barbara Bordo, Renee Prince; Mechanical Effects—Dave Hettmer; Assistant Director—Heather Ling; Production Coordinator—Laura Lutrell; Assistant Coordinators—Lynne Goldhammer, Rob Rinko; Production Assistants — Shana Babbs, Jay Veal; Gaffers — Rich Sands, Dave Amann; Key Grip — John Harlan; Stage Crew: Gary Drew, Fred Johnson, Bob Fisher, Tim Studley, Steve Bishart, Jeff Aherns, Ken Thompson, Dana Axelrod, John Aronson, Brian Tefoe, Larry McCarronJeff AhernsStage Managers — Issy Shabtay, Jeff Ahrens, Michael Carter; Editorial Supervisor — John Travers; Assistant — Shelly Adajian; Optical Supervisor — Spencer Gill; Payroll Service — All Payments Services; Camera Systems — Clairmont; Grip and Electric Equipment — J&L Service; Insurance — Great Northern Film Brokerage Corp.; Processing — Consolidated Film Industries; Post Production and Re-recording Facilities, Skywalker Sound, a division of LucasArts Entertainment Company. This film recorded digitally in a THX Sound System theater. *Army of Darkness*, the ultimate experience in medieval horror, was filmed in Acton, California, and Hollywood, USA. The producers wish to give special thanks to: The California State Film Commission; The City of Los Angeles. In remembrance of Irvin Shapiro. Clips from *Evil Dead II* 1987, Rosebud Releasing Corp. through the courtesy of the Paravision International Group. Color by Deluxe

SYNOPSIS: *Army of Darkness* is a very funny sequel to the *Evil Dead* horror series. In this film, Ash, an S-Mart department store clerk from the housewares division, is transported by an evil force back to either the Dark Ages or medieval Britain. The protagonist figures the time to be 1300 A.D. but he winds up at the castle of Lord Arthur. Arthur's advisor is called the Wiseman, but he looks like every other movie image of Merlin.

The storyline is that an evil force has been released by the discovery of a book called *Necronomicon Ex Mortis*. Arthur's time is besieged by strange beasts and demons so Ash must find the book in order to put all that to rest and return home. In *Evil Dead II* the evil had gotten into Ash's hand and his hand went bad, so he cut it off at the wrist with a chainsaw. Now he wears the chainsaw as a hand and totes a shotgun as well.

Arthur has just defeated and taken as prisoner Henry the Red, duke of Shale and lord of the Northlands. He captures Ash too. Back at his castle, Arthur has Ash thrown into a pit, which contains one of the evil beings.

With his chainsaw and Indiana Jones–style techniques, Ash temporarily defeats the creature and escapes the pit. He promptly knocks Arthur out and frees Henry and his men.

Presumably because he's out of gasoline for the thing, Ash abandons the chainsaw and constructs a mechanical hand for himself. Now ready for anything, he has a romantic night with the beautiful Sheila and in the morning heads out to locate the book. Finding it, he speaks the incantation incorrectly, thus releasing even more evil.

On his way back to the castle with the book, the evil catches up with him, gets inside him and clones the Evil Ash, who raises an army of dead warriors. He then has Sheila kidnapped and converts her into a witch. The army of the dead attack the castle and almost win but Duke Henry shows up with his forces to turn the tide of battle. The dead are routed, the book and Sheila are saved and Ash returns to his own time and his job at S-Mart.

Arthur and the Square Knights of the Round Table (1972)
51 minutes; Color; Cartoon; Copyright 1972, Southern Star Film Investments; Southern Star Sales; New Family Movies; Distributed by Simitar Entertainment, Inc.; Simitar item #6161

CREDITS: Voices — Lola Brooks, John Ewart, Kevin Golsby, John Meillon, M. O'Sullivan; Animation — Kevan Roper, P. Luschwit, Gus McLaren, G. M. Cooke, D. MacKinnon, S. Barry, Leif Gram, Ray Bartle, Jean Tych, Vivien Ray, John Burge, Eddy Graham; Backgrounds — P. Connell; Layout — C. Cuddington; Music — Clare Bail; Sound — R. Bowden; Camera — G. Sharpe; Checker — Zora Bubica; Scripts — Lyle Martin, Rod Hull, M. Robinson, John Palmer, A. Buzo; Director — Zoran Janjic; Producer — Walter J. Hucker

SYNOPSIS: *Arthur and the Square Knights of the Round Table* was an Australian television cartoon series. This 51-minute tape includes ten of the shorts, 7 of them approximately 7 minutes long, 3 of them a minute or less. A video tape released by Active Home Video in 1984 evidently had more of the series and ran

80 minutes. Unfortunately it is no longer available.

Aimed at young children, *Arthur and the Square Knights* are very silly, very simple productions. The animation style itself is reminiscent of the old *Rocky the Flying Squirrel* and *Rocky and Bullwinkle Show* cartoons, though these are much less sophisticated and include almost none of the adult humor that those programs incorporated. This tape apparently excerpts episodes from the midst of the series, since some of the characters are not introduced. The witch for instance is never named.

SEGMENT 1: "THE FLYING MACHINE"

The town crier of Camelot announces a contest. Whoever can build a flying machine will win a holiday to "historic Atlantis" and 1,000 crowns of spending money. The court jester makes a balloon that doesn't get off the ground. Merlin produces a helicopter which explodes. Lancelot's airplane looks so promising, however, that the witch has the Black Knight put her magic broom aboard the craft. The plane does fly, but with Lancelot and King Arthur aboard, the broom answers the witch's call and they crash outside of her mountain-top castle. The jester gets his balloon to work and rescues the King and his Knight.

SEGMENT 2: "THE GREAT JOUST"

Sir Sinister and Sir Dexter challenge sirs Lancelot and Gawain to a joust. Before the contest, the evil duo pour water on Lancelot's armor (causing it to fall apart from rust) and glue on Gawain's (making him nearly immobile) and by their trickery win the first round. Before the second round Sinister and Dexter convince the physical trainer of Camelot, Squire Fitzafiddle, to suggest to King Arthur that he order Lancelot and Gawain into a fitness program immediately. The plan backfires though; instead of exhausting the heroes, Lancelot and Gawain are strengthened and win the day.

SEGMENT 3: "KING'S DIET"

King Arthur is on a diet that he doesn't

like. He sneaks into the kitchen and steals some soup that is simmering in a large cauldron on the stove. It turns out to be the cook's laundry and Arthur turns green.

SEGMENT 4: "PINK IS IN"

Arthur's overbearing mother-in-law, Lady Gertrude, decides to sell her castle and move in with the kids. She immediately decorates Camelot in pink. Arthur hires the scariest outlaw in the forest to kidnap the woman. She of course decorates the outlaw's cave in pink. The outlaw offers to pay Arthur to take her back, but Arthur declines.

SEGMENT 5: "TIMBER"

Merlin warns that the coldest night in 30 years is about to fall. Everyone starts hunting for firewood. The witch sends the Black Knight to plant an exploding log among Lancelot's wood. All of the Black Knight's efforts fail and he winds up accidentally bringing the bomb back to the witch's castle. It explodes in her fireplace, destroying her home.

SEGMENT 6: "PLAY GYPSY, PLAY"

Guinevere throws a garden party and the witch and the Black Knight sneak in disguised as gypsies. The witch stirs up trouble between Arthur and Lancelot. When the two nobles decide to joust it out, Guinevere intervenes, making them sit down to tea. Things are patched up and they discover these are false gypsies when the Black Knight is unable to play the fiddle.

SEGMENT 7: UNTITLED SHORT

At the start of a new day, first the Queen, then Lancelot beat poor King Arthur into the castle bathroom.

SEGMENT 8: "THE JOKER"

Sir Percival the practical joker comes to court, aggravating everyone with exploding cigars, collapsing chairs, electric-eel-charged handshakes and other nuisances.

SEGMENT 9: "KNIGHT SCHOOL DROPOUT"

The witch discovers that the Black

Knight can't write and Lancelot is assigned to teach school that day.

SEGMENT 10: UNTITLED SHORT
Lancelot is bothered by a fly at bedtime.

Arthur and the Square Knights of the Round Table (1984)
Not viewed; 80 minutes; Color; Cartoon; Copyright 1984, Australia; Copyright 1990, United Kingdom; API Television

Same as previous entry with more episodes.

Arthur and the Sword see under Fables and Legends: English Folk Heroes

The Arthurian Tradition
Not viewed; 1 Compact disc; Films for the Humanities and Sciences #AUF6948; Available for Macintosh or Windows

SYNOPSIS: Examines the mythical and historical bases of the legends of King Arthur. Features include:

> Text of *Le Morte D'Arthur*
> > Text of *Idylls of the King*
> > Excerpts from: *Ruin of Briton* (Gildas), *The History of the Kings of Britain* (Geoffrey), *Life of Merlin* (Geoffrey) and *History of the Britons* (Nennius)
> > > Interactive
> > > Guides to Arthurian internet sites
> > > Interviews with Arthurian heroes
> > > Recreations of battles
> > > Accounts of Drustan, Hengist, Urien and others
> > > Theories of the Holy Grail and the Knights Templar
> > > Discourse by Nikolaievich Tolstoi
> > > Filmography
> > > Bibliography

Arthur's Departure see Ymadawiad Arthur

Arthur's Quest (2000)
Not viewed; Crystal Sky International

CAST: Eric Christian Olsen (Artie/King Arthur); Arye Gross (Merlin); Katie Johnston

(Gwen); Zach Gallagan (King Pendragon); Catherine Oxenberg (Morgana); Kevin Elston (Dark Knight); Clint Howard (Mr. Whitney); Gregory Poppen (Alley Thug); Brion James (Trent); J. F. Pryor (Slagador); Robby Seager (Young Arthur); Alexandra Paul (Caitlin Regal)
CREDITS: Director—Neil Mandt; Writers—Lance W. Dreesen, Clint Hutchison, Gregory Poppen; Camera—Anton Floquet

SYNOPSIS: To save a young King Arthur from the evil Morgana, Merlin sends Arthur to the America of the future. Years later, when Merlin goes to get Arthur, the boy has become a teenager and does not want to return to the past.

Artists at WGBH, Boston (1976)
Music Concerts; (*Tristan and Isolde* by Wagner); Copyright 1976, New Television Workshop

No further information available.

Artus, Merlin a Prchlici (1995)
Not viewed

Babylon 5: "A Call to Arms" (1998)
Approximately 120 minutes; Color; Live Action; Copyright 1998, Warner Bros. Pay TV, Cable and Network Features

CAST: Bruce Boxleitner (John Sheridan); Jerry Doyle (Michael Garibaldi); Jeff Conaway (Zack Allan); Carrie Dobro (Dureena Nafel); Peter Woodward (Technomage Galen); Tony Wood (Leonard Anderson); Tracy Scoggins (Elizabeth Lochley); Tony Maggio (Drake); Michael Harris (Bishop); Scott MacDonald (First Officer); Wayne Alexander (Drakh); Carlos Bernard (Communications); Burt Bulos (Navigation); Ron Campbell (Drazi); David Coburn (Minbari Ranger); Matt Gallini (Roff); Valeria Ghiran (ISN Reporter); Marjean Holden (Navigation); Endre Hules (Yuri); Tim O'Hare (First Mage); Tom Ramirez (Second Mage); LaRita Shelby-Mullen (Lynne); Kayla Spell (Sarah)
CREDITS: Music—Evan H. Chen; Editor—Skip Robinson; Production Designer—John Iacovelli; Director of Photography—Frederick V. Murphy II; Conceptual Consultant—Harlan Ellison; Co-Producer—Slip Beaudine; Executive Producers—Douglas Netter, J. Michael Straczynski; Produced by—John Copeland; Created by—J.

The cast of *Babylon 5*: (standing, left to right) Jerry Doyle (Garibaldi), Claudia Christian (Ivanova), Peter Jurasik (Londo), Mira Furlan (Delenn), Andrea Thompson (Talia Winters), Andreas Katsulas (G'Kar), Richard Biggs (Dr. Franklin), and (seated) Michael O'Hare (Sinclair).

Michael Straczynski; Written by—J. Michael Straczynski; Director—Michael Vejar; Associate Producer—Susan Norkin; Unit Production Manager—Skip Beaudine; 1st Assistant Director—Doug Wise; 2nd Assistant Director—David McWhirter; Casting—Fern Chapman, C.S.A., Mark Paladini, C.S.A.; Costume Designer—Tina Haatainen Jones; Visual Effects Produced by—Netter Digital Equipment; Supervising Animators—Harry Hendrickson, Tom Helmers; Systems Engineer—Larry Stanton; CG Design and Animation Team: Bill Arbanas, Tim Everitt, Jim Hoffman, H.W. Parker, Larry W. Bowman, Ed-

ward Helmers, Rich Jeffreys III, Andrew Romine; Visual Effects Supervisor—Steve R. Moore; Visual Effects Art Director—Timothy E. Earls; Compositors—Ken Busick, Kim Hoven Anderson; Concept Designs—Luc Mayrand; Movie Makeup Effects Created by—John Vulich, Optic Nerve-Studio; Special Makeup Effects Artists—Jerry Gergely, Gabriel De Cunto; Makeup Effects Supervisors—Jeff Farley, Mark Gabarino; Makeup Effects Sculptors—John Wheaton, Glenn Eisner; Art Director—Mark Louis Walters; Set Decorator—Jason Howard; Property Master—Dark Hoffman; Graphic Artists—Doreen Austria, Cathy

Coultas; Construction Coordinator — Curtis Laseter; Scenic Artist — Mathew Plummer; Costume Supervisor — Kim M. Holly; Key Costume — Linda Huse; Key Makeup Artist — Cinzia Zanetti; Department Head for Hair — Barbara Wilder Pearlman; Key Hairstylist — Kim M. Ferry; Hair and Makeup — Tegan Taylor; Camera Operator — Peter Kowalski; 1st Assistant Camera — Mike McEveety; Gaffer — Carlos Torres; Key Grip — Chris Nagle; Best Boy Electric — Nathaniel Roberts; 2nd 2nd Assistant Director — David Fudge; Special Effects Supervisor — Mike Del Genio; Stunt Coordinator — Kerry Rossall; Dolly Grip — Charles S. Lantz, Jr.; Best Boy Grip — John Schultz; Production Sound Mixer — Don H. Matthews, C.A.S.; Sound Designer — Harry Cohen; Sound Effects Editors — Elisabeth Flaum, Laura Pratt, Tim Walston; Dialogue Editors — Paul Curtis, John C. Stuver, MPSE; Re-recording Mixers — Marshall Garlington, Juan Peralta, Ken Teaney, C.A.S.; Sound Supervisor — Michael Payne; 1st Assistant Editor — John Burrus; Assistant Editor — Jennifer Vejar; Apprentice Editor — Maritza Suarez; Post Production Coordinator — Pam Oseransky; Production Coordinator — Celeste Healy; Script Supervisor — Kate Lewis; Production Accounting Services provided by Oberman, Tivoli & Miller, Ltd.; Production Accountant — Mike Hoover; Script Coordinator — Tracy Yates; Executive Producer's Assistants — Tracie Drenning, Karen Harrell, Joanne Higgins; Reference Editor — Fiona Avery; Producer's Associate — Jeffrey Willerth; Special Effects Contact Lens Consultant — Jonathan Gording, D.D.; Filmed with Panavision™ Cameras and Lenses; Color by Pacific Film Laboratories, Electronic Laboratories, Lases Pacific, MFDIA Corporation; Digital Sound and re-recording by IFX, Dolby Entertainment; Babylon 5 soundtrack album is available from Sonic Images Records, SI # B502-2; Babylonian Productions, Inc.; Warner Bros. Domestic Pay TV, Cable and Network Features; A Time Warner Entertainment Company

SYNOPSIS: The television science fiction series *Babylon 5* ran for five years, from 1994 through the end of 1998. The made for television movie *Babylon 5: A Call to Arms* is both the final episode of the original series and the introductory story to a spinoff series (see *Crusade* entry) scheduled to begin some time in 1999).

The whole series *Babylon 5* had Arthurian elements in it. The space station which gives the show its name became the center of an alliance of previously warring planets. They are drawn together to oppose an outside invader, the "Shadows." The character John Sheridan can be seen as the King Arthur of the tale. During the show's five-year run, there were two specifically Arthurian episodes, "Grail" and "A Late Delivery from Avalon" (see those entries).

"A Call to Arms" takes place several years after the events depicted in the last regular show of the series. Sheridan, now the president of the Alliance, goes with his old friend Garibaldi to a secret construction station orbiting Mars. Two new ships are nearing completion, destroyers named *Victory* and *Excalibur*. These ships combine the technologies of humans and two others races and are more sophisticated than anything else ever built.

Interrupting his inspection tour, a message comes in for Sheridan. Taking the message in a private office, the strange transmission hypnotizes the president for 20 minutes.

Shortly afterwards, while resting, Sheridan has a dream-like vision of standing on the surface of a burning, dead planet. A strange being called Galen is there as well. This Druidic figure has been watching Sheridan, literally in a crystal ball. He tells Sheridan that the dead world is the result of an experiment, a test of a weapon system. In tones reminiscent of Merlin's exhortations in the film *Excalibur*, Galen tells Sheridan, "Remember what you have seen."

Sheridan comes out of the trance determined to get to Babylon 5. Once there, he meets up with two others who were similarly visited by Galen. The upshot of Galen's purpose is to warn people that the evil Drakh, former allies of the Shadows, have decided to try to take over where the Shadows left off — namely in conquering the galaxy. The Drakh are in possession of a weapon left behind by the Shadows, a "Death Cloud" which is a planet destroying device. The planet that Galen showed his contacts was the test of the Death Cloud; the next target is Earth itself.

The two others who now team up with

Sheridan are Dureena Nafeel, an accomplished thief, and Captain Anderson of the ship *Charon*. Once clear on their mission, these three head back to Mars and hijack the two new destroyers. With Anderson at the helm of *Victory* and Sheridan commanding the *Excalibur* they first visit the planet they'd seen in their visions and confirm that it has been destroyed.

As they are about to leave the area, four Drakh ships approach and a running battle starts. *Victory* and *Excalibur* chase the Drakh vessels until they disappear into a "Null Field" in space. *Excalibur* follows them in and is immediately surrounded by a swarm of Drakh ships — the main attack fleet itself. Sheridan manages to get *Excalibur* out just ahead of the fast moving enemy. *Excalibur* and *Victory* make their best speed towards Earth and just ahead of the Drakh fleet, transmitting warnings as they go.

At Earth the battle is met. Things do not go well for the Earth forces and *Victory* is damaged. Sheridan determines to attack the center of the enemy's fleet — the planet destroyer itself. Finding its control center *Victory* moves in ahead of *Excalibur* but is almost completely disabled. Anderson sacrifices himself and his crew by ramming his ship into the control center, destroying it.

The Death Cloud launches its weapons randomly and ineffectually but it is rigged with a doomsday device. Though the enemy fleet departs, drones are released which blanket Earth with a sinister spray. Scientists analyze the spray and learn that it is a biogenic plague, a virus that will take five years to adapt to human beings. If a cure isn't found in that time, the entire population of Earth will die. The planet is quarantined.

Because the virus was designed by Shadow technology, there is no hope of developing a cure on Earth. The antidote must be found out in the galaxy somewhere. *Excalibur* is turned into a traveling research laboratory and Sheridan puts the resources of his White Star fleet at the disposal of this quest. "Legend says," Sheridan states, "that the real Excalibur would return in our greatest hour of need ... I guess this is it."

So the stage is set for the upcoming series *Crusade*. If this final battle against the Drakh was the equivalent of Arthur's Battle of Badon, then it seems Camelot will know no twenty or so years of idyllic peace. The knights of this Round Table are shipping out immediately on a Quest for a new Holy Grail — a cure for a plague.

Babylon 5: "Grail" (1993)

Television series episode; 1 hour; Color; Science Fiction/Live Action; Originally aired July 6, 1994; Copyright 1993, PTN Consortium; Copyright 1996, Time Warner Entertainment Co., LP Production #109

CAST: Michael O'Hare (Comdr. Jeffrey Sinclair); Claudia Christian (Lt. Comdr. Susan Ivanova); Jerry Doyle (Security Chief Michael Garibaldi); Mira Furlan (Delenn); Richard Biggs (Dr. Stephen Franklin); Andrea Thompson (Talia Winters); Stephen Furst (Vir); Bill Mumy (Lennier); Caitlin Brown (Na'Toth); Andreas Katsulas (G'Kar); Peter Jurasik (Londo); David Warner (Aldous Gajic); William Sanderson (Deuce); Tom Booker (Jinxo); Jim Norton (Ombuds Wellington); Linda Lodge (Mirriam Runningdear); Ardwight Chamberlain (Kosh); John Flinn (Mr. Flinn); Marianne Robertsons (Tech. #1)

CREDITS: Created by — J. Michael Straczynski; Director of Photography — John C. Flinn III, A.S.C.; Conceptual Consultant — Harlan Ellison; Co-Producer — Richard Compton; Producer — John Copeland; Written by — Christy Marx; Director — Richard Compton; Executive Producers — Douglas Netter, J. Michael Straczynski; Associate Producer — George Johnsen; Story Editor — Lawrence G. Ditillio; Music by — Christopher Franke; Music Performed by — Christopher Franke, The Berlin Symphonic Film Orchestra; Production Designer — John Iacovelli; Casting by — Mary Jo Slater, C.S.A.; Unit Production Manager — Kevin G. Cremin; 1st Assistant Director — John Radulovic; 2nd Assistant Director — Pamela Eilerson; Visual Effects Designed by — Ron Thornton; Visual Effects Produced by — Foundation Imaging; Computer Imaging Supervisor — Paul Beigle-Bryant; Visual Effects Producer — Shannon Casey; Visual Effects Supervisor — Mitch Suskin; Series Makeup Effects Created by — Optic Nerve Studios, Everett

Burrell, John Vulich; Art Director — Deborah Raymond; Property Master — Barbara Cole; Set Decorator — Nancy S. Fallace; Leadman — Jason Howard; Costume Designer — Ann Bruice; Costume Supervisor — Kim M. Holly; Key Makeup Artist — Mary Kay Morse; Key Hairstylist — Myke Michaels; Script Supervisor — Haley McLane; Camera Operator — Eyal Gordin; 1st Assistant Camera — Peter B. Kowalski; Gaffer — Marshall Adams; Key Grip — Rick Stribling; Special Effects by — Ultimate Effects; Stunt Coordinator — Kerry Rossall; Sound Mixer — Patrick Mitchell; Sound Design — Jon Johnson, M.P.S.E.; Re-recording Mixers — Terry O'Bright; Todd Orr; Sound Supervisor — Erin Hoien; Editor — Lisa M. Citron; Assistant Editor — Kathie Burr; Digital Effects Animation — Kevin Kutchaver; Post Production Coordinator — Susan Norkin; Production Coordinator — Chris O'Connor; Production Accounting Services Provided by — Oberman, Tivoli & Miller, Ltd.; Production Accountant — Sarah Fischer; Script Coordinator — Rebecca Langenfeld; Executive Producer's Assistant — Tracie Esparza; Producer's Assistant — Kelsey Kline; Filmed with Panavision Cameras and Lenses, 3D Visual Effects System; The Video Toaster Furnished by — Newtek, Inc.; Color by — Pacific Film Laboratories; Electronic Laboratory Laser-Pacific Media Corporation; Digital Sound and Re-recording by — EFX Systems, Dolby Surround

SYNOPSIS: The science fiction television series *Babylon 5* ran from 1994 through the end of 1998. "Grail" was number 15 of a total of 110 *Babylon 5* episodes, airing during the first season of the show's original run. (See also *Babylon 5*: "A Call to Arms" and *Babylon 5*: "A Late Delivery from Avalon.")

In "Grail," a holy man named Aldous Gajic arrives on the space station Babylon 5 from Earth, searching for the Holy Grail. Becoming embroiled with criminals and memory-sucking aliens, Gajic dies but not before passing his quest on to another.

Babylon 5: "A Late Delivery from Avalon" (1995)

Television series episode; 1 hour; Color; Science Fiction/Live Action; Originally aired April 22, 1996; Copyright 1995, PTN Consortium; Production #312

CAST: Bruce Boxleitner (Capt. John Sheridan); Claudia Christian (Comdr. Susan Ivanova); Jerry Doyle (Security Chief Michael Garibaldi); Mira Furlan (Delenn); Richard Biggs (Dr. Stephen Franklin); Bill Mumy (Lennier); Jason Carter (Marcus Cole); Stephen Furst (Vir); Jeff Conaway (Zack Allan); Peter Jurasik (Londo); Andreas Katsulas (G'Kar); Michael York (Arthur); Michael Kagan (Emmett Farquaha); Roger Hampton (Merchant); Dona Hardy (Old Woman); Michael Francis Kelly (Security Guard #1); James Kiriyama-Lem (Med Tech); Robert Schuch (Lurker); Jerry O'Donnell (Security Guard #2)

CREDITS: Created by — J. Michael Straczynski; Edited by — David W. Foster; Production Designer — John Iacovelli; Director of Photography — John C. Flinn III, A.S.C.; Conceptual Consultant — Harlan Ellison; Produced by — John Copeland; Written by — J. Michael Straczynski; Directed by — Michael Vejar; Executive Producers — Douglas Netter, J. Michael Straczynski; Associate Producer — George Johnsen; Music Performed by — Christopher Franke, The Berlin Symphonic Film Orchestra; Unit Production Manager — Skip Beaudine; 1st Assistant Director — Ronnie Chong; 2nd Assistant Director — David McWhirter; Casting — Fern Champion, C.S.A., Mark Paladini, C.S.A.; Costume Designer — Ann Bruice Aling; Visual Effects Designed by — Ron Thornton; Visual Effects Produced by — Foundation Imaging; Computer Imaging Supervisor — Paul Beigle-Bryant; Visual Effects Producer — Shannon Casey; On-Set Visual Effects Supervisor — Ted Rae; Matte Artist — Eric Chauvin; Senior Computer Animators — Adam "Mojo" Lebowitz, John Teska; Composite 2D Animator — Sherry Hitch; System Engineer — Steve Pugh; Series Makeup Effects Created by — Optic Nerve Studios, John Vulich; Makeup Effects Artists — Greg Funk, Will Huff, Fionagh Cush; Makeup Effects Supervisor — Mark Garbarino; Makeup Effects Sculptor — John Wheaton; Art Director — Roland G. Rosenkranz; Set Decorator — Alexandra Rubinstein; Property Master — Mark-Louis Walters; Graphic Artist — Alan Kobayashi; Construction Coordinator — Curtis Laseter; Costume Supervisor — Kim M. Holly; Key Costumer — Linda Huse; Key Makeup Artist — Cinzia Zanetti; Assistant Hair & Makeup — Kim M. Ferry; Key Hairstylist — Traci Smithe; Camera Operator — Peter B. Kowalski; 1st Assistant Camera — Wally Sweeterman; Gaffer — "The" John Smith; Key Grip — John Warner; Best Boy Electric — David H. Neale; Dolly Grip — Kenny Yakkel; 2nd 2nd Assistant Director — Douglas Corring; Special Effects by — Ultimate Effects; Special Effects Supervisor — Paul Sokol; Stunt Coordinator — Kerry Rossall; Sound

Mixer — Linda Coffey; Sound Designer — Paul Menichini; Sound Effects Editor — Michael Moser; Re-recording Mixers — Terry O'Bright, C.A.S., Keith Rogers; Sound Supervisor — John Caggiano; Post Production Supervisor — Susan Norkin; Assistant Editors — Jason Netter, John Burrus; Production Coordinator — Chris O'Connor; Script Supervisor — Haley McLane; Production Accounting Services Provided by — Oberman, Tivoli & Miller, Ltd.; Production Accountant — Mike Hoover; Script Coordinator — Carol Henry; Executive Producers' Assistants — Tracie Esparza, Joanne Higgins; Producer's Associate — E. J. Kavounas; Special Effect Contact Lens Consultant — Jonathan Gording, O.D.; Filmed with Panavision Cameras and Lenses; Lightwave 3D Furnished by — Newtek, Inc.; Color by — Pacific Film Laboratories, Electronic Laboratory Laser-Pacific Media Corporation; Digital Sound & Re-recording by — EFI, The Sound of Pictures, Dolby Surround

SYNOPSIS: Another Arthurian entry in the television science-fiction series *Babylon 5*. "A Late Delivery from Avalon" was number 57 of a total of 110 episodes, airing during the third season of the show's original run. (See also *Babylon 5: "A Call to Arms"* and *Babylon 5: "Grail."*)

In "A Late Delivery from Avalon," Michael York plays a passenger on a shuttle craft headed for the space station Babylon 5. During his trip he has a vision, or dream, of himself walking down a hallway toward a gleaming sword hovering in midair. Smiling, he grasps the weapon.

When the shuttle arrives at the station this character, clad in chainmail and cape, steps through a security gate with a sword at his side. Alarms go off and guards stop him. Unsheathing his sword to protect himself, he asks, "Have I been gone so long?" Further challenged, he declares himself to be Arthur, son of Uther Pendragon.

The station's doctor and another important regular character named Marcus happen to be passing by as this disturbance occurs. Marcus, being of British descent, immediately recognizes what is happening. He steps in to defuse the situation by kneeling before Arthur, stating that they were unprepared for his arrival and that he will notify Galahad, Lancelot and the rest. Arthur becomes angered, saying he knows those knights are all long since dead at the battle of Camlann and that he himself has come a long way through time, but that he is not mad. Marcus still is able to calm the man and lead him off to the medical lab for the doctor to examine him. (Arthur smilingly admits, "I've been poked and prodded by the nine sisters since the Year of Our Lord 515, what is one more?")

Security is unable to find any record of the man; he has no identification on him and no travel papers. In talking with the doctor, Arthur describes his memories of the battle of Camlann — how, as he lay dying, his brother Bedevere pulled him away from the people scavenging for valuables among the bodies. He tells of asking Bedevere three times to return the sword to the Lady of the Lake and of the arrival of a barge carrying three queens and the nine sisters to take him to Avalon.

Later, in a meeting with the captain of the space station, Marcus and the doctor each present their ideas about Arthur. Marcus is prone to believe the man, at least to some extent. He points out that they know of a race who have in the past kidnapped people and held them in stasis until a later time. The doctor disagrees, pointing out that Arthur's speech patterns and vocabulary are all wrong for an ancient Briton. He surmises that some trauma or breakdown has caused the man to take on King Arthur's identity.

Arthur escapes the medical lab and wanders about the station. He comes across an old woman, a member of a class of people called "lurkers," who has been mugged. The thugs stole her only photograph of her deceased husband because it was in a valuable frame. Arthur promises to get it back for her.

He does indeed find the culprits and, wielding his sword with no little skill, vanquishes them. Unfortunately ne'er-do-well reinforcements arrive. Luckily, one of the show's nonhuman regulars happens by and leaps to

Arthur's aid. This big fellow, named G'Kar, thoroughly enjoys the fight for such a good cause and he and Arthur return the photo to the old woman. Celebrating their victory at a bar, Arthur knights his new friend and G'Kar becomes the Red Knight.

Marcus finds them in the bar and convinces Arthur that he must return with him to the lab. G'Kar attempts to go along but is too drunk. G'Kar collapses unconscious on the floor. Arthur looks at him and quips that Gawain had a similar problem with drink and that many mornings they would take one look at him and call him the Green Knight.

The doctor finally digs out the truth about Arthur. His real name is David MacIntyre and he had been a gunnery sergeant aboard a ship that touched off a terrible war. When an alien vessel had approached his ship with its gun ports open, the ship's captain had misinterpreted this as hostility and ordered MacIntyre to open fire. Twenty thousand people died in the battle and MacIntyre had spent the rest of his life blaming himself. He equated the misinterpretation that started the space battle with the legend of a soldier at Camlann striking an adder accidentally, touching off that battle. On the anniversary of the space battle, this Arthur has returned to the region to unburden himself of guilt by giving his sword to the Lady of the Lake.

Marcus and the doctor end up getting one of their female associates on the station to act the part of the Lady of the Lake. Arthur solemnly gives her the sword and, freed of his self-imposed mental burdens, he is able to begin a therapeutic return to reality. Finally healed, he leaves Babylon 5 and goes to G'Kar's world, where he will help the resistance in a war.

The Ballad of King Arthur (1973)

Not viewed; Filmstrip; 80 frames; Color; 35mm, 33⅓ record included; Copyright 1973, Scholastic Magazines; The National Gallery of Art, New York; From the series Dreamers and Visionaries, Art and Man; Library of Congress

Call #CB 351; Library of Congress Catalogue #79730700/F; Dewey Decimal #940.1

SYNOPSIS: This is an introduction to Middle Ages studies, utilizing the legend of King Arthur.

Battlefield see Doctor Who: "Battlefield"

Beowulf see under Fables and Legends: English Folk Heroes

Beowulf and the Old English Tradition (1984)

Title on film: Beowulf and Old English Literature; 38 minutes; Color; Documentary; Copyright 1984, 1985, Films for the Humanities, Inc.; Video #AUF765

CREDITS: Produced by — Stephen Mantell; Written by — Carroll Moulton; Associate Producer — David Mantell; Art Research — Ann Priester

SYNOPSIS: This film is of interest because of its discussion of the history of English literature which led up to the Arthurian tales. Its main topic, obviously, is not Arthurian literature at all. It is mentioned, however, that it was a blending of mythical Celtic elements with Anglo-Norman literary versions that gave us the legends of Arthur and the Round Table.

The tape first reviews early British history. Despite 400 years of occupation, Romanization was never complete. In fact the Picts were never conquered at all. In time the Angles, Saxons and Jutes swept through the land while the Celts withdrew into Scotland, Wales and Cornwall. In the late 800s Old Norse was added to the linguistic and cultural mix with the absorption of the Danes and Vikings.

The discussion continues through the Norman Conquest and its ramifications, including the influence of French and Latin and the dialects of Middle English. It is pointed out that the anonymous author of Sir Gawain and the Green Knight wrote in a northwestern form of Middle English.

The Best of the Broadway Musicals: Original Cast Performances from The Ed Sullivan Show (1993)

56 minutes; Color, Black and White; Live Action; Copyright 1993, Sofa Entertainment; Walt Disney Home Video #2235; Buena Vista Home Video

CREDITS: Narrated by—John Raitt; Executive Producer—Andrew Solt; Produced by—Greg Vines; Edited by—Debra Sanderson, Stewart Schill, Leslie Tong; Written and Directed by—Andrew Solt; New Music by—Artie Butler; On-Line Editor—Charles Migel; Post Production Supervisor—Debra Sanderson; On-Line Assistant—Ray Wolf; Re-recording Mixer—Bob Manahan; Post Production Audio—Andrew Somers; Production Coordinator—Catherine DeMeis; Assistant to Mr. Solt—Donna Langley; Legal Clearances—Melody Siroty, Scott Cruchley, Media Rights, Inc.; Editorial Assistants—Kevin Cope, Les Hidvegi; Production Staff—Jenee Mendelsohn, Dave Moore; Restoration Consultant—David Crosthwait; Still Photographs—CBS Photo Archives Candillo, Irv Haberman, Romano, L. Lautenberger, Bob Stahman; Playbill is a registered trademark of Playbill, Inc., NYC, used by permission; We appreciate the talents of the many creative people who worked on *Toast of the Town* and *The Ed Sullivan Show* during its 23 years on the air, especially Producers—Marlo Lewis, Rober Precht; Directors—John Wray, Tim Kiley; Original Music Conducted by—Ray Bloch; Executive in Charge of Production—Steven L. Pollock

SYNOPSIS: This is a collection of 12 performances from Ed Sullivan's classic television shows. Spanning a period of 14 years, they include numbers with the original cast members from shows like *Oklahoma!* and *West Side Story*. The segment of note for this book is the appearance of Richard Burton and Julie Andrews singing "What Do Simple Folk Do" from the Broadway musical *Camelot*.

This is one of only a few tapes available with any footage of the two from that show. (See also the entries for *Julie Andrews Sings Her Favorite Songs, Lerner and Loewe Special, Broadway! A Musical History* and *The Very Best of the Ed Sullivan Show*. Unfortunately, this version of the Broadway show was never filmed; Richard Harris and Vanessa Redgrave starred in the subsequent Hollywood production of *Camelot* for the screen.

As for the scene for "What Do Simple Folk Do," the king and queen are both depressed. Arthur knows that Gwenevere is in love with Lancelot. Gwenevere is in agony over the affair herself. They are sitting silently in their chambers together when the queen asks the song title as a question. In the midst of it they manage to cheer up briefly and Burton does an uncharacteristic little dance step, quite a sight from the "famous Welsh Shakespearean actor," as Sullivan had introduced him.

Of other historical interest is Raitt's narrated prologue to the Burton and Andrews segment. He points out that *Camelot* was a favorite of the Kennedy White House and that the line "for one brief shining moment" would always be associated with Kennedy's time as president of the United States.

Best of the Fests, 1988: "Cerridwen's Gift" (1988)

90 minutes; "Cerridwen's Gift" segment: 10 minutes; Color; Animated still illustrations; Copyright 1986, Rose Bond; Copyright 1991, Picture Start, Inc.

CREDITS: Narrator—Fiona Ritchie; Musicians—Skip Paunti (fiddle), Michael Bigland (accordion), Timmy Hayes, Michael Dembraill (guitar, whistle, synthesizer); Engineer—Billie Osley; Recorded at—Nightnoise Studios, Portland, Oregon; Writing—Laurie Meeker; Sound Effects—Don Fibigen, C. Davis Weinber; Baby's Voice—Philip Stubbs; Consultant—Chris Caul; Optical Printing—Alpha Cine Lab; Film by—Rose Bond; Thanks to Jim Bleakfield, Norma Dreifser, Nancy Dawson, Dick Heduse, Joyce Janike, Melissa Mauland, Kent Pinlaski, Joanna Priestley, Bob Spielhelg, Elaine Velasquez, Bob Fencher, Carolyn Wood; Filmed by the Oregon Arts Commission and the Western States Regional Media Arts Foundation.; Award-winning short films from the Ann Arbor, Athens, Chicago International, CINE, Film Arts, New York Expo, Nissan FOCUS, Ottawa, Sinking Creek/Nashville, Student Academy Awards and U.S. Film Festivals

SYNOPSIS: *Best of the Fests, 1988* is a tape containing nine short films. The seventh entry on the tape is the 1986 film "Cerridwen's Gift," a ten-minute animated version of the tale of the birth of the Welsh bard Taliesin.

The narrator opens the film by describing Cerridwen as a woman learned in the three ancient arts of magic, enchantment and divination. She lived on an island with her young daughter and son. Her daughter was a pretty and happy little girl, but the boy was dark and brooding.

Rather than allow the boy to grow up rejected by people, Cerridwen determined to do something to give the boy some advantage. In her book of fairy magic she found the recipe for a brew, three drops of which would bestow upon the boy the gifts of poetic inspiration and prophecy.

Cerridwen prepared a cauldron. She called up spirits to bless the water, then set a fire beneath the cauldron, which was to burn for a year and a day. Gathering herbs and roots at the proper times and adding them to the brew by prescribed methods, Cerridwen spent the year devoted to the project. While she was about her other tasks, Cerridwen had her servant, Gwion Boch, stir the brew.

When the day finally came Cerridwen was exhausted and fell asleep. The brew erupted and three drops of it fell on Gwion's fingers. Cerridwen woke up in time to see Gwion eating the magical potion from his hand. Enraged, she started for Gwion, who promptly turned himself into a rabbit to escape. Cerridwen became a dog to chase him. Gwion jumped into the ocean and became a fish, Cerridwen, close behind, took the shape of an otter. When Gwion leaped from the water as a bird, Cerridwen followed in the form of a hawk. Gwion desperately transformed himself into a wheat seed, but Cerridwen became a hen and ate him.

Thinking she's won, Cerridwen returns to her own form, only to realize the seed is growing inside her. She decides to kill Gwion when he is born, but nine months later is unable to do so. The magic has transformed Gwion into a beautiful child with a shining brow. "Give him to his fate," she tells herself, and she places the infant in a leather-covered wicker basket. She throws the coracle into the weir of the River Dyvi near Aberystwyth.

The baby rested at the bottom of the waters for many years. An unlucky fisherman named Elphin lived in the area. One day a sorceress told him his luck would change if he fished the Dyvi weir. Snagging the coracle, Elphin found the child and named the boy Taliesin, which means "shining brow."

Like King Arthur, the Welsh bard Taliesin may be more legend than reality. Unlike Arthur, however, there are poems existing which are attributed to him. Though he is often placed in a time period just after the Arthurian years, Taliesin's legend has gradually come to be attached to Arthur's. Among the stories connecting the two is the poem *Preiddu Annwfn* in which Taliesin accompanies Arthur on a journey into the Otherworld.

Another is the continuation of the Cerridwen story. Elphin's luck did indeed change so much that he came to brag that he had a wife as good as any lady in King Arthur's court and a bard better than any of Arthur's. This of course caused a serious run-in with King Arthur, the result of which was Elphin's imprisonment. Taliesin's cleverness, trickery and skillful singing, however, saved the day.

While this film does not go into great detail and fails to extend the story of Taliesin's life, it does follow the liveliest part of the legend very closely. A few characters are missing for the sake of simplicity: Tegid Voel, for instance, Cerridwen's husband, and Morda, the blind man who Cerridwen had tend the fire. In the legends, Cerridwen is variously called a witch or a hag. Her appearance in this film as an attractive young mother in a red plaid skirt is certainly more appealing to modern viewers.

The Black Knight (1954)
85 minutes; Color; Live Action; Copyright 1954, Warwick Pictures

CAST: Alan Ladd (John); Patricia Medina (Linet); André Morell (Sir Ontzlake); Harry Andrews (Earl of Yeonil); Peter Cushing (Sir Pala-mides); Anthony Bushell (King Arthur); Laurence Naismith (Major Domo); Patrick Troughton (King Mark); Bill Brandon (Bernard); Ronald Adam (Abbot); Basil Appleby (Sir Hal); Thomas Moore (Apprentice); Jean Lodge (Queen Guinevere); Pauline Jameson (Countess Yeonil); John Kelly (Woodcutter); Elton Hayes (Troubadour); John Laurie (James); Olwen Brookes (Lady Ontzlake); David Paltenghi (High Priest)

CREDITS: Original Screenplay — Alec Coppel; Additional Dialogue — Dennis O'Keefe; Bryan Forbes; Music Composed by — John Addison; Played by — The Royal Philharmonic Orchestra; Conducted by — Muir Mathieson; Ballad "The Bold Black Knight"; Music by — Leo Maguire; Lyrics Composed and Sung by — Elton Hayes; Assistant Producer — Phil C. Samuel, B.S.C.; Director of Photography — John Wilcox; Production Supervisor — Adrian Worker; Art Director — Vetchinsky; Assistant Script Director — John Cox; Camera Director — Ted Moor; Costumes Designed by — Beatrice Dawson; Wardrobe Supervisor — John McCorry; Assistant Director — Phil Shipway; Costuming — Betty Harley; Technicolor Color Consultant — Joan Bridger; Editor — Gordon Pilkington; Makeup Artist — Fred Williamson; Hairdresser — Gordon Bond; Sound Recordists — Charles Knutt; J. G. Smith; Archery Expert — Georg Brown; Choreographer — David Paltenghi; Production — Arthur Alcott; Executive Producers — Irving Allen, Albert R. Broccoli; Director — Tay Garnett; Made at Pinewood Studios, London, England

SYNOPSIS: *The Black Knight* is reminiscent of a number of other Arthurian films and series, including *Knights of the Round Table, The Adventures of Sir Lancelot* and even the 1954 production of *Prince Valiant.* The filming, costuming, sets and acting styles are stereotypically "fifties."

The casting of the stony-faced Alan Ladd in the role of John/Black Knight brings an unusual flavor to the whole production. Ladd, better known for his roles in American Westerns, gives the film a "Shane Goes to King Arthur's Court" feeling.

At the castle of the earl of Yeonil, John, the blacksmith, has just put the finishing touches on a new sword he's made when the blustery Sir Ontzlake enters the shop. After testing its cutting powers, Ontzlake deems it a worthy blade. The fair Linet arrives as well, ostensibly to check on John's progress with the sword, which is to be a surprise for her father, the earl. It is obvious that there is an attraction between Linet and John.

The household repairs to the dining room where Ontzlake reports the news from Camelot. As the Viking raids continue, there is unrest at the court. King Mark is scheduled to leave Camelot the next day and Ontzlake states his distrust of Mark. Mark's court is "full of Saracens and the like," Ontzlake says.

After dinner Linet goes back to the smithy where she tries to express her feelings to John. John is resistant, citing their radically different stations in life. She breaks his resolve however and Yeonil and Ontzlake walk in to find them in a passionate embrace. Sending Linet to her chambers, Yeonil regretfully dismisses John from his employ.

Ontzlake, taking on the role of John's mentor, stays as John packs up to leave. The knight counsels John to be patient, implying that Arthur's rule will eventually make it possible for even a commoner to marry Linet. Ontzlake points out that he himself was not born to knighthood but achieved it through deeds. He hands John the recently completed sword and says, "You made it, now let it make you."

John rides out alone, unaware that horn-helmeted Vikings are attacking the earl's castle. He hasn't gone far though before he looks back and spots the smoke of the fires that the invaders have set. He immediately rides back but arrives too late. Lady Yeonil has been killed, the earl is severely injured and the attackers have gone.

John leaves again, chasing after the two leaders of the Viking attack. He witnesses them removing disguises. They're Saracens! When he follows them to Camelot itself, the culprits turn out to be none other than Sir Palamides and his assistant Bernard. John manages to get into the banquet hall and attack Palamides, but he is stopped by the rest of the knights.

No one but Ontzlake believes John's accusations of treason, but Arthur grants John three months of freedom to come up with proof. The news of the "Viking" attack at Yeonil arrives and Arthur calls all to arms. King Mark and Palamides ride out together. The two are in cahoots, of course, plotting the destruction of Arthur and Camelot.

In a break in the political machinations, John has a run-in with Palamides. He's nearly killed but Ontzlake stops Palamides. Ontzlake takes John under his wing and teaches him sword fighting, jousting and the proper use of daggers. Donning a new suit of armor, John heads off on his own to expose the plotting of Mark and Palamides.

The earl of Yeonil has gone mad at the loss of his wife. He rattles around his destroyed castle alone, not recognizing anyone. Linet thinks that John is a coward, having misinterpreted his rushing off after Palamides as fleeing the attack on her home. There is indeed trouble in Camelot.

Christianity worries King Mark, and he declares to Palamides that when Arthur is defeated, he will restore the old religion of the Druids. The false Vikings attack and wreck a new church, executing the monks before a firing squad of archers. Linet is captured and taken to Stonehenge to be sacrificed by the Druids to their Sun God.

The Black Knight arrives just in time to save her, after having sent word to Camelot for backup support. When the Knights of the Round Table arrive, they drive the Druids off, killing many of them, then proceed to tear down Stonehenge. The Black Knight drops Linet off at Yeonil, but she is promptly captured once more by Palamides.

Trying to find out the whereabouts of this pesky Black Knight, Palamides interviews Linet but she is uncooperative. He hands her over to the murderous Bernard for questioning. The Black Knight again arrives in the nick of time.

Next, John sneaks into Mark's castle, where he overhears Mark and Palamides planning a morning attack on Camelot. Palamides returns to Camelot and informs Arthur that his castle has been burned to the ground by the Vikings, led by none other than the Black Knight. The Black Knight picks that very moment to ride in to Camelot. He is immediately arrested and his identity is revealed. Arthur has him thrown in the dungeon.

Finally realizing her mistake, Linet goes to the dungeon and releases John. Ontzlake comes as well, giving John his sword. John informs Ontzlake, who in turn informs Arthur, of the dawn attack. As final proof of his claims, John kidnaps King Mark and places him in Arthur's bed. Palamides sends Bernard to kill Arthur and the sniveling Mark is killed instead. John kills Bernard and his good name is at last cleared.

In the morning the Saracens (disguised as Vikings still) attack, but instead of being assisted by Mark's forces as planned, they are met by Arthur's defenders. Archers, cavalry and foot soldiers meet in a huge battle outside the castle walls. John slays Palamides and the Saracens are soundly beaten.

As Sir Ontzlake predicted, John is knighted. Arthur offers him whatever boon he might ask and John requests Linet's hand. Happily, Arthur grants the wish.

For details about a nearly identical film, see *Siege of the Saxons.*

The Black Knight (1962)
Popeye Cartoon; Copyright 1962, King Features

No further information available.

The British Isles (1998)
PBS Documentary

No further information available.

Broadway! A Musical History (1988)
Vol. 1: "The Formative Years of Broadway," 110 minutes; Vol. 2: "The Revolution on Broadway," 114 minutes; Color; Documentary; Copyright 1988, Chesney Communications

CREDITS: Narrator — Ron Husmann; Author/Historian — Stanley Green, Author of *Broadway Musicals, Show by Show*; Historian — Gerald Bordman, Author of *American Musical Theatre*; Historian — Ethan Mordden, Author of *Broadway Babies*; Historian — Miles Kreuger, Author of *Showboat*; Musical Samples — Holly Saunders, Ron Husmann; No production credits listed on tape.

SYNOPSIS: *Broadway! A Musical History* is a five-volume set of video cassettes, each running approximately two hours. Designed as an instructional aid, the series is intended to be used in conjunction with Stanley Green's book *Broadway Musicals, Show by Show*.

Each volume consists of four segments. Volume 1 begins with a discussion of the first musical production performed in a theater on the corner of Broadway and Prince Street in Lower Manhattan in 1866. Carrying through to the late 1920s and early 1930s, all the major productions and the people responsible for them are examined. Social and political influences on the shows are also pointed out, from the effects of the Civil War to the post–World War I era.

In the fourth segment of volume 1, one hour and 50 minutes into the tape, Rodgers and Hart's musical adaptation of Twain's *A Connecticut Yankee in King Arthur's Court* is briefly mentioned. It is stated that the 1927-1928 season was the biggest in the history of Broadway. Among the unusually large number of new shows was Rodgers and Hart's *A Connecticut Yankee*, which turned out to be their biggest hit of the 1920s. The musical ran for more than a year, starring Constance Carpenter and William Gaxton. Two black-and-white publicity stills are pictured on the video, as well as a color photo of some playbills and programs from the show.

Volume 4, "The Revolution on Broadway," features a segment (second on the tape) titled "The Golden Era Continues." It includes a nine-minute look at the 1960 production of *Camelot* starring Richard Burton, Julie Andrews and Robert Goulet.

The bulk of the segment consists of Julie Andrews recounting anecdotes and ideas about the production. *Camelot* followed *My Fair Lady* on Broadway, which also starred Andrews. Because of that, it had the largest advance box office sales of any show up to that time.

While Andrews says she enjoyed doing the show very much, she does not feel that justice was done to T. H. White's book, on which it is based. White's *The Once and Future King* is described by Andrews as a massive, four-volume, 30-year work. Condensing it into a two-and-a-half-hour show was problematic, she says. Her main disappointment is with the second half of the production, when it switches from "fairy story" to "great drama and great seriousness." Andrews met White and describes him as a "dead ringer" for Ernest Hemingway and also as very Merlinesque. Her last comment is about how attractive Goulet's legs were in tights.

Robert Goulet also recounts an anecdote or two about the show but nothing revelatory. Several color stills of the original cast are shown.

The Brush in the Stone see The Adventures of Timmy the Tooth: "The Brush in the Stone"

Bugs Bunny in King Arthur's Court (1972)

26 minutes; Color; Cartoon; Copyright 1972, Warner Bros. Television; A Chuck Jones Enterprises Production; Ray Bradbury's name courtesy of Ray Bradbury; Color by Deluxe

CAST: Yosemite Sam (Merlin of Monroe, Baron of Yosemite); Daffy Duck (Arthur, King of England, etc.); Elmer Fudd (Sir Elmer of Fudde); Porky Pig (Varlet, Sir Loin of Pork); Bugs Bunny (Himself)

CREDITS: Voice Characterizations — Mel Blanc; Produced, Directed and Plagiarized by — Chuck Jones; Master Animation — Ben Washam, Virgil Ross, Phil Montore, Lloyd Vaughan, Ken Champin, Manny Perez; Music Composed and Conducted by — Dean Elliott; Key Assistant Animation — Marlene Robinson; Assistant Animators — Jean Washam, Joe Roman, Rochon, Woody Yocum; Editor — Sam Horta; Ink and Paint —

Daffy Duck as "Arthur, King of England, etc." chats with Bugs in *Bugs Bunny in King Arthur's Court.*
©1972, Warner Bros. Television, Chuck Jones Enterprises Production

Celine Miles; Camera — Animagraphics; Elegant Noodling — Linda Clough; Graphics — Don Foster; Production Assistants — Susan Charron, Marjorie Roach; Assistant to the Producer — Marian Dern; Production Manager — Mary Roscoe

SYNOPSIS: A cartoon adaptation of Mark Twain's *A Connecticut Yankee in King Arthur's Court*. This time, drastically off course in his tunneling, Bugs Bunny pops up in the vicinity of Camelot. "Never, never again do I take travel hints from Ray Bradbury," Bugs says. "Last time I took Bradbury's advice, I ended up in the twenty-fifth century as a Martian monocle on Mars," referring to Bradbury's science fiction work *The Martian Chronicles*.

In the meantime, Sir Elmer of Fudde is on a dragon hunt. In escaping Fudde, the dragon rushes past Bugs, singeing the bunny's whiskers. "Something wicked this way went," Bugs says, another reference to a Bradbury work *(Something Wicked This Way Comes)*.

Fudde takes the role of Sir Sagramore in capturing Bugs and bringing him to King Arthur. The bored king (Daffy Duck) sentences Bugs to death. True to Twain's story Bugs not only saves himself by predicting an eclipse but becomes the power behind the throne, stealing Merlin's thunder. Bugs starts an armor factory for endangered species — deer armor, squirrel armor and so forth, using the dragon as the power source. Ultimately Bugs pulls the sword from the stone and becomes King Arth-Hare.

For aficionados, this is not one of the better Bugs Bunny cartoons. In spite of the occasional adult joke, it lacks the energy, visual detail and sophistication of earlier incarnations of these classic characters. Even Mel Blanc's famous voice sounds tired and unenthusiastic throughout the film, approaching its old verve only with some of Porky Pig's incredible stuttering. But, for all of its slapstick nonsense, *Bugs Bunny in King Arthur's Court* is a fairly good children's version of Twain's original.

Bugs Bunny's Easter Funnies: "Knighty Knight Bugs" (1950)

50 minutes; Color; Cartoon; Copyright 1977, 1959, 1958, 1957, 1954, 1953, 1952, 1950, Warner Bros., Inc.; A DePatie-Freleng Production; Warner Bros. Animation, Inc.; Easter Sequences Produced by DFE Films

CREDITS: Executive Producer — Hal Geer; Supervising Director — Friz Freleng; Sequences Directed by — Friz Freleng, Chuck Jones, Robert McKimson; Voice Characterizations — Mel Blanc; Voice of Granny — June Foray; Animation, Stories, Backgrounds, Layouts and Artwork by Members of the Motion Picture Screen Cartoonists Local 839; Easter Story Written by — Friz Freleng, David Detiege; Directed by — Robert McKimson, Gerry Chiniquy; Easter Sequences Animation — Don Williams, Robert Richardson, Warren Batchelder, Bob Be Miller, John Gibbs, Nelson Shin, Norm McCabe, Bob Matz, Bob Bransford; Easter Sequence Layouts — Bob Givens; Easter Sequence Backgrounds — Richard H. Thomas; Easter Sequence Editor — Rick Steward; Title Design by — Arthur Leonardi; Music — Doug Goodwin, William Lava, John Seely, Milt Franklin, Carl Stalling; "Mister Easter Rabbit" Music by — Maddy Russell, Words by — Jack Segal

SYNOPSIS: *Bugs Bunny's Easter Funnies* is a series of excerpts from Looney Tune cartoons spliced together around an Easter story. It includes a two-minute segment of the cartoon "Knighty Knight Bugs." The entire six-minute version of "Knighty Knight Bugs" can be viewed on *Friz Freleng's Looney Looney Looney Bugs Bunny Movie*.

Bugs Bunny's Hare Raising Tales: "Knight Mare Hare" (1955)

45 minutes; Color; Cartoon; Copyright 1955/1988, Vitaphone Corporation and Merrie Melodies; A Warner Bros. Cartoon; Warner Home Video #11831; A Subsidiary of Warner Bros., Inc.; A Warner Communications Company; Warner Bros. Pictures Presents; Color by Technicolor

CREDITS: Story by — Tedd Pierce; Animation — Ken Harris, Ben Washam, Abe Levitow, Richard Thompson; Layouts — Ernie Nordli; Backgrounds — Philip DeGuard; Voice Characterizations — Mel Blanc; Music Direction — Milt Franklin; Directed by — Chuck Jones

SYNOPSIS: This is a collection of Bugs Bunny cartoons. The one to look for is entitled

"Knight Mare Hare," running from 9:15 to 16:24 on the tape.

In another takeoff on Mark Twain's *A Connecticut Yankee in King Arthur's Court*, Bugs takes the place of Hank Morgan. An apple falls on his head, sending him to the dream land of Camelot. An unusual cast of knights, like Sir O of K, Sir Osis of Liver and the Earl of Watercress, are after Bugs. However, not even a fire-breathing dragon is a match for Bugs's seltzer water and other antics.

A Peter Lorre–esque Merlin of Monroe enters into a magic powder contest with Bugs and loses. Bugs finally hits himself on the head with an apple to get back home.

Camelot (1967)

180 minutes; Color; Live Action; Copyright 1967, Warner Bros., Inc.; A Warner Bros./ Seven Arts Presentation; Warner Home Video #11084; A Subsidiary of Warner Bros., Inc.; A Warner Communications Company; Technicolor, Filmed in Panavision

CAST: Richard Harris (King Arthur); Vanessa Redgrave (Guenevere); Franco Nero (Lancelot du Lac); David Hemmings (Mordred); Lionel Jeffries (Pellinore); Laurence Naismith (Merlyn); Pierre Olaf (Dap); Estelle Winwood (Lady Clarinda); Gary Marshal (Sir Lionel); Anthony Rogers (Sir Dinadan); Peter Bromilow (Sir Sagramore); Sue Casey (Lady Sybil); Gary Marsh (Tom of Warwick); Nicolas Beauvy (King Arthur as a boy)
CREDITS: Director of Photography — Richard H. Kline, A.S.C.; Costumes, Scenery and Production Designed by — John Truscott; Sets and Art Direction — Edward Carrere; Film Editor — Folmar Blangsted, A.C.E.; Assistant Director — Arthur Jacobson; Musical Staging Associates — Buddy Schwab, Leo Shuken; Orchestrations — Jack Hayes, Peter King; Music Liaison by — Trude Rittman; Set Director — John W. Brown; Speech Consultant — Dr. Daniel Vandraegen; Sound by — M. A. Merrick, Dan Wallin; Makeup Supervisor — Gordon Bau, S.M.A.; Supervising Hair Stylist — Jean B. Reilly, C.H.S.; Miss Redgrave's Makeup by — Warner Bros. Cosmetics; Based on the Play *Camelot*; Book and Lyrics by — Alan Jay Lerner; Music by — Frederick Loewe; Directed by — Moss Hart; Produced on the Stage by — Jenny Productions; From *The Once and Future King* by T. H. White; Assistant to the Producer — Joel Freeman; Music Supervised and Conducted by — Alfred Newman; Associate — Ken Darby; Music by — Frederick Loewe; Screenplay and Lyrics by — Alan Jay Lerner; Produced by — Jack L. Warner; Directed by — Joshua Logan

SYNOPSIS: One of the most famous and longest running musicals of its day, the film *Camelot* was originally a Broadway play by Lerner and Loewe. Though the Broadway production was never filmed, some clips of the original stars doing short guest appearances do exist. The stage play starred Richard Burton and Julie Andrews. (See the entries for *The Best of Broadway Musicals, The Very Best of the Ed Sullivan Show, Lerner and Loewe Special* and *Julie Andrews Sings Her Favorite Songs*.)

Camelot the movie opens on the eve of Arthur's siege of Lancelot's castle. On this evening, a sad king sits wondering how it all began. Merlyn comes to him and says, "Think back," and until the final scene, the rest of the film is a flashback of the story of King Arthur, Guenevere and Lancelot.

Though claimed to be based on White's *The Once and Future King*, the film tracks just as strongly with Malory's version. The most obvious presence from White's story is the comical Pellinore. The dotty Pellinore vaguely remembers once having "spent a jolly fortnight with a lad named Wart." Lancelot's innocent conceit (at least at the beginning) is another humorous aspect to the movie.

As this story goes, the marriage between Arthur and Guenevere is an arranged one. Guenevere falls in love with a stranger, who has come upon her trying to escape from her journey to Camelot. It turns out to be Arthur, of course, but things quickly go awry. Once married, Guenevere never shows much more than a bemused tolerance for Arthur's dreams.

The biggest dream the king hatches is of a new order of chivalry in which might will be used for right. He puts out a call for knights to join him. One who comes is Lancelot. He and Guenevere promptly fall in love and Camelot begins to crumble before it has had much of a chance to begin.

Medieval artifacts designed by John Truscott for *Camelot*: (clockwise from top left) art-nouveau hour glasses, oil-burning lamp, planetary projector and pewter distillery.

Rumors of the affair between the queen and Lancelot are rife but Arthur will not recognize them. He banishes knights who make the accusation until Mordred forces the issue by catching the two red-handed.

Lancelot manages to fight his way out, but Guenevere is captured and condemned to burn at the stake for her treason and adultery. Lancelot returns with his men in the nick of time to save Guenevere and carry her off.

Richard Harris (middle) stars in Joshua L. Logan's *Camelot* (1967).

At this point the film returns to the night before the battle at Joyous Gard. Lancelot and Guenevere both approach Arthur and Arthur learns that Guenevere has joined a nunnery. Arthur declares the Round Table dead. The three say their sad goodbyes.

Just before dawn Arthur meets a young boy — Tom of Warwick — whom he knights and invests with the duty of telling the world the story of what Camelot once was.

Camelot (1967/1995)

227 minutes (feature: 180 minutes, extras: 47 minutes); Color; Live Action/Documentary; Digitally remastered; Widescreen (Letterbox); Copyright 1967, 1995, Warner Bros.; Warner Bros. Classics; Warner Home Video #12238

OPENING DOCUMENTARY: 10 minutes; "The Story of Camelot"; Copyright 1968, Warner Bros./ Seven Arts, Inc.; Produced by — Professional Film Services for Warner Bros./Seven Arts. This documentary is a behind-the-scenes look at the three-year making of the movie *Camelot*. It is followed by three theatrical trailers for the film.

CLOSING DOCUMENTARY: 26 minutes; "The World Premiere of Camelot"

CAST: Joshua Logan (1st Guest); Richard Harris (2nd Guest); Alan J. Lerner (3rd Guest); Jack L. Warner (4th Guest); John Truscott (5th Guest)

CREDITS: Produced and Directed by — Elliot Geisinger, Ronald Saland; Written by — Burt Sloane; Edited by — Hortense Beveridge; Associate Producer — Jay Anson; Post Production Supervisor — Howard Kuperman; Production Manager — John Quill; Special Sets by — Phil Abramson; Your Hosts — Fred Robbins, Lee Phillip of WBBM-TV CBS, Chicago; Produced for Warner Bros./Seven Arts by Professional Film Services; A J. P. Stevens and Company and famous.barr presentation

SYNOPSIS: The feature is followed by approximately six more minutes of theatrical trailers for *Camelot* and then this 26-minute

King Arthur was portrayed by Richard Harris in the 1967 film version of the Lerner-Loewe musical *Camelot*.

documentary of the premiere of the film. The trailers at the opening and close of the film become repetitive. The opening documentary is a glossy commercial production. The closing documentary is of note particularly for film buffs for its short interviews with a few giants of the film industry.

The cast, credits and synopsis for the film itself can be seen in the entry *Camelot* (1967) above.

Camelot (1982)

Not viewed; Copyright 1982, HBO Television

CAST: Richard Backus; Meg Bussert; Richard Harris; Barrie Ingham; Robert Muenz; James Valentine

CREDITS: Director — Marty Callner

SYNOPSIS: This cable television presentation by Home Box Office first appeared on September 26, 1982. It was HBO's airing of the Broadway revival of the famous Lerner and Loewe musical *Camelot*.

Camelot (1995)

48 minutes; Color; Documentary; Copyright 1995, Multimedia International and A&E Television Networks; Produced by Multimedia Entertainment, Inc., and Filmroos in Association with the Arts and Entertainment Network; Distributed by Multimedia Entertainment, Inc.; A&E Home Video

CREDITS: Executive Producer — Bram Roos; Producer — David M. Frank; *Camelot* Produced by — William Kronick; Supervising Producer — Lionel Friedberg; Coordinating Producers — Mark Finkelpearl, Michele Thibeault; Associate Producer — Jordan Friedberg; Music by — Vaughn Johnson; Art Consultant — Kathleen Ahmanson; Historical Consultant — Dr. Charles T. Wood; Editor — Duane Tudahl; Director of Research —

Tracey Benger; Art Supervisor — Karla Rose; Art Production — Susan Lutz; Researcher — Rachel Barouch; Production Assistants — Andrea C. Gargiulo, Stephen A. Ricci; Executive Assistant — Sylvia A. Ruiz; Post Production Supervisor — Liz Newstat; On-Line Editor — Jeff Winston; Field Producer — John Court; Camera — Tom Payne, Greg Bader, CGI Productions; Production Associates — Rebecca Meiers, David Schnier, Lisa Wiegand, Marty Polanski; Photos and Footage Courtesy — Loyola Marymount University, British Tourist Authority, Thames and Hudson, Excalibur Hotel, Las Vegas, Geoffrey Ashe, Leslie Alcock; Special Thanks to — The Swordsmen and New Riders of the Golden Age; Dr. Norma L. Goodrich; Dr. David Freke; Louise Bradbury; Dr. Harry Rutledge, AIA/Eastern Tennessee Society; Maryellen Saltmarch, Swan Hellenic; Dr. Susan Robinson, Loyola Marymount University; Dr. Hendrick Stooker, Occidental College; George Porcori, Pasadena Art College; The J. Paul Getty Center Research Library; Professor Leon Blevins; John Dickason, Director, The McAlister Library, Fuller Theological Seminary; Macmillan Publishing Company; Distant Lands Bookstore; Motion Control Camera — Zona Productions, The Ohio Pendragon Festival; Main Title by — Art F/X; Graphics by — Vision Art; Post Production Facilities — Varitel Video; Audio Post Production Facilities — Coley Sound; Audio Mixer — Bill Smith; Executive Producer for A&E Network — Michael E. Katz; Bonnie Wheeler, Editor, *Arthuriana*, Professor of English, Southern Methodist University; Geoffrey Ashe, Author, Glastonbury, England; Hosted by — Kathleen Turner; Narrators — Richard Kiley, Jean Simmons

SYNOPSIS: A part of the A&E television series *Ancient Mysteries*, this episode is divided into five acts. Each segment discusses a different aspect of the Arthurian legend and all are interspersed with historical information.

Act 1, "The Man and the Legend," gives the most hard historical data. Rome departed Britain around 410, and the Celts were left to defend against incursions of Angles, Saxons and Jutes. It wasn't until the Norman invasion of 1066 that Christianity was fully imposed on the British tribes.

The literature of the legends is also examined. Beginning with Geoffrey of Monmouth, the film runs through Chrétien, Malory and Tennyson. A claim is made that Geoffrey's book started the code of chivalry, leading eventually to the Geneva Conventions. Chrétien is credited with introducing Lancelot and profane love to the tales.

Lastly, the history of Tintagel is presented, with notes that sixth century commerce is evident archaeologically, predating the twelfth century castle ruins.

Act 2, "The Mist of Avalon," skips around a bit. It moves from the influence that forests had on Celtic folklore to the sixteenth century construction of the round table designed by Henry VIII. Finally, the "modest excavations" of the 18-acre hilltop fort at Cadbury Castle is discussed.

Act 3, "The Holy Grail," presents the traditions surrounding Joseph of Arimathea. Here it is said that Joseph came to Glastonbury 30 years after Christ's death carrying a chalice containing Christ's blood.

Act 4, "The Love Triangle," as might be expected, goes into the embroilment of Lancelot and Guinevere. It also mentions Malory and his eight-year incarceration in a London jail.

Act 5, "Once upon a Time," is most remarkable for an error. While discussing Guinevere in the nunnery, the picture on the screen is actually Perceval's sister Dindrane.

In all, the tape is an excellent overview of the history, archaeology, legends and literature of King Arthur.

Camelot (1997)

48 minutes; Color; Cartoon; Copyright 1997, Sony Wonder, a Division of Sony Music Entertainment, Inc.; Copyright 1998, Sony Music Entertainment, Inc.; Sony Wonder #LV49939; Golden Films

CREDITS: Screenplay — Peter S. Beagle; Producer — Diane Eskenazi; Director — Greg Garcia; Associate Producer — Darcy Wright; Production Coordinator — Rana Davis; Character Design — Len Smith; Background Design — Kathy Swain, Animation & Effects; "Merlin's Song": Lyrics — Merrill Farnsworth; Music — Bonnie Keen; Track Producer — Chris Davis; "Dreams of Avalon": Vocals — Scott Brasher; Lyrics — Merrill Farnsworth; Music Composer/Track Producer — Scott Brasher;

"Camelot": Lyrics — Merrill Farnsworth; Music — Scott Brasher; Track Producer — Chris Davis; Sound Mixer — Will Harvey; Foley Artist — Charlie Stockley; Sound Supervisor — Steve Limonoff; Music, Dialog and Effects Editor — Steve Limonoff; Audio Post Production — Music Annex; Video Post Production — Varitel; Editor — Tom Nichols; Colorist — Bob Campbell; Post Coordinator — Christine Odegard; Overseas Animation — Hong Ying Animation Co.; Overseas Director — Bobby Hsieh; Overseas Production Coordinators — Winnie Chaffee, Sharon Shen, Cathy Wang; Interpreter — Tom Pong; Track Reading — Charlie King, Toon Tracks, Glenwood Editorial; Color Keys — Diane Eskenazi, Rana Davis; Recording Studio — Music Annex; Dialogue Director — Diane Eskenazi; Library Music — Associated Production Music; Library Coordinator — Steve Appel; Prop Design — Steve Rabitich, Rana Davis; Story Board Slugging — Kyle James Walker; Executive Producer — Diane Eskenazi

SYNOPSIS: Of the cartoon versions of the King Arthur legend, Enchanted Tales' *Camelot* creates one of the more sophisticated storylines. Incorporating elements of both Malory and White along with some imaginative inventions, even the complex love triangle among Arthur, Guenevere and Lancelot is dealt with.

The film opens with Merlin saving the infant Arthur from the ravages of an unexplained battle. Taking the child to Avalon, Merlin calls on Vivienne to care for the child. This becomes something of a problem. The inhabitants of Avalon are a group of powerfully mystical women — Merlin's place among them, being a man, seems tenuous at best — and they argue with Vivienne that no mortal boy belongs there.

Vivienne is their leader, however, and her words finally convince them. They are to teach Arthur the ways and wisdom of Avalon and, when he comes of age, Vivienne says, "My sister Morgause will teach him the lessons of love."

As the young Arthur grows, Merlin turns him into a mouse, a bird, a dolphin, a fish, a dragonfly and a tree. Arthur learns the value of all of life and nature. When the time comes,

Arthur and Morgause fall in love and are wed. Soon after the marriage Merlin takes Arthur to a cave under Avalon. All the sorceresses are there and so too is a gleaming golden sword in a stone. Merlin explains that over the centuries no one has been able to pull the sword from the stone but Arthur manages it. Vivienne warns the young man that should he ever unsheathe the sword for an unworthy cause; it will turn to dust in his hands.

Next Merlin explains to Arthur that his destiny is to bring peace to Britain. In spite of his love for Morgause and Avalon, Arthur must leave to help mankind. Regretfully but with determination the young man sails a barge away from the invisible island to the shores of his homeland.

Arthur's first adventure in Britain is saving a damsel from a fire-breathing dragon. Killing the dragon, he wins Guenevere's heart and she goes with him as he travels the country gathering friends and knights to his cause. With Gawain, Palamedes and a few others, Arthur settles on Cornwall for the site of his castle. "Sometimes," he says, "from Cornwall you can see Avalon."

The small group begins building Camelot and, as word spreads that Arthur and his men are there to protect the weak, more help pours in. Once it is finished, more knights come to Camelot, Lancelot du Lac, son of King Ban of Benwick, among them. Arthur builds the Round Table and Merlin's spirit attends the first ceremony there, turning all the knights' swords to gold like Excalibur. The people are so happy that Arthur is elected king.

Arthur marries Guenevere and the work of quieting the land begins. Peace is finally achieved and to keep his warriors from boredom Arthur conducts tournaments and jousts. He begins to notice the looks that Guenevere casts toward Lancelot but puts the thought aside.

As Arthur becomes more and more involved in the matters of the kingdom, Guenevere and Lancelot meet surreptitiously with increasing frequency. In one scene Guenevere tells Lancelot, "After all, he's got Camelot and his eternal love for Morgause." On a court visit to the castle of Leodegrance the lovers are discovered by their host. Lancelot moves to kill Leodegrance, but Vivienne appears and stops him. She causes the poor fellow to forget what he saw so as to avoid trouble. As she disappears she says over her shoulder to Guenevere, "If you can't be faithful to Arthur, at least be kind."

One day at Camelot Sir Mordred of Avalon presents himself to the court. He is Arthur's son by Morgause and Arthur welcomes him happily. The young man soon becomes aware of the relationship between Lancelot and the queen. Only trying to help, he speaks of it to his father. Out of shame Arthur becomes angry with Mordred and sends the boy away. Mordred spreads word of the illicit affair of the queen, and Arthur is forced to allow Mordred to set a trap for the lovers.

In the classic scene of Lancelot fighting his way out of Guenevere's chambers, this film has Arthur coming to his assistance and allowing Lancelot and Guenevere to escape. Gareth, Bedevere, Palamedes and a number of others go to Joyous Gard to help Lancelot. Arthur is pushed into setting up camp outside of Lancelot's castle, but he meets with his old friend and they agree on a truce. Lancelot says he will go to a monastery.

In a scene reminiscent of one from the film *Excalibur*, Merlin comes to Arthur that night to give him words of encouragement. He tells Arthur that yes, Camelot has fallen in this age, but now there is a Camelot to remember and it will be built and fall over and over again through time. He also tells Arthur that he is and always will be a part of Avalon.

The following day, as Arthur and Lancelot are about to sign their pact, Mordred becomes angry that the queen's betrayal will go unpunished and he incites the final battle. In the melee someone mortally wounds Arthur. As the king lies dying he asks Mordred to "carry the peace of Avalon forward."

Merlin and Vivienne appear and in a swirl of fog they put Arthur's body on a barge to take him home to Avalon. Morgause is waiting for Arthur on the shore and, through the magic of the island, the king is revived. "He never gave up on people," the narrator states, "that's why he waits still on Avalon, to return when his time comes again. That's why he lives forever."

This cartoon is unusual for one intended for children. The affair between Guenevere and Lancelot is frankly presented but rationalized by the queen's knowledge of Arthur's immortal wife on Avalon. There are a number of such clever explanations of Arthurian legends in the film. That Avalon is a society of sorceresses is interesting in and of itself. The women meet and dance in a circle of stones that looks like Stonehenge. Merlin's secondary role in their midst is also a point of interest.

The softening of Mordred's illegitimate birth and of his character works well. It is explained by Merlin at one point that Mordred is acting out of love for his father, but that love can sometimes cause us to do terrible things. Though the cartoon introduces some very difficult concepts and a number of ideas not traditionally associated with Arthurian legend, it does make a very complete presentation of the story.

Camelot (1997)

50 minutes; Color; Cartoon; Copyright 1997, 1998, Anchor Bay Entertainment, Inc.; Library of Animated Video Treasures

WITH THE VOICES OF: Alistair Duncan; Robyn Moore; Lee Perry

CREDITS: Storyline — Roddy Lee, Roz Phillips; Screenplay — Paul Leadon; Music by — Tony King; Animation Director and Story Board — Richard Slapczynski; Timing — Geoff Collins; Background Design — Robert Qui; Character Design — Richard Slapczynski; Models — Cynthia Leech; Color Styling — Flaming Eyeball Productions, Ltd.; Track Breakdown — Dennis Collins; Animation Production — Colorland Animation Productions, Ltd.; Editors — Steven Turner, Marcus Bolton; Video Post Production — Acme Digital; Sound Mix and Post Sync Effects — Julian Ellingworth; Generic

Opening Music — Garry Hardman; Voice Track Direction — Peter Jennings; Recording Studio — Audioscapes; Production Consultancy — Different Film Productions PTY, Ltd.; Assistant to the Producer — Ruth Kuss; Production Consultant — Myles Spector; Production Manager — Roddy Lee; Production Accountant — George Conomos; Producer — Roz Phillips; Executive Producer — David C. Field; Produced by Burbank Animation Studios PTY Ltd., Sydney, Australia

SYNOPSIS: Reminiscent of Disney's *The Sword in the Stone, Camelot* is another cartoon look at how young Arthur came to be king. It literally opens on a dark and stormy night. The old king of Camelot, Gerdlach, lies dying in his bed attended by Merlin. In his final moments he worries that upon his death Camelot will be no more. He asks Merlin to bring his son to him.

Merlin brings the infant Arthur to his father and Gerdlach asks Merlin to take the boy to raise. He also gives Merlin his sword, Excalibur, to keep until the boy reaches the age of 12. Merlin accedes to all this and carries the child into the secret passages of the castle.

Using Supermanlike heat vision, Merlin lights a torch and burns an old lock off a door, carrying Arthur out of Camelot. The tunnel leads to Stonehenge, within sight of the castle. Merlin plants the sword into a stone there, then transports himself and the boy to his house in the trunk of a giant tree where they are awaited by the owl Terquin.

This Merlin wears a gigantic, flat-brimmed, conical witch's hat, complete with stars and half moons on it. He intermittently speaks with a decidedly French accent. "Gerdlach" is pronounced "guerre de lac," reminding one of Lancelot du Lac.

Among other magical paraphernalia housed in Merlin's abode is the Wizard Pool. This small stone cistern contains water through which Merlin is able to see the future and the past.

As time passes, Gerdlach's fears come true. Other kingdoms invade Camelot. Stonehenge becomes a refuge for the animals of Camelot and a playground for Arthur. One day a foundling girl, Cynthia, appears there, sleeping with her animal friends, a raccoon, a hedgehog, a bird and a mouse. Merlin takes Cynthia in and she and Arthur play together.

One day Cynthia unconsciously uses some sort of magic power to help get Arthur out of trouble. Shortly after that the Wizard Pool chooses Cynthia to become Merlin's apprentice. This is crushing to Arthur since he had always wanted to attain that position. Then, to add to the boy's misery, the pool predicts a new king coming to Camelot. Merlin tries to reassure the boy that a very important future is in store for him, but Arthur decides to leave.

Merlin tells Cynthia to follow Arthur and watch over him. He turns her into a falcon to make the job easier. As Arthur steps through the magic portal in one of the stones of Stonehenge, a young page witnesses the event. He also sees the falcon follow through the same rock. Arthur trips and his hand bumps the sword in the stone. The sword moves. The page knows that no one can move that sword, so he takes his incredible news to his lord, Sir Baldrick.

Baldrick doesn't listen to the page at first, but then a strange light emanates from Stonehenge. Looking out his castle window at it, Baldrick and the page hear the voice of Merlin. Merlin calls all of Camelot to meet at Stonehenge. At this meeting, Merlin charges all the clans of Camelot to choose their champions, who will seek to pull the sword from the stone.

The page finally gets through to Baldrick about Arthur having moved the sword. Baldrick wants the kingship for himself, so he captures Arthur. In the meantime, Cynthia has discovered that as a falcon she can talk with her animal friends. Together they follow Arthur into Baldrick's castle.

Arthur fails all of Baldrick's tests of strength. Convinced that his page lied and that Arthur is useless, Baldrick has Arthur thrown into a dungeon to be eaten by the dragon of the castle. Cynthia and her friends manage to free Arthur just as the dragon approaches.

Humphrey, the hedgehog, becomes the hero of the day when the dragon steps on Humphrey's quills and runs off. Arthur gets to Stonehenge just in time to remove the sword from the stone and be declared king of all Camelot.

Merlin retires and Cynthia becomes King Arthur's court magician. Arthur restores the old castle to its former glory, Humphrey is given a medal for bravery and Baldrick is banished. Arthur builds a Round Table so that no knight will ever again abuse his power and Terquin catches a 150-year cold from a mischievous dip he took in the Wizard Pool.

The departures from Arthurian tradition outnumber any consistencies with tradition in this film. Gerdlach, instead of Uther, being Arthur's father is one; Cynthia becoming Camelot's wizard under Arthur is another. Britain is never mentioned, only Camelot, as if *it* were the country. A baldric is an ornamented leather sword belt. No character named Baldrick figured prominently in any of the better-known literary versions of the legends.

Camelot, in spite of all that, is a better-than-average reworking of the story of Arthur. Leaning heavily on White's *The Once and Future King* and perhaps borrowing a bit from *The Sword in the Stone* from Disney, it's a charming version that should pique children's interest in the Arthurian tales.

Camelot: The Legend (1998)

70 minutes; Color; Cartoon; Copyright 1998, G. T. Merchandising & Licensing Corporation; Good Times Home Video #05-07342

FEATURING THE VOICES OF: Long John Baldry (Merlin); Gary Chalk (King Arthur, Bandit #1, Mason); Lee Tokar (Mordred, Bandit #2); Kathleen Barr (Guinevere, Griselda); Saffron Henderson (Morgan Le Fay); Scott McNeil (Lancelot, Bruce); John Murphy (Knight Commander); Jason Gray Stanford (Gilly); Doug Parker (Guard)

CREDITS: Executive Producers — Andrew Greenberg, Seth Willensen; Written by — Lisa Moricoh-Latham; Additional Writing by — Elizabeth Logan; Producer — William R. Kowalchuk; Associate Producer — Jean Rogers; Song and Music — Jim Latham; Director — William R.

Kowalchuk; Story Development — Michael Aschner; Story Editor — Elizabeth Logun; Historical Consultant — David Bourla; Casting — B.L.T. Productions; Voice Director — Doug Parker; Director's Assistant — Elizabeth Carol Savankoff; Production Assistants — Tanya Roberts, Sheila Rowan; Recording Facility — Griffiths Gibson & Ramsey Productions, Inc.; Recording Engineer — Johnny Q; Supervising Editor — W. R. Kowalchuk; Associate Editors — Jason W. Kowalchuk, Daniel Krause; Video Facility — Anderson Video, A Four Media Company; Sound Post Production — A. Backus Communications, Inc.; Supervising Sound Editor — Barry Backus; Track Readers — Dianne Dasko, Peter Mehrabian, Alan Henderson; Lip Assignments — Stuart Wenschlag; Dialogue Editor — Peter Mehrabian; Sound Effects Editors — Barry Backus, Ewan Deane; Foley Artist — Ian Mackie; Audio Re-recording Facility — Pinewood Sound Studios; Re-recording Mixers — Randy Kiss, Geoff Turner; Storyboard Supervisors — Jean Rogers, William R. Kowalchuk; Lip Chart Designer — Daniel DeSerrano; Character and Background Designers — Erik Dunn, Chantel A. Bryan, Suzanne Hirota; Animation Production Services — Colorland Animation Productions, Ltd.; Executive in Charge of Animation Production — Sally Huiling Luo; Animation Director — Bin Zhao; Layout Artists — Bin Zhao, Jiancheng Lei, Xuthua Chao, Jianfeng Huang, Ban Yu, Feng An; Animators — Bin Zhao, Xuhua Chao, Jianfeng Huang, Jin Xu, Xuli Gai, Xiaobin Yuan, Jianjun Lei, Liang Ge, Yong Wang, Xudong An, Hong Miao, Jiping Wang, Xin Jin, Ming Zhung, Bengin Den, Juan Qiu, Xingwu Zhang, Di Tao; Clean-up Artists — Bin Zhao, Xiage Du, Shenqhong Tan, Wei Gao, Gang Ren, Jin Xu, Qi Xu, Weiming Tan, Minggeng Jian, Kaisheng Song, Zhihong Xu, Min Chen, Ge Yang, Jingyi Yan; In-between Checkers — Wuming Xu, Scong Li, Ruyi Sheng, Yu Wang, Yehua Zhao, Junhua Yang, Hungtap Zhang; Background Artists — Weiming Hu, Jianshe Jin, Jingu He, Lung He, Shuanghua Xu, Gelin Ying, Zhongu Gao, Zhun Liu, Xiaqing Zhang, Zhongwei Shan, Wei Guo, Chunyang Chen, Benhuai Rao; Digital Painters — Yanging Lu, Jian Zhou, Guifang Yu, Qiong Fang, Mengqun Chen, Bixia Lin, Zhonlan Wu, Yue e Lin, Yuling Xiong; Final Checkers/Composition Digital Special Effects — Yitao Cai, Yaxian Lu, Weixiong Wong, Zhu He, Yingfang Lin, Fei Xue; System Administrator — Mulin Zhang; Legal Administration — Perkins Coie, LLP, Kelly J. Reinholdtsen, Esq.; Financial Administrator — Michael John Klein, CPA; Presented in Dolby Surround; Animation, Ink, Paint and Composite by

Colorland Animation Productions, Ltd.; Produced by Tundra Productions, Inc.

SYNOPSIS: Another cartoon version of the Arthurian story, seemingly aimed at five- to eight-year-old children. It runs a bit long for the age group's attention span, however, and although it has its own kind of charm, the unsophisticated cartooning does not help.

The film is introduced by a long written account. It tells of Arthur having pulled a sword from a stone to become king of England, of Morgan tricking him into fathering Mordred, of her schemes for placing Mordred on the throne and of Merlin's association with Arthur.

The action opens with Lancelot defeating the last of the worthy opponents at a joust in France and deciding to go to England to find King Arthur and Camelot. The scene switches to England, where Merlin, with his pet owl, Solomon, on his shoulder, begins recounting the tale of Camelot.

Arthur, Guinevere, Mordred and Merlin journey toward Cornwall, where Arthur has called a meeting of the leaders of England. His goal is to hammer out a unification of vying factions in the country. The group stops for the night at one of their castles along the way. Mordred sneaks out and sets a trap to be sprung the following day.

On the road again the next day, Mordred's henchmen attack and manage to capture Arthur and Guinevere. Mordred slips away to watch the melee. Lancelot arrives in time to help and the murderous conspirators are driven off. Arthur, suspecting a possible attack on Camelot, decides to return to his capital.

Mordred hightails it to his mother, Morgan. This fat, very ugly witch has been imprisoned by Merlin for 20 years in a cave. Oddly, Mordred is able to come and go, but Morgan cannot. In her cave she has a magic sword stuck in a stone table which projects televisionlike images of the events happening in the outside world. Eating popcorn while she watches, she claps her hands to turn the sword's projections on and off. She and her sniveling son make further plans to defeat Arthur.

At Camelot Arthur and Guinevere make plans for recruiting common workers into the brotherhood of arms. They decide to utilize one of their wedding gifts — a big round table — as the place to hold the meetings. Lancelot becomes instrumental in finding new knights and also begins teaching Guinevere to fight with a sword. Seeing the friendship between Lancelot and Guinevere, Morgan tricks them into meeting alone in the forest. The plan goes awry, but Mordred winds up kidnapping Guinevere.

Lancelot and Merlin rescue the queen and Lancelot escorts her back to Camelot. Merlin stays behind to fine-tune his spell on Morgan so that she can do no more damage. Just as Guinevere gives Lancelot a demure hug of thanks, Arthur and his knights ride up. Becoming jealously angry at what looks like his wife kissing Lancelot, Arthur orders them arrested. Lancelot gets away but Guinevere is locked in a tower at Camelot.

After cooling off Arthur finally realizes that his wife is true to him and he begs her forgiveness. They reconcile and come up with a plot of their own. They decide to fake the trial of the queen in order to draw out Mordred and his men. The plan works. Mordred attacks the prepared Camelot and Lancelot even shows up to turn the final tide of battle, driving Mordred off once and for all. All having ended well, Merlin completes his narration by stating that Arthur and Guinevere ruled happily, in peace, for many years.

Camelot: The Legend is interesting in spite of its shortcomings. In this age of high-tech 3-D computer graphics, the cartooning looks old-fashioned. It is a musical, but the story is only interrupted a few times for song-and-dance numbers. On the other hand, elements of the legends are introduced which don't normally appear in children's cartoons.

Though it is not explained in depth, the fact that Morgan tricked Arthur into fathering Mordred is taken from the Vulgate *Mort Artu* (though there it was Morgause). With Guinevere tied to a rock overhanging a deep pit in Morgan's cave, Lancelot uses his sword as a bridge to get to her. That scene is not unlike Lancelot's rescue of Guinevere from the land of Gorre in Chrétien's *Knight of the Cart*, in which he had to cross a perilous sword bridge to enter that kingdom. Morgan's imprisonment in a cave is a reversal of many versions of the legend in which it is usually Merlin who is doomed to that fate.

The film's smoothing over of the potential love triangle among Lancelot, Guinevere and Arthur contradicts almost all medieval and later versions. It is, however, a nice way of avoiding the complexities of that situation for a young audience. In light of that, however, one wonders at the inclusion of the Mordred indiscretion.

Though loaded with such details, there is enough silliness to get a few laughs out of kids. A drawn-out sneezing scene, some of Morgan's antics in her cave, a game of "damsel-toss" that gets properly squelched by the good Lancelot are among them. Camelot's bar, Ye Olde Knight Club, even gets transformed to Ye Olde Table Round when Arthur and Guinevere's Round Table is placed there.

The Centurians: "Merlin" (1986)

Cartoon; Copyright 1986, Ruby-Spears; No further information available.

Cerridwen's Gift see Best of the Fests, 1988: "Cerridwen's Gift"

The Changes (1975)

Not viewed; Copyright 1975, BBC

SYNOPSIS: A story of Merlin from the books by Peter Dickinson (*The Devil's Children*).

Les Chevaliers de la Table Ronde (1990)

Not viewed; Copyright 1990, Les Films du Jeudi, France

CAST: Maria Casarès; Alain Cuny; Mireille Delcroix; Alain Mace; Catherine Rétoré; Michael Vitold

CREDITS: Director — Denis Llorca

A Choice of Weapons (1975)

Originally: *Dirty Knights' Work*; 88 minutes; Color; Comedy/Murder Mystery; Copyright 1975, Warner Bros., Inc.; Paragon Video Productions; A Gamma III Release; A Weintraub-Heller Production

CAST: John Mills (Bertie Cook); Donald Pleasence (Sir Giles Marley); Barbara Hershey (Marion Evans); David Birney (Sir John Gifford); Margaret Leighton (Mrs. Gore); Peter Cushing (Sir Edward Gifford); Brian Glover (Sidney Gore); John Savident (Oliver Griggs); John Hallam (Sir Roger Moncton); Keith Buckley (Herald); Neil McCarthy (Ben Willoughby); Thomas Heathcote (Tramp); Bernard Hill (Blind Freddie); Alexander John (Lawyer); Diane Langton (Ruby); Una Brandon-Jones (Martha Willoughby); Brian Hall (Policeman with Alsatian); Peter Childs (1st Reagan Brother); John Bindon (2nd Reagan Brother); Brian Coburn (Lefty); Kevin Lloyd (Little Willie); Max Faulkner (Sir Harold Carslake); Bill Weston (Sir Anthony Beeson Whyte); Mike Horsburgh (Sir Thomas Hartwell); Marc Harrison (Boy John); George Sweeney (1st Lorry Driver); Harry Meacher (2nd Lorry Driver); Maurice Bush (3rd Lorry Driver); Romo Gorrara (1st Leather Jerkin); George Cooper (2nd Leather Jerkin)

CREDITS: Film Editor — Willy Kemplen; Music — Frank Cordell; Designed by — Edward Marshall; Screenplay — Julian Bond, Steven Rossen, Mitchel Smith; Story — Fred Weintraub, Paul Heller; Produced by — Fred Weintraub, Paul Heller; Director — Kevin Connor; Production Manager — Eva Monley; Production Services by — Plaza Productions; Consultant to the Producers — Tully Friedman; Location Manager — Arnold Ross; Assistant Director — Terry Clegg; Camera Operator — Derek Browne; Set Dresser — Josie McAvin; Casting Director — Mary Selway; Special Effects — Ian Wingrove; Continuity — Doreen Soan; Sound Recordist — John Bramall; Dubbing Editor — John Poyner; Dubbing Mixer — Doug Turner; 2nd Unit Cameraman — Jimmy Davis; Stunt Coordinator — Peter Brace; Wardrobe Supervisor — Rosemary Burrows; Construction Manager — Vic Simpson; Chief Makeup — Eddie Knight; Hairdresser — Ramon Gow; Stillsman — Keith Hamshere; Chief Electrician — Frank Heeney; Propman — Terry

Wells; Production Secretary — Sharon Gold; Assistant to the Producers — Barbara Weintraub; With Special Thanks to the Company of Knights; Suggested by — Terrence Marcel; Color by — Technicolor; Music Recorded — Olympic Sound Studios, Barnes; Re-recorded at — De Lane Lea, London; Filmed entirely on location in England by Combat Pictures, Ltd., London, England

SYNOPSIS: An unusually good cast for such an odd movie. The opening scene is of a knight riding across the English countryside. There is a shift to a gathering of knights escorting a prisoner to a jousting site. There it is announced that the Knights of Avalon have come together to witness this trial by combat. In spite of his objections the prisoner is put on a horse, handed a lance and forced to face a similarly mounted and armed knight. The prisoner is promptly unhorsed. Now fighting on foot but obviously completely outmatched, he is killed.

As the knights circle the body a man in twentieth century garb carrying a shotgun walks out of the woods and joins the scene. Shocked by the sight of the dead man, this fellow accuses the knights of having gone mad. The slayer of the prisoner argues that the dead man was a "murdering swine" whom the courts had let go and that justice has been done. The knights circle the man threateningly. He reaches for a sword and the entire group raises weapons against him. Afterward, the prisoner's body, wrapped in a red banner, is dumped from a car on a city street.

Switching to other events, John Gifford arrives in England from America. He is met at the airport by Bert Cook, who is the retired commissioner of Scotland Yard.

Cook takes Gifford to Scotland Yard. There is an extended slapstick scene of Cook wandering unannounced into the present commissioner's office and nearly destroying it. He lets pigeons in the window to feed them, moves the furnishings around, has a chart thrown on the commissioner's desk and breaks a number of knickknacks with mock clumsiness.

Griggs, the new commissioner, is unable to stop Cook. It turns out that Gifford's father has been murdered and he has come to find out what is being done and to hear the reading of his father's will. Cook, an old friend of the Gifford family, takes John to his own home where he tells John about an odd case he's following involving someone he calls "the red banner butcher."

Next Cook brings John to the Gifford estate where a lawyer is to do the reading. When they arrive they are greeted by none other than Sir Giles Marley, grandmaster of the Knights of Avalon, along with the whole contingent of knights. Gifford and Cook don't know anything about it, of course, but Marley is the knight who killed the prisoner earlier.

At this meeting we learn that John's father, Sir Edward, was the founder of the Knights of Avalon. During the reading of the will John has a flashback to his youth and growing up at the estate. His parents were divorced and his mother had returned to America. His father taught him archery, fencing and saber skills as well as the principles of chivalry. The audience now knows that it was John's father who came upon Marley just after he'd killed the prisoner.

So, all is revealed within the first twenty minutes. Marley has taken control of Gifford's group of medieval reenactors and puts them upon a twisted quest of righting the wrongs perpetrated by a justice system Marley believes to have gone awry. When the senior Gifford discovered them, he had to be killed. Their methods involve kidnapping criminals who've been released on technicalities, bringing them to the estate and killing them in jousts and sword fights.

The rest of the film rambles through Cook and John Gifford discovering the truth and defeating this gang of not-so-chivalrous knights.

Marley invites Gifford to Castle Mordred for a memorial joust in honor of his father. There Gifford meets Marion Evans, an attractive young lady working for Marley while she

studies architecture. Gifford winds up participating in the tournament and wins it. That
night there is a medieval feast in the castle.
Chatting with Marion, at one point Gifford
states, "I always thought King Arthur's court
was a real drag."

Clues begin to pop up; Cook gets to work
tracking down the culprits with John's help and
a series of fights and chase scenes ensue. More
criminals are killed by the gang and more comedy is introduced with the involvement of a
good, bad guy named Sidney Gore. Cook enlists Gore's help in digging up information and
all-out war starts. Gore is captured by the gang,
then Cook is captured, then so is Marion.

Predictably Griggs is a member of the dis-
honorable order of knights as well, so things
look hopeless with the commissioner of Scotland Yard co-opted. Gore escapes execution
and proves himself to be a mighty fighter,
killing Knights of Avalon everywhere he goes.
Marion becomes an invaluable ally in the escapes and chases. In the final battle all the
Knights of Avalon are defeated and Marley
dies, impaled on the spikes of a half-closed
portcullis. With Marley's body hanging
Christlike in the background, John's closing
remark is "Well, everyone has their hang-ups."

The Coming of Arthur (1973)

Not viewed; Filmstrip; Part 1: 54 frames, Part
2: 52 frames; Color; 35mm, 33⅓ 16-minute
(Part 1) and 17-minute (Part 2) records included; Copyright 1973, Imperial Film Company, Inc.; Released by Educational Development Corporation, Learning Resources
Division; Library of Congress Call
#PR5558.A3; Library of Congress Catalogue
#73736392/F/r882 (Part 1), #73736393/F/
r882 (Part 2); Dewey Decimal #821

SYNOPSIS: A study of the poetry of Tennyson's
Idylls of the King.

A Connecticut Yankee (1931)

98 minutes; Black and White; Live Action;
Copyright 1931, Fox Film Corporation; Re-
newed 1958, 20th Century–Fox Film Corpo-
ration, 1991, CBS/Fox Company; CBS Fox
Video, Fox Home Entertainment #1694; Re-
public Pictures Home Video #TW1694;
Adapted from Mark Twain's *A Connecticut
Yankee in King Arthur's Court*

CAST: Will Rogers (Hank Martin); William
Farnum (King Arthur); Frank Albertson (Clarence);
Maureen O'Sullivan (Alisande); Brandon Hurst
(Sagramore); Myrna Loy (Morgan Le Fay); Mitchell
Harris (Merlin)
CREDITS: Director — David Butler; Writer —
William Conselman (adaptation and dialogue);
Photography — Ernest Palmer; Sound — Joseph E.
Aiken; Settings — William Darling; Special Ef-
fects — Fred Sersen, Ralph Hammeras; Costumes —
Sophie Wachner

SYNOPSIS: Hank Martin — played by the
political satirist Will Rogers — is the prime
mover of the WRCO radio station in Hardale,
"the biggest little town in Connecticut." Interrupted during an evening program at the
station, Hank is called away to a spooky mansion to deliver a battery.

The scientist there believes that with his
radio reception gear he can tune in to the
sound waves of the past that continue in the
eternal ether. In trying to find his way to the
scientist's laboratory, Hank runs into several
people involved in a romantic plot.

With the new battery installed, the scientist does tune in to something — of course,
it's a broadcast of a part of the Arthurian legends. A lightning storm cuts loose, someone
knocks over a suit of armor and Hank is
knocked unconscious as it falls.

Hank dreams himself back to a Camelot
peopled by the odd characters who had
whirled around him just before his transportation. Sir Sagramore captures Hank and
takes him to the court of a sinister, brooding
King Arthur, who then begins plotting against
Hank with Morgan Le Fay and Merlin.

Hank gets involved with the romance between Clarence and Arthur's daughter, Alisande, and enlists Clarence as his assistant.
The two men get condemned to death. Using
his knowledge of a solar eclipse to get them
freed, Hank's incantation is "Property, farm
relief, freedom for Ireland and light wines and
beer!"

During the ceremony to knight Sir Boss, Hank says, "I'm like Mussolini — I don't want no title, I just like to be the boss."

Having won the good graces of King Arthur, Hank sets up a factory where he manufactures things that no one knows they'll need, but will be willing to pay dearly for. Camelot undergoes an incredible technological leap which includes a knights' armor car wash, an extensive phone system complete with switchboards and roller-skating secretaries, and a bathtub production line.

The story continues with a grisly gallows scene where many die before the denouement. Clarence comes to the rescue with a fleet of mini-cars, tanks, Thompson submachine guns and one of the first real helicopters.

The prime worth of this film is its historical value. Will Rogers became a national treasure. Any tapes of his performances are worth catching.

A Connecticut Yankee (1954)

Not viewed; Comedy; Copyright 1954, Kraft Theatre and ABC Television

CAST: Edgar Bergen; Sally Gracie; Victor Jory; Jack Livesey; Carl Reiner; Joey Walsh
CREDITS: Director — Fiedler Cook

SYNOPSIS: A comical made-for-television version of Mark Twain's novel.

A Connecticut Yankee (1955)

Not viewed; 90 minutes; Musical special; Copyright 1955, NBC Television

CAST: Eddie Albert (Martin Barrett); Boris Karloff (King Arthur); Janet Blair (Sandy); John Conte (Sir Kay); Leonard Elliott (Merlin); Gail Sherwood; Bambi Linn; Rod Alexander; Beverlee Dennis; Ray Drakerly; Robert Wright; Craig Timberlake; Lee Brown (Host)
CREDITS: Directors — Max Liebman, Bill Hobin; Writers — William Friedberg, Neil Simon, Will Glickman, Al Schwartz; Music — Richard Rodgers, Lorenz Hart; Dances Staged by — Rod Alexander

SYNOPSIS: Bringing song and dance to Twain's novel, this was a made-for-television version of Rodgers and Hart's 1927 Broadway musical of the same title.

A Connecticut Yankee in King Arthur's Court (1921)

Not viewed; 8 reels, 8,291 feet; Black and White; Silent; Copyright 1921, Fox Film Corporation

CAST: Harry Myers (Martin Cavendish); Pauline Starke (Sandy); Rosemary Theby (Queen Morgan Le Fay); Charles Clary (King Arthur); William V. Mong (Merlin the Magician); George Siegmann (Sir Sagramore); Charles Gordon (Clarence); Karl Formes (Mark Twain); Herbert Fortier (Mr. Cavendish); Adele Farrington (Mrs. Cavendish); Wilfred McDonald (Sir Lancelot)
CREDITS: Director — Emmett J. Flynn; Story — Mark Twain; Adaptation — Bernard McConville; Photography — Lucien N. Andriot; Film Editor — C. R. Wallace; Art Director — Ralph DeLacey; Assistant Director — Ray Flynn; Presenter — William Fox

A Connecticut Yankee in King Arthur's Court (1948)

108 minutes; Color; Live Action; Copyright 1948, Paramount Pictures, Inc.; MCA/Universal Home Video #80601; Color by Technicolor; Based on the Novel by Mark Twain

CAST: Bing Crosby (Hank Martin); Rhonda Fleming (Alisande); William Bendix (Sagramore); Sir Cedric Hardwicke (King Arthur); Murvyn Vye (Merlin); Henry Wilcoxon (Lancelot); Richard Webb (Galahad); Joseph Vitale (Sir Logris); Alan Napier (Executioner); Julia Faye (Penelope)
CREDITS: Screenplay by — Edmund Beloin; Director of Photography — Ray Rennahan, A.S.C.; Technicolor Color Director — Natalie Kalmus; Associate — Monroe W. Burbank; Art Directors — Hans Dreier, Roland Anderson; Special Photographic Effects — Gordon Jennings, A.S.C., Jan Somela, Irmin Roberts, A.S.C.; Process Photography — Farciot Edouart, A.S.C.; Set Decoration — Sam Comer, Bertram Granger; Assistant Director — Oscar Rudolph; Edited by — Archie Marshek; Costumes — Mary Kay Dodson; Men's Wardrobe — Gile Steele; Makeup Supervision — Wally Westmore; Sound Recording by — Harold Lewis, John Cope; Music Score — Victor Young; Vocal Arrangements — Joseph J. Lilley; Special Orchestral Arrangements — Van Cleave; Music Associate — Troy Sanders; Songs: Lyrics by — Johnny Burke; Music by — James Van Heusen; Produced by — Robert Fellows; Directed by — Tay Garnett

SYNOPSIS: Bing Crosby brings his lugubrious intonations to a musical version of Mark Twain's story.

Crosby plays Hank Martin who, in this incarnation of the tale, is an American blacksmith. Touring Pendragon Castle, he meets Lord Pendragon and tells his story.

While delivering a horse to a customer during a lightning storm, the horse spooked. Martin was knocked out and woke up in the year 528. Most of the details of the film follow the general outline of Twain's work.

In this variant of the tale, Hank and Alisande fall in love even though she is betrothed to Sir Lancelot. When Hank embarrasses Lancelot by using rodeo techniques in a joust, however, Alisande is offended and goes back to Lancelot.

A Connecticut Yankee in King Arthur's Court (1952)

51 minutes; Black and White; Live Action; Copyright 1952, CBS-TV; Westinghouse Studio One; Copyright 1983, 1996 Video Yesteryear; Video Yesteryear Recording #1086; A Video Images Presentation; Original live broadcast: May 19, 1952

CAST: Thomas Mitchell (The Boss, Hank Morgan); Boris Karloff (King Arthur); Berry Kroeger (Sir Sagramore); Salem Ludwig (Merlin); Loretta Day (Alisande); Robert Duke (Clarence)

CREDITS: Written for Television by — Alvin Sapinsley; Produced by — Donald Davis, Dorothy Mathews; Directed by — Franklin Schaffner; Settings by — Willard Levitas

SYNOPSIS: This version is a little-known production of Mark Twain's novel. The live performance is rough and unpolished but great to watch for nostalgia value. Karloff was 65 years old when he did this role.

Obviously done in a cramped television studio, there are no costume changes and no exterior shots. Occasional bumbled lines and blocked camera shots are amusing in and of themselves.

The script follows Twain's storyline very well considering the condensation that had to be done. One interesting variation is that

Arthur actually fights with two thugs Merlin has hired to kill him. He beats them and changes clothes with them to make his escape.

A Connecticut Yankee in King Arthur's Court (1969)

Not viewed; Filmstrip; 35 minutes, 41 frames; Color; Copyright 1969, Popular Science Publishing Company; Audiovisual Division; FOM Filmstrip #5018

SYNOPSIS: Discussion of chivalry, the Knights of the Round Table, sixth-century Britain and Mark Twain's interpretations thereof.

A Connecticut Yankee in King Arthur's Court (1970)

74 minutes; Color; Cartoon; Copyright 1970, Air Programs International; MGM/UA Home Video; An API Television Production

VOICES: Orson Bean; B. Llewellyn; B. Montague; R. Haddrick; J. Llewellyn; B. Senders; H. Morse

CREDITS: Animation — S. Barry, G. Cooke, P. L. Schwartz, D. MacKinnon, G. McLaren, J. Burge, P. Gardner, G. Perkins, L. Sharpe, J. Tych; Layout — C. Cuddington, M. Fredlund, R. Smit, M. Wedd; Assistants: Backgrounds — R. Zalondek; Editing — E. Graham; Editing — Rod Hay; Camera Director — Graham Sharpe; Timing Director — Leif Gram; Backgrounds — Ann Williams; Script — Michael Robinson; Music — Richard Bowden; Director — Zoran Janjic; Production — Walter J. Hucker

SYNOPSIS: A dated cartooning style but a good version of Twain's novel for kids. Hank Morgan is working in a steel mill this time and is hit on the head by a falling wrench. The rest of the film follows the standard form.

A Connecticut Yankee in King Arthur's Court (1978)

60 minutes; Color; Live Action; Copyright 1978, Metropolitan Pittsburgh Public Broadcasting, Inc.; *Once Upon a Classic,* a Presentation of WQED, Pittsburgh; The Mastervision Library of Arts, Humanities, Science, Sports and How Tos; Mastervision, Inc., #MAS 713; An Art-7 Film

CAST: Hosted by Bill Bixby; Richard Basehart (King Arthur); Roscoe Lee Browne (Merlin); Frederick Coffin (Sagramore); Tovah Fedshuh (Sandy); Paul Rudd (Hank); Dan Shor (Clarence)

CREDITS: Dramatized by — Stephen Dick; Produced by — Chiz Schultz; Directed by — David Tapper; Associate Producer — Lisa Cantini-Sequin; Production Associate and Script Supervisor — Joan Wood; Art Director and Set Designer — Cletus Anderson; Lighting Director — Frank Warninsky; Music Composed by — Alden Shuman; Music Arranged by — Roy Straigis; Casting Director — Shirley Rich; Costume Designer — Barbara Anderson; Assistant Director — Jill Philipson; Production Assistants — Jeff Ames, Tredessa Dalton; Technical Director — Ken Anderson; Audio Recording Supervisor — Gary Alper; Audio — Jack Arthurs, Dick LaSota; Camera — Art Vogel; Video — Tom Deluga; Editors — Nicholas Spies, Bob Walsh; Assistant Editor — Keneth Love; Videotape Editor — Bob Millslagle; Sound Editor — Nicholas Spies, David Stanton; Assistant Sound Editor — Bill Smales; Engineering Crew — Frank Colista, Don McCall, Ralph Seigler, Don Williamson, Bob Foreman, Dick Reschoff, Bob Vaugh; Technical Supervisor — Tom Stoffel; Key Grip — Joe Abeln; Grip Crew — Kathy Kearny, Wayne Morris, Jim Seech; Lighting Crew — Doug Coates, Nick Tallo; Production Coordinator — John Cosgrove; Prop Master — Mitchel Greenberg; Carpenters — Pat Gianella, Richard Karapandi; Painter — Russ Stang; Makeup — Bonnie Priore; Production Manager — Alan Brennecke; Post Production Supervisor — Christine Ochtun; Executive in Charge of Production — Dale Bell; Co-Producer — Shep Greene; Executive Producer — Jay Rayvid; Special Thanks to: The Fisher Scientific, Hartwood Acres, Allegheny County Department of Parks, The Lovelace Theater Company, The Pittsburgh Madrigal Society, The University of Pittsburgh

SYNOPSIS: A weak and silly permutation of Mark Twain's comic use of Camelot. This one has more elaborate costuming than usual. The main reason for watching it is to see Basehart as Arthur and Browne as Merlin.

A Connecticut Yankee in King Arthur's Court (1989)

95 minutes; Color; Live Action; Copyright 1989, Consolidated Productions; A Schaeffer Karpf Production in Association with Consolidated Family Home Entertainment Theatre #27577

CAST: Keshia Knight Pulliam (Karen); Jean Marsh (Morgana de la Fay); Rene Auberjonois (Merlin); Emma Samms (Guenevere); Whip Hubley (Lancelot); Hugo E. Black (Mordred); Bryce Hamnet (Clarence); Michael Gross (King Arthur); Berlinda Tolbert (Karen's Mother); Marissa Lindsay (Liz [Karen's Sister]); William Nunn (Schoolteacher); William Jongeneel (Angry Knight); Gardew Robinson (Peasant #1); Natasha Williams (Peasant #2); Bernard McKenna (Peasant #3); Camilla Dempster (Lady Courtier)

CREDITS: Music by — William Goldstein; Edited by — Rod Stephens, A.C.E.; Production Designer — Brian Eatwell; Director of Photography — Harvey Harrison, B.S.C.; Co-Producer — James Pulliam; Producer — Graham Ford; Based on the book by Mark Twain; Teleplay by — Paul Zindel; Directed by — Mel Damski; Casting — Susan Shaw (USA), Davis/Zimmerman (UK); Production Managers — Neville Thompson, Maria Ungor; Associate Producer — Adrienne Luraschi; *In Hungary and the UK*: First Assistant Directors — Graham Ford, Kevin Barker, Gabor Varadi; Second Assistant Director — Marta Kertesz; Third Assistant Director — Toby Ford; *In USA*: Unit Production Manager — Graham Ford; First Assistant Director — Bart Patton; Second Assistant Directors — Cathy A. Roszell, Tom Ruse; Costume Designer — May Routh; Additional Photography — William Wages (USA), John Wyatt (Hungary); Location Manager — Gyorgy Kuntner; Unit Managers — Karoly Rozsnyay, Istvan Nedeczky; Art Directors — Derek Nice, Tividar Bertalan; Set Dresser — Fereng Schoffer; Property Masters — Otto Mesterigs, Gabor Posevitz; Script Supervisor — Josie Fulford; Camera Operators — Gordon Hayman, Edwin Myers; Aerial Cameraman — Ray Andrews; Aerial Coordinator — Nick Phillips; Gaffer — Peter Sidlo; Key Grip — Tony Turner; Focus Pullers — Shane O'Neill, Britta Sell; Production Sound Mixer — Simon Kaye; Boom Operator — Tommy Staples; Makeup Supervisor — Peter Frampton; Makeup Artist — Otilla Pasztori; Ms. Pulliam's Makeup (USA) — G. Romania Ford; Chief Hairdresser — Sue Love; Hairdresser — Erzsebet Racz; Assistant Costume Designers — Joanna Eatwell, Timothy Dodd; Wardrobe Master — Gabor Csiszar; Stunt Coordinator — Gerry Crampton; Stuntman — Mark Newman; Special Effects — Gabor Budahazi; Pyrotechnician — Gyula Krasnayanszki; Construction Manager — Jozsef Bredl; Balloon Owner/Pilot — Giles Camplin; Still Photographer — Robert Szabo; Dialogue Coach — Wayne Slappy; Main Title Design — Randy Macdonald; Production Buyer — Shirley Spriggs; Armorer — Terry English; Assistant

KINGS. QUEENS. MURDEROUS MAGICIANS. THE STUFF OF DREAMS

But ten-year-old Karen Jones wasn't dreaming —
she was 5,000 miles and 1,500 years from home.

Connecticut Yankee
IN KING ARTHUR'S COURT

A NEW ADAPTATION OF THE CLASSIC MARK TWAIN NOVEL.

Consolidated

Ad slick for the 1989 NBC television movie *A Connecticut Yankee in King Arthur's Court*, starring Michael Gross and Keshia Knight Pulliam (courtesy CME Entertainment).

to the Producer — Damon Romine; Production Accountant — Con Cremins; Production Coordinator — Leila Kirkpatrick; Sound Editing — Echo Film Services, David McMoyler; Music Editing — DO-RE-MI Music; Assistant Editors — John Kawamoto, Shirley Stephens; Sound by — Ryder Sound Services, Inc.; Recording Mixers — John "Doc" Wilkinson, Douglas Turner, Grover Helsley; ADR/Foley Mixer — Troy Porter; "Cross My Heart" Performed by Tracie Spencer, Courtesy of — Capitol Records, Inc., by arrangement with Cema Special Markets. Words and music by Michael Jay. Copyright 1987 and 1989 by Ensign Music Corporation.; Eastman Color Stock by — Kodak; Processed by — Hungary Film Labs; Electronic Laboratory by — Pacific Video, Inc.; Cameras and Lighting by — ARRI, Munich; Music Performed by — Hungarian Opera Orchestra; Facilities by — Intercam and MAFILM, International Studios; Filmed on location in Hungary, United Kingdom, USA

SYNOPSIS: This version of Twain's novel is designed for five- to twelve-year-old girls. Keshia Knight Pulliam, one of the kids from the old Bill Cosby television sitcom, plays the main character, Karen.

The film opens in Karen's science class where, absent-mindedly copying notes from the blackboard, she jots down the solar eclipse date of June 21, 528. Later, when school lets out, Karen is condemned by her mom to be babysat by her older sister. Karen tags along to the sister's equestrian lesson, where she suckers a young fellow into letting her ride his horse. Of course, Karen has no riding experience, the horse bolts, she's thrown and knocked unconscious and it's off to the dreamland of Camelot.

A blond and beautiful Sir Lancelot captures Karen and brings her to King Arthur's court. On the way Karen meets Clarence, the page, and uses the "you're more like a paragraph" joke. The malleable Arthur is influenced by his knights (who sit at a square table) and the sinister Merlin into burning Karen at the stake.

Conveniently, Karen's backpack has made the trip with her and in it is an instant camera. The flash and the photos convince everyone that she has fantastic powers. Karen cuts a deal to be named prime minister, to receive a 1 percent commission on all profits and to provide Clarence with a blacksmith shop. She is dubbed Sir Boss, and Merlin and Mordred immediately begin plotting against her.

Morgana de la Fay arrives for a visit and begins plotting along with her son, Mordred, for the takeover of Camelot. In the meantime, Karen strikes up a relationship with Guenevere and her ladies-in-waiting. Using her tape recorder, she teaches them to dance, do karate moves and say things like "ciao baby."

Merlin sneaks into the blacksmith shop, where Karen is living with Clarence, to destroy the camera. Karen overhears Merlin and Mordred's plans to kill the king and his knights. She tells Guenevere who, in turn, talks Arthur into going among his people in disguise to learn their true feelings about his reign.

The unsuspecting Arthur tells his sister, Morgana, of the plan and Morgana arranges for the king to be taken while in his disguise. Karen accompanies Arthur on the expedition. Arthur sits at a round table in a pub and talks with some of the barflies, learning that Mordred has elevated the kingdom's taxes to 90 percent of all income.

Morgana's men capture Arthur and Karen and hold them to be beheaded the next day. Lancelot and the boys arrive on bicycles just in time to save them but Morgana gets away. Mordred challenges Karen to a joust. Lancelot takes up the gauntlet for her but is only able to beat Mordred because of Karen's trick of polishing Lancelot's armor so brightly that Mordred is temporarily blinded. In spite of that Mordred's men capture Arthur and Karen again and this time they're sentenced to burn at the stake.

Karen finally uses the solar eclipse trick to buy some time. In the ensuing battle, Guenevere uses karate, Arthur and Lancelot use their swords, and victory goes to the just.

During the fight Karen escapes to a field where Clarence is waiting with a hot air balloon. Rising through the air as Merlin casts his only spell that works, Karen sees Lancelot gazing lovingly at Guenevere. Merlin's sleeping spell hits Karen and she wakes up back in her own time. The movie closes with Karen's instant photo of a surprised Merlin falling in the grass as she, her sister and her mom head for home.

Connemara (1989)

Not viewed; Copyright 1989, Lapaca Productions, France

CAST: Charley Boorman; Bernard-Pierre Donnadieu; Dierdra Donnelly; Brigitte Marvine; Maurice O'Donoghue; Daragh O'Malley; Steven Rekap; Jean-Pierre Rives; Hervé Schmitz
CREDITS: Director — Louis Grospierre

SYNOPSIS: A permutation of the Tristan and Isolde legend. In this one, Tristan is Loup, Isolde becomes Sedrid. Loup is sent by his uncle, Mark, to accompany Mark's fiancée on her journey. The two fall in love and are discovered.

Crown and Country (1998)

PBS Documentary; No further information available.

Crusade (1999)

Thirteen 1 hour episodes; Color; Live Action; Copyright 1998, Warner Bros., Domestic Pay TV; Cable and Network Features; A Time Warner Entertainment Company; Babylon Productions, Inc.

CAST: (The following cast list is consistent throughout the series. Actors appearing in specific episodes are listed with those episodes.) Gary Cole (Capt. Matthew Gideon); Tracy Scoggins (Capt. Elizabeth Lochley); Daniel Dae Kim (Lt. Matheson); David Allen Brooks (Max Eilerson); Marjean Holden (Dr. Susan Chambers); Peter Woodward (Galen); Carrie Dobro (Dureena Nafel)
CREDITS: (The following credits listing remained relatively consistent throughout the series. A few changes may have occurred in specific episodes which are not accounted for here. The "Editor," "Writer" and "Director" credits, which changed more frequently are listed with each episode.) Music — Evan H. Chen; Production Designer — John Iacovelli; Director of Photography —

Frederick V. Murphy, II; Co-Producer — Skip Beaudine; Producer — John Copeland; Executive Producers — Douglas Netter, J. Michael Straczynski; Associate Producer — Susan Norkin; Unit Production Manager — Skip Beaudine; First Assistant Director — Carla McClosky; Second Assistant Director — David Fudge; Casting — Fern Champion, C.S.A., Mark Paladini, C.S.A.; Costume Designer — Randy Gardell; Visual Effects Produced by — Netter Digital Entertainment; Supervising Animator — Larry Bowman; CG Animation Team — Kevin Gendreau, Justin Hammond, Edward Helmers, Tom Helmers, Harry Hendrickson, Jim Holman; Playback Animator — Tim Petre; 3D Animation Producer — Terry Whiteside; Visual Effects Supervisor — Steve R. Moore; Visual Effects Art Director — Timothy M. Earls; Compositors — Ken Busick, Kim Hoven-Anderson; Conceptual Designers — Luc Mayrand; Makeup Effects Created by — John Vulich; Special Makeup Effects Supervisor — Shaun Smith; Key On-Set Special Makeup Effects Artist — Jerry Gergely; On-Set Special Makeup Effectgs Artist — Gabriel Decunto; Conceptual Designer/Makeup Effects Artist — John Wheaton; Makeup Effects Artist — Hiroshi Katagiri; Art Director — Mark Louis-Walters; Set Decorator — Jason Howard; Property Master — Dark Hoffman; Graphic Artist — Doreen Austria; Construction Coordinator — Curtis Laseter; Key Scenic Artist — Mattew Plummer; Costume Supervisor — Kim Holly; Key Costumer — Linda Huse; Key Makeup Artist — Conzia Zanetti; Key Hairstylist — Kim M. Ferry; Assistant Makeup — Denise Fischer; Camera Operator — Peter Kowalski; First Assistant Camera — Mike McEveety; Gaffer — Carlos M. Torres; Key Grip — Robert Devine; Best Boy Electric — Nathaniel Roberts; Dolly Grip — Charles S. Lantz, Jr.; Best Boy Grip — Reid Wheatley; Second Second Assistant Director — Bob Acosta; Special Effects Supervisor — Mike Del Genio; Stunt Coordinator — Kerry Rossall; Production Sound Mixer — Donald K. Matthews, C.A.S.; Sound Designer — Harry Cohen; Sound Effects Editors — Elisabeth Flaum, Rebecca Hanck; Dialogue Editor — John C. Stuver; Re-Recording Mixers — Michael Olman, Liz Sroka; Sound Supervisor — Michael Payne; Assistant Editors — Ben Stokes, Maritza Suarez, Jennifer Vejar; Post Production Coordinator — Janet Kasper; Production Coordinator — Celeste Healy; Script Supervisor — Kate Lewis; Production Accounting Services Provided by — Oberman, Tivoli & Miller, Ltd.; Production Accountant — Mike Hoover; Script Coordinator — Tracy Yates; Executive Producers Assistants — Tracie Esparza, Valeria Ghiran, Karen Harrell; Producers

Associates — Tracy Yates; Reference Editor — Fiona Avery; Special Effects Contact Lens Consultant — Jonathan Gording, O.D.; 3D Medical Animation Courtesy of — Blausen Medical Communications, Inc.; Technical Operations for NDEI — Larry Stanton; Technical Advisors — Jet Propulsion Laboratory, California Institute of Technology; Main Title Design by — Copeland/Straczynski; Filmed with Panavision Cameras and Lenses; Color by Pacific Film Laboratories; Electronic Laboratories; Laser Pacific Media Corporation; Digital Sound and Re-Recording by IFX

SYNOPSIS: *Crusade* was a spinoff from the television science fiction series *Babylon 5* (see two *Babylon 5* episode entries above). It was introduced in the film *Babylon 5: A Call to Arms* (see that entry above), which was also the final episode of the original show.

After that pilot movie, the producers had filmed 13 episodes of the new series with an understanding that the program would have a five-year run. Before *Crusade* was aired, however, the network involved backed out of the deal and announced the cancellation of the show. The initial 13 episodes were finally broadcast in the U.S. from June through September of 1999. The creator, J. Michael Straczynski, sought other support, including the SciFi Channel, with no success. *Crusade* picks up several years after the time of *Babylon 5*. An alien attack on Earth failed, however, before departing the aliens deployed over the Earth a "biogenic" plague. That virus will take five years to adapt to human biology and then if not stopped, kill the entire population of the planet. In *Crusade*, the crew of the ship *Excalibur* are assigned the duty of trying to find a cure for the virus among other worlds.

Babylon 5 contained Arthurian elements, but *Crusade* includes even more. With the whole Earth a potential wasteland, this science fiction quest for the Holy Grail of a cure for a plague is a fairly blatant connection to legend, as is of course the name of the space ship itself.

If the character Sheridan from the original series *Babylon 5* can be seen as a King Arthur figure, particularly as he becomes pres-

ident, the lead character of *Crusade*, Gideon, is more like the Dux Bellorum Arthur. Not only is the *Excalibur* a fully equipped scientific research vessel, but it is also loaded with the most lethal weaponry that the Earth Alliance has ever put together. Gideon as Captain of the *Excalibur*, is given carte blanche to go wherever and do whatever is necessary to achieve his goal.

Overdrawing the Arthurian influences in this show or *Babylon 5* would be a mistake, however. Straczynski's work is unusually literate for television science fiction. One of the most blatant examples is the name Gideon, taken from the Bible. This humble hero was chosen by God to take a band of 300 men selected from 32,000 to defeat the invading Midianite army of 135,000.

Tagging along with the *Excalibur* is the "Technomage" named Galen. These folks are the embodiment of the famous Arthur C. Clarke quote, "Any sufficiently advanced technology will appear to be magic." Galen is a loner, having been asked to leave the order of Technomages because of his too frequent contacts with humans. He pops in and out of events in *Crusade* much the way Merlin shows up at opportune times in Arthur's trials and tribulations.

The following are brief synopses of each episode of *Crusade*, along with special guest cast and writer, director, editor credits for those episodes.

EPISODE 1, "WAR ZONE"

GUEST CAST: Alex Mendoza (Trace Miller); Tim Thomerson (Senator McQuate); Chris Comes; Maggie Egan; Don Fischer; Mark Hendrickson; Elijah Majar; Rebecca Markham; Brook Parker; John Sanderford; Will Sclub; Otto Sturcke

EPISODE SPECIFIC CREDITS: Writer — J. Michael Straczynski; Director — Janet Greek; Editor — Michael B. Hoggan, A.C.E.

The new crew of the *Excalibur* is introduced. Hand picked by President Sheridan himself for the captain's seat is Matthew Gideon. This unconventional, almost rogue battleship captain, is felt to have the requisite improvisational skills and dangerous personality to get the job done. Much of Gideon's crew is selected for him by Earth Alliance military commanders, but two people Gideon himself insists on. The first is his own second in command, the telepathic Lieutenant John Matheson. The second is Dureena Nafeel, the thief whose incredible ingenuity and sheer determination got her to Mars to meet with Gideon.

The first mission given the *Excalibur* is to track down an Earth destroyer which at the end of the Drakh war had chased an escaping Drakh ship. Command believes the Drakh ship was forced down on the planet Ceti 4. *Excalibur* is to investigate in the hopes of learning something about the plague. As *Excalibur* departs, the small black craft of the Technomage Galen is seen surreptitiously following.

On Ceti 4 an archaeological exploration team led by Max Eilerson had been working when the Drakh ship crashed. Eilerson is of course a consummate archaeologist, but he also happens to be an expert linguist, capable of decoding and translating the most difficult languages. When the large crew of Drakh warriors surviving the crash begin advancing on the expeditionary team, they hide out in an ancient underground city after managing to get a distress signal transmitted.

Though Drakh reinforcements arrive, the *Excalibur* and Galen show up just in time. The Drakh ground troops are killed, the small space fleet driven off and the Drakh captain is captured, to be sent to Earth for interrogation and, somewhat vengefully, exposure to his own plague. The acerbic but obviously extraordinarily capable Eilerson is added to the crew of the *Excalibur*.

In the final scene some of the relationship between Galen and Gideon is revealed. Somehow nine years in the past, Gideon had been abandoned, left floating in space in an EVA (Extra-Vehicular Activity) suit. A Technomage ship rescued him just as he lost consciousness and Gideon now realizes it was Galen. Also realizing what an invaluable asset a Technomage would be to his mission, Gideon asks Galen to join them. Before he accedes, Galen quizzes Gideon with five questions which become the opening narrative of every episode: "Who are you? What do you want? Where are you going? Who do you serve? And who do you trust?"

EPISODE 2: "THE LONG ROAD"

GUEST CAST: Alison Lohman (Claire); Scott Petty (Lt. Meyers); Mike Scriba (Barkeep); Marhslal Teague (Captain Daniels); Edward Woodward (Alwyn)

EPISODE SPECIFIC CREDITS: Writer — J. Michael Straczynski; Director — Mike Vejar; Editor — Skip Robinson

An Agrarian, separatist colony of humans has for some 90 years existed in peace on the planet Regula 4. It was learned some time after their arrival there that a mineral in the planet's water has an antiviral capacity in the human metabolism. In fact, the folks on Regula 4 have developed a life span that averages 15 years longer than "Earth normal."

Until the quarantining of Earth due to the Drakh plague, this fact was little more than a curiosity to be looked into at some time. Now, however, there is an urgency to acquire the mineral and see if it might help fight the Drakh plague virus. A strip mining operation is established on the planet by the main village of the colonists since it is most concentrated there.

The *Excalibur* is called in to assist when mining operations are slowed by what is termed terrorism. The pranks that are the actual mystery are things like the appearance of a giant golden dragon (though it does no damage), the inexplicable disappearance of the engines of one of the shuttles (replaced by a mass of peanut butter) and other oddities.

The culprit turns out to be a former Technomage, Alwyn. Alwyn left the Order because he disagreed with their decision to relocate to a safer hiding place when the Earth war broke out. Though out of the brotherhood, he maintains all his powers and is using them to try to protect these people from the incursion of the outside universe and the destruction of their peaceful existence.

Conflicts and disagreements escalate almost to the point of a war the colonists have no hope winning. Alwyn finally realizes he has to stop the process and get both sides to work together. He places himself in the bowl of the mining excavation and using it like a transmission dish, gathers and magnifies his powers, threatening to blast the mining ship out of its orbit. This forces Gideon to fire the *Excalibur*'s monstrous main guns on Alwyn, eliminating him and fusing the entire mining site into a useless mass of glass.

The colonists are stunned by the loss of their mentor and come to their senses. The mine operators also see reason and the two factions make plans for cooperation. Happily Alwyn staged the event in such a way that he could escape, having realized also that it was time these people got on on their own. He says his goodbyes to Galen and disappears.

EPISODE 3: "THE WELL OF FOREVER"

GUEST CAST: Michael Beck (Mr. Jones); David A. Saunders (Navigation); Joe Wandell (Communications Officer)

EPISODE SPECIFIC CREDITS: Writer — Fiona Avery; Director — Janet Greek; Editor — Jeff Hodge

A Mr. Jones from the Bureau of Telepaths is brought aboard the *Excalibur* to perform a legally required periodic assessment of Lt. Matheson. This invasion is regarded by Matheson (and Gideon) with the same joy that a taxpayer would have for a call from the Internal Revenue Service. Gideon eventually tricks Jones into violating one of his own laws, eliminating the nuisance.

At the same time, Galen has discovered a long lost Technomage device which reveals the location of "The Well of Forever." Galen describes the place as a crossroads in hyperspace, similar in a sense of lay line points on Earth, Stonehenge and others. He says, however, that the Well is inconceivably more ancient, valuable and powerful. He later explains privately to Dureena that anyone who goes there can get answers — they "just have to listen and ask the right question" (shades of Parsifal?).

In spite of objections from his staff, particularly Eilerson, Gideon agrees to the diversion. The navigational controls of the *Excalibur* are merged with those of Galen's ship and they set off. Once there, Galen goes alone to the surface of the immense, peculiar artifact. Gideon orders everyone to stand by and he goes down by hismelf to find Galen.

The Well is actually a sort of mausoleum, holding the remains of and monuments to a race of unknown antiquity. Other races who have been able to find the place over the aeons have used it similarly. Galen has hijacked the *Excalibur* to fulfill a promise of his own, a promise to his wife to bury her there.

EPISODE 4: "THE PATH OF SORROWS"

GUEST CAST: Mark Blankfield (Jenson); Gary Graham (Bruder); Sophie Ward (Isabelle); Dawn Stern (Alison)

EPISODE SPECIFIC CREDITS: Writer — J. Michael Straczynski; Director — Mike Vejar; Editor — Jeff Hodge

As a vehicle for delving further into the backgrounds of several of the main characters of the show, in "The Path of Sorrows" the crew of the *Excalibur* find a strange creature on an isolated planet. Existing inside a kind of giant snow globe, this being is able to force out of anyone their deepest, most disturbing memories. Each time this happens, however, the creature tells the individual, "I forgive you."

Gideon brings the thing on board the ship and he, Matheson and Galen experience the creature's power. From Gideon we learn the details of his abandonment in space and why Galen happened to be there to save him. From Matheson we are shown the oppressions and responsibilities that telepaths have been forced to live through. And from Galen, we learn the details of his love, Isabelle, who died so tragically and whose loss Galen is still unable to cope with.

EPISODE 5: "PATTERNS OF THE SOUL"

GUEST CAST: Peter Deanda (General Thompson); Sharrise Baker (IPX Official); Brian Thompson (Robert Black); Eric Ware (Time); Scott Carollo (Colonist); Nancy Linehan Charles (Villager); Curt Lowens (Old One)

EPISODE SPECIFIC CREDITS: Writer — Fiona Avery; Director — Tony Dow; Editor — Skip Robinson

Earth Force orders the *Excalibur* to the planet Theta 49 to arrest and bring to Earth 30 people. These individuals rocketed off Earth at the time of the Drakh invasion and it is suspected that they are infected by the plague.

These renegades turn out to be a group of Earth Force soldiers who had volunteered for cybernetic enhancement experiments. They came to this planet to escape the imprisonment they had been forced into when Earth Force decided not to proceed further with the project. They indeed are infected by the Drakh virus, but it was Earth Force itself that contaminated a food shipment to them.

It is also found that a small tribe of people were on the planet before the cybernetic warriors. They are the last remaining group of Dureena's race, the only ones who survived an early Drakh invasion of their world.

Despising the duplicity of the politicians in Earth Force, Gideon decides to keep Dureena's people's existence a secret and he fakes the destruction of the renegades' ship. They are all left on the planet to continue their desired isolation from the outside and to hope for the cure to the plague.

EPISODE 6: "RULING FROM THE TOMB"

GUEST CAST: Alex Mendoza (Trace Miller); Juanita Jennings (Lieutenant Carr); John Novak (Dr. Alain Lebecque); Fred Estrada (Cultist #1); Mario Roberts (Passerby); Jason Rodriguez (Rivera); Harley Zumbrum (Bruiser)

EPISODE SPECIFIC CREDITS: Writer — Peter David; Director (John Copeland); Editor (Michael B. Hoggan, A.C.E.

The politicians feel that a huge conference about the plague is in order, so the base on Mars becomes host to the gathering. As prime off-world vessel involved in the search for a cure, *Excalibur* is ordered there and the ship's doctor, Sarah Chambers, is to be the keynote speaker. Captain Elizabeth Lochley from *Babylon 5* is there as well and the whole event turns into a security nightmare for the two captains.

The problem is a Doomsday cult that has a number of members present on Mars. One of them, a cleric who hears the voice of Joan of Arc, has decided to plant a bomb among the audience. Finding him and neutralizing the threat form the backdrop to a show that starts a romance between Gideon and Lochley as well as showing a humorous and human side to Eilerson.

EPISODE 7: "THE RULES OF THE GAME"

GUEST CAST: Timothy Landfield (Lorcan #3); Sal Landi (Rolf Mueller); Jamie Rose (Cynthia Allen); Jonathan Chapman (Lorcan Ambassador); Carl Reggiardo (Drazi Vendor); Kathe Weeks

EPISODE SPECIFIC CREDITS: Writer — J. Michael Straczynski; Director — Jesus Trevino; Editor — Jeff Hodge

The planet Lorca 7 comes to the attention of Gideon. The original population of the planet was destroyed by some unknown factor and the new residents are resistant to *Excalibur* and her crew coming anywhere near them. Gideon is on Babylon 5 trying to negotiate a landing.

Eilerson, in the meantime, has met with his ex-wife who has fallen prey to a loan shark. This sleazy character, named Rolf, not only is demanding exorbitant repayment from Eilerson's former spouse, but he is stalking her. The last straw is when Rolf kidnaps Eilerson's cat (whom his wife has custody of).

The two insufferably smug and insular Lorcan representatives on *Babylon 5* decide to eliminate their problem by killing Gideon and Lochley. The romance between the two captains reaches a crescendo after they manage to defeat the Lorcan criminals in a running battle. Similarly, but using his intelligence rather than brute force, Eilerson heroically defeats Rolf and saves both his cat and his ex-wife.

A special credit at the end of this episode reads, "In memory of Mr. Kitty, 1987 to May 17, 1999. Now Chasing Star Mice."

EPISODE 8: "APPEARANCES AND OTHER DECEITS"

GUEST CAST: Luanne Ponce (Janey); John Vickery (Mr. Welles); Wayne Wilderion (Kevin Sprach); Christopher Michael (Earth Force Captain)
EPISODE SPECIFIC CREDITS: Writer — J. Michael Straczynski; Director — Stephen Furst; Editor — Skip Robinson

Politicians decide that in order to convey a more positive image, the *Excalibur* and its crew need a face lift. They send aboard a representative and a decorator. In spite of this interference, the *Excalibur* finds a derelict alien vessel. It is littered with bodies of the crew, but one is still alive.

This one survivor is brought aboard *Excalibur* but dies before they are able to help him. In his death throes, the creature touches one of the medics and a race of predatory beings who exist in an energy form are transferred from his body to the crew of the *Excalibur*. Before they are able to take over the entire crew, Gideon is able to isolate them. The beings are finally defeated when it is discovered that they need oxygen and they are herded into a chamber that is evacuated of air. The show ends with Gideon donning, in disgust, his new uniform.

EPISODE 9: "RACING THE NIGHT"

GUEST CAST: Brenan Baird (Kulan); Madison Mason (General Miller); Neil Bradley (Drazi Ambassador)
EPISODE SPECIFIC CREDITS: Writer — J. Michael Straczynski; Director — Mike Vejar; Editor — Jeff Hodge

The *Excalibur* finds a dead planet. The cities are intact but the race that built them seems to have disappeared more than a thousand years ago. In one building they find fascinating hieroglyphs which Eilerson gets caught up in translating. They are a series of incomplete formulae for all sorts of incredible and advanced products, energy sources and so forth. While investigating these oddities, a crew member is mysteriously killed and disemboweled.

Shortly a squadron of alien vessels attacks the landing party. Gideon acts as a decoy to draw them off so the rest can safely return to *Excalibur*. Galen shows up just in time to rescue Gideon. In a private moment, Dureena approaches Galen, requesting to learn his skills. Galen refuses until she can rid herself of her rage and need for revenge for the loss of her race.

Galen sends what he calls a "homunculus" spell to the planet's surface. This is no diminutive man, but a full sized projection of himself. An alien ship is fooled by the thing, comes and guts it and flies off. By having watched through the homunculus's eye the crew is able to find the source of this strange activity.

The race that lived here was indeed infected by the Drakh plague. When they couldn't find a cure quickly, they put their whole population into cryogenic storage. One member of the populace is brought out of deep freeze every two years to do the grisly dissections of anyone drawn to the surface of their world, in the hope of finding a cure.

Gideon assures the present representative of that world that once *Excalibur* finds the cure, he will see to it that they pay the price for their criminal vivisection of so many beings over so many years.

EPISODE 10: "THE MEMORY OF WAR"

GUEST CAST: Susie Park (Sogayu); James Parks (Duncan); John Saint Ryan (Technomage); Ron Campbell (Belan); Dustin MacDonald (Guard); Maggie Egan
EPISODE SPECIFIC CREDITS: Writer — J. Michael Straczynski; Director — Tony Dow; Editor — Michael B. Hoggan, A.C.E.

Another dead planet with intact cities is located but Galen gives strong and repeated warnings that this is not a good place to go. He states that no one who's ever gone there has returned and that even Technomages have avoided the world for 100 years.

Disregarding Galen's words, Gideon leads a landing party and that night seven crew members are killed. In autopsying the corpses Dr. Chambers finds the cause is a nanotechnology virus; submicroscopic machines controlled by a central computer/power source invaded the landing party's nervous systems and made them kill one another. A signature on the minuscule items makes it obvious a Technomage constructed them.

Galen returns to the planet and finds tunnels below the surface. He tracks down the nanotechnology constructed replica of the original mage lurking there. They converse briefly, but the evil mage disappears. Galen next finds the power source and hurling his staff at it, destroys it.

Without their power source, the nanoviruses go dormant. Dr. Chambers recovers a quantity of them and from them, with the help of Galen, she is able to make a one-use inoculant against the Drakh plague. It only works, however, for 48 hours. The relationship between Galen and Dureena deepens when she risks her life returning to the collapsed caverns to recover Galen's staff.

EPISODE 11: "THE NEEDS OF EARTH"

GUEST CAST: Tony Amendola (Natchok Var); Bill Mondy (Nix); Mark Hendrikson; Peter Welkin; Tom Winer

EPISODE SPECIFIC CREDITS: Writer — J. Michael Straczynski; Director — Mike Vejar; Editor — Skip Robinson

The Rangers find some information for Gideon, but point out that to take advantage of it, he will have to break a lot of laws. A fellow named Natchok Var on Praxus 9 downloaded onto a data crystal, the entire history and record of his race, including cultural, scientific and medical data. Praxus 9 is not under the wing of the Earth Alliance and is outside of legal traffic lanes.

Gideon doesn't hesitate to go in spite of the moral questions involved. He and Dureena land on the surface, to battle its sand storms, toxic atmosphere and lightning storms. They make it to the domed city with a number of further difficulties and get Var out.

EPISODE 12: "VISITORS FROM DOWN THE STREET"

GUEST CAST: Josh Clark (Kendarr); Francoise Robertson (Lyssa); Harry Van Gorkum (Durkani); Robert Caso (Maintenance Man); Sandra Gonzalez (Maintenance #2); Eric Whitmore (Security #1); Camila Griggs (Security #2)

EPISODE SPECIFIC CREDITS: Writer — J. Michael Straczynski; Director — Jerry Apoian; Editor — Skip Robinson

This is the *Crusade* rendition of *The X Files*. The *Excalibur* picks up a distress signal and finds an escape pod floating derelict in space. It looks like the classic 1950s conception of a flying saucer from outer space. On board are two alien individuals, a man and a woman, both of whom are dressed in 20th century Earth suits and ties, and both of them speak English.

They are a couple of conspiracy theorists, convinced that travelers from Earth have been visiting their planet for hundreds of years, interfering and gradually taking over. They have evidence of sightings, abductions, even satellite photos of Mount Rushmore. Before long Special Agent Kendarr shows up from their planet.

The arguing and embroilment get to be too much for Gideon and he has them all taken into custody. He cuts the couple loose in their small craft after having his maintenance crews recharge and resupply it. Pumping Kendarr, Gideon gets the agent to admit that his planet used the existence of Earth as a scapegoat, blaming the aliens of Earth for all his own planet's internal problems. Gideon lets Kendarr go as well, but does a fly-by of the planet, dropping hundreds of probes to the surface containing proof of Earth's existence and complete transcripts of Kendarr's admissions.

EPISODE 13: "EACH NIGHT I DREAM OF HOME"

GUEST CAST: Richard Biggs (Dr. Stephen Franklin); Liz LaVoie (Carole Miles); Carl Reggiardo (Drakh)

EPISODE SPECIFIC CREDITS: Writer — J. Michael Straczynski; Director — Stephen Furst

(Some above details for episode 13 lost due to a defective tape.)

Excalibur is sent to meet with a destroyer and pick up two passengers. The passengers turn out to be a senator and a fellow named David Williams. The senator is carrying orders for Gideon, requiring him to take the *Excalibur* to Earth. No details of the mission are allowed to be revealed, even to Gideon as yet.

On arrival at Earth a space shuttle rises from the surface and ejects a life pod. The standing orders, due to the quarantine of the planet, are any craft at that altitude is to be shot down. Once the pod is clear, the shuttle explodes in space.

In the pod is Dr. Franklin, one of Earth's head researchers working on the problem of the plague. He is placed in the medical isolation chamber. Williams has volunteered to be infected by the plague so the doctor can monitor its initial attack on a human body. His fiancée was on Earth at the time of the Drakh war, he was on Mars. He wants to be with her and keep their wedding date.

The Crystal Cave see under *Deepak Chopra: Alchemy and the Crystal Cave*

Day for Knight see *Land of the Lost: "Day for Knight"*

Deepak Chopra: Alchemy and the Crystal Cave (1996)

Part 1: "Alchemy," 78 minutes; Part 2: "The Crystal Cave," 80 minutes; Color; Lecture and Reading; Copyright 1996, Infinite Possibilities Media, Inc.; Copyright 1997, Unapix Entertainment, Inc.; Infinite Possibilities International; A Mountain Drive Production; Based on Chopra's book *The Way of the Wizard*; Unapix Video #78011 (boxed set)

CREDITS: Special Appearances by — Joanna Cassidy, Robert Guillaume, Martin Sheen; Executive Producers — Sandra Hay, Marc Robertson; Co-Executive Producers — David Fox, Deepak Chopra, Richard Perl; Producer — Stanley Dorfman; Producer — Karen McCarthy; Director — B. C. Flood; Project Executive for KCET — Stephen Kulczycki; Executive in Charge of Production for Mystic Fire/Unapix — Karen Gnat; Lighting Designer — Simon Miles; Lighting Director — John Morgan; Production Designer — Naomi Slodki; Music Composer — Mark Wood; Unit Production Manager — Phil Silver; Production Supervisors — Seth Mellman, Dhari Gray; Associate Producer — Arielle Ford; Talent Coordinator — Apryl Rose; Talent Assistants — Ellen Spindell, Robert Seeley; Production Auditor — Pashu Dowthwaite; Technical Director — Terry Donohue; Script Supervisor — Stephanie Rondeau; Production Coordinators — Jason Rita, Patrick Dempsey; Camera Operators — Rob Bennett, Rocky Danielson, Dave "Boomer" Dougherty, Craig Peck, Danny Webb; Utility — Dean Ferzell, Wesley Landers; Video Control — Doug Decero; Video Tape Operator — Tom Rand; Teleprompter — John Cox; Gaffer — Richard Engel; Board Operator — Ron Vandervort; Electricians — Lex Crow, Scott Jones, Ron Miller; Audio Mixer — Rob Scott; Audio 2 — Paul Chapman; House PA Mixer — Patrick Baltzell; Set Decorator — Mathew Carey; Wardrobe Supervisor — Erin Rarrell; Assistant Wardrobe — Hayley Cecile; Caterer — Eva Parkinson; Craft Service — Bite Me [*sic*], Johnny Mendez; Production Assistants — Grainne Tiernan, James Gilbert, Tony Nassaney, Christian Fuhrer; Still Photography — Pablo Grodnitzsky; Post Production Services — Pacific Ocean Post; Off Line Editor — Tom Mitchell; On Line Editor — Randy Lowder; Audio Mixer — Mark Meyuhaus; Electronic Graphics — Mark Botello; Optical Effects and Titles by — Kristen Johnson; HAL Artist — Marla Carter; Wardrobe Provided by — Donna Karan; Special Artwork Provided by — Courtney Davis; Literary and Creative Artist's Agent for *The Way of the Wizard* — Muriel Nellis; Special Thanks to — Rita Chopra, Linda Livingston, Alan Kozlowski, Janet Robertson, Verna Jones; Dedicated to — Patricia Robertson

SYNOPSIS: On the old wall of Arthurian legend, Chopra hangs the even older tapestry of Vedic philosophy. Mainly using the characters of King Arthur, Merlin, Galahad and Percival, Chopra does an extraordinarily clever job of merging Vedic teachings with some aspects of the Arthurian story.

Chopra presents his material in lecture form. The guest stars do occasional readings to highlight points he is making. The readings are from Chopra's book *The Way of the Wizard* (see *Deepak Chopra: The Way of the Wizard*).

Chopra's thesis is that there is a wizard like Merlin within each of us. If we work our way through the seven stages of consciousness we can achieve the Holy Grail of true enlightenment. The two tapes in this boxed set say essentially the same things in only slightly different ways.

In "Alchemy" the emphasis is on Galahad and Percival trying to come to terms with what the Holy Grail might be. Both Arthur and Merlin give them advice at different points.

In "The Crystal Cave" the emphasis is on Merlin's teaching of the young King Arthur.

Deepak Chopra: "The Way of the Wizard" (1995)

68 minutes; Color; Lecture; Copyright 1995, Unapix; A Mystic Fire Video

CREDITS: Executive Producers — Sandra Hay, Marc Robertson; Co–Executive Producer — David Fox; Producer — Stanley Dorfman; Director — B. C. Flood; Project Executive for KCET — Stephen Kulczycki; Executive in Charge of Production for MoJo Productions — Mark Farrell; Production Manager — Dhari S. Gray; Line Producer — Dustin Nelson; Associate Producer — Arielle Ford; Executive in Charge of Production for Mystic Fire/Unapix — Karen Gnat; Lighting Designer — Simon Miles; Production Designer — Naomi Slodki; Makeup/Wardrobe — Erin Farrell; Staging Supervisor — Don Sparks; Technical Director — Dave Castaneda; Music Composed by — Wendell Yuponce; On-Line Editor — M. T. Badertscher; Assistant Editor — Dean Chu; Post Production Supervisor — Jeff Blodgett; Camera Operators — Scott Kaye, Craig Peck, Rob Bennett, Dave Dougherty; Key Grip — Richard Engle; Dolly Grip — Matt O'-Connor; Electrical Team — Ron Miller, Scott Jones, Ron Vandervort, Bill Davis, Van Johnson; Utility — Wesley Landers, Dean Ferzell; Video Control — John Palassio; Video Tape Operator — Steve Bires; Production Audio Mixer — Evan Adelman; Audio 2nd — Paul Chapman; PA Mixer — Steven Anderson; Post Audio Mixer — Mitch Dorf; Voice Over Artist — Randy Thomas; Creative Consultants — Linda Livingston, Janet Mills; Production Accountant — Teri Nassaney; Script Coordinator — Michelle Otto; Audience Coordinator — Elizabeth Fies; Assistant Production Coordinator — Cathleen Alexander; Set PAs — Alexander Boginovic, Jason Frasco, Brian Lipscomb, Charles Parrish, Kent Toussaint; Usher — Moksha LeBlanc; Post Production Facility — Pacific Ocean Post; Audio Facility — Pacific Ocean Post Sound; Special thanks to — Frank Calabrese, Alan Kozlowski, Jim Liati, Rose Bueno-Murphy, Richard Perl, Rita Chopra, Jody Singer-Kulezncki, Carol Meyers, Pamela Murphy

SYNOPSIS: Appealing to Westerners through mention of the wizard Merlin, Chopra, who has a charismatic, smiling demeanor, gives a wide-ranging lecture on how to attain Merlinlike spirituality. The steps one must take go from innocence through the birth of ego to achieving, giving, seeking and seeing until finally one may achieve the birth of spirit.

Synthesizing Vedic principles, pop science and medicine, Chopra's purpose is not the advancement of Arthurian education.

Chopra released another project with Arthurian allusions. See *Deepak Chopra: The Art of Spiritual Transformation*.

Delights and Dangers of Ambiguity (1992)

Lecture Documentary; Copyright 1992, KULTUR; No further information available.

Dirty Knights' Work see *A Choice of Weapons*

A Disney Christmas Gift: "The Sword in the Stone" (1982)

47 minutes; Color; Cartoon; Copyright 1982, Walt Disney Productions; Walt Disney Home Video

CREDITS: Executive Producer — William Robert Yates; Prepared for Television by — Ed Ropolo, Frank Brandt, Darryl Sutton, Joan Spollino; With the Talents of — Bobby Driscoll, Verna Felton,

Frances Langford, Ilene Woods; Song "You Can Fly"—Sammy Cahn, Sammy Fain; Additional Music by—John Debney; "On Christmas Morning": Lyrics by Linda Laury, Music by John Debney; Toys from the collection of the Walt Disney Archive; This program is the result of the talents of many creative people at Walt Disney Studios. The contribution of the Animation Staff is particularly appreciated; Color by Technicolor

SYNOPSIS: This video is a smattering of clips from eight Disney cartoons and cartoon movies, all relating to Christmas. The sixth segment on the tape is from *The Sword in the Stone*. The scenes included are Merlin rocketing off to Bermuda and young Wart pulling the sword from the anvil and stone. (See the entry for *The Sword in the Stone*.)

Disney's Halloween Treat: "The Sword in the Stone" (1984)

47 minutes; Color; Cartoon; Copyright 1984, Walt Disney Productions; Walt Disney Home Video

CREDITS: Executive Producer—Robert Yates; Prepared for Television by—Ed Ropolo, Frank Brandt, Darryl Sutton; With the Talents of—Bobby Driscoll, Peggy Lee; Featuring Bing Crosby relating *The Legend of Sleepy Hollow* by Washington Irving; Songs and Music—Sammy Cahn, Sammy Fain, Don Raye, Gene DePaul; Additional Music by—John Debney; "Disney's Halloween Treat": Lyrics by Galen R. Brandt, Music by John Debney; This program is the result of the talents of many creative people at Walt Disney Studios. The contribution of the Animation Staff is particularly appreciated. Color by Technicolor

SYNOPSIS: A collection of clips from Disney cartoons relating to Halloween. The first excerpt is from *The Sword in the Stone*. The scene presented is the wizards' duel between Merlin and Madame Mim.

Doctor Who: "Battlefield" (1989)

Television series episode; 90 minutes; Color; Science Fiction/Live Action; Original broadcast: September 1989; Copyright 1989, 1998, BBC; Distributed under License by BBC Worldwide, Ltd.; 20th Century–Fox Home Entertainment; CBS Fox Video; BBC Video #2775

CAST: Sylvester McCoy (The Doctor); Sophie Aldred (Ace); Jean Marsh (Morgaine); Nicholas Courtney (Brigadier Lethbridge-Stewart); James Ellis (Peter Warmsly); Angela Bruce (Brigadier Winifred Banbera); Christopher Bowen (Mordred); Marcus Gilbert (Ancelyn); Angela Douglas (Doris); Noel Collins (Pat Rowlinson); June Bland (Elizabeth Rowlinson); Ling Tai (Shou Yuing); Robert Jezek (Sergeant Zbrigniev); Dorota Rae (Lieutenant Lavel); Stefan Schwartz (Knight Commander); Paul Tomany (Major Husak); Marek Anton (The Destroyer)

CREDITS: Stunt Arranger—Alf Joint; Theme Music Composed by—Ron Grainer; Incidental Music—Keff McCulloch; Special Sound—Dick Mills; Production Manager—Ritta Lynn; Production Assistant—Rosemary Parsons; Assistant Floor Managers—Matthew Purves, Julian Hearne; OB Lighting—Ian Dow; Engineering Manager—Brian Jones; OB Sound—Martin Broadfoot; OB Cameramen—Paul Harding, Alan Jessop; Visual Effects Designer—Dave Bezkorowajny; Video Effects—Dave Chapman; Vision Mixer—Dinah Long; Graphic Designer—Oliver Elmes; Technical Coordinator—Richard Wilson; Camera Supervisor—Geoff Clark; Videotape Editor—Hugh Parson; Properties Buyer—Sara Richardson; Studio Lighting—David Lock; Studio Sound—Scott Talbott; Costume Designer—Annshia Nieradzik; Makeup Designer—Juliette Mayer; Script Editor—Andrew Cartmel; Production Associate—June Collins; Designer—Martin Collins; Writer—Ben Aaronovitch; Producer—John Nathan-Turner; Director—Michael Kerrigan

SYNOPSIS: *Doctor Who* was a campy British science fiction television series, which ran from 1963 to 1989. The Doctor, a Time Lord, traveled through time and the universe in a device called the Tardis, which looked like a police call box.

During that 26 years there were seven different Doctors. Written into the storyline of the series was the fact that occasionally the Time Lord would go into a state of regeneration and return with a completely different form and personality. This happened conveniently whenever a new actor took over the role.

The seventh and last of the television Doctors (one feature-length film about the Time Lord was made in 1996, introducing an eighth persona) was Sylvester McCoy. In the episode "Battlefield," which was divided into four parts, this Doctor meets up with Arthurian aliens.

The opening scenes of part one show a retired army brigadier working with his wife in their garden, army troops moving around a bucolic countryside, a sword hilt with a glowing jewel in its pommel and a sorceress's face in a crystal ball.

The Doctor and his female companion, Ace, receive an odd signal from Earth of the near future. Not sure if it's a summons or a distress call, they land to investigate. The Tardis appears in the woods several miles from Lake Vortigern and the Doctor and Ace hitchhike to the area that the signal came from. They get a ride from Warmsly, a local archaeologist who works for the Carbury Trust searching for King Arthur's final battle site.

The three approach the army convoy — a mobile nuclear missile launch group — and notice the odd sounds of space ships crash-landing on Earth. From the ships emerge armored knights carrying swords and ray guns.

Going to a local hotel for refreshment, the Doctor notices a scabbard hung on a wall. The blind wife of the owner of the hotel says there's something strange about the scabbard. She can "feel" its presence. It apparently is the only artifact that Warmsly has turned up in ten years of digging.

In the meantime, two factions of space knights have begun fighting each other. One knight is blown into the air by a grenade and lands in a barn on the hotel property. When our heroes investigate, the knight they find recognizes the Doctor as Merlin. He tells them that his people are here in answer to Excalibur's call and that this must be the time when Arthur will rise again.

Part two picks up with enemy knights appearing to capture the Doctor and his friends. The leader of this group is none other than Mordred. He too is convinced that the Doctor is Merlin. Ancelyn, the knight who fell through the roof of the barn, reminds Mordred

that Merlin defeated Mordred's mother, Morgaine, at Badon. Thus warned, the Doctor and company depart unscathed.

That night in a nearby castle, Mordred sets up an intergalactic transfer point and "biomass to biomass" calls to his mother: "To Avalon I summon thee." A stylishly armored and crowned Morgaine appears to a fanfare of lightning and smoke.

In the meantime the government has summoned a retired brigadier back to duty. It turns out he's an old friend of the Doctor's. The Doctor has Ace (who is something of an explosives expert) blast a hole in the ground at the archaeological dig and a tunnel is uncovered.

Ace and the Doctor enter the tunnel (which promptly closes up behind them) and find that it leads into a space ship at the bottom of Lake Vortigern. In the ship they find Arthur's body lying across a stone altar. In the stone is Excalibur. Just as part two ends, a ghostly snakelike monster attacks the two intruders.

At the start of part three, Ace manages to escape with Excalibur. The old brigadier shows up just in time to break the control box which activates the guardian snake and he and the Doctor make their way out of the ship.

Morgaine sends her men after the sword, then she and Mordred meet at the hotel. While they're there, one of the army officers shows up. Morgaine reads her mind to learn of the army's strength in the area. The process kills the woman. By way of apology, perhaps, Morgaine cures the blindness of the hotel owner's wife.

Battle finally erupts between the forces. Morgaine fails in her attempt to get the sword so, as a last resort, she summons the Destroyer.

Part four finally explains some of the goings-on. Morgaine has returned for her beloved Arthur and to get Excalibur, which is the key to her returning home.

Ace and the Doctor replace the sword in its stone, but Arthur does not rise. The Doctor removes the helmet from the armor to find inside only dust. There is, however, a note written by the Doctor himself from another time. It reads, "Dear Doctor, Arthur died in final battle. Everything else propaganda. P.S. Morgaine has the nuclear missile."

Morgaine's last desperate act is to threaten to explode the nuclear bomb. The Doctor manages to convince her that such a weapon is not an honorable thing to use. Morgaine is crushed when she learns that Arthur is dead. She and Mordred are locked up.

There is obviously no attempt here to represent either any historical aspect of the Arthurian story or any particular literary source of the legends. It is simply typical *Doctor Who* fun with time travel, aliens and monsters.

Don Quixote (1933)

76 minutes; Black and White; Musical; Copyright 1933, Nelson Films and Vandor Films; A Video Images Presentation; A Video Yesteryear Recording #3012

CAST (English Version): Feodor [sic] Chaliapin (Don Quixote); George Robey (Sancho Panza); Oscar Asche (Captain of Police); Donnio (Carrasco); Frank Stanmore (Priest); Miles Mander (The Duke); Walter Patch (Gipsy [sic] King); Sydney Fox (The Niece [Maria]); Emily Fitzroy (Sancho's Wife); Lydia Sherwood (The Duchess); Renée Valliers (Dulcinea); Genica Anet (Servant at Inn)
CAST (French Version): Mirielle Balin (The Niece [Maria]); Mady Berry (Sancho's Wife); Dorvill (Sancho Panza)
CREDITS: Based on the Novel by Miguel de Cervantes; Director — Georg Wilhelm Pabst; Writers — Alexandre Arnoux, Paul Morand; Producer — Georg Wilhelm Pabst; Music — Jacques Ibert; Camera — Nicolas Farkas; Film Editor — Hans Oser; Art Director — Andrej Andrejew

Synopsis: *El Ingenioso Hidalgo Don Quixote de la Mancha* by Miguel de Cervantes Saavedra first appeared in print in 1605. Part 2 of the tale, *Segunda Parte del Ingenioso Cavallero Don Quixote de la Mancha,* came out in 1615. The entire work has come to be known simply as *Don Quixote,* its author as Cervantes.

Cervantes' novel was a parody of the chivalric Arthurian romances which preceded it. Focusing on the character of an old man who has read too many of those romances and gone insane, it is a landmark work in Spanish and, indeed, world literature.

The story is about an impoverished gentleman who replaces reality with his idealization of the Arthurian legends some 1,000 years after the actual time of Arthur. Deciding to become a knight errant, he rides away from his home to seek adventure and right wrongs wherever he comes upon them.

This movie version of the story is unique. It is the only filmed appearance of Fyodor Ivanovich Chaliapin, a popular and world-famous Russian operatic bass at the turn of the century. The movie was filmed three times, once in German, once in French and once in English. As indicated by the cast listings above, several of the cast members were changed for the different versions.

The film opens as Don Quixote, reading in his barren room, dressed in near rags, is called to lunch. Distracted by the book in his hand and all the books around him, he has difficulty concentrating enough to respond. As he sings of love and knightly prowess, his niece, Maria, and her fiancé, Carrasco, listen from outside. Carrasco comments that the old man should be put in an asylum, but Maria defends her uncle, stating that he harms no one.

Carrasco and others in the town, including the priest and the local police, debate that point, realizing that Don Quixote has sold off all his land and most of his possessions in order to buy his books. A general consensus that he needs to be stopped seems to develop. Carrasco's main concern is that there will be no dowry.

One day a band of gypsies enters the town, announcing a street performance. Their trumpeter attracts Don Quixote's attention and he misinterprets the clarion call. "It is a sign," he says, "the trumpets of King Arthur call me!" His path is set. Donning scraps of disintegrating armor which he has collected, Quixote emerges from his room in glorious disarray.

He shows up at the gypsy's street entertainment, a play about a knight protecting a princess from a giant. When the mock giant calls on Merlin the Magician for assistance, Quixote leaps from the audience with drawn sword and attacks first Merlin, then the giant. Despite being dragged off, Quixote gets the gypsy king to knight him, much to the amusement of the audience. Before retiring, he chooses a street girl as his damsel, naming her Dulcinea.

The next morning, mounted on a horse and carrying a jousting lance, Quixote wakes his faithful friend, Sancho, and the two go off on the misguided quest. Quixote's first adventurous encounter is with an army of giants — actually, a herd of sheep being moved down the road. He attacks vigorously, scattering the flock and killing a few of them in the process. The shepherds, of course, are miffed and they carry the evidentiary corpses to the captain of police. An arrest warrant is issued for Don Quixote.

The knight's helmet having been damaged in the melee, he sends Sancho back for another. In the town Sancho learns that they are wanted men, but he manages to steal a barber's bowl before leaving. Carrasco and the priest in the meantime decide to go to the duke to plead for leniency for Don Quixote. The duke finds the old man interesting and determines to stage a farce rather than allow him to be arrested. In an aside he tells the priest to burn Quixote's books as an ultimate cure for their influence on the old man.

Back on the road, Quixote and Sancho come across some soldiers escorting prisoners to the galleys. Quixote, thinking them unjustly enslaved victims, manages to get them free but the brigands turn on Quixote and stone him. As he is injured, the police nearly capture the knight errant but the duke's "herald" arrives just in time with an invitation for the "Knight of the Mournful Countenance" to appear at court.

Deeply honored, Quixote sings to the assembled court of Dulcinea. Another fully armored knight arrives and claims that his lady is more beautiful. The duke suggests single combat to determine the truth and, incredibly, Quixote wins the day. But when he sees that the other knight is just Carrasco, Quixote realizes he has been made a fool and he sadly departs.

Riding with Sancho one more time into the countryside, he meets some farmers complaining of taxes and granary service prices. When Don Quixote spots the offending granary windmills, he envisions them as oppressing giants and immediately attacks. His lance and helmet catch in the latticework of one of the active mill's blades, and the old man is agonizingly spun round and round half a dozen times before workers manage to stop the mill.

The police arrive to carry Quixote off in an animal cage cart. He arrives to the laughter of the whole town but all fall silent when they see his stunned reaction to the bonfire that has been made of his beloved books. Quixote collapses and with his dying words apologizes to Sancho that their dreams will not be fulfilled.

By contemporary standards of long, lingering, emotional camera shots and more completely explicated character development, Pabst's *Don Quixote* might seem a cold, perfunctory presentation. Part of the charm of the film, however, is its spareness and brevity. All the human emotions are portrayed, if somewhat hurriedly. The musical format is almost an afterthought, occasional songs erupting nearly irrelevantly from one or two of the performers.

If nothing else, Chaliapin's age brought huge empathy to the role. He was 60 years old when he played *Don Quixote* and he died a scant five years after it was filmed. His haggard, craggy face is obviously not the result of makeup. His haunted, hollow eyes express more than mere role playing.

Dragon and Slipper see *Sarkany es Papucs*

Dragonheart (1995)
103 minutes; Color; Live Action and Computer Graphics; Copyright 1995, Universal City Studios, Inc.; Copyright 1996, MCA

Home Video, Inc.; MCA Universal Home Video #82826; Universal Pictures; A Raffaella De Laurentiis Production

CAST: Dennis Quaid (Bowen); David Thewlis (Einon); Pete Postlethwaite (Gilbert); Dina Meyer (Kara); Jason Isaacs (Felton); Brian Thompson (Brok); Lee Oakes (Young Einon); Wolf Christian (Hewe); Terry O'Neill (Bedefard); Peter Hric (King Freyne); Eva Vejmelkova (Felton's Minx); Milan Bahul (Swamp Village Chief); Sandra Kovacicova (Young Kara); Kyle Cohen (Boy in Field); Thom Baker (Aislinn's Chess Partner); Julie Christie (Aislinn); Sean Connery (Voice of Draco)

CREDITS: Director of Photography — David Eggby, A.C.S.; Co-Producer — Hester Hargett; Executive Producers — David Rotman, Patrick Read Johnson; Story by — Patrick Read Johnson, Charles Edward Pogue; Screenplay by — Charles Edward Pogue; Produced by — Raffaella De Laurentiis; Directed by — Rob Cohen; Casting by — Margery Simkin; Associate Producers — Herbert W. Gains, Kelly Breidenbach; Visual Effects Supervisor — Scott Squires; Dragon Designs by — Phil Tippett; Character Animation Supervisor — James Straus; Visual Effects Producer — Judith Weaver; Special Effects Supervisor — Kit West; Costume Designers — Thomas Casterlin, Anna Sheppard; Music Composed by — Randy Edelman; Edited by — Peter Amundson; Production Designer — Benjamin Fernandez; Unit Production Manager — Milan Stanisic; 1st Assistant Director — Herbert W. Gains; 2nd Assistant Director — Chitra F. Mojtabai; Effects Producer — John Swallow; Digital Effects Supervisors — Kevin Rafferty, Euan Macdonald; Visual Effects Art Director — Mark Moore; Stunt Coordinator — Paul Weston; U.K. Casting — Sheila Trezise; 2nd Unit Director of Photography — Buzz Feitshans IV; Supervising 2nd Editor — Richard L. Anderson; Re-recording Mixers — Bill Varney, Michael Casper, Daniel Leahy; Recordist — Charlie Ajar, Jr.; Sound Editors — Clayton Collins, Marla McGuire, Devin Joseph, David Williams; Effects Editors — Avram D. Gold, M.P.S.E., Michael Chock; ADR Supervisor — Andrew Patterson; ADR Editors — Eric Lindemann, Alan Nineberg, M.P.S.E., David Wittaker, M.P.S.E.; Special Sounds Designer — John Pospisil; Assistant Sounds Editor — Vanessa Lapato; Sound Assistants — Ralph L. Stuart, Jessica Goodwin; Foley Artists — Ken Dupva, M.P.S.E., David Lee Fein, M.P.S.E.; Foley Mixer — Rand K. Singer; Dragon Foley Artists — John Roesch, Hilda Hodges; Dragon Foley Mixer — Mary Jo Lang; Set Decorator — Giorgio Desideri; Supervising Art Director — Maria Teresa Barbasso; Art Director — Jan Svoboda; Assistant Set Decorator — Alberto Tosto; Assistant Art Director — Dusan Svoboda; Set Dressing Buyer — Peter Vojtech; Art Department Buyer — Miroslav Javorka; Set Dressing Carpenter — Gianfranco Masciotti; Production Manager, Slovakia — Viliam Richter; Unit Manager — Dubravko "Baja" Petrovic; Transportation Coordinator — Mladen Cernjak; Transportation Captains — Martin Stubniak, Zdenko Sertic; Location Managers — Dragan Josipovic, Marian Postihac, Damir Teresak; Assistant Location Managers — Vladimir Magal, Ivan Janovsky; Production Coordinator — Hilde Odelga; Script Supervisor — Nada Pinter; Supervising Accountant — Michael Menzies; Production Accountants — Eduardo de la Grana, Juraj Povazan, Terrence Dunn, Rudolph Ericman; Cashier — Iveta Mayerova; Production Coordinator, Slovakia — Andrea Lalakova; Assistant Production Coordinators — Sandra Odelga, Angela Jobbagyova, Henrietta Odelga; Production Liaisons — Golda Offenheim (U.K.), Steve O'Corr (U.S.); Set Coordinators — Zdravko Madzarevic, Dodo Banyak; 2nd 2nd Assistant Director — Hester Hargett; DGA Trainee — Seth Edelstein; Set Production Assistants — Nada Albert, Brano Binda; Assistant to Miss De Laurentiis — Daniel Hadl; Assistants to Mr. Cohen — David Henri, Astrid M. Gotuzzo, David Reeder; Production Secretaries — Nenia Petrivalska, Henrieta Mikulickova; Production Assistant — Marcela Svedova; Post Production Supervisor — Barbara Ostrowiecki; 1st Assistant Film Editor — John Taylor; Assistant Film Editors — Matthew Brockhoff, Aaron J. Yamamoto, Giorgio Conti, Lisa Cossettini; Negative Cutter — Theresa R. Mohammed; Color Timer — Mike Stanwick; Design of Titles and Credits — The Seiniger Advertising Group; Artwork Title Design — Cimarron Bacon O'Brien; Titles and Opticals — Pacific Titles; Camera Operators — Buzz Feitshans IV, Igor Meglic; Focus Pullers — Derry Field, Siljo Branko Knez; Clapper Loaders — Adrien Seffrin, Zoran Mikincic-Budin; Vistavision Focus Puller — Robert Stuard; 2nd Unit Clapper Loaders — Ladislav Gazo, Brigitte Rasine; Steadicam Operators — Denis Kington, Nigel Curtain; Video Operators — Juraj Bohus, Jaro Schnieber; Still Photographers — Ryan Nellis, Vaclav M. Polak; Unit Publicist — Ginger Corbett; Makeup Supervisor — Giannetto De Ross; Makeup Artist — Maurizio Silvi; Assistant Makeup — Eloisa De Laurentiis; Chief Hairdresser — Mireila De Rossi; Hair Artist — Angelo Vannella; Supervising Property Master — Ron Downing; Property Masters — Jiri Juda, Stano Mozny; Armorer — Scott Ellis; Assistant

Brother Gilbert (Pete Postlethwaite), Kara (Dina Meyer) and Bowen (Dennis Quaid) ride horseback in *Dragonheart* (1996).

Property — Jonathan Downing; Production Sound Mixer — Reinhard Stergar; Boom Operator — Robert Polich; Cableman — Juraj Oravec; Assistant Costume Designers — Nadia Vitali, Lubica Jar-jabkova; Principal Costumer — John Stuart Stowe; Head Wardrobe Mistress — Zdenka Bocan Kova; Wardrobe Mistresses — Snejzana Miric, Rudka Cillekova, Ludmilla Demovicova; Wardrobe Master

Tailor — Giovanni Indovino; Tailor — Vittorio Torrieri; Head Seamstress — Silvana Cocuccioni; Seamstresses — Anna Benicky, Renata Kerulova, Jana Jankova; Dyeing Workshop Supervisor — Gregorio Similli; Ager Dyers — Robert Bunca, Tomas Vidrman, Jan Csomor; Leather Workers — Pavol Koniar, Marcel Potocny, Peter Skrabalek; Textile Workers — Alzbeta Burianova, Ludmila Fintorova; Shoe Master — Oliver Csoka; Metal Worker — Alexander Gal; Wardrobe Assistants — Magdalena Biernawska, Paul Grabaczyk, Marianne Frank; Special FX Floor Supervisor — Trevor Neighbour; Special FX Workshop Supervisor — Trevor Wood; Special FX Coordinator — John Baker; Senior Special FX Technicians — Peter Fern, Terry Glass, Marijan Karoglan, Dragutin Poldrugac, John Hatt, Rodney Fuller, John Herzberger, Ken Gittens, Terry Cox; Special FX Technicians — Trevor Butterfield, George S. Vrattios; Special FX Riggers — Ron Skinner, Bob Schofield; Special FX Pyrotechnicians — Jozef Taptik, Alexander Mucha; Special FX Carpenters — Ignac Matula, Lubos Ac; Special FX Locksmiths — Stefan Vrbiar, Tibor Kalmar; Special FX Technicians — Ivan Balazi, Brano Masek, Peter Richter, Fedor Balazi, Jan Remay, Filip Remay, Ivan Kokavec, Roman Medzo, Milan Sulva, Jaroslav Kolenic, Michal Mikulic, Werner Mai; Gaffers — Robert A. Driskell, Jr., Fernando Massaccesi; Best Boy Electric — Vaclav Cermak; Electricians — Istvan Denc, Zeljko Vrscak, Julius Vardos, Vlado Bures, Ivan Konopasek, Vladimir Rauchbaur, Lubomir Dufek, Pavol Kalina, Miro Skuliety; Rigging Electricians — Dean Brkic, Vlad Ceh; Generator Operators — Harald Hauschildt, Martin Danisovsky, Lorre "Dugi" Vidic; Key Grips — Grahame Litchfield, Tony Cridlin; Best Boy Grip — Stefan Bleho; Grips — Stjepan Klen, Emil Tardik, Pavol Kovac, Vincent Roth, Jozel Zeman, Ivo Gresak, Pavol Dostal; Rigging Grips — William James Howe, Antun Gorisek; Greensman — Karal Czolle; Catering — Hren & Namic Catering; Set Dresser Draftsman — Peter Batogh; Draftsmen — Vlado Zelenka, Viera Dandova, Olga Malova, Barbora Krskova; Storyboard Artists — Nikita Knatz, W. Stewart Campbell, Joseph Musso, Tracey Wilson; Construction Coordinators — Fernando Valento, Rastislav Pauliny; Head Carpenter — Franco Fabietti; Carpenters — Renzo Corradi, Francesco Valento, Robert Szinghoffer, Branko Grajciar, Pavol Venglar, Vendelin Karlak, Stefan Cich, Csaba Szinghoffer, Alexander Mateffy, Attila Bittera, Karol Matis, Attila Porsok; Sculptor — Rafael Ablanque; Head Plasterers — Carlo Maggi, Galliano Donati; Plasterers — Ivano Ferrario, Peppino Luciani, Romano Sgoflon, Tito Cesare Serini, Domenico

Garitta, Ladislav Markic, Stefan Ziak, Stefan Potancok, Marian Skolar, Richard Bencik, Marcel Ziak, Jaroslav Holesa, Peter Sulik, Stefan Tesovik, Robert Duricko, Anna Holanova, Lydia Zvolenska, Peter Luknar, Denisa Ronecova; Head Painters — Marcello Turco, Vito Consoli; Painters — Tibor Alexy, Patrizia Nicoloso, Karol Branicky, Peter Ryhar, Stefan Budaj, Stano Liska; Leadman — Peter Lajas; Swing Gang — Karol Krajcik, Jan Ziska, Eugen Koszeghy, Peter Kusy, Karol Zelenay; Upholsterers — Marian Derda, Roman Albrecht, Ludvik Sury; Microlight Coordinator — Brian Johnson; Microlight Pilot — David Cook, Cook Flying Machines; Assistant Pilot — Jacob Cook; Visual Effects Coordinator — Mara Hamilton; Visual Effects Assistants — Pat Hadnagy, Buddy Quaid; U.S. Casting Assistant — Peggy McConnell; U.K. Casting Assistant — Katy Whiteley; Extras Casting — Eva Stefankovicova; Crowd Marshals — Frantiska Lajchova, Leo Stefankovic, Lenka Stefankovicova; Interpreters — Peter Petruna, Branko Jehlar, Andrej Otruba, Jolana Kadlecikova, Juraj Paulik, Lubomir Baluch, Martin Ragala, Andrea Benicky, Dagmar Cechova, Cyril Sikula, Robert Janal; Special Visual FX and Animation by Industrial Light and Magic, a Division of Lucas Digital, Ltd.; Visual FX Pre-Production Co-Supervisor — Alex Seiden; Supervising Digital FX Artist — Barry Armour; Supervising Character Animators — Rob Coleman, Doug E. Smith; Character Animators — Chris Armstrong, Patrick Bonneau, Sue Campbell, Michael Eames, Miguel Fuertes, Daniel Jennette, Julija Learie, Julie Nelson, Magali Rigaudias, Dan Taylor, Dennis Turner, Colin White, Linda Bel, David Beyers Brown, Lou Dellarosa, Jenn Emberly, Paul Hunt, Ken King, Robert Marinic, Steve Nichols, Trish Schutz, James Tooley, Tim Waddy, William R. Wright; Digital FX Artists — Kevin Barnhill, Steve Braggs, Russell Earl, Gerald Gutschmidt, Margaret Hunter, Jeff Light, Min, Patrick T. Myers, David Parrish, Amanda Ronai, Laurence Treweek, Andy Wang, Mike Bauer, Marc Cooper, Dan B. Goldman, Roger Guyett, Gregor Lakner, Erik Mattson, Curt Miyashiro, Patrick Neary, Tony Plett, Ben Snow, John Walker; Lead Digital Character Modeler — Paul Giacoppo; Digital Modelers — Wayne Kennedy, Tony Hudson, Bruce Buckley; Animation Software Development — Cary Phillips; Digital Texturing Paint Artists — Carolyn Rendu, Jean-Claude Langer; Digital Paint and Roto Supervisor — Sandy Houston; Digital Paint and Roto Artists — Donna Beard, Rebecca Heskes, Susan Weeks, Joanne Hafner, Jodie Maier, Heidi Zabit; 3D Camera Matchmove Supervisor — Keith Johnson; 3D Camera Matchmove Artists — Lanny

Cermak, Loring Doyle, James Hagedorn, Patrice dS. Saenz, Terry Chostner, Selwynn Eddy III, David Hanks, Marla I. Selhorn; Sabre Compositing Artists — Caitlin Content, Grant Guenin, Chad Taylor, Rita Zimmerman; Visual FX Coordinators — Andy Bronzo, Vicki Engel, Luke O'Byrne; Color Timing Supervisor — Kenneth Smith; Visual FX Editors — Greg Hyman, Bill Kimberlin; Production Assistant — Deborah Heller; CG Resource Assistants — Michael Corcoran, Robert Mendez; Scanning Operators — Randall K. Bean, Mike Ellis, John Wlisnant; Digital Continuity Editor — Angel Leaper; Visual FX Assistant Editor — Roberto McGrath; Chief Modelmakers — Jean Bolte, Richard Miller; Sculptors — Robert Cooper, Mark Siegel, Harold Weed; Mechanical Rig — Mike Mackenzie, Scott McNamara, Michael Steffe, Eben Stromquist; Negative Cutter — Doug Jones; CG Technical Assistants — Tom Fejes, Doug Smith, John Torrijos; Digital Frame Touch-up — Al Bailey, Scott Bonnenfant; Line-up — James Lim, Tim Geideman; Storyboard Artists — David Dozoretz, Jonathan Rothbart; Video Engineer — Fred Meyers; ILM Senior Staff — Patricia Blau, Jeff Mann, Gail Currey, Jim Morris; Dragon Animatics by — Tippett Studio; Producer — Jules Roman; Art Director — Craig Hayes; Character Designer/Sculptor — Peter Konig; Dragon Sculptor — Ron Holthuysen; Fabrication Casting — Danny Wagner; Animators — Adam Valdez, Blair Clark; Technical Supervisors — Steve Reding, David Valdez; CG Painter — Paula Lucchesi; Software Programming — Doug Epps; Motion Input Fabrication — Bart Trickel; Movement Input — Leonard Pitt; Coordinator — Sheila Duignan; Production Accountant — Suzanne Yoshii; Runner — Warwick Seay; Matte Paintings by — Syd Dutton, Bill Taylor, A.S.C., of Illusion Arts, Inc.; Illusion Arts Visual FX Crew; Matte Artists — Robert Stromberg, Mike Wassel; Digital Supervisor — Richard Patterson; Digital Compositing — David S. Williams, Jr.; Digital Animator — Fumi Mashimo; Matte Photography — Adam Kowalski; Production Manager — Catherine Sudolcan; Hammerhead Tracking — Rebecca Marie, Thad Beier; Digital Frame Enhancement by — Perpetual Motion Pictures; Visual FX Supervisor FMP — Richard Malzahn; Visual FX Producer FMP — Kimberly Sylvester; Orchestra Conducted by — Randy Edelman; Music Editor — Joanie Diener; Scoring Mixers — Elton Ahi, Dennis Sands; Orchestration — Ralph Ferraro; Orchestra Contractor — Sandy DeCrescent; Assistant Music Editor — Christine Cholvin; Music Preparation — Julian Bratolvubov; Scoring Crew — Tim Malone, Irl Sanders, Greg Dennen, Odile Simkin, Sue McLean, Jill Tengan, Mark Esaelman; Horse Master — Ivo Kristoff; Sword Trainer/Choreographer — Kiyoshi Yamazaki; Physical Trainer — John Lees; Stunt Players — Gerry Crampton, Zoltan Gulyaskiss; Borsel's Stunt Company — Peter Hric, Bustav Kyselica, Monika Fiserova, Michal Sandala, Branislav Martinak, Ingrid Vrabcova, Peter Prikler, Samuel Kalim, Mirolsav Bertovic, Lubomir Burco, Vladimir Kuna, Peter Rak, Lubomir Misak, Rastislav Kotula, Peter Plazak, Vladimir Furdik, Marek Toth, Daniel Zdenek, Pavol Osusky, Martin Uhrovcik, Jaroslav Sykora, Peter Olgay, Stanislav Satko, Jana Zvarikova, Peter Uhrovcik; Filmed at Koliba Film Studios, Bratislava, Slovakia, and on location throughout the Republic of Slovakia. Recorded at Universal Studios Sound Facility; Lighting and Grip Equipment by — Arri Rental, Munich; Insurance — Great Northern/Reiff & Associates; Video Facility — Encore Video; Travel Services — Susan Hasrris, Revel Travel Service; Icon Lights provided by Light and Sound Design, Inc.; The producers would like to thank the following costume houses for their participation in the making of this film: Pentor Films, Ltd., Warsaw, Poland; Angels and Bermans, London, United Kingdom; Cornejo, Spain; Gabriella Lo Far, Rome, Italy; Lodzkie Filmove Centrum, Lodz, Poland; Animales y Carruajes, S.A., Madrid, Spain; In loving memory of Irwin Cohen and Steve Price; MCA Soundtracks; Filmed with Panavision Cameras and Lenses; Color by Deluxe; Eastman Color Film; DTS Stereo; DTS Digital Sound; Country of first publication: USA; Draco Productions Limited is author of this picture for purposes of the Berne Convention and all national laws giving effect thereto.

SYNOPSIS: Dragonheart opens in A.D. 984 A knight named Bowen has been hired by a king to teach Prince Einon the arts of battle and knighthood. In a raid on a village, the king is killed and Einon is mortally wounded. The queen takes the boy to the cave of a dragon. The dragon saves the boy's life by giving him half of his own heart.

Bowen comes to see that Einon is essentially evil and blames the dragon for it. He leaves, swearing to kill all dragons he runs into.

The film then jumps ahead 12 years and we meet Brother Gilbert of Glocanspur. Gilbert is a wandering bard and monk who rides a mule named Merlin in search of Avalon. He witnesses Bowen kill a dragon and states

The last remaining dragon and a dragonslaying knight form an unlikely alliance in Rob Cohen's *Dragonheart.*

that Bowen's skills are worthy of King Arthur and the Knights of the Round Table. Bowen runs into the dragon who saved Einon and they battle to a stalemate. Finally declaring a truce, the two talk and decide to team up to stage fake dragon killings in order to earn a living. Bowen names the beast Draco.

The love interest in the story is a girl named Kara. She happens to be the young lady who wounded Einon years before. Einon subsequently killed her father so she has an abiding hatred for the new king. This foursome travels around for a bit until they get into trouble at one village. Snatching them out of that situation, Draco flies them to Avalon. There, at the tomb of King Arthur, Bowen hears the voice of Arthur. Bowen renews his knightly vows, then he, Draco and Gilbert go off with Kara to fight Einon.

In the last battle it finally becomes clear to Bowen that the only way Einon can die is if Draco dies. Their shared hearts connect them. Draco harasses Bowen to strike the fatal blow, but Bowen can only bring himself to do it when it is to protect Kara from the rampaging Einon. As the last of the dragons dies, so does Einon, and Draco's spirit is freed to take its place among the stars.

This movie is completely fanciful, of course, but its use of Arthurian elements is intriguing. The character of Gilbert brings to mind Gildas and/or Nennius, both early writers of British history who mention a person of one name or another who may have been the Arthur of legend. Gildas and Nennius were both clerics as well, but they pre-dated the time depicted in this film — Nennius by about 100 years and Gildas by much more.

Dragons themselves have a strong connection with Arthurian legend, particularly in some of the traditions about Merlin. When Vortigern was unable to construct a fortress, the young Merlin revealed to him the reason: two dragons, a red one and a white one, were locked in combat beneath the foundations, causing the walls to fall (see *Merlin of the Crystal Cave, Merlin and the Dragons* and *Excalibur*).

It was a bit surprising that among Draco's ramblings Merlin wasn't mentioned. The fact that Gilbert rode a donkey named Merlin bears no further analysis.

References to the "old code" of knighthood and chivalry are frequent throughout the film, harking back, of course, to the ideals of the Knights of the Round Table. But the biggest connection to Arthuriana is the visit to Avalon. The site is depicted as a ruined castle on a crag. A Stonehenge-like circle of stones forms the tomb and memorial to King Arthur. The image of Arthur appears from one of the stones and Arthur himself speaks to Bowen, reminding the knight of his vows and his duty to mankind.

If all of that weren't enough, the special effects used to create the dragon for this movie make seeing it a real treat. Sean Connery, who performed in two other Arthurian films *(see Sword of the Valiant and First Knight),* does the voice of Draco. The catlike dragon has many of Connery's facial expressions blended into an incredibly realistic scaled, winged beast right out of the pages of myth.

Duck to the Future: "Sir Gyro de Gearloose" (1987)

44 minutes; Color; Cartoon; Copyright 1987, Walt Disney Company; Walt Disney Home Video #768; Produced by Walt Disney Television Animation

CREDITS: Supervising Producer — Fred Wolf; Associate Producer — Tom Ruzicka; Director — Steve Clark; Story Editors — Tedd Anasti, Patsy Cameron; Written by — Mark Zaslove; With the Talents of — Hal Smith, Russ Taylor, Peter Cullen, Barry Dennen, Richard Erdman; Art Director — Brad Landreth; Associate Director — Skip Morgan; Key Layout Stylists — Michael Peraz, Ed Ghertner, Ed Wexler; Storyboard Design — Elizabeth Chapman, Thom Enriquez, Jan Green, Rob Laduca, Elyse Pastel, Monte Young, Rich Chidlaw, Steve Gordon, Chuck Harvey, Marty Murphy, Hank Tucker; Key Background Styling — Paro Hozumi, Lisa Keene, Gary Eggleston; Color Key Styling — Debra Jorgensborg, Jill Stirdivant, Jan Cummings; Character Design — Ron Scholefield, Jill Colbert, Ed Gombert, Toby Shelton; Overseas Animation Supervisor — Mike Reyna; Timing Directors — David Brain, Vincent Davis, Bob Zamboni; Dialogue Direction — Andrea Romano; Track Reading — Skip Craig; Production Manager — Olivia Miner; Assistant Director — Randy Chaffee; Post Production Coordinator — Ken Tsumura; Production Assistants — Barbara Brysma, Krista Bunn, Jacaleen Veber, Luanne Wood, Judy Zook; Managing Editor — Rich Harrison; Supervising Editors — Charlie King, Rober S. Birchard; Sound Effects Editors — Marc Orfanos, Craig Jager; Assistant Editors — Rick Hinson, Glenn Lewis; "Duck Tales" Theme Composed by — Mark Mueller; Music Composed and Conducted by — Ron Jones; Additional Music by — Tom Chase, Steve Rucker; Animation Production by — Wang Film Productions Company, Ltd., Cuckoos Nest Studio

SYNOPSIS: *Duck to the Future* is one of a series of tapes that are recordings of the *Duck Tales* television cartoon series. The title of the tape is also the title of the first cartoon on the video. Neither of them have anything to do with the second cartoon, "Sir Gyro de Gearloose," which is the subject of this entry.

There is very little of interest here, other than the creativity of the writers at coming up with comical alternative names for pseudo-Arthurian characters.

Gyro, the *Duck Tales* handyman, is depressed at doing nothing but fixing minor problems for folks and builds himself a time machine called the Sometime Tub. He goes off to the land of Quackalot (Camelot) and meets King Artie ("And I love to party. Arthur, that other king who lives over there, boy is he dull").

Moreloon the magician is threatened by Gyro's scientific abilities. He enlists the help of Lesdred to get rid of Gyro, but Lesdred double-crosses Moreloon and takes over the castle. To win the inevitable fight, Moreloon and Gyro build a giant electromagnet. The effects of this on armor can be imagined. Gyro returns to his normal environs a happier man.

Dying (1975)

Not viewed; 120 minutes; Color; Documentary; Copyright 1975, WGBH Boston in Association with Amberson Video, Inc.; Distributed by PBS Video

CREDITS: Produced and Directed by — Michael Roemer; Music — Ron Hays; Performed by — Boston Symphony Orchestra; Conductor — Leonard Bernstein

SYNOPSIS: An examination of the psychological aspects of facing advanced terminal cancer, both on the patients and their families. A moving montage of colors and shapes gives visual expression to the Prelude and Liebestod from Wagner's *Tristan und Isolde*.

The Empire Strikes Back see Star Wars: The Empire Strikes Back

England's Historic Treasures
Documentary; No further information available.

La Espada en la Piedra (1963)
79 minutes; Color; Cartoon; Copyright 1963, Walt Disney Productions; Distributed by Buena Vista Home Video; Walt Disney Home Video #229/73

WITH THE VOICES OF: Alberto Gavira; Luis Manuel Pelayo; Dagoberto de Cervantes; Salvador Najar; Maruja Sen; Carlos Petrel
CREDITS: Spanish Version Direction — Edmundo Santos

SYNOPSIS: This is the Spanish-language version of Disney's cartoon movie *The Sword in the Stone*. It is identical in every way to the original except that Spanish has been dubbed in. For the complete credits and synopsis, see the entry for *The Sword in the Stone*.

The Eternal Return (1943)
100 minutes; Black and White; Live Action; French with English subtitles; Copyright 1943, André Paulvé; Janus Films; Public Media/Home Vision #ETE020; A Films Incorporated Presentation

CAST: Madeleine Sologne; Jean Marais; Jean Murat; Junie Astor; Roland Toutain; Jeanne Marken; Jean D'Yd; Pieral; Le Chien Moulou; Alexandre Tignault; Yvonne de Bray
CREDITS: Un Film de — Jean Delannoy; Récit et Paroles de — Jean Cocteau; Musique de — Georges Auric; Image de — Roger Hubert; Decors de — Wakhevitch; Assistant du Metteur en Scène — Roger Calon; Script Girl — Jacqueline Chevillotte; Operateur — Marc Fossard; Photographe — Aldo; Regie Géneral — Theron; Ingenieurs du Son — Monchablon et Carrère; Montage — Suzette Fauvel; Maquettes des Costumes — Annen Koff; Administrateur — Gaston Goudard; Directeur de Production — Emile Darbon; Tourné aux Studios CIMEX de la Victorine a Nice sur systeme "Western Electric"; Une Production André Paulvé; Distribuée Par Discina, Paris, Bordeaux, Lille, Lyon, Marseille, Toulouse

SYNOPSIS: At the end of the opening credits is the following quotation:

Eternal Return, a title borrowed from Nietzsche, means that the same legends are reborn time and again without the hero's knowledge. Eternal return of simple circumstances is the base of all great love stories. (signed) Jean Cocteau.

A somewhat dated modernization of the Tristan and Isolde story, the film nonetheless wears well and follows the legend in impressive detail.

Patrick is an orphan being raised by his uncle, Marc. Marc is widowed, but Gertrude, Patrick's mother's sister, and Gertrude's husband also live with Marc. Gertrude has a son, Achille, who is 24 years old and a dwarf. With all these oddball relatives rattling around in the palatial house, Marc is going a bit mad from loneliness and frustration.

Patrick goes to find his uncle a beautiful young wife. He goes to an island that his uncle apparently owns. In a bar he comes across a drunk picking on a young woman. To stop the man, Patrick fights with him and winds up with a knife wound in the leg. The young woman, Natalie, takes him home to patch him up and they become silently attracted to one another.

Natalie is an orphan as well and was raised by a woman named Ann, who is versed in the uses of herbs and potions. It turns out the drunk in the bar (Morolt), is Natalie's fiancé.

Patrick talks Natalie into going to meet his uncle. Before she leaves, Ann gives Natalie a love potion. It is in a bottle marked "poison" so no one will touch it. Marc marries Natalie, but Gertrude becomes very concerned that Marc won't want her family in the castle anymore. She sets Achille to spying on Patrick and Natalie.

Alone in the house one day with Natalie, Patrick makes drinks. Achille pours what he thinks is Natalie's poison into their drinks, so they end up consuming the love potion. At

A tender scene from *The Eternal Return* (1943) (courtesy Public Media, Inc.).

with him to a mountain cabin. In the cold and the snow Natalie falls ill and Patrick leaves to get her some medicine. While he's gone Marc finds Natalie and takes her back to his castle.

Patrick goes to a friend in town who owns a car repair shop. He is convinced to stay there for a time. The friend has a sister, also named Natalie. The three are relatively happy for a time and this second Natalie falls in love with Patrick. Her brother harasses Patrick into marrying her.

Patrick takes the two of them to Ann's place on the island for the wedding but insists on seeing his first Natalie one last time. He wants to see for himself that his first love doesn't love him any longer. That night, outside the castle walls, Patrick calls at her window, not knowing that she's changed rooms. Distraught that she didn't respond to him, he and the second Natalie's brother head back to the boat.

Patrick's whistling outside awakened Achille, however. The dwarf takes one of his father's guns and shoots the departing Patrick in the leg. Escaping through a swamp, Patrick's friend gets him to the boat and back to the island. The wound, however, has become infected.

Knowing that he is dying, Patrick pleads for his friend to go to the first Natalie and bring her to him. He asks that they place a white scarf at the top of the mast of the boat if she is coming to him. The friend agrees, leaving Patrick in the care of Ann and his sister.

Growing increasingly feverish and ill, Patrick finally hears the motor of the return-

first only Natalie believes that the brew can have any effect but it becomes obvious to everyone that something is going on between them.

Setting a trap for the young lovers, Marc pretends to leave for three days. He parks his car down the road and walks back to the castle. Marc, Gertrude and Achille catch Patrick in Natalie's bedroom that very night. Marc tells Patrick to leave immediately and tells Natalie she will be escorted back to her island in the morning.

Patrick sabotages Gertrude's car, it breaks down and he intercepts them, taking Natalie

ing boat. He asks the second Natalie if she can see the scarf. The poor girl lies at first but, seeing the devastating effect this has on Patrick, she tells him the truth. It is too much for Patrick, however, and he dies before his one love can get to him. The first Natalie finds him, but it is too late. She lies down beside Patrick's body and dies.

Except for the changes of time and names, *The Eternal Return* is an exact retelling of the Tristan legend. In this film Tristan has become Patrick, the Natalies are Iseult and Iseult Blanchemains, and Achille is Melot. Kahedrin is here in the person of the second Natalie's brother. King Mark is Patrick's Uncle Marc, the Brangien of the legend is Ann. Even the island comes from the old legends in that Iseult was the daughter of the king of Ireland.

The only criticism that might be leveled at this film is the fact that the subtitles are so incomplete. There are large sections of dialogue with no translation. Anyone with an ear for French can pick up what is being said, but for those either out of practice or totally unfamiliar with the language, there is a real loss of some of the nuances of the script.

Even Knights Have to Eat see under ***King Arthur and the Knights of Justice***

The Evil Forest see ***Parsifal (1951)***

Excalibur (1981)

141 minutes; Color; Live Action; Copyright 1981, Orion Pictures Company; Copyright 1991, Warner Home Video, Inc.; A Subsidiary of Warner Bros., Inc., a Time Warner Company

CAST: Nigel Terry (King Arthur); Helen Mirren (Morgana); Nicholas Clay (Lancelot); Cheri Lunghi (Guenevere); Paul Geoffrey (Perceval); Nicol Williamson (Merlin); Robert Addie (Mordred); Gabriel Byrne (Uther); Keith Buckley (Uryens); Katrine Boorman (Igrayne); Liam Neeson (Gawain); Corin Redgrave (Cornwall); Niall O'Brien (Kay); Patrick Stewart (Leondegrance); Clive Swift (Ector); Ciarin Hinds (Lot); Liam O'Callaghan (Sadok); Michael Muldoon (Estamor); Charley Boorman (Boy Mordred); Mannix Flynn (Mordred's Lieutenant); Garrett Keogh (Mador); Emmet Bergin (Ulfus); Barbara Byrne (Young Morgana); Brid Brennan (Lady in Waiting); Kay Peterson (Aged Morgana); Eamoan Kelly (Abbott)

CREDITS: Directed and Produced by — John Boorman; Screenplay by — Rospo Pallenberg, John Boorman; Adapted from Malory's *Morte D'Arthur* by — Rospo Pallenberg; Production Designer — Anthony Praff; Director of Photography — Alex Thomson, B.S.C.; Film Editor — John Merritt; Original Music Composed and Conducted by — Trevor Jones; Costume Designer — Bob Ringwood; Associate Producer — Michael Dryhurst; Executive Producers — Edgar F. Gross, Robert A. Eisenstein; Creative Associate — Neil Jordan; Second Unit Director/Photographer — Peter MacDonald; Casting — Mary Setway; Camera Operator — Bob Smith; Assistant Editor — Michael Kelliher; Fight Arranger — William Hobbs; Choreographer — Anthony Van Laasi; Assistant Director — Barry Blackmore; Production Manager — Jack Phelan; Production Accountant — Arthur Tarry; Continuity — Jean Skinner; Art Director — Tim Hutchinson; Associate Art Directors — John Lucas, Bertram Tyrer; Set Decorator — Bryan Graves; Makeup — Basil Newall, Anna Dryhurst; Hairstylist — Ann McFadyen; Wardrobe Master — Daryl Bristow; Sound Editor — Ron Davis; Sound Mixer — Doug Turner; Dialogue Editor — Tony Message; Sound Recordist — Tom Curran; Assistant Sound Editor — Pat Brennan; Special Effects — Peter Hutchinson, Alan Whibley; Armor by — Terry English; Assistant Directors — Ted Morely, Andrew Montgomery, Robert Dwyer Joyce, David Murphy, John Lawlor; Production Assistants — Beryl Harvey, Marie McFerran; Location Manager — Kevin Moriarty; Camera Assistants — Mike Brewster, John Campbell, Peter Versey, Shane O'Neill; Camera Grip — Luke Quigley; Boom Operator — John Fortune; Special Effects — Gerry Johnston, Michael Doyle; Property Master — Bob Hedges; Production Buyer — Trisha Edwards; Property Men — David Boyer, Paddy Murray; General Assistant — Teissche Boorman; Assistant Accountant — Cam Cremins; Construction Manager — Joe Lee; Wardrobe Mistress — Janet O'Leary; Hairdresser — Anne Dunne; Electrical Supervisor — Jack Conroy; Electricians — Louis Conroy, Derek Hale, Terry Eille, Martin Holbend; Standby Crew — Barry Cunningham, Martin Forrestal, Terry Baker, Christy Yourell, Tom Lundy; Stillsman — Armond Stilgast; Modelmaker — Anthony Freeman; Scenic Artist — Merwyn Howe; Master Plasterer — Joe Lear; Mas-

Lobby card from John Boorman's *Excalibur* (1981).

ter Painter — Owen Marname; Transport Manager — Arthur Dunne; Armorers — Peter Leicht, Steve Tidiman, Nick Fitzpatrick; Horsemaster — Michael Rowland; The Riders — Philip Bernon, Richard Collins, Seamus Collins, Joe Cullen, Daithi Curren, Tony Doyle, Donal Fortune, David Gawaghan, Eddie Kennedy, Branco McLaughlin, Michael O'Farrell, Roy O'Toole; Stunts — Ken Byrne, Dominic Newill, Paul Kelly, Chris King, James McHale, Ed Mcshortall, Donal O'Farrell, Bernard O'Hare, Peter Spelman, Alan Walsh of the Irish Film Stunt Squad; Special Digital Effects — Wally Weevers; Special Photographic Effects — Oxford Scientific Films, Ltd.; Optical Effects and Titles — General Screen Enterprises, Ltd.; Cameras by — Arraflex; Color by — Technicolor; Ethnic Jewelry by — Liberty's, London; Sound Re-recording — Delta Sound, Ltd.; Music Recording — The Music Center; Music Recording Engineers — John Richards, Richard Lewzey; Prelude in *Parsifal*, Prelude in *Tristan und Isolde* and Siegfried's Funeral March from *The Ring* by Richard Wagner; Specially Recorded by — The London Philharmonic Orchestra; Conducted by — Norman Del Mar; "O For-

tuna" from *Carmina Burana* by Carl Orff, Copyright 1932, Munich, Germany; Leipzig Radio Symphonic Orchestra and Chorus; Conducted by — Herbert Kegel; Courtesy — Polygram Records; Thanks to: Board of Works, Robert Childers, Esq., The Powerscourt Estate, The Hon. Garth DeBrun, Mrs. Caroline Hamilton, The Earl of Heath; Filmed in the Republic of Ireland in Wicklow, Kerry, Tipperary and at the National Film Studios

SYNOPSIS: If *Excalibur* does nothing else for Arthurian film, it gives the subject an epochal feel. The dark, noisy and depressing movie seems to have been written around the stirring music of Richard Wagner and Carl Orff, which is used extensively.

Excalibur is based on Malory, but makes many departures from the traditional details. The opening essentially follows customary lines except that Uther receives Excalibur from Merlin and with it he makes peace with Cornwall. At the celebration feast, however, Uther lusts after Cornwall's wife, Igrayne. He gets Merlin to use magic so he can appear to Igrayne as her husband and that night begats Arthur upon her.

One oddity of the movie is that these medievally clad knights never seem to remove their armor. Even when making love to poor Igrayne (as her daughter, Morgana, looks on) Uther is fully encased in iron.

When Merlin comes to claim the infant Arthur, Uther chases after him but is ambushed. In his death throes Uther plunges Excalibur into a stone, declaring none shall wield it but himself. There it stays until Arthur comes to get it as a young man, to replace his foster brother Kay's sword, which was misplaced just before a tournament.

There is much consternation and disagreement over Arthur being named king. Uryens is the main dissident but even he is won over when Arthur defeats him at the siege of Cameliard. There Arthur meets Guenevere, the daughter of King Leondegrance of Cameliard. He falls in love with her despite Merlin's warnings.

Some time later Arthur comes across Lancelot, who does not recognize the king. Lancelot challenges Arthur to fight. Arthur accepts and, on the verge of humiliation at the hands of this foreign knight, he calls on the power of Excalibur. In doing so he injures Lancelot, winning the fight but breaking Excalibur.

At Arthur's realization that Excalibur is meant to "unite all men, not to serve the vanity of one man," the Lady of the Lake returns the repaired sword to him.

After another victory, Arthur declares his plans for a Round Table and a gathering of knights to meet there. He then sends Lancelot to escort Guenevere to Camelot for the wedding. Lancelot declares his eternal love to the girl and, as Merlin warned, the stage is set for disaster.

Morgana is present at the wedding feast and she talks Merlin into taking her under his wing. Lancelot spends most of his time away from Camelot to avoid Guenevere. He meets young Perceval on one journey and brings him back as a page.

Morgana begins to work her revenge by goading Gawain into accusing the queen of infidelity. Arthur can't champion Guenevere because he is the king and must judge her.

Sleeping in the forest, Lancelot is attacked by his own armor and stabbed through the side. No one shows up at the appointed jousting site to defend Guenevere's honor, so the page Perceval volunteers. Arthur knights him on the spot, but Lancelot arrives just in time to take the challenge. In spite of his wound he defeats Gawain.

While Lancelot and Guenevere are away consummating their love, Arthur has a conversation with Merlin about them. When Arthur asks if he must kill them, Merlin replies that he can tell Arthur no more, his time here is ended. "There are other worlds", he says, "this one is done with me."

Arthur finds Guenevere and Lancelot sleeping together in the forest. He drives Excalibur into the earth between them — much as Uther had done — and leaves it there as a sign to them. At the same time, Morgana, who by now has learned much of Merlin's dark arts, manages to trap the old wizard and lock him up forever in a crystalline limbo. Then Morgana goes to Arthur and magically charms him into thinking she's Guenevere, getting him to begat Mordred upon her.

Finally Arthur is struck down by a lightning bolt in his chapel. With these cataclysmic events, the land begins to die. In desperation Arthur decrees a quest to find the Holy Grail in order to restore things to normal.

The search goes on for years. Mordred and Morgana kill most of the Knights of the Round Table as they wander the world seeking the holy relic. Perceval, however, survives their perfidy, finds the Holy Grail and brings it to Arthur. Drinking from it, Arthur's life and will are renewed. In a nice summation he says, "Lancelot carried my honor, Guenevere my guilt, Mordred my sins. My knights fought my causes. Now, my brother, I shall be king."

Arthur puts out a call to arms, then goes to the nunnery where Guenevere has been living. To his surprise she has Excalibur and she gives it to him for this final battle against Mordred.

Next Arthur pays a visit to Stonehenge where the spirit of Merlin comes to him in a dream. As a spirit, Merlin assists in the effort to eradicate Arthur's enemies by tricking Morgana into destroying herself.

The final terrible battle is met. Even Lancelot comes out of his self-imposed retirement for the fight. Both sides annihilate each other and at last the two main antagonists come face to face. Mordred runs Arthur through with a spear, but Arthur is able to strike. Mordred's magical armor does him no good against Excalibur and he dies at his father's hand.

Perceval is with Arthur in his last moments, and he throws the sword back into the waters of the lake. The film closes with a ship carrying Arthur off, attended by three ladies.

This film could as well have been titled *Merlin,* for it is that character's thread which is strongest throughout the movie. In fact Merlin's is the most enjoyable and well-developed personality in the whole thing.

For Merlin to figure so strongly throughout the whole tale is one of many departures from Malory that Boorman and Pallenberg took in writing this screenplay. In Malory it is Nimue, one of the Ladies of the Lake, who has it in for Merlin. In a rather perfunctory manner she traps him under a big stone and leaves him there (book 4, chapter 1).

Uther wielding Excalibur is another major departure. Uther planting Excalibur in the stone is one more, although that particular adaptation does simplify the confusion that sometimes occurs over Arthur's involvement with more than one sword.

Perhaps the biggest difference from Malory is Arthur being equated with the wounded Grail King, or Fisher King, in *Excalibur.* Wolfram's version of this part of the legend (which pre-dates Malory by some 200 years) names Amfortas as the Fisher King, whose wound could only be healed by Perceval (or Parsifal) asking the right question. By the time Malory takes on the story there are two wounded kings, Pellam (book 2, chapters 15 and 16) and his son Pelles (book 17, chapter 5). Both of them are called the "Maimed King" in Malory.

Pellam is wounded in a fight with Balin, who wields the Sacred Spear, the very one used to pierce Christ's side on the cross. This wound to Pellam is the one known as the Dolorous Stroke. Pelles is wounded through both thighs by the same spear.

By contrast, in the film *Excalibur* Arthur is given the Dolorous Stroke by Heaven itself when a lightning bolt crashes through a stained glass window, smiting him. This probably comes directly, if in somewhat editorialized form, from book 13, chapter 7, of Malory. As the court sits at supper while a thunderstorm rages outside, a beam of sunlight seven times brighter than daylight enters the hall. The Grail floats in, covered by white samite, but none of them can see the Grail itself. Foods appear and the Grail vanishes. Arthur gives thanks and Gawain vows that on the following day he will begin his search for the Grail. One hundred and fifty Knights of the Round Table wind up following Gawain's lead. The strongest effect this has on Malory's Arthur is sadness at their departure and the feeling that most of them will die, ending the fellowship of the Round Table.

So, where Malory made two Grail Kings of Wolfram's one, Boorman and Pallenberg return the number to one again. They also simplify the tale by making Arthur the Grail King. Where Galahad healed Malory's Pellam, Perceval heals Arthur in *Excalibur.*

Excalibur (1981) see under *King Arthur and the Knights of the Round Table*

Excalibur (1982) see *Into the Labyrinth: "Excalibur"*

Excalibur: The Raising of the Sword (1982)

Not viewed; 16mm; Copyright 1982, Whaddon Boys Club Film Unit, Great Britain

CAST: Adrian Lester; Members of the Whaddon Boys Club Film Unit

SYNOPSIS: Merlin uses his powers to raise the sword from the lake.

The Excalibur Kid (1998)

90 minutes; Color; Live Action; Copyright 1998, The Kushner-Locke Company; Copyright 1998 Canarom Productions, Inc., and Castel Films, SRL; Full Moon Releasing; Pulsepounders! Item #7007

CAST: Jason McSkimming (Zack); Francois Klanfer (Merlin); Mak Fyfe (Arthur); Francesca Scorsone (Morgause); Natalie Eester (Gwynneth); Serban Celea (Sir Ector); Teodor Danetti (Old Man at Court); George Duta (Jeffy); Camelia Maxim (Gail); Claudiu Trandafir (Jim); Constantin Draganescu (Old Man with Cart); Julia Boros (Innkeeper); Adrian Ciobanu (King Carados); Vitali Bantis (Dolt 1); Marcelo Cobzariu (Dolt 2); Mihnea Trusca (Kay); Livia Timus (Nasty Man); Constantin Florescu (King Bans); Razvan Popa (Duke of St. Ives); Felix Totolici (Courtier 1); Enea Dabija (Courtier 2); Vlad Jipa (Courtier 3)

CREDITS: Casting — Marsha Chelsey, CDC; Costume Designer — Oana Paunescu; Music Composed by — Paul Inston; Production Designer — Ioana Corciova; Editor — Paul Winestock; Director of Photography — Viorel Sergovici, Jr.; Executive Producers — David M. Perlmutter, Lewis B. Chesler; Executive Producer — Vlad Paunescu; Executive Producers — Donald Kushner, Dana Scanlan; Producer — Chris Andrei; Written by — Antony Anderson; Director — James Head; Co-Producers — Gari Antal, Michael J. Mahoney; Production Manager — Irina Chirita; 1st Assistant Director — Cristian Ciurea; Script Supervisor — Cornelia Stefan; Slate — George Toader; Production Coordinator (Romania) — Marian Popescu; Production Coordinator (Canada) — Brenda Torrance; Makeup — Catalin Ciutu; Hairstylist — Carmen Tibuslea; Wardrobe Supervisor — Ana Ioneci; Dressers — Eli Calin, Carmen Ilie, Cristina Anton; Art Director — Viorel Ghenea; Assistant Art Director — Cristina Filimon; Property Master — Cristian Baluta; Props — Ghita Cosache, Nicolae Geroiu; Effects Props and Rigs — Ionel Popa; Props Studio — Mihai Alexandru; Construction Coordinator — Vlad Paun; Construction Supervisor — Szoli Szabo; Carpenters — Fratila Marin, Alexandru Constantinescu, Cristian Simon; Effects Supervisor — Daniel Parvulescu; 1st Assistant Camera — Ilie Georgica; Loader — Radu Nicolae; Key Grip — Gabi Postasu; Grips — Iona Matei, Constantin Rusetescu; Gaffer — Catalin Calin; Electricians — Cioc Pascu, George Stan, Nicu Botarlaianu, Paul Ticu; Generator Operator — Bebe Surgiu; Location Sound — Camil Silviu; Boom — Nicolae Perianu, Aurel Perianu; Video Assist — Bogdan Barbaslescu; Stills Photographer — Costin Doina; 2nd Assistant Director — Laurentu Maronnese; Assistant Director Trainee — Eduard Reghintovschi; Casting Coordinator (Romania) — Catalin Dordea; Extras Casting — Doru Bobesiu; Stunt Coordinator — Adrian Pavlovski; Stunts — Mihai Silviu, Radu Popescu, Mihai Maldea, Fane Ursu; Production Accountants — Chris Elkins, Donalda Palmer; Cashier — Diana Negoitescu; Transportation Coordinator — Ion Damion; Transportation Captain — Vlad Tomescu; Shipping and Customs — Toni Lakatos; Bidder — Cristian Bostanescu; Set Production Assistants — Bogdan Obrocea, Lucian Azoitei; Secretary — Lidia Cheinic; Production Secretary — Sanda Mihalache; Translator — Andreea Ciocan; Catering — Mirela Ionita, Oana Chitu; Post Production Supervisor — Lisa Kalushner; Post Production Coordinator — Brenda Torrance; Post Production — Eyes Post Group; Colorist — Sue Chambers; On-Line Editor — Frank Biasi; Post Production Audio — Trackworks, Inc.; Supervising Sound Editor — Steve Munro; Dialogue Editor — David Drainie Taylor; ADR Editor — Tim Roberts; Effects Editor — Colin Baxter; Foley Artist — John F. Thompson; ADR/Foley Recordist — Steve Pollett; Trainee Assistant Editor — Timothy Mehlenbaacher; Re-Recording Mixers — Steve Munro, Tim Roberts; Visual Effects by — Sundog Films, Inc.; Visual Effects Supervisor — Wayne Trickett, Doug Campbell, Mario Ferreira, Kent Ing, Dave Bachelor, Steve Gordon, Cisco Ribas, May Leung, Greg Astles; Visual Effects by — Aris Studios, Ionica Adriana, Sergin Negulici, Anca Ignatescu, Stefan Cios, Dana Palcu, Dragos Stanomir; Film Processing — The Lab in Toronto, Inc.; Insurance Provided by — B.F. Lorenzetti & Associates, Inc.; Production Financing Provided by — Equipcap Financial Corporation; Financial Legal Services Provided by — Heenan Blaikie; Completion Bond — Film Finances; Special Thanks to — Robert Beattie,

Annette Grot, Elizabeth McGuinness, Steve Ransohoff, Harian Freedman, Panasonic Canada, Inc.; Filmed on location in Romania at Castel Film Studio; A Canada-Romania Co-Production; Produced with the participation of the Government of Ontario; The Ontario Film and Television Tax Credit; Chesler Perlmutter Productions

SYNOPSIS: *The Excalibur Kid* is the story of a 15-year-old boy named Zack who is very upset with his parents because they are about to move the family to a new city. Arguing with them about it over breakfast one morning, he feels that he won't make the fencing team in a new school because it's too late in the year. Not getting the response from them he'd like, Zack storms out of the house, grabbing his foil on the way.

His little brother Jeffy follows him into the woods and tries to cheer Zack up, but it doesn't work. Zack just gets grumpier and even wishes he lived in medieval times, when things were simpler.

While this is going on, Morgause is watching. Having her own plans, she grants Zack's wish and brings him to her time of A.D. 486. Using various spells, Morgause gets Zack to pull Excalibur from the stone before young Arthur gets there. She pretends to be Zack's sister and wowing the young fellow with his new kingship, the two go to court together.

Merlin realizes that the young sorceress must have gotten her hands on the Dark Book. He goes to Zack, appearing in the form of a horse and convinces the boy that things aren't right. Zack helps Merlin try to convince Arthur that it is really he who should be on the throne. It all seems too ridiculous to Arthur though, and he ignores them.

Morgause indeed has the Dark Book and in a borrowing from *Excalibur*, she tries "the Spell of Making." It is such a powerful spell, however, that she decides to practice more with others before using it.

Things go along in this vein until Arthur is finally convinced of his rightful place. He with Excalibur, Zack with his foil and Merlin's

cloak of invisibility, and Merlin with all his magic take on Margause's evil minions. There is a battle between the wizards and finally Morgause is neutralized. Merlin determines to send Morgause to Orkney where King Lot can watch over her for a time. Zack is returned to his own time and though he maintains no memory of the incredible events he has been a part of, he seems to have become a happier, wiser individual for the experience.

This film takes a smattering of things from many sources, throwing them together to make a mildly humorous movie for kids. These folks were, however, familiar with many often overlooked particulars of the legends.

At one point for instance, while Zack is holding court with Morgause, "King Bans" and his brother Bors appear to warn him that six other kings are banding together against him. Ban and Bors are not usual inclusions in films, but indeed appear in the Vulgate Cycle and Malory.

The very use of the name Morgause is more accurate than most movies' use of Morgan or Mab. Morgause was traditionally the oldest of three sisters and in fact was said to have married King Lot who with her sired Gawain, Agravain, Gareth, Gaheris and Mordred. So, the fact that in *The Excalibur Kid* Merlin sends her to Lot is another indication of a knowledgeable writer.

The whole premise of the film is of course somewhat similar to Twain's *A Connecticut Yankee in King Arthur's Court*. Merlin's appearing as a horse, then later as a mouse would seem to come from White's *The Once and Future King*, though in the book it was young Arthur (or Wort), not Merlin, who was changed into several animals as part of his lessons. The battle between Morgause and Merlin is reminiscent of a similar scene in Disney's *The Sword and the Stone* cartoon classic and as already mentioned, the "Spell of Making" seems to come from Boorman's *Excalibur*.

Exploring the Celtic Lands: Landscape of Belief (1991)

28 minutes; Color; Documentary; Copyright 1991, R.T.E.; Copyright 1993, Films for the Humanities, Inc.; Films for the Humanities and Sciences #3848

CREDITS: Narrated by—Peadar Lamb; Written and Devised by—John Feehan; Music—John Feeley; Sound—Simon J. Willis; Sound Dubbing—Bob Bell, Terry Gough, Joe Ó'Dubhghaill; Editor—Amanda Sutton; Assistant Editor—James Dalton; Photography—Cian de Buitléar; Director—Paddy Breathnach; Series Producer—Éamon de Buitléar; The Producers Wish to Thank: Sealink Ferries, English Heritage, British Tourist Authority, Dublin, Orkney Tourist Board, The National Trust, Historic Buildings and Monuments, Scotland, Caledonian MacBrayne Ferries, Office of Public Works; Produced with assistance from AIB Group; An Éamon de Buitléar production for R.T.E.

SYNOPSIS: A thorough tour of ancient stone artifacts around Western Europe, including Brittany, Scotland, Ireland and the Hebrides. Stone circles, chamber tombs, passage tombs, portal tombs, hole stones and pillar stones are viewed and discussed.

Entirely logical and rational in presentation, the film evaluates these Stone Age and Bronze Age landmarks for what they are—namely tombs, religious celebration markers and ancient lunar and astronomical observatories.

It is made clear that these structures predate the Celtic move into the various regions by many centuries. The few Celtic marks on the land are called "tattoos" in the film. These are gigantic pictures carved on chalk hillsides.

Although a fascinating film, Arthurian content is minimal. One portal tomb in Ireland is tied to the Celtic legend of Grania and Dermot, which the film identifies as the source of the Tristan and Isolde story of later times.

Fables and Legends: English Folk Heroes (1986)

30 minutes each volume; Color; Still illustrations; Copyright 1986, Milliken Publishing Company; Copyright 1986, MCA Home Video, Inc.; Milliken Publishing Company and Donald Thomas Associates; MCA Home Video #VHS 80451, 80452

CAST: Phil Johnson; Joe Price; Roseanne Gauvin; Trevor Pollack; Brandon Pollack; Jennifer Roszell; Sarah Thompson

CREDITS: Producer—Donald Thompson; Director—Greg Beeson; Project Coordinator—David Hersk; Creative Director—Maria Ojile; Audio Engineers—Rob Rivard, Kevin Peterson, John Warner; Videotape—Craig Wolfe; Technical Directors—Phil Duff, Mike Miller; Set Design—Bob Bye; Camera—Craig Chapman, Joanne Babie, Pat Chuinard, Steve Norlin, David Trout, Colin Williams; Floor—Ron Westgaard, Bob Garvie; Milliken Editorial Staff—Cameron McKay

SYNOPSIS: As stated on the jacket, Milliken's *Fables and Legends* series is intended for children ages 12 and under. The opening format is of a modern family on a camping trip. Gathered around the campfire at night, they get the father to tell the stories on these tapes.

"Arthur and the Sword" is the first of two stories told in volume 1. The second is "Ivanhoe."

King Arthur is identified as "semimythical, probably a minor Roman or Saxon leader in the south of England." It is described how Uther maintained peace in Britain with the help of Merlin. The peace was destroyed, however, when Uther died, so Merlin and the archbishop agreed that one king had to be chosen. They gather all the knights and lords on New Year's Day at the Cathedral of Canterbury. Sir Ector, his son Kay, and his "stepson" Arthur, are among them and the familiar scenario of Kay's forgotten sword and Arthur's retrieval of the one in the stone is recounted.

Merlin reveals the truth of Arthur's lineage to Uther, the archbishop declares Arthur to be king and the coronation is held on Pentecost.

"The Table Round" is the first of two legends presented in volume 2. The second is "Beowulf."

In the version used in "The Table Round," the Round Table was a gift from Gwenevere to Arthur. It is stated that stories about the Knights of the Round Table are a mixture of many different tales with many levels of interpretation possible.

The conniving Morgan Le Fay, Arthur's sister, is described as never having accepted the true church. Instead she was a "false" Druid and perhaps more powerful than Merlin. Her evil son, Mordred, goes to Camelot and is accepted by Arthur.

Lancelot of the Lake comes all the way from France to join the Round Table. None of the other knights accept him until Arthur knights him. Lancelot goes off to aid King Pellus, whose castle is under siege, and is waylaid by the Black Knight (it is implied here that he is Mordred) and a group of Morgan's men. They capture Lancelot and bring him to Pellus. The Black Knight pretends to be Lancelot, but Pellus's daughter, Elaine, recognizes the truth.

Lancelot kills the Black Knight and stays for some time with Pellus. He and Elaine fall in love and marry, then Lancelot leaves for Camelot. Along the way he meets a beautiful maiden who gives him a drink of water. Unfortunately it's actually Morgan and the water causes Lancelot to forget everything that has happened to him on his mission to Pellus's castle. Elaine gives birth to Galahad just before dying of sorrow.

Fifteen years pass and we find a Round Table peopled with lying, grumbling knights who no longer go out on quests or do any real good. Merlin has disappeared and things aren't looking good for Camelot.

On the feast of Pentecost a hermit shows up with the young Galahad. Arthur recognizes the hermit's voice (Merlin?) and heeds his words. Galahad is the only one pure enough to fill the Siege Perilous and to take on the one and only quest that might save Camelot, namely, the recovery of the Holy Grail. Arthur knights the boy and Galahad leaves.

Galahad finds the Grail in a cave atop Mount Salvat, but it is too late to save Arthur's Camelot. "Time and the nature of men" have destroyed it.

The Faery Princess see under *Princess Gwenevere and the Jewel Riders*

La Femme d'à Côté see *The Woman Next Door*

The Ferocious Fathers see under *The Adventure of Sir Lancelot*

Feuer und Schwert: Die Legende von Tristan und Isolde see *Fire and Sword: The Legend of Tristan and Isolde*

Field Trip: "Sticks in Stones" (1998)

Television series episode #038; 30 minutes; Color; Live Action and Puppets; Television series, Episode #038; Copyright 1998, ProCreations/Western International Syndication

CAST: Talia Osteen (Charly); Andrew Jones (Zero); David Fedele (Pug); Michael Nozzi (Policeman); Ron Ship (Policeman); Juan Talamantez (Policeman); Tony "Tonan" Swatton (Himself); Patrick Lambke (Mordred); William Cory Hurt (Sir Galahad); Kristina Hagerty (Lady in Waiting); Michaela Nastasia (Guenevere); Additional Voices (Marcy Madden, Kara Nau).

CREDITS: Executive Producers—Chris Lancey, Jane Cohen; Producers—Scott Madden, Andrew Jones; Line Producer—Mirjam Schippers; Written and Created by—Andrew Jones, Scott Madden; Director—Scott Madden; Director of Photography—Rick S. Butler; Original Music—John Nau; Associate Director—Anne Rickey; Location Coordinator—Roderick Young; Sound Recorder—David Gekler; B-Camera Operator—Larry Farmer; B-Camera Sound Recorder—John Slocum; Gaffer—Roderick Young; Key Grip—Todd Appleman; Grips—Joe Thompson, Malakhi Simmons; Utility—Gordon Musgrove; Post Production Supervisor—Marcy Madden; Editors—Sibille Törber, Gary Laird; Post Production—KRAKATOA Entertainment; Sound Designer/Mixer—Todd Brown; Post Production Audio—KRAKATOA Entertainment; Sound Assistant—Ramy Sabry; Puppets by—The Jones Effects Studio; Project Supervisor—Connor McCullagh; Puppet Wardrobe—Paul McAvene, Scott Johnson, Mathew McAvene; Computer Animation—Blue Light Animations, Ed Rubin; Prop Master—Mike

Semon; Puppet Wrangler — Fred Cervantes; Hair and Makeup — Debra Hodgen; Production Staff— Juan Talamantez, Kevin Briles, Sanaa Seaton; Controller — Carren Jones; Additional Writing — Marcy Madden, David Fidele; Educational Consultant/Research — Ray Conser; Talent Provided by — Tory Christopher, Associated Artist Agency; Catering by — Nicelys Aussie Cafe; Medieval Wardrobe Provided by — English Rose Consulting, Cynthia Hawkins, Sword & the Stone; Title Sequence Created by — Gary Laird; Special Thanks to: Tony Swatton, Sword & the Stone, McKell Brockbank, Cynthia Hawkins, Nathan Hess, Suzanne Jacobs, Mathew Murphy, Jon Woodard, Sheri Boyd; Website Designed by — Chris Sherman, www.pugandzero.com; www.pugandzero.com produced in association with Allbittron Communications Company, Inc.

SYNOPSIS: *Field Trip* is an educational children's television series in which puppet characters interact with humans. The background to the series is the following: Twelve-year-old Charlotte Wells (nicknamed Charly) discovered a way to travel through time and space. She calls the device the "Exploragyzer." The first time she fired it up, two alien but friendly time travelers, named Pug and Zero, were trapped in our time. A third character, Scoop, is a pyramid-shaped flying camera from Zero's gadget bag who provides unusual visuals of the subjects at hand.

Charly traded the Exploragyzer for Pug's wrist modem, a Dick Tracy–esque communication device. Pug and Zero promptly disappeared into a quantum hole and are bouncing around (on field trips) to different interesting places in our time. Charly built another Exploragyzer and headed out to find the wayward pair.

Each episode of the show concentrates on one topic, providing basic information on the subject in a clear and entertaining way. The "Sticks in Stones" episode visits modern-day blacksmith Tony Swatton. In doing so, the story also centers on Arthurian legend and chivalry.

Pug and Zero pop out of the quantum hole and interrupt a sword fight between two knights, one in classic shining armor, the other in sinister black. A small crowd of folks in medieval garb are watching. The Black Knight turns out to be a grouchy Sir Mordred. Feeling insulted, he challenges Pug to a joust.

Misunderstanding the term, Pug accepts. One of Pug's many quips is that perhaps Mordred had a bad childhood. A lady in waiting presents Pug with the handkerchief of none other than Guenevere, stating that if he wins the joust, Guenevere will be Pug's lady. When Pug learns from Zero that jousting is fighting, not the "jesting" he thought it was, he loses some of his confidence.

The two make their way to Swatton's shop, the Sword & the Stone. Swatton, we learn, is one of only 12 blacksmiths in the world who create complete armor and other knightly accoutrements. He has provided arms and armor for such films as *Hook, Conan, Zorro* and *Batman and Robin*. The sympathetic blacksmith makes a magnificent sword (Excalibur?) for Pug and a full suit of armor. At the shop Swatton demonstrates the steps to make a sword, starting with steel flat stock, through the forging and finishing processes.

The two aliens meet Mordred at the appointed time but Zero trips and the sword flies through the air, implanting itself magically through an anvil sitting on top of a stone. As Pug, his back to the sword and stone, gamely tries to face down Mordred, a heroic knight pulls the sword out and grimly approaches. Mordred makes a hasty retreat. In awe, the alien crew asks, "Are you that Darth Vader guy?" "Our knight in shining armor?" "The once and future king?". Swatton who, having defeated Mordred, states, "Maybe it's time for the blacksmith to stand with the queen."

There are many more references to both Arthurian legend and the art of blacksmithing than are mentioned here. The show's website provides excellent age-appropriate bibliographical material for each episode. Links to Arthurian websites as well as Swatton's Sword & the Stone site are included. As Producer Scott Madden wrote, "We view our show as a vehicle for inspiration. We hope to plant seeds that will inspire further discovery in young minds."

Fire and Sword: The Legend of Tristan and Isolde (Feuer und Schwert: Die Legende von Tristan und Isolde) (1982)

84 minutes; Color; Live Action; Copyright 1985, New Horizons Picture Corporation

CAST: Peter Firth (Dinas); Leigh Lawson (Mark); Christoph Waltz (Tristan); Antonia Preser (Isolde); Vladek Sheybal (Andret); Walo Lüönd (Gorvenal); Kurt Raab (Ganelon); Christine Wipf (Brangäne); Rita Kail (Maid); Archie O'Sullivan (Old Baron); Brendan Cauldwell (1st Baron); Don Foley (2nd Baron); Dietrich Kerky (Denavolin); Anton Huber (Gondoin); Liam O'Callaghan (Morolt); Kerstin Dobbertin (Abess); Patrick Müllerschön (Perinis)

CREDITS: Photography—Aribert Hantke, Jacques Steyn, Pim Tjujerman, Des Whelan; Editor—Barbara von Weitershausen; Grip—Honorat Stangi, Helmut Glass, Christoph Fromm, Eugene Whelan; Gaffers—Hans Dreher, Hans Krügler, Wolfgang Geyer; Costumes—Ruth Gilbert, Renate Zimmermann, Horst Esser, Angelica Del Negro, Helen Curran; Art Department—Aribert Hantke, Claude Garnier, Mervyn Rowe, Dieter Bächie, Phillip Henderson, Tom Murphy, Helmut Glassmann, Christian Klein, Erich Kuster, John Burke, Eamonn O'Higgins; Research—Georg von Kieseritzky; Makeup—Jill Carpenter; Hairdressing—Renate Dreher; Still Photography—Norman Hargood; Horses—Mick Rowland, Franz Huber; Stunt Coordination—Hans Priegel; Catering—Margot RothKirch-Bächle, Katharina Preser; Guide Sound—Nicolai Müllerschön; Script Supervision—Helga Soboszek; Assistant Director—Christa Reeh; Producer—Peter Genée; Film Accountants—Kerstin Dobbertin, Daniel Ferrari, Heidi Huber; Associate Producers—Kevin Moriarty, Harald Kügler; Production Team—Peter Holder, Robert Dwyer-Joyce, Gay Brabizon, Rainer Kürzel, Margot Rothkirch-Bächle; Production Assistants—Bernd Grotzke, Volker Hannawacker; Secretaries to the Producers—Ulrike Ares, Laureen Stierle; Sound Mix—Peter Hillert; Editing—Barbara von Weitershausen, Moune Barius; Music—Robert Lovos; Screenplay—Max Zihlmann; Story by—Veith von Fürstenberg, based on legend; Directed by—Veith von Fürstenberg; A German-Irish Co-production Produced by Genée and von Fürstenberg Film Produktionsges, mbH

with Popular-Film, Hans H. Kaden, FFAT, DNS-Film, Dieter Geissler Filmproduktion GmbH ZDF and Don Gerghty Filmservices Ltd.

SYNOPSIS: A serious and grim rendering of the Tristan and Isolde legend, *Fire and Sword* is reminiscent in style of Bresson's *Lancelot of the Lake*. The movie combines beautifully stark filming with long, studied silences and some additional quirks.

Introductory text at the beginning of the film states:

> Through trial by combat God determines right from wrong and his judgment is revealed in the outcome. Morolt, the invincible Irish knight, wants to enforce Ireland's ancient right of tribute from Cornwall. Mark, king of Cornwall, who has no wife and no heirs has promised his throne to the man who defeats Morolt in single combat. The combat is to take place on the island of Saint-Samson. There will be no witnesses, only one knight will survive. Tristan, King Mark's beloved nephew, has accepted the challenge.

If one were not familiar with the legend, this film would be difficult to follow since so little else is explained. For instance, it is plainly shown that a chink has been broken from Tristan's sword after his fight with Morolt, but no further reference is made to that.

First Knight (1995)

134 minutes; Color; Live Action; Copyright 1995, Columbia Pictures Industries, Inc.; Copyright 1995, Columbia Tristar Home Video; A Zucker Brothers Production; Columbia Pictures, a Sony Pictures Entertainment Company; Columbia Tristar Home Video #71173

CAST: Sean Connery (King Arthur); Richard Gere (Lancelot); Julia Ormond (Guinevere); Ben Cross (Malagant); Liam Cunningham (Sir Agravaine); Christopher Viliers (Sir Kay); Valentine Pelka (Sir Patrise); Colin McCormack (Sir Mador); Ralph Ineson (Ralf); John Gielgud (Oswald); Stuart Bunce (Peter); Jane Robbins (Elise); Jean Marie Coffey (Petronella); Paul Kynman (Mark); Tom Lucy (Sir Sagramore); John Blakey (Sir Tor); Robert Gwyn Davin (Sir Gawaine); Sean Blowers (Sir Carados); Alexis Denisof (Sir Gaheris); Daniel Naprous (Sir Amant); Jonathan Cake (Sir Gareth);

Paul Bentall (Jacob); Jonty Miller (Gauntlet Man); Rose Keegan (Mark's Wife); Mark Ryan (Challenger); Jeffrey Dench (1st Elder); Neville Phillips (2nd Elder); Oliver Lewis (1st Marauder); Wolf Christian (2nd Marauder); Angus Wright (3rd Marauder); Jonathan Janes (1st Guard); Eric Stone (2nd Guard); Ryand Todd (Young Lancelot); Albie Woodington (Scout); Richard Claxton (Child); Dido Miles (Grateful Woman); Michael Hodgson (Young Man in Crowd); Susannah Corbett (Young Woman in Crowd); Susan Breslan (Wedding Guest); Kate Zucker (Flower Girl); Bob Zucker (Little Boy with Birds); Charlotte Zucker (Bread Vendor); Burt Zucker (Bread Vendor)

CREDITS: Casting — Mary Selway; Costumes — Nana Cecchi; Executive Producers — Gil Netter, Eric Rattray, Janet Zucker; Film Editor — Walter Murch, A.C.E.; Production Design — John Box; Director of Photography — Adam Greenberg, A.S.C.; Story by — Lorne Cameron, David Hoselton, William Nicholson; Screenplay by — William Nicholson; Produced by — Jerry Zucker, Hunt Lowry; Directed by — Jerry Zucker; Stunts — Kim Billings, Graeme Crowther, Sarah Franzl, Paul Heasman, Nick Hobbs, Sy Hollands, Rowley Irlham, Paul Jennings, Vincent Keane, Simone Le Lievre, Gerard Naprous, Miguel Pedregosa, Gary Powell, Jose Maria Serrano, Terry Walsh, Nick Wilkinson, Steve Dent, Joss Gower, Lyndon Stewart Hellewell, Diane Kelley, Les Maryon, Nigel Oliver, Eric Petch, Nosher Powell, Lee Sheward, David Ware, George Branche, Ken Buckle, Jamie Edgell, Steve Griffin, Paul Herbert, Billy Horrigan, Jazzer Heyes, Eddie Kidd, Peter Miles, Adrien O'Neil, Andreas Petrides, Dane Rawlins, Mark Southworth, Peter White; Unit Production Manager — Hunt Lowry; Associate Producer — Kathryn J. McDermott; 1st Assistant Director — Chris Carreras; 2nd Assistant Directors — Cliff Lanning, Richard Whelan, Jamie Christopher; Supervising Producer — Paul Hitchcock; Supervising Art Directors — Bob Laing, Michael White; Art Directors — Stephen Scott, Giles Masters; Set Director — Malcolm Stone; Chargehand Dressing Propmen — Stan Cook, Brian Humphrey; Senior Draughtsmen — Edward Ambrose, Jean Peyre; Scenic Artist — Steven Michael Sallybanks; Modeler — Michael Milford; Storyboard Artists — Martin Asbury, John Rose, Roger Deer; Script Supervisors — Angela Allen, June Randall; Camera Operators — Gordon Hasyman, Tim Ross; Focus Pullers — Michael Evans, Kenny Groom; Clapper Loaders — Dean Morrish, John Gamble; Camera Grips — Kenny Atherfold, Joe Felix; Standbys — Tony Westbrook, Gordon Izod, Brian Mitchell,

Ken Hawkey, Cornelius Murphy; Swordmaster — Bob Anderson; Stunt Coordinators — Greg Powell, Dinny Powell; Horsemaster — Steve Dent; Wardrobe Supervisor — Kenny Crouch; Set Wardrobe Supervisor — Annie Crawford; Assistant Costume Designers — Emanuele Zito, Mauritzio Basile; Costume Coordinator — Graham Churchyard; Set Wardrobe Mistress — Jo Korer; Set Wardrobe Master — Mark Holmes; Mr. Connery's Dresser — Hans G. Struhar; Ms. Ormond's Dresser — Nancy Thompson; Head Seamstress — Caroline Thorpe; Costume Cutter — Annie Hadley; Armor Maker — Terry English; Assistant Armor Maker — Pete Corrigan, Glen English; Chief Makeup Supervisor — Peter Robb-King; Chief Makeup Artist — Jane Royle; Makeup — Trefor Proud; Chief Hairdresser — Elaine Short; Hairdressers — Betty Glasow, Tracy Lee, Barbara Ritchie; Chief Lighting Technician — Chuck Finch; Best Boy — Billy Merrill; Rigging Gaffer — Simon Lucas; Electricians — Sam Bloor, Rocky Evans, Tom O'Sullivan, Toby Tyler, Fred Brown, Steve Finch, James T. Smart; Video Coordinator — Chris Warren; Video Assistant — Dave Holland; Special Effects Supervisor — George Gibbs; Gauntlet by — Jonathan Angell, Paul Knowles; Special Effects Floor Supervisor — John Evans; Special Effects Technicians — David Watson, Peter Skehan, Barry Whitrod, Roger Nichols, Digby Milner, Philip Knowles, Paul Dimmer; Production Supervisor — Alexander deGrunwald; Production Coordinators — Janine Lodge, Bi Benton; Production Secretary — Marianne Jenkins; 2nd 2nd Assistant Director — Joshua Robertson; Production Accountant — Mike Smith; Assistant Production Accountant — Linda Bowen; Assistants to Mr. Zucker — Leslie Maier, Katie Locke; Assistant to Mr. Hitchcock — Lidia Likes; Assistant to Mr. Geer — Lucy Darwin; Assistant to Mr. Connery — Rhonda Tollefson; Location Manager — Chris Brock; Location Manager, Wales — Alan James; Prop Master — George Ball; Standby Propmen — Graeme Purdy, Steven Payne, Wesley Peppiat; Standby Propman, Weapons — Clive Wilson; Sound Mixer — Colin Charles; Boom Operator — John Samworth; Floor Runners — Emma Griffiths, Simon Downes, Susan Wood, Hazel Waite; Unit Nurse — Nicky Gregory Jarvis; Casting Assistant — Emma Buckley; Publicist — Sue D'Arcy; Still Photographer — Frank Connor; Technical Advice — John Waller; Construction Manager — Tony Graysmark; Assistant Construction Manager — Peter Williams; Re-recording Mixers — Walter Murch, C.A.S., Gary Gegan, Mathew Iadarola; Associate Film Editor — Joe Wood, Jr.; 1st Assistant Editors — Derrick

Mitchell, Catherine Chase; Assistant Editor — Tom Barrett; Apprentice Editor — Kimberley A. Jorgensen; Associate Editor, London — Les Hodgson; Assistant Editor, London — Kerry Kohler; 1st Assistant Editor, London — Daniel Farrell; 2nd Assistant Editor, London — Lucy Mannsell; Supervising Sound Editor — John Morris; Sound Editors — Michael Magill, Ian MacGregor-Scott, Noah Blough, David Van Slyke, Richard Burton, Cindy Marty, Allison Fisher; Music Editor — Kenneth J. Hall; ADR Supervisor — Kimberly Harris-Rivolier; ADR Editors — Ulrika Akander, Beth Bergeron; Assistant ADR Editor — Laura P. Krasnow; Foley Supervisor — Christopher Flick; Foley Artists — Alicia Stevenson, John Cucci; 1st Assistant Sound Editor — Paul Camy-Parsons; Assistant Sound Editors — Tricia Linklater, Thomas P. McNamara; Visual Effects Coordinator — Dennis Lowe; Catering by — Silent Movies; Unit Drivers — Dave Manning, Mark Davies, Billy Castille, Peter Graorac; 2nd Unit Director — Arthur Wooster; 1st Assistant Director — Terry Madden; 2nd Assistant Director — Mark Layton; Script Supervisor — Caroline Sax; Camera Operator — Martin Hume; Focus Puller — Timothy Wooster; Clapper Loader — Sean Connor; Camera Grips — Harry Eckford, Philip Kenyon; Hairdresser — Annie Townsend; Gaffer — Mickey Wilson; Chargehand Standby Propman — Simon Wilkinson; Special Effects Floor Supervisor — Terry Glass; Floor Runner — Sara Desmond; Costumes Manufactured by — Puggero Peruzzi for Costumi D'Arte, Rome, Florence; Miniature Construction — The Magic Model Company; Main and End Titles Designed by — Nina Saxon Film Design; Opticals by — Pacific Title; Negative Cutter — Superior Film Service, Inc.; Color Timer — Dale Grahn; Titles by — Cinema Research Corporation; Digital Film Services by — Cinesite Digital Film Center Digital Effects Supervisor — Gareth Edwards; Digital Effects Producer — Sharon Lark; Senior Compositor — Mark Nettleton; Senior Animator — Bill Scanlon; Digital Effects and Animation — CFX Associates, London, Craig Zeronni, Chris Briscoe; Animation Visual Effects by — Available Light Limited; Animation Design and Supervision — John T. Van Vliet; Additional Digital and Visual Effects by — D-Rez, Hollywood; Soundtrack on — Epic Soundtrax; Orchestrations by — Alexander Courage; Music Recorded and Mixed by — Bruce Botnick; Los Angeles Master Chorale — Paul Salamunovich; Columbia Pictures is the author of this film (motion picture) for the purpose of copyright and other laws.; Filmed at Pinewood Studios, London, England; Filmed with Arriflex 535 Cameras and Zeiss Lenses, Supplied by Media Film Service, London; Prints by Technicolor; Filmed on location in the United Kingdom; Thanks to the Gwynedd Film Office, Wales

SYNOPSIS: A King Arthur story with no mention of Excalibur or Merlin is hard to imagine, but *First Knight* is just that. This freely adapted version includes comic book–style armor, a Guinevere who comes from Lyonesse and many other nontraditional details.

Lancelot is an itinerant freelance who makes his living not by jousting but by trick sword fighting. (In fact, there isn't a single joust in this movie.) While he is bopping around the countryside dispensing jazzed-up samurai-style fencing lessons and friendly advice, Guinevere is having troubles on the home front. Her father is dead, and the job of ruling Lyonesse has fallen to her. One day her soccer game is interrupted by supplicants from one of her villages. It seems a villain named Malagant has intentions of taking over Lyonesse and he's been marauding through the land at will.

Guinevere's counselors advise her to accept King Arthur's proposal of marriage as a wise and prudent move. She happens to like the old king, whom she met as a young girl, so she packs up and heads for Camelot.

Malagant attacks her entourage on the road and the escort Arthur has sent is outsmarted by the ne'er-do-well. In a chase scene Guinevere is forced to jump from her carriage. She is almost captured but Lancelot happens to be in the neighborhood and rescues her.

Finding himself alone with Guinevere, Lancelot flirts persistently. Though attracted to this dashing vagabond, Guinevere remains relatively demure, making Lancelot promise never to kiss her again. He promises to kiss her only if she asks.

As friendly search parties approach to find Guinevere, Lancelot goes off by himself. Guinevere is brought to Camelot and is welcomed to the walled city with great pageantry.

Some time later Lancelot makes his way to Camelot and comes upon a contest going on

Richard Gere, Sean Connery and Julia Ormond star in *First Knight*.

in the great square. A gigantic mechanical gauntlet has been set up. Whoever makes it through the thing will receive a kiss from Arthur's fiancée. All the other hearties who try it wear huge pads to protect themselves from the swinging blades and other hazards, but Lancelot hops onto the thing in just his street clothes and is the only one to make it all the way through.

As if putting on such an impressive display weren't enough to catch Arthur's eye, Lancelot then gallantly declines the kiss (especially when he sees the distress on Guinevere's face). Arthur invites Lancelot to stay on.

Malagant shows up at Camelot to discuss a plan with Arthur. Evidently before he went bad Malagant had been first among the Knights of the Round Table. Now in his black bad-guy's armor he proposes splitting Lyonesse with Arthur. The good king says no and declares war on Malagant.

Malagant has Guinevere kidnapped. With ropes, pulleys and a horse on shore, he turns a rowboat into a speed boat for the coup. Guinevere is locked into an oubliette in a dark crumbling castle, but with tremendous bravery and acrobatics Lancelot rescues her once more.

To Guinevere's surprise, Lancelot accepts a seat at the Round Table. The wedding finally occurs and Malagant takes Lyonesse. Arthur rides out with his army and drives the enemy out of Guinevere's lands.

Ultimately Lancelot determines that things are just too awkward between himself and Guinevere. He decides to leave Camelot and goes to Guinevere to say goodbye. As a last farewell, Guinevere asks for that promised kiss but, as fate would have it, Arthur walks in on them at the critical moment. Everything goes down the drain.

His trust in them destroyed, Arthur is

forced to try them publicly for treason and adultery. In the middle of the trial Malagant attacks Camelot itself. Caught off guard, the place is surrounded and everyone is captured. Arthur howls his defiance and calls everyone to fight. He is mortally wounded but all the warriors and citizens of Camelot spring to action.

Lancelot is in the thick of the fight from the beginning and winds up pitted against Malagant. Malagant manages to gain an advantage, disarms Lancelot and is about to strike when Lancelot spots another sword within reach. It seems to be Arthur's, which the king dropped when he was wounded, but it's hard to say since all the Knights of the Round Table carry identical weapons.

In any case, this sword glints oddly when Lancelot picks it up and he is imbued with an energy and speed that we haven't seen before. He kills Malagant handily and the enemy attack collapses.

On his deathbed Arthur declares Lancelot his "first knight" and leaves the care of Camelot in his and Guinevere's hands. In the closing scene Arthur is given a classic Viking funeral. His body is placed on a sailboat, which is set afire as it drifts off into a spectacular sunset.

Very little of any classic versions of the stories of either Arthur, Lancelot or Guinevere have been used in this movie. Only the barest skeleton of the original tale is present — that Arthur was king of Camelot, that something happened between Lancelot and Guinevere and that Arthur was killed by someone whose name began with an *M*.

For starters, there is the matter of Lyonesse. In Malory, Dame Lyonesse of the Castle Perilous was Lynet's sister. Besieged by the Red Knight of the Red Lands, Dame Lyonesse is rescued by Gareth and winds up marrying him. Other traditions have it that Lyonesse was a land beyond Cornwall which had sunk into

the sea. Tennyson wrote that Arthur's final and fatal battle occurred at Lyonesse.

The matching armor and weaponry of the Knights of the Round Table in *First Knight* is pretty fanciful stuff. Arthur and his men include as part of their uniforms strange little six- or eight-inch shields mounted on their left shoulders. The most fanciful armor of all, though, is worn by Malagant's horse. It and Malagant's sword look like items out of a Conan story. Tiny handgun-sized crossbows are another interesting addition to the armaments of *First Knight*.

Malagant himself, at least, comes from traditional versions, though his name has been modified. In Malory, he was Meliagaunt and his name has also been spelled Meleagaunce, among other variations. In Welsh, the character was Melwas.

Malagant's kidnapping of Guinevere tracks with a number of permutations of the story, but his killing of Arthur does not. That deed has traditionally been the role of Mordred, Arthur's illegitimate son.

The Fisher King (1991)

137 minutes; Color; Live Action; Copyright 1991, Tristar Pictures, Inc.; Columbia Tristar Home Video #70613

CAST: Jeff Bridges (Jack); Robin Williams (Perry); Mercedes Ruehl (Anne); Amanda Plummer (Lydia); David Pierce (Lou Rosco); Michael Jeter (Homeless Cabaret Singer); John de Lancie (TV Executive); Ted Ross (Limo Bum); Lara Harris (Sondra); Warren Olney (TV Anchorman); Frazer Smith (News Reporter); Kathy Najimy (Crazed Video Customer); Harry Shearer (Sitcom Actor Ben Starr); Melinda Culea (Sitcom Wife); James Remini (Bum at Hotel); Mark Bowden (Doorman); John Ottavino (Father at Hotel); Brian Michaels (Little Boy); Jayce Bartock (First Punk); Dan Futterman (Second Punk); Bradley Gregg (Hippie Bum); William Jay Marshall (Jamaican Bum); William Preston (John the Bum); Al Fann (Superintendent); Stephen Bridgewater (Porno Customer); John Heffernan (Stockbroker Bum);

Opposite: **The Red Knight stalks Parry (Robin Williams) through the streets of New York City in** *The Fisher King.*

Chris Howell (Red Knight); Richard La Gravanese (Strait Jacket Yuppie); Anita Dangler (Bag Lady); Mark Bringelson (Drooler); Johnny Paganelli (Pizza Boy); Diane Robin (Receptionist); John Benjamin Red (Motorcyclist); Lisa Blades (Perry's Wife); Christian Clemenson (Edwin); Carlos Carrasco (Doctor); Joe Jamrog (Guard); Lou Hancock (Nurse); Adam Bryant (Radio Engineer); Paul Lombard (Radio Engineer); Caroline Cromelin (Radio Show Call-in); Kathleen Bridget Kelly (Radio Show Call-in); Patrick Fraley (Radio Show Call-in)

CREDITS: Casting — Howard Feuer; Costume Design — Beatrix Pasztor; Music — George Fenton; Editor — Lesley Walker; Production Designer — Mel Bourne; Director of Photography — Roger Pratt, B.S.C.; Written by — Richard LaGravanese; Produced by — Debra Hill and Linda Obst; Director — Terry Gilliam; Associate Producer — Stacey Sher; Unit Production Manager/Associate Producer — Anthony Mark; First Assistant Directors — David McGiffert, Joe Napolitano; Second Assistant Director — Carla Corwin; Second Second Assistant Director — Cynthia A. Potthast; Script Supervisor — Marion Tumen; Art Director — P. Michael Johnston; Set Decorator — Cindy Carr; Art Department Assistant — Anne Harmon; Set Designers — Jason R. Weil, Rick Heinrichs; Model Consultants — Bill Cruse & Co.; Leadmen — David C. Potter, Kristen Kelly; Property Master — Larry Clark Bird; Assistant Property Masters — Ken Zimmerman, David Aaron; Camera Operator — Craig Haagensen; First Assistant Camera — Nicholas J. Masuraca; Second Assistant Camera — Gregory D. Walters, Chuck Whelan; Assistant Film Editor — Jeremy Hume; Assistant Film Editors, U.S.A. — Edward Stabile, Tara Timpone; Second Assistant Film Editor — Tullio Brunt; Apprentice Film Editor, U.S.A. — Tristan Brighty; Sound Editor — Peter Pennell; Assistant Sound Editor — Stefna Borges; Dialogue Editor — Alan Paley; Assistant Dialogue Editor — Andrew Melhuish; Foley Editor — Bob Risk; Assistant Foley Editor — Steve Maguire; Music Editor — Kevin Lane; Music Consultant — Ray Cooper; Sound Mixer — Thomas Causey; Boom Operators — Joseph F. Brennan, Richard Kite; Re-recording Mixers — Paul Carr, Robert Farr; Video Assistant Operator — Neil S. Buckhantz; Post Production Supervisor — Sharre Jacoby; Chief Lighting Technician — James Plannette; Lighting Technicians — R. Michael Dechellis, John Gutierrez; Rigging Gaffer — Andy Nelson; Electrical Best Boy — Paul Ary; Best Boy — Roger Blauvelt; Key Grip — Marty Eichmann; Second Grip — Stephen V. Isbell; Dolly Grip — Antonio V. Garrido; Grips — Patrick Shaun Bard, William R. Taylor, Paul David Williams; Creative Special Effects Consultant — Robert E. McCarthy; Special Effects Supervisor — Dennis Dion; Special Effects — Dan Sudick; Costume Supervisor — Joie Hutchinson; Costumer — Linda Louise Taylor; Assistant Costume Supervisor — Randy Starck; Red Knight Costume Designed by — Keith Greco, Vincent Jefferds; Wardrobe Assistant — Rainer Judd; Key Makeup Artist — Zoltan Elek; Key Hairstylist — Lisa Joy Meyers; Stunt Coordinator — Chris Howell; Choreographer — Robin Horness; Location Manager — Bill Bowling; Assistant Location Manager — James R. Maceo; Special Projects — Barry Rosenbush; Publicity — Susan Pile; Still Photographers — John Clifford, Stephen Vaughn; Transportation Coordinator — Edward F. Voelker; Transportation Captain — James W. Roberts; Construction Coordinator — Richard Dean Rankin; Construction Foreman — David B. Brenner; Maco Lighting Technician — Ron Kunecke; Production Coordinator — Pam Cornfeld; Production Secretary — Sharyn Shimada; Production Accountant — Margaret A. Mitchell; Assistant Accountants — Veronica Claypool, Gary McCarthy, Jr.; Assistant to Robin Williams — Marsha Williams; Assistant to Debra Hill — Valencia Giacco; Assistant to Lynda Obst — Carmen B. Weets; Assistant to Terry Gilliam — Yvette S. Taylor; Assistant to Anthony Mark — Ann Weiss–La Gravanese; Casting Assistant — Alishan Coker; Production Assistants — Mark Galley, T. R. Jones, Travis Keyes, Barbara Lampson, Amy Love, Nicole Miller, Ellie Smith, Michael Viglietta; DGA Trainee — Margaret Piane; DJ Consultant — Stephen Bridgewater; News Report Supervisor — Nancy Platt Jacoby; Horses Owned and Trained by — James Zoppe; Animal Colorist — Douglas J. White; Artwork Donated by — Sy and Jessica Sher; Post Production Facilities — Prominent Studios; Re-record at — Roger Cherrill's Ltd., London; Title Design by — Chris Allies; Opticals and Visual Effects by — Peerless Camera Co.; New York Unit: Assistant Unit Production and Location Manager — Mark A. Baker; Set Decorators — Kevin McCarthy, Joseph L. Bird; Chargeman Senior Artist — Michael Zansky; Property Master — Tom Wright; Assistant Property Master — Thomas A. McDermott; First Assistant Camera — Jonathan T. Ercole; Second Assistant Camera — John Gambria; Sound Mixer — Dennis Maitland II; Boom Operator — John K. Fundus; Cableman — Stephen Scanlon; Video Assistant Operator — Richard Mader, Jr.; Chief Lighting Technician — Kenneth R. Connors; Rigging Gaffer — Robert G. Connors; Key Grip — Michael

Parry (Robin Williams) is terrorized by visions of the Red Knight in *The Fisher King*.

Miller; Second Grip — Thomas J. Jirgal; Grips — Jimmy Finnerty, Jr., Robert Miller; Special Effects Supervisor — Edward Drohan; Costumer — Mary Coleman-Gierczak; Makeup Artist — Craig Lyman; Additional Location Manager — Mark L. Rhodes; Assistant Location Managers — Ann F. Markel, Lawrence P. Ganem; Assistant Production Accountants — Desiree Perri, Mark J. Levenstein; Extras Casting — Todd Thaler; Transportation Captain — John Leonidas; Construction Coordinator — Ed Ferraro; Second Second Assistant Director — Cyd Adams; DGA Trainee — Rebecca Saionz; Production Office Coordinator — Jackie Martin; Production Secretary — Jeanne Chrzanowski; Production Assistants — Tristan Bourne, Pierre Cailliarec, Todd M. Camhe, Patrick D. Garrison, Maureen Garvey, Kathleen Kelly, Timothy C. Lee, Jason Mark, Carrie Rudolf, John Rybacki; Special Thanks to — The Arthur Company, Caballero Home Video, Major Soccer League, Members Only, Metropolitan Transportation Authority, Miele Appliances, Inc., New York Post, Radio and Record, KFI Radio, KQLZ Pirate Radio, Billboard Magazine; Copyrights Courtesy of — BPI Communications, Inc.; Tape Material from *Jeopardy* Courtesy of — Jeopardy Productions, Inc.; Original soundtrack album available on MCA records, tapes and CDs.; Additional Orchestrations — Jeff Atmajian; Synth Programming — Adrian Thomas; Music Scoring Mixers — Keith Grant, Simon Smart, Gerry O'Riorden; Music Recorded at — C.T.S. Studio, London, England; "How About You": Written by — Ralph Freed, Burton Lane; Produced by — Ray Cooper, George Fenton; Whistled and Sung by — Harry Nilsson; "Chill Out Jack": Written by — Cave Samrai, Richard Williams, Peter Harvey, Johnny Templeton; Performed by — Trip; Courtesy of — MCA Records; "Hit the Road Jack": Written by — Percy Mayfield; Performed by — Ray Charles; Courtesy of — Ray Charles Enterprises, Inc.; "I Wish I Knew": Written by — Harry Warren, Mack Gordon; Performed by — John Coltrane; Courtesy of — MCA Records; "I'm Sorry": Written by — Ronnie Self, Dub Allbritten; Performed by — Brenda Lee; Courtesy of — MCA Records; "Lydia the Tattooed Lady": Written by — E. Y. Harburg, Harold Arlen; "The Power": Written by — Benito Benitz, John Garrett III, Toni C., Robert Frazier, Mark James; Performed by — Chill Rob G; Remixed by — Kevin Lane; Courtesy of — Wild Pitch Records, Ltd.; "Rose's Turn": Written by — Stephen Sondheim, Jule Styne; "Some People": Written by — Stephen Sondheim, Jule Styne; "You're Having My Baby": Written by — Paul Anka; Color by Technicolor; Lenses and Panaflex Cameras by Panavision

SYNOPSIS: *The Fisher King* is set in modern-day New York City. Wise-cracking radio talk show host Jack Lucas unintentionally gives some bad advice on the air to one of his callers. The disturbed caller takes Jack's remarks seriously, walks into a restaurant and kills seven people with a shotgun.

Jack is so devastated by the news of this slaughter that he drops his rising career, begins drinking heavily and hides from the world. He moves in with a sympathetic girlfriend who owns a video store. Living off of her generosity, his depression deepens until he decides to commit suicide.

Literally on the brink of his attempt, he is attacked by a couple of punks. Out of nowhere a band of street people appears to save him. Led by Perry, who yells, "In the name of Blanche de Fleur, unhand that errant knight!" the derelicts drive the punks off and take Jack to their hideout. In a drunken stupor Jack passes out.

He awakens the next day in Perry's abode, which is the boiler room of a building. During their ensuing conversation, Jack learns that this lunatic is searching for the Holy Grail. Perry had a vision of angels, who told him to look for it on page 33 of the February 1988 issue of *Progressive Architecture* magazine.

In the background of a photo on that page is a bookshelf on which stands a silver trophy cup. The photo is of a wealthy New Yorker named Langdon Carmichael, who Perry is convinced possesses the Grail. He is also convinced that Jack is "the one" sent by the angels to recover the Grail.

Subsequently Jack learns that Perry's real name is Henry Sagan and that he was a college professor whose thesis was "The Fisher King: A Mythic Journey for Modern Man." Perry and his wife were in that ill-fated restaurant the night one of Jack's callers went berserk. Perry's wife was killed by a shotgun blast to the head as she sat across the table from Perry.

Now, in his deranged state, Perry's recurring hallucination is of a Red Knight on horseback hunting him through the city. This incredible figure, spouting balls of fire, with its grotesque red armor and sprays of barbs and stalks is the psychic embodiment of the image of Perry's wife's head exploding before his eyes. The shock of her violent and horrific death has been translated into the Arthurian legends which once filled Perry's other life. When reality threatens, this apparition appears and drives Perry back into a safer world of madness and forgetfulness.

Jack, as a means to forgive himself, as a penance for what he feels was his sin, determines to help Perry. In one of his lucid moments, Perry recounts to Jack the story of the Fisher King, a man who was wounded so deeply that the wound would not heal. Only when an innocent, ignorant fool helps the Fisher King does he finally heal.

So, the scene is set. Perry is both Perceval, the seeker of the Grail, and Parsifal, the innocent fool, who through pure trust heals the Fisher King. Jack is both the deeply wounded Fisher King and the Galahad of the story, he who must ultimately achieve the Grail. Though for the moment he cannot accept the love of the world around him, whether from this derelict or from his girlfriend, Jack nonetheless is seeking to find that ultimate answer that will absolve him of that ultimate sin.

A long sequence about the love involvements of the two protagonists is interrupted when Perry finds it all too much and the Red Knight returns. Perry loses touch completely and runs off, only to be beaten by the same punks who beat Jack. Now comatose in a psychiatric ward, there seems to be no hope of recovery for Perry.

This setback spurs Jack to abandon his own reticence. He dons a street person's rags and makes a heroic illegal entry into the wealthy old man's home to steal the Grail. While Jack is in the room, Carmichael dies. The torch or, in this case, the Grail, has been passed. Jack brings it to Perry and Perry is healed.

There is an abundance of foul language in this film and a couple of embarrassingly irrel-

evant nude scenes. Despite these Hollywood film prerequisites, *The Fisher King* presents an intriguing modernization of the legend.

The legend of the Holy Grail can be interpreted in many ways and this film has picked one that works well for its purpose. The simple lesson that Jack finally learns is that love for other human beings is essential to a whole life. Money, career, image and all the other aspects of society have no importance when one finds oneself faced with the essentials of one's existence. This interpretation ignores God and the other Christian traditions that the legends of the Holy Grail are built around, but that seems to be another of those Hollywood prerequisites. Yet one more bit of drivel is the fixation Hollywood has for the ennobling of bums and street people. But if one keeps in mind a sort of Buddhist outlook, that we and everything else in the universe are parts of the Godhead, then even this film has not wandered too far off the path.

The Flintstones: "Time Machine" (1964)
Cartoon; Copyright 1964, Hanna-Barbera; No further information available.

For Whom the Bell Trolls see under Princess Gwenevere and the Jewel Riders

För att Inte Tala om Alla Dessa Kvinnor see All These Women

The Formative Years of Broadway see under Broadway! A Musical History

Four Diamonds (1995)
Not viewed; Color; Live Action; Copyright 1995, Disney Studios

CAST: Thomas Guiry (Chris/Sir Millard); Kevin Dunn (Chris's Father/Charles the Mysterious); Jayne Brook (Chris's Mother/Wise Hermit); Sarah Rose Karr (Chris's Sister/Stacia Swan); Christine Lahti (Doctor/Queen Raptemahad)

CREDITS: Original Story by—Chris Millard; Director—Peter Werner; Script Writer—Todd Robinson

SYNOPSIS: *Four Diamonds* is a Disney Channel production from an original story by and based on the real life of Chris Millard. Millard died of cancer at age 14 in 1972. During his battle with the disease, for an English assignment he wrote a short story about a young squire who seeks to become one of King Arthur's knights.

Fractured Fairy Tales (1961)

Not viewed; 4½-minute episodes; Cartoon; Copyright 1961, Association of Television Production

VOICES: Edward Everett Horton (Narrator); June Foray (Several Characters); Daws Butler (Several Characters); Bill Scott (Several Characters); Julie Bennett (Fill-in, 3 episodes); Paul Frees (Fill-in, 5 episodes)

CREDITS: Producers—Jay Ward, Bill Scott, Peter Peach, Bud Bourley; Executive Producer—Ponsonby Britt; Writers—Chris Hayward, Chris Jenkins, Lloyd Turner, George Atkins, Al Burns; Animation—Gamma Productions

SYNOPSIS: "Fractured Fairy Tales" were 4½-minute segments of the *Rocky and His Friends* and *The Bullwinkle Show* television cartoon shows. Ninety-one episodes of "Fractured Fairy Tales" appeared between 1959 and 1961. The shows appear as reruns occasionally but are not currently available on video tape. Of special interest are episode 12, "Tom Thumb"; episode 16, "Sir Galahad"; episode 28, "Tom Thumb (Tiny Tom)" and episode 53, "Thom Tum."

Frank and Ollie (1995)

Not viewed; 90 minutes; Color; Documentary; Copyright 1995, Walt Disney Productions/Theodore Thomas Productions; Distributed by Buena Vista Pictures

CAST: Frank Thomas; Sylvia Roemer; John Culhane; Jeanette A. Thomas; Andy Gaskill; Oliver M. Johnston, Jr.; John Canemaker; Marie E. Johnston; Glen Keane

CREDITS: Director—Theodore Thomas; Written by—Theodore Thomas; Photography—Erik Daarstad; Music—John Reynolds III; Film Editing—Kathryn Camp; Producers—Kuniko Okubo, Theodore Thomas; Foley Artist—Greg Barbanell; Additional Photography—Josh Bleibtreu; Production Assistant—Greg Cannone; Makeup Artist—Cindy Costello; Production Assistant—David Eggleston; Dolby Stereo Consultant—Thom "Coach" Ehle; Production Stills—Carla Fallberg; Supervising Sound Editor—Marc Fishman; Music Recording—Scott Fraser; Re-recording Mixer—William Freesh; Sound Effects Editor—Tim Gedemer; Foley Mixer—Brian Geer; Assistant Editor—Suzy Gilbert; Production Assistant—Peter Hutcheson; Location Mixer—Ken King; Makeup Artist—Oona Lind; Production Stills—Karen Quincy Loberg; Production Assistant—Peter Mauro; Electrician—Chris O'Neil; Assistant Camera—Marie Pedersen; Gaffer—Simone Perusse; Assistant Camera—Cal Roberts; 2nd Assistant Camera—Shauna Roberts; Sound Services Manager—Paul Rodriguez; Color Timer—Walter Rose; Sound Effects Editor—Ann Scibelli; Re-recording Artist—Tony Sereno; Grip—Michael Shore; Gaffer—Scott Spencer; Electrician—Georgia Tays; Re-recording Mixer—Ken Teaney; Assistant Camera—Amanda Thompson; Post Production Assistant—Eric Trueheart; Production Assistant—Mike West

SYNOPSIS: Contains information on and an excerpt from *The Sword in the Stone*.

Friz Freleng's Looney Looney Looney Bugs Bunny Movie: "Knighty Knight Bugs" (1981)

80 minutes; Color; Cartoon; Copyright 1981, Looney Tunes; Warner Home Video #11142; A Subsidiary of Warner Bros. Inc.; A Time Warner Company; Warner Bros. Pictures; Technicolor

CREDITS: Produced and Directed by—Friz Freleng; Voice Characterizations—Mel Blanc; Additional Voice Characterizations—June Foray, Frank Nelson, Frank Welker, Stan Freberg, Ralph James; Music by—Rob Walsh, Don McGinnis, Milt Franklyn, Bill Lava, Shorty Rogers, Carl Stalling; Film Editor—Jim Champin; Executive Producer—Hal Geer; Story—John Dunn, David Detiege, Friz Freleng; Sequence Directors—David Detiege, Phil Monroe, Gerry Chiniquy; Associate Producer—Jean H. MacCurdy; Production Design—Cornelius Cole; Layouts—Peter Alvarado, Robert Givens, Michael Mitchell; Backgrounds—Richard H. Thomas; Animators—Warren

Batchelder, Charles Downs, Marcia Fertig, Bob Matz, Manuel Perez, Virgil Ross, Lloyd Vaughan; Assistant Animators — Alfred Abranz, William Exter, Terrence Lennon, Karenia Haber, Allen Wade, Jane Nordin, Paulette Downs, Edward Faigan, Sonja Ruta, Robert Shellhorn, Susan Sugita, Ronald Wong; Animation Checking — Dora Yakutis; Final Checking — Val Vreeland; Production Assistants — Kathleen Helppie, K. Ray Iwami; Ink and Paint — C&D Ink and Paint; Camera — Nick Vasu, Inc.; Sound Effects Editor — Jim Graziano; Special Optical Effects — Pacific Title; Music Produced by — Screen Music West; Negative Cutter — Maarlene New; Classic Cartoons: Stories — John Dunn, Warren Foster, Friz Freleng, Tedd Pierce; Animation — Ted Bonnicksen, Ken Champin, Arthur Davis, Emery Hawkins, Bob Matz, Virgil Ross, Peter Burness, Gerry Chiniquy, Lee Halpern, Art Leonardi, Manuel Perez; Layouts — Hawley Pratt; Backgrounds — Boris Gorelick, Paul Julian, Tom O'Loughlin, Irv Wyner; Editor — Teg Brown; Color by Technicolor; Previous Copyrights: 1941, 1942, 1952, 1954, 1955, 1956, 1957, 1958, Vitaphone Corporation, 1962, 1963, Warner Bros. Pictures, Inc.; Distributed by Warner Bros., Warner Communications Company

SYNOPSIS: "Knighty Knight Bugs" (six minutes), the first offering in this collection of cartoons, is a classic of Looney Tunes slapstick animation with Bugs Bunny as the court jester at Camelot.

King Arthur tells the gathered knights that the Black Knight has stolen the "singing sword." Sir Osis of Liver and Sir Loin of Beef aren't up to the challenge, so Arthur sends Bugs to recover the sword.

Yosemite Sam is the Black Knight. His not-so-trusty steed is a fire-breathing dragon that keeps sneezing, appropriately setting fires on the Black Knight. Bugs quickly recovers the sword and a long chase follows. Of course, poor Yosemite Sam is never a match for the wiles of Bugs Bunny.

Full Circle see under *Princess Gwenevere and the Jewel Riders*

Gargoyles (1994)

Episodes 30 minutes each; Color; Cartoon; Copyright 1994–1997, Buena Vista Television

(The following is a combined cast and credit listing)

WITH THE VOICES OF: Thom Adcox-Hernandez (Lexington); Edward Asner (Hudson); Brigitte Bako (Angela); Keith David (Goliath, Morgan); Bill Fagerbakke (Broadway); Jonathan Frakes (David Xanatos); John Rhys-Davies (Macbeth); Salli Richardson (Elisa Maza); Laura San Giacomo (Fox); Marina Sirtis (Demona); Frank Welker (Bronx, Boudicca); Thomas F. Wilson (Matt Bluestone); John St. Ryan (King Arthur); Jeff Bennett (Brooklyn, Owen, Magus, Maol Chalvin); Ian Buchannan (Constantine); J.D. Daniels (Tom); Sheena Easton (Finella); Gerrit Graham (Guardian); Morgan Shepard (King Kenneth); Kath Souci (Princess Katherine, Weird Sisters, Mary); Ruben Santago Hudson (Gabriel); David Warner (Archmage)

CREDITS: Supervising Producers — Frank Paur, Greg Weisman; Produced and Directed by — Dennis J. Woodyard; Associate Producer — Lisa A. Salamone; Story Editor (Brynne Chandler Reaves); Written by — Lydia C. Marano; Voice Casting and Dialogue Director — Jamie Thomason; Animation and Timing Directors — Carole Beers, Burton Medall, Daniel De La Vega, Barbara Dourmashkin Case, Mitch Rochu; Storyboard — Patrick Archibald, David Prince, Debra Pugh, George Booker, Victor Cook, Douglas Murphy; Character Design — Greg Guler, Kenny Thompkins; Key Layout Design — Don M. Cameron, Nicola Cuti, Ted Blackman; Prop Design — Paul Scarzo; Key Background Stylists — William J. Dely, Garry Eggleston, Donna Prince, Kim Spink, Robert Schwefer, Leonard Robledo; Color Key Stylists — Marta Gludkowska, Robert Draper Koblin, Janet Cummings; Storyboard Revisions — Eddy Houchins, Pat R. Achasin, Melissa Suber, Craig Kemplin, Bob Zambuni; Production Manager — Kevin Traxler; Overseas Animation Sueprvisor — Henry Neville; Continuity Coordinator — Myoung Smith; Talent Coordinator — Julie Morgavi; Music — Carl Johnson; Title Theme — Carl Johnson; Animation Production — Koko Entertainment Co., Ltd.; Animation Directors — Sun Hee Lee, Bek Yub Sung, Dung Ho Kim; Layout Artists — Kyung Young Bae, Myung Sub Jung, Myung Jung Yo; Animators — Young Chul Park, Ki Huhynag; Heads of Background — Yung Hwan Oh, Seung Duk You, Kyung Ho Park; Head of Camera — Seong Il Choi, Seung Duk You; Additional Production Facilities — Dong Yang Animation Co., Ltd., Anima Sam Won Co., Ltd., Seoul Movie Co., Ltd.; Supervising Film Editor — Robert S. Birchard; Assistant Film Editors — Shannon Scudder-Pudleiner, John Royer; Pre-Production Film Editor — Monte Bramer; Post Production Supervisor — Jeffrey Arthur; Sound Dubbing Supervisor — Mark Von Der Heide; Tracker Reading — Skip Craig; Lip Sync — Erik Peterson; Production Mixer — Deb Adair; Dialogue Editors — Chris Eaton, Elliot Anders; Dialogue Production Assistant — Mark Cabellero; Re-Recording Mixers — James Hudson, Bill Klepnick, Ray Leonard, Melissa Gentry-Ellis; Sound Design — Paca Thomas, Phyllis Ginter; Dialogue Editing — Melissa Gentry-Ellis; Music Editing — Marc Perlman; Scoring Music Editor — Liz Lachman; Production Assistants — Tanja Kunubutch, Tom Pantewski, David Witting; Script Coordinators — Monique Beatty, Denise Byrne, Leonard Jernnigan; Art Coordinator — Melinda Cisueroz; Administrative Coordinator — Johanne Beaudoin; Script Supervisor — Anita Lish; Story Coordinator — Nanci Schwartz; Assistant Ppost Production Supervisor — Steve Werner; Post Production Coordinator — Keith Yeager; Post Production Assistant — Andrew Sorcini; Shipping Coordinator — Craig Simpson

SYNOPSIS: *Gargoyles* was a cartoon series which ran from October of 1994 to February of 1997. A total of 78 episodes were produced, four of which were distinctly Arthurian: "Avalon," Parts One, Two and Three, and "Pendragon."

Arthur and Merlin were mentioned in another episode, "A Lighthouse in Time," but that is not covered here due to its lack of further detail. Two other episodes, "The Gathering," Parts One and Two, focus on the visit of Oberon and Titania, the King and Queen of Avalon, to New York. Since no further particularly Arthurian slant is involved, these two shows are also skipped here.

Briefly, the Gargoyles were a race of beings existing in Dark Ages Europe and are brought back to life in the present. Turning to stone in daylight, active at night, they become involved in all sorts of adventures and situations from meeting the Golem to contending with the real Macbeth. The clan of one Gargoyle named Goliath now lives in New York City, doing what they can to protect the people there and trying to improve relations between humans and Gargoyles. In the three "Avalon" episodes, they team up with King

Arthur to do battle with the Archmage who seeks to conquer Avalon.

"AVALON" PART ONE

A man in a full suit of armor poles a boat up to a wharf in New York City. As he walks the streets, a group of muggers try to take advantage of him, but he holds his own against them, until the police show up. Recognizing other "guardians," the armored fellow gives himself up to the officers and is brought to jail.

Elisa, a friend of Goliath's and a young gal very sympathetic to the Gargoyle cause, works at the police station. When the armored man is brought in, he asks for the Gargoyles and Goliath in particular. Elisa manages to arrange his release and a meeting with Goliath.

He turns out to be Tom, one of the original Guardians of the eggs of Goliath's clan. Tom was a young boy when the eggs were moved to the island of Avalon to protect them. He has come from Avalon to seek Goliath's help. The Archmage, already an evil wizard, has managed to acquire all three powerful artifacts: the Grimoram which is a book of ancient spells, the Eye of Odin, a jewel that gives the wearer vast powers and the Phoenix Gate an amulet that enables the bearer to travel through space and time at will. The Archmage intends to take over Avalon to complete his quest for ultimate power.

Goliath and Elisa don't hesitate for a moment, but join Tom and board his boat. Tom poles the vessel out into the water, speaks an incantation and they glide off into the mist.

"AVALON" PART TWO

The Archmage attacks the group the moment they arrive at Avalon. He appears as a sand monster on the beach. No matter what they do, he keeps reforming. Finally, he stops and informs them that at dawn he will kill them all.

By now of course, Goliath's clan's eggs have hatched and grown up. One of them, Angela, is Goliath's daughter. All of the clan gathers to help in the fight.

A dawn attack by the Archmage will mean that the Gargoyles are all in their stone state and out of any fight. Goliath knows they have to avoid that and that they are nearly powerless in any event against the Archmage. He takes Angela with him to try to get the Eye of Odin and the Phoenix Gate to even the odds. Before leaving, he tells Elisa to try to come up with a backup plan in case his doesn't work out. Elisa begins by asking about the "sleeping king" of Avalon.

"AVALON" PART THREE

The wizard Magus takes Elisa to the Hollow Hill to wake the sleeping king. It is no easy task, with guardian knights and other magical protections to make their way through, but eventually Arthur is roused from his centuries of slumber and brought into the plans for battle.

Being a natural leader and the best fighter and strategist the world has known, once apprised of the situation, Arthur begins assigning missions. Goliath will go after the Archmage, Magus will take on the Weird Sisters and Arthur will do combat with Demona and Macbeth. The clan members are divided up amongst them and they all head out. The battle is fierce but ultimately the Archmage is utterly destroyed.

Goliath, Angela and Elisa board a boat to head back but Arthur decides to see the new world for himself. He poles off from Avalon on his own.

"PENDRAGON"

Avalon doesn't simply release one, it sends people on quests. Goliath, Angela and Elisa traveled much of the world before returning to Manhattan. It was some time too before Arthur found his way to London. On an unexpectedly dark and stormy night, he finds his way back to an abbey. Breaking in, he finds also the Stone of Destiny which once held Excalibur.

Griff, the resident protector Gargoyle, meets him and helps Arthur decipher the rid-dle the Stone presents Arthur. The Stone stated that it would take Arthur to Excalibur if he can state where it is. Griff remembers a riddle he'd heard about the sword, "Isle of towers, glass and stone, pure white lilies speak her name. Blood red bane in Dragon Stone, Excalibur waits for him alone."

The isle of towers of course is Manhattan, so off Arthur and Griff are carried on an adventurous hunt for the sword. The ebon glass in an emerald frame turns out to be the lake in Central Park. Arthur goes there, finding the pure white lilies and he calls the Lady of the Lake. Even she, however, seems intent on testing Arthur rather than simply handing over Excalibur. After Arthur beats the Lady's water beast, she tells him where to look.

The Dragon Stone is just that, a stone in a large garden carved in the shape of a dragon. And in that stone is a sword. Another warrior from the past beats Arthur to the sword. MacBeth snatches the blade and he and Arthur fight over it, until the Dragon awakens. They both fight the beast, but it launches itself into the air with them clinging to it. Finally Arthur realizes that the red stone in the middle of the dragon's chest must be where the true Excalibur is hidden. Smashing the huge gem with his mace, sure enough, he pulls forth Excalibur. The dragon disintegrates and Macbeth kneels to King Arthur.

Gawain and the Green Knight (1973)

Not viewed; 35mm, 10 reels, 8,370 feet; 93 minutes; Color; Live Action; Copyright 1973, United Artists/Sancrest; Library of Congress Call #CGB5757–5761 (reference print); Library of Congress Catalogue #92509955/MP/r93

CAST: Murray Head (Gawain); Nigel Green (Green Knight); Geoffrey Bayldon (The Fool); Robert Hardy (Sir Bertilac); Ciaran Madden (Linet); Anthony Sharp (The King); Ronald Lacey (Oswald); Murray Melvin (Seneschal); David Leland (Humphrey); Willoughby Goddard (Knight); Richard Hurndall (Bearded Man); Tony Steedman (Fortinbras); George Merritt (Old Knight); Peter Copley (Pilgrim); Pauline Letts (Lady of Lyonesse); Geoffrey Bayldon (Wiseman); Jerald Wells (Sergeant); Jack Woolgar (Porter); Michael Crand (The Giant)

CREDITS: Director—Stephen Weeks; Writers—Philip Green, Stephen Weeks; Music—Ron Goodwin; Director of Photography—Ian Wilson; Art Director—Anthony Woollard; Producer—Philip Breen; Editor—John Shirley; Additional Dialogue—Rosemary Sutcliff

Gawain and the Green Knight (1991)

76 minutes; Color; Live Action; Copyright 1991, Thames Television; Copyright 1992, 1993, Films for the Humanities and Sciences

CAST: Malcolm Storry (The Green Knight, The Red Lord); Valerie Gogan (The Lady); Jason Durr (Sir Gawain); Marc Warren (Arthur); Martin Crocker (Knight); Patrick Moore (Knight); Stephen Tiller (Knight); Marie Francis (Guinevere); Jonathan Adam (Ferryman); Michael Povey (Blacksmith); Gethin Mills (Blacksmith's Son); Sally Mates (Woman in Black); Shay Gorman (Chamberlain); Arthur Kelley (Older Servant); Nigel Cairns (Younger Servant); John Lyons (Woodman); George Sweeney (Guide)

CREDITS: Original Music—Walter Fabeck; Music Consultant—Robert King; Performers of the Period Music—The King's Court; Boy Treble—Aidan Oliver; Music Executive—Joyce Sharpen; Movement—Geraldine Stephenson; Casting Director—Elizabeth Sadler; Senior Booking Assistant—Vickey Moore; 1st Assistant Director—Peter Errington; Floor Assistant—Sara Valentine; Location Supervisor—Chrissie Cocks; Location Manager—Barry Millar; Stage Manager—Auriole Lee; Makeup Design—Carol Cooper; Makeup Artists—Hazel Weatherly, Lesley Faulkner; Costume Design—Jennie Tate; Costume Assistants—Mandy Harper, Verity Hawkes; Graphic Design—Ethan Ames; Production Buyer—Ronnie Urquhart; Props Charge Hand—Ian Coward; Location Effects—Mick Brady; Editing Assistants—Rupert Miles, Sarah Rains; Camera Operator—Graham Whittaker; Focus Puller—Philip Conn; Camera Grip—Peter Durbin; Gaffer Electrician—Bill Chamberlain; Period Music Recording—Richard Bradford; Dubbing Editor—Colin Ritchie; Dubbing Mixer—Richard King; Boom Operator—Tom Buchanan; Sound Recordists—Chris Ashworth; Production Assistant—Mary Crewe; Videotape Editor—Alan Ritchie; Film Editor—Trevor Waite; Lighting Cameraman—Jim Howlett; Production Design—Jane Krall; Design Assistant—Carol Sanders; Executive Producer—Ian Martin; Producer and Director—John Michael Phillips

SYNOPSIS: A nicely put together rendition of the classic fourteenth century poem of the same title, this movie presents a convoluted story of magic, courtly love, honor and human imperfection.

The first 20 or 25 minutes of the film are a series of time shifts that jump back and forth between the present of Gawain's journey to meet with the Green Knight and the past events that led up to his trip. Each scene shift is a juxtaposing of occurrences on Gawain's trip with past events.

Eating a horrid-looking stew in a peasant's house on the road, Gawain remembers the feast in Arthur's court, which was the beginning of the story. As he tries to sleep, his armor hanging from the ceiling and thumping gently in a breeze, he thinks back to the sounds of hooves clattering up to the doors of Arthur's hall. Crossing on a barge in a dense fog, the bargeman's comments about never having heard of Green Chapel evoke images of the Green Knight entering Arthur's hall. This apparition, covered in leaves, branches and vines, glowed with a green light.

Riding through a forest at night Gawain pictures the huge battle ax that the Green Knight carried as he proposed his "Christmas game." As a blacksmith works on the eye slits of Gawain's helmet, the young knight pictures how the Green Knight's eyes flared red when, stunned by the Green Knight's strangeness, not one of Arthur's knights came forth to accept his challenge. Finally Arthur himself stepped forward but, embarrassed that his king should have to do so, Gawain took his place.

The Green Knight's proposition was that Gawain could have one stroke at his neck with the ax. However, the Green Knight claimed the right to an equal blow at Gawain on New Year's at a place of his choosing, the Green Chapel. A dislodged rock rolling along the ground calls up Gawain's memory of the head of the Green Knight rolling on the floor of Arthur's castle.

Gawain being lost in another forest is contrasted with a scene of the Green Knight's body struggling to retrieve its head. Finally, Gawain's arrival in the far north country elicits the memory of the Green Knight's body, carrying its living head as it rode out of the court.

This repeated flashback technique is potentially confusing (especially for younger viewers, though this is certainly not meant as a children's film) and a bit overly complicated, but it is interesting nonetheless. It cinematically mirrors the end structure of the original poem, in which Gawain and the Red Lord live out juxtaposed events over the course of three days.

Gawain's arrival at the Red Lord's castle marks the end of the flashback sequences. He is greeted with hospitality, bathed, fed and given clean clothes. During an evening Christmas service, with dancing and games afterward, it becomes obvious that Gawain and the Red Lord's wife find each other attractive. After the guests have gone, Gawain tells the Red Lord of his covenant with the Green Knight. The Red Lord tells Gawain that he can guide him to the Green Chapel, but he insists that, since New Year's is three days away, Gawain stay on until then.

In his turn, the Red Lord strikes a deal with Gawain. He will go out hunting while Gawain rests at the castle and the two agree to give each other whatever they win each day.

On the first day, the Red Lord's wife enters Gawain's chamber and wakes him. With cheerful banter and charming verbal fencing, she seeks further attentions from Gawain and winds up kissing him on the forehead before leaving. Later in the day, the Red Lord returns from his hunt with a deer, which he gives to Gawain. Bound by his agreement, Gawain must give the lord that which he had won and so he kisses the Red Lord on the forehead.

A bit surprised, the Red Lord asks, "A comely kiss. Where did you win that within these walls?" Gawain points out their deal did not include revealing their sources.

On the second day, the lady returns to wake Gawain, this time more insistent and finally critical of Gawain for not speaking with her of love. Planting a kiss on each of his eyes, she departs. That evening the lord returns with only a boar to give Gawain, but receives from Gawain the two kisses. Tension builds.

On the third morning the lady asks if the reason for Gawain's rejection is a love at home. When he says no, she is hurt and angered but she asks for a last kiss and kisses him on the cheek. Then she asks for a token to remember him by but Gawain states that he has nothing to give her. The lady says that, in that case, she will give him something and offers a ring. Gawain refuses it, so the lady offers instead a green silk girdle belt from under her mantle.

At first Gawain refuses this too, but then the lady tells him that it has the power to protect anyone wearing it from any harm by another. Thinking of his impending confrontation with the Green Knight, Gawain accepts the gift, but the lady begs him not to tell her husband of it. In leaving she kisses Gawain on the lips.

That evening the Red Lord returns with only a small pelt. Gawain gives the Red Lord the requisite kiss, which does nothing to improve Gawain's comfort level as guest in the house. After supper Gawain asks if he can still have a guide to the Green Chapel and the Red Lord grants the request.

Gawain and the guide leave in the morning. Eventually they reach a cliff on the edge of a valley. This is as far as the guide will go, but he tells Gawain that the thing he seeks is in the valley. Gawain descends and finds the Green Chapel, which is more of a cairn than a chapel. He calls for the Green Knight and the mysterious fellow appears.

As sworn, Gawain kneels and presents his neck to the Green Knight's ax blade. The Green Knight feints a stroke and Gawain flinches. The Green Knight ridicules Gawain for this but Gawain points out that once his head is chopped off, there's no healing. The Green Knight swings the ax a second time, then a third. The third stroke is a real one, but only scratches Gawain's neck.

The Green Knight says his ax has tried Gawain twice with no effect, but the third time cut him because of Gawain's not having mentioned the sash. Chagrined, Gawain says, "That lie has lessened me." The Green Knight nods in agreement and tells Gawain to keep the sash as a reminder of his own imperfection. Then, before Gawain's eyes, the Green Knight transforms into the Red Lord.

Gawain is humbled even further, but the Red Lord invites him to a feast. Gawain declines and returns to King Arthur's court. There, Arthur has green sashes made for all of his knights and, in a formal ceremony, invests them all into the noble order of the silken sash. Gawain's closing thoughts are that he recognizes that he has met his master and that his master has invested him with the emblem of imperfect man.

Geoffrey Chaucer and Middle English Literature (1985)

35 minutes; Color; Documentary; Copyright 1985, 1993, Films for the Humanities, Inc.; Films for the Humanities and Sciences #ASJ906

CREDITS: Produced by — Stephen Mantell; Written by — Carroll Moulton; Narrated by — Protase Woodford; Associate Producer — John Pozzi; Cameraman — Richard Dallett; Editor — Paul Greene; Sound Mix — Dick Baxter

SYNOPSIS: An examination of the evolution of literature and literary forms in medieval England, this film's main concern is with the innovations Chaucer, though the discussion of the use of Arthurian legends is worth noting.

It is pointed out that after the Norman Conquest, French language and thought had a marked effect on Anglo-Saxon poetry. The absorption of Norman words and philosophies changed how stories were told, moving the English language from Old English to Middle English and the literature of Britain from old epic forms to the romance and dream vision.

Courtly love and chivalric codes replaced tales of ancient heroes. Around 1200 the priest Layamon wrote the first English source for legends about King Arthur, though his *Brut* is called relatively primitive. By 1375 an anonymous poet had written *Gawain and the Green Knight,* a combination of medieval romance, legend and psychology.

While there are a number of other fourteenth century poems about King Arthur, Lancelot and Galahad, this production states that one of the greatest literary achievements in prose was Malory's *Morte D'Arthur*. This was also one of the first books ever printed in English.

Prime examples of the dream vision genre are *Piers Plowman* and *The Pearl*. Where most dream vision poems were heavily allegorical, *The Pearl* took a somewhat different tack. Written by the same anonymous poet who wrote *Gawain and the Green Knight, The Pearl* resembles lyric poetry more than any other form.

From here the film moves into its discussion of Chaucer. Born in the 1340s, Chaucer was at various times a soldier, a diplomat and a government official. His own evolution as a writer followed lines of development similar to the culture around him, for he began by writing romances. However, after an extended trip to Italy, the effects of the early Italian Renaissance and men like Boccaccio became obvious. Chaucer's later writings, particularly his masterpiece, *The Canterbury Tales,* introduced realism and fiction to English literature.

Ginevra (1992)

Not viewed; Copyright 1992, Theuring-Engström Productions, Germany

CAST: Michèle Addala; Christian Koch; Serge Maggiani; Amanda Ooms; Zacharias Preen; Gerhard Theuring; Diego Wallraff

CREDITS: Director — Ingemo Engström

SYNOPSIS: An actress calling herself Guinevere has a nervous breakdown and becomes torn between her love for a doctor, Luc, and a painter, Arthur.

Good King Arthur (1967)

Not viewed; Filmstrip; 67 frames; Color; 35mm, 12-minute record and guide included; Copyright 1974, Moreland-Latchford, Ltd.; From the series "Famous Stories of Great Courage"; Library of Congress Call #PZ8.1; Library of Congress Catalogue #75735195/F/r88; Dewey Decimal #389.2

SYNOPSIS: An overview of the story of King Arthur.

Good Knight MacGyver see MacGyver: "Good Knight MacGyver"

Goodknights (1994)

Not viewed; 5 minutes; 35mm; Color; Cartoon; Copyright 1994, Hungary

CREDITS: Director — Zoltan Lehotay; Animator — Zoltan Lehotay; Designer — Zoltan Lehotay; Producer — Andras Erkel; Writer — Andras Erkel; Music — Ga'bor Presser

SYNOPSIS: A story of Camelot in decline. Arthur is senile, Merlin no longer believes in magic and Lancelot is getting old.

Grail see Babylon 5: "Grail"

Great Castles of Europe: "The British Isles" (1992)

75 minutes; Color; Documentary; Copyright 1992, 1994, The Learning Channel

CREDITS: Executive Producer — Tom Okkerse; Series Editor — Mark Verkerk; Director — Mark Verkerk; Producer — Ellen Kaptijn; Writer — James Barrat; Director of Photography — René Heijnen; Narrator — Larry Lewman; Music — Bernhard Joosten; Camera Assistant/Sound Recordist — Jum Festen; Grip Assistant/Gaffer — Roel Vos; Research Assistant — André Eilander; Production Assistants — Ineke Meter, José Vander Ven, Irma van Zand; Location Equipment — Cameo Equipment, TV Support Equipment; Film Laboratory — Cineco; Post Production Facilities — Valkieser Group; Film to Tape Transfer — Hendrik Wingelaar; Senior Editor — Oscar de Waard; On-Line Editors — Herman Ansink, Halbo van der Klaaw; Animation/Graphics/Titles — Andrea Alfaro Casarin, Anita Levering, Wijnand Ott; Color Grading — Hendrik Wingelaar; Narration Recording —

Roland House; Sound Editing and Mixing — Rob van Schoonderwalt; Post Production Coordinator — Karin van der Beck, Myriam Blom; Production Manager — Agaeth van Oosten; Financial Controller — Theo Okkerse. We gratefully acknowledge the collaboration of the following institutions: Bunratty Castle, The Ringfort of Cathair Bhaile Clan Mhargaishe, University of Utrecht, Amsterdam Free University; Special Thanks to: Liz Broderick, Michael Cleary, Patrick Crowe, Sean Kelly, Nandi O'Sullivan, Dr. R. J. van der Spek, Grania Weir, Tom Cassidy, John Collins, Professor Dr. D. R. Edel, Mr. & Mrs. Tom Neylon, Tom Sheedy, Paul Tuohy, Hugh Weir; For The Learning Channel: Concept by — John Ford, Mike Quattrone; Production Manager — Dawn Sinsel Quattrucci; Production Assistant — Kevin Tao Mohs; Series Editor — Eleanor Grant; Executive Producer — Mary Ellen Iwata; Produced for The Learning Channel by European Media Support, Hilversum, The Netherlands

SYNOPSIS: This Learning Channel production covers three castles on the British Isles: Warwick, Glamis and Bunratty. Each is interesting but Warwick is of particular interest to Arthurian study.

As the tape points out, the coat of arms of the earls of Warwick (a bear and staff) has been in use since the time of "Arthgillis, a knight of Arthur's Round Table." (The spelling is mine from the pronunciation of the narrator.) Arthgillis, or Artgualchar, or Artegall, is said to have been the first earl of Warwick. His name does crop up in Geoffrey of Monmouth's work and much later in Grafton's (sixteenth century).

The bulk of the discussion of Warwick Castle deals with Sir Guy of Warwick, who was one of England's mightiest fighters. He attained the earlship through marrying the earl's daughter and outliving the old man.

Glamis Castle inspires details of the Christianization of Scotland with the arrival of Fergus from Ireland around A.D. 710 Shakespeare's Macbeth is set in Glamis. The hauntings of the ghost of Lady Glamis (who was killed by James V in 1540 for witchcraft) are discussed.

The discussion of Bunratty Castle in

Ireland brings up the fact that the Romans never set foot on Irish soil. The heyday of Ireland ended with the Viking invasions in the late 700s. The throwing off of the Viking control by Brian Boru is mentioned as in Henry VIII's mandate for the destruction of all ring forts and crannogs.

Great Moments in History: "A Visit with King Arthur" (1983)

Subtitle: *Whatever Happened to Chivalry?*; 30 minutes; Color; Puppets; Copyright 1983, Coombe-Grove Productions, Inc.; The Bridgestone Group; Diamond Entertainment Corporation; TAV/ATI Videos, Agapeland Home Video

CAST: Toby Turtle (Himself); The 5th Street School Players (Themselves); Marty Allen (King Arthur); Dian Hart (Miss Twiddle)
CREDITS: Produced by — William David, Tom Bruner; Created by — William David; Music and Lyrics Composed and Arranged by — Tom Bruner; Directed by — Denny Fisher; Associate Producer — Sandy Shapiro; Written by — William David, Richard Ellis; Puppets Designed and Built by — John Brunner, Vivian Brunner; Puppeteers — John Brunner, Vivian Brunner, Mary Johnston, John Patrick; Voices of Laura and Penelope — Jackie Ward; Voices of Oliver and Conrad — Rick Segall; Voice of Toby — Stan Farber; Scenic Designer — Kelly Ray; Production Assistant — Sindy Bregman; Wardrobe — Muriel Sachs; Casting — Debbie Cope; Lighting Director — Dennis Weiler; Stage Manager — Hugh Atkins; Makeup — Wendy Osmundson; Technical Director — Frank Bronell; Video Engineer — Lance A. Wandling; Audio Engineer — Otto Svoboda; Camera — Manuel Zuma, Jim Velarde, Joe Chess; Video Tape Operator — Richard Strock; Key Grip — Luke Lima; Grips — Perry Suen, Matt Karhan, Paul Grenville; Video Tape Editors — Michael Polito, Richard Uber; Video Tape Operator — Mark Blackford; Post Production — Premore, Inc.; Executive Producer — Justin-Pacific Corporation

SYNOPSIS: A truly abysmal little production that seems to say boys can be rude, King Arthur was a boor and we should all try to get along with each other.

This film, one of a 13-tape series, only vaguely connects anything to the title they picked. The 5th Street School Players are a bunch of puppet characters. The puppets are well made, but the puppeteering, script and ideas are some of the worst one is likely to run across anywhere.

In "A Visit with King Arthur," Laura (a dog, perhaps?) wants Toby Turtle to throw his coat over a puddle so she won't get her feet wet. Toby has to think about it and Laura wonders where chivalry has gone.

During the first 15 minutes, Laura explicates her terrible plight. She talks to Miss Penelope, a giraffe, then sings a song about how words can be misunderstood. She then falls asleep and dreams of Camelot.

Comedian Marty Allen appears as King Arthur. His main contribution is the statement "Women should be fetching and schlepping." Laura sings a song about rumors, then she wakes up and decides that chivalry wasn't all it's cracked up to be.

Why these people decided to pick on King Arthur for this is hard to say. No personal affront to Mr. Allen is intended here, but if a denigration of the traditional Arthurian image was the goal, Allen was a good choice.

The Green Knight see under King Arthur and the Knights of the Round Table

Guinevere (1993)

93 minutes; Color; Live Action; Copyright 1993, Hearst Entertainment Productions, Inc., Copyright 1993, Alexander/Enright and Associates; Weintraub/Kuhn Productions; Distributed by Simitar Entertainment, Inc. Item #5133

CAST: Sheryl Lee (Guinevere); Donald Pleasence (Merlin); Noah Wyle (Lancelot); Sean Patrick Flannery; Brid Brennan (Morgan); James Faulkner (Malgon[?]); Constantine Gregory (Leodogan); Martin East (Gawain); Ben Pullen (Kei); Andrius Bobrovas (Perceval); Kestas Jakstas (Yvain); Anton Lesser (Envoy); Bruce Liddington (Swordsmith); James Greene (Bishop); Regina Share (Kaethi); Laura Girling (Guinevere's Mother); Saulius Sipras (Damon); Jonas Pakulis (King Stater); Ramunas Abukevicius (King Urian); Irena-Marija Leonaviciute (Midwife); Eva Dubey (Female Student); Ervinas Peteraitis (Carpenter); Gediminas Storpirstis (Rider); Anaya Vasara (Princess); Nanute Juronyte (Vivian); Vytas Sapranaukas (Leodogan's Aide); Sarunas Puidoks (Servant)

CREDITS: Music — Johnny Harris; Editor — Eric L. Beason; Production Designer — Matthew C. Jacobs; Director of Photography — Gabor Szabo, H.S.C.; Produced by — Joi Broido; Television Story and Teleplay — Ronni Kern; Based on the novels by Persia Woolley; Director — Jud Taylor; Executive Producers — Les Alexander, Don Enright; Line Producer — Gideon Amir; Casting — Lynn Kressel, C.S.A.; Production Manager — Regina Buteikyte; Assistant Director — Tania Jakovleva; Script Supervisor — Kathleen Mulligan; London Casting — Suzanne Crowley, Gilly Poole; Art Decorator — Galius Kilicus; Property Master — Algis Budzinskas; Sound Mixer — Stephen M. Zelenko; Stunt Coordinator — Gerry Crampton; Costume Designer — Jill M. Ohanneson; Hair — Rose Bologa; Makeup — Rachel Kick; Production Coordinator — Veronica Alweiss; Gaffer — Tibor Weber; Key Grip — Algis Zitkevicuis; V.P. Post Production — Paul D. Goldman; Assistant Editor — Lewis Chioffi; Apprentice Editor — Nicole Schubert; Supervising Sound Editor — Burt Weinstein; Color Timer — Dan Muscarella; Color and Opticals — CTI; Titles — Jeanne Beveridge; Film Transfer — Fred Eldridge; Audio Post Production — Larson Sound Center; Re-Recording Mixers — David E. Fluhr, C.S.A., Melissa S. Hofmann, C.S.A.; Executive in Charge of Production — Mel A. Bishop; Lietuvos Kino Studios

SYNOPSIS: *Guinevere* was a made for television movie based on the trilogy of novels by Persia Woolley (*Child of the Northern Spring*, 1987, *Queen of the Summer Stars*, 1990, and *Guinevere: The Legend in Autumn*, 1991). Taking a strongly feminist angle, this film makes Guinevere something more than just the power behind the throne.

In an opening narration Guinevere says, "They say Britain's greatest age began when Arthur pulled the sword from the stone. They got the story only part right. History is written by men and there is much in life that they ignore." She goes on to state that her mother died when she was five years old and that she was sent by her father to a "sanctuary of the old religion" in the North. There, among other royal children in similar protective holding, Guinevere was singled out for special treatment by the young priestess Morgan Le Fay. The special treatment involves schooling in subjects usually reserved only for men, including languages, the sciences and knife and sword fighting.

Another youngster raised at the sanctuary by Le Fay, but one of unknown ancestry is a fellow named Lancelot. Le Fay saved the infant Lancelot from drowning in a lake (thus presumably his full name, "du Lac") and became almost a mother to him. Of Lancelot, Guinevere says, "He was my hero. He was my friend." By the time they are adolescents Guinevere and Lancelot have fallen in love.

An elderly traveler shows up at the sanctuary, with stories of a new High King of Britain. He meets Guinevere in the woods and conducts a sort of interview with her. She reveals her thoughts on the unification of Britain and the need for her father's kingdom, Camelot, to be the focal point of a new peace and equality in the land.

Upon the old man's departure, Le Fay rails against the whole male dominance of politics, war and the country. She of course hates the coming of Christianity, with its male God overshadowing the Goddess. She hates the decline of women's influence and power with the rise of all the new "heroes." But most of all she hates the upstart Arthur, her half brother, born to her mother out of the rape by Uther Pendragon. Le Fay's goal is to destroy Arthur and make Lancelot and Guinevere King and Queen of Britain.

Le Fay binds herself and the two lovers in a blood ceremony, committing them to marriage upon Guinevere's next menstrual cycle. Lancelot is very accepting of this prospect, but Guinevere has doubts. First she wishes to get her father's approval, but more importantly she wants to learn what this Arthur actually stands for. Against Le Fay's wishes Guinevere rides for home.

Guinevere arrives to find nothing but trouble in Camelot. King Malgon of Gaul is visiting her father, seeking Guinevere's hand and threatening war if he is refused.

An aside here. The spelling of "Malgon" may not be correct. The names of the first six members of the cast listed above were given in the film's opening credits, but their characters' names were not — which is also the reason for the question mark in the cast listing. "Malgon" is what the pronunciation of the names sounds like in the film, but the character is probably modeled on Meliagaunt or Meleagaunce, the knight who in Malory and other versions, kidnapped Guinevere.

In any case, rather than give up his daughter or his kingdom to this would-be usurper, Leodogan chooses war. The first encounter goes poorly and many of Leodogan's men are killed or wounded. During a respite in the battle, six warriors arrive to offer their assistance. In the next fight the six newcomers make a considerable difference and the enemy is driven off but Leodogan is mortally wounded.

Out of deep gratitude for their having saved her land, Guinevere offers the leader of the knights errant any boon he could request. He asks for her hand in marriage. It is only then that he is introduced as Arthur Pendragon. This fortuitous turn of events is too good to pass up and Guinevere accepts the proposal.

In a heart to heart discussion with Guinevere, Merlin makes clear to her his own involvement in the political machinations and he helps to prepare her for her new position as High Queen. It is at this time that he says to her, "Though men desire you for your lands and your great beauty, I have chosen you for your mind."

Guinevere is stunned to see Merlin turn up for the coronation ceremony in Roman Catholic bishop's robes. He states that in the end, all the gods are the same god. The Cardinals who arrive, however, force Guinevere to give up her personal dagger. Merlin assures her that just as Arthur has Gawain as a protector, she will have a champion as well. In fact, to keep peace with the High Priestess of the old religion, they are accepting as Guinevere's guardian a man sent by Morgan Le Fay.

As other preparations continue for the big event, a carpenter is seen in the middle of constructing a table for the gathering. Guinevere stops and gives him a couple of suggestions, the last of which is to make it round.

It is no surprise to the audience that the protector who arrives from Le Fay's sanctuary is Lancelot. Lancelot desperately tries to convince Guinevere to leave with him, but she refuses to abandon her responsibilities in trying to end the wars throughout Britain.

Guinevere is soon pregnant by Arthur. She accompanyies him on a campaign to quell yet another civil war, and the royal couple are invited to a nearby castle for a night. There Le Fay has laid a trap for Arthur, getting him into her bed and also becoming pregnant by him. She also poisons Guinevere, but the queen escapes Le Fay and gets help in time to deliver a healthy baby girl. She gives the infant to the midwife, making the woman swear to protect the child and never tell where it came from.

Guinevere is unable to have more children but she and Arthur come to terms over his infidelity and agree to make Britain their family. Arthur sends Lancelot off to put down an Irish incursion and Arthur goes off on a six-month campaign in Gaul but is captured by Malgon. Guinevere abandons her peaceful stance and takes up the standard of the Warrior Queen to try to rescue Arthur.

Before departing, Guinevere and Merlin speak one last time. He assures the queen that her daughter is safe and well. He tells Guinevere that the girl will one day, as Arthur did, return to save Britain. The obviously ailing advisor tells her that they will meet again.

A peasant army joins her, but Guinevere's forces are not enough to hope to defeat Malgon and the other four kings who have joined him. Though his own battered army is three days behind him, Lancelot shows up just in time to lend his assistance. Guinevere sets up a ruse making her peasant force look more formidable than they are, particularly with the renowned Lancelot at their head. She addresses the rebelling group, giving them the opportunity to act as and indeed be, one people. King Urian is the first of Malgon's followers to throw down his sword.

Arthur and the other prisoners are freed and the victorious Queen brings them home to Camelot. Guinevere's closing words are, "And so Lancelot left, Merlin died, but Arthur and I endured. Peace came to Britain and with it prosperity and Camelot became a beacon to all people, in all lands, for all time."

Evidently no sequel film was intended, though the number of unresolved threads would make it an easy possibility. The completed Round Table is never seen in the film, nor are there any Knights of the Round Table mentioned. Le Fay's pregnancy by Arthur is never mentioned further and neither is Guinevere's daughter. Lancelot's self-imposed banishment is left hanging so, in spite of the many changes wrought here on traditional legend, some essentials remain as possible fulfillments of the accustomed disastrous conclusions.

Gumby: The Movie (1966)

90 minutes; Color; Claymation; Copyright 1966, Clokey Films; Copyright 1995, Premavision, Inc.; Kid Vision, Warner Vision Films; A Premavision Production

Voices: Charles Farrington (Gumby); Charles Farrington (Claybert); Charles Farrington (Fatbuckle); Charles Farrington (Kapp); Art Clokey (Pokey); Art Clokey (Prickle); Art Clokey (Gumbo); Gloria Clokey (Goo); Manny LaCarruba (Thinbuckle); Alice Young (Ginger); Janet MacDuff (Gumba); Patti Morse (Tara); Bonnie Randolph (Lowbelly); Bonnie Randolph (Farm Lady); Ozzie Ahlers (Radio Announcer)

CREDITS: Written by — Art and Gloria Clokey; Music Score by — Jerry Gerber; Editor — Lynn Stevenson; Associate Producer — Kevin Reher; Produced by — Art and Gloria Clokey; Director — Art Clokey; Storyboards and Script — Art Clokey; Set Breakdown — Gloria Clokey, Holly Harman; Trimensional Animation — Stephen Buckley, Dan Mason, Mike Belzer, Angie Glocka, Peter Kleinow, Tony Landati, Ken Willard, Art Clokey, Kurt Hanson, Harry Walton; Computer Motion Control — Dan Mason; Editing — Lynn Stevenson, Marilyn McCoppen; Editing Consultant — Joe Clokey, Jora Clokey, Peggy Connell; Model Sculpturing — Tom Rubalcava; Model Construction — Dennis Yasukawa, Earle Murphy; Puppets and Costumes — Cora Craig, Tom Rubalcava, Gloria Clokey, Janet MacDuff, Holly Harman, Mindy Beede-Harman; Sets and Backgrounds — Holly Harman, Bonnie Liebhold, Dennis Yasukawa, Janet MacDuff, Dan Morgan, Mary Bradley; Character Molds — Cora Craig, Tom Rubalcava, Shawn Nelson; Stage Manager — Jim Belmessieri; Armature Construction — Kurt Hanson; Animated Effects — Tom Rubalcava; Animation Assistants — Tansy Brooks, Dan Mason, Dennis Yasukawa; Animation Consultant — John R. Dilworth; Optical Effects — Image FX, Harry Walton; Additional Effects — Interformat, Michael Hinton; Music Score — Jerry Gerber, Marco Co–Marco d'Ambrosio; Music Consultant — Eric Levin; Sound Effects — Wave Group Sound; Sound Design/Mixer — James Allen; Assistant Engineer — Al Anderson; Sound Track Mixing — Russian Hill Recording; Sound Engineer/Mixer — Jeff Kliment; Assistant Engineer — Scott Strain; Additional Sound Effects — Kim Christianson, Bob Olsson, Andy Wiskes; Sound Transfers — Skywalker Sound, NT Audio Visual, John Seifert; Background Voice Effects — David Archer, Lillian Nicol, Rick Warren; Voice Coach — Dallas McKennon; Dialogue Recording — The Plant — Ann Fry, Jeffrey Norman; Dialogue Recording — Focused Audio — Jeff Roth; Dialogue Editing — Pamela Pittman, Susan Quinn, Pamela Z; Film Laboratory — Monaco Labs, Jim Moye; Video Transfers — Monaco Video, Ann O'Toole, Pacific Ocean Post, Thomas Mitchell; End Credits — Interformat, Michael Hinton; Negative Cutting — Negative Image, Judy Epstein; Research — Sausalito Public Library, Sausalito Fire Department, Institute for Advanced Psychology, Keith Harray, Research Director; Production Materials — Santa Clara Foam, Jerry Haug, Scott Harman; Animation References — Name That Tune Galleries, Craig Wolfe, Film Art Galleries, Aron Laikin; Production Accounting — Kevin Reher, Don Hedrick; Excerpt from original Gumby Adventure Series — "The Glob"; Songs: "Take Me Away": Lyrics — Gloria Clokey; Music — Ozzie Ahlers; Vocalist — Melissa Kary; Lead Guitar — Craig Chaquico; Rhythm Guitar — Lorin Rowan; Keyboards — Ozzie Ahlers; Bass — Ozzie Ahlers; Percussion — Ozzie Ahlers; Recorded at Focused Audio, San Francisco; Remix Engineer — Jim Reitzel; Published by — Premavision/Misticaro Music, BMI; Produced by — Ozzie Ahlers; "Rockin' Arc Park": Music — Ozzie Ahlers;

Guitars—Craig Chaquico; Keyboards—Ozzie Ahlers; Bass—Ozzie Ahlers; Percussion—Ozzie Ahlers; Recorded at Focused Audio, San Francisco; Engineer—Jeff Roth; Remix Engineer—Jim Reitzel; Published by—Premavision/Misticaro, Music, BMI; Produced by—Ozzie Ahlers; "This Way and That": Lyrics—Gloria Clokey; Music—Ozzie Ahlers; Vocalist—Kirby Coleman; Guitars—Vernon Black; Keyboards—Ozzie Ahlers; Bass—Ozzie Ahlers; Percussion—Ozzie Ahlers; Recorded at Laughing Tiger Studio, San Anselmo, California; Engineer—Jim Reitzel; Produced by—Ozzie Ahlers; "He Was Once": Lyrics and Music—Pete Kleinow; Vocals—Ann Clokey and Friends; Produced by—Clokey Productions, Ruth Goodell; Recorded at—Audio FX Co., Hollywood; End Credit Visuals—New Gumby TV Series; Kinesthetic Film Forces—Stavko Vorkapich, "Greatest Motion Picture Artist of the 20th Century"; Thanks to: City of Sausalito, California, Martin Luther King Jr. School; *Gumby: The Movie* (also iknown as *Gumby 1*) is dedicated to Sri Sathya Sai Baba. "Love All, Serve All"

SYNOPSIS: Gumby and his sidekick, Pokey, come to Earth as a couple of *2001*-style monoliths. They're actually just members of a band, called the Clayboys, looking for new concert ideas. After a couple of odd adventures, the gang settles down to serious searching.

Their search method is to meld into books. In a book about farms they find a bunch of people about to lose their farms to the Easy Loan Company, so they decide to do a farm benefit concert.

For some reason the dog, Lowbelly, cries pearl tears that are worth $2,400 each. And something about the music at the concerts makes him cry more than ever. Antagonists called Block Heads kidnap the dog and the chase is on.

As part of the rescue, Gumby melds into a *Knights of the Round Table* cassette. He acquires a suit of armor from the blacksmith there but fails to pull a sword from a stone. His evil robot duplicate does get the sword and chases Gumby around the Round Table hall. Galahad gives Gumby his sword, but Gumby loses the fight with the robot. He escapes with a crossbow.

The bad robot follows Gumby into a *Star Wars*–like setting called the Battle of the Nebula. In the battle Gumby gets a light saber and destroys the robot's sword, then a fireman defeats all the robots by spraying them with water. The dog cries lots of valuable tears at seeing the *Gumbymania* video the gang has produced and at a picnic the riches are given to the about-to-default farmers.

Neither Camelot, Excalibur, King Arthur nor any Arthurian characters, other than Galahad, are named in this movie. Galahad seems to be a favorite of the creators of Gumby (see *Gumby's Supporting Cast*).

The sword involved will be assumed by most children to be Excalibur. The association with Arthur's sword coming from a stone is so often misrepresented that any involvement of the Lady of the Lake is by and large forgotten. As usual, little is explained, so the use of this sword from the stone for evil purposes raises no questions in most viewers' minds.

For those unfamiliar with Gumby, he was a very early television animated character. Consisting of clay figures laboriously filmed in stop-action technique, *Gumby* was a charming kids' series. "Dragon Witch" was actually produced in 1956.

Gumby's Supporting Cast: (1967)

45 minutes; Color; Claymation; Copyright 1967, Clokey Productions, Inc.; Copyright 1987, F.H.E. (Family Home Entertainment); Lorimar Telepictures; F.H.E. Family Home Entertainment

CREDITS: Oddly, none given on this tape.

SYNOPSIS: A collection of seven Gumby claymations. The first one is titled "Dragon Witch." Gumby doesn't appear in this segment, but Henry Bear stars as the savior of a witch who's about to be eaten by her dragon because she didn't feed it that day. Dressed in armor, Henry says, "Sir Galahad couldn't do this."

"Dragon Witch" was actually produced in 1956.

Hanya, Portrait of a Pioneer (1984)

57 minutes; Color; Documentary; Copyright 1984, 1988, University Foundation, California State University, Chico; A Dance Horizons Video; Princeton Book Company

CREDITS: Introduced by—Julie Andrews; Narrated by—Alfred Drake; Executive Producer—Marilyn Cristofori; Producer—Nancy Mason Hauser; Director—John C. Ittelson; Editors—Nancy Mason Hauser, Peter Kirby, Scott Burrows; Narrative Script—Jack Carroll; Still Photographs—"Trend and Six Portraits," Barbara Morgan; Production Crew—Larry Schmunk, Wayne Leathers, Kenneth M. Yas, Tim Broderick, Valorie Wiggins; Tape Operators—Rose Calabrese, Bob Gingg, Mitch Wolf; Graphics Operator—Sherrie Lucas; Production Assistants—Judith Olmsted, John Crawford, Marie Bardin, Mark Hansen; Creative Advisors—Jack Carroll, Harold Lang; Research—Vicki Marie Hatch; Production Secretary—Arnelle Runnells; Rehearsal Dance Sequence, "Get Me to the Church on Time": Michael Blake, Janis Brenner, Betsy Fish, Robert McWilliams, Margaret Morris, Michael Podolski, Danial Shapire, Joanie Smith of the Murray Louis Dance Studio; Excerpts from "Jocose," "Capers" and "Ratta" Performed by Don Redlich Dance Company—Kathryn Appleby, Jim Clinton, Robyn Cutler, Ruth Davidson; Post Production Facilities—Video Transitions; Film Clips Provided by: Leonard Aitkin Film Productions, Library of Congress, Special Collections, Tutt Library, Colorado College, Mills College, Sullivan Productions, Lincoln Center Dance Collection, Murray Louis; Additional Photographs from the Personal Collections of: Hanya Holm, Eve Gentry, Crandall Diehl, Alwin Nikolais, Glen Tetley, Harold Lang, Mary Anthony and Special Collections, Tutt Library, Colorado College, Lincoln Center Dance Collection; Original Music—Kenny Davis, piano, Marguerite Heart, percussion; Special Thanks to: The Nikolais-Louis Foundation for Dance, The Colorado College, General Electronics Systems, Inc., Sony Video Utilization Services, Robert J. Bakke, Douglas B. Jacobs, Margery Turner, Emily Sutton; This program was made possible by grants from: The Ford Foundation, The National Endowment for the Arts, The Capezio Foundation, The Martinson Foundation, The Jerome Robbins Foundation

SYNOPSIS: Hanya Holm was one of the earliest proponents of modern or expressionist dance. Born in 1893 in Germany, she emigrated to the United States several years before the American entry into World War II. She choreographed, among other things, the original Broadway production of *Camelot.*

Educated in a convent, she trained for music but switched to dance early on. With other dance world luminaries she established a dance instruction school at Bennington College. From 1941 to 1983 her headquarters was Colorado College.

One minute into the tape there is a ten-second clip of Richard Burton and Julie Andrews dancing to the number "What Do Simple Folk Do" from the Broadway musical *Camelot.* Forty minutes into the tape there is a more complete two-and-a-half-minute clip of the same sequence. One can see why Burton never achieved fame as a dancer.

These clips are from a performance Burton and Andrews did on *The Ed Sullivan Show* in 1960. Lerner and Loewe's Broadway production of *Camelot* was never filmed. Two appearances on the Sullivan show are the only existing footage of the famous musical that was later made into the movie musical *Camelot,* starring Richard Harris and Vanessa Redgrave.

Hercules: The Legendary Journeys: "Once Upon a Future King" (1999)

Television series; Approximately 60 minutes; Color; Live Action; Copyright 1999, Studios USA Television Distribution, LLC; Renaissance Pictures; In Association with Studios, USA

CAST: Kevin Sorbo (Hercules); Tamara Gorski (Morrigan); Neill Rea (King Arthur); Sara Wiseman (Mab); Tim Faville (Young Merlin); Norman Forsey (Old Merlin); Asa Lindh (Lady of the Lake); Wayne Peters (Albion); Graham Smith (Baker); Michael Garnet-Holt (General Gwain); Emlyn Williams (Trevis); Andrea Bryce (Teacher); Steve Isherwood (Soldier #1); Wayne England (Soldier #2); David Bolton (Knight #1); Geoff Snell (Headmaster)

CREDITS: Producer—Bernadette Joyce; New Zealand Producer—Chloe Smith; Consulting Producer—Gerry Conway; Co-Producer—Patrick Moran; Producer—Paul Robert Coyle; Producers—Gene O'Neill, Noreen Tobin; Co-Executive

Producer—Liz Friedman; Co-Executive Producer—Eric Gruendemann; Co-Executive Producers—Roberto Orci, Alex Kurtzman; Created by—Christian Williams; Written by—Gene O'Neill, Noreen Tobin; Directed by—Mark Beesley; Executive Producers—Sam Raimi, Robert Tapert; Unit Production Manager—Eric Gruendemann; First Assistant Director—George Lyle; Second Assistant Director—Louise Marinovich; Director of Photography—John Mahaffie; Edited by—Steve Polivka, A.C.E.; Production Designer—Robert Gillies; Costume Designer—Ngila Dickson; Music by—Joseph Lo Duca; U.S. Casting by—Beth Hymson-Ayer, C.S.A.; Extra Casting Director—Tracy Hampton; Stunt Coordinator—Peter Bell; Second Unit Director—Wayne Rose; Camera Operator—Phil Samuels; Gaffer—Benare Mato; Key Grip—Geoff Jamieson; Wardrobe Design—Janis MacEwan; 2nd Unit Assistant Director—Rachel Heath; 2nd Unit Director of Photography—Rick Allender; Digital Matte Printer—George Ritchie; 3-D Artists—Thomas Reimann, Tim Capper; Digital Post Supervisor—Fiona Webb; Visual Effects—Flat Earth, Doug Beswick, Kevin Fletcher, Kevin O'Neil; 3-D Supervisor—Everett Burrell; 3-D Modeling and Animation—John Gibbons; 3-D Composite Supervisor—Mark Tiway; Digital Matte Paintings—Phil Cabanard; Digital Compositing—Eric Retshard, Owen Hammer, John Gest Anderson, David Rednoir; Flat Earth VFX Coordinator—Omar McClinton; Supervising VFX Coordinator (NZ)—George Port; Visual Effects Consultant—Kevin Blank; Visual Effects Editor—Jody Fedele; VFX Coordinators—Joe Conway, Martin Lam; Sound Recordist—Mike Westgate; Script Supervisor—Britta Johnstone; Makeup/Hair Supervisor—Annie Single; Mechanical Effects Supervisor—Ken Durey; Locations Manager—Sally Sherratt; Unit Manager—Marco Majorana; Studio Manager Assistant—Petelo Fanene; Prosthetic Technician—Mark Irvine; Art Directors—Jennifer Ward, Nigel Tweed; Art Department Coordinator—Pip Gillings; Construction Manager—Phil Chitty; Scenic Artist—Phil Radford; Set Dresser—Vivienne Kernke; Prop Master—Grant Vesey; Production Accountant—Keith Mackenzie; Production Coordinators—Jane Lindsay, Moira Grant, Phee Phanshell; Writers' Assistant—Stephanie C. Meyer; Creative Associate—Teresa Rowlee; Post Production Sound—Digital Sound and Picture; Post Sound Supervisor—Kelly Vendever; Rerecording Mixer—Bill Smith; ADR Supervisor—Tim Boggs; Action Pack Theme by—Ray Bunch; Supervising Music Editor—Philip Tallman; Music Editor—M.K. Broek; Assistant Film Editor—Mel Friedman; Post Production Supervisors—D. Gunther Tarampi, Robert B. Geth; Post Production Coordinator—Edwin B. Stilter; Supervising Executive for the Action Pack—Alex Beaton; Many Giant Steps were taken during the production of this motion picture. However, none for mankind. Sound track available on Varese Sarabande Records, Inc.; Filmed entirely on location in New Zealand; Visual Effects by Flat Earth Productions, Inc.

SYNOPSIS: "Once Upon a Future King" was the 100th episode of the television series *Hercules: The Legendary Journeys*. It aired originally on April 26, 1999, during the show's fifth season. The program took Hercules far beyond the expected 12 labors into conflicts with gods, goddesses, demigods, centaurs, Amazons, outlandish warriors from outlandish lands and a panoply of imaginative monsters. Full of facetious humor, *Hercules: The Legendary Journeys* made no claim at accuracy of any kind, but instead had a lot of fun putting the mythical hero into unusual situations.

This particular episode opens in A.D. 500 in Camelot. But this Camelot is battle-scorched, with bodies lying everywhere. Through the carnage saunters a merciless Arthur, accompanied by the sorceress Mab. The two enter the castle, in one of the rooms of which rests a stone with a sword in it. An elderly Merlin awaits them there.

It's obvious that Merlin doesn't approve of this evil Arthur's actions or his association with Mab but he does nothing to prevent Arthur from approaching the sword. He in fact has placed a spell on the sword. When Arthur touches the hilt, he and Mab are hurled back 1,000 years. Since Merlin can't change Arthur's ways, he has sent him back to someone who can.

Arthur and Mab appear in the castle among barbarians. Arthur immediately kills their leader and sets about making plans for taking over the kingdom. Mab on the other hand wants to try to figure out how to return to their own time.

While that is going on, the very much younger Merlin finds Hercules and pleads with the hero to accompany him on a ship bound for Britannia. All Hercules needs to hear is that thousands of lives are at stake and they head off.

Landing at Britannia, Hercules runs into an old friend, Morrigan. Morrigan had appeared in several earlier episodes of the show. She had been a destructive demigod associated with the isle of Eire. Hercules had visited Eire to help a beleaguered band of Druids. Through a complex set of circumstances, Morrigan was turned from evil to good to become a guardian of the Druids and Eire and she even struck up a romance with Hercules.

To stop this ruthless Arthur from moving out of Britannia and attacking Eire, Morrigan teams up with Merlin and Hercules. Even though Arthur seems bad, Merlin has a vision of the people of Britannia bowing to him as if he is a hero. Morrigan scoffs at the idea, but Hercules is more philosophical about it. They head out to find the errant time traveler.

Mab, in the meantime, has convinced Arthur that Merlin is probably somewhere around. Arthur has ordered the armies to search for the young wizard. Then she takes Arthur to the voluptuous Lady of the Lake to acquire Excalibur. The Lady heeds the summons, but doubts that this can be Arthur, since it is 1,000 years early. Arthur shows her a unique birthmark on his neck to convince her, and she tosses him the sword. Mab and Arthur move off to find Merlin.

They do find him, but Merlin's associates prove to be more than they can handle. Mab captures Merlin and disappears with him while Hercules captures Arthur and takes Excalibur.

The sword comes in handy when some of Arthur's soldiers waylay the group. Using the sword variously as a bat, a club and a post to spin on, Hercules' irreverent comments are, "Hmm, solid construction, handles well, turns on a dinar." Then, in stopping a quartet of the soldiers from escaping, Hercules puts a small round stone on the ground and taking a big round swing with Excalibur, smacks the stone

towards them. The rock hits the closest man, whose body in turn knocks down the remaining three. Hercules says, "Four! I knew this thing would slice."

Throughout their tussles and adventures, Hercules lectures Arthur on the finer points of leadership. By the time they get to the castle and Hercules tricks Mab into revealing that she is only after power and couldn't care less about Arthur, Arthur realizes he's been on the wrong path.

In her final attempt to get Excalibur for herself, Mab conjures up a giant Black Knight. Arthur, Merlin, Morrigan and of course Hercules all perform heroically in fighting the thing. Finally Hercules uses the knight's own shield as a sort of discus to cut off his head. The knight's body falls on Mab, presumably crushing her.

The group returns to the castle and goes to the room where the stone is. Hercules plants Excalibur in it, Arthur thanks them all, touches the hilt and is returned to his own time.

Before airing, this episode had been titled "A Greek Hero in King Arthur's Court." It can be seen as a convoluted reworking of Mark Twain's *A Connecticut Yankee in King Arthur's Court*, but since it is Arthur himself who travels back in time any connection with Twain's work is minimal at best.

Highway to Heaven: "A Divine Madness" (1984)

Television series; Approximately 60 minutes; Color; Live Action; Copyright 1986, Michael Landon Productions, Inc.

CAST: Michael Landon (Jonathan Smith); Victor French (Mark Gordon); Jonathan Frakes (Arthur Krock, Jr.); Ellen Maxted (Linda Krock); Scott Stevenson (Dr. Bob Halstead); Jean Allison (Gwen Halstead); William Edward Phipps (Carl); Ron Moody (Arthur Krock, Sr.)

CREDITS: Executive Producer — Michael Landon; Director — Michael Landon; Writer — Dan Gordon; Casting — Susan McCray; Associate Producers — Marvin Coil, Gary L. Wohlleben; Music — David Rose; Director of Photography —

Brianne Murphy, A.S.C.; Art Director — Geo. B. Ghan; Editor — Jerry Taylor, A.C.E.; Set Decorator — Lowell Chambers; Production Manager — Kent McCray; Assistant Director — Reid Rummage; Second Assistant Directors — Brad Yacobian, Jack Willingham; Camera Operators — Kenneth Hunter, S.O.G., Mike Meinarous, S.O.G.; Key Grip — Ron Housiaux; Gaffer — Lon Massey; Script Supervisor — Erika Wernher; Location Manager — John Warren; Property Master — Dean Wilson; Makeup — Allan Snyder; Hair Stylist — Lillian Barb; Men's Costumer — Bob E. Horn; Women's Costumer — Linda Taylor; Special Effects — Gary L. Crawford; Construction Foreman — Wallace Graham; Transportation Coordinator — Clyde Harper; Music Editor — Tom Gleason; Color Timer — Dennis McNeill; Negative Cutter — Kay Suffern; Sound Recording — Anthony F. Brissinger, M. Curtis Price, C.A.S.; Production Coordinator — Gary Wohlleben; Orchestra Manager — Charles M. Price; Photographed with Panavision Equipment

SYNOPSIS: *Highway to Heaven* was a television series which ran from 1984 to 1988. Landon played an angel in human form named Jonathan Smith, wandering the Earth helping people in need. A normal human named Mark Gordon is his partner and traveling companion. "A Divine Madness" was episode #7 of a total of 108, from the show's first season.

In this episode Arthur Krock, Sr., is a successful retirement age construction company owner. He spent his life building his business kingdom but neglected his family. He had promised his wife that he would build her a castle in which they would live happily ever after. He did build the castle but when his wife died, he went into a depression so deep that he took on the persona of King Arthur. Dressing in full chain mail, robes and a crown, Arthur stays in his home living out his fantasy and hiding from the world.

His son Arthur, Jr., or Art, is running the business and Art's sister Linda takes care of their father. Art has learned all the hard-nosed business tactics his father demonstrated while he was growing up, as well as his father's past disregard for more human concerns.

A conflict arises when Gwen Halstead, the mother of a local veterinarian, refuses to give up her property so that the Krock empire can take over her land for a $20 million building project. Gwen has taken on 200 stray dogs along with a number of other animals and cares for them in the well equipped animal hospital. Art has gotten a court order to demolish the Halstead property and proceed with construction.

Enter Angel Jonathan Smith, taking a job as a handyman for Arthur, Sr. Smith convinces Gwen to talk to Krock senior and the old man is stunned that a Gwenevere has returned to him. Her petition for aid, however, scares him. He resists leaving his house to go into the world where he knows he will be laughed at.

That night Smith finds the old gentleman brooding on the castle roof. He tells him that if he does not do battle the next day, then he is no king. Krock removes his crown and prays out loud, "Grant me courage to go out into the world and never let the jeers of those who laugh at me drown out the voice of truth you plant in all men. Give me courage to dream dreams and strength to make them real and if this be madness, let it only serve your purpose and I'll envy no man the world calls sane." A distant lightning bolt is the sign that bolsters Krock's courage and he replaces the crown on his head.

The next day a bucket loader shows up at the Halstead house. But King Arthur arrives as well, in full plate armor, mounted on his horse Galahad, carrying a lance. He attacks this dragon, and damages it enough to stop it. The construction crew leader, a man named Carl who has worked for Krock for 30 years, tells the men that if that's what his old friend wants, then they'll leave the site.

Krock's son is of course furious and he gets an attorney to force his father into a competency hearing. Krock decides that Smith will serve as his defense attorney and through a couple of small miracles Smith wins the sympathy of the judge. The clincher, however, is when Krock stands before his son in court, having declared publicly that he had been wrong to ignore the love of his family to tend only to business, and now declares his love for his son. Arthur junior breaks down and the case is dismissed.

At a gathering back at the Krock castle after the trial, the senior Arthur appears for the first time in 20th century street clothes. He and Smith share a heartfelt farewell and Smith and Gordon drive off to their next involvement.

Each episode of *Highway to Heaven* is something of a tear-jerker, this one no less than the others. Though a bit maudlin, Landon produced a series of shows that present some very old-fashioned, very fine ideas and principles.

The Holy Grail
A&E documentary; No further information available.

The Holy Grail (1997) see *Legends of the Isles: "The Holy Grail"*

The Holy Quest: In Search of Biblical Relics: "Castle of the Holy Grail" (1996)
42 minutes; Color; Documentary; Copyright 1996, Films for the Humanities and Sciences; Copyright 1996, Newbridge Communications, Inc.; Item #6532

CREDITS: Co-Production of NCRV — Holland, WDR — Germany, BRTN — Belgium, The Learning Channel, CoBofund; Producer — Roel Oostra — CTC; Camera — Ruud Denslagen; Sound — Paul Cresset; Narration — Douglas Kline, Jennifer Eory; Script Supervisor — Marissa DeMatteo; Editors — Erwin Nagel, Richard Tramontana; Director — Roel Oostra; Historian — Walter Birks; Author — Christian Bernadac; Church Historian — Prof. Gilles Quispel; Historian — Anne Brenon; Historian — Michel Rocquebert; Author — Yves Rouquette; Historian — Prof. Karl Huser

SYNOPSIS: The fascinating connection between Arthurian legend and the "heretical" sect of Catharism is one of the subjects of this documentary. The film concentrates heavily on the history of the Cathars and the crusade of extermination carried out against them in the thirteenth century by the Roman Catholic church. It also examines some relatively modern appearances of Catharism and Grail legends, primarily in the work of Otto Rahn and his involvement with Heinrich Himmler and Nazi Germany.

The Grail castle spoken of in this film is Montsegur, site of the final conflict between the church and the Cathars. The documentary begins, however, with an examination of the legends about Joseph of Arimathea. His founding of Glastonbury and especially the discovery of King Arthur's grave there are, the narrator states, things to be treated "with some cynicism." The fact that the discovery was made shortly after a disastrous fire at the abbey is reviewed. Revenues from tourists enabled the abbey to be rebuilt.

Further inferences are made that Joseph of Arimathea is not likely to have visited Britain at all. It is offered that this legend may come from a time when monks were traveling between Egypt and Ireland and may be based on a different person, whose name was confused with Joseph's but who was in fact a Coptic.

Next an outline of Cathar history is reviewed. Since Cathars believed that the Supreme Being created matter but that a lesser god created man, the imposition of monotheistic Christianity by Constantine the Great was a death knell for the sect. Christians who leaned toward the Roman bureaucratically organized church began persecuting these other Christians and within 100 years the Cathars were nearly wiped out. Some migrated to Armenia and hid there for nearly 500 years, but around A.D. 1000 they were driven out of there as well. Moving into western Europe they were able to find followers in many places but in southern France they became particularly influential. There, in an atmosphere of intellectual freedom, their ideas flourished until they once again attracted the attention of the powerful Roman Catholic church.

It is exactly at this time that Grail legends erupt on the scene. Historians interviewed for the film make the case that these stories served as propaganda to mobilize the knights of the north against the Cathars. That the Grail might be in the possession of heretical polytheists was strong incentive to go questing. By the early 1200s it was an all-out crusade. In 1209 papal legates unleashed an army of French, Dutch, Frisians and Germans on a town that harbored around 200 Cathars. Twenty thousand people were slaughtered.

Cathars were burnt at the stake by the hundreds. Twenty years of this crusading weakened Cathar spirit, but the Inquisition broke it. The ten-month siege of Montsegur was the climax of the conflict. Finally, 220 Cathars surrendered and were burned at the stake. Three are said to have escaped, with the Grail of course.

The last segment of the documentary deals with the occultism that grew from the search for an Aryan heroic age by Nazi Germans of the twentieth century. Himmler's attempt to blend Grail legends with Gnostic and Cathar ideas, among others, and the Nazi portrayal of Hitler as a Parsifal figure are discussed.

I Was a Teenage Thumb (1963)

Not viewed; Color; Cartoon; Copyright 1963, Warner Bros.

VOICES: Mel Blanc (George Ebeneezer Thumb, Ralph K. Merlin, King Arthur); Julie Bennett; Ben Frommer; Richard Peel

CREDITS: Director — Chuck Jones; Assistant Director — Maurice Noble; Writers — John Dunn, Chuck Jones; Original Music — William Lava; Editor — Treg Brown; Animators — Bob Bransford, Ken Harris, Tom Ray, Richard Thompson; Background Artist — Philip DeGuard; Layout Artist — Robert Givens

SYNOPSIS: Merlin, King Arthur and Sir Mordred all appear in this short Tom Thumb story. George and Prunhilda Thumb wish for a child. Merlin stops by and grants their wish. Tom is born and winds up at King Arthur's court.

In Search of Biblical Relics: Castle of the Holy Grail see The Holy Quest: "In Search of Biblical Relics: Castle of the Holy Grail"

In Search of History: "The Holy Lance" (1997)

Approximately 60 minutes; Color; Documentary; Copyright 1997, A&E Television Networks; The History Channel

CREDITS: Executive Producers — Craig Haffner, Donna E. Lusitana; "The Holy Lance" Produced by — Peter Doyle; Narrator — David Ackroyd; Senior Producer — Rhys Thomas; Coordinating Producer — Lois Yaffee; Co-Producer — Wayne Gray; Music — Christopher I. Stone, Zeljko Marasovich; Segment Producer — Margaret Haddad; Editors — Steve Pomerantz, Kevin Brown; Director of Photography — Steve Gray; Cameras — Paul Dougherty, Steve White, Jarid Johnson; Researchers — Peter Krajewski, Teri Scott; Production Coordinator — Louis C. Tarantino; General Counsel — Shinaan S. Arankowsky; Post Production Supervisor — Eric Lindstrom; Post Production Coordinator — Robert Senkel; Post Production Assistants — Ronnie Krondal, Peter Krajewski; Production Assistants — Andrew Nock, Tom Martin, Bryan T. Schmidt, Valerie Sheldon; Field Audio — Steve Wytas, Steve Gray, Tom Staton, Alex Winck; On Line Supervisor — Eric Lindstrom; Post Production Audio — Craig Plachy, Ron Miller; Composite Editor — Joseph R. Dalby; Post Production Services — Matchframe Video; Motion Control Photography — Zona Productions, Inc.; Period Music — RCM; Performed by — The Ensemble de Medici; Electronic Graphics — Leigh Thomas; Graphic Design — Bughouse Design; In Search of History Special Production Unit: *For FilmRoos:* Post Production Supervisors — Felicia Lansbury, Douglas Brooks West; Script Supervision — Michael Birnbaum; Executive Consultant — Arthur Canton; Footage Researcher — Paul Heet; Production Assistant — Karla Rose; Post Production and Audio Facility — Tell-a-Vision Post; Video Compositor — Eric Noth; Editor — Michael Hall; Assistant Editor — Jesse Murray; Graphics — Jonathan Curtis; Audio Mixer — Michael Simpson; Post Production Supervisor — Florence B. Savoye; Main Title Theme — 615 Music; Main Title Design — Hothaus Design; *For the History Channel:* Supervising Producer — Beth Dietrich; Executive Producers — Abbe Raven, Beth Relick Wright, Charlie Maday; Artwork Footage Courtesy of — Art Resource

Archive, The Bettmann Archive, German Information Center, The National Gallery, Washington, D.C., Quelinberg Castle, Irish National Heritage, Archive Photo, Dover Publications, German Tourist Board, NorthWind Picture Archives, English Heritage, BBC Worldwide Americas, Archive Films; Special Thanks — Michelle Brue, Krystina Jaslewycz, Anna Chachulska, Dominican School of Philosophy and Theology, Dr. Kathleen Irwin and The Encyclopedia of Biblical Tradition in the Arts, Colleen O'Connel, Facts-on-File, Wolfgang Fritz, Howard A. and Emajean Jordan Buechner, Kreismuseum, Wewelsburg, Mr. Brebeck, Kunstihistorisches Museum, Malcollm Billings, Majorie Weeke and Archbishop Foley, Nurenberg Castle, Professor Jan Oftrowski, Wawel Royal Castle, Krakow, Poland, Stuart Russell, Vatican Commission for Social Communications, A production by Greystone Communications, Inc., for The History Channel; Credited within the film — S. Thomas Parker, Professor of History, North Carolina State, Father Michael Morris, O.P., Ph.D., Dominican School, Berkeley, Professor Herman Fillitz, former First Director, Kunsthistorisches Museum, Vienna, Robert Benson, Professor, Medieval Historian, UCLA

SYNOPSIS: Though "The Holy Lance" makes no direct mention of Arthurian legend specifically, this documentary does point out the use of the lance in the Parsifal story, particularly Wagner's opera. The film gives an excellent overview of the legends and history surrounding the lance which may have pierced Christ's side on the cross. This lance eventually was incorporated into a fair amount of Arthurian literature as well as several films (see for instance, *Perceval le Gallois*, and the *Parsifal* opera entries).

All four of the Gospels make mention of a centurion being present at Christ's death. However, only John (19:34) tells of the Roman using his lance to pierce Christ's side. In a much later apocryphal text, this soldier is given the name Longinus.

The film explains that a nearby armory would have been the place the lance was deposited. This armory was seized when Jews took Jerusalem over in A.D. 66 though traditions state that the lance was hidden away and protected. In A.D. 135, in his efforts to eradicate Christianity, the Emperor Hadrian had Jerusalem destroyed. From then on myths and stories about the lance grew and spread.

Though the next written record of the lance in Jerusalem comes from the account of a Pilgrim in the sixth century, the Emperor Constantine the Great is involved with fourth century developments of the story. Immediately after a tragic embroilment which culminated in the execution of her favorite grandson, Helena, Constantine's mother, made a pilgrimage to the Holy Land. She had a number of churches built and is credited with having found the true cross and many other sacred artifacts including the nails from the cross. Constantine had some of the nails reforged into a crown, others into a new lance, which he kept at Constantinople.

From then on there was a proliferation of holy relics, lances included. In A.D. 614 during the Persian capture of Jerusalem the tip of the lance of Longinus was said to have been broken off and stolen. In 1097, while besieged in Antioch, the first Crusaders discovered another lance. Yet another, the Lance of St. Maurice was at one time in the possession of Henry I.

Nineteenth century romanticism is said in the film to be typified by the works of Richard Wagner. The holy lance is a central part of his opera *Parsifal*. Adolf Hitler viewed a performance of *Parsifal* in 1912 and in 1938 claimed the Lance of St. Maurice for the Third Reich, taking it from Vienna to Nurenberg. It was recovered by U.S. forces in 1945 and returned to Vienna.

The broken lance shaft held at the Vatican is said to be from the lance of Longinus.

In Search of History: "The Knights of Camelot" (1997)

43 minutes; Color; Documentary; Copyright 1997, A&E Television Networks; The History Channel; A&E Home Video

CREDITS: Executive Producer — Bram Roos; Series Producer — David M. Frank; *The Knights of Camelot* Produced by — William Kronick; Narrator — David Ackroyd; Supervising Producer — Lionel Friedberg; Coordinating Producers — Mark Finkelpearl, Michele Thibeault; Associate Producer — Jordan Friedberg; Music — Vaughn Johnson; Art Consultant — Kathleen Ahmanson; Historical Consultant — Dr. Charles T. Wood; Editor — Duane Tudahl; Director of Research — Tracey Benger; Art Supervisor — Karla Rose; Art Production — Susan Lutz; Researcher — Rachel Barouch; Production Assistants — Andrea C. Gargiulo, Stephen A. Ricci; Executive Assistant — Sylvia A. Ruiz; Post Production Supervisor — Elizabeth Newstat; On-Line Editor — Jeff Winston; Field Production — John Court; Camera — Thomas Payne, Greg Bader, CGI Productions; Production Assistants — Rebecca Meiers, David Schnier, Lisa Wiegand, Marty Polanski; *In Search of History* Special Production Unit; For Film Roos; Post Production Supervisor — Felicia Lansbury, Douglas Brooks West; Script Supervision — Michael Birnbaum; Executive Consultant — Arthur Canton; Footage Researcher — Paul Heet; Production Assistant — Karla Rose; Post Production and Audio Facility — Tell-A-Vision Post; Video Compositor — Eric Notti; Assistant Editor — Jesse Murray; Graphics — Jonathan Curtis; Audio Mixer — Michael Simpson; Post Production Supervisor — Florence B. Savoye; Main Title Theme — 615 Music; Main Title Design — Hothaus Design; For The History Channel: Supervising Producer — Beth Dietrich; Executive Producers — Abbe Raven, Beth Reuck Wright, Charlie Maday; Footage and Artwork Courtesy of — Loyola Marymount University, British Tourist Authority, Thames and Hudson, Excalibur Hotel, Geoffrey Ashe, Leslie Alcock; Special Thanks to — The Swordsmen and New Riders of the Golden Age, Ohio Renaissance Festival, Dr. Norma Lorre Goodrich, Dr. David Freke, Dr. Susan Robinson, Loyola Marymount University, Dr. Hendrick Stooker, Occidental College, George Porcari, Pasadena Art College, The J. Paul Getty Center Research Library, John Dickason, Director, The McAlister Library, Fuller Theological Seminary, Macmillan Publishing Company, Distant Lands: A Travelers Bookstore, Pasadena; Motion Control Camera — Zona Productions; Main Title by — Art F/X; Graphics — Vision Art; Post Production Facilities — Varitel Video; Audio Post Facilities — Coley Sound; Audio Mixer — Bill Smith; Production by Film Roos, Inc., for The History Channel

CREDITED WITHIN THE FILM: Jeremy Adams, Professor of History, Southern Methodist University, Charles T. Wood, Professor of History, Dartmouth College, Bonnie Wheeler, Editor, *Arthuriana*, Professor of English, Southern Methodist University, Alan Lupack, Curator, The R. H. Robbins Library, University of Rochester, Geoffrey Ashe, Author

SYNOPSIS: *The Knights of Camelot* is a recycled version of the 1995 documentary *Camelot. Camelot* was a production of the A&E series *Ancient Mysteries* (see entry for *Camelot*, Documentary, 1995). It was originally hosted by Kathleen Turner and narrated by Richard Kiley and Jean Simmons. *Camelot* was divided into five acts and ran slightly longer than *The Knights of Camelot*. This latest version eliminates the subdivisions and has a new narrator but follows the same outline.

The tape covers the history, archaeology, legends and literature surrounding King Arthur and is a good overview and introduction to the topic. Highlighted are the works of Geoffrey of Monmouth, Chrétien de Troyes, Malory and Tennyson.

In Search of King Arthur see *King Arthur and the Legends of Glastonbury*

In the Shadow of the Raven (I Skugga Hrafsina) (1988)

Not viewed; Copyright 1988, Sandrews

CAST: Reine Brynolfsson (Trausti); Tinna Gunnlaugsdottir (Isolde); Egil Olafsson (Hjorleif); Sune Maangs (The Bishop); Helgi Skulason

CREDITS: Director — Hrafn Gunnlaugsson; Executive Producers — Katinka Farago, Klas Olofsson; Writer — Hrafn Gunnlaugsson; Cinematographer — Esa Vuorinen; Music — Hans-Erik Philip

SYNOPSIS: The Tristan and Isolde legend transplanted to medieval Iceland. In this film, however, Trausti (Tristan) kills Isolde's father.

Indiana Jones and the Last Crusade (1989)

126 minutes; Color; Live Action; Copyright 1989, Lucasfilm Ltd., Paramount Pictures; Copyright 1995, Paramount Pictures; A Paramount Communications Company; A Gulf & Western Company; A Steven Spielberg Film; Paramount Video #31859

The Grail Knight (Robert Eddison) in *Indiana Jones and the Last Crusade* (1989).

CAST: Harrison Ford (Indiana Jones); Sean Connery (Professor Harry Jones); Denholm Elliott (Marcus Brody); Alison Doody (Elsa); John Rhys-Davies (Sallah); Julian Glover (Walter Donovan); River Phoenix (Young Indy); Michael Byrne (Vogel); Kevork Malikran (Kazim); Robert Eddison (Grail Knight); Richard Young (Fedora); Alexei Sayle (Sultan); Alex Hyde-White (Young Henry); Paul Maxwell (Panama Hat); Mrs. Glover (Mrs. Donovan); Vernon Dobtcheff (Butler); J. J. Hardy (Herman); Bradley Gregg (Roscoe); Jeff O'Haco (Half Breed); Vince Deadrick (Rough Rider); Marc Miles (Sheriff); Ted Grossman (Deputy Sheriff); Tim Hiser (Young Panama Hat); Larry Sanders (Scoutmaster); Will Miles (Scout #1); David Murray (Scout #2); Frederick Jaeger (WWI Ace); Jerry Harte (Professor Stanton); Billy J. Mitchell (Dr. Mulbray); Martin Gordon (Man at Hitler Rally); Paul Humpoletz (German Officer at Hitler Rally); Tom Branch (Hatay Soldier in Temple); Graeme Crowther (Zeppelin Crewman); Luke Hanson (Principal SS Officer at Castle); Chris Jenkinson (Officer at Castle); Nicola Scott (Female Officer at Castle); Louis Sheldon (Young Officer at Castle); Stefan Kalipha (Hatay Tank Gunner); Peter Pacey (Hatay Tank Driver); Pat Roach (Gestapo); Suzanne Roquette (Film Director); Eugene Lipinski (G-Man); George Malpas (Man on Zeppelin); Julie Eccles (Irene); Nina Almond (Flower Girl)

CREDITS: Costumes Designed by — Anthony Powell, Joanna Johnston; Production Designer — Elliot Scott; Director of Photography — Douglas Slocombe; Editor — Michael Kahn, A.C.E.; Music — John Williams; Executive Producers — George Lucas, Frank Marshall; Story by — George Lucas, Menno Meyjes; Screenplay by — Jeffrey Boam; Produced by — Robert Watts; Directed by — Steven Spielberg; Casting by — Maggie Carter, Mike Fenton, C.S.A., Judy Taylor, C.S.A., Valorie Massalas; 2nd Unit Directors — Michael Moore, Frank Marshall; Associate Producer — Arthur Repola; United Kingdom Production Crew: 1st Assistant Director — David Tomblin; Production Supervisor — Patricia Carr; Production Manager — Roy Button; 2nd Assistant Directors — Lee Cleary, Patrick Kinney; United States Production Crew: Production Managers — Joan Bradshaw, Ian Bryce; 1st Assistant Director — Dennis McGuire; 2nd Assistant Director — Artist Robinson; Sound Design — Ben Burtt; Mechanical Effects Supervisor — George Gibbs; Visual Effects Supervisor — Michael J. McAlister; Stunt Coordinator — Vic Armstrong;

Financial Comptroller — George Marshall; Additional Photography by — Paul Beeson, B.S.C.; Production Coordinators — Carol Regan, Maggie Tyler; Script Supervisor — Nikki Clapp; 3rd Assistant Director — John Withers; Camera Operators — Mike Roberts, David Worley; Assistant Cameramen — Martin Kenzie, Simon Hume; Dolly Grips — Colin Manning, John Flemming; Video Assistant Technician — Ian Kelly; Sound Mixer — Tony Dawe; Boom Operator — John Samworth; Sound Maintenance — David Brill; Supervising Art Director — Fred Hole; Art Director — Stephen Scott; Set Decorator — Peter Howitt; Production Illustrators — David Jonas, Ed Verreaux; Senior Draughtsman — James Monahan; Draughtsman — Peter Russell; Construction Manager — Alan Ecoth; Property Master — Barry Wilkinson; Scenic Artist — Brian Bishop; Supervising Decor & Lettering Artist — Steve Hedinger; Supervising Sculptor — Fred Evans; Production Buyer — David Lusby; Research — Deborah Fine; Assistant Special Effects Supervisor — Joss Williams; Special Effects Floor Supervisor — Dave Watking; Senior Special Effects Technicians — Alan Barnard, John F. Brown, Terence Glass, Paul Knowles, Brian Morrison, Peter Pickering, David M. Watson, Robert Bromley, Michael Dunleavy, David Knowles, Kenneth Morris, Roger Nichols, Neil Swann, Paul Whybrow; Special Effects Technicians — Jonathan Angell, George Chamberlain, Peter Fern, David Hunter, Stephen Lloyd, Anton Prickett, Peter White, Tim Willis, Trevor Butterfield, Michael Dawson, Darrell Guyon, Brian Unce, Alan Poole, Peter Skehan, Andrew Williams; Specialist Senior Wire Technician — Bob Wiesinger; Chargehand Riggers — Special Effects — Dave Skinner, Sid Skinner; Special Effects Electronic Engineer — Stuart Lorraine; Wardrobe Supervisor — Ron Beck; Wardrobe Mistress — Janet Tebrooke; Wardrobe Master — Colin Wilson, Sr.; Makeup Supervisor — Peter Robb-King; Chief Makeup Artists — Jane Royle, Pauline Heys; Mr. Connery's Makeup Artist — Ilona Herman; Chief Hairdresser — Colin Jamison; Hairdresser — Janet Jamison; Chief Makeup Artist, Prosthetics — Nick Dudman; Unit Publicist — Susan D'Arcy; Publicity Assistant — Rebecca West; Stills Photographer — Murray Close; Production Accountant — Michele Tandy; Assistant Production Accountant — Betty Williams; Assistant Accountant — Allan Davies; Accounts Assistant — Deborah Leakey; Assistant to Mr. Spielberg — Deborah Fletcher; Secretary to Mr. Spielberg — Lil Hevman; Assistant to Mr. Marshall — Barbara Harley; Assistant to Mr. Watts — Barbara Margerrison; Animal Consultant — Mike Culling; Camel/Horsemaster — Bronco McLoughlin; Chief Wrangler — Juan Cruz; Mr. Ford's Stand-in — Jack Dearlove; Mr. Connery's Stand-in — Roy Everson; Location Manager, Germany — Helmut Fodschuk; Vehicle Maintenance — Dave Eickers; Armorers — Simon Atherton, Bapty & Company; Unit Nurse — Li Chin Tye; Physiotherapist — Andre van Commenee; Trainer — Fran Horneff; Supervising Stand-by Propman — Joseph Dipple; Chargehand Dressing Propmen — Bernard Hearn, Charles Iker, Reg Wheeler; Prop Storeman — Tommy Ibbetson; Stand-by Propman — Paul Cheesman; Assistant Construction Manager — Fred Wyatt; HOD Carpenter — Frank Henry; HOD Painter — Mike Sotheran; HOD Rigger — Paul Mitchell; Supervisor Stagehand — John Tregear; Construction Buyer — Sydney Wilson; Stand-by Carpenter — Peter Mann; Stand-by Plasterer — Denis Brown; Stand-by Painter — Terry Weaver; Stand-by Rigger — Tom Lowen; Stand-by Stagehand — Peter Wells; Location Security Provided by — Berman and Ely, Inc.; Associate Editor — Colin Wilson; Assistant Editors — Patrick Crane, Nick Moore, Andrew McRitchie, Carin-Anne Strohmaier; Music Editor — Kenneth Wannberg; Orchestrations — Herbert Spencer; Music Contractor — Meyer Rubin; Post Production Provided by — Sprocket Systems, a Division of Lucasfilm, Ltd.; Re-recording Mixers — Ben Burtt, Gary Summers, Shawn Murphy; Supervising Sound Editor — Richard Hymns; Supervising ADR Editor — C. J. Appel; Dialogue Editors — Karen Spangenberg, Michael Silvers, Gloria D'Alessandro; Sound Effects Editors — Ken Fischer, Teresa Eckton, Sandina Bailo-Lape, David Stone; Assistant Sound Editors — Ewa Sztompke, Gwendoly Yates, E. Jean Putnam, Bob Marty, E. Larry Oatfield, Kris Handwerk Wiskes; Foley Artists — Dennie Thorpe, Marne Moore; Foley Recordists — David Slusser; ADR Assistant — Jil-Sheree Bergin; Music Scoring Mixer — Dan Wallin; ADR Mixer (U.S.) — Charleen Richards; ADR Mixer (U.K.) — Lionel Strutt; Color Timer — Jim Schurmann; Negative Cutting — Sunrise Film, Inc.; Laboratory Consultant — Michael O. Crane; Titles and Opticals — Pacific Title; Second Unit (London): 1st Assistant Director — Gareth Tandy; 2nd Assistant Director — Nick Heckstall-Smith; 3rd Assistant Director — Adam Amner; Script Supervisor — Marilyn Clarke; Camera Operators — Wally Byatt, Derek Browne; Focus Pullers — Keith Blake, Keith Thomas; Clapper Loaders — Nigel Seale, Richard Brierley; Grips — Gary Hutchings, Derek Russell; Camera Maintenance — Norman Godden; Video Assistant Technician — Peter Hodgson; Special Effects Supervisor — Terry Schubert; Gaffer — Steve Kitchen; Chief Hairdresser — Hilary Haines; Chargehand Standby Propman — Simon Wilkinson; Stand-by Propman — Peter Williams; Stand-by Carpenter — Robert Eames; Stand-by Plasterer — Michael Melia; Stand-by Painter — John Hurley; Stand-by Rigger — Simon Alderton; Stand-by Stagehand — Tony Driver; Spain: Production Manager — Denise O'Dell; 1st Assistant Directors — Carlos Gil, Jose Luis Escolar; Unit Manager — Diego G. Sempere; Location Manager — Alfredo Belinchon; Production Coordinators — Margarita McDermott, Trilby Norton; 2nd Assistant Director — Javier Chinchilla; 2nd Assistant Director — Yousaf Bohkari; Art Director — Benjamin Fernandez; Set Decorator — Julian Mateos; Wardrobe — Andres Fernandez; Chief Makeup Artist — Eddie Knight; Production Accountant — Antonio Garcia; Unit Doctor — Raul De La Morena; Italy: Location Manager — Christopher Hamilton; 1st Assistant Director — Gianni Cozzo; Art Director — Guido Salsilli; Accountant — Enzo Sisti; Jordan: With Thanks to Their Majesties King Hussein and Queen Noor and the People of the Hashemite Kingdom of Jordan.; Jordan Contact — Mounir Nassar, International Traders; United States: Production Executive — Kathleen Kennedy; Production Coordinator — Lata Ryan; Assistant Production Coordinator — Susan Spencer Robbins; Location Manager — Bruce Rush; Additional Photography by — Robert Stevens; Director of Photography, 2nd Unit — Rex Metz; Camera Operator — Norm Langley; 1st Assistant Photographer — Lou Nemeyer; 2nd Assistant Photographer — Pattie Harrison; Panaglide Operator — Ray Stella; Panaglide Assistant — Clyde Bryan; Sound Mixer — Willie Burton; Boom Operator — Marvin Lewis; Cable Man — Robert Harris; Art Director — Richard Berger; Set Designer — Alan Kaye; Set Decorator — Ed McDonald; Lead Man — Bill Gay; Co–Lead Man — Ron Chambers; Set Dresser — Joe Mendoza; Property Master — Louis Fleming; Assistant Props — Michael Carrillo; Special Effects Supervisor — Mike Lantierri; Costume Supervisor — Eddie Marks; Costumer — Tony Scarano; Makeup Artist — Kathy Elek; Hair Stylist — Robert Stevenson; Unit Publicist — Anne Reilly; Still Photography — Bruce Talamon; Production Accountant — Cheryl Stone; Assistant to Mr. Marshall — Mary T. Radford; Assistant to Mr. Lucas — Jane Bay; Assistant to Mr. Reppla — Robin Skelton; Production Assistant — Jim Langlois; Transportation Coordinator — Steve Collins; Transportation Captain — Russ McEntyre; Period Cars — Unique Movie Cars, Mario Sciortino; Wrangler — Corky Randall; Horse Wranglers —

Gene Walker, Dick Rust; Animal Trainers — Sled Reynolds, Boone Narr; Snake Wrangler — David McMillan; Construction Coordinator — Jerry Fitzpatrick; Gaffer — Pat Kirkwood; Best Boy/ Electrician — Ted Schwimmer; Key Grip — Gene Kearney; Dolly Grip — Don Hartley; Greensman — Don Glasshoff; First Aid — Todd Adelman; Craft Services — Tim Gonzales; Caterers — Gala Catering, Inc., Fred Gabrielli; Extras Casting — Sally Jackson; Location Security — Bill Werner; Aerial Unit: Director of Photography — Peter Allwork; Aerial Camera Assistant — Mathew Allwork; Aircraft Coordinator/Chief Pilot — Tony Bianchi; Pilots — Jonathan Whaley, Jacques Bourret; Pilot/Engineer — Donald Taviner; Aerial Fixed-Wing Aircraft — Bianchi Aviation, Film Services, Salis Aviation; Visual Effects Produced at Industrial Light and Magic, a Division of Lucasfilm, Ltd., Marin County, California.; Visual Effects Producer — Patricia Blan; Visual Effects Art Director — Steve Beck; Optical Photography Supervisor — John Ellis; Visual Effects Editor — Michael Gleason; Model Shop Supervisor — Michael Fulmer; Makeup Effects Supervisor — Stephen Dupuis; Matte Painting Supervisor — Mark Sullivan; Animation Supervisor — Wes Takahashi; Stage Managers — Ed Hirsh, Brad Jerrell; Camera Operators — Peter Daulton, Kim Marks, Patrick Sweeney, Pat Turner; Camera Assistants — Sel Eddy, Ray Gilberti, David Hanks, Jo Carson; Production Coordinator — Melissa Taylor; Optical Camera Operators — James Lim, Jon Alexander, Jim Hagedorn, Kenneth Smith, Don Clark, Tom Smith; Optical Lineup — Bruce Vechitto, Peg Hunter, David Kasppman, Brad Kuehn, Lori Nelson, Mike Cooper; Optical Processing — Tim Geideman, Bob Fernley; Assistant Effects Editor — Terry Peck; Matte Photography — Wade Childress, Harry Walton; Matte Model Artist — Paul Huston; Matte Artist — Yusei Uesugi; Model Makers — Charlie Bailey, Steve Gawley, Paul Kraus, Blair Clark, Ira Keeler, Richard Miller; Donovan's Digital Compositing — Les Dittert, Doug Smythe, Sandra Ford; Puppet Engineers — Kelly Lepkowsky, Marc Thorpe, Mike Jobe, Don Bies; Makeup and Clothing Effects — Lauren Vogt, Lauren Wohl, Steve Anderson, Anne Polland, Victoria Lewis, Kim Smith, Ease Owyeung; Animation Camera Operators — Charlie Clavadetscher, Eric Swenson, Bruce Walters; Animators — Sean Turner, Chris Green; Roto Scopers — Tom Bertino, Joanne Hafner, Jack McGovan, Rebecca Petrulli, Barbara Brennan, Sandy Huston, Ellen Mueller, Terry Sittig; Stage Technicians — Bill Barr, Robert Finley, Jr., Dave Heron I. J. Van Peere, Jr., Dick Cova, Joe Fulmer, Ross

Lorente; Production Assistant — Penny Runge; Stunts — Dickey Beer, Graeme Crowther, Martin Grace, Wayne Michaels, Rocky Taylor, Jordi Casares, Hubie Kerns, Steve Kelso, Bob Jauregui, Luis Miguel Arranz, Stuart Clarke, Nrinda Dhudwar, Billy Horrigan, Eddie Powell, Tip Tipping, Richard Cruz, Chuck Waters, Jeff Jensen, Fred Hice, Jose Maria Serrano, Simon Crane, Jim Dowdall, Wendy Leech, Terry Richards, Malcolm Weaver, Steve Lambert, Sean Lane, Roy Clarke, Pat Brymer, Gabe Cronnelly, Nick Gillard, Bronco McLoughlin, Tony Smart, Miguel Pedregos, Mike McGaughy, John Hatley, Paul Lane, Ignacio Carreno; "You're a Sweet Little Headache": by Leo Robin & Ralph Rainger; Performed by Benny Goodman; Courtesy of RCA Records, Cassettes & CDs; "Just a Gigolo": by Leonello Casucci & Julius Brammer; Courtesy of Chappell & Company; Photographed at Cannon Elstree Studios, Borehamwood, England, and on location in Spain, Italy, Germany, Petra-Jordan, Colorado, Utah, New Mexico, Texas and California.; Based upon characters created by George Lucas and Philip Kanfanan.; The Producers Wish to Thank: Samuelson Lighting, D&D International Transport, Location Facilities, Rafeel Hostelenia International, S.A. , Location Caterers, Istec-Aerial Camera Systems, Audiolink, Ltd. , The Travel Company, Renown Freight, Ltd. , The Tank Museum, Bovington Camp, T.L.O. Film Services, Bickers Action Enterprises, Ltd. , Turk Film Services, Ltd. , The Colorado Film Commission, The Cumbres & Toltec Scenic Railroad, Chama, New Mexico, Russ Fischer, The Utah Film Commission, The Moab Film Commission, Arches National Park, Moab, Utah, Paul Guraedy, The National Park Service, The New Mexico Film Commission, The Texas Film Office, The Amarillo Film Office, Bonne Redford, Martin Cohen, Brad Goodman; Re-recorded in a THX Sound System Theatre; ADR by Warner Hollywood Studios and Mayflower Recording, Ltd.; Music Recorded at Lorimar Studios; Personal Training for Harrison Ford — Body by Jake, Inc.; Originated on Eastman Color Film from Kodak; Color by Rank Laboratories; Prints by DeLuxe; Filmed with Panavision Cameras and Lenses; Dolby Stereo in Selected Theatres; Soundtrack album available on Warner Bros. records, tapes and compact discs.

SYNOPSIS: "The Arthur legend. I've heard this bedtime story before" is Indy's comment early in *Indiana Jones and the Last Crusade*. If he doesn't ever come to believe in King Arthur, by the end of the story the famous character certainly believes in the Holy Grail.

That's about the extent of truly Arthurian content in this movie. The bulk of the film is a series of captures of and escapes by the protagonists as they race against Nazis and other unsavory types for the Grail. Hitler's minions want the Grail's power to aid their quest for world domination. The evil Donovan wants it for eternal life for himself. Indy just wants to find his dad.

The film's opening is a look back at Indiana Jones as a young boy. Accoutrements like his famous hat and whip are explained with run-ins with bad guys trying to steal the Cross of Coronado.

After a while we move forward to the "present" of the 1940s. Indy meets a wealthy antiquarian named Donovan. From a dig somewhere north of Ankara this fellow has acquired a broken sandstone tablet with partial directions to the Grail's location. Indy learns from Donovan that his father has disappeared in Venice. The senior Jones, a lifelong Grail scholar, was there tracking down further clues about the artifact.

The story that the father and son team unearth is of three brothers who went on one of the Crusades together. They discovered the Holy Grail and one of them remained with it while the other two trekked to bring the news to Christendom. One brother died on the trip but one made it back. His tomb in Venice holds the key to the rest of the map to the Grail.

In Venice on the trail of his father, Indy finds the tomb, then has to contend with the Brotherhood of the Cruciform Sword. This group, modern-day Grail knights, is sworn to protect the whereabouts of the Grail. When it turns out that the seductive Dr. Elsa Schneider is a Nazi, the adventures begin. Indy is off to Austria, then Berlin, then the Hatay empire. There are horse chases, foot chases, airplane and zeppelin chases and a tank chase. Finally the good guys and the bad guys all get to the sanctuary of the Grail. Indy is forced to make it through the traps that protect the Grail when Donovan shoots his father. Only the Grail's healing power can save the senior Jones. Indy is followed by Elsa and Donovan.

The last of the three brother knights is in the Grail chamber, still waiting after 700 years. The charming old man no longer has the strength to protect the Grail, but he warns Indy of the dangers. Donovan ignores the warnings, is given the wrong cup by Elsa, and dies horribly after drinking from it. Indy finds the right one and heals his father with it.

Elsa's greed gets the better of her and she dies trying to remove the Grail from the sanctuary. In the end the Grail and the knight remain behind as the Joneses and their friends ride off into the sunset — literally.

The deepest that this adventure movie gets into Grail tradition is a couple of comments about the inner search that we all must make to find peace or whatever it is we might be looking for.

Neither Indy nor his dad is a holy man in any sense of the term. The father's quest is to keep the power of good from the clutches of evil. Indy's quest is a more nineties kind of thing — a pop psychology need to "talk" to his dad. It seems he doesn't think his father paid enough attention to him while he was growing up. The old man brushes that off humorously when Indy is at a loss for words at the question, "So what do you want to talk about?"

But the Indiana Jones movies aren't meant to be edifying, they're just fun-to-watch adventures.

Into the Labyrinth: "Excalibur" (1982)

Not viewed; British television episode; Color

CAST: Howard Goornay (Bram); Simon Henderson (Terry); Ron Moody (Rothgo); Pamela Salem (Belor); Lisa Turner (Helen); Simon Beal (Phil); Chris Harris (Lazlo)
CREDITS: Director — Peter Graham Scott; Producers — Patrick Dromgoole, Peter Graham Scott; Original Music — Sidney Sager; Designer — John Reid

SYNOPSIS: *Into the Labyrinth* was a British television series which ran from 1981 to 1982. It's 21 episode titles were 1. "Rothgo," 2. "The Circle," 3. "Robin," 4. "Masrur," 5. "Conflict," 6. "Revolution," 7. "Minotaur," 8. "The Calling," 9. "Treason," 10. "Alamo," 11. "Cave of Diamonds," 12. "Shadrach," 13. "Siege," 14. "Succession," 15. "Lazlo," 16. "Dr. Jekyll and Mrs. Hyde," 17. "Eye of the Sun," 18. "London's Burning," 19. "The Phantom of the Opera," 20. "Xanadu" and 21. "Excalibur."

The premise of the show was that three youngsters find and free from imprisonment the wizard Rothgo. They join him in a search through time to battle the evil witch Belor. Though none of the series was viewed for this book and though it is never wise to assume anything, it does not seem unreasonable to surmise that the 21st episode, "Excalibur," had something to do with King Arthur.

Isolde (1989)

Not viewed; Copyright 1989, Norsk Film Productions/The Danish Film Institute

CAST: Claus Flygare; Kim Jansson; Pia With
CREDITS: Director — Jytte Rex

SYNOPSIS: Another setting of the Tristan and Isolde legend in modern times. Isolde is a librarian caught between an ex-husband and a murderous lover.

Ivanhoe see under *Fables and Legends: English Folk Heroes*

Jack the Giant Killer (1962)

95 minutes; Color; Live Action and Animated Puppets; Copyright 1962, Zenith Pictures; Copyright 1990, MGM/UA Communications; United Artists; MGM/UA Home Video

CAST: Kerwin Mathews (Jack); Judi Meredith (Princess Elaine); Torin Thatcher (Pendragon); Walter Burke (Carna); Don Beddoe (Imp); Barry Kelley (Sigurd); Dayton Lummis (King Mark); Anna Lee (Lady Constance); Roger Mobley (Peter); Robert Gist (Scottish Captain); Tudor Owen (Chancellor); Ken Mayer (Boatswain)
CREDITS: Screenplay by — Orville H. Hampton, Nathan Juran; From a Story by — Orville H.

Hampton; Production Supervisor — Ben Hersh; Unit Production Manager — Ralph Black; Assistant Director — Richard Moder; Script Supervisor — Sam Freedle; Property Master — Art Cole; Special Effects — A. J. Lohman; Sound — John Kean; Rerecording — Buddy Myers; Sound Effects Editor — Don Hall, Jr.; Art Director — Edward G. Boyle; Makeup by — Charles Gemora, Frank McCoy; Hair Stylist — Louise Miehle; Men's Wardrobe — Bucky Rous; Women's Wardrobe — Sabine Manela; Costumes by — David Berman; Music Editors — Lloyd Young, Sid Sidney; Technicolor; Director of Photography — David S. Horsley, A.S.C.; Special Photographic Effects in Fantascope by — Howard A. Anderson; Film Editor — Grant Whytock, A.C.E.; Stop Motion Animation by — Wah Chang, Gene Warren, Tim Barr; Effects Animation by — Lloyd L. Vaughan; Music Composed by — Paul Santell, Bert Shefter; An Edward Small Production; Associate Producer — Robert E. Kent; Directed by — Nathan Juran

SYNOPSIS: A strange conglomeration of things come together in this film.

The late (eighteenth century?) accretion to Arthurian legend of Jack the giant killer is addressed in a film that attempts Ray Harryhausen–quality special effects.

The movie opens with a statement that this legend was born more than a thousand years ago in Cornwall, England, near Land's End. The Black Prince, Pendragon, master of all witches and giants, was exiled by the wizard Hurla to an uncharted island.

Interestingly, the king of Cornwall is Mark. This Mark, unlike the one of Tristan and Isolde legends, is not only happily married, but he has a beautiful daughter named Elaine. The film opens at her birthday celebration, to which Pendragon comes disguised as "Prince Elidorus." Pendragon's gift to Elaine is a little demon in a box which that night turns into a giant and carries the princess off.

Cormoran, the giant, makes the mistake of trying to pass through Jack's farm on his way back to his master. Jack kills the giant, saving Elaine. When King Mark and his men finally catch up, the king is so pleased that he knights Jack and charges him with escorting his daughter to the safety of a convent in Normandy.

As luck would have it, Elaine's lady-in-waiting is a spy for Pendragon, so the evil one learns of their plans immediately. Elaine and Jack sail for Normandy on a decidedly eighteenth century, three-masted, full-rigged ship. Phosphorescent witches take over the ship in midvoyage, kidnap Elaine and throw Jack overboard.

Praying to Isis, using the sacred orb of Egypt, Pendragon turns Elaine to evil. Then he goes to King Mark and gives Mark one week to abdicate the throne.

In the meantime Jack and the ship's captain's son have survived the attack on the vessel and are picked up by an affable Viking named Sigurd. Sigurd not only sailed with Erik the Red, but he also has a leprechaun in a jar. The leprechaun suckers Jack into releasing him in exchange for three magic coins. This crew sails to Pendragon's island.

The first obstacle Jack faces is a small *Wizard of Oz* lookalike army of soldiers who spring up from the dragon's teeth that Pendragon throws at him. There are other problems to overcome, but Jack rescues Elaine from the "little Roman temple" where Pendragon has her ensconced. All it takes is breaking a mirror and she's as good as new.

In the final battle Pendragon turns himself into a dragon which Jack kills. Jack and Elaine are free to go off together, the leprechaun heads for his beloved homeland in his seven-league boots and all is well.

This film is a classic case of the misinterpretation of the name Pendragon. Etymologically it may come from a combination of the Latin prefix *pene*, signifying next to the last, and dragon, traditionally believed to have come from the Welsh *dragwn*, meaning dragon or leader. If *pen* is thought of as head or highest, then *pendragon* becomes "highest leader." However, the Latin implication also makes sense when one considers the fact that it is Uther, Arthur's father, who is usually called Pendragon, next-to-the-last leader, with Arthur being the last of the spirited Celtic leaders in England before the Anglo-Saxon takeover.

Here, *pendragon* becomes "ultimate dragon," or ultimate evil. It works well in the context of the film and makes for a lot of great effects possibilities.

Tying it all to Cornwall and King Mark makes the story all the more tantalizing for Arthur buffs, but using any strict or scholarly analysis, there isn't much here to bear fruit.

Jewel Quest see under *Princess Gwenevere and the Jewel Riders*

John Steinbeck (1995)

45 minutes; Color; Documentary; Copyright 1995, Gédéon/France 3; Copyright 1996, Films for the Humanities and Sciences

CREDITS: Written by—Michel Le Bris; Director—Alain Gallet; Cameraman—Roland Thépot; Assistant Directors—Sébastion Degenne, Joshua Philips; Rostrum Camera—Bruno Abate, Franck Nourrisson; Editor—Bénédicte Mallet; Narrator—Nick Calderbank; Researcher—Deborah Ford, for Le Chaînon Manquant; Translator—Michael Westlake; Sound Engineer—Edward Pelicciari; Production Manager—Anne Moullahem; Production Assistant—Caroline Ronzier Joly; Post Production—France 3, West Rennes Bretagne; Film Archives; Pathé; Image Bank; Lobster; NBC News Archives; KIT Parker Productions; SVT; National Archives; Photographic Archives; Center for Creative Photography, Tucson; Steinbeck Research Center, San Jose; California Views; Monterey Public Library; John Steinbeck Library, Salinas; Le Figaro; Library of Congress, Washington; Quotes and excerpts from *East of Eden, The Long Valley, Burning Bright, To a God Unknown, Cannery Row, A Life in Letters, Tortilla Flat* foreword, Modern Library edition (1937) and Nobel Prize speech; With thanks to: Mrs. Elaine Steinbeck, California Rodeo, Salinas, John Defloria, Fisherman, Monterey, Mike Weber, Lake Tahoe, Mrs. Julie Fallowfield, Brandon Jamieson, New York, Don Elliot, CL Glot, Centre de L'Imaginaire Arthurien, Compex, Mrs. J. S. Gamble, Salinas, Mrs. Susan Shillinglaw, San Jose, Camp Richardson Resort, MacIntosh and Otis, New York, Caymus Vineyards; For France 3—Bernard Rapp, Florence Maurow, Sophie Humarau; Production Coordination—Marie-Dominique Bernoux; With the participation of Centre National de la Cinématographie and the support of Procirep; Producer—Anne-Françoise de Buzareingues; Executive Producer—Stéphane Millière; A Gédéon/France 3 Coproduction

SYNOPSIS: John Steinbeck (1902–1968) is one of the best-remembered American writers of the twentieth century. His stories of the lives of simple people became some of the most popular works of their time. Though often panned by critics in his lifetime, a number of his works have become literary classics, the most famous being *The Grapes of Wrath* for which he won the Nobel Peace Prize in 1962.

Frequently writing of the hardships faced by migrant farm workers, ranch hands, vagrants and other down-and-outers, it comes as a surprise to many that one of Steinbeck's ongoing interests and influences was the legends of King Arthur.

This biographical film points out that from childhood, Malory's *Morte D'Arthur* was one of Steinbeck's favorite books. Steinbeck's childhood was filled with stories of questing relatives as well. Both grandfathers, whom he spent considerable time with, had emigrated to America. His maternal grandfather had come from Ireland at the age of 17 and traveled across the country to California with the pioneering wagon trains. Steinbeck's Lutheran paternal grandfather left Düsseldorf on horseback to evangelize in Palestine before he came to America.

Steinbeck himself led a restless life. Even though he attended Stanford University, he resisted his parents' wishes for a professional career. Taking jobs on boats, farms and ranches, he spent much of his time with the migrants he wrote about so well.

As he became financially successful with his writings, Steinbeck was able to extend his travels across the country and around the world. He lived in New York and Paris, and late in life he spent a year in Britain working on his planned Arthurian saga.

Steinbeck's major Arthurian work was never completed, but Arthurian themes run through much of his writings. One short novel in particular, *Tortilla Flat*, was intentionally patterned on the Knights of the Round Table. A film version of the novel was made in 1942, starring Spencer Tracy (see entry for *Tortilla Flat*).

Johnny Mysto, Boy Wizard (1996)

87 minutes; Color; Live Action; Copyright 1996, Kushner-Locke Productions; Copyright 1997, Paramount Pictures; Paramount Home Video #837963

CAST: Toran Caudell (Johnny Mysto); Russ Tamblyn (Blackmoor); Michael Ansara (Malfeasor); Amber Rose Tamblyn (Sprout); Ian Abercrombie (Merlin); Patrick Renna (Glenn); Pat Crawford Brown (Margaret Lattamer); Jack Donner (King Arthur); Magda Catone (Rose); Sarah Haseltine (Andrea); Eric Countryman (Bunko); Cezarara Dafinescu (Griselda); Razvan Ionescu (Lead Soldier); Stefan Velniciuc (Second Soldier); Claudiu Romila (Third Soldier); Dan Victor (Guard); Theodore Daneth (Village Elder); Dan Marariu (Dwarf); Traian Zecheru (Peasant); George Danila (Peasant with Pig); Catalina Mustata (Guinevere); Doru Ana (Trooper); Petre Moraru (Johnny's Dad); Manuela Ciucur (Johnny's Mom); Gabriel Mican (Bunko's Crook); Igor Harnoff (Bunko's Crook); Razvan Catian (Bunko's Crook); Margaret Tate (Andrea's Friend); Ady Kuchok (Andrea's Friend); Madalina Constantinescu (Andrea's Friend)

CREDITS: Casting—Bob MacDonald, C.S.A., Perry Bullington, C.S.A.; Visual Effects Supervisor—Al Magliochetti; Costume Designer—Oana Paunescu; Music—Joseph Williams; Production Designer—Vali Calinascu; Editor—Carol Oblath; Director of Photography—Viorel Sergovici; Produced by—Mark Headley; Producer—Vlad Paunescu; Executive Producers—Peter Locke, Donald Kushner; Written by—Benjamin Carr; Director—Jeff Burr; Supervising Producer—Harlan Freedman; Associate Producer—Melanie Weiner; Production Supervisor—Gabi Antal; Unit Production Manager—Cristina Dobre; 1st Assistant Director—Cristian Ciurea; 2nd Assistant Director—Catalin Ciutu; Production Coordinator, Romania—Rachel Gordon; Production Coordinator, U.S.—Kevin Mueller; Script Supervisor—Ana Tarina; Casting Coordinator—Iulius Liptac; Extras Coordinator—Koseghi Arpad; Stunt Coordinator—Doru Dumintrescu; Animal Wrangler—Stefan Brandes; Production Accountants, Romania—Toni Lakatos, Cristiana Lakatos, Troaca Victorita; Production Accountant, U.S.—Chris Elkins; Production Assistants—Stefan Angheluta, Marius Nicolescu; First Camera Assistant—Gigel Dumitrescu; Second Camera Assistant—Lucian Iordache; Still Photographer—Dragos Popescu; Gaffer—Colin Constantin; Best Boy—Tanase Marcel; Electricians—Alaexandru Nicolae, Stan George, Ion Marcu, George Ursescu; Generator Operator—Bebe Surugiu; Key Grip—Dan Nicolae; Grips—Postasu Gabriel, Marcu Laurentiu; Art Director—Viorel Ghenea; Set Decorator—Ica Varna; Property Master—Ionel Popa; Property Assistants—Doicescu Cornel, Valentin Dumitru; Scenic—Stefan Ionci; Assistant Costume Designer—Mihaela David; Costumers—Hilda Canciu, Doina Raduciu; Wardrobe, U.S.—Karen Mann; Key Hair and Makeup—Mihai Stanescu; Special Makeup Effects—Dana Busoiu; Pyrotechnics—Petre Constantin; Sound Mixer—Dragos Stanomir; Boom Operator—Radu Nicolae; Boom Man—Nicolae Perianu; Interpreter—Ana Maria Uceanu; Catering—Mirela Dabija, Carmen Sercaianu; Drivers—Gabi Dinu, Gheorghe Mirea, Gabi Stojan, Alfred Bauer, Gheorghe Ciocariea, Mihai Surugiu, Vali Georgescu; Production Consultant—Gregory Everage; Assistant to the Director—Jerry Lentz; Post Production Supervisor—Harvey Greenberg; Post Production Coordinator—Kevin Mueller; Assistant Editor—Daniel Tivin; Post Production Assistant—Adam Severin; Second Post Production Facility—Coley Sound Productions; Audio Supervisor—William Smith; Sound Design Editors—Glen Auchinache, Angelo Palazzo; ADR Mixer Editor—Yuri Reese; Dialogue Editors—Dov Schwarz, Steven Coker; Foley Mixer—Lorita De La Cerna; Foley Walkers—Anita Canella, Dustin O'Halloran, Rick Owens, Gregory Louden; Re-recording Mixers—William Smith, Joe Barnett, Yuri Reese; Special Visual Effects—Eye Candy; Digital Compositing Supervisor—Al Magiochetti; Digital Animation Supervisor—Todd Sheridan Perry; Digital Morph Supervisor—Cain Cross; Digital Artists—Jennifer A. Champagne, Michael Hoover; Title Design—Billy Shane; Digital Title Effects—Crainroyer Studios; Video Post Production Services—Sunset Post, Inc.; Colorist—Adam Adams; On-Line Editor—Rich Uber; Film Lab—4 Media Film Laboratories; Video Services—Encore Video; Stereo Consultants—Daniel W. Victor, Jr., Fred Rivas; Executive in Charge of Post Production—Bob Wenokur; Special Thanks—Jay Woelfel, Kristi Keller-McHugh, Nora Ferris, Matt Coleman, Dave Parker, Dona Fischer, Nora Nash; "Do You Believe in Magic": Performed by—Toran Caudell; Music and Lyrics by—Michael Ross; Bond Company—Film Finances; Production Counsel—Law Offices of Alan Abrams; Insurance Provided by—AON/Albert G. Ruben & Company; Research—Joan Pearce Research Associates; Travel Arrangements Made by—Hoffman Travel; Shipping—Showfilm; Executive in Charge of Production—Reid Shane; Filmed at Catel Studio, S.R.I., Bucharest, Romania; Recorded by—Ultra Stereo

SYNOPSIS: To the numerous film versions of *A Connecticut Yankee in King Arthur's Court* can be added *Johnny Mysto, Boy Wizard*. This low-key rendition takes a couple of new twists and introduces characters not seen elsewhere. Though Twain's work is not cited as the source, this film is based on his original idea of sending someone from the present back to King Arthur's Camelot.

The first scene is of a platoon of sword-wielding, chainmail-clad soldiers chasing a little girl through the woods. She manages to get to the ruins of a stone building, finds a particular rock, slides it out of the way and climbs into a hole in the ground. Pulling the rock back over her head, she proceeds down a stone spiral staircase into Merlin's underground lair.

The prize that the girl has carried to Merlin is a mirror. "Sprout," as Merlin calls her, informs him that the soldiers are everywhere. Merlin reverently takes the mirror and, as he chants, "Oh, glass of Avalon, I bid thee wake," he pulls magical lightning from the air, activating the mirror. The mirror's reflective surface becomes a liquid through which Merlin puts his hand.

Next Merlin tells Sprout to put the mirror in a place of safety. He says the only hope for saving the land is that a hero will come who may not be born for another 1,000 years.

Cut to the present, where young Johnny Mysto is putting on a backyard magic show. Despite the help of his younger sister, Andrea, and his heavyset friend, Glenn, Johnny's tricks bomb. In the small audience are a bully named Bunko and three of his cronies. They jeer at Johnny's efforts and the entire audience leaves grumbling.

Discouraged, Johnny and Glenn watch television that night. Johnny's hero, the magician Blackmoor is on and Johnny follows his act studiously, trying to duplicate the man's every move. The two boys decide to go to the local theater where Blackmoor is appearing, to see if the magician might give Johnny some pointers.

Blackmoor, it turns out, is on the skids.

A bit inebriated and in a foul mood, he at first dismisses Johnny, giving the boy a book and cynically telling him that whatever he wants to learn is in there. Seeing how crushed the boy is, Blackmoor finally softens and rummages through his things. He finds a manila envelope and removes a massive ring from it. He tells Johnny that it's the ring of Astarte and that it will help Johnny's magic.

Once on his finger, the ring's powers actually do come to life. Every trick Johnny tries works perfectly and then some. He is able to pull a seemingly infinite number of scarves from his mouth. He pours water into a folded newspaper and for the first time doesn't spill a drop. At the next backyard magic show, his tricks amaze the audience but Johnny becomes a little worried when he can't seem to control the number of rabbits that come from his hat. As a finale, he puts his sister in a box and makes her disappear. The real trouble starts when he is unable to bring her back.

Panicky, the boys go back to see Blackmoor. He's drunk again but Johnny uses the magic of the ring to sober him up. They explain the situation and Blackmoor digs up the manila envelope the ring was in. It had been sent to him by one Margaret Lattamer, who had been kind enough to put her return address on the envelope.

Finding Lattamer, they learn that the ring had been in her family for 1200 years. She says that the only person who can help them is Merlin. Retrieving a magic scroll from her basement, she says it will take Johnny where he needs to go.

Johnny's parents are on vacation at the Grand Canyon and their housekeeper, Rose, is watching over him and Andrea. He says that Andrea has to be back home by supper time or Rose will discover their problem. Lattamer assists Johnny in transforming Glenn into the likeness of Andrea and Glenn is sent back to Johnny's house in her place.

Blackmoor puts his hand on Johnny's shoulder, Johnny puts his ringed hand on the magic scroll and the two are transported back in time. They pop out of the mirror in the woods and make their way to Sprout's village.

An evil fellow named Malfeasor has imprisoned King Arthur and Queen Guinevere. He is in possession of a duplicate of Johnny's ring. With its power he is working to destroy the land. He even manages to capture Merlin before Johnny can get to Camelot.

Once there, however, the battle is met. Blackmoor finds Excalibur and uses it to defeat Malfeasor's accomplices. In a final showdown Johnny combines the power of the ring with Excalibur to kill Malfeasor.

Restored to their thrones the grateful Arthur and Guinevere greet the three adventurers. Arthur dubs Johnny and Blackmoor knights. Merlin bequeaths the other ring and his magic scrolls to Sprout and instructs her to pass them on from daughter to daughter. Keeping his ring, Johnny returns to the present with Blackmoor. He retrieves his sister from the ether and restores Glenn to his normal appearance, all just in time, as his parents return from vacation. The final scene is of Johnny on television performing magic with Blackmoor.

Johnny Mysto, Boy Wizard is a children's movie that manages to avoid becoming as obnoxious as it might have. While the children are the central focus of the film, it is not at the cost of the intelligence or dignity of every adult around them.

As in the film *A Young Connecticut Yankee in King Arthur's Court,* it's something of an accident that a young boy becomes the hero whom Merlin awaits. However, this Merlin is very much alive in his time, not the disembodied image of a face floating on the surface of water. King Arthur is once again an aged fellow, even balding, but he and his queen are not introduced to the viewers until the very last moments of the movie.

The similarities go on, but the differences are more numerous. The connection to Arthurian legend is scant, whether routed through Twain or not. Malfeasor replaces Morgan and just who he is is never really explained. Simply a wizard gone bad, one supposes (with a name based on *malfeasance*, how good can you be?), although at one point Sprout calls his troops "the devil's soldiers." There are three robotlike creatures that do Malfeasor's bidding, which Blackmoor destroys with Excalibur. They are never explained either, nor are they listed in the film's credits.

The dual rings are an even more remote addition to the story. Blackmoor calls his the ring of Astarte but Merlin never reiterates the name. Astarte was a Semitic goddess of love and fertility, making this an unusual possession for Merlin.

The Jousters (1989)

Not viewed; 16 minutes; Copyright 1989

CAST:/CREDITS: John Muccigrosso

SYNOPSIS: A story of two boys who, having heard tales of Sir Lancelot, pretend to be knights and have an adventure in a real castle.

Julie Andrews Sings Her Favorite Songs (1989)

60 minutes; Color; Live Performance; Copyright 1989, Thirteen/WNET and Greengage Productions, Inc.; Questar Home Video #2278

CREDITS: Directed for the Stage by — Michael Kidd; Musical Conductor — Ian Fraser; Set Designer — Roman Johnston; Lighting Designer — John Rook; Original (Special) Music and Lyrics by — Larry Grossman, Buzz Kohan; Directed by — Dwight Hemion; Produced by — David Horn; Written by — Buzz Kohan; Associate Producer — Patricia Ryan; Production Manager — Susan Benaroya; Production Supervisor — Mitch Owgang; Audio Producer — Douglas Nelson; Edited by — John Carral; Stage Supervisor — John W. Bradley; Technical Consultant — John B. Field; Associate Director — Ellen Brown; Script Supervisor — Kristine Fernandez; Graphic Design — B. T. Whitehill; Producer for the Julie Andrews Tour — Gerald T. Nutting; Photographs Provided by the Billy Rose Theatre Collection of the New York Public Library.; Special Thanks to: The Historic Wiltern Theatre, Los Angeles, California; Executive Producer — Jac Venza; A production of Thirteen/WNET in association with Greengage Productions, Inc.; Distributed by Questar Video, Inc.

SYNOPSIS: More than 47 minutes into the tape, Andrews sings "How to Handle a Woman" from the Broadway play *Camelot*. A few minutes later, she sings a bit of the title song from the same play.

The bulk of the performance is songs from her many other plays and movies, interspersed with superficially autobiographical tidbits.

A Kid in King Arthur's Court (1995)

90 minutes; Color; Live Action; Copyright 1995, Alpine Releasing Corporation & Trimark Pictures, Inc.; Buena Vista Pictures Distribution, Inc., Walt Disney Pictures in Association with Tapestry Films and Trimark Pictures; Walt Disney Home Video #5938

CAST: Thomas Ian Nicholas (Calvin Fuller); Joss Ackland (King Arthur); Art Malik (Lord Belasco); Paloma Baeza (Princess Katie); Kate Winslet (Princess Sarah); Daniel Craig (Master Kane); David Tysall (Ratan); Ron Moody (Merlin); Barry Stanton (Blacksmith); Michael Mehlnan (Shop Owner); Melanie Oettinger (Peasant Woman); Rebecca Denton (Washer Woman); Michael Kelly (Apprentice); Louise Rosner (Lady-in-Waiting); Paul Rosner (Peasant Boy); Béla Unger (Head Guard); Shane Rimmer (Coach); Tim Wickham (Ricky Baker); Daniel Bennett (Howell); Debora Weston (Mom); Vincent Marzello (Dad); Catherine Blake (Maya); J. P. Guerin (Umpire)

CREDITS: Executive Producer — Mark Amin; Co-Producers — Andrew Hersh, Jonathon Komack Martin; Casting by — Allison Gordon-Kohler (USA), John and Ross Hubbard (U.K.); Production Designer — Lászlo Gárdónyi; Music by — J. A. C. Redford; Edited by — Michael Ripps, Anita Brandt-Burgoyne; Director of Photography — Elemér Ragályi; Written by — Michael Part, Robert L. Levy; Produced by — Robert L. Levy, Peter Abrams, J. P. Guerin; Directed by — Michael Gottlieb; Associate Producer — Megan Ring; Line Producer — Louise Rosner; Stunt Players — Béla Unger, László Mecseki, Sandor Bertalan, László Imre, László Román, Tamás Vavrik, János Oláh, Sándor Boros, Peter Kantona, László Szili, Károly Medriczky, István Szimár, Levente Lezkák; 1st Assistant Director — Gábor Gajdos; 2nd Assistant Director — Andrea Albert; Script Supervisor — Julia Betik; Production Coordinator —Ágnes Komlóssy; Production Secretary — Csilla Ott; 3rd Assistant Director — Kati Csényi; Assistant to the Producers —

Claire Sutherland; Unit Manager — László Gojdár; Location Organizer — László Roráriusz; Production Assistant — Gábor Lettner; Art Director — Béata Vaurinecz; Set Dresser — István Tóth; Assistant Set Dresser — András Maros; Additional Set Dresser — János P. Nagy; Property Master — Zoltán Tóth; Additional Property Assistant — Imre Nagy; Storyboard Artist — Kevin Farrell; 1st Assistant Camera — András Váradi; 2nd Assistant Camera — Németh Fereng; Camera Leader — Tóreky Attila; Additional Operator — Tamas Sas; Unit Still Photography — Tamás Kende; Gaffer — Miklós Hajdú; Best Boy — György Berghopper; Electricians — Péter Fundéliusz, Sándor Szikszó, György Budai; Key Grip — Imre Sisa; Grips — Gyula Peterdy, Tibor Putnoki; Sound Recordist — Ottó Oláh; Boom Operator — Attila Madaras; Special Effects Coordinator — Fereng Ormos; Special Effects Technician — Gábor Balogh; Pyrotechnic Engineer — Gyular Krasnyánszky; Pyrotechnician — Attila Varsányi; Construction Coordinator — Béla Péterdi; Construction Crew — Attila Olah, László Asztalos, Jenó Kiss, István Harta; Costume Designer — Mária Hruby; Wardrobe Master — György Homonay; Wardrobe Mistress — Zsóka Hóka; Costume Dressers — Mari Balázs-Piri, Gábor Szabó; Key Makeup Artist — Julia Vitray; Assistant Makeup Artist — Györgi Filts; Key Hair Stylist — Bogyó Kajtár; Additional Hair and Makeup — Ildiko Makk, Mariann Hufnáger, Anna Tesner, Noémi Czako; Local Casting — Magic Media, Ltd.; U.K. Assistant Casting — Mary Maguire; U.K. Casting Assistant — Lisa Anne Porter; Extras Coordinator — Erzsébet Gáspár; Production Cashier — Margit Bácsi; Location Security — Iván Barkovics; Catering — Béla Dévényi; Interpreter — Judit Sági; Transportation Coordinator — Katalin Pintyé; Drivers — Csaba Fargó, Zoltán Danó, Csaba Annus, Gabor Luleczky, Andras Greznevecs, János Oravecz, Pal Nyerges; Stunt Coordinator — Béla Unger; Post Production Supervisor — Sherwood Jones; Trimark Production Supervisor — Cami Winikoff; Trimark Post Production Supervisors — Richard Jordan, Bruce Eisen; Trimark Legal/Business Affairs — Peter Block; Trimark Production Controller — Carole J. Meyer; Film Conforming by — John Travers, Kristopher Lease, Douglas Haines; ADR Supervisor — Louis Elman; ADR Mixer — Henry Dobson; ADR Facility — Magmasters, London; Sound Post Production — Soundfirm, Australia; Sound Mixed by — Roger Savage, Steve Burgess; Sound Editors — Gavin Myers, Gareth Vanderhope, Martin Bayley, James Harvey; Editing Coordinator — Peter McBain; Foley by — Gerard Long, Steve Burgess; Assistant Mixer — Paul Pirola; Color by — Technicolor; Color Timer — Dale Grahn; Negative Con-forming Services — Magic Film and Video Works, Marie-Hélène Desbiens, Barbara Solorio, Natalie Tezai, Syd Cole; Dailies by — Metrocolor London, Ltd., Foto-Kem Laboratories; Dailies Telecine — Molinare, Ltd.; Titles by — Title House; Visual Effects; Westbury Design and Optical; Matte Artist — Cliff Culley; Optical Effects — Neil Culley; Title House; Executive Producer — Keith Allan; Optical Supervision — Dave Gregory; Digital Effects — Title House Digital; Digital Artists — Dragon, Robert Lakstigala; The Post Group; Executive Producer — Mark Franco; Visual Effects Supervisor — Cosmo P. Bolger, Jr.; Digital Effects Composing — Peter Sternlicht; Film Recording — Karen Skouras; Film Scanning — Chris Kutcka; Effects Animation — Robert Scopinich; Post Production Coordinator — Tim Belcher; OCS/Freeze Frame/Pixel Magic; Digital Effects Supervisor — Ray McIntyre, Jr.; Digital Effects Coordinator — Phillip O'Hanlon; Digital Artist — Jim Gorman; Digital Technician — Victor DiMechina; Legal Services Provided by — Manatt, Phelps & Phillips; Camera Equipment — FGV Schmidle, Munich; Insurance Broker — RHH/Albert G. Ruben; Music Editors — Mark Green, David Gates; Supervising Orchestrator — Thomas Pasatieri; Orchestrators — Eric Schmidt, Carol Johnson, Larry Kenton, Christopher Guardino; Supervising Copyists — Ross & Audrey de Roche; Music Engineer — Eric Tomlinson; Music Production Coordinator — Juraj Durovi_; Performed by — The City of Prague Philharmonic; Music Recorded at — Smécky Studios, Prague; Concert Master — Bohumil Kotmel; Musician Contractor — Rudolph Wiedermann; Music Mixed at — Lansdowne Studios; "Third Eye" performed by Feel, Courtesy Red Engine Music (ASCAP), ©1994.; The producers wish to thank the following: The Reebok Company, The Coca-Cola Company, Hillerich and Bradsby Co., Bill Williams, Swiss Army Knife/Forchner Group, Joe Boxer, Transatlantic Media Associates, Ralph Russo and Hilton International, TravelCorps, Gateway 2000, The Harmonica Store, Hacker Electronics, Laser Toner and Computer Supply, Marla Scarnechia, Robin Hanna, Mark Fleischer, Esq., Laurence Marks, Esq., Patricia Hartling, James E. Keegan, David Ginsburg, László Helle, Debbie Albert, Peter Robey, Kevin O'Shea, Mr. Norwin Ricardo and Citco Banking Corporation, Steve Hardie, Natan Zahari, Barbara Feinstein, Lisa Mattinson Part, Nicholas Akira Part, Sally B. Merlin, Dr. Francisco Merino, Grace G., Julia G., Doran Clark, Natalie Abrams, Lisa Coburn, Andy Hill, Sam Bernard, Jennifer Shankman, Elizabeth Aiko Mi-dori Part, Steven E. De Souza, Lawrence Block, Alessia Gottlieb, Sarah G., Fabienne Guerin, Katharine Abrams, Jules Levy, Michael Levy and Samuel L. Clemens; Filmed entirely on location in Hungary and England

SYNOPSIS: This time Twain's *A Connecticut Yankee in King Arthur's Court* becomes a teenager's love story. Camelot is in ruins and the spirit of Merlin awakens to find a champion to salvage the kingdom. Poor Merlin seems to be trapped in a well — his face appears in the water there.

The chosen one is a boy from present-day America, Calvin Fuller. Calvin's biggest problem in life is that although he's on a baseball team called the Knights, he's a lousy player. An earthquake sends him back to Camelot.

The situation Cal finds there is grim. King Arthur has grown old and tired. Gwenevere has passed away and the king is raising their two daughters, Sarah and Katie, by himself. Lord Belasco is conniving to take over the kingdom. Arthur has committed his daughter Sarah to marry the winner of a rigged tournament but Sarah loves Master Kane, the local martial arts instructor.

Compact disc players and roller blades replace the lower-tech paraphernalia of Twain's original story. Cal and Katie fall in love, Belasco kidnaps Katie, Arthur and Cal rescue Katie and Arthur is revivified. The king opens the tournament to everyone and, appropriate to the nineties, it is Sarah, disguised as the Black Knight, who saves the day.

When everything is straightened out in Camelot, Cal has to leave. Returning to the present just in time to take a last swing at the baseball, Cal notices that the name of his bat is Excalibur. Then he sees Katie and Arthur in the stands — in modern garb, of course. What more could a young fellow ask for?

This film is no truer to Twain's novel than that book was to any of the Arthur legends. Cal, Sarah, Katie, Belasco and others are all inventions for this film. Twain, of course, invented many characters for his satirical story, but he also retained dozens of the originals from Malory.

Kids of the Round Table (1995)

89 minutes; Color; Live Action; Copyright 1995, Melenny Productions; Cabin Fever Entertainment, Inc.; Malofilm Communications in Association with Melenny Productions; Cabin Fever Entertainment's Timeless Adventures; Cabin Fever Video Item #155

CAST: Johnny Morina (Alex); Maggie Castle (Jenny); Christopher Olscamp (Norman); Justin Borntraeger (James "Scar" Scarsdale); Billie Coyle (Ronnie); Jeoffrey Graves (Buck); Malcolm McDowell (Merlin); Peter Aykroyd (Alex's Father); Mélany Goudreau (Waitress Cindy); James Rae (Sheriff Ferguson); Jamieson Boulanger (Luke); Roc Lafortune (Gil); Michael Ironside (Butch Scarsdale); René Simard (Stu); Melissa Altro (Heather); Barbara Jones (Mrs. Ferguson); Charles Powell (State Trooper)

CREDITS: Production Designer — Michel Marsolais; Costume Designer — Hélène Schneider; Film Editor — Gaétan Huot; Director of Photography — Roxanne di Santo; Music Composed by — Normand Corbeil; Line Producer — Ann Burke; Screenplay by — David Sherman; Based on an Original Story by — Robert Tinnell; Produced by — Richard Goudreau; Directed by — Robert Tinnell; Stunt Coordinator — Stéphane Lefebvre; Stunts — Marc Desourdy, Gina Duhamel; Produced with the Participation of Telefilm Canada and the Government of Quebec Income Tax Credit Program for Films.; Screenplay Consultant — Richard Goudreau; Casting — Andrea Kenyon, Myriam Vezina; Associate Producer — Kami Asgar; Production Manager — Anne Burke; Location and Unit Manager — Marie-Claude Filteau; Production Coordinator — Hélène Valois; Travel Coordinator — Diane Goudreau; Production Secretary — Manon Lavoie; Production Administrator — Alain-Louis Pharand; Public Relations — Lise Dandurand, Annie Tremblay; First Assistant Directors — James Rae, André Martin; Second Assistant Director — Richard Bouchard; Script Supervisor — Esther Coté; Story Boards — Luc Savoie; Assistant Art Director — Alain Clouatre; Prop Master — Francois Locas; Medieval Props — Thérèse Dion; Assistant — Ann St.-Denis; Head Carpenter — Marcel Blondeau; Carpenter — Edouard Faribeau; Laborers — Éric Gagné; Swing Gang — Randy Cyrenne, Martin Migneault, Alain Deniger; Head Painter — Véronique Pagnoux; Painters — Louise Tremblay, Caroline Morneau, Martin Morneau; On-Set Special Effects Supervisor — François Locas; Head Wrangler — Normand Trahan; Head Wardrobe — Denise Canuel; Dresses — Suzie Coutu, Yves Robillard; Makeup and Hair Stylist — Camille Bélanger; Assisted by — Christine Laurin; First Assistant Camera — Yvan Bourdages; Second Assistant Camera — Yoan Cart; Additional Camera Assistant — André Beaulieu, Josée Deshaies, Jeff Patenaude, Bill St.-John; "B" Camera Operators — Yvan Bourdages, Josée Deshaies; Steadicam Operator — Yvan Bourdages; First Assistant Steadicam — Denise Noel-Moster; Still Photographer — Jan Thijs; Los Angeles Crew: Production Manager — Jeffrey Jarrett; Assistant Camera — David Dowell; Gaffer — Karen Roseme; Production Assistant — Eddie Nicholas; Opening Title Sequence — Robert Tinnell, Richard Goudreau; Cinematography — Roxane di Santo; Art Director — Michel Marsolais; First Assistant Camera — René D'Aigle; Second Assistant Camera — Nicolas Luca; Edited by — André Corriveau; Sound Recordist — Julian Ferreira; Boom Operator — Sylvain Vary; Gaffer — Denis Paquette; Best Boy — Michel Caron; Electrician — Jacques Tremblay; Generator Operators — Yves Paquette, Kenneth McKenzie, Yves Ouimet; Key Grip — Normand Guy; Second Grip — Gilles Mayer; Additional Electricians — Francois Lefebvre, Benoit "Bean" Sévigny; Assistant to Mr. Simard — Jocelyne Gergeron; "Making of…" — Brent Radford, Jason Cavalier; Production Assistants — Michel Beauregard, Marc Filteau, Carl Richer, Denis Deschamps, Melany Goudreau, Saguay Lecor; Craft Services — Suzanne Filteau, Dimetri Bouet-Collin; Driver — Nicola Sisto; Post Production Supervisor — Caroline Grisé; Assistant — Victor Rego; Assistant Editors — Alain Reinhardy, Sylvain Lebel; Editing Suite — Création Montage; Work Print Confirmation — Isabelle Levesque, Benoit Falardeau; Supervising Sound Editor — Arun Majumdar; Dialogue Editor — Steven Gurman; Additional Dialogue Editing — Patrice Rivard; Assistant Dialogue Editor — Glenn Tusman; Apprentice Dialogue Editor — Peter Hay; Foley Artist — Serge Godier; Additional Foley — Monique Vezina; Foley Recordist — Daniel Bisson; Foley Recording Studios — Modulations, Inc.; Post Production Sound Services — Premium Sound 'n' Picture; Additional Dialogue Recording: Montreal — Cinelume Montreal; Director — Arthur Holden; Recordist — Michel Laliberté; Los Angeles ADR Recording — John Brasher and Associates Studios; Re-recording Mixer — Hans Peter Strobl; Assistant — Martin Cazes; Mixing Studio — Marko Films; Negative Cutting — Claudette Champagne, Diane Leroux; Color Timing — Vladimir Zabransky; Laboratory Coordinator—André Gagnon; Laboratory—Sonolab; Video Transfer—CME; Titles and Opticals—Film Opticals; Optical Effects Supervisor—François Aubry; Legal Counsel—Sander H. Gibson; Legal Assistant—Patricia Bradley; Grip and Electrical Equipment—Cinepool, Inc.; Camera Rental—Location, Michel Trudel, Inc.; Weapons Supplied by—Code Blue, Andrew Campbell; Generator Rental—Yves Paquette; Stock—AGFA Motion Picture Film; Insurance—B. F. Lorenzetti and Associates, Inc.; Music Composed by—Normand Corbeil, Les Éditions Clavicorde, S.O.C.A.N.; Music Editor—Michel Gauvin; Score Produced and Mixed by—Normand Corbeil; Score Recorded at—Les Productions, Clivicorde, Montreal; Songs: "Say It Ain't So Joe": Lyrics and Music by—Murray Head; Performed by—Murray Head; Courtesy of Polygram Special Projects/A&M Records and Island Records, divisions of Polygram Group Canada, Inc.; "Little Kid Blues": Lyrics by—Tony Roman; Music by—Jerry De Villier, Jr.; Performed by—Angelo Finaldi, Jerry De Villier, Jr.; J.D.Jr. Music—S.O.C.A.N.; "Rap for Alex": Lyrics by—Ossey Aeline; Music by—Jerry De Villier, Jr.; Performed by—Ossey Aeline; J.D.Jr. Music—S.O.C.A.N.; "Tamy's Party": Lyrics by—Tamy Peddle; Music by—Jerry De Villier, Jr.; Performed by—Tamy Peddle; J.D.Jr. Music—S.O.C.A.N.; "Nonstop Fun": Lyrics and Music by—Jerry De Villier, Jr.; Performed by—Jerry De Villier, Jr.; J.D.Jr. Music—S.O.C.A.N.; The Producers Wish to Thank the Following: Characteric de France, Collège de Saint-Césaire, Dr. Francis Gorsalla, Heuriste Vaudreil, Gascon and Associates, Groupe Yoga Adhara, Int., Hélène de Chaplain Restaurant, Hudson's Police Department, Kevin Reed, La Cordét, LCT Radio Service, Le Valet de Coeur, Madame Margaret Laginodiére, Simon Laginodiére, Maison de l'Artisan, Maison de l'Assrazonie, Met Tech, Mobilier Le Patrimoine, Morgan Arboretum Sainte-Anne-de-Bellevue, Norco Cycles Inc., Oasis, Parc des Iles, Ile Sainte Hélène, Montreal City, Paul Gregoire, Rons Foods, Sainte-Césaire Presbytery, Ted Newsome, Town of Hudson, Town of Rougemont, Town of Saint-Césaire and Its Residents, The Wilson Family; Special Thanks: Guy Clotier, Noèl Cormier, Eric Rournier, Roger Khayat, Jan Mc-Callum, Magella Methot, Pierre René, Tony Roman, Michael Gornick, Joëlle Levit, René Malo, Eric Normandin, Jean-Guy Rolliard, Desert Music Pictures, Lenny Jo Goudreau, Louis Laverdiere, Maria Melograze, Kerry O'Quinn, Georges A. Romero, Mr. and Mrs. Robert O. Tinnell, and Romeo Goudreau; Photographed with Arriflex Cameras and Lenses; Filmed entirely on location in Montreal, Quebec, and Los Angeles, California; Foreign Sales Malo Film Inc., a Division of Malo Film Communications

SYNOPSIS: *Kids of the Round Table* is one of the better live-action Arthurian films for children to be cranked out lately. Unfortunately its reliance on the Hollywood prerequisites of crudity, obscenity and adult vacuity detracts from an otherwise excellent story idea.

The main character, a youngster named Alex, has become enthralled with the legends of King Arthur. Alex and a group of friends have built themselves a castle in the woods, complete with a Round Table. Among the crew is Jenny, a girl Alex obviously has a crush on. They wear homemade armor, stage battles and have meetings.

"Scar" Scarsdale is an older kid who shows up one day with his rowdy friends to chase the reenactors away. While escaping the attack, Alex falls down a hillside into a mysterious glade and finds himself face to face with Excalibur in a stone. He pulls it out easily and none other than Merlin appears.

Merlin explains to Alex that no, the world doesn't need another king, this is America. He says that Alex didn't find the sword, it found him. Merlin's job is to teach Alex how to use the power of the sword. He also warns Alex that no one must ever see the sword.

Alex brings Excalibur home and hides it in his bed. He then rushes off for a dinner engagement with his father at a swanky restaurant. It's made apparent that Alex lives in a single-parent home, that his mother left and that Dad isn't around too much.

The next scene is on a basketball court at school. Alex is confronted by a big handsome new kid named Luke. Alex apparently has been the champ in his grade, but Luke is a lot better and beats him.

Later Alex heads for the castle and finds Scar and his cronies there, picking on the rest of the members of the Round Table. Alex tussles with the bully and is knocked to the ground. Silently calling on the power of Excalibur, Alex leaps up, thrashes Scar and chases the bullies off. Alex then dubs Luke a knight of the group, but notices Jenny eyeing Luke appreciatively.

That night Alex goes to Merlin to tell of his victory and Merlin philosophizes about fighting. He warns Alex that to misuse Excalibur would be to lose Excalibur.

Next we meet Scar's father, Butch Scarsdale, an ex-convict who now runs a village flower shop. He has two pals with him and they speak of coming up with a plan.

In the meantime, at school Jenny sends a note to Alex, which he reads when he gets home. In it Jenny asks Alex if he thinks that Luke might like her. She says she likes Luke a lot. Alex is crushed. Merlin comes to his room that night and Alex asks him what to do. Merlin states that he doesn't know, but that he'd fallen in love once. "The young woman locked me in a cave for 800 years," Merlin says. Merlin leaves Alex with words of hope, but they do little good.

On his next meeting with Luke, Alex calls on the power of the sword again and pommels Luke. Jenny yells, "I hate you for this!" The dejected Alex goes to find Merlin, but his mentor has vanished. Panicked, Alex runs home but the sword is gone as well.

At this point the film begins to lose its unique quality. Butch and his two followers hatch a plot to rob a bank, then kidnap the sheriff's wife and daughter (Jenny) to get away.

The criminals are morons who can't get anything right. It's Jenny's birthday and the house is full of kids when the robbers arrive. Alex arrives late to find the hostage situation in progress. He lures two of the criminals into the barn and captures them there. When Butch, the ringleader, comes out of the house the whole gang waylays him by throwing apples. An apple to the man's groin (this incident seems to be a requirement for kids' movies) stops him until Jenny's father, the sheriff, gets there to take him away.

Much shortened here, the segment after the robbery goes on too long. The slapstick and idiocy don't connect with the rest of the film at all.

Alex winds up the hero and learns the difference between right uses and wrong uses of power. The three friends come to a happier resolution than Arthur, Gwenevere and Lancelot did. It's a shame the creators couldn't find a better way to get there.

Despite that, *Kids of the Round Table* is an effective blending of Twain's *A Connecticut Yankee in King Arthur's Court* and more traditional versions of the tale. Setting the meaning of the legend in the present is a nice twist that works well. "Perhaps it is all a dream," says Merlin at one point, "but does that matter?" Indeed.

King Arthur (1961) see *Peabody's Improbable History: "King Arthur"*

King Arthur (1964) see *Mr. Magoo's Literary Classics: "King Arthur"*

King Arthur (1983)

Not viewed; Filmstrip; 59 frames; 35mm with teacher's guide; Copyright 1983, Simon and Schuster, Inc., New York, for Young American Films; From the series Golden Classics, based on Golden Stamp Classics

CREDITS: Terry Anne White; Shane Miller

King Arthur (1997) see *Legends of the Isles: "King Arthur"*

King Arthur: From Romance to Archaeology (1975)

22 minutes; Color; Documentary; Copyright 1975, University of Toronto

CREDITS: Narrated by—Paul Soles, John Cartwright; Written and Researched by—James Carley; Consultant—Lynette Olson; Graphics—Linda Staats; Photography—Julias Van Stokkam; Cameras—Dan Elsliger, Bill Morris; Audio—Gerard Beckers; Video—Terry Marks; Videotape—Jim Alston; Technical Director—Michael

Daroalay; Production Assistant — Lydia Manget; Production Director — Maxine Hemrend; Produced by the Center For Medieval Studies in cooperation with the Media Centre, University of Toronto; Acknowledgments: The Trustees of the British Museum, London, The Bodleian Library, Oxford, The Metropolitan Museum of Art and The Cloisters, New York, Thomas Fisher, Rare Book Library, University of Toronto, University College, Cardiff, A. G. Rigg, Toronto, Miss Joan B. Tanner, Somerset, Miss Kara Pollitt, Devon, The Camelot Research Committee

SYNOPSIS: Though more than 25 years old as of this writing, *King Arthur: From Romance to Archaeology* remains one of the best documentaries on the subject. In scholarly fashion the tape first examines the few historical records that exist on Arthur, then covers the major archaeological findings related to Arthur and Camelot in Britain.

The only sources quoted are those considered to be histories. No references are made to the more purely romantic writers like Wolfram, Chrétien or even Malory. It is pointed out that, other than the few mentioned historical writers, there has been major interest in establishing any truth behind the legends of King Arthur only recently, in the twentieth century.

The tape opens with a quote from Geoffrey of Monmouth, who wrote *Historia Regum Britanniae* (History of the Kings of Britain) around A.D. 1136. In it, he speaks of the worldwide renown that King Arthur achieved, with peoples as far away as India and Egypt knowing stories of the British warrior king.

The film quotes Saint Gildas, who wrote *De Excidio Britanniae* (The Ruin of Britain) sometime in the mid–sixth century. Although he mentioned no individual by the name of Arthur, he did speak of the battle of Mount Badon, or Badon Hill, which later came to be associated with Arthur.

The first historical mention of Arthur is by Nennius in his early ninth-century work, *Historia Brittonum* (History of the Britons). Nennius claimed that Arthur killed 900 of the enemy single-handedly at Mount Badon. The narrator points out that, as unlikely as this detail is, Nennius was nonetheless seeking to achieve some historical veracity in his writings.

The final major historical reference noted in the film is William of Malmesbury's *Gesta Regum Anglorum* (Deeds of the English Kings), written in the twelfth century. William posits that Arthur served King Ambrosius, the last of the Roman Britons. William also maintains the tradition of Arthur's Herculean killing spree at Mount Badon.

Noting that we have no more historical evidence about Arthur than existed in the twelfth century, the tape next moves on to the archaeological evidence. Even here, though, it is stated that there have been no archaeological finds that positively link the name Arthur to any specific date. What have been found are signs that a major resistance to invasion did occur in southwestern England during the time period in which Arthur is thought to have lived. Digs at two sites are described in detail: South Cadbury Castle and Glastonbury Abbey.

At South Cadbury a major excavation was undertaken for five seasons between 1966 and 1970. On the steeply banked and defensively ditched hill were found ruins of a major fortification made up of stone foundations with wooden parapets. The size of the fortification and the number of buildings indicate a massive emplacement of troops. The crucial finds were shards of pots and wine jars, which have been dated to the late fifth and early sixth centuries. These match the types of shards found at Tintagel, the reputed birthplace of Arthur.

The discussion of Glastonbury begins with a quote from Gerald of Wales, who wrote of a visit he made to the abbey in 1190 or 1191. Monks at the abbey had unearthed what was said to be the grave of King Arthur. Gerald wrote of the hollow oak that held the bones and of the inscribed lead cross that was in the grave.

Since that discovery Glastonbury has

come to be thought of as Avalon, the fog-shrouded island where the king was taken to either heal from his wounds or go to his final rest. The film states that during the fifth and sixth centuries, Glastonbury was in fact an island created by the flooding of surrounding areas.

Glastonbury Tor is visible from Cadbury Castle and the film states that it may well have been an outpost for that large fort. Additionally excavations at Glastonbury have turned up Celtic-style chapels and mausoleums dating from the same period as the hill fortifications of Cadbury.

The hard evidence shows that Cadbury could well have been the place that came to be called Camelot. If nothing else, it is the location of a huge fortified center of resistance to invaders.

Complementarily, the long-established religious traditions centering on Glastonbury make it the likely site of Avalon. It is reiterated, however, that no hard evidence exists to place anyone called Arthur at either of these locations.

The first portion of the video includes photos of the original manuscripts quoted and associated later artwork. The second part of the tape uses film of the sites in question both as they stand now and during excavation. Also shown are excellent drawings of what the structures may have looked like when intact 14 centuries ago.

King Arthur: His Life and Legends (1995)

50 minutes; Color; Documentary; Copyright 1995, A&E Television Network; A&E Biography with Jack Perkins; A&E Home Video #14040

CREDITS: Produced and Directed by — Sue Hayes; Legends Narrated by — Mike Grady; Program Narrated by — John Shrapnel; The producers wish to thank: CADW Welsh Historic Monuments, Cardiff Castle, English Heritage, Glastonbury Abbey, Gothic Image, Ltd. , Hampshire County Council, King Arthur's Great Halls, J A & E Montgomery, Ltd., National Trust (Wessex Region), Willa and Leonard Sleath, The Dean and Canons of Winchester, The Dean and Canons of Windsor, The Wallace Collection, Tintagel Castle, Wilkinson Sword, Ltd., Winchester City Council; Archives and Stills: The Bayeux Tapestry (eleventh century) by special permission of the City of Bayeux, Bridgeman Art Library, London, Hulton Deutsch Collection, Ltd., Trustees of Lambeth Palace Library, Mary Evans Picture Library, Quintessa Art Collection, Ltd., Range/Bettmann; Camera — Graham Maunder; Sound — Peter Vasey; Stills Photography — Ian Jones, Matt Prince; Rostrum Camera — Ivor Richardson, Ken Morse; Graphics — Emir Hasham; Illustrators — Amanda Cameron, Stephen Gooder; Editor — Guy Savin; Dubbing Mixers — Nick Rogers, Mark Parry; Music — Michael Tauben, Simon Benson; Production Secretary — Janne Schack; Production Assistant — Katharine Babington; Additional Research — Liz Boggis; Line Producer — Carol Rodger; Associate Producer — Vincent Beasley; Executive Producer — Rod Caird; A&E Manager Documentary Programming — Bill Harris; A&E Executive Producer — Michael Cascio; A Satel Documentary Production for A&E Television Networks

SYNOPSIS: An unusually well done documentary, lavishly illustrated with art stills and reenactment sequences, this film takes a rational look at the legends surrounding King Arthur and why they developed the way they did.

Aside from the narrators, four experts discuss various aspects of the legends. Their names don't appear in the regular credits. They are Dr. Juliette Wood of the Folklore Society, Dr. Robert Dunning, historian, Professor Stephen Knight, literary historian, and David Edge of the Wallace Collection

Extensive paraphrasing of Malory and other sources are used to describe critical segments of the legends. Included, for instance, are accounts of Arthur's mysterious birth, the illegitimate birth of Mordred, the Grail myths, Lancelot and Galahad.

Malory is called the most complete history of Arthur, but just as much attention is paid to the importance of Chrétien de Troyes and Geoffrey of Monmouth. Geoffrey's work, the *History of the Kings of Britain,* was the first major piece to include the Welsh poet Myrddin (as Merlin) with the Arthurian saga.

It is stated that the greatest turning point in the development of the Arthurian legends was the Norman Conquest of 1066. After that, as various leaders tried to establish their legitimacy by tying their ancestry to Arthur, embellishments to the legends grew.

Chrétien, writing in the late twelfth century, introduced stories of individual knights and the ideas of chivalry and courtly love. Chrétien's Lancelot is described as a "French lounge lizard" and a medieval replacement for the earlier Welsh champion, Bedevere.

A large section of the film is devoted to Galahad and the Grail, including a discussion of the confusion over just what the Grail is. At various times it has been considered to be a stone, a platter, the chalice from Christ's Last Supper or the cup that caught his blood from the cross (or both).

The main thrust of the tape is expressed by each of the experts. Essentially, there probably was some historical figure upon whom the Arthur legends are based, but it is impossible to pin down a specific individual. As time goes on more characters and events have been added to the story and what little existed of any original tale has become more and more remote.

The accumulation of medieval warpings of the legends that began with Chrétien have little to do with what a historical Arthur would have been like. As Wood points out, Arthur came to represent what is best of the battle leader, the Christian knight, later, the Victorian Christian and now, the New Age mystic.

King Arthur: The Legend and the Land (1991)

2 Video cassettes; Approximately 15 minutes each; Color; 1st tape: Still illustrations; 2nd tape: Documentary footage; One-page study and teacher's guide included; Copyright 1991, Educational Video Network; #249 V

TAPE 1: "THE LEGEND"

CREDITS: Author — Shirley Dye; Artwork — Julie Cornah, Jenni Longshore, Shirley Dye; Script Editor — Gary Edmondson; Videographer/Video Editor — Brian Kaspar; Technical Consultant — Henry H. Brown, Jr.; Audio — Marilyn Cowart; Narration — Thomas F. Soare, Ph.D.

SYNOPSIS: Created as a teaching film, *King Arthur: The Legend and the Land* gives an overview of the Arthurian story based essentially on the Malory version. Fifth graders would seem to be the ideal target audience. The tape is a bit simplistic for high school students and a little too fast paced for younger children.

In the presentation, Uther makes his deal with Merlin so that he can have Igraine. Arthur is born, taken by Merlin and raised by Ector. Uther dies, leaving no known heir, and civil wars break out.

When Arthur comes of age, Merlin has the archbishop of Canterbury gather all the worthy men of the country to determine a king. At the Christmas assemblage, a sword in a stone (no mention of an anvil here) is discovered but no one is able to pull it out. At the New Year's tournament, Kay loses his sword and Arthur retrieves the one from the stone, making Arthur the main contender for the throne.

Arthur picks 12 knights and goes to Caerleon, where he is besieged by dissenters. He manages to win that battle, then moves on to save Leodegrance from a siege, where he meets Guenevere.

After many further battles, Arthur is crowned in London. While quelling other rebellions Arthur's sword breaks and Merlin takes him to the Lady of the Lake, where the new king acquires Excalibur. He finally brings peace to the land, marries Guenevere and establishes the Round Table.

Lancelot and Guenevere have their affair but this film's telling of it has Arthur catching them in the act himself. Arthur condemns Guenevere to death, Lancelot rescues her and Guenevere goes to a convent. Lancelot retreats to France, where Arthur attacks him, having left Mordred in charge back in Britain. Mordred kidnaps Guenevere and assumes the throne. Arthur returns to do battle with the usurper, kills Mordred and receives a mortal wound himself.

As he lies dying, Arthur has Bedevere throw Excalibur back into the water from which it came (which Bedevere is reluctant to do). A black barge with three queens aboard arrives to carry Arthur off to Avalon.

TAPE 2: "THE LAND"

CREDITS: Author — Shirley Dye; Photographers — Shirley Dye, Eddie L. Dye; Script Editor — Gary Edmondson; Videographer/Video Editor — Brian Kaspar; Technical Consultant — Henry H. Brown, Jr.; Audio — Marilyn Cowart; Narration — Thomas F. Soare, Ph.D.

SYNOPSIS: The second tape of this set is a filmed tour of many of the important sites throughout England that are associated in one way or another with King Arthur. Several of the sites visited are not in other similar documentaries.

The first scenes are of the ruins of the twelfth century castle at Tintagel. This site of the reputed birthplace of Arthur includes archaeological evidence of a monastery which pre-dated the castle. The old Roman buildings of London are viewed, which certainly existed in the time of Arthur.

The home of the Roman 2nd Legion in Caerleon, Bodman Moor and Dozmary Pool, all in Wales, are each shown. Dozmary Pool is said to be where the Lady of the Lake appeared.

Malory placed Camelot at Winchester, but Cadbury also has strong claims as the site, and both places are shown. Dover, from which Arthur may have set sail to attack Lancelot, is included, as are Camelford and the river Camel, near which the fateful battle of Camlann may have occurred.

Also seen are Glastonbury Abbey, which is thought to be Avalon as well as the burial place of Arthur and Guenevere; St. Michael's Mount, which figures in the Tristan and Isolde legend; Chester, which is claimed by the ninth century author Nennius to be the site of one

of Arthur's 12 major battles; and Windsor, where in 1344 King Edward III formed a new chivalric order — the Royal Order of the Garter — modeled after Arthur's Round Table tradition.

King Arthur and His Country (1984)

Alternate Titles: *King Arthur and His Country — Southern England* and *King Arthur Country and Southern England*; 31 minutes; Color; Documentary; Copyright 1984, Finley Holiday Film Corporation

CREDITS: Narration — Stephen Vergo; Screenwriters — Robert D. Ellis, Bill D. Finley; Photography — Sandra Armenta, Ronald W. Rickard; Optical Effects — Sins' Animation; Video Titles — Foto-Tonics; Laboratory — Foto-Kem; Video Transfer — United Video; Produced with the Cooperation of the British Tourist Authority

SYNOPSIS: This work is emblazoned with one title on the video box, a different title on the cassette, and still a third title on the film itself. As this confusion might imply, the film doesn't quite know what it wants to be. Part tourist temptation, part travelogue, part historical documentary, it doesn't do too well at any of it.

The following, however, are some of the more interesting statements made in the film:

"Now … we know that the great and mighty Arthur did exist…. His name was probably Arturius and he was probably Christian."

"In 1191 Glastonbury Tor was established as the island of Avalon and as the location of the actual grave of Arthur and Gwenevere."

"It was Bedevere who threw Arthur's sword into the water after the battle with Mordred."

The first half of the tape gives these and other statements in rapid-fire succession. The second half is a general travelogue of towns and other places associated with Arthur, including Plymouth, Land's End and St. Michael's Mount.

If nothing else, it's refreshing to come across a definitive statement about Arthur's existence.

King Arthur and His Country—
Southern England see *King*
Arthur and His Country

King Arthur and the Knights of Justice (1992)

22 minutes each volume; Color; Cartoon; Copyright 1992, Golden Films Finance Corporation II; Copyright 1995, Sony Music Entertainment, Inc.; Bohbot Entertainment; Creativite and Developpment, S.A.; C&D/ Golden Films; Family Time Video #LV49559, #LV49564, #LV49565, #LV49566

CAST: Kathleen Barr, Michael Beattie, Jim Byrnes, Garry Chalk, Michael Donovan, Mark Hildreth, Lee Jeffrey, Willow Johnson, Andrew Kabadas, Scott McNeil, Venus Terzo

CREDITS: Executive Producers—Diane Eskenasi, Allen Bohbot, Jean Chalopin, Abi Arad; Written by—Jean Chalopin; Directed by—Stephan Martiniere, Charlie Sansonetti; English Story Adaptation by—Jack Olesker; Producers—Allen Bohbot, Diane Eskenasi, Xavier Picard, Mark Taylor; Coordinating Producers—Terry Lee Torok, Victor Villegas; Animation Production—KKC&D, Asia; Production Director—Shigeo Koshi; U.S. Production Director—Toshiyuki Hiruma; Animation Producer—Hiroshi Saotome; Production Coordinators—Seuchi Kikawada, Katsuya Shirai, Yasue Oki, Hakuchin Kim; Art Director (Animation Staff)—Kazusuke Yoshihara; Layouts—Lin Oda, Nobuko Shinohara, Studio Imagine, Yumera Company; Art Director (Pre-Production Design Staff)—Stephan Martiniere; Character Designers—Pascal Morelli, Stephan Martiniere, Didier Cassegram; Props Designer—Frederic Blanchard; Backgrounds Designers—Vincent Gassier, Stephen Martiniere; Color Key (Char Props)—Claude Morelli; Storyboards—Herve Bedard, Pascal Morelli, Remy Brenot, Richard Danto; Color Backgrounds—Florence Breton; Production Coordinators—Saud Asseti, Jill Gray, Kazumi Sawaguchi, Robert Winthrop; Animation Checking—Network of Animation, Inc.; Voice Direction—Michael Donovan; Casting—BLT Productions, Ltd., Michael Donovan, Victor Villegas; Talent Coordinator—Gail L. Hackaray; Recording Engineer—Marcel Duperreault; Track Assembly—Dick & Roger's Sound Studio, Ltd.; Exposure Sheet Timing and Direction—Bill Reed; Storyboard Timer—Jeff Hall; Track Reading—Peggy Denbaugh; Dialogue Transfer Services Provided by—Ryder Sound Services; Post Production—AB Production, Metropolitan Entertainment; Post Production Supervisor—Yannick Heude; Audio Supervisor—Jacques Siegal; Video Supervisor—Jean-Marc Fonseca; Post Production Supervisors—Aban Patel, Suzanne Remiot; Music Production—Saban International, Paris; For Bohbot Communications Distribution Sales: Adrien Seixas; Program Development—Jan Teich; Artistic Development—Lon Martin; Bohbot Entertainment, Inc. in Association with the Centre National de la Cinematographie.; Créativité & Développment

SYNOPSIS: This was a made-for-television cartoon series of the same caliber as *Princess Gwenevere and the Jewel Riders*. This one, however, is aimed at boys and so incorporates a lot more violent action and more strange creatures. The series opens with the statement, "And then from the field of the future a new king will come to save the world of the past."

Each tape is a single 22-minute episode. The credits remain consistent for each tape.

VOLUME 1: "OPENING KICKOFF"

Merlin narrates, saying that the Camelot he knew is no more. The evil Lord Viper ravages the land, Morgana has consigned Arthur and the Knights of the Round Table to the Cave of Glass and Viper is attacking Camelot itself. One of Viper's warlords, a flying fellow named Blackwing, captures Guinevere and carries her to Castle Morgana.

Merlin's magic grows weak as he tries to defend Camelot by himself. Out of the Round Table rises the ghostly image of a lady. She tells Merlin that somewhere in the future are 12 good men. Merlin goes off to search for them.

Meanwhile, back at the football game, Arthur King is the quarterback of the Knights professional football team. The rest of the guys have names like Trunk and Brick and Lug. On the bus trip to their next game a storm drives them off the regular road. They crash into the wall of an old tunnel and mysteriously find themselves at the Round Table.

The magic of the Round Table arms them all with modern and stylized suits of armor and weapons. They fight Lord Viper immediately and win the first battle.

VOLUME 2: "THE SEARCH FOR
     GUINEVERE"

First, it should be pointed out that this is
no ordinary armor these Knights of Justice
have. Each has a different beast on his shield,
which becomes a real beast when he is in battle. Arthur King's is a dragon. Serendipitously,
the symbol of Excalibur on Arthur King's
breastplate becomes the real Excalibur when
he needs it.

In this episode, the Knights of Justice ride
off to find Guinevere. Morgana captures two
of them — Lance and Trunk — and Arthur goes
alone to save them. He fights a giant bat, finds
his boys and Guinevere and frees them. They
escape Castle Morgana. Trunk's ram emblem
turns into a giant mountain goat to help things
along.

They battle through the warlords and
make it back to the Round Table. Guinevere
notices that this guy looks like her Arthur but
acts differently. During the celebration of their
return, Merlin warns the new Arthur that they
must yet find the magic keys so the team can
return to its own time.

VOLUME 3: "EVEN KNIGHTS HAVE TO
     EAT"

It is revealed that each of the Knights of
Justice must have his own Key of Truth to get
back to the present. Merlin's falcon has located
one of the keys, but Camelot is surrounded by
the armies of Lord Viper's warlords.

Using life energy–sapping magic to create a tunnel of light out of Camelot and past
their enemies, Merlin sends the boys on their
way. At the tunnel exit they have to fight their
way through more of the warlords' men.

Coming upon a village, Arthur finds
farmer Orin is being harassed by three trolls.
He helps the farmer but lets the trolls go. The
warlords kidnap Orin's wife, Kate, and Arthur
and the knights attack to save her. The trolls
help by capturing warlords in their underground tunnels.

Finally they find the key they came after,
but when one of the guys grabs it the thing

melts away. It was Arthur's key, and the wrong
person touching it destroyed it.

VOLUME 4: "QUEST FOR COURAGE"

Princess Krislyn comes to Camelot to ask
for help. Rikus, her father, is being held captive by a sea serpent. Though she has her own
magical powers, she cannot defeat the thing
alone. Arthur gathers the knights and Krislyn
wraps them in a spell of invisibility so they
can pass through the ranks of the warlords,
who are attacking the castle. An accident reveals them and they fight their way to a village.

At the village the children help the
Knights of Justice, but the adults are all afraid
to fight the warlords. Arthur decides to leave
the knights at the village to help defend it and
to go on with Krislyn by himself. Krislyn tells
Arthur that she's leading him into a trap — the
sea serpent is in the cave at Queen Morgana's
command to get Arthur and Excalibur. Arthur
goes anyway and with the help of the dragon
from his shield he defeats the sea serpent and
frees Rikus.

Back at the village, the children once again
fight alongside the knights, but this time the
adults find their courage and the warlords are
driven off. Rikus and Krislyn decide to live at
the village to help defend against future attacks.

King Arthur and the Knights of the Round Table (1981)

60 minutes each volume; Color; Cartoon;
Copyright 1981, ZIV International, Inc.; Family Home Entertainment; Video #5000020,
#5000021

CREDITS: Executive Producers — Max J. Rud-
erian, Irv Holender, Ronald Ruderian; Production
Supervisor — Matt Steinbuch; Production Associ-
ate — Alan Letz; Video Presentation by — Jim Terry
Productions; King Arthur Theme Song Music and
Lyrics by — Shuki Levy, Haim Saban; Production
Assistance — Steve Fogelson, Bill Sussex, Susan
Christison, Chris Denes; A presentation of ZIV In-
ternational, Inc., in cooperation with TOEI Ani-
mation Company, Ltd.

SYNOPSIS: Each of these two tapes contains three episodes of a cartoon series that,

despite major departures from tradition, wind up being fairly good. There are some character improvisations which are curious but the basics of the Arthur legend are preserved.

Why the character changes were made is hard to say. Someone called Malisa sort of replaces Morgan Le Fay or (Morgause or Morgana) as the wicked sorceress. There is also a King Lavik introduced to the mix, perhaps as a means of avoiding the tale of adultery that surrounds Arthur's birth.

There are some other confused elements but this series retains so much of the flavor of Arthurian legend that they are forgivable.

These cartoons outstrip most other cartoon versions by a country mile.

VOLUME 1, EPISODE 1: "KNIGHTS OF THE ROUND TABLE"

We find Uther blissfully married to Igraine and it's little Arthur's third birthday party. Among the gathered nobility is one grumbler, King Lavik, who doesn't particularly care for Uther. Enter Malisa, a sorceress bent on the destruction of Uther's line and the capturing of any power she can acquire. In a tête-à-tête with Lavik, she suggests that he use King Ban's sword to kill both Uther and Arthur.

Merlin had prophesied these kinds of troubles. Sure enough, a bunch of black knights, who look like ninjas, attack. Presumably these are Malisa's forces come to create the distraction Lavik will need to perform the dastardly deed.

Igraine manages to escape with Arthur, but not before Lavik succeeds in killing Uther, using King Ban's sword. Merlin takes Arthur and places him with Ector to be raised safely away from assassination attempts.

Some time later the scene at the cathedral is played out. Lavik is among those who try to pull the sword from the stone but only Arthur succeeds. Ector then informs everyone that Arthur is actually the son of Uther of *Camelot* (emphasis mine). Leodegrance and his daughter, Gwenevere, are attending the event.

Arthur and the young lady catch each other's attention.

VOLUME 1, EPISODE 2: "THE GREEN KNIGHT"

Picking right up where episode 1 left off, Lavik insists on a rematch at the sword-in-the-stone contest. The archbishop declares Arthur the king of Camelot, but not yet of Britain. Someone named Peter comes to the cathedral, but nothing more is said of him in this segment.

After the day's excitement it's determined that Arthur might as well reclaim his true home, so he goes to Camelot. Once on the premises and particularly when he is near the Round Table, the memories of his infancy begin to return to Arthur. But those black-armored ninjas attack, distracting everyone.

Out of a mysterious fog comes a Green Knight who turns the tide of battle and Malisa's men are driven off. As soon as the fight is over, the Green Knight vanishes again.

VOLUME 1, EPISODE 3: "THE KNIGHT OF THE LAKE"

The title presumably refers to Lancelot du Lac, who appears in this episode simply as Lancelot, son of King Ban. Malisa appears again to Lavik, stirring him once more to nefarious activity.

In the meantime Gwenevere goes to Camelot for a visit and the black knights attack again. This time Lancelot saves Arthur from a sticky spot, but Arthur still thinks that it was Lancelot's father, King Ban, who killed his own father, Uther. The two boys tussle over the accusation but stop and decide to go to Merlin to learn the truth.

VOLUME 2, EPISODE 4: "THE KNIGHT OF THE HARP"

On their way to find Merlin those danged black knight ninjas attack Arthur and Lancelot again. The Green Knight shows up just in time to lead them to safety, then fades out of the picture again.

Shortly thereafter a fellow who calls himself Tristram of the Harp saunters onto the scene. Riding a horse as he plays his little harp, he seems an affable enough sort, so Arthur and Lancelot let him tag along as they continue their journey.

Soon they come upon a band of highway robbers who've set up a roadblock to waylay travelers. And — who would have guessed?— the black knight ninjas are there to help too. Tristram's harp doubles as an effective bow for shooting arrows, Malisa's men are driven off and the highway robbers are defeated.

VOLUME 2, EPISODE 5: "PRINCE CHRISTOPHER"

This segment comes out of left field, not connecting with much of anything before or after it. Lavik is holding this little fellow's mother hostage. Lavik evidently threatened Christopher's father with war if she didn't come willingly — which she did. Chris runs away and finds the appropriate help.

VOLUME 2, EPISODE 6: "EXCALIBUR"

Again on their way to find Merlin, Arthur and Lancelot run into the Green Knight. This time the mysterious benefactor stops them and challenges Arthur to a joust. The reasons for the test of combat are obscure and they are made even less understandable when Arthur loses but the Green Knight tells him Merlin's whereabouts anyway.

In any event they finally find Merlin, and Arthur and Lancelot are reconciled. We also learn that Arthur is 16 years old now and that Tristram is the son of the king of Cornwall.

Merlin sends Arthur to get Excalibur and a special shield with which he will be able to defeat Malisa and Lavik. Arthur finds the right lake, goes out on a boat and experiences a harrowing ride through a whirlpool. Vivien, the Lady of the Lake, gives Excalibur to Arthur.

King Arthur and the Legends of Glastonbury (1983)

Alternate Titles: *In Search of King Arthur; The Land of Castles*; Not viewed; 60 minutes; Color; Documentary; Copyright 1983, New Horizons Television

King Arthur and the Magic Sword (1956)

Not viewed; Filmstrip; Color; 35mm, with phono disc; Copyright 1956, 1967, Society for Visual Education

King Arthur and William Tell (1971)

Not viewed; 2 Filmstrips; 116 frames, 148 frames; Color; 35mm, 2 records (10 minutes, 12 minutes), teacher's guide included; Copyright 1971, McGraw Hill Book Company; From the series Filmstrip Cinema; From the series Mr. Magoo's Literature Series; Library of Congress Call #PZ8.1; Library of Congress Catalogue #72732887/F; Dewey Decimal #808.3

King Arthur Country and Southern England see *King Arthur and His Country*

King Arthur, the Young Warlord (1975)

90 minutes; Color; Live Action; Copyright 1975, Heritage Enterprises, Inc.; Copyright 1995, Colossal Entertainment; Heritage Enterprises, Inc., in Association with HTV, Ltd.

CAST: Oliver Tobias (King Arthur); Jack Watson (Llud); Michael Gothard (Kai); Brian Blessed (Mark of Cornwall); Peter Firth (Corin); Gila (Rowena); Rupert Davies (Cerdic); George Marischka (Yorath); Donald Burton); Michael Graham-Cox); Norman Bird

CREDITS: Executive Producer — Patrick Dromgoole; Produced by — Peter Miller; Written by — Terence Feely, Robert Banks Stewart; Directed by — Sidney Hayers, Patrick Jackson, Peter Sasdy; Theme Music by — Elmer Bernstein; Incidental Music and Orchestration by — Paul Lewis; Production Supervised by — William Kronick, William Cartwright; Production Executive — Julian J. Ludwig; Associate Producer — John Peverall; Production Manager — Keith Eaton; Fight Manager — Peter Bayham; Assistant Director — Stuart Freeman; Art Director — Doug James; Cameramen — Bob Edwards, Graham Edgar; Camera Operators — Brent Morgin, Roger Pearce; Sound Recordists — Mike Davey, Gordon Kethro; Set Dresser — Ken Bridgeman; Wardrobe — Audrey MacLeod; Makeup —

Christine Pennwarren; Editors — Barry Peters, Don Llewellyn, Terry Maisey, Alex Kirby; Set Design — Dan Perth; Post Production Services — Neiman Tilly Associates; Prints by — Movielab

SYNOPSIS: An interesting attempt at a plausible interpretation of what the King Arthur of legend might have really been like. This film takes a realistic look at tribal living in fifth- or sixth-century Britain and what contact with the Saxons and Jutes may have been like; it even comes up with a possible basis for the legend of the sword in the stone.

Originally produced as a 24-episode television series, this film is made up of five episodes somewhat raggedly edited together. A documentary-style narrative doesn't quite succeed at smoothing over the rough transitions between segments and the viewer has the impression of missing something in the characters' development. This, however, is inevitable when a series is chopped down so far.

Despite these flaws the film does piece together a look at a young tribal leader beginning to forge a union between the warring factions of his homeland. In many of its details, the film also demonstrates the writers' above-average knowledge of the material.

The first section of *King Arthur, the Young Warlord* deals with Arthur's initial efforts to draw the Celtic tribes together. He feigns his own death and the tribal leaders are invited to the funeral ceremony. Once at Arthur's village, they are all captured. Arthur presents himself and forces them to listen to his plan of cooperation. He explains that only together can they defeat the marauding Saxon enemy, Cerdic.

As a demonstration of what he is saying, Arthur has had a boulder placed on top of a sword. Anyone, Arthur declares, who can lift the sword over his head will lead them. Individually none of the leaders can move the stone but when Arthur has them each place a hand on it and push together, he snatches the sword from beneath it.

Some are convinced and some aren't. Mark of Cornwall is the most resistant to Arthur lording it over him and the debate continues right up until Cerdic attacks. With Arthur's sly leadership, though, the Saxons are driven off and the tribal chieftains are more willing to try Arthur's ways.

The next segment is a little morality play that demonstrates Arthur's fairness and wisdom. A young boy named Corin shows up at the village saying that he wants to learn to fight well. His people are constantly being harassed by the Picts and he will take what he learns back to his village to teach his people.

It turns out the boy is actually after revenge. He witnessed Arthur kill his father and Corin has come not only to learn to fight, but to kill Arthur. Arthur does teach the boy to fight. He also teaches Corin that Mordor, his father, was not killed without reason. Mordor had been attacking Arthur's territories and was simply killed in battle. Corin rides home a potential future ally.

The third portion of the movie is a comedy about a wedding. It's explained that Arthur has had girlfriends but one in particular is special to him. Princess Rowena, daughter of Yorath the Jute, seems to be the girl for him, though he isn't planning to marry just yet.

Mark of Cornwall, however, has proposed marriage and Rowena has accepted. Mark's main goal is to gain the land that will be Rowena's when her father dies. Arthur learns that Yorath doesn't want this wedding either so they make a deal. If Arthur can break up the wedding, Yorath will do more to plug the gaps in his borders through which invaders have been entering.

For the sake of the wedding the normally boorish Mark is acting ridiculously genteel. To expose him for the pig he really is, Arthur does all sorts of things to goad Mark into anger. Finally Mark snaps and attacks Arthur with his sword. While defending himself Arthur maneuvers near Rowena, then allows Mark to knock the sword from his hand. Rowena steps in to "save" Arthur's life and that's the end of Mark's plans for marriage. Arthur pledges his fidelity to Rowena.

The fourth story is of a raid Arthur tricks

Mark into helping him with. Arthur, Kai and Llud were captured by Saxons and only Arthur was able to escape. He gets Mark to provide a boat and men by telling him that they're after a trove of jewels and precious metals at the Saxon stronghold. By the time Mark finds out he's really on a rescue mission it's too late to turn back. They do save Kai and Llud and get away, only to learn that there actually was a cache of plundered treasure at the Saxon camp.

In the final episode Arthur tries to make peace with Cerdic. Yorath the Jute actually leads the way. He has become war weary and makes a truce with Cerdic. When Arthur learns that a huge force of Scots have sailed to attack Britain he decides this may be the time to do the same.

After exchanging gifts Cerdic and Arthur meet at Yorath's compound. They talk and come to an agreement to live and let live. During the festivities word comes that the entire Scottish fleet has been lost at sea in a huge storm. Just when everything seems to be working out an accident sets their men to fighting. A couple of people are killed and the peace talks break down. Both Arthur and Cerdic leave but they keep each other's gifts as tokens of this first step toward peace.

King Arthur, the Young Warlord is an intriguing film despite its weaknesses. Though a good deal of nonsense is mixed in, there are enough details and theorizations about the Arthurian era to pique one's interest.

The sword under the stone is a good example. If the drawing of Excalibur from a stone or an anvil or both is a legend which is based on fact, then the idea portrayed in this movie is as good a supposition as any about the legend's roots.

One of the Celtic tribal leaders who joins with Arthur is Ambrose. This particular fellow dresses in Roman military garb, looking more like a centurion than a Celt. He tries to get his men to march and act like Romans. His name harks back to the Latin Ambrosius Aurelianus, which comes from both history and some versions of Arthurian legend.

Ambrosius is identified by Nennius as the child who Vortigern intended to sacrifice in order to stabilize the foundations of a fortress that kept collapsing. Geoffrey of Monmouth, on the other hand, held that Ambrosius was Merlin and that Ambrosius Aurelius (note the different spelling) was Uther's brother. Gildas has an Ambrosius Aurelianus battling the Saxons. With these three ancient authors' writings as source material, some modern Arthurian scholars think that Ambrosius may have been the Arthur of legend.

On the surface it seems that the writers of this film are referring to Geoffrey's Ambrosius. His Roman inclinations and warlike demeanor fit the bill. He even invokes the god Mithras before he attempts to move the stone off the sword. Placing him in the same generation as Arthur does not track with the tradition of him being Uther's brother, of course, but once again, the filmmakers are presenting alternative theories for the bases of many things.

There is another equally interesting connection. The names Ambrosius and Aurelianus occur in Roman history during the occupation of Britain. At one point they occur simultaneously, though they are two different personages.

Saint Ambrose or, more correctly, Ambrosius (c. 339–397 A.D.) was the highly influential bishop of Milan during the reigns of Gratian, Valentinian II and Theodosius the Great. One of several things Bishop Ambrosius is known for is his single-minded campaign against pagan religions. In fact, by 391 Theodosius officially banned all pagan worship in the Roman empire.

One of Ambrosius's most vociferous enemies was Quintas Aurelius Symmachus, a renowned orator of the time and an opponent of Christianity. The point, vague as it might seem, is that during the period of Roman collapse and withdrawal from Britain, there were two men debating the merits of two different religious systems. One was Ambrosius, a Christian. The other was Aurelius, an anti-

Christian. That the names come together could be a symbolic personification of the conflict between Christianity and the old gods of both the Roman Empire and Britain itself.

Movies like *Excalibur* and others treat more directly the conflict between the old gods and the new. *King Arthur, the Young Warlord* merely calls this one character Ambrose.

One more such reference is Arthur's foster father. This man is traditionally known as Ector but in *King Arthur, the Young Warlord* he is Llud. Llud is not a name commonly associated with Arthurian stories but Lludd, or Nudd, is a figure from Cymric or Gaelic legend. In Welsh legend he is known as Nudd of the Silver Hand, connecting him to Nuada of the Silver Hand. This leader of the Danaans lost a hand in battle and had it replaced with a silver one. In the tale of Enid and Geraint he is the father of Edeyrn, a knight who jousts with Geraint.

Llud in *King Arthur, the Young Warlord* is not just Kai's father and Arthur's foster father. He also has a silver hand and forearm, which he uses to good effect in fights.

There are many other points of interest in the film. Merlin is not mentioned at all, though I do not know if he ever came up in the original television series. There is no Gwenevere either, but instead we have Rowena. This woman is the daughter of Yorath the Jute rather than of Hengist the Saxon as she appears in Geoffrey's writing.

There are none of the medieval influences so typical in Arthurian film — no full suits of armor, no jousting lists, no picture-book castles. The villages are made of simple wooden structures with thatched roofs. The costumes are more appropriate to the historical period, including leather tunics studded with small iron plates. There are no lances, but there are spears, axes and swords.

King Arthur Was a Gentleman (1942)

95 minutes; Black and White; Live Action/Musical; Copyright 1942, Gaumont British Picture Corporation, Ltd.; A Gainsborough Picture; General Film Distributors, Ltd.; Sinister Cinema

CAST: Arthur Askey (Arthur King); Evelyn Dall (Susan); Anne Shelton (Gwennie); Max Bacon (Maxie); Jack Train (Jack); Peter Graves (Lance Elliot); Vera Frances (Brownie); Brefni O'Rorke (Duncarron); Ronald Shiner (Sergeant)

CREDITS: In Charge of Production — Maurice Ostrer; Original Story and Screenplay by — Marriott Edgar, Val Guest; Directed by — Marcel Varnel; Produced by — Edward Black; Music by — Manning Sherwin; Lyrics by — Val Guest; Orchestrations — Bob Busby; Musical Direction — Louis Levy; Photography — Arthur Crabtree; Editing — R. E. Dearing; Cutting — Alfred Roome; Art Direction — John Bryan; Sound Supervision — B. C. Sewell; Made at the Gaumont British Studios, London

SYNOPSIS: A lighthearted raise-the-morale British WWII production which blends some silliness about King Arthur and Excalibur with the war effort and some songs.

Singing recruitment posters open the show, then we move on to the action. Susan Ashley, a gal in the service evidently working the chow lines, telegraphs her boyfriend that she's got a five-day pass before she ships out to the war. Her boyfriend is Arthur King, a reservist working as a mapmaker at Whitehall. Arthur is a milquetoast kind of fellow, obsessed with King Arthur.

There's another song when Susan arrives at Whitehall. Susan and her friend Gwennie get a bit mixed up at the outset. Susan forgot her pass and borrows Gwen's. They get arrested for that violation by the military police at a club.

Gwennie's father happens to be the local magistrate. Judge Duncarron lets them sit in jail overnight, but has them released the next day. Arthur threatens to turn the judge in for abusing his power unless the judge helps him get out of the reserves and into active duty with the Fusileers.

That patriotic goal achieved, Arthur soon drives his barracks mates nuts with his constant talk about King Arthur. There's a long slapstick bit of Arthur trying to learn to drive a small armored vehicle.

A work crew unearths an old sword and they have fun fooling Arthur into believing that it's Excalibur. They even use the PA system one night to have the voice of the Lady of the Lake convince Arthur that it's genuine.

Possession of the sword gives Arthur's confidence a tremendous boost. Soon after arriving at the front he uses the sword to capture three German soldiers. With life going so well, Arthur decides to propose to Susan, but she turns him down.

Disappointed, Arthur figures that history must be repeating itself and that he should instead marry Gwennie. He sneaks off to the women's barracks and promptly gets arrested.

Susan and Gwen visit him in the brig to tell him their mutual friend Lance is missing. The girls break him out of jail and they go to find Lance.

After the completion of the heroic rescue, the guys tell Arthur that the sword was a hoax. Susan assures him, however, that she's his girl. Happy at last, Arthur throws the sword into the lake, only to see a hand appear out of the water to catch it.

King Arthur's Camelot: King Arthur and the Knights of Justice (1997)

70 minutes; Color; Cartoon; Copyright 1997, UAV Corporation; UAV Entertainment #1338

SYNOPSIS: *King Arthur's Camelot* is a tape reissuing three episodes from the 1992 television cartoon series *King Arthur and the Knights of Justice*. Included on the tape are "Quest for Courage," "The Search for Guinevere" as well as "Warlord Knight," which was not included in the original 1995 video issue by Family Time Video. (For cast, credits and synopses of the series and the first two episodes, see the entry for *King Arthur and the Knights of Justice*.)

Another tape, *Return to Camelot* (see that entry) includes three more episodes, one of which, "The Way Back," is also a new release from the TV series.

The "Warlord Knight" episode of *King*

Arthur's Camelot is the story of how Lancelot fell into the River of Forgetfulness and was almost co-opted by Viper and Morgana. Retrieved from the river by the evil warlords, he is convinced for a time that he's one of them. Sent to Camelot to lower their defenses, Lancelot, Morgana and the warlords are nearly successful, until the magical Lady of the Round Table restores Lancelot's memory. The tide of battle is turned and Camelot is saved.

A Knight in Camelot (1998)

90 minutes; Color; Live Action; Copyright 1998, Disney Enterprises, Inc.; ABC Television; Rosemont Productions International, Inc.; Walt Disney Television

CAST: Whoopi Goldberg (Vivien Morgan); Michael York (King Arthur); Amanda Donohoe (Queen Guinevere); Ian Richardson (Merlin); Simon Fenton (Clarence); Paloma Baeza (Sandy); James Coombes (Sir Lancelot); Robert Addie (Sir Sagramour); Lukács Bicsey (Slave #1); Gobi Csizmodia (Mistress of Wardrobe); Gobi Fon (Mistress of Chamberpot); John Guerrasia (Bob); Pál Mokrai (Slave Driver); Paul Rogan (Sandy's Father); Steven Speirs (Chief Armorer); Mariann Szaky (Mistress of Ceremonies); Béla Unger (Sheriff)

CREDITS: Music Composed by — Patrick Williams; Edited by — Benjamin A. Wiessman, A.C.E.; Production Designer — Peter Mullins; Director of Photography — Elemér Ragályi; Produced by — Nick Gillott; Co–Executive Producer — Joe Wiesenfeld; Executive Producer — Norman Rosemont; Teleplay — Joe Wiesenfeld; Inspired by Mark Twain's *A Connecticut Yankee in King Arthur's Court*; Director — Roger Young; Casting — Beth Charkham; Unit Production Manager — Dusty Symonds; First Assistant Director — Simon Hinkly; Second Assistant Director — Sallie Hard; Set Decorator — István Tóth; Property Master — István Balogh; Script Supervisor — Lisa Vick; Production Coordinator — Zsuzsa Varadi; Hungary Casting — János Perjés; Costumes — Barbara Lane; Makeup — Kati Jakáts; Whoopi Goldberg's Makeup — Mike Germain; Hair — Gabriella Németh; Whoopi Goldberg's Hair — Julia Walker; Hungary Production Manager — József Cirká; Production Sound Mixer — Tony Dowe; Post Facilities and Visual Effects — Hollywood Digital; Post Production Sound — Buena Vista Sound; Presented in Dolby Surround Sound

Main cast of *A Knight in Camelot*: (left to right) Ian Richardson (Merlin), Robert Addie (Sir Sagramour), Simon Fenton (Clarence), Whoopie Goldberg (Vivient Morgan), Amanda Donohoe (Queen Guinivere) and Michael York (King Arthur).

SYNOPSIS: *A Knight in Camelot* is Disney's fifth Arthurian film and third production of a version of Twain's *A Connecticut Yankee in King Arthur's Court* (see entries for *The Sword in the Stone, Unidentified Flying Oddball, Four Diamonds* and *A Kid in King Arthur's Court*).

A Knight in Camelot breaks no new ground in *Connecticut Yankee* adaptation. It seems to have been quickly thrown together in order to take advantage of current interest in Arthurian legend.

Following closely on the heels of Warner's *Quest for Camelot* among others, *A Knight in Camelot* displays none of the originality of Disney's first two offerings. Neither the appearances of stars Michael York as King Arthur and Whoopi Goldberg as Vivien Morgan nor the colorful costuming hide the fact that this is a weakly conceived rehash of the story.

A Knight in Camelot bears a strong resemblance to two previous *Connecticut Yankee* adaptations, neither of them Disney productions. The casting of a black female (Goldberg) in the anchor role and her use of modern music, slang and frequent wisecracking is a near duplication of the 1989 Consolidated/Schaeffer Karpf production *A Connecticut Yankee in King Arthur's Court* starring Keshia Knight Pulliam. The prancing and irreverence of the role seem more appropriate to the youngster Pulliam than to the considerably older Goldberg.

Goldberg plays a scientist who has designed an expensive experimental machine. With funding for her experiments about to run out, she fires up the machine before it's actually ready. This angle was first used for an Arthurian story by the 1966 television show *Time Tunnel* (see entry for *The Time Tunnel: "Merlin the Magician"*), an Irwin Allen production.

A Knight in Camelot is a made-for-television movie (though it will undoubtedly appear on video) which originally aired on November 8, 1998, on the *Wonderful World of Disney* program. As Walt Disney used to do himself, the current president of the corporation opens the show with a brief introduction. Michael Eisner's 30-second commentary points out that in "the great age of castles," real life was not like in fairy tales. He states that most people slept on benches or floors, never bathed, had no plumbing or garbage collection, never ate fresh foods, never went to school and were married by age 14.

These themes are included in the film itself. Goldberg makes repeated comments about how badly the populace of Camelot smells. Once in Arthur's good graces, she is assigned three ladies-in-waiting, one of whom is the mistress of the chamberpot.

When at one point she is riveted into her armor, the standard practice according to the royal armorer, she realizes she has to go to the bathroom. Informed that she must do that in the armor, she's taken to "the knights' closet" where, as she makes all the appropriate facial expressions of evacuative relief, a torrent of water is poured on her rump.

The standard film variations on Twain's theme are used in *A Knight in Camelot*. A modern person is transported back into Arthur's Camelot, is captured by Sir Sagramore, is saved from being burned at the stake by predicting a solar eclipse and becomes Sir Boss. Sir Boss then tries to make improvements around the land but ultimately fails and finally returns to the present.

Major changes in this permutation are a focus on fresh vegetables, criticism of slavery and a discussion that even paid work can seem like slavery. As in *A Kid in King Arthur's Court*, the Merlin of *A Knight in Camelot* turns out to have been the real cause of Goldberg's time travel. His motive was to get Arthur back on the right track in leading his country. Goldberg's character ends up permanently leaving even her own time to travel the universe with Merlin.

Knight Mare Hare see Bugs Bunny's Hare-Raising Tales: "Knight Mare Hare"

The Knight of the Harp **see under**
*King Arthur and the Knights of the
Round Table*

The Knight of the Lake **see under**
*King Arthur and the Knights of the
Round Table*

The Knight with the Red Plume **see
under** *The Adventures of Sir
Lancelot*

Knightriders (1981)

145 minutes; Color; Live Action; Copyright
1981, United Films Distribution Company;
United Artists Corporation; Best Film and
Video #909

CAST: Ed Harris (Billy); Gary Lahti (Alan);
Tom Savini (Morgan); Amy Ingersoll (Linet); Pa-
tricia Tallman (Julie); Christine Forrest (Angie);
Warner Shook (Pippin); Brother Blue (Merlin);
Cynthia Adler (Rocky); John Amplas (Whiteface);
Don Berry (Bagman); Amanda Davies (Sheila);
Martin Ferrero (Bontempi); Ken Foree (Little
John); Ken Hixon (Steve); John Hostetter (Tuck);
Harold Wayne Jones (Bors); Randy Kovitz (Punch);
Michael Moran (Cook); Scott Erineger (Marhalt);
Maureen Sadusk (Judy Rawls); Albert Amerson
(Indian); Ronald Carrier (Hector); Tim Dileo
(Corn Cook); David Early (Bleoboris); John Har-
rison (Pellinore); Marty Schiff (Ban); Taso N.
Stavrakis (Ewain); Robert Williams (Kay); Molly
McCloskey (Corn Cook's Woman); Judy Barrett
(Musician Trio); Ian Gallacher (Musician Trio);
Donald Rubinstein (Musician Trio); Jim Baffico
(Lester Dean); Iva Jean Saraceni (Helen Dean);
Chris Jessel (Boy Billy); Bingo O'Malley (Sheriff
Rilly); Nann Mogg (Mrs. Rilly); Nancy Hopwood
(Sam); Victor Pappas (Photographer); Stephen
King (Hoagie Man); Tabitha King (Hoagie Man's
Wife); Jennifer Davis (Baby in Stroller); Hugh Rose
(Jess). With appearances by: William Bardwell,
Greg Besnax, Nancy Blum, Elva Branson, Leilani
Cataldi, Sal Carullo, Mark Carson, Nancy Chesney,
Tommy Lafitte, Gary Leventhal, Tom Madden,
Rick Marchisto, Jim McKissock, Ann Muffty, Chris
O'Connor, Ramona Zini, Ramona Dowrak, Julia
Dunster, Patrick Dunster, Cliff Forrest, George
Jaber, Jeannie Jeffries, Janet Kennedy, Louis Koep-
per, Jeff Paul, Joseph F. Pilato, John Mark Ridings,
Joe Shelleby, Mark Tierno, Fred Tietz, Bobbi Van
Eman

CREDITS: Production Design — Cletus Ander-
son; Editors — George A. Romero, Pasquale Buba;
Production Manager — Zilla Clinton; Stunt Coor-
dinator — Gary Davis; Music by — Donald Rubin-
stein; Associate Producer — David E. Vogel; Direc-
tor of Photography — Michael Gornick; Executive
Producer — Salah M. Hassanein; Produced by —
Richard P. Rubinstein; Written and Directed by —
George A. Romero; Stuntmen: Gary Davis, Tim
Davison, Art Fredenburgh, Pat Green, Freddie
Hice, John Hately, Steve Holladay, Richard Hum-
phreys, Gary Hymes, John Meier, R. A. Rondell,
Reid Rondell, Scott Wilder, David Zellitti; 1st
A.D. — Pasquale Buba; Assistants to the Producer —
Donna Siegal, Debra Shala; Camera Operator —
Michael Gornick; Sound — John Butler; Drivers —
Carl Augenstein, Jim Forrester; Key Grip — Nick
Mastandrea; 1st Assistant Camera — Tom Duben-
sky; Location Manager — Leslie Chapman; 2nd
A.D.s — Clayton Hill, John Roddick; Production
Coordinator — Marie Fiduccia; Script Supervisor —
Sandra Jetton; Still Photography — James Hamil-
ton; 2nd Unit Cameramen — Russell Rockwell, Ed
Marritz; 2nd Assistant Editors — Tony Buba, Rich
Dwyer, Nick Mastandrea; Grips: Joe Abeln, Salah
Hassanein, Lenny Lies, Chad Stockdale, Richard
Dwyer, Brian Haughin, Richard Ricci, Nick Talio;
Boom — Richard Sieg; Makeup — Jeannie Jeffries
Brown; Makeup Assistant — Liz Augenstein; Hair-
styling — Luigi Caruso, Mick Lanzino; Local
Casting — Sharon Ceccati; Casting Assistant — Jim
Wilhelm; Publicity — Pickwick, Mastansky, Keo-
nigsberg, Ann Thompson, Reid Rosefelt; Location
Publicist — Susan Vermazen; Transportation Coor-
dinator — Peter Levy; Motorcycle Coordinator —
Simon Manses; Mechanics — Bruce Gantenbein,
Jimmy Stephenson; Special Effects — Larry Roberts;
Orchestra Conducted by — Emmanuel Vardi;
Music Supervisor — David Franco; Solos by —
Eddie Daniels, Bill Frisell, Peter Gordon, Gordon
Gottlieb, Paul Johnson; Recorded at — Media
Sound Studio, N.Y.C.; Recording Engineer — Fred
Christie; Remixer — Jeree Records; Engineer —
Don Garvin; "The Father Be a Wanderer": Music,
Lyrics and Sung by — Donald Rubinstein; "Signi-
fying Monkey": Music and Lyrics by — Oscar
Brown, Jr.; Additional Arrangement — Michelle
Camillo; Music Copying — Wedo's; Assistants to
the Production Manager — William Brewer, Bruce
Miller, Christine Oagley; Construction Coordina-
tor — Ed Fountain; Properties Master — Michael
Gorman; Properties Mistress — Virginia E. Hil-
dreth; Scenic Painter — Ellen Hopkins; Costume
Construction Coordinator — Barbara Anderson; Set
and Props — Bruce Moore, Martin Giles, Roderick

Mayne, Michael McMackin, Johnny Gilles, Jim Feng; Wardrobe — Claudia Stephens Anderson, Alison Todd, Nancy Palmatier, Elizabeth Murray, Kathy Grillo, Lynne Nelson, R. A. Graham, David Velasquez, Patricia Risser, Howard Kaplan, Emily Harris, Ainslie Bruneau; Production Assistants — Robert Bremseln, Jeff Fisher, Marc Malloy, Debbie Pinthus, Debbie Wian, Medinah Davis, Daryne Chauver, Todd Hill, Mary McCloskey, Brian Sullivan, Jack Walworth; Production Coordinator — Curtis Sayblack; Accounting Assistants — Tina Cardonell, Claire McCoy, Kathleen Viskovicz; Accounting — Al Wyle, C.P.A., Charles Forman, C.P.A.; Office Manager — Vince Survinski; Production Secretary — Jean Bremseth; Locations — Wayne McCoy; Insurance — Rogal Co.; Beeper Communications — Page America, Inc.; Film Labs — Technicolor Precision; Equipment — Roessel Cine Photo Tech; Opticals — Select Effects, Inc.; Dubbing — Laurel Communications; Dubbing — Michael Gornick; Cutting Services — Forces, Inc.; Negative Cutting — Production House of Pittsburgh; Produced With the Cooperation of — Pennsylvania Film Commission, Fran & Don Porter, Citizens of Fawn Township, Pennsylvania, Irvin Shapiro

SYNOPSIS: A quirky film about a group of modern-day performers who travel the countryside putting on medieval/Arthurian–style jousts and battles on motorcycles.

Led by the older Billy, or King William, the group seems like a throwback to the hippies of the 1960s. All of them are societal dropouts of one form or another, seemingly with no place else to go. The charismatic Billy not only holds them together but provides an anachronistic ideal for them to live up to.

Setting their show up at county fairs or Renaissance festivals, these motorcycle warriors wear costumes of armor complete with plumes and chivalric insignia. They use actual weapons, like maces, swords and even jousting lances, though the lances are sawed through so as to break easily.

Billy and his queen, Linet, preside over the motorized tournaments from their thrones. In addition to the knights, with names like Bors, Kay and Ewain in the troop there are jesters and jugglers, a blacksmith, a mechanic and others. A hip harmonica-playing Merlin is Billy's faithful mystical advisor and also the group's medical doctor.

The film opens as preparations are being made for a show. Some dissension occurs over Morgan wanting to use a heavy solid mace in the tournament. Kay, in particular, feels that it is too potentially lethal but for some reason Billy allows its use.

The Arthurlike Billy is beset by two handicaps; one is mental, the other physical. He has frightening nightmare visions of a raven and is convinced that the black bird somehow spells his doom. Like the Fisher King of Arthurian legend he also suffers from a wound that never seems to heal. His left shoulder was injured in a previous encounter on the field of battle. To top it all off, Morgan is vying to become the new king. If he wins all of his battles in the shows, he rightfully can be crowned.

As the show and the fighting proceed Morgan defeats all comers including Kay, Billy's staunchest defender. Despite his bad shoulder, Billy accepts the challenge and does battle with Morgan. Billy is soundly beaten but his knights rescue him before he is forced to yield. Billy's shoulder is injured again and Merlin stitches him up.

During a run-in with a corrupt deputy sheriff, Billy clarifies his principles for himself and his crew. Refusing to pay off the policeman, he bullheadedly will not yield to injustice or anything else that would corrupt the ideals of the chivalric code he chooses to live by. Falsely accused of drug possession, Billy and one of the knights are imprisoned and the knight is viciously beaten by the deputy. They are released by the sheriff the next day.

Simultaneously there is contention over publicity for the troop and more glamorous and remunerative television and Las Vegas show deals. Billy sticks to his principles and won't allow any of it.

The troop breaks up over the disagreements. Many of the knights and their girlfriends ride off to take advantage of the more tempting offers or just to clear their heads.

Billy maintains the camp, waiting for his lost sheep to return.

After they taste the freedoms and complications of the outside, all of the crew returns and all grudges are dropped, all disputes forgiven. A final melee is held and Morgan wins the field. His work with the knights done, Billy steps down from the throne, crowns Morgan and leaves.

Billy is followed by one of his admiring former knights but this Bedeverelike character neither speaks to nor interferes with him on this last journey. Billy's first solitary act is to find the abusive deputy sheriff and publicly thrash him. His second act is to find a little boy to whom he had wrongheadedly refused to give an autograph at one of the shows. Billy gives the boy his sword and in this, the dying king himself, rather than Bedevere, throws Excalibur into the lake of the future.

Riding off once more Billy fantasizes being a real knight on a real horse and swerves into the path of an oncoming tractor trailer. The film closes after a tearful, rain-soaked funeral for Billy, with the troop driving through the countryside, headed for the next show.

Knights and Armor (1994)

100 minutes; Color; Documentary; Copyright 1994, A&E Television Networks; SATEL DOC, a SATEL Documentary Production; In Association with A&E Networks; A&E Home Video

CREDITS: Co-produced by Muse Film and Television; Landshut Festival Footage Directed by Bayley Silleck; Archives; Antikvarisk-Topografiska Arkivet, Stockholm; The Archbishop of Canterbury and the Trustees of Lambeth Palace Library; Biblioteque Nationale, Paris; Bridgeman Art Library, London; The Bayeux Tapestry (eleventh century) by Special Permission of the City of Bayeux; The British Library; The British Museum; Cadw: Welsh Historic Monuments, Crown Copyright; College of Arms; Corpus Christi College, Oxford; The Dean and Canons of Windsor; Dorling Kindersley; ET Archive; Giroudon, Paris; John Pickthorn; Librairie Droz, S.A., Geneva; National Museums and Galleries on Merseyside; Oxford University Press; Quintess Art Collection, Ltd.; Winchester City Council; The producers would like to thank: Consultant — Dr. Malcolm Vale, Consultant on William Marshal — Professor David Crouch, Christopher Gravett, Charlie Hayes, Sir Edward Heath, The Officers and Soldiers of the Household Cavalry Mounted Regiment, Ian Jones, Professor Dr. Peter Krenn, The Nottingham Jousting Association, Dr. Matthias Pfaffenbichler, William R. Raiford, Master Joseph Robinson, Colonel Jonathan Trelawny, Dr. Robert Unwin, Dr. Juliet Vale, Arms and Archery, Abbaye Royale de Ponterraud, Battle Abbey, English Heritage, Battle Abbey School, Buckingham Palace, Chapter House, English Heritage, Le Château de Chinon, Le Château de Tancarville, Chepstow Castle, City of London School, College of Arms, Dean and Chapter of Canterbury, Dean and Chapter of Westminster, H.M. Tower of London, The Heraldry Society, Kunsthistorisches Museum, Vienna, The Landeszeughaus, Graz, The Royal Armouries, The Royal Parks, Spink and Son, Ltd., St. George's Chapel, Windsor Castle, The Temple Church, Tintern Abbey, The Wallace Collection; Narrator — Nick Chilvers; Lighting Camera — Mike Coles; Additional Lighting Camera — Michael Miles; Camera Assistants — Richard Comrie, Ben Philpott; Sound — Keith Rodgerson; Lighting Gaffer — Nick Green; Additional Lighting Gaffers — Martin Hack, Paul Toley; Grips — John Abrahams, Alfred Hiebner, Robin Stone; Rostrum Camera — Ken Morse; Dubbing Editor — Steve McGorry; Dubbing Mixer — Michael Narduzzo; Illustrator — Stephen Gooder; Original Music Performed by — Kithara, Shirley Rumsey, Christopher Wilson; Location Manager, Austria — Cäcilia Meisel; Location Manager, France — Anne-Marie Leblic; Production Secretary — Janne Schack; Stills Research — Rebecca Jones; Line Producer — Andren Sprunt; Film Editor — Graham Shipham; Executive Producer for A&E — Michael E. Katz; Executive Producer — Rod Caird; Producer — Sue Hayes; Director — Andy Stevenson

SYNOPSIS: An outstandingly informative tape on the title topic, this is a complete view of what armor, jousting, chivalry and knighthood developed into over the centuries.

This tape makes clear that the formalized jousting made so familiar by Malory and, more recently, by Hollywood did not exist in King Arthur's time. In the twelfth century, however, tales of King Arthur pervaded the world of knights. As the tales of King Arthur and the Knights of the Round Table mutated over the centuries, they became the ideal for knights and sovereigns.

Tournaments came to be called Round Tables. Even in the fifteenth and sixteenth centuries Arthur's battles were still being reenacted. Arthur's was the ideal court, the model of excellence from a chivalric past.

In reality tournaments and melees were simply practice for battle in the eleventh and twelfth centuries. There were no safety precautions — real weapons were used. People were killed as whole villages sometimes were pitted against each other. The loss of the lives of both men and valuable horses became more and more of a concern.

By the beginning of the thirteenth century, as tournaments grew into a spectator sport, the church tried to ban them. Christian burial was refused to anyone who participated. Knights would go to France to keep up the activity, which was also becoming a way to earn a living.

In 1194 King Richard I of England introduced a licensing system. Five sites were approved for holding tournaments, entrants had to pay fees and no foreign knights were allowed to participate.

In the thirteenth century nonlethal weapons were introduced. Over the next hundred years many safety innovations were incorporated into the armor and techniques of competition, many of which are described and illustrated in this documentary.

The documentary addresses the development of heraldry and the life of William Marshal (1145–1219), who the archbishop of Canterbury described as "the best knight who ever lived." The history of the Royal Order of the Garter is traced, as is the story of the Knights Templar.

Finally, the documentary addresses the demise of this form of warfare, which came about because of the spread of the use of gunpowder in the sixteenth century.

Knights Must Fall (1949)

Not viewed; 7 minutes; Color; Cartoon; Copyright 1949, Warner Bros.

CREDITS: Director — Friz Freleng; Voice Characterizations — Mel Blanc; Writer — Tedd Pierce; Music — Carl Stalling; Animators — Ken Champin, Gerry Chiniquy, Manuel Péréz, Virgil Ross; Backgrounds — Paul Julian; Layouts — Hawley Pratt

SYNOPSIS: Bugs Bunny fights Sir Pantsalot of Drop Seat Manor.

The Knights of Camelot see In Search of History: "The Knights of Camelot"

The Knights of the Kitchen Table see Read On, Cover to Cover: "The Knights of the Kitchen Table"

Knights of the Round Table (1944)

Not viewed; 89 minutes; Copyright 1944, New World/Priority; No further information available. Listing found in Los Angeles Public Library PAC.

Knights of the Round Table (1953)

106 minutes; Color; Live Action; Copyright 1953, Loew's, Inc.; Copyright Renewed 1981, Metro-Goldwyn-Mayer Film Company; Copyright 1993, MGM/UA Home Video; MGM/UA and Turner Entertainment Company; MGM/UA Home Video #M300399

CAST: Robert Taylor (Lancelot); Ava Gardner (Guinevere); Mel Ferrer (Arthur); Anne Crawford (Morgan Le Fay); Stanley Baker (Mordred); Felix Aylmer (Merlin); Maureen Swanson (Elaine); Gabriel Woolf (Perceval); Anthony Fornwood (Gareth); Robert Urquhart (Gawaine); Niall MacGinnis (Green Knight); Ann Hanslip (Nan); Jill Clifford (Bronwyn); Stephen Vercoe (Agravaine)

CREDITS: Screenplay — Talbot Jennings, Jan Lustig, Noel Langley; Based on Sir Thomas Malory's Le Morte D'Arthur; Music — Miklos Rozsa; Directors of Photography — F. A. Young, Stephen Dade; Art Directors — Alfred Junge, Hans Peters; Costumes Designed by — Roger Furse; Film Editor — Frank Clarke; Photographic Effects — Tom Howard; Makeup — Charles Parker; Produced by — Pandro S. Berman; Directed by — Richard Thorpe

Movie still from *Knights of the Round Table*, directed by Richard Thorpe.

SYNOPSIS: If the Victorians could have made a movie of King Arthur, this would have been it. Pretty costumes (especially for the horses), pretty sets, stiff acting and enough changes to Malory's details to satisfy the most particular of censors. Despite being a film that seems to try to out-Malory Malory, *Knights of the Round Table* is a workmanlike and at some points interesting rendition of the tales.

The tone is set by the opening narration:

> It befell in the old days that Rome at need withdrew her legions from England. Then stood the realm in great darkness and danger for every overlord held rule in his own tower and fought with fire and sword against his fellow. Then against these dark forces rose up a new force wherein flowered courtesy, humanity and noble chivalry.

King Arthur in this version springs full-grown to the cause, brought by Merlin as an adult to the place where Excalibur is embedded through an anvil on a stone. He vies only

with Mordred for the honor of the crown, but Mordred does not accept the fact that pulling the sword means anything. Since there is objection, the high diplomat of the land, Merlin, decides that Arthur must prove himself further. There will be a meeting of all the kings at the "circle of stones."

In the meantime a happy and tuneful Lancelot has come seeking Arthur. Riding alone through some woods he comes across a young damsel — the fair Elaine — who says she is waiting there for the knight of her dreams to come and carry her off. Lancelot takes her with him but they are ambushed by five of Mordred's soldiers who are actually after Arthur.

Lancelot takes them on and is doing fine, but Arthur comes along and joins in the fight. They win over the brigands but Lancelot insists that the stranger must answer his challenge as punishment for interfering with

Ava Gardner plays Guinevere and Robert Taylor is Lancelot in 1953's *Knights of the Round Table*.

Lancelot's battle. The two men don't introduce themselves until they've fought to exhaustion, neither able to get the upper hand. Lancelot pledges eternal fealty to his lord; Arthur pledges eternal friendship.

Just then Perceval, Elaine's brother, happens by. By way of introduction he mentions that he will seek the Holy Grail. Additionally, Perceval requests that Arthur take him to Camelot where he can train and become worthy of his quest.

The next major encounter is at Stone-

The costumes in *Knights of the Round Table* (1953) were designed by Roger Furse.

henge where Merlin presides over the meeting of the kings of England. They are to determine who will lead them and Mordred is uncategorically opposed to Arthur's claim. Mordred has on his side Mar, the king of the Picts, and a number of others. Things become so lively that Lancelot has to cover Arthur's escape. So much for diplomacy.

Mordred and Arthur prepare their armies for war, but they wait out the long cold winter. Finally the day of battle comes. Even Merlin is in full armor and chainmail. Through superior tactics and cleverness Arthur wins the day and Mordred is driven off.

Returning to Stonehenge the kings of the land are more amenable this time to Arthur's supremacy. However Lancelot refuses to believe any remorse on Mordred's part. He wants the traitor banished forever. As the adversaries come to blows Arthur stops them and the new king chides Lancelot for not accepting his forgiving of Mordred. Incensed, Lancelot swears never to follow Arthur so long as Mordred is part of his court. The French knight leaves by himself.

During his wanderings Lancelot comes upon a castle where an unnamed knight holds a damsel captive. Lancelot challenges the man for the woman, wins and requires the recreant knight to take the damsel to Camelot. He rides on alone once more.

The wedding of Arthur and Guinevere finally occurs and Lancelot shows up just in time to be forgiven by Arthur and to be declared the queen's champion. Mordred and Morgan Le Fay witness the attraction between the knight and the queen and the plotting begins.

Luckily Merlin overhears the schemes of Mordred and Morgan and he is able to stave off disaster — at least for a time. His suggestion to Guinevere that Lancelot should marry is taken, but not before Lancelot requests of Arthur that he be sent to the north to defend the land against the Picts. Arthur grants the knight's wish and Lancelot, his new wife, Elaine, Gareth, Gawaine and a portion of the army move to the hinterlands.

Lancelot is so successful at keeping the Picts at bay that Mordred and Morgan see another opportunity for their plans. They convince Mar, the Pictish king, to sue for peace. Their goal is to get Lancelot back to Camelot where he is sure to eventually commit some faux pas with the queen that will spell his doom.

Elaine has become pregnant with the Galahad of the future, Perceval continues to receive signs of his otherworldly mission and Merlin continues his wise counsel to the consternation of Mordred and Morgan. They finally can tolerate the old wizard no more and do away with him.

Elaine dies in childbirth, Galahad is sent to Lancelot's father for upbringing and Lancelot returns to Camelot. Guinevere goes to her champion's room one night and Mordred sends his men after her to trap the two together. Lancelot fights his way out, brings the queen to safety and returns to Arthur to try to oil the waters.

Arthur banishes Lancelot and commits Guinevere to the nunnery at Amesbury. This incites Mordred further, making his argument easy since Arthur has contradicted his own laws, which state that such high treason requires execution. War is inevitable.

Arthur and Mordred's armies meet under a flag of truce, but the peace talks are tenuous at best. In the famous incident used in many Arthurian as well as other legends, the agreement is that no sword shall be unsheathed. A snake surprises one of the standing knights. The man reacts unthinkingly, draws his sword to kill it and the battle is met.

Arthur is mortally wounded. As he lies dying Lancelot shows up. Arthur forgives the knight, renews their brotherhood and asks Lancelot to tell Guinevere that he loves and forgives her as well. Arthur asks Lancelot to throw Excalibur into the sea, then he dies.

Lancelot and Perceval walk to a point of land and Lancelot throws the sword into the water. The two next visit Guinevere and Lancelot delivers the king's message. The closing scene is of Lancelot and Perceval in the hall of the Round Table. Lancelot is contrite for his sins and the destruction of the fellowship Arthur had created, but Perceval is taken with another vision. This time he not only hears the voice of God, but he sees an image of the Grail. The heavenly voice assures Perceval that all is not lost; that fellowship, chivalry and goodness will not perish from the Earth, that Galahad will be pure and that Lancelot is forgiven.

That such a film could avoid the more titillating aspects of the Lancelot and Guinevere story is not surprising when the era it was made in is considered, a time in this country when illicit affairs and other aberrations from the norm were frowned on.

However, that Merlin's magical powers were ignored is surprising, particularly in a Hollywood film. In *Knights of the Round Table* Merlin is an elder statesman, a father figure to all the young hot-blooded upstarts around him. But he is not a wizard, not a sorcerer. If nothing else, this bit of realism in the film lends an aspect of thoughtfulness to the writing of the screenplay.

There are lots of inconsistencies here. On the one hand, the Pictish king, Mar, appears at Stonehenge in full medieval armor. However, his men fight Lancelot in the north dressed in animal skins, bare-chested and vulnerable. Merlin is Arthur's prime source of wisdom, yet when he is killed, there is no further mention of him at all. No funeral, no grieving, not even a comment.

Knights of the Round Table, like many another film, tries to cover the whole of the King Arthur story in two hours or less. There are bound to be such twitches and jerks.

Knights of the Round Table (1981) see under *King Arthur and the Knights of the Round Table*

Knights of the Square Table; or, The Grail (1917)

Not viewed; 16mm (original is 35mm nitrate); 4 Reels, 1,078 feet; Black and White; Live Action; Copyright 1917, Thomas A. Edison, Inc.; Distributed by K-E-S-E Service; Conquest Program; Library of Congress Call #FLA1588-1591 (reference print); FRA4045-4048 (duplicate negative); FRA4049-4052 (archive positive); Library of Congress Catalogue #MP73073000

CAST: Paul Kelley (Pug Haddon); Yale Boss (David Scudder); Thomas F. Blake (Detective Boyle); James A. Wilder (Scoutmaster); Andy Clark ("Chick"); Donald McClellan (Billy); George Romaine (Haddon); John Tausey (Mickey); Ernest Mann (Galahad); Charles Mussett (King Arthur); Arthur Dennis (Sir Launfal); Clarence Dervin (The Leper)

CREDITS: Director—Alan Crosland; Scenery—Sumner Williams; Story—James A. Wilder; Camera—Philip Tannura

SYNOPSIS: The leader of a gang of juvenile delinquents uses the story of the Holy Grail as the basis for naming his gang—the Wharfrats Motherless Knights Erring of the Square Table. In a run-in with a troop of Boy Scouts, the gang learns that scouts aren't so bad after all and they all join the more civilized organization.

Knighty Knight Bugs see *Friz Freleng's Looney Looney Looney Bugs Bunny Movie: "Knighty Knight Bugs"*

Lady Lilith see under *The Adventures of Sir Lancelot*

The Lady of the Lake (1986)

Not viewed

CAST: Carolyn Davies (Guinevere)

Lancelot: Guardian of Time (1999)

85 minutes; Color; Live Action; Copyright 1999, Alpine Pictures, Inc.

CAST: Marc Singer (Lancelot du Lac); Claudia Christian (Katherine Shelley); John Saxon (Wolvencroft); Jerry Levine (Michael Shelley); Adam Carter (Arthur); Robert Chapin (Sir Gawain); Jack Barrett Phelan (Blackpool); Leonard Auclair (Merlin); Christal Chacon (Liz Marshal); C. C. Pulitzer (Lady Vivian); Zach Ward (A.J.); Marc Hart (Joe); Jeff Madick (Ricky); Larrs Jackson (Workman); Michael Sanders (Man on Bench); Kevin Abercrombie, Wayne Kohanek, Luke LaFontaine, Terence Rotolo, Robert Chapin, Kim Koscki, Nick Plantico, Lason Singer (Stunt Gargoyles); Tommy Novrian, Robert Sherman, Tommy Taretta, Xuyen Valdivia, William Ward (Additional Gargoyles)

CREDITS: Casting—Don Barns; Music—Ralph Rieckerman; Costume Designer—Judi Jensen; Production Designer—Robert E. Hummel; Visual Effects Supervisor—Robert Chapin; Editor—John Rosenberg; Director of Photography—David M. Rakoczy; Screenplay—Patricia Monville; Story—Ryan Carroll; Associate Producer—Bob Sherman; Executive Producers—Paul L. Miller, Roland Carroll, Ryan Carroll, Greg Cozine; Producers—George Peirson, Jed Nolan; Director—Rubian Cruz; Creative Consultant—John Rosenberg; Production Manager—Patricia Monville; First Assistant Director—Gregory Allen Webb; Second Assistant Director—Christopher A. Pavlu; Script Supervisor—Jan McWilliams; Stunt Coordinator—Robert Chapin; First Assistant Camera—Christopher Taylor; Second Assistant Camera—Jad Carmona; "B" Camera Operators—David Forfiri, Jason D. Libretta, Thomas Myrdaht; First Assistant "B" Camera—Fae Moore, Eulanda Bailey, Robert Burnette; Production Sound Mixers—Gerald B. Wolfe, Chris H. Leplus; Boom Operators—Scott Delgado, Eulanda Bailey; Gaffer—Steve R. Bentley; Best Boy Electric—Robert Bonilla; Set Electrician—Doug I. Heute; Key Grip—Jeffrey Michael Ross; Best Boy Grip—Michael Gearhart; Grip—Sean McArthur; Additional Grip Electric—James F. Brown, Jarrod Nettler, Adam Horak, Roger Morrissey, Chris Waisanen; Set Decorator/Props—Michele Kohse; Assistant Set Decorator—Alex Klyusner; Set Construction—Aaron Hummel, Kevin Hummel, Paul Braccili; Art P.A.—David Reynolds, Fred Jacobs; Costume Supervisor—Jenna Kautzky; Set Costumer—Nancy Bernal; Costumer—Essey Jenson, Liesel Gatcheco; Key Makeup Artist—Palah Sandling;

Key Hairdresser — Laura Markert; Gargoyle Makeup — Darren Perks, Shapeshifter, Make-Up FX; Assistant to the Producers — Valeri A. Landers; 2nd 2nd Assistant Director — Elana Karstofsky, Greta Ibranossian; Key Production Assistant — Ryan B. Kugler; Set Production Assistants — Dana Lynch, Jesse Nicely, Brian Abrams, Matt Kertzman, Cody Schoersiegel, David Gadarian; Special Effects Coordinator — Nick Plantico; Pyrotechnic Effects Supervisor — George Phillips; Special Effects Technician — Corey Roberts; 2nd Unit Photography — Gerald D. Wolfe; Location Manager — J.T. Recker; Assistant Locations — Lisa Livote; Production Coordinator — Tommy G. White; Assistant Coordinator — Chad Lageose; Still Photographer — Eric Lasher; Transportation Coordinator — Buffalo Bill Freeman; Transportation Captain — Rocky Choquette; Drivers — Joe Jones, Jim Helton, Gary Nielsen, Clint Wise; Boss Animal Wrangler — Sammy Thurman Brackenbury; Wranglers — Jess Brackenbury, Bobby Linn, Mark Toogood; Craft Services — Vivian Chan & Assoc.; Caterer — Mark Geroge, World Class Catering; Casting Associates — Jennifer Buttell, Ryan B. Kugler; Extras Casting — Charles Matthews Casting; Stand-in for Marc Singer — Matt Farnsworth; Stand-in for Claudia Christian — Jeannette Papineau; Set Medics Provided by — Affordable Services Agency, Rescues Unlimited; Set Medics — Maureen Clawson, Anush Sarabahksh; Set Security — Tysen L. DeJohnette, James V. Thompson, Burton Franks; Extra Set Security — C.A.S.T. Security, Inc.; Public Relations — Charles Barrett, The Barrett Company; Trade Coordinator — Elliott Metz; Production Accountants — P. K. Hammond, IV, Narciso Natera; Producer Post Production — John Rosenberg; Post Production Supervisors — George Peirson, Jed Nolan; Assistant Editors — Eugene Spektor, Michael Rosenberg; Avid Assistants — Craig Large, Linda Sundlin; Editorial Intern — Ashley Lund; CGI Artists — William Ward, Nicole Gray; Avid 3D Effects — John Rosenberg; Post Production Sound — Private Island Trax; Supervising Sound Editor — Michael McDonald; Dialog Editors — Phillip Moran, Christopher Jacobson, Michael McDonald; ADR Recordists — Mark Meyers, Michael McDonald; Assistant ADR Recordist — San Kim; ADR Editors — Christopher Jacobson, Sang Kim; Sound Design and Sound FX Editors — Michael McDonald, Christopher Jacobson, Sang Kim, Bryan Foster, Chris Anderson; Additional Sound FX Editors — John Sanacore, Bobby Solakov; Foley Artists — Tracy Burns, Danny Hartigan; Foley Recordists — Mark Meyers, Michael McDonald; Foley Editors — Sang Kim, Bryan Foster;

Re-Recording Mixers — Michael McDonald, Eric Fahlborg, Christopher Jacobson; Online Editorial Services — Straightline, Jason Neal; Alpine Production Associates — Sean Borzage, Neil Kaufman, Jack Larson, John Bunzel, Bernard Natalino, Judy Cruzen; Payroll Services — Pas Payroll; Production Insurance — Max Behm & Assoc.; Camera and Lenses Provided by — Hollywood Camera; Camera Dollies — Chapman Leonard Studio Equipment; Editing Equipment Provided by — Alpine Post, Midtown Video, Straightline; Animals Provided by — Wild Bunch Livestock; Special Thanks to — Marc Singer, Debbie Glovin, The Computer Film Company, Five Star Parking, Venice, California; "Send Me an Angel" Performed by the Scorpions, Copyright 1990, Rodulf Schenker/Klaus Meine/Pri Music (ASCAP); This film was shot on location in California at: Iverson Movie Ranch, Calamigos Ranch, Los Angeles Natural History Museum, Dockweiler State Beach, Stoger Seed Company, Alpine Pictures; American Humane Society was present on set to monitor the animal action. No animal was harmed in the making of this film. Developing and telecine by Four Media Company; Eastman Kodak

SYNOPSIS: *Lancelot: Guardian of Time* pits Merlin against another wizard before any of the potential sorceresses (Niniane, Vivian, Morgan Le Fay, or Mab, among others depending on which version one is reading or viewing) have become a problem.

The evil Wolvencroft has acquired a couple of magic black crystals which allow him to move through time. His convoluted plan is to go back in time to 15 years before Camelot and kidnap the young squire Arthur. Then taking him to the distant future of our present, he will have Arthur pull Excalibur from the stone in the wrong era. This will completely change history, creating centuries of chaos and somehow will give Wolvencroft ultimate power.

Merlin selects as his agent the good Sir Lancelot. He sends Lady Vivian ("Merlin's Witch," according to Gawain, "my Guardian Mother," according to Lancelot) with a note for Lancelot asking if he'll take on a vital quest. Vivian also gives Lancelot a magic ring through which Merlin can track Lancelot's whereabouts. And finally she gives the hero "the Sword of Glamis." No explanation is given but it is doubtful that this sword is intended in the film to be an artifact of the yet to be born Scottish thane Macbeth.

Gawain accompanies Lancelot on the first stage of the quest and they both appear at the castle Ravenskeep. Here Wolvencroft and his assistant Blackpool have young Arthur captive. Wolvencroft's little gargoyle minions keep Gawain occupied while Lancelot enters the castle and nearly succeeds at stopping the wizard's escape. Instead, Lancelot is carried into the future along with Wolvencroft, Blackpool and Arthur.

Wolvencroft sets himself up as a special guest curator at the Los Angeles Natural History Museum. Here he awaits the delivery from Britain of the stone with the famous sword still in it. Lancelot fetches up on a nearby beach where he finds a young man named Michael Shelley who is readily swept up by the knight's story. Mike takes Lancelot home to meet his sister Katherine, an attractive gal who pines for the days of heroes who cherish their women and in fact has written a book titled *Men of Romance: Myth and Reality*.

Though not completely swayed by the wild sounding tale, Katherine at least goes along to see what might happen. The three make a foray into the museum to try to find Arthur but Wolvencroft stops them. With gargoyles prancing around and Tyrannosaur skeletons attacking Lancelot, Katherine becomes a true believer. They escape and return to the Shelleys' home.

That evening Merlin communicates with Lancelot. Noon of the following day is the crucial hour at which Wolvencroft must have Arthur pull the sword from the stone. Not only must Lancelot prevent that, but he must get one of the black crystals in order to get himself and Arthur back to Ravenskeep. Katherine also has a brief conversation with Lancelot, primarily wondering if the knight has anyone waiting for him back in Camelot. Lancelot assures Katherine that were he free to love a maiden, it would be someone like herself.

The next day is full of action, all successful for the powers of good. Lancelot stops the wizard-controlled Arthur from pulling Excalibur from the stone, he grabs one of the crystals and disappears with Arthur back into history. Wolvencroft chases after them and fights with Lancelot, but he turns out to be no match for the pure knight. Lancelot destroys the second crystal which in turn destroys Wolvencroft.

Back in present day California, the tearful Katherine goes home, already missing Lancelot. But she finds a rose, Merlin's magic ring, a gauntlet and a note. The notes says, "...put the ring on and I will find you..." and is signed Lancelot du Lac. The moment she places the ring on her finger she is whisked to Camelot and met by Lancelot. Happily, she rides off with him.

Lancelot and Elaine (1909)

Not viewed; Copyright 1909, Vitagraph

CAST: W. Blackton; Leo Delaney; Charles Kent; Paul Panzer; Florence Turner
CREDITS: Director — Charles Kent

SYNOPSIS: Elaine falls in love with Lancelot when she nurses his tournament wounds. When he reveals his love for Guinevere, Elaine dies of a broken heart.

Lancelot and Elaine (1970)

Not viewed; Filmstrip; 57 frames; Color; 35mm; Copyright 1970, Brunswick Productions; Released by Educational Record Sales; From the series Our Heritage from Victorian England; Library of Congress Call #PR5559E.2; Library of Congress Catalogue #72736470/F; Dewey Decimal #821

SYNOPSIS: Focuses on Lancelot and Elaine from Tennyson's *Idylls of the King*.

Lancelot du Lac (1974)

Not viewed; 35mm Filmstrip; Copyright 1974, Bodleian Library

Lancelot du Lac (1974) see *Lancelot of the Lake*

Lancelot of the Lake (Lancelot du Lac) (1974)

80 minutes; Color; Live Action; Copyright 1974, Mara Films Laser Productions, O.R.T.F., France, GERICO Sound, Italy; Copyright 1995, New Yorker Films Artwork; New Yorker Video #17495; French with English subtitles

CAST: Luc Simon (Lancelot du Lac); Laura Duke Condominas (La Reine [The Queen]); Humbert Balsan (Gauvain [Gawain]); Vladimir Antolek-Oresek (Le Roi [The King]); Patrick Bernard (Mordred); Arthur de Montalembert (Lionel); Charles Balsan; Christian Schlumberger; Joseph Patrick Le Quidre; Jean-Paul Le Perlier; Marie Louise Buffet; Marie Gabrielle Cartron; Antoine Rabaud; Jean-Marie Begar; Guy de Bernis; Phillippe Chleq

CREDITS: Written and Directed by — Robert Bresson; Director of Photography — Pasqualino de Santis; Set Design — Pierre Charbonnier; Music by — Philippe Sarde Editions Yanne; Sound by — Bernard Bats; Mixer — Jacques Carrere; Cameramen — Jean Chiabaut, Mario Comini, Dominiques Le Rigoleur; Editor — Germaine Lamy; Special Effects — Alain Bryce; Costumes — Grès; Jewelry by — Cartier; Hairstyles by — Carita; Production Director — Michel Choquet; Executive Producers — Jean-Pierre Rassam, François Rochas; Eastman Color; Paris Studio Cinema

SYNOPSIS: Among the best of the artistically rendered versions of the legends, *Lancelot of the Lake* is also the most bleak and grim of them. Filmed with stark clarity, sounds are heavily emphasized — the clanking of armor, horses' hoofbeats and whinnyings, off-camera activities. The actors deliver their lines with emotionless severity.

The film opens with the return of the Knights of the Round Table from a failed two-year search for the Holy Grail. Merlin died before the quest began. Perceval has disappeared and Lancelot, in black armor, has vowed to be Guinevere's lover no longer.

So many knights have died on the quest that Arthur plans to close the Round Table room. He wonders if it is God's punishment that they are so stricken. He instructs his remaining knights to stay at arms, drop their quarrels and perfect themselves.

In spite of his vow, Lancelot meets twice with Guinevere in a loft. Guinevere refuses to cease the relationship and will not deny their love. Although Lancelot has offered his friendship to Mordred, Mordred spies on the two. He finds one of Guinevere's scarves in the loft.

Gawain warns Lancelot that many of the knights are siding with Mordred, including Gawain's own brother, Agravain. Two knights arrive as messengers from Escalot, requesting a tournament. Arrangements are made for the event to occur in two weeks. The knights set to honing their skills.

Lancelot and Guinevere meet in the loft again. Guinevere says that someone has taken her scarf. Lancelot removes his armor and they embrace as Mordred and his men watch through a window. Guinevere asks Lancelot to come to her room tomorrow during the tournament. Lancelot, however, dons a suit of white armor and goes to the tournament. In the meantime Mordred informs Arthur of Lancelot and Guinevere's love while Gawain denies it.

The conditions for the tournament include sharpened points but weakened lances. Except for the playing of bagpipes at each challenge, the tournament goes on in silence. Lancelot wins eight bouts and leaves the field but, bleeding heavily from his wounds, he falls from his horse somewhere in the woods.

Carmaduc and Bohort go looking for him to no avail. There is a rainstorm that night and the next day, finding his tattered flag, they believe Lancelot to be dead. Guinevere waits for Lancelot in the loft. Gawain goes to her, trying to talk her out of staying there, but she says she knows Lancelot lives. Arthur comes to her but she sends him away as well.

Finally Lancelot returns to carry off Guinevere and, fighting his way out, he wounds Gawain and kills Agravain. Gawain tells Arthur that Lancelot didn't know it was him and that his heart is with Lancelot.

Arthur and his men move to recover the queen. Arthur offers to end the bloodshed and take Guinevere back but is refused. Gawain however is able to talk sense to Lancelot and he returns to Arthur with Guinevere. News comes that Mordred has taken the castle and will challenge Arthur. Lancelot and his men join Arthur to fight Mordred. No one survives the final battle in the forest. The film ends with Lancelot's riderless horse running through the woods.

The Land of Castles see King Arthur and the Legends of Glastonbury

Land of the Lost: "Day for Knight" (1991)

Television series episode; 45 minutes; Color; Live Action and Puppets; Copyright 1991, Krofft Entertainment, Inc.; Copyright 1992, Krofft Entertainment, Inc.; Copyright 1993, Worldvision Home Video, Inc.; Worldvision Catalog #8033

CAST: Timothy Bottoms (Tom Porter); Jennifer Drugan (Annie Porter); Robert Gavin (Kevin Porter); Bobby Jacoby (Balin); Shannon Day (Christa); Ed Gale (Tasha); Danny Mann (Voice of Tasha); Tom Allard (Shung); Brian Williams (Keeg); R. C. Tass (Nim)

CREDITS: Produced by — Sid & Marty Krofft; Executive Producer — Jerry Golod; Producers — Len Janson, Chuck Menville; Co-Producers — Charles Chiodo, Stephen Chiodo, Edward Chiodo; Supervising Producer — Randy Pope; Written by — Jules Dennis, Richard Mueller; Directed by — John Carl Buechler; Music — Kevin Kiner; Director of Photography — Tony Cutrono; Production Designer — Gene Abel; Story Editors — Len Janson, Chuck Menville; Costume Designer — Greg LaVoi; Casting — Jean Scoccimarro; Production Supervisor — Rick Blumenthal; 1st Assistant Director — Jan Ervin; 2nd Assistant Director — Tony Schwartz; 2nd 2nd Assistant Director — Scott Harris; Stunt Coordinator — Bobby Porter; Set Decorator — Lauree Slattery; Property Master — Richard Wright; Set Dresser — Yuki Nakamura; Art Coordinator — Gregg Edler; Script Supervisor — Wayne Damore; Sound Mixer — Rick Wadde; Boom Operator — Brydon Baker; Still Photographer — Joel Sussman; Assistant to the Producers — Beth Cardenas; Key Makeup — Susan Reiner; Hair Dresser — Malcom McAlpine; Special Effects Makeup — Joe Podner; Production Coordinator — Jessica Budin; Assistant Production Coordinator — Skip Dominick; Costume Supervisor — Carma Huelle; Assistant Costume — Kendra Krofft; 1st Assistant Camera — Jerry Gorman; 2nd Assistant Camera — Brenda Ryan; Key Grip — Rodney French; Gaffer — Michael Stringer; Best Boy Grip — Matthew Craven; Best Boy Electric — Greg Beebe; Location Transportation — John Barbee; Transportation Captain — Mike Painter; Lead Carpenter — Lee Borisof; Construction Foreman — Simon Loftus; First Aid — Scott Rudolph; Production Accountant — Benj Whithouse; Unit Publicist — Joe Parker; Editors — Ron Halpern, David Burghardt, Booey Kober; Post Production Supervisor — Michael Lander; Post Production Coordinator — Katy Orman; Assistant Editor — Paula Jacobson; Post Audio Facility — Coley Sound; Special Visual Effects Produced by Chiodo Brothers Production, Inc.; Production Manager — Neil Lundell; Creature Shop Supervisor — Bart J. Mixon; Puppet Coordinator — Norman Tempia; Director of Photography — Victor Abdalov; Animation Coordinator — Jene Omens; Animators — Kim Blanchette, Justin Kohn, Mark Lougee; Republic Pictures; A Subsidiary of Spelling Entertainment Group, Inc.; Worldvision Enterprises, Inc.; Not affiliated with World Vision International, a religious and charitable organization.

SYNOPSIS: *Land of the Lost* was a television series that originally aired for three seasons from 1974 to 1976. Fifteen years later it was revived with a new cast and ran for two seasons in 1991 and 1992. There were 26 episodes in the second incarnation of the show. The seventh episode was "Day for Knight."

The premise of the show is that a father and his two children are on vacation. They are caught in an earthquake and fall into a time vortex. The strange world they find themselves trapped in is populated by dinosaurs, lizard people and other strange creatures. Like *Lost in Space*, another television series which also had a borderline Arthurian episode, (see *Lost in Space*: "The Questing Beast"), *Land of the Lost* is a takeoff on the *Swiss Family Robinson* story.

The main human characters are Tom Porter, the father, Kevin and Annie, his kids, and Christa, the mysterious cave girl who was raised by the monkey people. The lizard people are called Sleestaks, Annie has a pet baby dinosaur named Tasha and a family friend is the monkey person Stink.

In "Day for Knight," the time vortex opens and a young man from King Arthur's court steps into the Land of the Lost. Wearing a leather tunic, chainmail and a huge helmet, he becomes a heroic figure to the young girls when he causes a couple of invading Sleestaks to run off.

Tensions run high as Kevin becomes threatened by this new addition to the group. Because of his teenage crush on Christa he becomes jealous of Sir Balin. All is resolved however when Kevin and Balin combine forces to save Christa from a rogue tyrannosaur. Balin winds up confessing that he is nothing more than the squire to one of King Arthur's real knights. He had merely borrowed his master's helmet and sword to see what they felt like when he was overtaken by the time vortex.

The vortex opens once again and Balin determines to go back to Britain. Before leaving, however, he gives Kevin his mace as a token of their friendship.

The whole of book 2 of Malory's *Le Morte D'Arthur* is about Sir Balin, a knight who King Arthur had had in prison. Few if any similarities can be seen between that Balin and the young character in "Day for Knight."

Malory's Balin was an unfortunate soul who took a magical sword from a damsel who turned out to be not so well meaning. He wound up cutting off the head of the Lady of the Lake — in King Arthur's presence, no less — and later dealt King Pellam the Dolorous Stroke. This is the wound that would not heal until Galahad came along on his Grail quest. Ultimately Balin and his brother, Balan, not recognizing each other, fight to the death and Merlin buries them.

The young Balin of "Day for Knight" mentions no brother, but we may well be seeing a youthful Balin before he becomes Malory's calamitous knight. Other than the name, only two other comparisons are possible. This television Balin does take a sword not originally his with which to go adventuring. He also cuts off the head of a Sleestak bat-tle-ax, though it's doubtful that this was intended as a stand-in for the Lady of the Lake.

The Last Defender of Camelot see The New Twilight Zone: "The Last Defender of Camelot"

The Last Enchantment (1995)

Not viewed; 47 minutes; Color; Copyright 1995, Havas Productions; Distributed by Havas Productions

CAST: Dusty Baker (Executioner); Jeromia Catt (Jeromia the Polisher); Al Chicotel (Bedwer); Mark Kidd (Sir Prize); Chad Knauer (Jive Talker); Mike Wade (Arthur); Dan Work (Merlin)
CREDITS: Director — Dan Work; Writer — Dan Work; Costume Design — Mandi Work; Film Editing — Dan Work; Production — Havas; Camera Earl — e. o. pearl

Lauritz Melchior in Opera and Song, Vol. 2 (1950)

47 minutes; Black and White; Live Performances; Copyright 1950, 1951, 1952, The Voice of Firestone; Copyright 1990, 1991, Video Artists International; VAI #69124

CREDITS: Narrator — Martin Bookspan; Announcer — Hugh James; The Firestone Orchestra: Conductor — Howard Barlow; Production Coordinator — Allan Altman; Produced by Video Artists International in association with New England Conservatory
SYNOPSIS: From 1949 to 1963 the Firestone Tire and Rubber Company sponsored a weekly telecast of live musical performances. This tape highlights the appearances of the Danish tenor Lauritz Melchior.

Twenty-four minutes into the tape the February 12, 1951, telecast includes Melchior singing "In Fernam Land" from Wagner's *Lohengrin*. This five-minute solo is from act 3 of the opera. In it Lohengrin reveals his identity and background. (See the entry for *Lohengrin*, Bayreuth, 1982.)

The Legend of Arthur (1985)

Subtitle: *The True Legend of King Arthur*; 26 minutes; Color; Documentary; Copyright

1985, Libraprim, S.A., Geneva; Copyright 1986, 1993, Films for the Humanities, Inc.

CREDITS: A Film for the Humanities Presentation; Libraprim presents; Ancient Books in the French Language: Legends; Filmed and Produced by — Jaques Sandoz; Assisted by — Yves Bernard, Rafael Navarro; With Commentary by — Eliot W. Evans; Additional Commentary by — Jaques Sandoz; English Translation by — Jean Michel Fueter; Commentary and Quotations Said by — David Egli, Harold Frankel; Music Composed and Conducted by — Louis Crelier; We are thankful to the Abbey of Glastonbury (England) and to the Leeds Castle Foundation (England) representing Camelot.; Additional Music by — Henry Purcell (King Arthur); Original Music Recorded at Studio Prisme (Lausanne) with the Participation of the Collequim Academicum (Geneva); Musical Editions — Louis Crelier; Post Production — Stratis, S.A. (Geneva)

SYNOPSIS: The film opens with the story of Joseph of Arimathea bringing 11 disciples and the Holy Grail to England. Less well known details are given, including the fact that Joseph had been a metalsmith and had traveled to Cornwall before to trade for tin.

Traditions about other relics of Christ are also discussed, including. the story that Joseph carried two vials in the Chalice, one containing Christ's sweat, the other filled with Christ's blood. Both of these, along with the Grail, were thrown down a well at Glastonbury, which is now known as the Chalice Well.

Joseph is also said to have made a staff from the thorn tree from which Christ's crown of thorns was made. He planted the staff at Glastonbury and the tree that grew from it is said to be the same one that exists there today.

The documentary places the birth of Arthur at around 480 A.D. at Tintagel, his defeat of the Saxons at Mount Badon in 520 and his death at around 540. It states that he and Guenevere were buried at Glastonbury, which at the time was an island.

It also recounts that in 1191 Henry II charged the abbot of Glastonbury with ex-

huming Arthur's bones. A monk evidently had a vision as to where to look. Upon digging, a stone lid, the famous lead cross and, 16 feet farther down, the bones of the legendary king and his queen were found.

The literature of the legends of Arthur is cited throughout the film. From Christian's [sic] story of Perceval, the *Red Book of Wales,* to Wolfram's *Titurel* and *Parzival* and Malory's contributions, an overview of the seminal works is included. Mention is even made of the Palladin (or Palladienne, etc.) story.

The later political machinations surrounding Arthur also are pointed out. Edward I's reexhumation of Arthur's bones occurred in 1278. Henry VII's claims of Arthurian descent were made in 1485. Finally, in 1539, the dissolution of Glastonbury was ordered by Henry VIII during his wranglings with the Catholic church.

The Legend of Percival (1993)

Color; 30 minutes; Illustrated Narrative; Comes with 15-page instruction guide; Copyright 1993, Gateway Films and Joan Thiry; A Gateway Films/Vision Video Release

CREDITS: Executive Producer — Joan Thiry; Producer — Ken Curtis; Director/Camera — Judith Bost; Editor/Foley Artist — J. Stockton; Narration — Stephen Titra; Written by — Joan Thiry, James Robertson; Original Music Composed and Performed by — Stephen Titra; Original Art — Robert Robertson

SYNOPSIS: As explained in the accompanying instructional guide, the version of the Percival legend presented on this tape is based primarily on the writing of Wolfram Von Eschenbach. For ease of pronunciation, however, the names from Chrétien were retained.

One of King Arthur's best knights, Gahmuret, is killed in battle, leaving behind a wife and young son. The wife, Heart Sorrow, takes their son, Percival, to Wales where the boy is raised in isolation in a forest.

Some years later several of Arthur's

Opposite: **Illustrations from** *The Legend of Percival* **(1993) (courtesy Joan Thiry; Robert Robertson, artist; Stephen Titra, photographer).**

knights pass by and stop to chat with Percival. The boy determines to become a knight of the Round Table himself, much to his mother's grief. On his departure, she gives the "innocent fool" the well-intended advice that will be part of his many problems over the years.

Percival encounters the Maiden of the Tent, the Red Knight, the maiden who hadn't smiled in six years, Gournemonde, Blanche Fleur and Amfortas, the Fisher King. He sees the Grail but fails to ask the crucial question. He receives his magical sword, comes upon the maiden with the fallen knight who tells him about Amfortas's woes, then runs across the Maiden of the Tent again (who informs him of the secrets of his sword).

The tape recounts the story of Percival's trance over spots of blood in the snow, his battle with three of Arthur's knights and his appearance at King Arthur's court. There Kundry finds Percival and her words send him on his quest once more. After many years Percival loses track of his purpose. Finally, he meets some pilgrims on Good Friday, joins with them and meets the hermit who repairs his sword and reinstills Percival with the ardor and spirit required to continue into his future.

Interestingly, the tape ends here. The instructional pamphlet points out that there are several endings to the legend, some with Percival finding the Grail, others with Percival's son, Lohengrin, finding the Grail.

The narration on the tape goes into much more detail than is presented here. Gateway Films/Vision Video is a Christian video supplier. The accompanying printed supplement points out a number of discussion and study topics possible, using the Percival legend as a basis.

The Legend of Prince Valiant (1991)

66 minutes; Color; Cartoon; Copyright 1991,1992, Hearst Entertainment Distribution; Copyright 1992, Video Collection International, Ltd. (packaging design); IDDH Groupe Bruno Rene Huchez; Video Collection International, Ltd. (Britain, PAL format)

#VC1231; Pacific Arts Video #70001 (no longer available)

CAST: Robby Benson (Prince Valiant); Tim Curry (Sir Gawain); Samantha Eggar (Queen Guinevere); Michael Horton (Arn); Noelle North (Rowanne); Alan Oppenheimer (Merlin); Efrem Zimbalist, Jr. (King Arthur); James Avery; Dorian Harewood

ADDITIONAL VOICES: Marnie Mosilman; Peter Renaday; Dan Gilvezan; Mona Marshall; Patrick Fraley; Stu Rosen

CREDITS: Developed for Television and Produced by—David J. Corbett; Story Editor—Dianne Dixon; "The Dream" Written by—Dianne Dixon; "The Journey" Written by—Dianne Dixon; "The Blacksmith's Daughter" Written by—Chris Webber, Karen Wilson; Associate Producer—Mary C. Corbett; Line Producer—Gwen Sandiff Wetzler; Storyboard—Vincenzo Tippett; Storyboard Cleanup—Cesar Magsombol, Alete Estes, Lynn Hunter Yago, Gerald Forton; Original Model Designs—Jesse Fenn Santos; Additional Model Designs—Paula LaFond, Phillipe Mignon, Shayne Poindexter; Color Key—Isabelle Massenet, Allyn Conley; Background Layout—Jim Alles, Jesse Fenn Santos; Background Color—Barbara S. Schade, June Mieu; "The Dream" Animation Sequence—Neil Affleck; Assisted by—Anthony Stanley, Tom Yasumi; Chess Sequence—Magic Shadows, Inc.; Voice Direction—Stuart M. Rosen; Music Composed, Performed and Produced by—Exchange, Steve Sexton, Gerald O'Brien; Lyrics by—Marc Jordan; Performed by—Marc Jordan, Amy Sky; Post Production Audio—Advantage Audio, Jim Hodson, Bill Koepnick, Marc Perlman; Dialogue Recording and Editing—Screenmusic Studios, Deb Adair, Chris Eaton; Production Manager—Mary Katherine Moore; Production Auditor—Loretta Abata Elliott; Production Assistants—Andrew J. Leith, Stuka Kepel; Production Supervisors—France: Scott LaBarge, Korea: Mike Kaweski; Production Secretaries—Peggy Fansone, Lisa Larrick; French Production Adapter—Bruno Rene Huchez; Supervising Producers—Rene Huchez, Barham Rohani; Production Managers—Pierre Metais, Caroline Gruicheux; Production Supervisor—Jean Marc DesRosiers; Animation Production—Sei Young Animation Co., Ltd.; Animation Direction—Dae Jung Kim, Michel Lyman, Ron Myrick, Maria Dail, Mike Kaweski; Executives in Charge—Choi An Hee, Cho Jung Jin; Hearst Entertainment Distribution; Production Executive—Austin Hearst; Educational Consultant—John Arnold; Completion Bond Arranged by—Films Garantie

Finance; Executives in Charge of Production for the Family Channel — Terry A. Bolwick, James J. Ackerman; Executive Producers — William E. Miller, Jeffrey Schon; A production of Hearst Entertainment Distribution, Inc. and IDDH Groupe Bruno Rene Huchez, in association with the Family Channel, Inc., POLYPHON Film und Fernsehgesellschaft mbH and Sei Young Animation Company, Ltd.; Created for television by Hearst Entertainment Distribution, Inc. Trademarks in *The Legend of Prince Valiant* and its characters owned by King Features Syndicate Division, the Hearst Corporation.

SYNOPSIS: Loosely based on the comic strip by Hal Foster, *The Legend of Prince Valiant* was a fanciful cartoon series created for television. The series originally consisted of 26 episodes of approximately 22 minutes each. This tape includes the first three episodes; the rest have not been released on video. Further information is included at the end of the synopses.

EPISODE 1: "THE DREAM"

The story begins as Valiant's father prepares his castle for a siege. The hurried preparations are shown in some detail as doors, gates and shutters are closed, men deployed to their stations, women and children hidden away in safe rooms within the castle. Despite all this, the invading army outnumbers them three to one and the castle is quickly taken over.

The royal family escapes by boat and is caught in a terrible storm at sea. They are shipwrecked on an island inhabited by cavemanlike barbarians. They put up such a noble and brave front against impossible odds that the wild men choose not to keep them captive, but take them to an island of their own instead. Though isolated and filled with strange creatures, the place provides everything they need. They build a small village for themselves.

Valiant begins having a recurring dream vision of an unheard-of place called Camelot and a king named Arthur, who will start a new order of chivalry and honor. Despite his father's objections, Valiant leaves alone to find his destiny with the Knights of the Round Table.

EPISODE 2: "THE JOURNEY"

Alone in his rowboat for four days, Valiant is ill-prepared for life in the wilderness. Having gone the whole time without any food, he runs into a fisherman named Arn. As Arn is instructing the young prince in the mysteries of fishing an aquatic dinosaur attacks them. The two succeed in killing the beast and seem to be becoming friends, but Val sees a strange glow through the forest. Thinking it might be Camelot, he leaves without knowing Arn is following.

Val runs into a barbarian in the forest and they fight. The prince nearly beats the man to death but as Arn catches up Val realizes the wrong he is doing. He determines to return the comatose fellow to wherever he came from. With Arn's help he straps the giant to a pair of long poles and, hefting him onto their shoulders, the two search for the man's village.

The man's mother, it turns out, is a witch. She ties the adventurers up and pours a potion down Val's throat. It causes Valiant to have a vision of Camelot in ruins. After the effects of the potion wear off, the witch releases the two and sends them on their way.

EPISODE 3: "THE BLACKSMITH'S DAUGHTER"

Never one to be discouraged, Valiant posits that since the witch chose a vision of the end of Camelot as her revenge for the injury done her son then Camelot must actually exist. He and Arn continue on their way.

Coming to Bridgeford, they find Sheriff Robert harassing the people of the town. When this rowdy good-for-nothing and his men go after a beautiful young woman, Valiant steps in. He beats Robert in a sword fight and Robert swears revenge.

The girl is Rowanne, daughter of Cedric, the blacksmith. Thankful for the help Val gave his daughter, Cedric puts the travelers up for the night. Cedric is confident that his friendship with Baron Duncan, Robert's brother, will protect them against any petty trouble from Robert. But blood is thicker than water and Duncan backs Robert's efforts to take Rowanne to be his wife.

Rowanne helps Val and Arn escape, then with her parents' blessing and to avoid Duncan's revenge, she leaves to join Valiant on his quest. Catching up with them, she tells them that she intends to become the first female knight of the Round Table.

Original episode list: 1. "The Dream," 2. "The Journey," 3. "The Blacksmith's Daughter," 4. "The Kidnapping," 5. "The Trust," 6. "The Finding of Camelot," 7. "The Gift," 8. "The Singing Sword," 9. "The Trust Betrayed," 10. "The Secret of Perilous Garde," 11. "The Return," 12. "The Visitor," 13. "The Awakening," 14. "The Guardian," 15. "The Trap," 16. "The Turn of the Wheel," 17. "The Competitor," 18. "The Road Back," 19. "The Fist of Iron," 20. "The Waif," 21. "The Dawn of Darkness," 22. "The Battle of Greystone," 23. "The Reunion," 24. "The Choice," 25. "The Triumph," 26. "The Dream Come True."

Legend of the Holy Rose see *MacGyver: "Legend of the Holy Rose"*

Legends of the Isles: "Merlin the Wizard" (1997)

52 minutes; Color; Documentary; Copyright 1997, Emdee Productions, Acorn Media

CREDITS: Special Thanks to — Eamonn Corrigan, Crag Caves, Castleisland, English Heritage, Jim Fitzpatrick, Eric Maddern, Trinity College, Dublin, Welsh Historic Monuments; Produced with the support of investment incentives for the Irish Film Industry provided by the Government of Ireland.; Narrator — Bosco Hogan; Character Voice — Jonathan Ryan; Expert Commentary: Historian — Geoffrey Ashe; Druid — Ken Bailey; Writer — Count Nikolai Tolstoy; Research Assistants — Chris Jarvis, Tom O'Neill; Rostrum — Edd Condon; Graphic Design — Ian Jacobs; Electrical Facilities — Cine Electric, Ltd.; Electrician — Stephen Bruan; Lighting Cameraman — Peter Robertson; 2nd Unit Camera — Peter Dorney, Claran Kavanagh; Camera Assistant — Russell Glesson; Sound Recordist — Brendan Campbell; Music by — Dave Foden; Production Coordinator — Tanya Gillen; Production Assistant — Annmarie Fitzpatrick; Dubbing Facility — Moynihan Russell; Dubbing Mixer — Cecily Loughman; Post Production Facilities — Screen Scene; On-Line Editor — Mark Nolan; Editor — Isobel Stephenson; Script Editor — Ed Fields; Writer — Eric Maddern; Produced by Emdee Productions and the Learning Channel in association with RTE; For the Learning Channel: Production Assistant — Charlie Foley; Executive Producer — Sandra Gregory; For Emdee Productions: Production Manager — Patricia Grennan; Executive Producer — Maria Anderton; Director — Stephen Rooke

SYNOPSIS: "Merlin the Wizard" is the fifth episode of the 12-part made-for-television series *Legends of the Isles*. The series is available as a six-volume set or as individual tapes. Each tape contains two episodes, each episode runs for approximately 26 minutes.

"Merlin the Wizard" describes three interpretations of the personage of Merlin. The first, the legendary figure, is the one most familiar to modern readers and the one portrayed most often in films. This traditional version of Merlin goes back to the fifth century. It begins with the high king of Britain (the tape doesn't mention Vortigern specifically) trying to build a castle.

When the castle walls will not stand, the king's advisors tell him to find a fatherless boy. They tell the king that the blood of the child can be used to stop the crumbling of the structure. A young Merlin is brought to the king, but before he is sacrificed the boy reveals to the king the cause of the building failure.

A pond beneath the castle contains two jars. In the jars are two dragons, one red and one white. When released, the dragons fight but ultimately the red one drives the white dragon away. Merlin then prophesies that the red dragon represents Britain, the white, her enemies.

As Merlin matures his powers grow. He is called upon to build a monument to the fallen leaders of Britain. By his magic Merlin brings stones from Ireland and constructs Stonehenge.

Next the tape describes how "a besotted British king asked Merlin to cast a spell so he could lie with another man's wife." Oddly this second king in Merlin's life is not named either. The *Historia Regum Britanniae* by Geoffrey of Monmouth is cited in the film as one of the primary sources of information on Merlin. Geoffrey names both the high king mentioned above and the "besotted" king as Vortigern and Uther, respectively.

In any event, Arthur is the result of that illicit union and Merlin brings him to Wales to be raised. Merlin devises the test of the sword in the stone and when Arthur reaches the age of 15, he is made king. Merlin becomes King Arthur's chief advisor during the 20 years of peace that follow.

The second view of Merlin examined by this film is the historical Merlin. It is pointed out that 14 years after his *Historia Regum Britanniae* Geoffrey wrote the *Vita Merlini*. Merlin, however, is very different in this second work. He is high priest and poet to King Gwenddolau, the "last of the pagan kings" of Scotland. When Gwenddolau loses the battle of Arthuret, Merlin goes mad and goes to live in the forest.

Although, as the film points out, much of Geoffrey's work is fictional, it is thought that his biography of Merlin is based on genuine historical material. *The Lives* of Saints Sampson and Kentigern both mention a visionary, who may have been the actual Merlin.

This historic Merlin, however, would have lived after the time of Arthur. It is suggested that only in much later medieval times were the facts of his existence overlaid onto the legends of King Arthur.

Finally the narrative posits a third aspect to Merlin: that he may have been one of, if not the last of, the Druid priests. Rome had sought to wipe out Druidism and was nearly successful. However, Merlin may have been part of a Druidic revival after Rome's departure from Britain. The film states that "surviving poems by Merlin" tell of him communing with animals and performing other acts and ceremonies that are consistent with what is known of Druid practice.

Essentially the film concludes that there was an individual named Merlin (or Myrddin) who lived at the close of the pagan era. Romanticism has erroneously placed him alongside King Arthur.

Legends of the Isles: "King Arthur" (1997)
52 minutes; Color; Documentary; Copyright 1997, Emdee Productions, Acorn Media

CREDITS: Special Thanks to — Corridors of Time, English Heritage, Sam Humphries, The National Trust, Trinity College, Dublin, Welsh Historic Monuments; Produced with the support of investment incentives for the Irish Film Industry provided by the Government of Ireland.; Narrator — Bosco Hogan; Character Voice — Jonathan Ryan; Expert Commentary; Writer — Caitlin Matthews; Historian — Geoffrey Ashe; Research Assistants — Miranda Driscoll, Chris Jarvis; Rostrum — Edd Condon, Kieran Kavanagh; Graphic Design — Ian Jacobs; Electrical Facilities — Cine Electric, Ltd.; Electrician — Stephen Bruan; Lighting Cameraman — Peter Robertson; Camera Assistant — Russell Glesson; Sound Recordist — Brendan Campbell; Music by — David Foden; Production Coordinator — Tanya Gillen; Production Assistants — Shane Duggan, Annmarie Fitzpatrick; Dubbing Facility — Moynihan Russell; Dubbing Mixer — Cecily Loughman; Post Production Facilities — Screen Scene; On-Line Editor — Mark Nolan; Editor — Isobel Stephenson; Script Editor — Ed Fields; Produced by Emdee Productions and the Learning Channel in association with RTE; For the Learning Channel: Production Assistant — Charlie Foley; Executive Producer — Sandra Gregory; For Emdee Productions: Production Manager — Patricia Grennan; Executive Producer — Maria Anderton; Director — Stephen Rooke

SYNOPSIS: "King Arthur" is the eighth episode of the 12-part made-for-television series *Legends of the Isles*. The series is available as a six-volume set or as individual tapes. Each tape contains two episodes, each episode runs for approximately 26 minutes.

The "King Arthur" segment begins with a brief review of the legendary version of the Arthur story. As described in this tape, Merlin cast a spell so that the high king could lie with another man's wife. The resulting child was Arthur, whom Merlin took away to be raised by others.

Years later as the high king lay dying, he drove his sword into a stone, declaring that only the one who could pull it out would be the next king. This contradicts the version cited in the episode "Merlin the Wizard" in which it is stated that Merlin created this test.

With no leader Britain fell prey to barbarian invasions until Arthur finally came of age and pulled the sword from the stone. The legendary versions of Arthur's reign include the formation of the Knights of the Round Table, the founding of Camelot and the rise of chivalry.

The downfall of Camelot is attributed to the fact that Arthur failed to follow Merlin's advice on one occasion. In deciding to marry Gwenevere Arthur sealed his kingdom's fate, opening the door to the treachery and betrayal brought about by the love affair between the queen and Lancelot.

Next the tape delves into the possibility that Arthur may have existed. Following the departure of the Roman legions there was an influx of Saxons. History does point to someone having at least temporarily stopped them. "In the book of complaints by a fifth-century monk," the narrator says, the final battle at Badon is described, but no leader is named.

It is not until the ninth century that the name Arthur is used by the monk Nennius. In the twelfth century Geoffrey of Monmouth wrote a "history" which included so much mythical lore surrounding Arthur that it can hardly be called a history at all.

The film presents views of Tintagel Castle, but points out that the castle is actually a twelfth-century ruin and is not likely to have been Arthur's birthplace. It shows Cadbury Hill, suggesting that this is the probable site of the battle of Badon. While Cadbury may have been the site that came to be known as Camelot, archaeology has shown that during the late fifth and early sixth centuries many old Roman sites and other ancient hill forts were restored and reoccupied.

The narration explains that Lancelot was purely the invention of medieval French writers, but that it was Geoffrey who first accused Gwenevere of adultery. Geoffrey, however, held that Mordred was the culprit. There is a Medraut in older Welsh annals but he is not characterized as Arthur's enemy.

Geological evidence has shown that during the sixth century Glastonbury Tor was actually an island. This tends to support the tradition that the hill was the island of Avalon. The narrator discusses the conundrum of the "discovery" of Arthur and Gwenevere's grave at Glastonbury Abbey. The abbey had recently suffered a damaging fire. Finding King Arthur's tomb was, if nothing else, a great publicity move which garnered many pilgrims and contributors to the rebuilding of the place.

A political aspect to the discovery of Arthur's body is brought up that most other documentaries don't mention. Since the Norman Conquest, the threat of Arthur's return may have been viewed as a potential rallying point for native Britons. The finding that he was indeed dead would conveniently eliminate any such hope.

Other than a few minor inconsistencies, the only glaring fault with this episode is a common one. As in most films the reenactors who provide visual background to the narration are all armored in medieval, not sixth-century, accoutrements.

Legends of the Isles: "The Holy Grail" (1997)

52 minutes; Color; Documentary; Copyright 1997, Emdee Productions, Acorn Media

CREDITS: With Special Thanks to — Corridors of Time, Nanteos Manor, National Museum of Ireland, The National Trust, Trinity College, Dublin, Welsh Historic Monuments; Produced with the support of investment incentives for the Irish Film Industry provided by the Government of Ireland; Devised by — Cormac Larkin; Narrator — Bosco Hogan; Character Voice — Jonathan Ryan; Expert Commentary: Writer — Count Nikolai Tolstoy;

Historian — Geoffrey Ashe; Research Assistants — Chris Jarvis, Tom O'Neill; Rostrum — Edd Condon; Graphic Design — Ian Jacobs; Electrical Facilities — Cine Electric, Ltd.; Electrician — Stephen Bruan; Lighting Cameraman — Peter Robertson; Camera Assistant — Russell Glesson; Sound Recordist — Brendan Campbell; Music by — Dave Foden; Production Coordinator — Tanya Gillen; Production Assistants — Shane Duggan, Annmarie Fitzpatrick; Dubbing Facility — Moynihan Russell; Dubbing Mixer — Cecily Loughman; Post Production Facilities — Screen Scene; On-Line Editor — Mark Nolan; Editor — Isobel Stephenson; Supervising Writer — Ed Fields; Writer — Niall Murphy; Produced by Emdee Productions and the Learning Channel in association with RTE; For the Learning Channel: Production Assistant — Charlie Foley; Executive Producer — Sandra Gregory; For Emdee Productions: Production Manager — Patricial Grennan; Executive Producer — Maria Anderton; Director — Stephen Rooke

SYNOPSIS: "The Holy Grail" is the ninth episode of the 12-part made-for-television series *Legends of the Isles*. The series is available as a six-volume set or as individual tapes. Each tape contains two episodes, each episode runs for approximately 26 minutes.

As described by the narrator, the legend of the Grail begins in A.D. 63 with Joseph of Arimathea, "the disciple of a crucified carpenter." Joseph is said to have brought the Grail to England from the Holy Land, establishing a religious center at Glastonbury.

After Joseph a line of guardians kept the Grail through the centuries. During the reign of King Arthur the Grail was kept in a fortress, guarded by a worthy knight. This knight abandoned his duty to the Grail for the love of a woman and as a result received a mortal wound. Through the power of the Grail he could not die. Only when fishing could he forget his pain and thus he became known as the Fisher King.

Because of his failure, all the countryside around the Grail Castle became a wasteland. It was prophesied that an innocent knight would come along and ask a certain question, the mere asking of which would heal the wound and restore life to the wasteland.

In the meantime a widow lived in the wilderness with her last surviving child, a boy named Parsifal. Seeking to keep him from the harms of life, she taught him nothing of the outside world. One day Parsifal saw three knights and decided he wanted to become a knight himself. He left his mother to go to Camelot, leaving her to die alone of a broken heart.

Parsifal learned the ways of chivalry and the knights' code of silence (in order not to appear ignorant of anything), then set out to find his mother once more. He got lost in a mysterious fog and came upon the Fisher King. At the king's castle, Parsifal witnessed a strange ceremonial procession led by a damsel carrying the Grail. From the Grail a huge feast came forth. Parsifal also noticed that the king was in pain, but said nothing for fear of seeming ignorant.

Parsifal fell asleep and woke up to find the Grail Castle empty. As Parsifal left the castle it disappeared. He conversed with an old witch who told him that all is lost because he foolishly didn't ask the question. Next Parsifal learned how his mother died. In his rage and shame Parsifal turned against God and wandered the land aimlessly for many years.

After experiencing all the ills that his mother had sought to keep him from, Parsifal comes upon a holy man. This man tells Parsifal that the Fisher King is Parsifal's uncle. Parsifal repents his sins and regains his innocence. He finds the Grail Castle once more and asks the question, "What ails thee, uncle?" The wound is healed and the wasteland restored to its natural state.

Next the film asks if the legend of the Grail could be true. It states that though Chrétien de Troyes was the first to make the legend famous in his twelfth-century writings, he only wrote of a magical chalice. It was Cistercian monks whose versions of the story made the chalice the one Christ drank from at the Last Supper.

These medieval writers Christianized stories that historians agree are rooted in much older Celtic tales from Britain and Ireland. During the age of the plague and the Crusades, the story of the Grail grew from parable to propaganda, justifying holy war.

The narrator states that Celts escaping Britain during the early Roman advance migrated to Brittany. Their legends of magic cauldrons and horns of plenty are the ones that were transmuted into the story of the Grail.

Though this film does not break any new ground, it does describe one tradition that is not usually included in other documentaries on the subject. In the sixteenth century, Henry VIII broke with the Roman church. In the face of persecution, the monks of Glastonbury Abbey fled to Nanteos Manor, taking with them the Grail. When the last of the monks died, the Grail was entrusted to the lord of Nanteos Manor and it was kept there for some 400 years.

The last lord of Nanteos Manor died in 1952 and that Grail has since disappeared. The approximately 5-inch-diameter cup of dark olive wood was in poor condition, but a photo was taken of it and is included on this tape.

Legends of the Isles: "Stonehenge" (1997)

52 minutes; Color; Documentary; Copyright 1997, Emdee Productions, Acorn Media

CREDITS: With Special Thanks to — Trinity College, Dublin, The National Trust; Produced with the support of investment incentives for the Irish Film Industry provided by the Government of Ireland; Devised by — Cormac Larkin; Narrator — Bosco Hogan; Expert Commentary: National Museum of Ireland — Pat Wallace; Stone Circle Builder — Ivan MacBeth; Writer — Count Nikolai Tolstoy; Research Assistants — Miranda Driscoll, Chris Jarvis, Tom O'Neill; Rostrum — Edd Condon; Graphic Design — Ian Jacobs; Electrical Facilities — Cine Electric, Ltd.; Electrician — Stephen Bruan; Lighting Cameraman — Peter Robertson; Camera Assistant — Russell Glesson; Sound Recordist — Brendan Campbell; Music by — Dave Foden; Production Coordinator — Tanya Gillen; Dubbing Facilities — Moynihan Russell; Dubbing Mixer — Cecily Loughman; Post Production Facilities — Screen Scene; On-Line Editor — Derek Stonebridge; Editor — Gareth Young; Writer — Mike Dunstan; Supervising Writer — Ed Fields; Produced by Emdee Productions and the Learning Channel in association with RTE; For the Learning Channel: Production Assistant — Charlie Foley; Executive Producer — Sandra Gregory; For Emdee Productions: Production Manager — Patricia Grennan; Executive Producer — Maria Anderton; Director — Stephen Rooke

SYNOPSIS: "Stonehenge" is the tenth episode of the 12-part made-for-television series *Legends of the Isles*. The series is available as a six-volume set or as individual tapes. Each tape contains two episodes, each episode runs for approximately 26 minutes.

As this tape points out, Stonehenge's main connection to Arthurian legend or romance is through Merlin. A twelfth-century tale, the narrator says, speaks of Merlin building Stonehenge using his magical arts. He is said to have constructed it from stones brought from Ireland.

It is supposed to be a monument to fallen British leaders, perhaps the victims of the "night of the long knives." (This was one of Hengist's plots for Saxon domination of Britain described first by Nennius in his *Historia Britonum*. Hengist had his men slaughter Vortigern's retinue during an ostensibly peaceful meeting.) Other stories tell of Merlin using Stonehenge for mysterious ceremonies.

The only part of these legends that is supported by archaeology is the fact that the massive stones were indeed transported to their present location on Salisbury Plain from somewhere else. The "blue stones," for instance, which were the first of the gigantic blocks to be erected, evidently were quarried in South Wales, some 125 miles away.

That, however, is as close as one can come to actually connecting Merlin to the great stone circle. Archaeological evidence shows that construction of Stonehenge began around 3,000 B.C. and that the first stone blocks were brought in around 2150 B.C.

The film does a credible job of reviewing the general history of all of the stone circles and similarly dated burial mounds that exist throughout the islands. Their possible uses as accurate celestial observatories and their apparent ties to ancient Earth and Sun deity worship are thoroughly discussed.

The above-mentioned connection to Merlin is, however, the extent of this film's examination of Stonehenge in Arthurian literature and legend.

Leonard Bernstein's Young People's Concerts: "What Is a Melody?" (1960)

107 minutes; Black and White; Prerecorded television broadcast before a live audience; Copyright 1960, 1962, Columbia Broadcasting Systems, Inc.; Copyright l990, 1993, Video Music Education, Inc.; Sony Classical Presentation; Sony Home Video #57440

CREDITS: Produced and Directed by — Roger Englander; Script by — Leonard Bernstein; Assistant to the Producer — Mary Rogers; Assistant to Mr. Bernstein — Jack Gottlieb; Assistant to the Director — John Corigliano, Jr.; Associate Director — Alvin R. Mifelow; Technical Directors — Sandy Bell, Ted Miller; Lighting Director — Gene Ulrich; Production Supervisor — Herman Glazer; Music Coordinator — John McClure; For the New York Philharmonic — Carlos Moseley, William Weissel, Clara Simons; For Philharmonic Hall — John Totten; Presented by — Video Music Education, Inc.; Executive Producer — Harry Kraut; Associate Producers — Louis Landerson, Marie Carter; Program Restoration — Gary Bradley, Michael Bronson, Thomas P. Skinner, John Walker, Elaine E. Warner; For the New York Philharmonic — Stephen Samas, Albert K. Webster, Frank Milburn, Allison Vulgamore; Distributed by — BETA Film GmbH; Executive in Charge — Klaus Hallig

SYNOPSIS: This tape consists of two recordings of a series of 1960s television broadcasts. They were filmed live at Lincoln Center in New York City.

The first segment, "The Sound of an Orchestra," discusses how each of the different instruments contribute to the effect of the whole orchestra. This section has no Arthurian content.

In the second portion of the tape, "What is a Melody?" (originally broadcast December 21, 1962), Bernstein explains the difference between a musical theme and the short repetitive melody that people are used to from popular music. In describing the construction of a piece of music from motive to phrase to sentence and so on, one of his prime examples is the Prelude to *Tristan and Isolde* by Richard Wagner.

Bernstein further points out that Wagner didn't use "tunes" to create melodies in his operas, but built directly from motives. The basic building blocks of the *Tristan und Isolde Prelude* are two four-note motives linked together at the last note of the first and the first note of the second. With harmony added underneath the theme created by the motives, a melody emerges though there is no "tune" anywhere in the piece.

Bernstein describes the Prelude as "one long passionate melody for almost ten minutes," building to a "hair-raising climax," which is created by counterpoint — another musical device which he clearly and thoroughly explains.

Lerner and Loewe Special (1996)

52 minutes; Black and White; Television special; Copyright 1996, Hollywood's Attic; Classic TV

CAST: Starring in order of appearance — Maurice Chevalier; Richard Burton; Julie Andrews; Robert Goulet; Stanley Holloway. Featuring Frances Sternhagen; Woodrow Parfrey; John Becher; John Harmon; Charles Nelson Reilley as "George"

CREDITS: Executive Producer — Norman Rosemont; Musical Director — Franz Allers; Music Arranged by — Robert Russell Bennett, Luther Henderson; Musical Continuity by — Trude Rittman; The Merrill Station Voices; Choreography by — Carol Haney; Art Director — Gary Smith; Costumes by — Alvin Colt; Makeup — Robert Phillippe; Hair Styles — Ernest Adler; Unit Manager — Richard K. Swicker; Video — Arnold Dick; Audio — Jim Blaney; Lighting Directors — Phil Hymes, Fred McKinnon; Associate Director — Robert Hopkins; Production Assistant — Patti Reuben; Technical Director — O. Tamburri; Associate Producer — Chiz Schultz; Produced and Directed by — Norman Jewison; An Alfred Production

SYNOPSIS: This is one of only three tapes with footage of Richard Burton and Julie Andrews doing scenes from the Broadway production of *Camelot.* Hosted by Maurice Chevalier, this was originally a television special. It includes scenes and songs from *Camelot, My Fair Lady, Paint Your Wagon* and *Gigi.*

At the 16-minute point on the tape Burton performs the scene of the knighting of Lancelot. When the ceremony is over, King Arthur is left alone in the hall. He soliloquizes about his agony over loving both Gwenevere and Lancelot but knowing that they are in love with each other. The scene on the tape runs for approximately 7 minutes and 30 seconds.

At the 30-minute point Chevalier does a rendition of the song "Camelot."

The Lesser Breed see under *The Adventures of Sir Lancelot*

Little Norse Prince Valiant (1968)
Alternate Titles: Prince of the Sun: The Great Adventure of Horus; (Taiyo no oji: Horusu no Daiboken); Not viewed; 16mm; Color; Cartoon; Copyright 1968, Tôei Dôga, Co.

CREDITS: Director — Isao Takahata; Writer — Kazuo Fukazawa; Producer — Isao Takahata; Music — Yoshio Mamiya; Camera — Jiro Yoshimura; Scene Design — Hayao Miyazaki; Animator — Yasua Otsuka; Art Director — Maji Urata

The Live Short Films of Larry Jordan (1988)
45 minutes; Color; Art/Live Action; Copyright 1988, Larry Jordan; Presented by Facets Multimedia, Inc.

CREDITS: The filmmaker received a production grant from the American Film Institute in association with the National Endowment for the Arts

SYNOPSIS: Included on this tape are three short films by noted film artist Larry Jordan. The third selection, *Magenta Geryon: A Film Concert,* is a three-part movie set to the music of three different composers. The second section, "In a Summer Garden," uses the music of Delius and is 16 minutes long.

"In a Summer Garden" consists of scenes in a beautiful garden with a small gazebo. There are many close-ups of lovely, fully blooming flowers of many colors. There are also shots of bees in the flowers. At one point a woman wearing a summer dress and a large sun hat, carrying a basket, walks from left to right, entering the garden. We never see the woman's face.

There are scenes of numerous bees on a single blossom, a black kitten frolicking around, the woman, back to the camera, puttering. At one point she is sitting on a bench with her basket of flowers; she gets up, picks a white bloom and smells it. She exits the garden.

The Facets Multimedia online catalogue description of this film states, "'In a Summer Garden' explores the mystery roots of the filmmaker's own passion for the world of bright blossoms, the mystical rose and the ancient gardens of Beardsley and King Arthur."

Lohengrin (1907)
Not viewed; Black and white; Silent; German

CAST: Henny Porten

Lohengrin (1936)
Not viewed; Black and White; Copyright 1936, Ventria, Italy; Distributed by Eia

CAST: Vittorio DeSica; Sergio Tofano
CREDITS: Nunzio Malasomma

Lohengrin (1947)
Not viewed; Black and White; Copyright 1947, Gennaro Proto, Italy

CAST: Antonio Cassinelli; Michele Malaspina; Jacqueline Plessis
CREDITS: Director — Max Calandri

Lohengrin (Bayreuth, 1982)
110 minutes; Color; Opera; Translation Copyright 1971, Lionel Salter; Copyright 1982, Unitel; Copyright 1989, Philips Classics Productions; Polygram Music Video/Philips Video Classics #070 511-3

CAST: Siegfried Vogel (King Heinrich); Peter Hoffman (Lohengrin); Karan Armstrong (Elsa von

Brabant); Leif Roar (Telramund); Elizabeth Connell (Ortrud); Bernd Weikle (Herald); Toni Krämer (Noble); Helmut Pampuch (Noble); Martin Egel (Noble); Heinz-Klaus Ecker (Noble); Natuse von Stegmann (Page); Irene Hermmann (Page); Patricia Lampert-Bucher (Page); Elke Burkert (Page)

CREDITS: A Production of Unitel Film und Fernsehproduktionsgesellschaft mbH and Company, Munich; Adaptation and Subtitling by — David Hogarth; Musical Director — Woldemar Nelsson; Staged and Directed by — Götz Friedrich; Stage Design — Günther Uecker; Costumes — Frieda Parmeggiani; Bayreuth Festival Chorus; Chorus Master — Norbert Balatsch; Bayreuth Festival Orchestra; Video Director — Brian Large; Artistic Supervision — Wolfgang Wagner

SYNOPSIS:
ACT 1

King Heinrich has come to Brabant to raise men for his army. After a nine-year peace, Hungary is about to attack. Count Friedrich of Telramund tells the king that as he lay dying, the duke of Brabant entrusted him with the care of his children, Elsa and Gottfried.

One day Elsa took Gottfried for a walk and the boy disappeared. Telramund states that Elsa seemed guilty, that he renounced his marriage claim on her and married Ortrud instead. He then accuses Elsa of killing Gottfried so that she might have sole claim on the land. He asks the King to judge his cause.

The king calls on Elsa who says she has had a vision of her champion: a knight in gleaming armor carrying a sword and a gold horn. King Heinrich declares a trial by mortal combat to learn God's will and the Herald calls for Elsa's champion. Finally on the third call Elsa adds her prayers to the summons and a knight arrives in a boat drawn by a swan.

This knight promises to champion and marry Elsa if she will vow never to ask his name, his lineage or where he came from. She agrees, the knight defeats Telramund, though he doesn't kill him, and there is great joy at the couple's happiness.

ACT 2

Just before dawn Telramund and Ortrud are arguing outside the castle. Telramund rages at her evil nature, stating it was she who told him Elsa had drowned her brother. Ortrud in turn calls Telramund a coward and uses her sorceress's power to prophesy that if the knight's name and lineage were revealed or if he were to lose even a single drop of blood, he would lose his power. Excited at the prospect of regaining his honor, Telramund swears with Ortrud to get revenge.

Elsa appears on her balcony and she and Ortrud converse. Invoking the power of the old gods, Ortrud wins Elsa's trust and Elsa invites her to accompany her to the cathedral for the wedding. As the sun rises, they enter together while Telramund watches from the shadows. "Thus," he says, "ruin enters that house."

On the morning of the wedding the herald announces the king's decree that Telramund is banned and disgraced for seeking God's justice with false intent. He also declares that the good knight shall rule over Brabant. The knight rejects the title of duke, but accepts "protector." In the meantime Telramund has talked four men into helping him against the knight.

Elsa and her bridal procession enter. Ortrud interrupts, telling everyone that Elsa can neither name her husband, prove his noble birth nor tell where he started his journey from. The knight asks Elsa if her heart has changed but she doesn't answer. Telramund appears and accuses the knight of sorcery and demands that he reveal his name. The knight refuses, stating that he must only answer such questions from Elsa.

Telramund and Ortrud both try to convince Elsa to get a drop of the knight's blood. The knight sends them away and the procession continues into the church.

ACT 3

In the bridal chamber Elsa cannot resist trying to find out her husband's name. She presses so hard that the knight is about to speak but he is interrupted when Telramund and his men break in. The knight kills Telra-

„Das süsse Lied verhallt,
Wir sind allein, zum ersten Mal allein
Seit wir uns sah'n!"

3362/6. Aus Oper Lohengrin.

3. AKT.

Antique German photo postcard from Wagner's opera *Lohengrin*. The line at the bottom is translated as: "The sweet song fades, we are alone, alone for the first time since we met."

"No need to thank me, my dear swan" — German postcard from Wagner's opera *Lohengrin*.

mund then, taking his ring back from Elsa, says he will reveal all to the assembled court.

Before the king and all the nobles, the knight finally tells his tale. He describes Monsalvat, a fortress standing where no mortal dwells. There a shining temple houses the Holy Grail. The knights who guard the Grail are protected by its power so long as their names are unknown. It is the Grail that sent him, the knight says, and Parsifal was his father. His name, he tells them, is Lohengrin, and he must now return to the Grail.

The swan reappears. Lohengrin leaves his sword for victory for Brabant, his horn to call for aid and his ring to be remembered by. Ortrud rushes in, declaring that it was her own sorcery which turned Gottfried into a swan. Lohengrin prays and the swan is transformed back into Gottfried.

Lohengrin disappears. Elsa collapses. Silently, the boy holds up the sword.

Lohengrin (The Met, 1986)

220 minutes; Color; Opera; German with English subtitles; Copyright 1986, The Metropolitan Opera Association; Bel Canto, Paramount Home Video #12610; A Gulf and Western Company

CAST: Anthony Raffell (The King's Herald); John Macurdy (King Henry); Leif Roar (Telramund); Eva Marton (Elsa); Peter Hofmann (Lohengrin); Leonie Rysanek (Ortrud); Charles Anthony (Noble); John Gilmore (Noble); John Darrencamp (Noble); Richard Vernon (Noble); George Caputo (Page); Matthew Dobkin (Page); Melissa Fogarty (Page); Gary Lorentzson (Page); Timothy Murtha (Page); Elizabeth Rogers (Page); Zachary Taylor (Page); Dana Watkins (Page); Christian Collins (Gottfried)

CREDITS: Conductor — James Levine; Production — August Everding; Set Designer — Ming Cho Lee; Costume Designer — Peter J. Hall; Lighting Designer — Gil Wechsler; Chorus Master — David Stivender; Musical Preparation — Walter Taussig, Max Epstein, Philip Eisenberg; Assistant Stage Directors — Phebe Berkowitz, Pamela McRae; Stage Band Conductor — Gildo Di Nunzio; Prompter — Philip Eisenberg; The Metropolitan Opera Orchestra; Personnel Manager — Abraham Marcus; Concert Master — Guy Lumia;

Librarian — John Grande; The Metropolitan Opera Chorus; Stage Managers — Stephen A. Brown, Stanley Levine, Stephen R. Berman, William McCourt; Stage Operations: Master Carpenter — Stephen Diaz; Master Electrician — Sander Hacker; Properties Master — Arthur Ashenden; Wig and Hair Stylist — Nina Lawson; Makeup Artist — Victor Callegari; Wardrobe Mistress — Millicent Hacker; This stage production of *Lohengrin* was made possible by a gift from the FAN FOX and Leslie B. Samuels Foundation, Inc., Mr. and Mrs. Samuel L. Tedlow and the Metropolitan Opera Guild.; The revival was made possible in part by a gift from the estate of John Henry von Hasseln.; Executive Producer — Michael Bronson; Producer — Samuel J. Paul; Directed by — Brian Large; Associate Producer — Karen Adler Barbosa; Associate Director — Jay Millard; Engineer in Charge — Mark Schubin; Lighting Consultant — John Leay; Audio Director — Jay David Saks; English Subtitles — Sonya Haddad; Senior Technician — Ron Wasburn; Technical Director — Emmett Longhran; Audio Supervisor — Bill King; Audio — Michael Shoskes, Mel Becker, Robert M. Tannenbaum; Video — William Steinberg, Paul Ranieri; Camera — Bill Akerlund, John Feher, Jake Ostroff, Ron Washburn, Juan Barrera, Manny Gutierrez, David Smith; Videotape — Alan Buchner; Electronic Graphics — Karen McLaughlin; Television Stage Managers — Terrence Benson, Lee Iglesias, Martha Yates; Score Reader — Richard Rondeau; Production Assistant — Bonnie Stylides; Production Secretary — Elizabeth J. Michel; Production Facilites — Unitel Mobile Video, Record Plant Studios, Home Video Post Production; Video — Alfred Muller, Nexus Productions, Inc.; Audio — Vin Gizzi; This television production was made possible by a major grant from the Texaco Philanthropic Foundation, Inc.; Additional funding was made possible by Pioneer Electronic Corporation, the National Endowment for the Arts and the Charles E. Culpeper Foundation.; From a live broadcast, January 10, 1986

SYNOPSIS: This is one of the more straightforward presentations of a Wagner opera. Without exotic sets, modernized costumes or added-on scenes, this production of *Lohengrin* retains a classic look. For a complete synopsis of each act of Wagner's *Lohengrin,* see the entry for *Lohengrin* (Bayreuth, 1982).

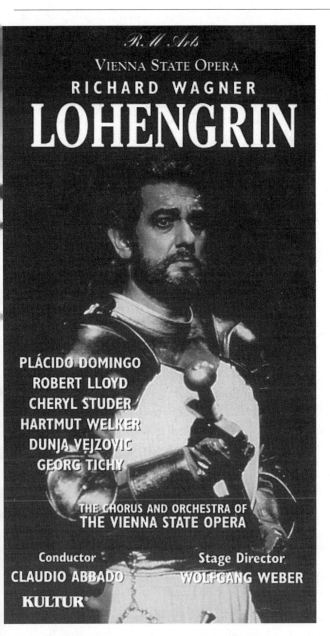

Video cassette art of the Vienna State Opera's 1990 production of *Lohengrin* (courtesy Kultur Video).

Lohengrin (Vienna State Opera, 1990)

223 minutes; Color; Opera; German with English subtitles; Copyright 1990, RM Arts; KULTUR Video #0003

CAST: King Henry (Robert Lloyd); Lohengrin (Placido Domingo); Elsa of Brabant (Cheryl Studer); Frederick of Telramund (Hartmut Welker); Ortrud (Dunja Vejzovic); The King's Herald (Georg Tichy); Bojidar Nikolov (Brabantian Count); Franz Kaseman (Brabantian Count); Claudio Otelli (Brabantian Count); Peter Köves (Brabantian Count); Silvia Panzenböck (Page); Ingrid Sieghart (Page); Ulrike Erfurt (Page); Johanna Graupe (Page); Renate Polacek (Lady of Honor); Gretchen Eder (Lady of Honor); Elisabeth Kudrna (Lady of Honor); Eva-Maria Thor (Lady of Honor); Karl Scheiner (Count Godfrey, Elsa's Brother

PLACE: Antwerp

TIME: First half of the tenth century

CREDITS: Orchestra of the Osterreichische Bundestheater; Conductor — Ralf Hossfeld; The Chorus of the Vienna State Opera; Chorus Master — Helmuth Froschauer; The Orchestra of the Vienna State Opera; Conductor — Claudio Abbado; Set Design — Rudolf Heinrich, Reinhard Heinrich; Producer — Wolfgang Weber; Directed for Television by — Brian Large; Production Assistant — Bruno Berger; Technical Manager — Hans Langer; Lighting Designer — Robert Stangl; Property Master — Pantelis Dessyllas; Head of Wardrobe — Alice M. Schlesinger; Makeup — Willi Riede; Camera — Helmut Fibich, Walter Hendl, Wolfgang Hirschl, Hans Victor Keppler, Peter Parth, Walter Rektorik, Gertraud Vala; Vision Mixer — Gerhard Braunsberger; Lighting — Rudolf Widmar, Franz Straub; Vision Control — Sylvia Keller, Christian Bruss; Videotape Editors — Wolfgang A. Hermann, Johannes Burkl; Sound — Gregor Hornacek, Peter Zwingelsberger, Niki Neuspiel; Audio Director — Miroslav Svoboda; Production Manager — Walter Marek; Assistant to the Director — Barbara Matula; Production Director — Ernst Neuspiel; Coordinating Producer — Gerald Szyszkowitz; Executive Producer — Franz Kabelka; Produced by ORF/BR/RM Arts in association with the Vienna State Opera and Pioneer LDC, Inc.; Distributed Worldwide by RM Associates

SYNOPSIS: One of the nice features of this version of *Lohengrin* is that it has some of the most complete subtitling of any of the operas. In the duets, for instance, both parts are written on the screen. Though a bit more of a reading strain, it makes the story more complete. These tapes are of a live performance before an audience, complete with curtain calls.

On the other hand, one is not apt to see worse swordfight choreography than here. Opera of course is focused on music, but there was apparently almost no time at all spent on making this part of the scant action even slightly realistic. The big draw to this performance is Placido Domingo's appearance as Lohengrin. A favorite opera tenor, his fame is perhaps second only to that of Luciano Pavarotti.

See the description of each act of *Lohengrin* at the entry for *Lohengrin (Bayreuth, 1982)*.

Lohengrin (Bayreuth, 1990)

215 minutes; Color; Opera; German with English subtitles; Copyright 1990, Unitel; Copyright 1993, Philips Classics Productions

CAST: Paul Frey (Lohengrin); Cheryl Studer (Elsa); Gabriele Schnaut (Ortrud); Ekkehard Wlaschiha (Telramund); Manfred Schenk (King Henry); Eike Wilm Schulte (Heerufer); Clemens Bieber (Vier Edle); Peter Maus (Vier Edle); Robert Riener (Vier Edle); Heinz-Klaus Ecker (Vier Edle); Rachel Robins (Edelknaben); Natue Von Stegmann (Edelknaben); Katalin Benei (Edelknaben); Akiko Makiyama (Edelknaben); Sarah Fulgoni (Edeldamen); Kriemhild Stettner (Edeldamen); Helen Lawson (Edeldamen); Isolde Claassen (Edeldamen); Martin Beier (Edeldamen); Yehudit Silcher (Edeldamen); Kristina Gloge (Edeldamen); Philippa Thompson (Edeldamen)

CREDITS: Conducted by — Peter Schneider; Staged and Directed by — Werner Herzog; Stage Design and Costumes — Hennin Von Gierke; Chorus Master — Norbert Balatsch; Orchestra and Chorus of the Bayreuth Festival; Video Director — Brian Large; Artistic Supervision — Wolfgang Wagner; Technical Director — Walter Huneke; Lighting — Manfred Voss; Costume Realization — Heike Ammer, Renate Stoiber; Makeup — Inge Landgraf, Hans-Rudolf Müller; Musical Assistance — Ed Spanjaard, Johannes Mikkelsen, Theodor Gress, Helmut Weese; Lighting — Heinz Müller-Grassmann; Assistant Directors — Charles Ebert, Hartwolf Stipetic; Choral Assistance — Milan Maly, Julius Asbeck, Michael Graves; Technical Director (Video) — Dieter Grohmann; Audio Producer — John M. Mordler; Sound — Gernot R. Westhäuser, Josef Wanninger, Andreas Stange, Werner Roth; Film Editor — Inge Marschner; Videotape Editor — Ivo Taschner; Production Managers — Ingunn Sievers, Franco Pizzorno; Executive Producer — Horant H. Hohlfeld; Translation — Lionel Salter; Adapted by — David Hogarth; Subtitling — Paola Simonetti; A production of Unitel Films — und Fernseh — produktionsgesellschaft mbH & Co., Munich

SYNOPSIS: A typically well done Bayreuth production of *Lohengrin* with some atypical stage effects. Though this one was obviously performed strictly for the cameras, Bayreuth's stagings always give the feeling of a live-audience presence.

Also typical of Bayreuth, there is little or no deviation from Wagner's storyline. The major differences between this and other versions of *Lohengrin* are in the above-mentioned effects. Particularly noteworthy are the almost imperceptible merging of painted scenes into actual stage settings, the cloud tunnel effect marking the approach of the swan-drawn boat and the shoreline scene in act 2.

Act 1 has the troops of Brabant gathered on a snow-covered field to welcome King Henry. A nine-year truce with Hungary is at an end and the Hungarians are preparing to attack Germany. Henry is traveling the country to gather his army together. He finds Brabant in disarray and without a leader. Questioning Frederik of Telramund the king learns that young Gottfried, the rightful heir to the throne of Brabant, has disappeared under mysterious circumstances and Frederik accuses Gottfried's sister, Elsa, of killing the boy.

The king has Elsa brought before him but she offers no defense. The king decides that she must choose a champion to defend her honor against Telramund's accusation and the herald calls for her knight. After some delay a boat towed by a swan arrives carrying a knight who takes Elsa's cause under the condition that she never ask of him his name, his lineage or where he came from. Elsa agrees, the two vow their love for each other and the knight defeats Telramund in single combat.

In marked contrast with the quality of the rest of the film, this fight and the swords used by the two men are the worst parts of the movie. The knight's sword is an over-long wavy-bladed thing that looks like it came from a Conan movie. Telramund seems to wield a gnarled old tree branch rather than a sword. The fight itself consists of the knight fanning the air three times in slow motion with his silvery blade and Telramund falling to the ground, defeated but unharmed.

In act 2 it is revealed that Telramund's wife, Ortrud, has been the one goading him on in this venture. She is something of a sorceress who is greedy for the power that will come from her husband being the king of Brabant. She calls on the old gods to help her defeat this mysterious knight. Her plot involves turning Elsa against her vow never to ask the knight's name. She and Telramund continue their efforts right to the door of the church as the wedding procession enters.

Act 3 opens in what is usually the bridal chamber but in this version becomes a green field. The wedding bed, with its swan headboard, sits in the middle of a circle of stones under the open sky. The knight and Elsa have a long discussion in which Elsa is unable to resist asking the fatal questions. Before he can answer though, the knight is attacked by Telramund and his men. The knight kills Telramund, then tells Elsa that he will reveal all but only before the gathered court and the king.

In the final scene the knight tells the story of Monsalvat, a castle far away where is kept the Holy Grail. He tells everyone that he is one of the Grail's knights, that his father is Parzival and that his own name is Lohengrin. Because he has revealed all of this he must leave but before going he frees the swan from the golden chains binding it to the boat. The swan turns out to be the young Gottfried, trapped in swan form by the conniving Ortrud. Lohengrin declares Gottfried the true leader of Brabant and as the Grail knight departs, the opera ends with Elsa and Ortrud reaching for each other in silence.

Lon Chaney: Behind the Mask, Volume 5

Double Feature: *The Shock* and *The Light of Faith*; *The Light of Faith*— 30 minutes; Silent; B&W, Tinted; Live action; Originally, 1922; Copyright 1995, Film Preservation Associates; A Kino International Release

CAST: Lon Chaney (Tony Pantelli); Hope Hampton (Elaine)

CREDITS: Director—Clarence Brown; Musical Setting—Hank Troy; Restored Version Produced by—Adam Reilly; Scenario by—Clarence Brown, William Dudley Pelley; Based on Pelley's story; Photographed by—Alfred Ortlieb, Ben Carre; Music Arranged and Directed by—Robert Israel; Digitally Mastered from archival prints; Featuring musical sound tracks; Special contents of this edition ©1995 Film Preservation Associates; Presented by Select Safety Film Service, Providence, R.I. (1922); *The Light of Faith* is abridged from *The Light in the Dark*

SYNOPSIS: *Lon Chaney: Behind the Mask* is a series of eight video tapes available from Kino International. *The Shock* and *The Light of Faith* is volume five of the series. *The Light of Faith* stars Lon Chaney in one of the most unusual Grail stories on film in which the Holy Grail finds its way to America in the 1920s.

Chaney, known as the "Man of a Thousand Faces," is best remembered for roles he took on as horribly disfigured characters. *The Hunchback of Notre Dame* (1923), *The Phantom of the Opera* (1925), and *Where East Is East* (1929) are just a few examples. Less well remembered are a number of films in which he portrayed criminals. None of Chaney's "bad guys," however, were all bad. As Chaney himself is quoted as saying on the back of this video tape's jacket, "I have dozens of letters from convicts … and all say the same thing: that they appreciate my characters because no matter how evil they are, there is always some redeeming spot of good in them."

In *The Light of Faith*, Chaney's Tony Pantelli is just such a character, a thief with a heart of gold. The story opens with a young lady making her way up a sidewalk to the front steps of a rooming house. The landlady shows her to a one-room flat and takes the girl's last dollar as payment. On entering the building, the girl attracted the eye of the other roomer in the house, Tony. He debates knocking on her door, but looking at his own ragged appearance, thinks better of it.

In the meantime, as the titles in the film put it, "Across the ocean in Southern England, Warburton Ashe is trying to forget that he's an unhappy man." We find Ashe bird hunting with a dog and valet. They stop to rest and Ashe pulls a letter out of his jacket pocket. Shown on the screen the letter closes, "...and neither lawyers nor detectives are able to find her. Come back and help, Warburton, like a man. Affectionately, your sister, Bernice."

Suddenly, Ashe's dog points, then runs off into the woods. Following the dog, Ashe is led into the ruins of an old stone building. The dog digs and turns up a large dirt-encrusted cup. Ashe takes the thing with him. He and his valet stop in at a pub on the way home that evening and one of the old fellows there states that it reminds him of tales of the Holy Grail. Ashe decides that he will catch the first boat back home.

The girl, meanwhile, has been unable to find work. Exhausted, she collapses on the steps. Tony hears the noise and finds her prostrate in the hall. Holding her, he finds a business card in her otherwise empty purse, which conveniently popped open in the fall. The card is from J. Warburton Ashe and the address on it is 990 Fifth Avenue. Tony carries the girl up to her bed. The landlady comes along and fusses about while Tony disappears, then returns with a tray full of food. A doctor is called and he determines that the girl has either been working too hard or is worrying about something.

The titles state, "Followed days when an overwrought mind drifted into delirium." Tony tries everything to cheer the girl up. One day he brings her a newspaper and some flowers. Before she notices the flowers, the girl reads the headline in the paper: "Is the Holy Grail in New York?" and the subheading, "Did J. Warburton Ashe, fleeing from Haunting Memories of a Dead Love, find the Phantom cup of Lord Tennyson's poem in an English wood?" She collapses on the pillows on her bed.

Tony reads the headlines and asks, "Say, what is this Holy Graill, anyway?" The girl begins the story with "Tradition says that the cup from which the Master drank at the Last Supper was carried to Britain where it disappeared, and none could find it. At last, in the reign of King Arthur...." The scene shifts to King Arthur's time. We see Galahad (Ashe of course) sitting by a pond where a beautiful maiden (the girl) soon joins him. She tells Galahad of a dream she had the night before. Now the scene switches to the maiden asleep in bed. A shaft of moonlight comes through her window, waking her up. Down the moon beams, as if floating in a soap bubble, hovers the Holy Grail. It slides closer to the maiden's outstretched arms, but disappears before reaching her.

The maiden tells Galahad, "Thou art the Knight, dear Galahad, to find the Holy Grail and all the world be healed." The maiden next renounces the world until Galahad's return, cuts her hair and braids from it a girdle for his sword. Arriving at the abbey to say goodbye, Galahad vows never again to seek her until he finds the Grail. And so, he fights his way through a hundred lands, this "White Knight" as the film calls him and indeed finds the Grail. Galahad returns on a snowy Christmas eve and brings the Grail to the abbey. There, the glowing cup is set upon an altar and people come from all around to be healed.

Now cognizant of the cup's powers, Tony decides on a rash course of action. He goes to Ashe's home to get the Grail to heal this girl he's obviously fallen in love with. Ashe asks if it is Elaine who sent him (finally we know her name!), but Tony won't reveal where she is. Ashe of course is not about to be intimidated by this ruffian and attempts to use a pistol to be rid of Tony, but Tony knocks Ashe out with one punch. Tony steals the Grail from Ashe's mantle, sneaks it up to Elaine's room and convinces her, in spite of her resistance, to touch the glowing Chalice.

The Grail does its work and Elaine is healthy once more, but her heart is still broken by the rift between herself and Ashe. Tony sneaks into her room again the next day, to get the Grail and return it to Ashe's home, but the police are waiting for him.

Tony is taken to night court. Just as Ashe is about to identify the culprit, the judge interrupts and asks to see the Grail. When he is told that it glows in the dark and works miracles, the judge has the lights turned off. Sure enough, the Grail glows and a moonbeam comes in the window, illuminating the Grail and Ashe himself. The heavenly light has a deep impact on Ashe. When the trial starts up again he says he was mistaken, that Tony is not the man.

Ecstatic that her man has freed the good-hearted Tony, Elaine goes to Ashe and they look lovingly upon one another. Tony watches ruefully and when they notice him he smiles, puts on his cap and slowly departs.

The ending is no surprise, though in spite of one's happiness for Elaine and Ashe, the melancholy of Tony's life is oppressive. This back street Galahad is no pure White Knight, but he has his moments. Chaney's Tony is reminiscent of many vaudevillian characters, sad clowns like Chaplin and later television personalities like Red Skelton's mimings as well as Jackie Gleason's.

Tony's exit from the final scene is made all the more poignant by director Clarence Brown's use of light. As Tony stops outside the courtroom doors, he is silhouetted in one of the translucent panels. He lights up a cigarette and just as he exhales a puff of smoke, the silhouette of a police officer appears in the other pane. The officer waves Tony away from the doors, and the sad Tony wanders off.

Some of the charm of silent films are the exaggerated, now stereotyped motions and actions the actors incorporated into their techniques. Elaine's fall down the rooming house staircase is of course preceded by the classic back of the hand to the forehead maneuver. The eyelash battings and flutterings, the clasped hands over the heart, the heavily made up wide-eyed looks directly into the camera lens, all are here in this short film.

The story itself is a charmer as well. That the Holy Grail should be found by an American (albeit one with a very British sounding name) and brought to the States to heal a love gone sour is unique.

Lost in Space: "The Questing Beast" (1967)

Approximately 1 hour; Color; Live Action; Copyright 1967, Space Productions; 20th Century–Fox Television, Inc.

CAST: Guy Williams (Prof. John Robinson); June Lockhart (Maureen Robinson); Mark Goddard (Maj. Don West); Marta Kristen (Judy Robinson); Angela Cartwright (Penny Robinson); Billy Mumy (Will Robinson); Jonathan Harris (Dr. Zachary Smith); Bob May (Robot); Dick Tufeld (Voice of Robot); Hans Conreid (Sir Sagramonte); Sue England; Jeff County

CREDITS: Creator/Producer — Irwin Allen; Writer — Carey Wilbur; Director — Don Richardson; Associate Producer — William Faralla; Story Editor — Anthony Wilson; Director of Photography — Frank Carson; Music — Cyril Mockridge; Music Supervision — Lionel Newman; Production Supervisor — Jack Sonntag; Production Associate — Hal Herman; Unit Production Manager — Ted Butcher; Post Production Supervisor — George F. Swink; Art Directors — Jack Martin Smith, Robert Kinoshiten; Set Decorators — Walter M. Scott, James Hassinger; Costumes Designed by — Paul Zastupnevich; Film Editor — Frederic Baratta; Special Photographic Effects — L.B. Abbott, A.S.C.; Makeup Supervision — Ben Nye; Hairstyling — Margaret Donaovan; Production Coordinator — Les Warner; Supervising Sound Effects Editor — Don Hall, Jr.; Sound Effects Editor — Frank White; Theme — Johnny Williams; Executive in charge of production for Van Bernard — Guy Della Cioppa; Color by DeLuxe; Assistant Director — Gil Mandelik; Supervising Music Editor — Leonard A. Engel; Music Editor — Joseph Ruby; Post Production Coordinator — Robert Mintz; Astronomical Photographs Copyright 1959 by The California Institute of Technology; An Irwin Allen Production in association with Jodi Productions, Inc., 20th

Century–Fox Television, Inc., and CBS Television Network; William Self in charge of Production; Filmed at the Hollywood studios of 20th Century–Fox Television, Inc.

SYNOPSIS: *Lost in Space* was a television series that ran for three seasons from 1965 to 1968. Loosely based on *The Swiss Family Robinson* by Johann David and Johann Rudolf Wyss, this show placed the Robinsons in the future of 1997 aboard the spaceship *Jupiter 2*. This first colonization effort to Alpha Centauri is sabotaged by a spy from a foreign country. The spy gets trapped on board, the ship's navigational system is damaged and the family and their tagalong nemesis go adventuring through the universe.

"The Questing Beast" was the 17th episode of the second season. A space knight named Sir Sagramonte stops at the planet the Robinsons currently inhabit. Sagramonte is after a dragon which he finally corners in this show. Finding out that the thing is an intelligent female, he decides not to kill her.

Though it could be argued that this episode's story bears similarities to Cervantes' *Don Quixote* the Arthurian references are far stronger. It is a "questing beast" in Malory (book 1, chapter 19) that King Pellinore is after, though this strange animal is no dragon. From its belly came the sound of 30 baying hounds. After Pellinore's death Sir Palomides took up the hunt.

The space knight, Sagramonte, seems to have taken his name from Arthurian tales. The name is nearly identical to that of a knight of the Round Table known in Malory as Sagramore le Desirous. This fellow appears in four of Chrétien's stories as Sagremor the Unruly. Oddly, in nearly all of the films that are based on Twain's *A Connecticut Yankee in King Arthur's Court*, it is Sir Sagramore who captures the Yankee and takes him to Camelot. Twain, however, wrote of Sir Kay the Seneschal capturing the man from the future, not Sagramore.

Lovespell (1979)

91 minutes; Color; Live Action; Copyright 1979, Clar Productions; Continental Video #1019 (no longer available)

CAST: Richard Burton (King Mark); Kate Mulgrew (Isolt); Nicholas Clay (Tristan); Cyril Cusack (Gormond of Ireland); Geraldine Fitzgerald (Bronwyn); Niall Toibin (Andred); Diana van der Vlis (Alex); Niall O'Brien (Gorvenal); Kathryn Dowling (Yseult of the White Hand); John Jo Brooks (Father Colm); Trudy Hayes (Anne); John Scanlon (Bishop); Bobby Johnson (William the Guard); John Labine (Eoghanin)

CREDITS: Costume Designer — Mary O'Donnell; Production Designer — John Lucas; Casting — Shirley Rich; Title theme composed and arranged by Paddy Moloney and played by The Chieftains; Editor — Russell Lloyd, A.C.E., G.B.T.E.; Director of Photography — Richard H. Kline, A.S.C.; Executive Producer — Thomas H. Ryan; Writer — Claire Labine; Producers — Tom Hayes, Clair Labine; Director — Tom Donovan; Editorial Consultant — Ralph Rosenblum; First Assistant Director — Barry Blackmore; Unit Production Manager — Peter Holder; Assistant Producer — Douglas Hughes; Continuity — Pat Rambaut; Assistant Editors — Ben Gibney, Robert Dwyer-Joyce; Assistant Editor — Bill Parnell; Camera Operator — Al Bettcher; Focus Puller — David Fitzgerald; Clapper Loader — D. Whetan; Gaffer — Jack Conroy; Electricians — Derek Hide, Tommy Durnam, Joe Goodwin; General Operator — John Cohen; Chief Grip — Luke Quigley; 2nd Grip — John Murphy; Stand-by Rigger — Pascal Jones; Stagehand — Jimmy Lowe; Dubbing Editor — Peter Best, G.B.T.E.; Assistant Dubbing Editors — Pat Brennan, Chris Lloyd; Sound Mixers — Tom Curran, Liam Saurin; Makeup — Ron Berkeley; Assistant Makeup — Alan Golgoss; Hairdresser — John Havelin; Construction Manager — Tommy Bassett; Stand-by Carpenters — L. O'Toole, Eddie Humphries; Changehand Carpenter — Benny McLaughlin; Changehand Painter — Owen Mumane; Set Decorator — Arden Cantley; Dressing Props — Kevin Hudson; Stand-by Props — P. J. Smith, Bobby Dunne; Falconer — Dr. Heinz Meng; Peregrine Tiercels — Adam's Brother, Prince Albert; Unit Publicity — John Scanlon, Maeve Fitzgibbon; Still Photographer — William Eddy; Production Accountant — John Moore; Production Secretary — Marie McFerran; Account Secretary — Anna Hayes; Catering — Matt Dowling; Irish Casting — Nuala Moiselle; Location Rushes — Annie Furlong; Projectionist — Paddy Byrne; Film Rushes — Skyway Intercity Couriers; Assistant to

Richard Burton — Robert Wilson; Transport Captain — Arthur Dunne; Drivers — Jackie Dunne, Michael Gilligan, Sunny O'Brien, Frank King, Martin Murphy, Peter Hill, Seamus McCabe, Jimmy Doyle, Johnny Gilbert, James Hurley; Heavy Transport — Jimmy Lowe; Special Transport — Paul Wolfe, Currency Advisor — John Crowley; Titles — G.S.E., Ltd.; Additional Music — Film Sounds, Inc.; Film processing at — Rank Film Laboratories, Limited; Dubbing at — National Film Studios of Ireland; Lenses and Panaflex Cameras by — Panavision; Filmed entirely on location in the Republic of Ireland; Special thanks to Joseph Condon, curator, Caher Castle, Bob Brown, the Scariff Dramatic Society, the Board of Works, the Captain and Crew of the Gull Marne and to the people of the Republic of Ireland, particularly of Caher Co., Tipperary, Corofin Co., and Oughterard Co. Galway

SYNOPSIS: "It is believed that in Cornwall in the sixth century, there ruled a king named Mark whose warrior nephew Tristan was his adopted son and heir. The story of these two men and the Irish princess Isolt has been told in many forms and variations for fourteen hundred years..." Those words open the film *Lovespell* and indeed, this movie adds another variation to the legends of Tristan and Isolde. It in fact reverses many of the elements of the traditional stories.

Perhaps the most surprising switch in *Lovespell* is the very beginning when King Mark pays a personal visit to Gormond of Ireland. We learn that Morholt, Gormond's brother-in-law, has been killed by Mark's nephew Tristan. The giant warrior, as Mark calls Morholt, stole much from Cornwall in his rampages and Mark is seeking a reckoning. Gormond states that Morholt probably stole as much from him as from Cornwall and he would just as soon give all that is in Morholt's coffers to Mark. However, with advancing age Gormond is concerned about the disbursement of his properties and wealth, particularly in providing for his daughter Isolt after his death. He tells Mark to give him an estimate of his losses and they will be gladly repaid.

Isolt is summoned and Mark is immediately taken with the younger woman. She too

is delighted to learn that her detestable uncle is no more. When she hears that Tristan was severely wounded in the battle and seems not to be healing, she tells Mark to send him to her, that she is a healer.

During his short visit Mark and Isolt strike up a real friendship and on his departure they exchange heartfelt gifts. Mark, however, comes away with a much deeper interpretation of their easy conviviality and by the time he reaches home he has determined to ask for Isolt's hand in marriage.

The only potential stumbling block that Mark can see is his word to Tristan. He realizes that since adopting Tristan and declaring him his heir, the young man would have the right to object to Mark's marriage. Should Mark have children by Isolt, Tristan could be denied an inheritance. Mark actually asks Tristan's approval but Tristan makes no objection at all.

Wounded but by no means bedridden, Tristan is glad to go to Ireland for Mark to convey the marriage request and perhaps be healed as well. There is an instant spark of attraction between Isolt and Tristan which only grows as they become more intimate through her ministrations.

Gormond counsels Isolt to accept Mark's proposal, but by the time they are due to leave for Cornwell, Bronwyn, their old serving lady, has seen the dangerous attraction between the young couple. She has concocted and gives to Isolt a love potion which she insists that Isolt drink with Mark as soon as she arrives in his home.

On board the ship what little will power the two had breaks down completely and Tristan and Isolt consummate their love. The very night they arrive in Cornwall, Tristan finds his way to Isolt's room. Isolt takes out the potion, pours it and drinks it with Tristan instead of Mark.

In spite of all this the marriage between Isolt and Mark does take place. Their relationship deteriorates rapidly, however, when Isolt has no skill to be a loving wife with so much passion being spent on Tristan. Mark eventually catches them together and condemns Tristan to death. Isolt runs off and a friend helps Tristan escape. Tristan finds Isolt and the two try to get away but Mark and his men soon catch up with them.

Relenting somewhat, Mark banishes Tristan and brings Isolt home. Tristan goes to Brittany only to be attacked and mortally wounded. The sympathetic connection between the lovers is such that Isolt falls ill and takes to her bed. Tristan gets word to Isolt that he needs her, but she is too ill to make the journey. Amazingly, Mark sails to Brittany to bring Mark back. He tells Isolt that if Tristan is alive on his return he will have a white sail on the boat. If not, the sail will be shrouded in black.

On the way back to Cornwall Tristan tells Mark the whole truth of his involvements with Isolt. Mark, incensed, makes it clear to Tristan that he only planned to bring him to Isolt in order to save her life. He has no intention of letting her go. His rage is such, howver, that he goes on deck, followed by Tristan, and cuts the rope holding the black shroud above the sail. Isolt, who has dragged herself out to watch the ship approach, sees the sail go black and falls from the cliff to the rocks below.

Having witnessed her fall, Tristan hurls himself overboard. In a last act of compassion Mark dives in after him and tows him to shore. Tristan struggles towards Isolt, and then just reaching her, the lovers die together.

MacGyver: "Good Knight MacGyver" (1991)

Television series episode; Approximately 60 minutes; Color; Live Action; Copyright 1991, Paramount Pictures, Inc.

CAST: Richard Dean Anderson (Angus MacGyver); Dana Elcar (Pete Thornton, King Arthur); Bruce McGill (Jack Dalton); Tim Winters (Merlin); Lynne Harbaugh (Cecilia); Robin Strasser (Morgana); William H. Bassett (Ian M'Iver); Christopher Neame (Duncan); Colm Meaney (Irwin Malcolm); Christopher Collet; Peter Vogt; Mark Holton; Harry Victor; David L. Considine (Balladeer); Nolan Hamings (Page)

CREDITS: Writer — John Considine; Director — Michael Vejar; Executive Producers — Henry Winkler, John Rich, Stephen Downing; Co-Producer — John Sheppard; Coordinating Producer — Thomas R. Polizzi; Creative Consultant — Rick Mittleman; Executive Story Consultant — Brad Radnitz; Story Consultant — John Considine; Associate Producer — Sara Thornberg; Music — Ken Harrison; Theme — Randy Edelman; Casting — Mark Tillman, C.S.A.; Casting Associate — Russell Gray; Director of Photography — Jack Whitman; Production Designer — Reg Raglan; Editor — Ron Binkowski; Unit Production Managers — Joseph M. Ellis, David Menteer; First Assistant Director — Jerry Fleck; Second Assistant Director — Tomaz Remec; Art Directors — Robb Bacon, Stephen M. Berger; Set Decorator — Charles Pierce; Special Effects — Henry Millar; Script Supervisor — Jan Rudolph; Costume Supervisor — Tommy Welsh; Costumes — Bernadette O'Brien, Robert Moore, Jr., Danielle Veber-Feller; Makeup — Marvin Westmore; Hairstylist — Vivian McAteer; Stunt Coordinator — Vince Deadrick, Jr.; Location Manager — Michael Jarvis; Property Master — Dean Wilson; Sound Mixer — James LaRue; Music Editor — Steve Danforth; Production Coordinator — Rosie Dean; Supervising Sound Editor — Thierry Couturier; Post Production Facility — Modern Videofilm; Visual Effects Supervisor — Elan Soltes; Visual Effects Animator — Adam Howard; Camera Equipment by Otto Nemenz International, Inc.; A Henry Winkler/John Rich Production in association with Paramount, a Gulf & Western Company

SYNOPSIS: *MacGyver* was an adventure series that ran on television for seven seasons, from 1985 to 1992. "Good Knight MacGyver" was a two-parter (episodes 132 and 133) from the seventh season, airing in November 1991.

"Good Knight MacGyver" is an adaptation of Twain's *A Connecticut Yankee in King Arthur's Court*. MacGyver goes to a genealogist where he learns that his ancestry is traceable back to the seventh century. During that time one Ian M'Iver (the name changed over the centuries) had been wrongly accused of something and died in prison.

After leaving the genealogist's office, MacGyver sees a planter box about to fall on a fellow in a tuxedo on the sidewalk ahead of him. Racing to push the man out of the way, the box hits MacGyver instead, knocking him unconscious. MacGyver wakes up in Arthur's Britain.

In fact, he wakes up at a joust between Sirs Duncan and Galahad. Duncan injures Galahad, MacGyver takes his place and uses a rope as a lasso since he has no armor or weapons. This doesn't win him the friendship of Duncan of course. Presented to King Arthur, MacGyver learns that Ian M'Iver has been accused of having sided with Arthur's half sister, Morgana, in her plots to destroy Arthur.

Trying to figure out who this stranger is, Arthur declares a battle of magic between Merlin and MacGyver. MacGyver wins by lighting a match. A short time later Arthur collapses. Recognizing the symptoms of poisoning, MacGyver saves the king's life. In gratitude Arthur tells MacGyver he must be knighted and must ride with Merlin to stop Morgana. Morgana has let word out that she will test a new weapon she has acquired on Cecilia, Galahad's betrothed, whom she holds captive.

Duncan interferes, however, by "discovering" evidence that Merlin poisoned Arthur. Merlin is tied up in his own quarters pending a trial and MacGyver goes there to analyze the poison. Using materials at hand, MacGyver determines that it is a "binary poison," one that is not supposed to exist for another 1,000 years. The ore it's made from comes only from Scotland, Caledonia, or, as Merlin and everyone else call it, Morgana Country.

At a meeting of the Knights of the Round Table, Duncan stirs them up against Merlin. The wizard is tied to a stake to be burned, but MacGyver shows up just in time with a makeshift fire extinguisher. He exposes Duncan as the traitor and Duncan escapes. Arthur knights MacGyver and gives him a gift — a necklace with a metallic tube containing "the Royal Favor, reserved only for Knights of the Round Table." Arthur sends MacGyver and Merlin to rescue Cecilia and stop Morgana.

The two find Morgana's Cave of Darkness where they are promptly trapped by Duncan. Morgana appears, however, to kill Duncan and leave Merlin and MacGyver hanging, literally, over a pit of lava, ending part 1.

Part 2 opens with MacGyver saving them by using his Swiss Army knife as a climbing device. They make their way to Morgana's castle, sneak inside and find her laboratory. The supplies that are there are all the components for making gunpowder. The heroes find Cecilia, but she won't leave unless they help the fellow in the next cell. It's Ian M'Iver. They release him from his chains, but he dies. Ian did, however, leave some writing on his prison wall — a message for his son, Angus.

Morgana catches the three of them and locks them in the cell. Using Merlin's odd assortment of supplies, the quill stays and silk from Cecilia's dress and Merlin's wine skin, MacGyver manufactures a kite, a balloon and some hydrogen. He also has Merlin cut his cape into a single long strip, using MacGyver's Swiss Army knife. Merlin is so fascinated with the scissors incorporated in the knife that MacGyver gives it to him as a token of friendship.

As MacGyver constructs his equipment, Morgana experiments with her gunpowder and a blunderbuss she has. She tries it out on one of her own guards, killing the man.

Floating the kite out the cell window with the balloon and attaching it to the long strip of cloth from Merlin's cape, MacGyver rigs the door lock with some gunpowder. The kite attracts and conducts lightning down the cloth, blasting the cell door open and starting a fire. The three are almost out of the castle when Morgana catches up with them, wielding her gun. She fires it at MacGyver, hitting him in the forehead. The blast knocks her backwards into her lab, and all the powder there explodes, killing her in the process. MacGyver collapses as Merlin and Cecilia come to his aid.

The scene dissolves and MacGyver wakes up lying on the sidewalk, a paramedic flashing a light in his eyes to check for signs of consciousness. A crowd is gathered around him, the tuxedoed man he saved and his weddinggowned bride among them. MacGyver's boss (who had accompanied him to the genealogist) looks just like King Arthur, the bride like Cecilia and the medic looks like a beardless Merlin. In fact he is using the scissors of a Swiss Army knife to trim the tape on a bandage he has put on MacGyver's cut forehead. MacGyver reaches into his pocket and pulls out the amulet necklace that King Arthur had given him. End of part 2.

Though obviously based on Mark Twain's *A Connecticut Yankee in King Arthur's Court*, no mention of that is made in the credits to "Good Knight MacGyver." Perhaps it was thought that since they ranged far enough away from Twain's original it was unnecessary.

Indeed, other than the basic premise of someone from the present being transported back to Camelot, very little of Twain's work is evident here. MacGyver is the ideal Hank Morgan, an extremely ingenious individual, thoroughly familiar with modern technologies and sciences. However almost none of the rest of the *Connecticut Yankee* story is transferred to the adventure series episode. MacGyver does not seek to improve the lives of the people of Britain. His only goals are to rescue Cecilia and his family's good name.

MacGyver: "Legend of the Holy Rose" (1989)

Television series episode; Approximately 60 minutes; Color; Live Action; Copyright 1989, Paramount Pictures, Inc.

CAST: Richard Dean Anderson (Angus MacGyver); Dana Elcar (Pete Thornton); Bruce McGill (Jack Dalton); Lise Cutter (Zoe Ryan); Robin Mossley (Alexander Shannon); Michael Ensign (Professor Wycliff); Tony Perez (Estebar); Judd Omen (Shiva Luca); Christopher Neame (Erich Von Leer); Sheila Paterson (Cleaning Lady); Christopher Gaze (Cabbie); Claire Brown (Eunice); Gerry Bean (Afiniman); Kevin Hayes (Newscaster); Stephen Dimopoulous (Pilot); Vladimir Kulich (Mammon); Pedro Salvin (Worker)

CREDITS: Writer — Stephen Downing; Director (Part 1) — Michael Coffey; Director (Part 2) — Charles Correll; Executive Producers — Stephen Downing, Henry Winkler, John Rich; Supervising Producer — Michael Greenburg; Co-Producer — Hudson Hickman; Coordinating Producer — John B. Moranville; Created by — Lee David Zlotoff; Executive Story Consultant — Rick Drew; Executive Story Editors — John Sheppard, Chris Haddock; Story Editor — Paul Margolis; Associate Producer — Thomas R. Polizzi; Music — Dennis McCarthy; Theme — Randy Edelman; Casting — Victoria Burrows, C.S.A., Mark Tillman, Susanne McLellan; Director of Photography — William Gereghty; Production Designer — Rex Raglan; Editor (Part 1) — Brad Rines; Editor (Part 2) — Jana Fritsch; Post Production Supervisor — Mike Eliot, A.C.E.; 1st Assistant Director (Part 1) — Bill Mizel; 1st Assistant Director (Part 2) — Peter Dash Kewytch; 2nd Assistant Directors — Paul Etherington, Craig Matheson; Location Manager (Part 1) — David Keiss; Location Manager (Part 2) — Bruce Brownstein; Special Effects — Henry Millar; Script Supervisor — Candice Field; Set Decorator — D. Fauquet-Lemaitre; Construction Coordinator — Charles Leitrants; Costume Department Supervisor — Tommy Welsh; Assistant Costume Designer — Stephanie Nolin; Key Grip — R. K. Hill; Gaffer — Len Wolfe; Special Thanks to Riane Eisler, Center for Partnership Studies; Stunt Coordinator — Vince Deadrick, Jr.; Property Master (Part 1) — Dean Wilson; Property Master (Part 2) — Pat O'Brien; Makeup — Jan Newman; Hairstylist — Michael Ross Pachal; Sound Mixer — Eric Batut; Music Editor — Steve Danforth; Assistant to Mr. Downing — Sara Thornberg; Production Office Coordinator — Valerie Gray; Supervising Sound Editor — William H. Angalora; Post Production Facilities — Modern Videofilm; Lenses and Cameras by — Panavision; Filmed on location in British Columbia, Canada; British Columbia Film Centre; The Bridge Stages; Production Executive — Robert Frederick; Henry Winkler/John Rich Productions in association with Paramount, a Gulf & Western Company

SYNOPSIS: *MacGyver* was an adventure series that ran on television for seven seasons, from 1985 to 1992. "Legend of the Holy Rose" was a two-part episode which aired in August 1989 (episodes 84 and 85). Angus MacGyver was a sort of super secret agent working for The Phoenix Foundation, an outfit dedicated to righting wrongs without having to go through the red tape of governmental involvement. MacGyver's claim to fame was a combination of athletic abilities and incredible mechanical ingenuity.

In this episode, MacGyver returns home from a difficult rescue in Colombia and prepares for a vacation. He wakes up in the morning to discover that his houseboat has been cut adrift. The culprit turns out to be Zoe Ryan, an old friend from childhood who is now an associate professor of archaeology. On a field trip to Greece she discovered a clue to the location of the Holy Grail, and with the threat of leaving him adrift, she coerces MacGyver into helping her find the artifact.

MacGyver's initial reaction to her claim is "Indiana Jones already did that. I saw the movie!" (see entry for *Indiana Jones and the Last Crusade*), but after further encouragement he consents. The clue that Zoe found is what looks like a large, cast-metal soup bowl with ancient writings worked into the rim. It is called Diana's Mirror. The Mirror was made by Ambrose, the most famous alchemist of the twelfth century. Having translated the writings on its rim, Zoe believes the second of three pieces to the puzzle of the Grail's location is in an old abbey in London.

The other parts of the puzzle are the Scepters of the Triple Deity and the Holy Rose. Zoe's mentor, Professor Wycliff, produces an ancient book that describes the whole story. The three sets of artifacts will lead to a temple in which Ambrose hid the Holy Grail. The Grail itself, or Cauldron of Regeneration is explained to be related to Diana and the Triple Goddess.

Trouble begins almost immediately. The wealthy rogue who funded Zoe's trip to Greece is a nefarious character named Von Leer. With spies everywhere, he knows the value of the Mirror and wants it and the Grail for himself. Zoe's apartment is torn apart by Von Leer's men, but they don't find the Mirror. Retrieving it, Zoe and MacGyver depart for the abbey in Britain.

They find the place, though the structure is now Bodin's Chamber of Torture, a museum of old interrogation devices. Finding a baptismal font in the building, MacGyver fits the Mirror into it and, using it as a kind of key, re-leases a mechanism which ejects the three Scepters. Unfortunately Von Leer has Professor Wycliff under his thumb and, having learned of Zoe and MacGyver's plans, he and his minions arrive, take Zoe captive and steal the Scepters and the Mirror. They tie MacGyver beneath a swinging knife-edged pendulum and leave. Thus ends part 1.

Part 2 opens with MacGyver's ever-creative escape from the pendulum. He trails Wycliff and Von Leer, recovers the artifacts and rescues Zoe. Reading the further information provided by the three Scepters, Zoe determines that the next key to the puzzle, the Holy Rose, is located somewhere near Cherbourg, France. Chartering a plane she and MacGyver locate a Stonehengelike ruin. The three Scepters fit into one of the rocks and unlock a hidden chamber containing the Holy Rose.

This item is a sphere made of five petals of gold. Inside it is a gigantic ruby. They find another carved stone into which the Mirror fits, as well as the Holy Rose and the three Scepters. All these pieces work together in such a way that light is reflected from the Mirror into the Holy Rose. MacGyver explains in amazement that Ambrose created a "light pump," or a ruby laser. The light bounces around inside the Rose, is amplified by the ruby, then emitted and focused by the lenses in the handles of the Scepters. When they activate the device the laser beam focuses on a rock wall and a hole explodes open (the rock was no doubt impregnated with gunpowder, surmises MacGyver) creating an entrance to the chambers in which Ambrose hid the rest of his treasures.

Still hot on their trail Von Leer arrives just as MacGyver and Zoe discover the Holy Grail itself. In the ensuing conflict one of Von Leer's men reveals himself as a member of the Brotherhood of Hashishim and he tries to take the Grail. Believing the dust within it to be the Philosopher's Stone, a cure for everything, he pours it over himself after Von Leer shoots him. He dies in spite of his fanatical hopes,

Von Leer is killed by the laser beam and the whole chamber of treasures explodes, leaving Zoe with the original clue artifacts and the Holy Grail.

Though Holy Grail stories are now most frequently associated in some way with King Arthur and the Knights of the Round Table, this episode of MacGyver is remarkable for its avoidance of that connection. Tying it loosely instead to Diana and Triple Goddess myths, legends and beliefs, it avoids any Christian influence. No mention is made of Christ, Joseph of Arimathea, the Holy Lance or any of the other accoutrements of the more or less standard version.

References to a Cauldron of Regeneration are certainly valid, however, since it wasn't until Robert de Boron's trilogy of poems (late twelfth to early thirteenth century) that the Grail was specifically defined as the cup holding Christ's blood. Before that, the Grail, or any *graal*, was a platter or dish used in processional presentations of foods. *Graal* is a French word, so the MacGyver connection to France is easily made. Cauldrons of plenty and cornucopias, which appear in the art and legends of many cultures, may be the basis for the associations with the Holy Grail.

Oddly, the Grail that Zoe ends up with looks much more like the traditional cup that we think of today. The Mirror of Diana would have made more sense in light of the other references the show chose to make about the Grail.

Medieval Realms

Not viewed; 1 Compact Disc; Minimum system requirements: 386SX, 2Mb RAM, SVGA graphics, MS-DOS 3.0, Windows 3.1, Windows-compatible mouse, CD-ROM drive, no Macintosh format available at time of this writing; Features include 623 written sources 1066–1500; many extracts from many sources; 35 extracts in the original Middle English with modern translations; and sound clips, including one from *Gawain and the Green Knight*

Merlin (1992)

Alternate title: Merlin: The True Story of Magic; 112 minutes; Color; Live Action; Copyright 1992, October 32nd Productions, Ltd.; Copyright 1994, Hemdale Home Video, Inc.; Hemdale Home Video #7210

CAST: Nadia Cameron (Crystal of the Lake); Rodney Wood (Merlin); Richard Lynch (Pendragon); Peter Phelps (John Pope); James Hong (Leong Tao); John Ireland (Mr. Dobson); Desmond Llewelyn (Professor Mycroft); Robert Padilla (Black Eagle, Red Hawk); Zuzana Rzerska (Alice); Gary Crader (Gary Edward); Chris Tilloch (Hotel Receptionist); Gordon Sterne (Mr. Adams); Petra Tomasovicova (Pendragon's Receptionist); John Stewart (Angry Miner); Pavel Prager (Billy); Alastair Cumming (Doctor); Milos Pieter (2nd Doctor); John Stone (Mordred); Glen Jacobson (Mine Foreman)

CREDITS: Director — Paul Hunt; Writers — Paul Hunt, Nick McCarty; Director of Photography — Gary Graver; Music — William Campbell, Jr., Michael O'Donnell II; Production Design — Chris Tilloch; Film Editor — Phil Sanderson; Executive Producers — Cristina Collins, Peter Collins; Producers — Paul Hunt, Peter Collins; Associate Producer — Natalia Tomasovicova; Story — Paul Hunt, Nick McCarty; Screenplay — Nick McCarty; Action Sequences Directed by — John Stewart; Costumes Designed by — Zoenek Sansky; Created and Produced by — Peter Collins, Twickenham Film Studios; Additional Direction — Gary Grader; Unit Manager — Andrei Suplinsky; Additional Cinematography — Paul Hunt; Sound Recordist — Paul LeMare; Special Effects Pyrotechnics — Marian Polakovic, Ron Home, Kevin MacCarthy, Bruno Stemple, Jozef Tapak; Stunt Coordinators — John Stewart, Jiroslad Tomesa; Stunt Doubles (Pope) — Stanislad Janos; Laser Effects — Laser Creations, London; Production Secretary — Petra Tomasovicova; Horse Wranglers — Marian Le-Brocke, T. J. Ziska Brataslada; Horse Trainer — Marian Poline; Snake Wranglers — Vaclad Tomisovsky, Victor Camod; Bug Wrangler — Vladaslad Dorecky; Catering — Vladamir Matus; Greenwich Observatory Unit; Production Manager — Vincent O'-Toole; Director of Photography — Gary Cramer; Focus Puller — Keith Thomas; Gaffer — Stephan Foster; Best Boy — Gary Donohue; Sound Recordist — Paul Le Mare; Makeup and Hairdressing — S. Cristy MacLeod; Post Production Supervisor — Phil Sanderson; Supervising Sound Editor — Peter Best, A.M.P.S.; Associate Sound Editors — John Ireland, A.M.P.S., Colin Miller; 1st

Assistant Picture Editor — Bob Barchley; Assistant Sound Editors — Robert Mullen, Robert Ireland, Bill Barringer; ADR Editor, USA — Blake Le Mare; ADR Editor, Australia — Helen Brown; Re-recorded by — Gerry Humphreys, Dean Humphreys; Re-recorded at — Twickenham Studios, London; ADR Studio, USA — Directors Sound, Burbank; Casting — Cristina Collins, SSS, London; Publicity and Promo Materials by — The Creative Partnership; Color by — Metrocolor; Additional Processing by — Film and Photo Design, London; Music Recorded at — Bluebird Sound Studios, Shepperton; Financial Services — Barclays Bank, PLC; Insurance Services — Speare & Co., L.A.; Legal Advisors — Bernard Donnenfield, Natalia Tomasovacova, Johnathan Cameron; Worldwide Distribution by Shining Armor Communications, Ltd.; A United Film Makers Release

SYNOPSIS: In a fractured, disjointed film Merlin's daughter, Crystal of the Lake, is reincarnated in modern times to once more protect the sword of power from the evil intentions of Pendragon. Mixing elements of Arthurian legend, oriental mysticism, astrology and modern pyrotechnics *Merlin* leaps through three eras of history to create a nonsensical story.

In the opening, Merlin explains that this particular sword was forged by Beltane the smith and tempered by Merlin himself. Merlin places the sword in a stone in a field. Pendragon, the son of Mordred, is the personification of evil who searches through time for the sword. There are three objects of power: a jewel, a dagger and the sword. If all three are possessed together, ultimate power over the universe can be achieved.

However, the true purpose of the sword is for John Pope to use it to protect Crystal while she fends off Pendragon. In addition to John Pope, an old fellow named Leong Tao is always around to help the girl. No explanation is given for his presence in Dark Ages Britain, but he is a handy man to have on the side of good.

These four characters, Pendragon, Crystal, Pope and Tao, are reincarnated in different times to continue their battle for the items mentioned above. After their introduction in Britain, they show up next in a wild west American setting. In the gold-mining town of Lansdown, California, they fight a major battle and despite the help of a Native American chief and expert bowman, they are all killed.

Next they pop up in modern times to return to Lansdown and fight once more. This time the Native American has been reincarnated with them, but Pendragon seems closer to winning.

Luckily, Merlin is sleeping on a throne in an incredible underground temple in the nearby hills. His invaluable assistance comes just in the nick of time. At one point the body of the evil Mordred is reawakened to enter the fray.

That should give an adequate impression of the confused nature of the plot line of this film. Details of the story are added throughout, as if afterthoughts. Leaps back and forth through time, in and out of flashbacks and from location to location become exhausting.

No attempt is made to rationally connect these characters with the Arthurian tales they come from. No mention is made of Arthur, in spite of a sword in a stone and Mordred's existence. That Pendragon is chosen as the name for the enemy of the protagonists is nothing but further obfuscation, as is the rainbow coalition of American Indians, Kung Fu masters and so on.

Merlin (1998)

Made-for-television mini-series; 174 minutes (plus 19-minute "making-of" section at end); Color; Live Action; Copyright 1998, National Broadcasting Company; Copyright 1998, RHI Entertainment; A Hallmark Entertainment Production for NBC Entertainment; NBC Home Video

CAST: Sam Neill (Merlin); Helena Bonham Carter (Morgan Le Fay); Sir John Gielgud (King Constant); Rutger Hauer (Vortigern); James Earl Jones (The Mountain King); Miranda Richardson (Mab/Lady of the Lake); Isabella Rossellini (Nimue); Martin Short (Frik); Paul Curran (Arthur); Lena Heady (Guinevere); Jeremy Sheffield (Lancelot); Mark Jax (King Uther); John McEnery (Lord Ardente); Thomas Lockyer (Cornwall); Jason Done

(Mordred); Billie Whitelaw (Ambrosia); Daniel Brocklebank (Young Merlin); Agnieszka Koson (Young Nimue); Emma Lewis (Elissa); Justin Gurdler (Young Galahad); Roger Ashton-Griffiths (Sir Boris); Nicholas Clay (Lord Leo); Sebastian Roché (Gawain); Rachel Colover (Lady Igraine); John Turner (Lord Lot); Keith Baxter (Sir Hector); Janine Eser (Lady Elaine); Peter Woodthorpe (Soothsayer); Robert Addie (Sir Gilbert); Nickolas Grace (Sir Egbert); Peter Benson (1st Architect); John Tordoff (New Architect); Timothy Bateson (Father Abbott); Alice Hamilton (Young Morgan Le Fay); Peter Eyre (Chief Physician); Vernon Dobtcheff (1st Physician); Peter Bayliss (2nd Physician); Talula Sheppard (Lady Friend); Dilys Lane (Gudrun); Jeremy Peters (Village Chief); Joseph Mawle (Village Man); Camilla Oultram (Young Girl at Fair); Susan Rayner (Village Woman); Charlotte Church (Singer)

CREDITS: Costume Design — Ann Hollowood; Production Design — Roger Hall; Director of Photography — Sergei Kozlov; Visual Effects Supervisor — Tim Webber; Music — Trevor Jones; Editor — Colin Green; Line Producer — Chris Thompson; Executive Producer — Robert Halmni, Sr.; Producer — Dyson Lovell; Teleplay — David Stevens; Peter Barnes; Story — Edward Khmara; Director — Steve Barron; U.S. Casting — Lynn Kressel, C.S.A.; U.K. Casting — Noel Davis; 2nd Unit Director — Tim Webber; 1st Assistant Director — Gareth Tandy; 2nd Assistant Director — Rebecca Tucker; 3rd Assistant Director — Toby Hefferman; Script Supervisor — Jean Bourne; Location Manager — Chris Brock; Financial Controller — Andy Hennigan; Stunt Coordinators — Gerry Crampton, Terry Walsh; Production Coordinator — Paula McBreen; Production Sound Mixer — Peter Glossop; VFX Coordinator — Matthew Cope; Camera Operator — Mike Frift; Focus Pullers — Simon Mills, Martin Shepherd; Clapper Loaders — Catherine Frift, Helen Williams; Grip — John Payne; Video Operator — Nick Coward; Digital Video Effects — Framestore (London), Tim Greenwood, Pedro Sabrosa, Sirio Quintivalle, Martin Parsons, Tim Keene, George Roper, Murray Butler, Oliver Bersey, Andrew Daffy, Fiona Wilkinshaw; Creature Effects and CGI Dragon — Jim Henson's Creature Shop; Supervising Art Director — John King; Set Decorator — Karen Brookes; Assistant Set Decorator — Sonja Klaus; Art Director — Mike Boone; Scenic/Matte Artist — Brian Bishop; Stand-by Art Director — Frederic Evard; Makeup and Hair Designer — Aileen Seaton; Makeup and Hair Artists — Jane Walker, Norma Webb, Kylie Marr; Makeup/Hair, Sam Neill — Nuala Conway; Prosthetics Designer — Mark Coulier; Prosthetics Artist — Amber Sibley; Costume Design Assistant — Justine Luxton; Wardrobe Supervisor — Daryl Bristow; Set Supervisor — William Steggle; Wardrobe Mistress — Charlotte Finlay; Sound Maintenance — Shaun Mills; Sound Assistant — Stephen Gilmour; Gaffer — Eddie Knight; Best Boy — Stewart Monteith; Electricians — John Turner, George White, Stuart Reid, Peter Casey; Stand-by Props — Warren Stickley, Mitch Niclas; Property Master — Burce Bigg; Property Storeman — Ray Rose; Dressing Props — Peter Bigg, Edward Stickley; Stand-bys — Paul Nott-Macaire, Norman North, John Wright, Dean Norgate; SFX Supervisor — Richard Conway; Senior SFX Technicians — Darrell Guyon, Sam Conway, Terry Bridle, Dave Eltham; SFX Trainee — Ceri Nicholls; Additional SFX Staff — Alan Perez, Andrew Thompson, Caroline Roemmele; Assistant Location Managers — Simon Marsden, Robin Higgs; Location Assistant — Nick Waldron; Animal Coordinator — Helen Holdcroft; Conceptual Artist — Dermot Power; Draughtspersons — Peter Dorme, Margaret Horspool, Paul Kirby; Junior Draughtsperson — Andrew Thompson; Chief Sculptor — Andrew Holder; Storyboard Artist — John Greaves; Construction Manager — Dennis Bovington; Supervising Carpenters — Leon Apsey, Brian Blues, Mick Hedges; Supervising Painter — Christopher Mason; Supervising Rigger — Iain Lowe; Supervising Plasterer — Terry James; Assistant to Dyson Lovell — Bryon Fear; Assistant to Steve Barron — Louise Kramskoy; Assistant Production Coordinator — Ruth Breslaw; Production Assistant — Jonathan Pilcher; Illustrator — Alan Lee; Unit Nurse — Pat Barr; Additional Casting — Harry Audley, Oded Levy; Assistant Accountants, Rita Kozma, Tina McConnell, Fry Martin; Transport Captain — Gerry Gore; Horse Masters — Gerard Naprous, Daniel Naprous; Associate Editors — Kevin Lester, David Yardley; Assistant Editor — Dominic Strevens; Post Production Sound — Movietrack/Goldcrest, Tim Lewiston, Elaine "Chuck" Thomas, Rocky Phelan, Vicky Brazier; Re-recording Mixer — Paul Carr; Music Realized by — Janice Graham, Geoff Alexander, Kipper, Edmund Butt, Wayne Morley, Philip Todd, Simon Rhodes, Gareth Cousins, Julian Kershaw, Tony Stanton, Andrew Glen; Performed by — The London Symphony Orchestra; Music Coordinator — Victoria Seale; Original Soundtrack Available on Varese Sarabande Compact Discs; Legend Advisor — Loren Boothby; Research — Andrea Barron; Creative Concept Art — Vonn Stropp; CGI Griffins — BUF-France; Additional Composites — Mill Film, MPC, CFC; Second Unit: Action Director—Arthur Wooster; 1st Assistant Director— Terry Madden; 2nd Assistant Director—Richard Styles; 3rd Assistant Director—Jonathan Scott; Script Supervisor—Sarah Hiach; Utility Stand-ins—Alan Meacham, Debbie Hanney; Stills Photographer—Oliver Upton; VSFX Cameraman—Stefan Lange; Title Sequence—Tim Osborne; Floor Runners—Tamana Bleasedale, Fiona Gosden; Filmed on location in Wales and at Pinewood Studios, London, England; Thanks to the Corporation of London

CREDITS: For "The Magical Making of Merlin"; Writer/Producer—Russ Patrick; U.K. Crew—Mark Rivers, Steve Taylor, Roger Penny, Darrell Briggs, Roger Burgess; U.K. Directors—Rob Done, Colin Burrows, David Castell; Special thanks to the cast and crew of *Merlin*; "The Magical Making of Merlin" ©1998, Hallmark Entertainment

SYNOPSIS: As distributed by NBC Home Video, *Merlin* comes as a two-tape set along with a 243-page book, *The Shooting Script: Merlin*. Part 1 is 87 minutes long; part 2, including the segment "The Magical Making of Merlin," runs for 106 minutes.

A two-part television mini-series, *Merlin* is a special effects tour de force. It is a fantasy version of the whole Arthurian saga, similar in scope to Boorman's *Excalibur*. In fact, it one-ups Boorman in that *Merlin* goes all the way back to before even Uther, to Uther's father, King Constant. Focusing on Merlin, of course, the film opens with King Constant's demise at the hand of Vortigern and winds up just after Arthur's death.

Merlin is the narrator of the tale. A very aged wizard speaks directly to the camera, wondering where to begin the story. One of his opening lines is "King Constant was the first Christian king of England." Shortly after Vortigern's usurpation, civil war tears the country apart, then the Saxons come. These invaders rampage across the countryside destroying Christian churches as well as pagan places. At this point it is stated that only one being could save the land, Queen Mab of the old ways.

Summoned by the cries of the few who remember her, Mab, garbed all in black, emerges from a stone. She immediately contacts her sister, The Lady of the Lake. Unfortunately the Lady of the Lake will not assist Mab in fighting against the change toward Christianity and the loss of the pagan religions. Mab swears to create a powerful leader, a wizard, to bring the people back.

By magically impregnating an unnamed woman, Mab creates Merlin. Merlin's mother dies at his birth and Mab leaves the infant to be raised by a former worshiper, Ambrosia. This feisty and independent woman rears the child, agreeing to turn him back over to Mab when the time is right.

The film then jumps forward to Merlin's teenage years. Waking up in the woods one day, Merlin finds he's being observed by a beautiful young lady and her traveling companions. Introduced as the Lady Nimue, the girl informs Merlin that they are on their way to Lord Lambert's castle and have become lost. For the price of a kiss, Merlin gives them directions and warns them that the woods are dangerous and to stick to the path.

Nimue promptly falls into a bog. Hearing her cries for help, Merlin comes to the rescue. In the frenzy of the moment Merlin is suddenly able to cause a tree branch to grow enough for Nimue to grasp it and thus be pulled from the sinkhole. The day's events mark the beginning of the love between Merlin and Nimue and the time that he must depart Ambrosia to return to Mab.

A white horse arrives to carry Merlin "home" to Mab's domain. This horse's name, incidentally, is Rupert and he is an intelligent creature who speaks with Merlin. At the border of the fairy kingdom, Frik, Mab's faithful but much abused assistant, meets Merlin to guide him to her castle. This pointy-eared, elfin shape-shifter becomes Merlin's primary tutor in the ways of magic while Mab observes and tends to her machinations.

To both Frik's and Mab's disappointment, Merlin does not like magic. He only achieves the second of the three levels of wizardly skill before his lessons are interrupted. The Lady of the Lake appears to Merlin, informing him that Ambrosia is dying. The youthful magician leaves immediately to be with her. Before he gets to Ambrosia's hut, however, Mab visits the old woman and in an argument with her over Merlin, injures Ambrosia enough to speed the woman's death. Merlin arrives just in time to hold his "aunt" and hear Ambrosia's last words as she dies.

Thus is set Merlin's eternal enmity for Mab. Burying Ambrosia, he swears that he will only use his magic to destroy the fairy queen.

In the meantime Vortigern has been trying to build a fortress, but the thing collapses repeatedly. Having learned that King Constant's son, Uther, is returning from Normandy to try to make claim to the throne of Britain, Vortigern is holding Nimue hostage as a guarantee that her father, Lord Ardente, remains faithful in his military support. Mab tells Vortigern's soothsayer to find a man with no human father and mix his blood with the mortar of Vortigern's fortress. Then she leads him to Merlin.

Taken before Vortigern to be killed, Merlin describes the trouble with the construction as a stream beneath the foundations. He also has a vision of a red dragon — representing Uther — defeating Vortigern's white dragon. Impressed with Merlin's prophesying Vortigern imprisons the wizard.

Nimue convinces Vortigern to release Merlin from his cell in exchange for his advice and the two are reunited for the first time since the incident at the bog. In a romantic aside Nimue tells Merlin the story of Joseph of Arimathea carrying the Holy Grail to the island of Avalon. Merlin puts the tale aside as a pretty story, but Nimue states that the man who finds the Grail will bring peace to the land.

Mab reenters the scene with a proposal to Vortigern. She wants Merlin back and in exchange for him will tell Vortigern how to defeat Uther. Vortigern agrees and for starters Mab tells him to sacrifice Nimue to the Great Dragon. Vortigern claims he can't do that for fear of losing Lord Ardente's forces. Mab has

Frik appear as a soldier/messenger with the news that Ardente has already defected.

Nimue is tied to a stake in front of the Great Dragon's cave, Merlin to a tree on a hilltop overlooking the scene. The dragon emerges and when it threatens Nimue, Merlin cuts loose his powers. Still tied to it, Merlin uproots the tree and strikes the dragon with it. As Merlin stumbles, the dragon redirects its attention toward Nimue. Merlin finally frees himself from the ropes and causes vines and plants to entrap the dragon, but not before it is able to send a blast of flame at Nimue. Merlin is unable to curb the blast completely and Nimue's face and neck are severely burned.

Merlin carries Nimue to Avalon for the monks and sisters to heal her. He swears to destroy Mab and goes to the Lady of the Lake for help. Though critical of his efforts, the Lady of the Lake gives Excalibur to Merlin.

At Winchester, Merlin convinces Uther that even though it's winter, Vortigern is about to attack. With this warning and Merlin's aid in planning the battle, Uther is successful at defeating Vortigern's army. Merlin wields Excalibur during the fight and personally defeats Vortigern. Only after the battle does he give the sword to Uther.

Uther crowns himself and immediately lusts after Igraine, the wife of Cornwall; they are among the crowd who've come for the coronation. A young and evidently congenitally deformed Morgan Le Fay, the daughter of Cornwall and Igraine, is there to witness the goings-on.

Uther asks for Merlin's help in winning Igraine and the wizard refuses, advising the king against the adultery. When Uther says he'll use Excalibur in a war on Cornwall, Merlin tricks him into handing him the sword. Merlin stabs Excalibur into a rock, awakening the Rock of Ages. This huge, reclining, basaltic figure chats briefly with Merlin, curious about what is going on. When Merlin explains, the Mountain King promises to hold the sword "until a good man comes along" to claim it, as Merlin has requested.

Merlin wanders off for a time but upon returning finds that Uther has been laying siege to Tintagel, Cornwall's nearly impregnable castle. Hundreds have died for Uther's lust. In desperation Merlin agrees to help Uther, but only on the conditions that he gets to keep the son that will be conceived and that Cornwall is unharmed. The deal is made, Merlin causes Uther to take on the appearance of Cornwall and the false king has his way with Igraine. However, he betrays Merlin's trust by having Cornwall killed.

Morgan is present when Uther comes to her mother. She is able to see that it is indeed Uther and not her father. In spite of her objections and attempts to warn Igraine, however, the little girl is taken out of the room.

Not long afterward, Mab sends Frik to win Morgan over. Frik awes the child with his magic abilities and gets her to place one of Mab's enchanted stones in the infant's crib.

Merlin has Arthur raised by Sir Hector, but it is Merlin who over the years tutors the child in morality and ethics. When Arthur is a young man, Uther goes mad and kills himself. Merlin takes Arthur to the Mountain King, where despite Mab's appearance and attempted interference, Arthur pulls the sword from the Rock's clenched fist.

Over Uther's bier the lords of Britain argue as to whether this boy can really be king. Arthur unsheathes Excalibur and spins it over his head, cutting the burning tips off the candles of two candelabras. As just the flames magically rise through the air, many in the court become convinced. Lot, however still resists and in the company of a number of other lords, he leaves, declaring war. This in spite of the fact that his son, Gawain, has pledged himself to Arthur.

Morgan, now a teenager, has another visit from Frik. This time Frik follows through on a previous promise, namely to make Morgan beautiful. For some reason, however, her incredible lisp remains. Though she tells Frik she wants the throne Frik tells her that her son might attain it.

Inevitably Arthur must face Lot on the battlefield. As the two armies range opposite each other, Arthur rides out alone to speak with Lot. He hands Excalibur to Lot, telling him if he is truly worthy of it, then take it and kill him. Lot raises the sword, but feels its magic and is converted. The war does not happen and the troops celebrate. Circling around Arthur the men listen as the young king speaks of their equality and the noble lives they will lead with him in Camelot.

That night Frik brings Morgan to Arthur, introducing her as Lady Marie. They make love and Mordred is conceived. While her servant is performing his task, Mab herself visits Nimue on Avalon. She offers to restore Nimue's beauty if Nimue will take Merlin with her to a place Mab has created for them in which they can live out their lives in happiness. Nimue is tempted, but knowing Merlin's commitment to righting the wrongs that are going on, she declines.

Arthur finds himself a wife — Guinevere, the daughter of Lord Leo. Mordred grows unnaturally quickly and learns incredible skills and strength under the tutelage of Mab and Morgan. Arthur decides to go in search of the Holy Grail.

Merlin consults with the Lady of the Lake about who to leave in charge of Camelot in the king's absence. She tells him the right man is at Joyous Gard. Going there, Merlin finds Lancelot, his wife, Elaine, and their son, Galahad. Of course Merlin assumes Lancelot to be the correct choice and Elaine encourages the good knight to go off on his "last great adventure."

In spite of Merlin's warnings, Lancelot and Guinevere fall in love. Mab uses her magic to reveal the fact to Elaine who in turn dies of a broken heart. Her body floats on a barge to Camelot. By this time Mordred has reached his full powers.

Mab takes Mordred with her over Morgan's protestations. In the argument between the two women, Mab causes Morgan to take a fatal fall. The spell of magic broken, Morgan returns to her deformed appearance. Holding her in his arms, Frik, who has always loved Morgan, tells her as she dies that she is as beautiful as ever. Mab removes all of Frik's magical powers and fires him from her employ.

Finally, after years of questing, Arthur and his men return to find the construction of Camelot complete. However, the great hall is filled with somber lords and ladies as Mordred informs the king of the indiscretions that have occurred while he was away.

Backed into a corner by logic and the law, Arthur is forced to have Guinevere tried for treason and burned at the stake. He and Merlin watch the execution from a window, but Merlin is unable to allow it to continue. As the flames rise around the queen, Merlin causes a rain shower, slowing the conflagration. Lancelot rides into the courtyard, hacking his way through the crowd to free Guinevere and carry her off. And so, Merlin says, "They rode out of my story and into legend."

As Mordred incites his faction of lords against Arthur, Nimue calls on Mab to accept her deal. Mab tells Merlin that Nimue awaits him and Arthur tells Merlin the lords don't want him involved in the battle with Mordred, so the wizard decides to retire. He finds Nimue in a glowing, idyllic glade hidden in a cliffside cavern. He is relatively happy for a time but, as the battle between Mordred and Arthur begins, Merlin is able to sense the goings-on and becomes disquieted.

The desperation of the fight comes home to Merlin and he leaves Nimue to return to the real world. He arrives at the battlefield to find Mordred dying in Mab's arms and Arthur mortally wounded. As he dies Arthur charges Merlin with returning Excalibur to the Lady of the Lake.

In a last consultation with an obviously weakening Lady of the Lake, Merlin learns that, indeed, Galahad was the man she meant as the one to protect Camelot.

Merlin goes to Camelot and finds the equally weakening Mab at the Round Table. A crowd is present to witness the confrontation. In a battle-of-the-wizards Merlin is able to hold his own and Mab becomes exhausted. Merlin and the assembled court turn their backs on her, Merlin stating that they will simply forget her. The fairy queen evaporates. Galahad returns alone with the Holy Grail and peace is restored to the land.

The film cuts to the "present" of Merlin's narration. He is an old beggar, telling his tale for donations. The people disperse, but one remains behind. Frik, old now too, greets Merlin and the two reminisce briefly. Frik has brought Rupert the talking horse with him and tells Merlin that Rupert can take him to Nimue, who still waits for him. Mab's spells are coming apart and Merlin's love is no longer trapped. Merlin and Nimue are reunited and, as his last act of magic, Merlin restores them to their youth.

Merlin retains the basics of Arthurian traditions, but makes many departures from them as well. Most notably unique to this film are Mab, Frik, Ambrosia, Rupert the talking horse and the special effects.

Connecting Mab or Queen Mab to King Arthur and Merlin is unusual, to say the least. Though probably rooted in Celtic folklore (the Welsh word *mab* means youth or child), she is better known from Shakespeare's play *Romeo and Juliet* and Drayton's poem *Nymphidia*. In *Romeo and Juliet* Mab is called the fairy's midwife; in *Nymphidia* she is the wife of Oberon, king of the fairies.

Frik is perhaps a construct just for this film. His character fits well within the plot of the movie but is irrelevant from an Arthurian standpoint. Though dwarves, giants and magical beings figure in some versions of the legends, Frik's extraordinary powers and heavy involvement with every aspect of the story is unique to this film.

Ambrosia seems to be a blending of legend with history and imagination. In Gildas and Bede, Ambrosius Aurelianus is the last of the Romans left to defend Britain from Saxon invasions. Nennius names Ambrose as the person we normally think of as Merlin. By the time Geoffrey of Monmouth writes a version of the story, Aurelius Ambrosius is the brother of Uther and Constans. So there is plenty of room for adaptation. Making an Ambrosia the foster mother of Merlin at least ties a version of an old name back in with the legend.

Little needs to be said about a talking horse. One is only grateful that a different royally associated name wasn't chosen, like Edward, for instance.

The special effects and computer-generated imagery in *Merlin* are extraordinary. The Lady of the Lake appears as an ethereal, floating woman with a necklace of tiny live fish. Credibly nasty-looking griffins attack Merlin and Arthur at one point. The busy little fairies at Mab's command are quite a sight. All in all, an unusually extensive production for television.

One character in *Merlin* who is consistent with the legends but is portrayed in a refreshing manner is Vortigern. The humor given to the part is good to see for a change.

The usual inferences that Vortigern was either a complete idiot or a totally evil individual follow traditions established by all the early chroniclers. This Vortigern, however, is able to crack a wry smile at his own simplistic philosophizing or even laugh at a well-placed insult directed at him. One particular line given to Vortigern sums up his (and, in a sense, all of the Arthurian figures') place in history rather nicely. Merlin has just delivered his vision of the dragons at the site of Vortigern's collapsing fortress. Vortigern has decided to hold on to Merlin for future use and the news that Uther is on the march necessitates prompt action. Vortigern knocks Merlin unconscious, criticizing the wizard for his slowness. Vortigern expounds that his enemies all think before they act, but "I act before I think. That's why I always have the advantage."

As for other aspects of the film, *Merlin* is an interesting effort. As mentioned above, it tracks relatively well with early writings, like those of Bede, Nennius and Geoffrey. It manages to avoid turning totally medieval in at least the superficial features, like armor and architecture.

Ambrosia's hut is a construction of sod and thatch. Camelot, though built of stone, has none of the gilt and crenellation that occurs in other films. There are no knights clad in full body armor in the thirteenth century style, but many are in leather with metal plates attached. Uther and his men are panoplied in full Roman harness, a shock but a possibility. If nothing else, the disparity in styles earmarks the transitional stage this period of time represents.

"The Magical Making of Merlin" segment at the end of the NBC Home Video tapes is fun to watch but not revelatory. There are the requisite soundbite-style "interviews" with the director, executive producer and several of the stars of the film. All of these serve to promote the television movie without managing to increase anyone's knowledge about the film or its subject matter.

Superficial details are given about the numbers of CGI (computer-generated images) scenes included, certain aspects of the difficulties in building artificial animal models, etc. The relative weather conditions in Wales during the outdoor filming, the enthusiasm of the crew and the level of medieval literary education that at least two of the stars received are also mentioned.

One of the most interesting tidbits of information garnered from the segment is the use of a "periscopic" camera on tracks in certain close-up scenes. The other is the statement that the roles of Mab and Frik are "deliciously campy."

Merlin: The Magic Begins (1997)

Not viewed; Color; Live Action; Copyright 1997, Seagull Productions/KMG; Kaleidoscope Media Group; Wynn Entertainment; Cromwell Productions

CAST: Jason Connery (Merlin); Deborah Moore; Gareth Thomas (Blaze); Graham McTavish; Fiona Kempin; Gordon Hall; John Woodford; Chick Allen; Finn Begbie; Peter Begbie; Rosie Begbie; Katrina Boyd; Michael Boyd; Andy Bryden

SYNOPSIS: *Merlin: The Magic Begins* is a made-for-television two-hour pilot with, as of this writing, 22 one-hour follow-up episodes. It was being aired in October and November 1998 in 62 percent of the U.S. and no word is currently available as to whether the series will be picked up for broadcast.

It is the story of the young Merlin just learning his powers. Uther Pendragon has been removed from his throne at the hands of King Vidus, his advisor, Rengal, and Saxon mercenaries. Merlin struggles to save the king, the land and Nimue.

Merlin: The True Story of Magic see *Merlin (1992)*

Merlin and the Dragons (1990)

27 minutes; Color; Cartoon; Copyright 1990, 1991, 1995, Lightyear Entertainment, L.P.; Lightyear Video #54003-3; A Joshua M. Greene Production

CREDITS: Based on the Illustrations of—Alan Lee; Narrated by—Kevin Kline; Music by—Michael Rubini; Executive Producer—Arne Holland; Producer—Joshua M. Greene; Original Story by—Jane Yolin; Based on *Vita Merlini, Historia Brittonum* by Nennius and; *Historia Regum Britanniae* by Geoffrey of Monmouth.; Art Direction and Story Board—Dennis J. Woodyard; Animation Director—Hu Yhong; Design—Aland Lee, Robert Gould; Character Design—Nicholas Filippi, Edward Lee, Dennis J. Woodyard; Background Design—Jeff Gatrall, Robert Stuhmer, Michael Zoderozny; Animation Layout—Nina Bafaro, Nicholas Filippi, Jeff Gatrall; Color Models—Chelsea Animation; Shanghai Animation Film Studio; Production Manager—Huanghong Mei; Translator—Cai Yizhu; Layout Design—Wong Jin, Wong Jia Shi; Background Design—Li Ming; Key Animators—Chen Yu, Qina Yao, Xin Pang, Ge Yan, Jion Xiu, Wong Jin, Gu Lin Long, Xu Zhu Ming, Huong Wen Ping; Background Artist—Li Ming, Wang Jia Shi, Dai Da; Camera—Jiam Yon Y, Wang Fu Kang; Assistant Camera—Zhu Yi Ping, Qiu Xiao Ping; Editor—Mo Pu Zhong; Checking—Qian Pie Qin; Produced in Association with—Hi-Tops Video, Media Home Entertainment, Dutton Children's Books, WGBH Boston; With assistance from the National Endowment for the Humanities; Special Thanks to—Ziou Ke Qin; Production Supervision—Robert Mandell, New Frontiers Productions; Executive in Charge of Production—Eleanor Kearney

SYNOPSIS: As noted in the credits, this story, written by Jane Yolin, is based on the works of Nennius and Geoffrey of Monmouth. Yolin's children's book makes for an excellent kids' film that depicts some very old versions of Merlin's life.

The film opens shortly after young Arthur has been crowned. Having nightmares about not being able to hold the sword, the boy goes to Merlin for solace. Merlin tells Arthur a story.

Cover art from *Merlin and the Dragons* (1990) (courtesy Lightyear Entertainment, L.P.).

Once a young boy named Emrys lived in North Wales. He was having strange dreams and visions. An old wise man was his friend and one day Emrys found a star book in the old man's cottage. Emrys predicted an eclipse, and although he was only nine, everyone began to think that Emrys was evil.

When Emrys was 12 years old, Vortigern, fighting under the banner of the Red Dragon, unjustly took over the kingdom. Vortigern had a mighty tower built, but the walls collapsed. He forced the villagers to rebuild it, but it crumbled again. When the tower fell a third time, Vortigern's magicians told him that he must find a fatherless boy who was spawned by a demon. He must sprinkle the boy's blood on the stones of the tower.

The villagers suggested Emrys, but Emrys had a vision and told Vortigern that two huge breathing stones holding two dragons were in a pool under the tower.

They broke the dragons free. One was white, one red. The white dragon killed the red one and Emrys told Vortigern that this was a sign that Vortigern would die soon. The two rightful kings of the land arrived — Ambrosius and Uther Pendragon.

Merlin tells Arthur that Uther was Arthur's father, then he shows Arthur a dragon's tooth and Arthur realizes that Emrys was Merlin.

Merlin and the Sword (1983)

Original title for television: *Arthur, the King*; 95 minutes; Color; Live Action; Copyright 1983, Comworld Productions; Copyright 1994, GoodTimes Home Video Corporation; Copyright obtained by Jadran Film, Zagreb, Yugoslavia; c/o Films Around The World pursuant to foreclosure sale 8/11/86; A Martin Poll Production in Association with Comworld Productions; GoodTimes Home Video #9202

CAST: Malcolm McDowell (King Arthur); Candice Bergen (Morgan Le Fay); Edward Woodward (Merlin); Dyan Cannon (Cathryn Davidson); Joseph Blatchley (Mordred); Rupert Everett (Lancelot); Rosalyn Landor (Gwenevere); Liam Neeson (Grak); Patrick Ryecart (Gawain); Philip Sayer (Agravain); Ann Thornton (Lady Ragnell); Lucy Gutteridge (Niniane); Dennis Lill (King Pellinore); John Quarmby (Sir Kai); Michael Gough (Archbishop); Milance Avramovic (Gorgo); Terry Torday (Enchanted Queen); Mary Stavin (Princess); Carole Ashby (Princess); Alison Worth (Princess); Peter Blythe (Guide); Pat Starr (Woman Passenger); Marie Elise (1st Court Lady); Maryan D'Abo (2nd Court Lady); Tina Robinson (3rd Court Lady); Pia Constance-Churcher (Barge Lady); Linda Fontana (Barge Lady); Christine Hunt (Barge Lady); Cia Ford (Barge Lady); Miro Pfeiffer (Undead Knight); Vlado Spindler (Boatman); Mise Martinovic (Niniane's Father); Tom Vakusic (Ragnar)

CREDITS: Music by — Charles Gross; Director of Photography — Denis Lewiston; Production Designer — Francisco Chianese; Costume Designer — Phyllis Dalton; Editor — Peter Tanner; Produced by — Martin Poll; Written by — J. David Wyles; Narration by — John Smith; Directed by — Clive Donner; Associate Producer — David White; Production Supervisors — Douko Buljan, John Chulay; Production Coordinator — Roy Parkinson; Production Secretary — Nada Pinter; Co–Associate Producer — Kathryn Stellmack; Casting Director — Rose Tobias Shaw; 1st Assistant Director — Ray Corbett; Continuity — Nikki Clapp; Sound Recording — David Hildyard; Production Managers — Emil Bolanac, Paolo Fabbri; Assistant to the Producer — Olgo Pogostin; Production Accountant — Maureen Holmes; Master of Weapons — Jack Barry; Stunts Coordinator — Petar Buntic; Sound Editors — Doug Grindstaff, Gil Marchant, Gordon Daniel; Re-recorded at — Goldwyn Sound Facilities; Chief Makeup Artist — Giancarlo Del Brocco; Chief Hairdresser — Ida De Guilmi; Wardrobe Master — Marko Cerovac; Art Director — Dusko Jericevic; Key Grip — Marijan Marcijus; Set Dresser — Stanislav Dobrina; Supervising Electrician — Derek Gattrell; Focus Operator — Zoran Veselic; Assistant Editor — Marcel Durham; Makeup Consultant — Barbara Daly; Hairdressing Consultant — Michael Rasser; Processed by — Jadran Films and Rank Film Laboratories, Ltd.; Wigs by — Simon; Optical Effects by — Optical Film Effects, Ltd., Pinewood, England; Practical Special Effects by Effects Associates, Pinewood, England; Executive in Charge of Production — Matthew N. Herman; Filmed on Location in Yugoslavia and England; Pinewood Studios, England; Production Facilities by Jadran Film

SYNOPSIS: *Merlin and the Sword* is a modernized *Connecticut Yankee in King Arthur's Court,* but instead of leading to a Sir Boss scenario it has Merlin give us a flashback to a more traditional Camelot than Twain's.

A gal from New York, Cathryn, is visiting England. On a guided tour of Stonehenge she wanders from the group and hears some voices. She stumbles, falls down a tunnel and meets Merlin and Niniane. The three chat for a bit and Merlin conjures up the "inner sight" to recount the story of how he and Niniane happen to be stuck where they are.

The usual assortment of characters are there, in more or less typical roles but there are some twists. Morgan Le Fay is as evil as ever, but in this version she is a queen of Gaul. Gawain and Agravain are part of Arthur's entourage. Mordred is Morgan's nephew in this film and as evil as his aunt. Niniane comes to Camelot with King Pellinore (her own father is too old and busy) and she and Merlin promptly fall in love. Lancelot arrives also and is declared by Arthur to be Gwenevere's champion.

One of the most interesting additions to the cast are the Picts. The Pictish leader, Grak, kidnaps Gwenevere, ensconcing her for a time in his castle until Lancelot comes to rescue her.

Another unique — at least for films — addition to the mix is Lady Ragnell. Gawain's chivalrous marriage to this loathsome but heroic lady (Ragnell is known in legend as the Loathsome Lady) is her miraculous salvation.

In what looks like a transmutation of the Gawain and the Green Knight story, Arthur at one point is confronted by an Undead Knight raised by Morgan. He cuts off the creature's head and the armored body wanders off.

In the meantime, Morgan has captured Niniane's father. She takes Niniane to her castle and demands — with the threat of killing her father — that Niniane neutralize Merlin's power. In order to save her father Niniane learns Merlin's most powerful spell and locks him in his cave forever, but she is caught there as well.

Of course the Gwenevere-Lancelot problem erupts when Gawain and Agravain stumble upon the pair in delicto (if not flagrante). Agravain does some further spying on them,

Mordred takes the information to Arthur and, in a very Shakespearean scene, winds up stabbing the king.

The trapped Lancelot beats most of Agravain's 20 men. Gawain comes along to help and kills his traitorous brother. Morgan confronts Lancelot in the great hall and calls up a dragon. A fearsome fight ensues.

The entire film is interspersed with breaks back to the "present." Our New York visitor either listens to discourses from Merlin and Niniane or debates with them about the events they've witnessed. During this particular interlude, she convinces Merlin to use his astral body to go back and help Lancelot. In doing so, Merlin defeats the dragon, then calls on the power of Excalibur to kill Morgan. Merlin tells Lancelot that Camelot is dead and charges him to find the castle of the Holy Grail, to "seek the greater good."

It is Lancelot who takes the sword in the end. Arthur's body is placed on the barge to be carried to Avalon. In another shift to the present, Merlin and Niniane are reconciled to their fate. However, Cathryn tells them that they can break the spell, that Love cancels all curses. They go back but Cathryn cannot return with them. She awakens back at Stonehenge, with a scrap of Merlin's robe as a souvenir of her adventure.

Merlin and the Toothless Knights (1974)

Copyright 1974, I.D. Television, Britain; No further information available.

Merlin, Arthur and the Holy Grail (1998)

78 minutes; Color; Documentary; Copyright 1998, Emdee Productions, Ltd.; Copyright 1998, Acorn Media (packaging); Distributed exclusively by Acorn Media; The Learning Channel

Synopsis: This tape gathers the three primarily Arthurian episodes from the series *Legends of the Isles*. Included from that video collection are the episodes "Merlin the Wizard,"

"King Arthur" and "The Holy Grail." Each segment is approximately 25 minutes long and is reproduced in its entirety, including all the credits (see the entries for *Legends of the Isles*).

Evidently because only brief mention of Merlin is made in it, the "Stonehenge" episode is not included on this tape.

Merlin el Encantador (1976)

Not viewed; 2 Filmstrips; Part 1: 108 frames; Part 2: 110 frames; Color; 35mm, 2 audio cassettes (30 minutes each), teacher's guide included; Spanish; Copyright 1976, Walt Disney Educational Media Company; From the book by T. H. White; Library of Congress Call #PC4112.7; Library of Congress Catalogue #76732202; Dewey Decimal #372.6

Merlin of the Crystal Cave (1991)

159 minutes; Color; Live Action; Copyright 1991, British Broadcasting Corporation and BBC Enterprises, Ltd.; Noel Gay Television for BBC Television in Association with BBC Enterprises, Ltd.; CBS Fox Video #5840

CAST: George Winter (Merlin); Robert Powell (Ambrosius); Trevor Peacock (Rolf); Sam Hails (Arthur); Thomas Lambert (Child Merlin); Jody David (Boy Merlin); Benedick Blythe (Camlach); John Phillips (King Dafydd); Kim Thomas (Ninianne); Hefin Clarke (Dinias); Sam Dastor (Alun); Betty Marsden (Moravic); Mark Williams (Cerdic); Mark Collingwood (King Gorlon of Lanascol); Jonathan Copestake (Messenger); Julie Neubert (Queen Olwen); Don Henderson (Galapas); Christopher Quinn (Mabon); Gawn Grainger (Hanno); Davyd Harries (Marric); Peter Layton (Porter); Roger Alborough (Uther); Gordon Gostelow (Old Man); Mike Shannon (Black Beard); Jon Finch (King Vortigern); Emma Sutton (Queen Rowena); John Bennett (Maugan); Lewis Jones (Magician); Eamonn Collinge (Magician); Robert Brown (Gorlois); James Cormack (Foreman); Anthony Murray (Vortigern's Soldier); Alan Biars (Vortigern's Soldier); David Kelly (Poet); and the people of North Wales

CREDITS: Based on the Novel by — Mary Stewart; Adapted for Television by — Steve Bescoby; Music Composed and Conducted by — Francis Shaw; Orchestra — The Munich Symphony Orchestra; Casting Director — Jane Davies; Graphics — Andrew Smee; Visual Effects — Stuart Murdoch; Stunt Arranger — Gareth Milue; Property Master — Paul Purdy; Scenic Artist — Steven Sally-banks; Set Dresser — Amanda Ackland-Snow; Art Director — Dennis DeGroot; Costume Designer — Michael Burdle; Makeup Designer — Ann Buchanan; Makeup Assistant — Emma Bailey; Production Team — Celia Z. Bargh, Penelope Chong, Sarah Hutton, Barry Robinson-Wilson, Gary Beckerman; Grip — Alan Tabuer; Technical Director — Jeff Jefferey; Gaffer — Tony Hughes; Sound Recordists — Derek Williams, Ken Campbell; Cameraman — Ron Green; Special Effects Editor — Simon Brewster; On-Line Editor — Jeremy Adair; Off-Line Editor — Greg Harris; Dubbing Mixer — Mike Erander; 2nd Assistant Directors — Jane Cotton, Kerry Waddell; Production Assistant — Helen Drake; Production Manager — Jane Denholm; Location Manager — Julian Scott; 1st Assistant Director — John C. Cox; Lighting Designer — Peter Middleton; Production Designer — James Dillon; Line Producer — Hillary Bevan Jones; Executive Producers — Bill Cotton, Maurice Taylor; Producer — Shaun Sutton; Director — Michael Darlow

SYNOPSIS: For a made-for-television film, *Merlin of the Crystal Cave* is a terrific rendering of Mary Stewart's novel of the same title. A departure from the norm, this story leans heavily on the writings of Gildas, Bede, Nennius and Geoffrey of Monmouth rather than on Malory. An interpretation of the politics leading up to the time of Arthur, the film opens with the boy Arthur pulling Caliburn from the stone (on which are inscribed the words "Mithrea Invicto"), but continues as a reminiscence by Merlin. Riding off to rest after getting Arthur to the stone, Merlin's helper, Rolf, gets Merlin to recount how it all began.

As Merlin tells it, 100 years after the Roman withdrawal from Britain, Vortigern seized the throne. The rightful heirs, Ambrosius (or the Celtic Emrys) and his brother, Uther, escape to Brittany where they await an auspicious time to return and reclaim their heritage.

In order to quell civil wars, Vortigern enlists the aid of Hengist, most powerful of the Saxons. During a spy mission to Britain Ambrosius is wounded by Vortigern's mercenaries and found near death by Ninianne. She secretly nurses him back to health and they fall in love. Ambrosius has to return to Britanny so he is unaware of the birth of a son, who Ninianne names Merlin Emrys.

As a young boy Merlin discovers a cave and an old man who lives there named Galapas. Galapas teaches the young Merlin all sorts of things, from engineering to discovering his innate magical and visionary powers.

When the local king, Dafydd dies, Camlach takes over and immediately begins plotting against Vortigern. Planning to join Vortimer, one of Vortigern's sons in insurrection, Camlach also has it in for Merlin. Merlin manages to get away and winds up with his father in Brittany.

By the time Merlin becomes a young man, he has determined to help his father and Uther return to Britain. He and Rolf cross the channel to do some spying. Merlin finds Vortigern trying to build a fortress, but the walls will not stand. He convinces the superstitious Vortigern that dragons beneath the foundations are the cause and that they are a sign of danger. He scares Vortigern into fleeing to Caerleon, where Ambrosius is able to defeat him.

It is decided to restore the Giant's Dance at Amesbury as a monument to the Britons who died fighting the Saxons. Uther and Merlin go to Ireland to stop Gilam before the Irish can combine forces with Vortimer. It is there that Merlin finds the great stone he wants for the monument.

Vortigern and Camlach die and Uther becomes king.

Merlin the Magician see The Time Tunnel: "Merlin the Magician"

Merlin the Wizard see Legends of the Isles: "Merlin the Wizard"

Merlin's Magic Cave (1977)

89 minutes; Color; Cartoon; Copyright 1977, World TV Company; Copyright 1981, Century Video Corporation; Embassy Home Entertainment #7657

CREDITS: Narrator — Nicole Richards; Producers — Mike Haller, Yuji Tanno; Executive Producer — Century Video Corp.; Written by — Michael Haller; Music — Jamie Legon; Animation Services — Renan Productions; Voices — Nicole Richards, Lucy Holtzendorf, Mark Baldwin, Ann Fitzgerald; An International Media Group Production

SYNOPSIS: At the opening of *Merlin's Magic Cave* a cartoon narrator introduces herself, "Hello, my name is Morgan, and it's time for me to take you to Merlin's cave." As she is wearing a halloweenish witch's hat and a long gown, one might take her for a young Morgan Le Fay but the tape gives no further identification.

Morgan goes on to explain that Merlin was a great wizard "who served in King Arthur's court long, long ago." As she speaks, a couple of still illustrations of Merlin are shown. She says that when Merlin wasn't busy giving advice to kings and princes, he loved to tell stories to the children of the land. The children asked Merlin to hide the stories in a secret place and Morgan says she found the cave and the stories.

From here an adult narrator takes over, introducing each of eight traditional tales from around the world. All of them are done with cartoon characters. They are *Gulliver's Travels* by Jonathan Swift (England), *The Magic Pony* from Russia, *The Seal Skin* from Iceland, *The Monkey's Liver* from Thailand, *Thumbelina* by Hans Christian Andersen (Denmark), *The Wolf and the Seven Kids* by the Brothers Grimm (Germany), *The White Browed Dog* from Russia and *The Three Wishes* from England.

No further mention is made of Merlin or King Arthur.

Merlin's Magic of Learning (1979)

Not viewed; 15 minutes; Copyright 1979, Journal Films; No longer available. The distributor has archived copies, but says they are of unusually poor quality both in production values and content.

SYNOPSIS: Merlin brings three students to a magical world to encourage learning.

Merlin's Magical Message (197?)

Not viewed; 7 minutes; Color; Copyright 197?, Professional Research, Inc.; Library of Congress Call #RK63; Library of Congress Catalogue #85700539/F; Dewey Decimal #617.6

SYNOPSIS: Another use of Arthurian characters to promote dental health (see *The Adventures of Timmy the Tooth*).

Merlin's Shop of Mystical Wonders (1995)

92 minutes; Color; Live Action; Copyright 1995, Berton Films; Copyright l996, Santelmo Entertainment; Brencam Entertainment; A Berton Films Production; A Kenneth J. Berton Film; Monarch Home Video #7509

CAST: Ernest Borgnine (Grandfather); George Milan (Merlin); Bunny Summers (Zurella); John Terrence (Jonathan Cooper); Patricia Sansone (Madeline Cooper); Bob Mendelsohn (David Andrews); Mark Hurtado (Grandson); Julia Miller (Antique Store Clerk); Ben Sussman (Peddler in Park); Randy Chandler (Burglar); Vicki Saputo (Susan); Bruce Perry (Pete); Struan Robertson (Michael Andrews); Madelon Phillips (Psychic); Barry Chandler (Man in Car); J. Renee Gilbert (Grandma); Nicholas Noyes (Nicholas); Hillary Young (Nicholas's Mother); Olwen Morgan (Mrs. Johnson); Angeles Olazabaf (Girl on Bike); Kristi Berton (Sarah); Sheena (Miffy); Herself (Sparkle)

CREDITS: Executive Producers — Rose Ciolino, Grace Beretta; Directors of Photography — Michael Gfelner, Tony Martin; Associate Producers — Randy Chandler, Joe Baldanzi, Jr., Judith Chipalla, Jose Vergelin; Music by — Todd Hayen, Frank Macchia; Written, Produced and Directed by — Kenneth J. Berton; Line Producers — Kevin Dean, Stefan Rudnicki; Production Coordinator — Jamie Foley; Production Managers — Julie Baker, Kristi Berton; 1st Assistant Directors — Stacey Baily, Stefan Rudnicki; 2nd Assistant Directors — Jeremy Rubin, Ned Netterville; Production Assistants — Chuck Lewis, Cindy Moon, Kimberly Roseberry, Jane Foster, Ned Netterville, Chris Laro; 1st Assistant Camera — Chuck Baker, Scott Papera, Ron Hirshman, Val Camp; 2nd Assistant Camera — Laura Curry; Production Sound Recordist — Walter Andrews; Boom Operators — George Flores, Ted Harris; Gaffers — Mark Fraser, Keith Morgan, Jennifer Perkins; Best Boy Electrician — Alex Jawurski; Best Boy Grips — Frederico Capulino, Leslie McAlpine; Key Grips — Jim B. Irons, Richard A.

Ludt; Grips — A. J. Gilbert, Ian Anderson, Ken Herling, Richard Wood, David Stern; Production Designers — Lee Sjostrom, Melodie Eunist; Art Director — Laura Chariton; Set Construction — Randy Chandler, Joe Baldanzi, Nick Plantic, Scott Anderson, Chris Maggard, Judith Chipallo; Post Production Supervisor — Chic Ciccolini; Editor — Kenneth J. Berton; Assistant Editor and Avid Advisor — Jeffrey Belton; On-Line Technician — Keith Fernandes; Special Mechanical Effects — C.A.N. International, Nick Plantico, Scott Anderson, Chris Maggard; Music Orchestration — Todd Hayen, Frank Macchia, Ron Goldstein; Music Preparation — Janice Hayen; Music Assistant — Lisette Morton; Post Production Services — Post Plus, Inc., Firewater Films, Varitel Video, Beverly Hills Video Group; Post Sound Design — Track Design, Richard Allen; Sound Effects — Randy Chandler, Leonard Marcel; Additional Dialogue — Dina Sherman, Toni La Monica; Makeup Effects — Doug White Effects, Makeup Effects Lab; Makeup Effects Supervisor — Howard Tsuruba; Lead Sculptor — Jeremy Aiello; Makeup — Hillary Young, Adam Brandy, Lee Sjostrom; Props — Thornbird Arms; Pyrotechnics — Paul Sokol; Script Supervisors — Walter Hurd, Jon Valencia; Casting — Bebe Herman; Titles — CFI, Jeanne Beveridge, Hal Cohen; Cameras Provided by — Panavision; Film Lab — Four Media, Image Transform; Additional footage from *The Devil's Gift* courtesy of Windridge Productions; Special Thanks to: Chic Ciccolini, R. C. Nields, Richard Allen, Doug White, Anthony & Karen Hurtado, Calistoga Water, Hostess, Bud's Best Cookies, Inc., Organic Milling, California Snack Foods, Susana Mountain Water, Ocean Spray, Coca Cola, Hansens Natural, Creative Entertainment Services, Premier Entertainment Services, Dina Sherman, Michael Gfelner, Randy Chandler, Jeremy Rubin

SYNOPSIS: A little boy staying with his grandfather is watching a horror movie on television. Lightning knocks the power out and the grandfather entertains the lad with a couple of stories about Merlin the sorcerer. But these tales are not from King Arthur's time as the grandfather points out, but of when Merlin came to present-day California.

Merlin and his wife, Zurella, set up a curio shop on a trendy California street. But this shop is unique — much bigger on the inside than the entrance would have one believe. There are caves and rock gardens in the shop and a pool of water. In the middle of the place stands a ten-foot-tall rock with a bejeweled sword sticking out of it.

The first customer to wander into this strange store is a little boy whose mom meets a couple of friends on the sidewalk in front of the shop. While he chats with Merlin and Zurella his mom learns that her friend and her husband are unable to have any kids. The friend's husband, Jonathan Cooper, is a journalist who has come to check out the place for an article on the new store.

He's an obnoxious lout who doesn't believe anything Merlin says. Zurella talks Merlin into sending his book of magic home with the man. In the meantime Mrs. Cooper charms and is charmed by Zurella. Zurella gives her a magical wishing stone and we are led to believe that Mrs. Cooper wishes for a baby.

Mr. Cooper starts trying out the spells from the book and they all work. Unfortunately each time he uses one he ages. By the time he realizes the damage he's done to himself he's aged 15 years. Desperately searching through the book he finds a rejuvenation spell and casts it. It backfires on him and he becomes an infant, inadvertently granting Mrs. Cooper's wish.

The second story begins with a burglar breaking into Merlin's shop. Merlin's pet dragon, Gwendolyn, scares the miscreant off, but not before he manages to swipe a toy monkey.

To Merlin's chagrin, this happens to be the toy in which Morgana, the evil sorceress, has imprisoned an evil spirit. Merlin has to get the thing back.

The thief sells the monkey to another shop where it is bought by a woman as a birthday gift for a little boy. As soon as the monkey is in the boy's house, things start dying — plants, flies and the last straw is when the family dog is killed mysteriously.

The dad hires a psychic who tells him that it's the monkey causing all the troubles and that it must be gotten rid of. He tries to do so but it finds its way back. Merlin arrives in the nick of time to save everyone and he takes the evil toy away.

References to Arthurian themes are almost nonexistent in this film. The whole thing is about magic and the use of Merlin is simply to make something familiar the basis for it all.

The grandfather telling these stories states that Merlin left King Arthur's time to come to the present to reintroduce magic to the modern world. Excalibur shows up in Merlin's shop, though no character says anything about the sword. It's just there in the stone. Finally, the dragon's name, Gwendolyn, harks back to the name Gwenevere but this is not a very complimentary connection.

The Mighty (1997)

107 minutes; Color; Live Action; Copyright 1997, Miramax Films

CAST: Harry Dean Stanton (Grim); Gena Rowlands (Gram); Elden Henson (Maxwell Kane); Douglas Bisset (Homeless Man); Joe Perrino (Blade); Dov Tiefenbach (Doghouse Boy #1); Michael Colton (Doghouse Boy #2); Eve Crawford (Mrs. Donelli); Kieran Culkin (Kevin Dillon); Sharon Stone (Gwen Dillon); John Bourgeois (Mr. Sacker); Bruce Tubbe (Officer); Rudy Webb (Mr. Hampton); Ron Nigrini (Man in Diner); Nadia Litz (Girl in Diner); Gillian Anderson (Loretta Lee); Meatloaf (Iggy); Serena Pruyn (Girl in Hall); Telmo Miranda (Boy in Hall); Jordan Hughes (Denardo); Jennifer Lewis (Mrs. Addison); Bryon Bully (Fat Boy); Charlaine Porter (Girl with Limp); James Gandolfini (Kenny Kane); Lisa Marie Chen (Girl in Cafeteria); Lisa Mininni (Cashier); Ann Chiu (Nurse); Carl Marotte (Doctor); Nora Sheehan (Policewoman); Sophie Bennett (Little Girl); William Van Allen (Laundry Worker)

CREDITS: Costume Designer — Marie Sylvie Deveau; Casting — Barbara Cohen, Mary Gail Artz; Music — Trevor Jones; Editor — Martin Walsh; Production Designer — Caroline Hanania; Director of Photography — John De Borman, B.S.C.; Co–Executive Producer — Chaos Productions; Executive Producers — Bob Weinstein, Harvey Weinstein, Julie Goldstein; Co–Producer — Don Carmody; Produced by — Jane Startz, Simon Fields; Based on the novel *Freak the Mighty* by Rodman Philbrick; Screenplay — Charles Leavitt; Director — Peter Chelsom; Helicopter Pilot — David

William Paris; Stunt Coordinator — Rick Forsayath; Stunt Performers: Ron Bell, Matt Birman, C. J. Fidler, Erin Jarvis, Steve Lucescu, Sue Parker, Robert Racki, Anton Tyukodi, Dan Belley, Mary Ann Boyles, Jason Guja, Jamie Jones, Dwayne McLean, Ed Queffelec, Brian Renfro, Peter Szko; Production Manager — Joseph Boccia; First Assistant Director — David Webb; Second Assistant Director — Bruno Brynlarski; Production Associate — Liz Amsden; Art Director — Dennis Davenport; Set Director — Cal Loucks; Camera Operator — Perry Hoffman; First Assistant Camera — Michael Hall; Second Assistant Camera — Russell Bowie; First Assistant "B" Camera — Claran Copelin; Script Supervisor — Susanna David; Production Coordinator — Tammy Quinn; Assistant Production Coordinator — Elizabeth Senyi; Location Manager — Debra Beers; Assistant Location Manager — Beverly Kolbe; Sound Mixer — Bruce Carwardine; Boom Operator — Peter Melnychuk; Post Production Supervisor — Isabel Henderson; Associate Film Editor — Jacqueline Carmody; First Assistant Editor — Lynne Warr; Assistant Editor — Justin Green; Apprentice Editor — Aaron Nicolaides; Supervising Sound Editor — Paul Clay; Recording Mixers — Patrick Cyccone, Christian Minkler; Property Master — Tory Bellingham; Gaffer — Scotty Allan; Key Grip — Mike Kirilenko; Assistant Costume Designer — Jay DuBoisson; Key Makeup Artist — Christine Hart; Makeup Artist for Ms. Stone — Toni Walker; Key Hairstylist — Jennifer O'Halloran; Hairstylist for Ms. Stone — Toni Walker; Wig Coordinator — Deborah Wolksi-McNulty; Storyboard Artist — Gary Thomas; Assistant Art Directors — Andrew Stern, Mike Shocrylas; Prosthetic Appliances — FX Smith; On-Set Dresser — Arline Smith; Special Effects Coordinator — Michael Kavanagh; Assistant Special Effects Coordinator — Danny White; Construction Coordinator — Jim Halpenny; Transportation Coordinator — Nick Sweetman; Transportation Captain — Grant Volkers; Production Accountant — Irene Phelps; Assistant to Mr. Chelsom — Varina Bleil; Assistants to Ms. Startz — Deborah Devgan, Amanda Ansorge, Gillian MacKenzie; Assistants to Mr. Fields — Simone Stock, Emilie Sennebogen; Assistants to Ms. Goldstein — Michelle Sy, Meighan Dobson; Assistants to Harvey Weinstein — Rick Schwartz, Denise Doyle, Eli Holzman, Barbara Schneeweiss; Assistants to Bob Weinstein — Louis Spiegler, Michael Neithardt; Assistant to Ms. Stone — Brady Kuhlman; Art Department Coordinator — Tanit Ann Mendes; Art Department Assistant — Tim Brooks; Unit Publicist — Prudence Emery; Still Photographer — Kerry Hayes; Toronto Casting — Ross Clydesdale, C.D.C.; Casting Associates — Lynda Halligan, Karen Meisels; Wardrobe Mistress — Karen Renaut; Costumer — Robert Roberts; Costumer for Ms. Stone — Oda Groeschel; Leadperson — Dan Wladyka; Buyer — Linda McClelland; Assistant Property — Deryck Blake; Best Boy Electric — Ian Scott; Rigging Gaffer — Gary Deneault; Electricians — Paul Bolton, Gord Eldridge, Brian Woodroof; Generator Operator — Alan Angus; Best Boy Grip — Ron Yolevsky; Dolly Grip — Candide Franklyn; Rigging Grip — Roy Elliston; Grips — Glen Goodchild, Sam Turturicci; Camera Trainees — Tara Yates, Bob Standish; Video Assistant — Tim Davis; Third Assistant Director — Mary Sylwester; Locations Assistant — Ron Tailleur; Production Office Assistant — Paul Hiscock; Key Set Production Assistants — Robin Reelis, Cassandra Cronenberg; Post Production Assistant — Joseph Virzi; Head Carpenter — Steve Elliston; Assistant Head Carpenter — Rob Bonney; Scenic Artist — Tim Murton; Assistant Scenic Artist — Ian Nelmes; Head Painter — Rob McEune; Assistant Head Painter — Randy Ross; On-Set Painter — Brad Francis; Head Driver — Ron Hilts; Drivers — John Cocks, John Coles, Dave Cotton, Bill Jackson, Joe Muscat, Brian O'Hara; Catering — By David's; Craft Service — Starcraft; Stand-ins — Craig McGlauchlin, Corey Wood; Stand-in for Ms. Stone — Rose Heeter; Security for Ms. Stone — Kristin Marshall, Dave Reilly; Tutor — Laurel Bresnahan; Post Production Supervisor, U.K. — Stephen Law; Assistant Editor, U.K. — Andy Yuncken; Assistant Editor, Toronto — David McGroarty; Trainee Editor, Toronto — Shelley Croft; Dialogue Editors — Bob Goold, Vanessa Lapato; Effects Editor — Sam Gemette; ADR Editor — Tally Paulos; Sound Assistants — Paul Tinta, Chris Winter; ADR Mixer — Dean St. John; ADR Recordist — Joseph L. Bosco; Foley Artists — Casey Troutman, Jim Bailey; Dub-Stage Re-recordists — Frank Fleming, Brian Pierret; Dolby Sound Consultant — Thom "Coach" Ehle; SDDS Consultant — Benjamin Ing; ADR Group Voice Casting — Loop Troop; Sound Re-recorded at — Four Media Sound; Sound Editorial Services — Multimedia Sound; Supervising Music Editor — Jim Harrison; Assistant Music Editor — Richard Harrison; Music Editing — Segue Music; Temp Music Editor — Paul Rabjohns; Music Recorded and Mixed by — Simion Rhodes; Additional Mixing — Gareth Cousins; Synthesizers Performed by — Trevor Jones; Synthesizers Programmed by — Gareth Cousins, Kipper; Orchestrations — Trevor Jones, Geoff Alexander, Julian Kershaw; Music Performed by the London Symphony Orchestra; Leader — Gordon Nikolitch;

Additional Music Leader — Gavyn Wright; Conductor — Geoff Alexander; Orchestral Contractor — Isobel Griffiths; Ewi Played by — Phil Todd; Acoustic Guitar — Craig Ogden; Piano — Gwen Mok; Electric Guitar — Clem Clempson; Harmonica — Mark Feltham; Uileann Pipes — Paul Brennan; Electric Violin — Dermot Crehan; Percussion — Paul Clarvis; Singers — Miriam Stockley, Janet Mooney, Lance Ellington, Phil Nichol; Conductor — Geoff Alexander; Music Preparation — Tony Stanton, Bill Silcock; Music Coordinator for CMMP — Victoria Seale; Music Clearances — Jill Meyers; Music Recorded and Mixed at Air Lyndhurst and Abbey Road Studios, London; Synthesizers Recorded at — CMMP Studio; Studio Monitoring by ATC Loudspeaker Technology; Color by — Deluxe Laboratories; Color Timer — Bob McMillian; Negative Cutter — Gary Burritt; Titles and Opticals — Howard Anderson Co.; Title Designer — Charles McDonald; Optical Supervisor — Mike Griffin; Optical Line-up — Richard Eberhardt, Bernie Reilly, Leilani McHugh, Alex Cano; Title Camera — Thane Berti; Optical Camera — Steve Mayer; Digital Visual Effects by — Digiscope; Executive Producer — Mary Stuart-Welch; Effects Producer — Lorraine "Deedle" Silver; Digital Artists — Tony Deryan, Naomi Sato; Digital Imaging — Scott Crafford; Digital Visual Effects by OCS/Freeze Frame/Pixel Magic; Digital Supervisor — Raymond McIntyre, Jr.; Digital Coordinator — Dave Fiske; Digital Visual Effects and Animation by C.O.R.E. Digital Effects; Animation Directors — John Mariella, Aaron Linton, Suzanne Shortt, Jihyung Sung, Bradley Wilderson; Production Manager — Sara Fillmore; Cincinnati Unit: Production Manager — Sanford E. Hampton; Second Assistant Director — Jeff Shiffman; Production Coordinator — Taci M. Dunn; Assistant Production Coordinator — Iris Hampton; Location Manager — Deirdre Costa; Local Casting — D. Lynn Meyers; Aerial/Second Unit Cameraman — Michael Kelem; Aerial/Second Unit Camera Assistant — Daniel Larkin; Second Unit Assistant Camera — Dean Michael Simmon; Loader — Richard Fredette; Video Assistant — Kevin P. Boyd; Best Boy Electric — Quincy Koenig; Electricians — Tim Gendele, Jim Butler; Genny Operator — Ron Sabarsky; Best Boy Grip — Matthew Jennings; Grips — Jerry Tisdale, Jim Harrington, Randall Roman, Chris Athy; Model Helicopter Operator — Wendell Atkins; Boom Operator — Joel C. Trent; Set Dressers — Jack Hering, Jeff Zink; Set Costumer — Robin Fields; Props Assistant — Paula D. Collins; Key Set Production Assistant — Gina K. Frosini; Set Production Assistants — Andrew J. Madewell, Karen Usher, Mark Vise, Thomas "Shane" Reed; Office Production Assistants — Nora Martini, David S. Pensak; Transportation Coordinator — Don Retzer; Transportation Captain — Marvin Hacker; Catering — The Chafer Caterer; Craft Service — Debby A. Blome; Line Producer — Jason Clark; Production Manager — Brian Campbell; Director of Photography — David Dunlap; Production Designer — Tony Cowley; Art Director — Paul Austerberry; Extras Casting — Jane Rogers; Assistant Costume Designer — Michele Harney; Key Grip — Wayne Goodchild; Gaffer — Bob McRae; Makeup Artist — Christine Hart; Location Manager — David Banigan; Property Master — Christopher Greggie; Script Supervisor — Blanche McDermaid; Sound Mixer — Owen Langevin; Boom Operator — James L. Thompson; Special Effects Coordinator — Martin Malivoire; Transportation Coordinator — Neil Montgomerie; Driver/Captain — Gerry Savoy; Head Driver — Andrew Star; Stunt Coordinator — Charles Picerni; Visual Effects Coordinator — Eric Allard; Production Coordinator — Beverly Sutton; Co-Coordinator — Glennis Bastien; Production Assistants — Brad Milburn, Michelle Bridgman; Production Accountant — Heather McIntosh; Assistant Accountant — Sarah Thornton; "The Mighty": Written by — Sting, Trevor Jones; Performed by — Sting; Sting appears courtesy of A&M Records; "Folkloric": Written by — Alfred Kluten; Courtesy of Associated Production Music; "Don't Count Me Out": Written by — K. Perry; Courtesy of Zomba Music Services; "Strip Bar Style": Written by — Peter Haycock; Courtesy of Ark 21 Records; "Todo en la Vida se Paga": Written by — Steven John; Courtesy of Zomba Music Services; "Let the Good Times Roll": Written by — Leonard Lee, Shirley Goodman; Performed by — B. B. King; Zucchero; B. B. King appears courtesy of MCA Records; Zucchero appears courtesy of Mercury Records; "Jingle Bells": Arranged by — John D'Andrea; Performed by — Pat Boone; Courtesy of MCA Records; Under license from Universal Music Special Markets; Soundtrack Available on Pangaea Records; Camera and Location Equipment Supplied by — William F. White, Ltd.; Studio Services Provided by — Cinespace Studios Management; Production Insurance Provided by — Aon/Ruben-Winkler

SYNOPSIS: *The Mighty* is a film which incorporates Arthurian themes into modern life in a completely unique fashion. Based on the young reader's novel *Freak the Mighty* by Rodman Philbrick, it is a story about two 13-year-old boys and their brief but intense friendship.

Maxwell Kane is a giant of a boy who has been labeled as learning disabled. His father is in prison for having murdered his mother and Max lives with his grandparents. Kevin Dillon and his mother, Gwen, move into the neighborhood one summer. Kevin suffers from Morquio's Syndrome, a disease which causes severe skeletal deformity and internal organ complications. With his tiny, twisted body and leg braces, Kevin is labeled a freak.

Kevin is a voracious reader who seems to know everything. He also is a wise-cracking jokester who never holds his tongue. Compared to the reticent Max, he's a genius. Partly because of the sameness of their situations of being outcasts and partly because of their extreme differences they become a perfect team. Kevin's wit, imagination and excitable curiosity fill gaps in Max's life. Max's physical stature and willing acceptance do the same for Kevin.

The boys' relationship gets off to a rocky start when school opens and then Kevin is assigned to tutor Max in reading. He gives Max his own copy of James Knowles's *King Arthur and His Knights* to read. The ice is broken, however, at a fireworks show at a local carnival one night. Kevin has paid Max to take him to the event, but by the time of the fireworks display the crowd is so packed together that Kevin can't see a thing. On an impulse, Max picks Kevin up and puts him on his shoulders.

After the fireworks Max and Kevin are spotted by the members of a street gang whom they've already had run-ins with. Still on Max's shoulders, Kevin guides him like a horse, trying to evade the hoodlums, but they end up trapped at the edge of a pond. Kevin convinces Max to walk into the water.

Max finally heads out into the pond and the leader of the gang follows with a knife. The mud at the bottom makes it impossible for Max to go too far, but it's far enough to stop the attack. In an effort to free his legs from the

muck Max squats down, immersing the two of them completely. This impromptu baptism marks the beginning of Max and Kevin's new existence.

In the next days, Max and Kevin venture into the world of their neighborhood together, Kevin always on his friend's shoulders. Because of Kevin's fascination with the legends of King Arthur, they begin to see these outings as quests.

In one imaginative flash, a man lying in a doorway is transformed into a resting knight, complete with full chainmail and emblazoned tunic. The boys stop at a local restaurant to buy a candy bar at the counter and witness a punk roughing up a girl. The symbiotic pair step over and there is a momentary view of a chainmail-clad knight on a charger. They chase the punk off and the girl thanks them.

Then follows one of the most stirring of the Arthurian scenes in the film. Reveling in their newfound friendship and purpose, Max, with Kevin on his shoulders, walks across an old city bridge. Four of King Arthur's knights appear beside them, two on either side, riding along in silence with the boys.

The next quest Kevin launches them on proves more dangerous. There is a purse snatching and Kevin witnesses the culprit jam the purse down a storm grate. He cajoles Max into accompanying him to retrieve it. Donning costumes (in spite of Max's objections) and equipped with all sorts of paraphernalia, the two sneak out in the middle of the night to perform their good deed.

Using rope and a fire escape as a crane, they manage to lift the huge grate and Max climbs down to get the purse. Unfortunately the street gang also shows up to reclaim the prize and they threaten to beat the two heroes with bats and chains. When Kevin is cornered, Max goes berserk.

With Herculean strength, Max lifts the storm grate and uses it as a shield against the bats. In another imaginative flash, the grate becomes a real knight's shield, the bat appears as a sword striking it. Max's rage and superhuman aspect panic the gang and as they run off he hurls the storm grate after them.

Once things have settled down, Kevin digs a wallet from the purse, which is filled with money and the I.D. of its owner, one Loretta Lee. The next day they return the purse to its owner, thinking they're acting in a properly chivalrous fashion. Loretta and her husband, Iggy, live in a rundown tenement building. They turn out to be old acquaintances of Max's father. Recognizing Max, Iggy tries to pump the boys for information and scares them. In another display of his strength, Max nearly rips their door off its hinges to make his escape.

Things go from bad to worse. Max and his grandparents are notified that Max's father is being released from prison. The news sends them into paroxysms of fear. Shortly after that Kevin chokes on his lunch at school and the momentary airway blockage not only puts him in the hospital for two weeks, but worsens his systemic condition.

Although physically weakened by the incident, Kevin is released from the hospital eventually. On a winter's outing together, Kevin guides Max to a medical research center. Kevin tells Max that in about a year he will be the first human to be fitted with a bionic body. He claims to have been under the center's care for some time and they are almost ready to do the transplant. Max has a hard time grasping it all, but ultimately accepts his friend's story.

Then on Christmas Eve, the senior Kane shows up in Max's room and kidnaps the boy. Stealing a pickup truck, he takes his son to the tenements where Iggy and Loretta live and ties Max up in a temporarily unoccupied apartment. He tries to convince Max that he didn't kill his mother but Max, petrified, can only grimly go along with whatever the fiend is up to.

In the meantime Max's disappearance has been discovered and the police notified. Kevin, however, sneaks out on his own to track his friend down. At a particularly difficult mo-

ment in his journey, the silent, mounted knights appear.

Loretta sympathizes with Max and tries unsuccessfully to slip him a pair of cutters. Kane discovers the ruse and attacks Loretta, strangling her. Max's childhood memories flood back, the image of Kane strangling his mother clear now in his mind. Kevin shows up with a squirt gun filled with vinegar and pepper and sprays Kane's eyes in time to help Max and Loretta. Max breaks free of his bonds, picks Kevin up and crashes through a flimsy wall to the sunshine outside. As Kane gives chase, the police are there to put him back into custody.

Kevin's Christmas gift to Max is a thick journal that he made himself. The blank pages puzzle Max, but Kevin tells him to fill the book with their adventures. Words, Kevin says, are pieces of a picture, sentences are pictures and one just uses one's imagination to connect them together.

During the night, Kevin dies. Distraught and unbelieving, Max races to the medical research center and learns that there is no plan to give Kevin a mechanical body. It was simply a hopeful story Kevin had made up for himself.

Max goes into a deep depression, refusing to come out of his room for days. He finally does though and one day runs into Loretta. She asks him what he's up to and Max says, "Nothing." "Nothing's a drag," Loretta says, "think about it." Max does think about it and her few simple words wake him up.

In the closing scene, Max takes one of Kevin's favorite items outside. It's a rubber-band–powered model ornithopter, which Max winds up and releases into the sky. As it slowly flies off, higher and higher, the mounted knights appear again, watching the artificial bird, smiling.

Mr. Magoo's Literary Classics: "King Arthur" (1964)

50 minutes; Color; Cartoon; Copyright 1964,1984, Paramount Communications Company; UPA Video #12854

WITH THE VOICES OF: Jim Backus as Mr. Magoo; Howard Morris; Marvin Miller; Everett Sloane; Julie Bennett

CREDITS: Adapted for Television by — Sloan Nibley; Executive Producer — Henry G. Saperstein; Supervising Director — Abe Levitow; Story Editor — George Gordon; Sequence Director — Gerard Baldwin; Animation Director — Bob McKimson; Music by — Carl Brandt; Animation — John Walker, Bob Bransford, Phil Duncan, Marvin Woodward, Herman Cohen; Production Design — Tony Rivera; Titles — Jacques Rupp, Don Morgan; Color Styling — Robert Inman; Character Design — Lee Mishkin, Bob Dranko; Editorial — Sam Horta, Carl Bennett, George Probert, Wayne Hughes, Helen Wright; Camera — Max Morgan, Bill Kotler, John Folk, John Nelson, Dennis Cook; Production Manager — Earl Jonas; Production Coordinator — George Grandprè; Checking — Grace McCurdy; Ink and Paint — Auril Thompson; A Henry G. Saperstein Production by UPA Pictures, Inc.

SYNOPSIS: In the 25-minute "King Arthur" segment of this tape, Mr. Magoo plays Merlin. Bad kings are threatening the good King Uther's realm. In order to save the infant Arthur from possible assassination, Uther gives the child to Merlin to raise until he's old enough to take the throne. Merlin finds an infant too much to handle, so he gives Arthur to Ector to raise with Ector's own boy, Kay.

Years later, the evil Pellinore attempts to pull the famous sword from the stone, but can't. Arthur succeeds, Merlin reveals the truth of Arthur's heritage and the coronation is set for Sunday.

Arthur wants 50 knights for his Round Table. He chooses Leodegrance's daughter, Guenevere, to marry and sends Lancelot to get her. Pellinore tries to block the way, Merlin gets the Lady of the Lake to give Arthur Excalibur and Arthur defeats Pellinore.

For his fans Mr. Magoo makes a charming Merlin. For Arthur buffs, this tape is most interesting for its departures from the most commonly accepted versions of the legends.

The most glaring mistake is right at the opening when Magoo narrates, "back in medieval times … London in the third century." This has to be the only adaptation that dates Arthur 200 years before the Roman departure from Britain.

Mr. Merlin (1981)

Not viewed; 30-minute episodes; Color; Live Action; Copyright 1981–1982, Columbia Pictures Television/Larry Larry Company

CAST: Clark Brandon (Zachary Rogers); Barnard Hughs (Max Merlin); Elaine Joyce (Alexandra); Jonathan Prince (Leo)

CREDITS: Effects — Bill Millar; Cinematography (pilot) — Chuck Arnold; Cinematography (series) — Ronald W. Browne; Music — Ken Harrison; Production Design — Ross Bellah, Robert Purcell; Costume Design — Grady Hunt; Film Editor (series) — Kenneth R. Koch; Film Editor (pilot) — Robert R. Shugrue; Executive Producers — Larry Rosen, Larry Tucker; Special Visual Effects — Dina Burkett, Bill Millar; Camera Operator (pilot) — Jonathan West

SYNOPSIS: Merlin reincarnated as an auto mechanic? This short-running television series included one episode entitled "A Moment in Camelot" (January 6, 1982).

Monty Python and the Holy Grail (1974)

90 minutes; Color; Live Action; Copyright 1974, National Film Trustee Company, Ltd.; Krypton International Corporation; RCA/Columbia Pictures Home Video #92253; Columbia Pictures Home Entertainment; From Cinema 5; Python (Monty) Pictures, Ltd., in Association with Michael White

CAST (This section does not appear on the film, but anyone familiar with the Python troupe will recognize the following actors and their multiple roles): John Cleese (Guard #2, Customer, Black Knight, Villager #3, Sir Lancelot, French Guard, Tim the Enchanter); Graham Chapman (King Arthur, Middle Head); Terry Gilliam (Patsy, Old Man); Michael Palin (Guard #1, Dennis, Villager #2, Narrator, Sir Galahad, Right-Hand Head, Head Knight Who Says Nee, Father, 2nd Brother); Eric Idle (Mortician, Villager #1, Sir Robin, Guard, Concorde, Roger the Shrubber, Brother Maynard); Terry Jones (Woman, Sir Bedevere, Left-Hand Head, Prince Herbert)

CREDITS: Written and Performed by — Graham Chapman, John Cleese, Eric Idle, Terry Gilliam, Terry Jones, Michael Palin; With — Connie

Members of the famed comedic troupe in *Monty Python and the Holy Grail*.

Booth, Neil Innes, John Young, Carol Cleveland, Bee Duffell, Rita Davies; Also Appearing — Avril Stewart, Sally Klinghorn; Also Also Appearing — Mark Zuccio, Menuko Fornier, Sandy Rome, Joel Flynn, Leanine Ward, Sally Cocombe, Yvonne Dick, Fiona Gordon, Jody Lama, Sylvia Tayler, Mary Allen, Elizabeth Cameron, Sandy Johnson, Renaldo Squire, Alison Walker, Anna Lanki, Vivienne McDonald, Daphne Darling, Gloria Graham, Tracy Scadden, Joyce Fulmer; Camera Operator — Howard Atherton; Camera Focus — John Wellard; Camera Assistant — Roger Pratt; Camera Grip — Ray Hall; Chargehand Electrician — Terry Hunt; Lighting — Telefilm Lighting Service, Ltd., Andrew Ritchie & Son, Ltd., Technicolor; Rostrum Cameraman — Kent Houston; Sound Recordist — Garth Marshall; Sound Mixer — Hugh Strain; Boom Swinger — Godfry Kirby; Sound Maintenance — Phillip Chubb; Sound Assistant — Robert Doyle; Assistant Editors — John Mister, Brian Peachey, Alexander Campbell Askew, Nick Gast, Danielle Ko; Sound Effects — Ian Crafford; Continuity — Penny Eyles; Accountant — Brian Brockwell; Production Secretary — Christine Watt; Property Buyer — Brian Winterborn; Property Master — Tom Raeburn; Property Men — Roy Cannon, Charlie Torbe, Mike Kennedy; Catering — Ron Hellard, Ltd.; Vehicles — Budget Rent-a-Car, Ltd.; Assistant Art Director — Philip Cowlam; Construction Manager — Bill Harman; Carpenters — Nobby Clark, Bob Devine; Painter — Graham Bullock; Stagehand — Jim N. Savery; Rigger — Ed Sullivan; With special extra thanks to: Charles Knode, Brian McNulty, John Cahill, Peter Thomson, Scott Cable, Valerie Chartican, Drew Mars, Scott Smith, Charles Cocker, Brian Macnaghan, Scott Bunnell, Bernard Pelanger, Alcine McAlpine, Hugh Boyle, Dave Tayler, Gary Cooper, Peter Sanders, Ian Staghead, Vaughn Millard, Hamish MacDonners, Terry Macnic, Fawn O'Pierce; Made entirely on location in Scotland; Songs — Neil Innes; Additional Music — De Wolfe; Costume Designer — Hazel Pethig; Production Manager — Julian Doyle; Assistant Director — Gerry Harrison; Special Effects — John Horton; Choreography by — Leo Kharibian; Light Director and Period Consultant — John Waller; Makeup Artists — Pearl Rashbass, Pam Luke; Special Effects Photography—Julian Doyle; Animation Assistance—Lucinda Cowell, Kate Hepburn; Lighting Cameraman—Terry Bedford; Designer—Roy Smith; Editor—John Hackney; Executive Producer—John Goldstone; Producer—Mark Forstater; Directed by—Terry Gilliam and Terry Jones

SYNOPSIS: The quintessential spoof of Arthurian film and legend from the British comedy group Monty Python. The movie opens (ostensibly) in England, A.D. 932. Out of a fog trots King Arthur, not on horseback but on foot, pretending he's on a horse. He's followed by Patsy, his servant, who clacks together two coconut halves to make hoof noises.

Touring the countryside to get a feel for what's going on, Arthur comes across some peasants in a field of muck. One of the peasants gives Arthur an intellectual run for his money in political debate. "Strange women lying in ponds ... distributing swords is no basis for a system of government.... You can't expect to wield supreme executive power just because some watery tart threw a sword at you."

Arthur's next big encounter is with a Black Knight who is guarding a bridge. Anyone who wants to cross has to fight him first. Arthur is forced into combat and hacks the knight's limbs off one by one. The knight remains belligerent as Arthur trots off, ignoring the yelling torso.

There are further incredible adventures and asides: wandering monks, a witch trial, a song-and-dance number at Camelot, a chat with God, who tells the group to find the Holy Grail, and the siege of a French castle, including the construction of a sort of Trojan Horse that's a bunny rabbit.

The seeds of this Camelot's disintegration are planted when there is a break from the past. A "famous historian" doing a television documentary is cut down by a knight. Police begin searching for the killer.

Galahad sees the Grail as it hovers over the Castle Anthrax where dwell eight score beautiful young blondes and brunettes, all between the ages of 16 and 19½. He is saved from

their clutches and the group moves on to battle the knights who say Nee, to ruin the wedding of Prince Herbert and finally to meet the great enchanter, Tim.

In any other movie, this would be Merlin, and Tim looks and acts a bit like the Merlin in the film *Excalibur,* which was released seven years after the Python effort.

Tim leads the searchers to Caer Banough, a cave which is protected by a killer rabbit. This vicious, flying carnivore ("with huge pointy teeth") manages to kill Gawain, Hector, Bors and some others before it is stopped by the Holy Hand Grenade of Antioch.

Unfortunately the police are drawing nearer. In fact they hear the explosion of the hand grenade. In the meantime, on one of the cave walls Arthur and company find written the last words of Joseph of Arimathea.

As the group moves on to the Bridge of Death, the police find the carnage at the cave entrance. Arthur and Bedemeer come to a lake where a dragon ship takes them to the Castle Arrrg. The French are there and Arthur is driven off by their insults and spattered offal.

Back on shore Arthur calls up a huge army to help him attack the castle, but the charge is interrupted by the arrival of the police. Arthur and Bedemeer are hauled off in paddy wagons.

The Moon Stallion (1978)

95 minutes; Color; Live Action; Copyright 1978, 1985, 1990 British Broadcasting Corporation and BBC Enterprises, Ltd.; Distributed by BFS Video #99835; A BBC-TV Production in Association with Sudfunk Stuttgart; TABU

CAST: Sarah Sutton (Diana); David Haig (Todman); James Greene (Professor Purwell); John Abineri (Sir George Mortenhurze); David Pullan (Paul); Caroline Goodall (Estelle); Joy Harington (Mrs. Grookes); Peter Morley (Sam); Green King (Michael Kilgarriff)

CREDITS: Fight Arranged by—John Morgan; Music—Howard Blake; Graphic Designer—Karen Morley; Costume Designer—Judy Pepperdine; Makeup Artist—Viv Gunzi; Photography by—Ian Hilton; Sound—Doug Mawson; Film Editor—

Bill Wright; Production Assistant — Ian M. Fraser; Producer's Assistant — Anne Duffey; Designer — Roger Cann; Executive Producer — Anna Home; Director — Dorothea Brooking; Videotape Editor — Albert Bourne; Adapted for BBC Video by — Katrina Murray; Written by — Brian Hayles

SYNOPSIS: An intriguing blend of Arthurian legend and other lore of ancient Britain. Set around the turn of the century, the film concentrates on myths surrounding the Moon Goddess, Diana, the mystical Moon Stallion and the Chalk Horse of Uffington.

A blind girl named Diana travels with her brother and father to the home of a friend of her father. The men are preoccupied with research on locating the site of King Arthur's battle at Mount Badon. They theorize that Arthur was a Celtic cavalry warlord and place the battlefield somewhere nearby.

In the meantime strange things begin happening to Diana, who can sense the presence of the real white stallion that haunts the area. A stableman named Todman notices the strange connection with the girl. He is in cahoots with another character to capture the stallion, but Todman has his own plans as well. He's a "horse whisperer," able to communicate with animals.

Diana has a vision of King Arthur and winds up riding the white stallion to Weiland Smithy where Weiland the Green King guards the sacred iron. Diana's blind innocence awakens the Green King, who also happens to be the priest and consort of the Moon Goddess. This is what Todman is after. He challenges the Green King to hand-to-hand combat but, because he cheats, the Moon Stallion kills him.

Le Morte d'Arthur: The Legend of the King (1993)

50 minutes; Color; Documentary; Copyright 1993, Discovery Communications, Inc.; A Presentation of Discovery Productions in Association with Cronkite-Ward; The Discovery Channel Collector's Edition Great Books; Films for the Humanities and Sciences #ASJ5214

CREDITS: Dedicated to the memory of Maureen Schoos; Narrated by — Donald Sutherland; Written and Directed by — Dale Minor; Producers — Dale Minor, Linda Duvoisin; Series Producer — Jonathan Ward; Executive Editor — Walter Cronkite; Executive Producer — Tim Cowling; Cinematographer — Ian Savage; Editor — Loye Miller; Music — Frank Ferucci; Associate Producer — Pamela Deutsch; Coordinating Producer — Maureen Schoos; Additional Camera — Hugh Hood, Gary Griea, Chuck Levy, Michael Miles, Terry Morrison, Alan Palmer; Sound — Ann Evans, Glenn Marullo, Graham Ross, Dennis Towns, Mace Williams; Gaffers — Bob Waybright, Nick Green, Lance Phox; Production Manager/ U.S. — Rana Whited; Production Manager/U.K. — Irina Mishina, John Purdie; Research — Karen Gilmore; Stock Footage Research — Virginia Gray, Lorena Parlee; Unit Manager — Christine Thornhill; Production Assistant — Amanda Lowthian; AVID Editor — Ben Howard; D-1 Post Production — Roland House, Inc.; On-Line Editor — Ralph Quattrucci, III; Audio Mix — Michael David; Audio Editing — John Boren, Mark Haskins; Color Correction — Sue Roche, Tanya Roland, Fitz Rola; Feature Film Footage; *Monty Python and the Holy Grail* — Python (Monty) Pictures, Inc.; Robin Hood — 20th Century–Fox Film Corp.; The Empire Strikes Back — Lucasfilm, Ltd.; The Return of the Jedi — Lucasfilm, Ltd.; Merlin and the Sword — Jadran Films, Inc.; Star Wars Theme — Warner-Chappell Music, Inc.; Additional Stock Footage — Archive Films, Inc., Hearst Metrotone, Inc., Mr. Geoffrey Ashe, Streamline Productions, Inc., Worldwide Television News, Inc., J. Walter Cheroff Co.; Choir Music — Christ College, Brecon Chamber Choir, St. Matthew's of the Apostle Cathedral Choral; Art and Photographs: The Newberry Library, The National Gallery of Scotland, The Walker Gallery of Art, The Oak Ridger, King Features Syndicate, Neuschwanastein Castle, Bavaria, Lady Lever Gallery, Eastman Kodak Company, The Gradford Gallery, The Tate Gallery, The Forbes Magazine Collection, Minneapolis Institute of Arts, Mr. Barry Moser, Pennyroyal Press, Fine Art Society, London, Mr. Julek Heller, Dragons World, Ltd., Still from *The Sword and the Stone* courtesy the Walt Disney Company; "The Passing of Arthur," "The Parting of Lancelot and Gwenevere," "King Arthur" and "Lancelot and the Pale Nun" by Julia Margaret Cameron, courtesy the Royal Photographic Society, Bath; Special Thanks: Renaissance Pleasure Fair, San Bernadino, California, Metropolitan Museum of Art, Winchester Cathedral, British Library, Tower of London, Glastonbury Abbey, Pierpont Morgan Library, Mackenzie Smith Medieval Arms and Armor, Bath Spa Museum, Warwick Castle; Consultants: Mr. Geoffrey Ashe, Mr. Peter Fields, Mr. Norris Lacey, Ms. Freya Reeves; Produced in cooperation with the Center for the Book, Library of Congress; For Discovery Productions: Executive in Charge of Production — Clark Bunting; Co-Productions — Denise Baddour; Program Enterprises — Tom Porter; Associate Producer — Holly Barden Stadtler; Production Manager — Linda Guisset; Executive Producer, the Learning Channel — John B. Ford

SYNOPSIS: This one was actually produced in association with Films for the Humanities and Sciences. Although it appeared in a more popular forum than their typical efforts (Discovery Channel), it retains most of the qualities usually associated with FFH productions.

Perhaps the greatest value this documentary has is as a filmed record of four of the leading living Arthurian scholars. As noted in the credits, Geoffrey Ashe, Norris Lacey, Peter Fields and Freya Reeves each explicate various aspects of Arthurian legend and archaeology as it is currently understood.

Glastonbury Abbey, Cadbury Hill, archaeology, even armor manufacturing are discussed in this film. Unlike many other tapes on the subject, this one dares to enter the realm of women's studies as they apply to medieval literature and Arthurian legend. It is pointed out that Lancelot is a late French "import" to the story, mostly from Chrétien. The women of Malory's time, arranged marriages and courtly love are discussed as they relate to the versions of the legend that come down to us now.

George Lucas's *Star Wars* story, which involves another adaptation of the father-son conflict seminally presented in Arthurian legend, is discussed and Lucas is interviewed.

Another feature of the documentary is a discussion of the trivialization of Arthurian matters. The first "modern novel," *Don Quixote,* is pointed out as having been a spoof of the questing knight. Mark Twain's *A Connecticut Yankee in King Arthur's Court* introduced another comical element as did the ex-

treme example of *Monty Python and the Holy Grail.* Worse yet, perhaps, are the goings-on at Las Vegas's Excalibur Hotel and Casino.

The Mortaise Fair see under The Adventures of Sir Lancelot

The Muppet Babies: "The Pig Who Would Be Queen" (1988)

Cartoon; Copyright 1988, Marvel/Jim Henson Productions; No further information available.

Mysterious Places of England (1995)

60 minutes; Color; Documentary; Copyright 1995, Atlas Media Corporation; Goldhil Video

CREDITS: Narrator — Peter Thomas; Directed by — Bruce David Klein; Written by — Maria Lane, Bruce David Klein; Director of Photography — Kate Compel; Audio — Bruce Land; Production Coordinator — Aliyah Silverstein; Post Production Supervisor — Louis Germano; Edited by — Louis Germano, Kate Compel, E. Weston Brown III; Sound/Editing Facilities — Aurora-4 Video; Narration Recording — Alan Cagan Studios; Music Composed and Performed by — Gary Fitzgerald; For the Travel Channel: Executive Producer — Dalton Delan; Senior Producer — Phil Frank; Managing Producer — Paul Iacono; Executive in Charge of Production — Char Serwa; Program Executive — Patricia Newi; For the Travel Channel, U.K. — Christopher Roudette; Special Thanks, Stonehenge; English Heritage, Sharan White, Devizes Museum/The Wiltshire Archaeological and National Historical Society, Julian Richards ,Christopher Chippindale; Special Thanks, Glastonbury; Lydia Lite, Geoffrey Ashe, Kathy Jones, Glastonbury Abbey, Oshia Drury, St. John's Church, University of Avalon, The Chalice Well; "Mystical Spiral" courtesy of Silver on the Tree, Copyright Silver Branch Productions/Glastonbury, England; Special Thanks, Land's End; Nicholas Johnson, Cornwall County Archaeology, Ian McNeil Cooke, Martin Hunt, Adventureland "Connect with Nature," Connecticut Audubon Society, Penzance and District Museum and Art Gallery, Hamish Miller, Cheryl Straffon; Associate Producer — Richard Poggioli; Producer — Maria Lane; Executive Producer — Bruce David Klein; Produced by — Atlas Media Corporation

SYNOPSIS: A superficial and exceedingly repetitive treatment of three major areas of ancient British legend and archaeology. Stonehenge, Glastonbury and Land's End are examined with the main concentration being on mysticism. The healing powers of the Chalice Well are talked about extensively, a group of women sing and dance, invoking the goddess, a dowser researches lay lines.

Whether presenting Stonehenge, Hole Stones at Land's End or any number of other old structures, the narrator asks the same questions over and over again: "Who built these? How did they live, think and feel about themselves and each other? Why did they build them?" Good questions but no answers are given.

Most noteworthy for Arthurian study is the segment on Glastonbury. The ubiquitous Geoffrey Ashe briefly discusses the legend and likely time frame of King Arthur. In speaking of the ostensible discovery of Arthur and Gwenevere's grave at Glastonbury Abbey, Ashe notes that the abbey had suffered a lot of damage during a fire in 1184 A.D. The grave was conveniently found during the rebuild in 1191, creating a great deal of added revenue from sightseers and pilgrims.

Unsatisfying factually, this tape does however provide well-filmed views of some ancient and rarely seen artifacts.

The Natural (1984)

138 minutes; Color; Live Action; Copyright 1984, Tri-Star Pictures; Tri-Star–Delphi Productions; Columbia Tri-Star Home Video

CAST: Robert Redford (Roy Hobbs); Robert Duvall (Max Mercy); Glenn Close (Iris); Kim Basinger (Memo Paris); Wilford Brimley (Pop Fisher); Barbara Hershey (Harriet Bird); Robert Prosky (The Judge); Richard Farnsworth (Red Blow); Joe Don Baker (The Whammer); John Finnegan (Sam Simpson); Alan Fudge (Ed Hobbs); Paul Sullivan, Jr. (Young Roy); Rachel Halls (Young Iris); Robert Rich III (Ted Hobbs); Darren McGavin (Gus Sands [for some reason not included in the opening or closing credits, though the character is prominent in the film]); The New York Knights: Michael Madsen (Bump Bailey); Jon Van Ness (John Olsen); Mickey Treanor (Doc Dizzy); George Wilkosz (Bobby Savoy); Anthony J. Ferrara

(Coach Wilson); Philip Mankowski (Hank Benz); Danny Aiello III (Emil Lajong); Joe Castellano (Allie Stubbs); Eddie Cipot (Gabby Laskow); Ken Grassano (Al Fowler); Robert Kalaf (Cal Baker); Barry Kivel (Pat McGee); Steven Kronovet (Tommy Hinkle); James Meyer (Dutch Schultz); Michael Starr (Boone); Sam Green (Murphy); Additional Knights: Martin Greg, Richard Oliveri, Duke McGuire, Kevin Lester, Robert Rudnick, Joseph Mosso, Lawrence Conzens, Stephen Pollichik, Joseph Charboneau, Ken Kamholz); Sibbi Sisti (Pirates Manager); Phillip D. Rosenberg (Pitcher Youngberry); Christopher B. Rehbaum (Pitcher John Rhoades); Nicholas Koleff (Umpire Augie); Jerry Stockman (Umpire Babe); James Quamo (Memorial Game Umpire); Joseph Strand (Final Game Home Plate Umpire); James Mohr (Al); Ralph Tabakin (Al's Customer); Dennis Gould (Carnival Boy); Joshua Abbey (Home Plate Photographer); Gail Vance (Maid at Party); George Scheitinger (League Official); Peter Poth (Dr. Knobb); Bernie McInerney (Hospital Doctor); Elizabeth Ann Klein (Stern Nurse); Charles Sergis (Newsreel Narrator); Edward Walsh (Newsreel Presenter); Buffalo Swing (Nightclub Band); "Star Spangled Banner" Performed by Kate Smith, Courtesy RCA Records

CREDITS: Production Consultants — Malcolm Kahn, Robert Bean; Music by — Randy Newman; Edited by — Stu Linder; Production Designer (LA) — Angelo Graham; Production Designer (NY) — Mel Bourne; Director of Photography — Caleb Deschanel; Executive Producers — Robert Towne, Philip M. Breen; Based on the Novel by — Bernard Malamud; Screenplay by — Roger Towne, Phil Dusenberry; Produced by — Mark Johnson; Directed by — Barry Levinson; Associate Producer — Robert F. Colesberry; Art Director (LA) — James J. Murikami; Art Director (NY) — Speed Hopkins; Costume Designer — Bernie Pollack; Costume Designer for Ms. Close, Ms. Basinger, Ms. Hershey — Gloria Gresham; Production Executive — Patrick Markey; Creative Consultant — Ted Bafaloukos; Unit Production Manager — Robert F. Colesberry; 1st Assistant Directors — Chris Soldo, Patrick Crowley; 2nd Assistant Directors — Tom Davies, Carol Smetana; Casting by — Ellen Chenoweth; Set Director — Bruce Weintraub; Camera Operator — Craig Denault; Assistant Cameraman — Alan Disler, Bob Brown; Additional Casting — Lisa Clarkson, Louis Giaimo; Production Accountant — Nellie Nugiel; Additional Unit Production Manager — Peter Burrell; Assistant Production Manager — Thomas A. Razzano; Production Sound by — Jeff Wexler, Chris McLaughlin,

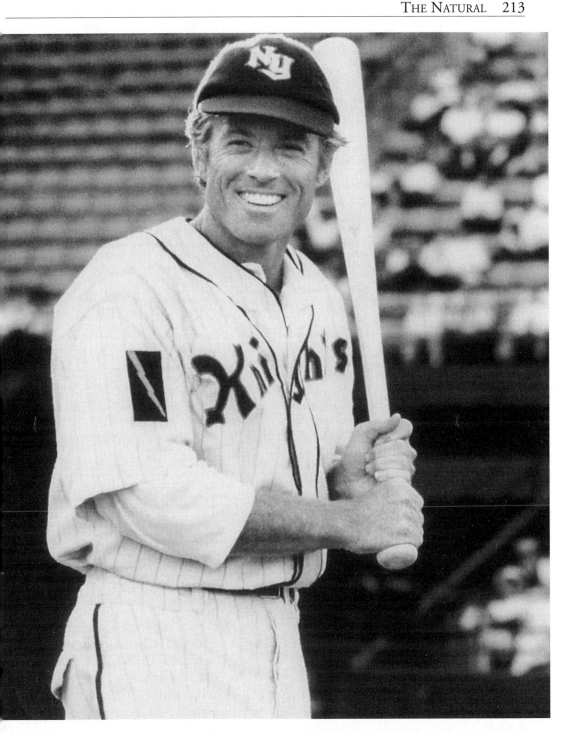

Robert Redford as Roy Hobbs in *The Natural* (1984).

James Stuebe; Re-recording Mixers — Christopher Jenkins, Jason Alexander, Larry Stensvold; Additional Editors — T. Battle Davis, Andy Blumenthal, Jere Huggins; Assistant Editor — Liza Randol; Orchestrator — Jack Hayes; Music Editor — Joe Tuley; Supervising Sound Editor — Bill Phillips; Sound Effects Editors — Hal Saunders, Andrew Patterson, Jimmy Ling; Assistant Sound Effects Editor — Michael A. Warner; Property Manager — Barry Bedig; Assistant Property Manager — Stan Cockerell; Gaffer — Gary Holt; Key Grip — Clyde Hart; Script Supervisor — Ana Maria Quintana; Makeup Artists — Gary Liddiard, Thomas Hoerber; Hair Stylist — Bernadette Parker; Costume Supervisor — Jules Melillo; Costumers — James Tyson, Steve Ellsworth, Sue Moore, Francine Jamison; Location Managers — Gary Staneck, Stratton Rawson, Lynn Goldman; Extras Casting — Mary Jo Markey, Una McClure; Production Office Coordinator — Shelley Honis; Assistant Production Office Coordinator — Judith Brown; Publicity Coordinator — Patricia Newcomb; Publicist — Ann Guerin; Still Photographers — Brian Hamill, Jurgen Wollmer, Steven Vaughan; Lead Men — Dan May, Chris Butler; Set Dressers — Casey Hallenbeck, John Sweeney; Painter — Roger Dietz; Special Effects — Roger Hansen; Assistant to Mr. Levinson and Mr. Johnson — Susan Moore; Assistant to Mr. Redford — Robbi Miller; Assistant to Mr. Duvall — Debbi Taylor; Negative Cutter — Donah Bassett; Construction Coordinator (NY) — Joe Accord; Construction Coordinator (LA) — Robert Mueller; Transportation Coordinator — Richard Mercier; Driver Captain — Dennis C. Ward; Baseball Trainers — Anthony J. Ferrara, Ken Hendler; Baseball Consultants — Gene Kirby, Richard Cerrone; Production Assistants — Neil Kirk, Christine Baer, Taine Riggio, Kristina Loggia, Nin Kostroff, Ralph Cavallaro, Jay Scherick; Researcher — Logan Payne; Furs by — Alixandre Furs; Lighting Equipment by — Hollywood Rental Co., Inc.; Filmed in Part at — Laird International Studios; Post Production Facilities — Market Street Studios, Venice, California; *Life* title and format used with permission of Time, Inc.; Original soundtrack album available on Warner Bros. records and tapes.; The filmmakers wish to thank Buffalo Mayor Jimmy Griffin, the New York State Office of Motion Picture and Television Development and especially the people of the city of Buffalo for their generosity and assistance in the making of this motion picture.; Processed by — Du Art Labs; Prints by — Technicolor; Lenses and Panaflex Camera by Panavision

SYNOPSIS: In Hollywood film terms, *The Natural* might be described as Parsifal playing baseball in the 1940s. Actually the main character, Roy Hobbs, is more like the Fisher King, Amfortas, Parsifal, Perceval, King Arthur and Galahad all rolled into one.

The Holy Grail that Hobbs seeks at the beginning is fame and achievement in his beloved sport. The Grail that he achieves in the end is very different, one which involves honor and love.

As a young boy growing up among the farms of the American heartland, Roy Hobbs discovers that he has a gift for baseball. His father encourages the boy to play ball but warns him, "Rely too much on your own gift and you'll fail." This is as close to a spoken religious reference as there is in the film, but many visual references to a guiding hand follow.

When Roy is still a youngster his father dies, collapsing under a tree in their yard. Some time later a lightning bolt splits the tree in two. Roy takes a chunk of wood from the tree and hand carves his own baseball bat from it. He burns the name "Wonder Boy" and a lightning bolt on the finished bat.

Not a lot is explicitly stated in the movie, but presumably just after high school a scout spots Roy and he is offered a slot with the Cubs baseball team. Roy packs to leave immediately, but first in the dark of night sneaks to his girlfriend's house to say goodbye.

On the train trip to Chicago, Roy meets a couple of people who wind up changing his life forever. His scout first introduces him to a newspaper sports columnist named Max Mercy. Mercy is in the middle of reading an article about a mysterious serial killer who has shot two athletes, killing them with silver bullets. Hobbs also meets a Babe Ruth like figure nicknamed "The Whammer." Harriet Bird, a beautiful camp follower, is also aboard; she seems to be following the Whammer.

The train stops at a local carnival and a bet is made that Hobbs can't strike the Whammer out with three throws. To the amazement of everyone the greenhorn does it. Harriet's attention shifts from the Whammer to Hobbs. On their arrival in Chicago she invites young Hobbs to her hotel room. He's barely in the door before she shoots him.

The film then jumps ahead 16 years to Knight's Field, New York. Hobbs has resurfaced, walking in on the hard-luck major league team managed by Pop Fisher. Fisher's assistant is another old timer, Red Blow.

To anyone familiar with Grail legend these names might seem a bit much. Pop Fisher—The Fisher King. Red Blow—the Wound, the Dolorous Stroke and other references. Traditionally it is the Fisher King who suffers from the wound that won't heal except by the influence of the Holy Grail. Yet in this movie it is Hobbs, the innocent fool, the Parsifal figure, who has received the wound both physical and psychic from which it is so hard to recover.

To reinforce the identity of Hobbs as a Parsifal figure, note that he entered into the world of baseball an innocent, the innocent fool who doesn't ask the right question, as we see in Wagner's Parsifal. He was stopped before he could get started in the sport, just as Parsifal is forced to leave the Grail Castle for his lack of probity.

Parsifal wandered for years before returning to claim his place at the Grail Castle. So too with Hobbs, who for 16 years disappeared from the scene only to pop up again, older but wiser.

Fisher can't believe that he's been saddled with such an old geezer for his team so he ignores Hobbs for a long time. The moment finally arrives though when Fisher is forced to see that Hobbs is an extraordinary batter. He adds Hobbs to the team's active roster and the team's fortunes immediately change.

In his first appearance in a major league game the harbinger lightning bolt flashes in the sky and Hobbs literally smashes the cover off the baseball. He becomes an instant celebrity.

In awe of this new hero and his now-famous bat, "Wonder Boy," the team's bat boy approaches Hobbs. They become friends and Hobbs promises to help the boy make a bat of his own.

However, the forces of evil have been unleashed as well. It is learned that old Pop Fisher has been ill-used by the owner of the team, the Judge. Fisher had gotten into some kind of financial bind and sold 10 percent of his shares to the Judge, giving the Judge legal control of the team. But, the side bet is that if the team wins a pennant Fisher can buy his shares back and regain total control—winner take all. Obviously, the Judge and his men have a vested interest in the team losing.

The first ploy used by the Judge and his partner, Gus, is to throw a girl at Hobbs—Memo Paris. As soon as Hobbs starts spending time with this woman his play goes downhill and the team goes into a slump.

Just in the nick of time Iris, Hobbs's hometown sweetheart, shows up at one of the games. The mere presence of this lady in white brings Hobbs back to his senses. She's not married, but has a son. The implication is that the boy is Hobbs's.

As Hobbs returns to his winning ways, the Judge and Gus try to buy him, offering him $20,000 to throw the games. Hobbs refuses, but at the same time his old wound comes back to haunt him. At a party one night Hobbs collapses. It looks like Memo has poisoned him at Gus's order, but that point is not made clear. In any event Hobbs is hospitalized on the eve of the most important games of the season.

The doctors pump his stomach and find the silver bullet that has been lodged there all these years. Apparently his stomach has deteriorated to such a dangerous degree that exertion could kill him. Hobbs sneaks off to the game anyway.

In classic baseball-movie style, it all comes down to one man. The Knights are losing 2–0, there are two men on base and it's the bottom of the ninth inning. Of course Hobbs is up. Blood is evident, oozing from his side. The count goes to two balls, two strikes. A lightning bolt flashes, Hobbs swings and his bat breaks!

The bat boy gives Hobbs his own bat and with it Hobbs hits the winning home run, the ball exploding the stadium lights into a fireworks victory display. The closing scene is of Hobbs and his son playing catch in those hometown wheat fields, Iris looking on happily.

Though this film retains many of the sequences and much of the storyline of the book it is based on, it also makes some major changes. The most glaring difference is that Bernard Malamud's novel *The Natural* does not have a happy ending.

In the novel, the all-too-human Roy strikes out on that fateful last at-bat. Neither does he win the girl in the end. Iris is not a hometown sweetheart in the novel, just a woman who is attracted to Roy. She does become pregnant by Roy but that occurs during Roy's late-in-life comeback, not in the distant past of their youths.

Neither is Roy's youth the idyllic thing presented in the film. Malamud depicts Roy's mother as a hooker who drives his father into alcoholism. Roy lives with a grandmother for a time, then in orphanages.

Taking another angle on things, much can be made of the names Malamud chose for this story. The name of the team — the Knights — needs no explanation. That Roy inscribed a name on his bat tracks with the fact that many swords in Arthurian literature had names.

Pop Fisher reminds one of the Fisher King, but in the film the team manager has no unhealing wound. The character makes more sense in the novel because he suffers from what is described as a sort of "athlete's foot on his hands." This miserable affliction causes him to bandage his fingers and the bandages ooze with pus and rot. When Hobbs puts the team on a winning streak, Fisher's hands heal up.

Judge Goodwill Banner, the owner of the team, has perhaps the most obvious name of all the characters. Though he is known only as "the Judge" in the movie, his function is the same in both film and novel. He is the evil one, the one who destroys, or bans, good will.

The name for the natural himself, Roy Hobbs, is not such an obvious one. *Roy* is a derivative of Rex, or king. *Hobbs* however is not so easily connected to Arthurian legend, though it may make some sense as applied in this story.

A first interpretation might be that Hobbs is a shortening of the word *hobbled*. It can't be denied that poor Roy Hobbs is initially handicapped by his own innocence and inexperience. Later he is further hobbled by his poor choices in life and his bad luck.

Another interpretation might connect the name to Thomas Hobbes (1588–1679), the seventeenth-century English philosopher and political theorist. Though presented in earlier works, Hobbes's ideas on the human condition and solutions for attaining peace and security were most completely and maturely explicated in his *Leviathan,* published in 1651.

Essentially Hobbes spoke of natural rights rather than natural laws. Man, Hobbes said, has the right to self-preservation and therefore does not have to follow natural laws if those laws are destructive to his security. However peace is impossible if those laws are not generally followed. The best way Hobbes felt this end could be achieved would be if man submitted totally to the determinations of some agreed-upon sovereign power. That sovereign would wield absolute power and be answerable only to God. By definition, then, the sovereign could not be unjust to his subjects since they had agreed to his power.

What is conveniently (for the sovereign) eliminated here is any incentive for a sovereign to act humanely or even morally. This is anathema to anyone imbued with the principles of Western democratic republicanism. And it is exactly the fix Roy Hobbs finds himself in when he signs the Judge's contract to play for the Knights.

Judge Banner, the owner of the team, is in effect the sovereign of that little world. Anyone signing a contract with that organization puts himself at the mercy of Goodwill Banner. Since Banner's machinations are not intended for the benefit of the team but for his own financial gain, the effects of his rule are bad for the psyches and morals of his subjects — particularly Roy.

The final shame in the novel is when Roy agrees to the Judge's deal to throw the last game of the series. For money Roy will throw away honor and betray his friends and teammates. In the end Roy cannot keep that devil's bargain and tries to turn things around again. Hollywood lets the effort work and in the movie Roy ends up the heroic savior. Malamud however did not. Malamud's Roy tries to win the game but fails and is implicated in an investigation by the Baseball Commission.

So Malamud could well have been demonstrating the deleterious effects of Hobbes's theories with a Hobbs of his own. Roy Hobbs is a natural at baseball and a natural man. Though given freedom of choice Roy doesn't necessarily do what's best for himself—his choosing to stay involved with Memo instead of Iris is a case in point. However Roy's involvements with the Hobbesian sovereigns of the world turn out to be much more destructive.

One can engage in similarly convoluted analyses of the other characters' names. Red Blow was mentioned briefly above. Iris could represent Blanchefleur of Arthurian legend, the mistress of Perceval. Their floral appellations make an easy connection.

Known for a humorous bent to his writing, Malamud surely meant to raise a chuckle with many of these names. One of the best examples might be the reporter's, Max Mercy, for it is mercy that he lacks.

To go too much further with name analysis becomes a bit tenuous. Memo Paris, for instance. There was a Paris in some versions of Arthurian legend, notably in *Culhwch and Olwen* and in *Ly Myreur des Histoires*. In the latter Paris was a king. In the former he was a friend of Arthur's who received as a gift from Arthur the daughter of the regent of a land Arthur had conquered. Memo is dangled in front of Roy as just such a prize should he agree to the Judge's shady deal.

Her first name is even more doubtfully connected to Arthuriana. Homonymically, Melot (if one gives it a French pronunciation), is the closest one can probably come. Melot was the dwarf in Gottfried von Strassburg's

Tristan (thirteenth century) who spied on Tristan and Iseult for King Mark. Replace the *m* sound in the middle of Memo with the *l* sound of Melot and there you might have it. It's more likely that Malamud meant something else by the name Memo, if he meant anything at all.

As I said, tenuous at best. Without having made a full study of Malamud and the depth of his interest in and knowledge of Arthurian subjects, this becomes guesswork, entertaining as it might be.

Other interpretations are certainly possible. Roy's bat being made from the heart of the lightning-struck tree can easily be viewed as the pulling of Excalibur from the stone. This leads one in completely different directions than examined above, though they might be just as plausible.

The New Adventures of a Connecticut Yankee in King Arthur's Court (Novye Prikluchenia Janke Pri Dvore Korola Artura) (1987)

Not viewed; Copyright 1987, Dovzhenko Studios

CAST: Albert Filozov; Evdoka Ghermanova; Mark Gres; Alexander Kaidanovsky; Sergei Koltakov; Anastasia Vertinskaya
CREDITS: Director — Viktor Gres

SYNOPSIS: In a Soviet-produced musical version of Mark Twain's novel *A Connecticut Yankee in King Arthur's Court,* an American pilot crashes and finds himself in Arthurian Britain. His attempts at modernizing Camelot are rejected, Lancelot defeats him in combat and he returns to the present.

The New Twilight Zone: "The Last Defender of Camelot" (1986)

Not viewed; Television series episode; 60 minutes; Color; Science Fiction/Live Action; Copyright 1986, CBS, Inc.; CBS Entertainment Productions in Cooperation with, Persistence of Vision; Library of Congress Call #2826; Library of Congress Catalogue #91727079

CAST: Richard Kiley; Jenny Agutter; John Cameron Mitchell; Norman Lloyd; Anthony LaPaglia; Don Stark

CREDITS: Writer — Roger Zelazny; Teleplay — George R. R. Martin; Director — Jeannot Szwarc; Producer — Harvey Frand

SYNOPSIS: Based on a science fiction short story of the same title by Roger Zelazny, this episode of *The New Twilight Zone* depicts Lancelot, Merlin and Morgana as having survived into the present day. Merlin had gone insane during Arthur's reign and Morgana had managed to trap him to save mankind from his diabolical plans. However, it's time for Merlin to reawaken and Morgana and Lancelot to team up to prevent him from trying to take over the world.

Northern Exposure: "Wake Up Call" (1992)

Approximately 60 minutes; Color; Live Action; Copyright 1992, Universal Studios

CAST: Rob Morrow (Joel Fleischman); Paul Provenza (Phillip Capra); Teri Polo (Michelle Capra); Barry Corbin (Maurice Minnifield); Janine Turner (Maggie O'Connell); John Corbett (Chris Stevens); Darren E. Burrows (Ed Chigliak); Peg Phillips (Ruth-Anne Miller); John Cullum (Holling Gustav); Cynthia Geary (Shelly Tambo-Vincoeur); Elaine Miles (Marilyn Whirlwind); Morty the Moose (Morty the Moose); Graham Green (Leonard Quinhagak); Andreas Wisniewski (Arthur); William J. White (Dave the Cook); Robrt Nicholson (Customer)

CREDITS: Writers — Diane Frolov, Andrew Sneider; Director — Nick Marck; Executive Producers — Joshua Brand, John Falsey; Associate Producer — Martin Bruestle; Second Unit Director/Associate Producer — Alan Brent Connell; Director of Photography — Frank Prinzi; Film Editor — Adam Wolfe; Music — David Schwartz; Costume Design — Katharine Bentley; Chief Lighting Technician — Scott Williams; Key Grip — Scott Hillman; Camera Operator — David J. Frederick; Art Director — Kenneth J. Breg; Property Master — Sean E. Markland; Production Sound Mixer — Robert Marts; Script Supervisor — Barbara A. Brown; Production Coordinator — Yvonne Yaconelli; Location Manager — J. Daniel Dusek; Transportation Manager — Russ Powell; Makeup Supervisor — Joni Meers; Hair Stylist — Rebecca Lynne; Set Decorator — Gene Serdena; Seattle Casting — Patti Carns Kalles, C.S.A.; Supervising Sound Editor — William Angarola; Music Editor — Allen K. Rosen; Music Consultant — John McCallough; Assistant Editor — Pamela Ziegenhagen; Extras Casting — John Vreeke; Post Production Supervisor — Joe Lazarov; Post Production Coordinator — Steve Turner; Title Design — Kathie Broyles; Assistants to Executive Producers — Denise Dobbs, Alix Hauser; Re-Recording Sound Mixers — Peter Cole, Gary Gegan, Anthony D'Amico; Post Production Sound Services provided by Sky Walker Sound; A division of Lucas Arts Entertainment Company; Color by Pacific Film Laboratory; Electronic Laboratory Services by Laser Pacific; Excerpt from "Renascence" by Edna St. Vincent Millay Copyright 1917, 1945 by Edna St. Vincent Millay; Finnegan Pinchuk; Falahey/Austin Street Productions in association with Universal Television

SYNOPSIS: *Northern Exposure* was a television series which ran from 1990 to 1995 and is currently being rerun on the A&E network. It was about a young doctor from Flushing, New York, who is assigned as a general practitioner to Cicely, Alaska, for four years to complete the terms of his medical school scholarship.

The quirky show incorporated many references to legends and literature, Arthurian themes among them. Two episodes in particular are of interest here (though there may be more). One had a regular character, Ed, wondering about his parents and witnessing a strange man appear and disappear several times. Another regular, Maurice, asks Chris if he is familiar with the Arthurian legends and then expounds on a story about Sir Gawain losing his nerve. According to this recounting, Gawain is only able to return to his former self by sleeping with a woman.

Another episode, titled "Wake Up Call," is a sort of ode to spring. The program examines how various members of the town act and react to the burgeoning of the world around them as winter disappears and new growth is on the verge of sprouting.

Maurice seems to get grouchy, frustrated with the same old coffee at the diner, the same old music at the radio station, his own same old after shave lotion. He winds up cleaning out his attic and finding the things left to him by his grandfather. Among them are the old man's pipe, his kilt and a set of bagpipes. Maurice happily, if nostalgically, reminisces.

Young Shelley erupts with an odd skin condition. Dr. Fleischman is unable to do anything for her. However, Leonard Quinhagak, a Native Alaskan healer happens to be in town observing Fleishman's practice. In a conversation with him, Shelley discovers that she is simply shedding her old skin and within a short time she is radiant again.

While this and other subplots play themselves out, the town is being pestered by a bear that saunters around at night rattling people's garbage cans. One night it wakes Maggie up in overturning hers. Maggie has been feeling exceedingly lonely, but the next day she gets stuck while driving on a logging road. A tall woodsman with long blond hair appears and helps her get out of the rut. She drives off nervously, watching him in her mirror.

That night clattering garbage cans wake her up again. Going outside, she is greeted by the man from the woods who happens to be walking by. He suggests jovially that perhaps the bear is looking for her and introduces himself as Arthur. He declines an offer to come in, compliments her beautiful eyes, then leaves.

The next day Maggie goes out to the woods and finds Arthur standing in a river. He catches a fish with his bare hands. She is amazed and she runs over to him. In conversing, Arthur tells Maggie that he lives alone, but learned all he knows of fishing and such things from his mother. Maggie accepts his invitation to see his home and he carries her across the river.

Arthur's home is a cave. It is stocked with berries and other items from the woods for food, and mead that he makes himself for drink. They dine by candlelight, then dance in silence. Arthur tells Maggie that the first time he saw her, he realized what was missing from his life.

The following day Maggie shows up in town in high spirits. Later she returns to Arthur's cave but finds it empty. A brown bear exits the cave, turns and looks at Maggie, then moves off into the forest.

Various theories have cropped up over the years that a Celtic bear god tradition may have influenced elements of the story of Arthur. These ideas are based primarily on tantalizing but not necessarily valid etymological twistings (the Latin "arctos" or the Welsh "arth" for instance) of the name Arthur. Right or wrong, it is still fun to think that an incarnation of the good king can show up in modern Alaska to help a damsel in distress.

Opening Kick-Off see under King Arthur and the Knights of Justice

Outside Time (1991)

Television mini-series; No further information available.

Parsifal (1904)

Not viewed; 611 feet; Black and White; Silent; Copyright 1904, Edison Film Company

CAST: Adelaide Fitz-Allen (Kundry); Robert Whittier (Parsifal)

CREDITS: Director — Edwin J. Porter; Scenery — Harley Merry; Cameraman — Edwin S. Porter; Location — Brooklyn, NYC

SYNOPSIS: Eight scenes from Wagner's opera with elaborate sets, exaggerated gesturing and some trick photographic work. Each scene was filmed, titled and copyrighted separately.

Parsifal (1912)

Not viewed; Black and White; Silent; Copyright 1912, Ambrosio Films

CREDITS: Director — Mario Caeserini

SYNOPSIS: Based on Wagner's opera, the story of Parsifal taking his place as a Grail knight.

Parsifal (1951)

US title: The Evil Forest; Not viewed; Spain: 95 minutes; USA: 79 minutes; Opera;

Spanish with English subtitles; Copyright 1951, S. Huguet, Spain; Copyright 1955, Studio Films, Inc., USA

CAST: Nuria Alfonso (Rage); José Bruguera (Titurel); Carmen De Lirio (Pride); Tony Domenech (Gluttony); Alfonso Estela (Anfortas); Ricardo Fusté (Alisan); José Luis Hernández (The Son); Angel Jordán (Roderico); Rosa Monera (Sloth); Elena Montevar (Envy); Teresa Planell (The Old Woman); Félix de Pomés (Klingsor); Josefina Ramos (Lust); Gustavo Rojo (Parsifal); Carlo Tamberlani (Gurnemancio); Ludmilla Tchérina (Kundry); Jesús Varela (The Dwarf); Carmen Zaro (Greed); Victoriano González; Rosa Manero; José Manuel Pinillos; Teresa Planells; José Tusset; Lupe De Molina

CREDITS: Directors — Daniel Mangrané, Carlos Serrano de Osma; Writer — Carlos Serrano de Osma; Story — Daniel Mangrané; Continuity — Francisco Naranjo; Dialogue — José Antonio Pérez Torreblanca; Cinematography — Cecilio Paniagua; Music — Richard Wagner; Film Editing — Antonio Cánovas; Producer — Daniel Mangrané; Musical Adaptation — Ricardo Lamotte de Grignon; Conductor — Ricardo Lamotte de Grignon; Special Effects — Daniel Mangrané; Music Editor — Enrique Ribo

Parsifal (1953)

Not viewed; Copyright 1953, Cine-Español

CAST: Gustavo Rojo; Ludmilla Tcherina
CREDITS: Director — Gustavo Rojo

SYNOPSIS: Set in fifth century Spain, this version of the Parsifal story is influenced both by medieval literature and Wagner's opera. Parsifal seeks and finds the Holy Grail in an effort to quell barbarian invasions of his homeland.

Parsifal (Bayreuth, 1984)

232 minutes; Color; Opera; German with English subtitles; Copyright 1984 Unitel; Copyright 1991, Philips Classics Productions; Translation Copyright, Lionel Salter; A Production of Unitel Film und Foruschproduktionsgesellschaft mbH & Co., Munich; From the Bayreuth Festspielhaus; Philips Video Classics #070510-3

CAST: Bernd Weikl (Amfortas); Matti Salminen (Titurel); Hans Sotin (Gurnemanz); Siegfried Jerusalem (Parsifal); Leif Roar (Klingsor); Eva Randova (Kundry); Toni Krämer (1st Knight of the Grail); Heinz Klaus Ecker (2nd Knight of the Grail); Marga Schiml (1st Squire); Hanna Schwarz (2nd Squire); Helmut Pampuch (3rd Squire); Martin Egel (4th Squire); Norma Sharp (Flower Maiden); Carol Richardson (Flower Maiden); Hanna Schwarz (Flower Maiden); Mari Anne Häggander (Flower Maiden); Marga Schimt (Flower Maiden); Margit Neubauer (Flower Maiden); Hanna Schwarz (Alto Solo)

CREDITS: Conducted by — Horst Stein; Production and Stage Design — Wolfgang Wagner; Costumes — Reinhard Heinrich; Choreographic Assistance — Riccardo Duse; Bayreuth Festival Chorus; Chorus Master — Norbert Balatsch; Bayreuth Festival Orchestra; Production Assistance — Peter Windgassen; Video Director — Brian Large; Artistic Supervision — Wolfgang Wagner; Subtitling by — Mary Adams; Makeup — Willi Klose, Inge Landgraf, Hans-Rudolf Müller; Technical Director — Walter Huneke; Lighting — Manfred Voss; Musical Assistance — Jeffrey Tate, Jacqueline Richard, Helmut Weese, Heinz Müller-Grassmann, Maximilian Kojetinsky, Konrad Leitner, Paul Herz; Choral Assistance — Milan Maly, Julius Asbeck, Ernst Dunshirn; Assistant Director — Steffen Tiggeler; Sets, Decoration and Projection Assistance — Michael Teitjens; Camera — Oskar Herting, Wolfgang Fritzberg, Dieter Schmidt, Andreas Dorner, Günther Mohn, Horst Thomas; Film Editor — Michael Becker; Film Engineer — Jörg Hildbrand; Lighting Engineer — Horst Biedermann; Videotape Editor — Joachim Meißner; Sound — Gernot R. Westhäuser, Hartmut Tscharke, Josef Wanniger; Audio Producer — Dr. Rudolf Werner; Technical Supervisor — Walter Conrad; Executive Producer — Horant H. Hohlfeld

SYNOPSIS: As one might expect of a Bayreuth Festspielhaus production, this is one of the purer, more clearly delineated versions of Wagner's Parsifal on film. Bayreuth after all is where Wagner settled to build his ideal opera house. The organization that functions there to this day is devoted to the preservation of Wagner's works. The staging is relatively simple and the story sticks to Wagner's original more precisely than other performances.

Wagner intended Parsifal as a consecrational festival opera and further intended that it be performed only at Bayreuth. The first time it was performed outside of Bayreuth was in New York in 1903.

While the Christian theme of redemption is paramount in the story, it is interesting to note that many other elements merge in Wagner's works. Act 2 of *Parsifal*, for example, and indeed the character of Klingsor are taken almost directly from Buddhist traditions surrounding Buddha and Mara.

Nordic myths, psychiatry and many other influences are noted in Wagnerian operas. It would take extensive space to go into all of them. Suffice it to say that Wagner read widely and stated that his *Parsifal* was nothing like Von Eschenbach's poem.

The opening scene of *Parsifal* is of Gurnemanz awakening the guards by the sacred lake outside the castle of Montsalvat. Amfortas, the wounded keeper of the Grail, is carried to the lake for his bath. It is mentioned that Gawain has gone off without permission to seek more remedies for Amfortas. Kundry, the strange wild woman, arrives from Arabia with another possible cure. Nothing works.

Gurnemanz recounts how Titurel, Amfortas's father, received the holy relics of the Grail and the Spear from angels. To Wagner in these operas, the Grail is both the cup from which Christ drank at the Last Supper and the chalice in which his blood was collected from the cross. Titurel then built the castle to protect them and the Knights of the Grail became a brotherhood of devotion to the relics.

One of them, Klingsor, sinned in some far-off land and was thrown out of the brotherhood. Klingsor built his own castle and using evil magic turned a desert around the castle into a garden where he grew "infernally" beautiful women.

Klingsor lusted after the relics. With the power of his sorcery he was able to steal the Spear. Amfortas tried to recover it but Klingsor wounded him with it. The wound does not heal and Amfortas wishes only for death.

Amfortas prays and receives a holy message: "Enlightened through compassion, the innocent fool, wait for him, the appointed one."

A wounded swan is brought to the assemblage and everyone is shocked that one of the creatures of the sacred forest has been shot with an arrow. Parsifal is brought in and he brags of his deed until the awfulness of his crime is explained to him. Shamed, he breaks his bow.

When questioned Parsifal seems to know nothing except that his mother's name is Heart's Sorrow. Kundry however knows all about him and tells how Parsifal's father was killed in battle and that Heart's Sorrow is also dead.

Gurnemanz takes Parsifal to the Grail Castle, where the boy witnesses a gathering of the brotherhood for the performance of the holy offices. The Grail is uncovered and at the end of the ceremony glows with holy light. Parsifal fails to ask the crucial question that Gurnemanz expects of him.

Act 2 opens at Klingsor's castle with the sorcerer preparing for Parsifal's arrival. He summons Kundry. Parsifal fights his way into the castle, defeating all of Klingsor's men. The women of the castle try to tempt Parsifal into sin. Parsifal is able to resist until one of them chases off the rest. This is Kundry in her seductive persona, under Klingsor's control.

Kundry tells Parsifal that his mother died of grief at his departure and Parsifal is devastated by the realization. Kundry gives him his "first kiss of love," but Parsifal throws her off. He then is stricken with the pain of Amfortas's wound.

Seeing that Parsifal is awakening to holiness, Kundry desperately tries to get him to lie with her. When Parsifal refuses she calls for Klingsor who appears with the Spear. Klingsor hurls the Spear at Parsifal but Parsifal catches it and Klingsor's power is broken.

Act 3 picks up years later. A bearded and black-armored Parsifal shows up at the sacred grove, where Gurnemanz and Kundry are conversing. It is Good Friday.

Parsifal still has the Spear. Gurnemanz describes how Amfortas is worse than ever and no longer performs the holy office. Kundry washes and anoints Parsifal's feet, Gurnemanz washes and anoints Parsifal's head and he declares Parsifal the new king of the Grail Castle.

They go to the castle where Amfortas performs the office one last time, then begs the knights to kill him. Parsifal stops them, then heals Amfortas with a touch of the Spear. Parsifal then takes over the office and the Grail shines brilliantly as he carries it around the hall.

Parsifal (Berlin, 1993)

244 minutes; Color; Opera; Copyright 1993, Metropolitan; Copyright 1994, Teldec Classics International; A Time Warner Company; Teldec Video #4509-92788-3

CAST: Poul Elming (Parsifal); Waltraud Meier (Kundry); John Tomlinson (Gurnemanz); Falk Struckmann (Amfortas); Günter von Kannen (Klingsor); Fritz Hübner (Titurel); Carola Höhn (Klingsor's Flower Maiden); Brigitte Eisenfeld (Klingsor's Flower Maiden); Carola Nossek (Klingsor's Flower Maiden); Borjana Mateewa (Klingsor's Flower Maiden); Elvira Dreßen Laura Aikin (Klingsor's Flower Maiden); Peter Bindszus (Knight); Gerd Wolf (Knight); Peter Menzel (Esquire); Andreas Schmidt (Esquire); Efrat Ben-Nun (Esquire); Elvira Dreßen (Esquire); Rosemarie Lang (Alto Voice)

CREDITS: Staged by — Harry Kupfer; Stage Design — Hans Schavernoch; Costumes — Christine Stromberg; Staatsoper Unter Den Linden; Staatskapelle Berlin; Deutscher Staatsoper Choir; Choir Director — Ernst Stoy; Conductor — Daniel Barenboim; Sound Recording Supervision — Helmut Mühle; Sound — Christian Feldgen, Christoph Franke, Hartwig Nickola; Camera — Erwin Tischler, Helmut Heine, Angelika Katzer, Markus Schmidt-Märkl, Gabriele Heimlich, Ingrid Jänicke, Manfred Schebsdat; Video Editor — Peter Rump; Score Reader — Iman Soeteman; Video — DEWE Television; Executive Producer — Ingrid Windisch; Video Director — Hans Hulscher

SYNOPSIS: The Berlin State Opera version (under the direction of Harry Kupfer) of Wagner's *Parsifal* remains essentially true to Wagner's libretto, but uses extensive innovations in set design and decoration. The Grail Castle is transformed into a gigantic gleaming steel structure. The passage in and out of the castle, which is also the passage between the worlds of the Grail knights and Klingsor's kingdom of evil, is an enormous circular bank vault–type door.

During different scenes various kinds of lighting play across the sheer walls of the edifice. Sometimes the source is reflected light but more often it is a complex array of lights set into the walls themselves.

As mentioned above, the story remains the same as it is traditionally presented. Parsifal, a youth raised in isolation by a widowed mother, goes off on his own to join some passing knights. In the original poem, written by Wolfram Von Eschenbach, the knights were members of Arthur's Round Table but no mention is made of that by Wagner.

Unwittingly Parsifal wanders into the environs of the Grail Castle. At the Grail Castle are housed and guarded two relics of Christ — the Holy Grail itself and the Spear which was used to pierce Christ's side on the cross. The Grail knights are a brotherhood of chivalrous men devoted to the protection of these sacred objects.

On the grounds of the Grail Castle, Parsifal innocently kills a swan. This breech brings him to the attention of Gurnemanz, one of the Grail knights who tends the king of the castle, Amfortas.

Amfortas suffers from a wound that won't heal, one inflicted on him by an evil sorcerer named Klingsor. Klingsor was once himself a Grail knight but, having committed some sin, was removed from the brotherhood of the Grail. Klingsor subsequently set up a kingdom of his own. Jealous of the Grail knights, Klingsor managed to snatch the Spear. When Amfortas sought to retrieve it, Klingsor wounded him with it and Amfortas cannot be released from the pain until the Spear is restored.

Gurnemanz takes Parsifal under his wing and brings the boy to the Grail Castle to witness a mass. When the Grail is revealed and glows with holy light, Parsifal is expected to ask a crucial question, but in his youthful ignorance and innocence fails to do so. In disgust Gurnemanz dismisses Parsifal from the great hall and the boy wanders off on his own again.

Some time later a slightly more worldly, or at least a somewhat more experienced, Parsifal battles his way into Klingsor's castle.

Klingsor's flower maidens show up as faces on many television screens embedded in the steel wall. A very real Kundry debates long and hard with Parsifal but he resists her temptations. When it becomes obvious he is going to be unable to corrupt Parsifal, Klingsor hurls the Sacred Spear at him. Parsifal catches it and with its power destroys Klingsor.

Years later, on Good Friday, a silent and dark-robed Parsifal appears at the Grail Castle. Gurnemanz and Kundry greet him and Gurnemanz is stunned to recognize Parsifal and the fact that the once-innocent fool carries the Spear. He and Kundry wash and anoint Parsifal's feet and head. Gurnemanz declares Parsifal the king of the Grail Castle. Parsifal baptizes Kundry amidst a long dissertation on absolution and redemption.

The three go to the castle where the failing Amfortas exhorts the knights to relieve his suffering by killing him. Parsifal stops them, touches Amfortas with the Spear and the wound is healed.

Parsifal sets the Spear with the Grail, the objects rise above their heads, Amfortas collapses and, as the film ends, Kundry, Gurnemanz and Parsifal are left standing alone.

Parsifal (The Met, 1993)

266 minutes; Color; Opera; German with English subtitles; Copyright 1993, Metropolitan Opera Association, Inc.; Deutsche Grammophon

CAST: Waltraud Meier (Kundry); Siegfried Jerusalem (Parsifal); Bernd Weikl (Amfortas); Franz Mazura (Klingsor); Kurt Moll (Gurnemanz); Jan-Hendrick Rootering (Titurel); Gweneth Bean (A Voice from Above); Heidi Grant Murphy (Esquire); John Horton Murray (Esquire); Bernard Fitch (Esquire); Paul Groves (Knight of the Grail); Jeffrey Wells (Knight of the Grail); Heidi Grant Murphy (Flower Maiden); Korliss Uecker (Flower Maiden); Kaaren Erickson (Flower Maiden); Gwynne Geyer (Flower Maiden); Jane Bunnell (Flower Maiden); Wendy White (Flower Maiden)

CREDITS: The Metropolitan Opera Orchestra; Conductor — James Levine; Production — Otto Schenk; Set and Projection Designer — Günther Schneider-Siemssen; Costume Designer — Rolf Langenfass; Lighting Designer — Gil Wechsler; Stage Director — Phebe Berkowitz; The Metropolitan Opera Chorus; Chorus Master — Raymond Hughes; The Metropolitan Opera Ballet; General Director — Joseph Volpe; Artistic Director — James Levine; Video Director — Brian Large; Audio Producer — Jay David Saks; Executive Producer — Peter Gelb; Musical Preparation — Walter Taussig, Philip Eisenberg, Dennis Giauque, Susan Webb, Franz Vote; Assistant Stage Directors — Laurie Feldman, Peter McClintock; Stage Band Conductor — Walter Taussig; Prompter — Philip Eisenberg; German Diction Coach — Irene Spiegelman; Children's Chorus Director — Elena Doria; Executive Director/External Affairs — Marilyn Shapiro; Artistic Administrator — Jonathan Friend; Technical Director — Joseph Clark; Labor Operations Director — Pamela Rasp; Coordinator/Artistic Relations — Charles Riecker; Orchestra Personnel Manager — Robert Sirinek; Concert Master — Raymond Griewek; Librarian — John Grande; Ballet Mistress — Diana Levy; Ballet Stage Managers — Stephen A. Brown, Gary Dietrich, Thomas H. Connell III, Raymond Menard; Master Carpenter — Stephen Diaz; Master Electrician — Sander Hacker; Properties Master — Edward McConway; Wig and Hair Stylist — Magda Szayer; Makeup Artist — Victor Callegari; Wardrobe Mistress — Millicent Hacker; Costume Shop Head — Richard Wagner; Producers — Daniel Anker, Suzanne Gooch; Associate Director — Carol Stowe; Engineer-in-Charge — Mark Schubin; Assistant Producer — Susan Erben; Technical Supervisor — Ron Washburn; Technical Director — Emmett Loughran; Audio Supervisor — Bill King; Audio — Michael Shoskes, Mel Becker, Paul Cohen, Robert M. Tannenbaum; Video — William Steinberg, Paul Ranieri, Susan Noll; Camera — William Akerlund, John Feher, Michael Lieberman, David Smith, Juan Barrera, Manny Gutierrez, Jake Ostroff, Ron Washburn; Videotape — Alan Buchner; Crane Technicians — Rob Balton, Jasper Johnson; Cam Remote Technician — Steve Search; Television Stage Manager — Terence Benson; Music Associate — Karen McLaughlin; Production Assistant — Jessica Ruskin; Production Aide — Dan Gabriel; Additional Editing — Gary Bradley; Audio Post Production — Vin Gizzi; Production Facilities — Unitel Mobile Video, Terry Adams, Jim Will, Remote Recording Services, Inc., David Hewitt, Phil Gitomer; Video Post Production — Alfred Muller, Nexus Productions, Inc.; In Memory of Cynthia Wood; A Metropolitan Opera Television Production; The Metropolitan Opera Association

SYNOPSIS: A clear presentation of Wagner's *Parsifal* without the complication of modern artistic interpretation. Some few details are missing that show up in other adaptations. For instance in the Met's production, Kundry does not fly through the sky on her arrival in act 1 as she seems to in at least one other version. If anything, the Met's performance is the more realistic for this kind of change.

There are some very well done scene changes and the scenery itself is plausible stuff. The costumes are appropriate for the story, though with a minimum of armor. In fact the only armor seen in the film is on Parsifal himself when he returns in act 3 and even then it consists only of a helmet and shield.

The storyline doesn't stray from the original. In act 1 Gurnemanz, the eldest of the Grail Knights of Monsalvat, says morning prayers and awakens the forest guards. Kundry arrives on foot, bearing a salve of balsam from far off Arabia for the wounded Amfortas. Amfortas is the son of Titurel, the founder of the Grail brotherhood. Titurel had received from angels the holy relics of the Grail and the Spear which had been used to pierce Christ's side on the cross.

It was Titurel who built the Grail Castle at Monsalvat and gathered worthy knights to protect the relics. As he became older, his son, Amfortas, took over as king of the castle. One of the knights, Klingsor, strayed into evil magic and managed to steal the Spear. During an attempt to regain the Spear, Amfortas was seduced by Kundry (who intermittently falls under Klingsor's spells when she's not helping the Grail knights) and then wounded by Klingsor who was wielding the Spear. Since the wound comes from the Holy Spear, only the Holy Spear can heal it. Amfortas, Gurnemanz and the brotherhood know this and they

know that they cannot defeat Klingsor and his magic. Only a prophesied "innocent fool" can save the king.

It's mentioned that Gawain has gone off again to seek other medicines for Amfortas. Here is another small departure from other versions of the opera. Most other performances include a seemingly irrelevant discussion of the fact that Gawain has done this without Amfortas's permission. Amfortas typically becomes angered at his knight's apparent disobedience, but none of that occurs here.

Amfortas is carried to the sacred lake for a soothing bath. While all are present, a youth inexplicably shoots a swan out of the sky with a bow and arrows he made himself. Everyone is enraged with the boy for desecrating the sacred grove and its animals. The boy sees no wrong in the act but when Gurnemanz questions him, he is unable even to account for his own name.

The ever-mysterious Kundry recognizes the fellow as the son of Herzeleide and Gamuret. Gamuret was killed in battle and the sorrowing Herzeleide brought her son up in total isolation, hoping that the boy would thus avoid a similar death by violence.

Seeing that this youth might be the prophesied innocent fool, Gurnemanz takes the boy with him and the rest of the group to the castle. There the brotherhood assembles in the great hall and Titurel harasses Amfortas into celebrating the Grail ritual once again. Gurnemanz finds that the boy seems to show no understanding of what he has seen and in disgust sends him away.

Act 2 switches to Klingsor's castle where the magician summons Kundry and puts her once again under his power. The innocent youth attacks the castle, his prowess routing Klingsor's knights. The boy enters Klingsor's magic garden where the flower maidens try unsuccessfully to draw the boy into sin. Finally Kundry goes to him and attempts the same thing herself. She tells the boy his name is Parsifal and tries to weaken him with the story of his mother's death.

She also informs him that she was present when Christ was crucified and that she mocked the savior on the cross. She was thus condemned to seek him "from world to world" for redemption. Parsifal is able to resist her, however, so Klingsor steps in. The wizard hurls the Spear at the boy but Parsifal catches it and with the holy relic's power he destroys Klingsor's realm.

Act 3 opens some years later in the sacred lands around Monsalvat on Good Friday. Gurnemanz, now living as a hermit, finds Kundry sleeping in a field of flowers. He revives her and as they chat Parsifal returns, still carrying the Spear. They anoint his feet and head and Gurnemanz declares him king of Monsalvat. Parsifal baptizes Kundry and the three go to the castle.

Titurel is dead and Amfortas is seeking death. With the Spear Parsifal heals Amfortas. The new king uncovers and raises the glowing Grail. Kundry dies freed from sin and the choirs sing praise to the redeemer.

Parsifal (Syberberg, 1982)

255 minutes; Color; Opera; Copyright 1982, TMS Films, München; Copyright 1988, Corinth Films, Inc.; KULTUR #1195; A Corinth Films Release; Triumph Films, a Columbia Pictures Film Company

CAST: Armin Jordan (Amfortas [Sung by Wolfgang Schöene]); Martin Sperr (Titurel [Sung by Hans Tschammer]); Robert Lloyd (Gurnemanz); Michael Kutter (Parsifal 1); Karin Krick (Parsifal 2 [Sung by Rainer Goldberg]); Aage Haugland (Klingsor); Edith Clever (Kundry]Sung by Yvonne Minton]); Rudolph Gabler (Gralsritter [Sung by Gilles Cachemaille and Paul Frey]); Urban von Klebelsberg (Gralsritter); Bruno Romani-Versteeg (Gralsritter); Monika Gaertner (Knappen [Sung by Christer Bladin, Tamara Hert, Michel Roider, Hanna Schaer]); Thomas Fink (Knappen); David Meyer (Knappen); Judith Schmidt (Knappen); Klingsor's Zaubermädchen — Hochste und Mitlere Hölben ([Sung by Britt-Marie Aruhn, Jocelyne Chamonin, Tamara Hert, Gertrud Oertel, Eva Saurova, Hanna Schaer] Anahita Farrochsad, Miriam Feldmann, Johanna Fink, Alexandra Grünberg, Claudia Schumann, Anya Toelle, Stephanie Cörler, Catharina Klemm, David Luther, Caroline Riollot, Sofia Romani, Balthasar Thomass, Vivian Kintisch, Martina Lanzinger, Atonia Preser, Catharina Preser, Bettina Stiller, Annette Woll, Eva Kessler, Sabine Kückelmann, Isabelle Malbrun, Guillemette Riollot, Ina Schröter, Sophie Von Uslar); Altstimme aus der Höhe (Gralsträgerin Synagoge der Glaube); Amelie Syberberg (Sung by Gertrud Oertel); Chor der Prager Philharmonie; David Luther (Kind Parsifal)

CREDITS: Orchestre Philharmonique de Monte Carlo; Musikalische Leitung — Armin Jordan; Musikaufnahmen — Erato, Paris, Michel Garcin, Jean-Pierre Brossmann, Pierre Lavoix, Jérôme Paillard; Mischung Dolby Stereo — Pierre Lavoix, Jérôme Paillard; Filmmischung — Milan Bor; Kamera — Igor Luther; Ausstattung-Architekt — Werner Achmann; Skulpturen — Rudolf Vincent Rotter; Puppen — Atelier Stummer & Buchwald; Kunstmaler — Johann Ploner; Modelle — Flo Nordhoff; Requisite — Peter Dürst, Rüdiger Wagner; Kostüme — Veronika Dorn, Hella Wolter; Kostüme Kundry — Moidele Bickel; Garderobe — Horst Kutzbach, Marion Siekmann; Masken — Edwin Erfmann, Brigitte Raupach, Josianne Deschamps; Tonbearbeitung — Ed Parente; Studio Ton — Norbert Lill, Peter Rappel; Standfotos — Natalie Mayer, Hans Peter Litscher; Script — Gretl Zeilinger; Kamera Assistenz — Marion Sloboda, Peter Kalisch; Musiktechnische Beratung — Bruce Cohen; Synchrondirigenten — Bruce Cohen, Michael Zilm; Aufnahmeleitung — Ike Werk, Lothar Schilling; Regie Assistenz — Wolfgang Schrötter, Helga Asenbaum (Studio), Hans Kunitzberger (Ausstattung), Hans Peter Litscher (Paris) Guy Patrick Sainderichin (Paris); Kunstlerische Mitarbeit — Bernard Sobel; Schnitt — Jutta M. Brandstaedter, Marianne Fehrenberg; Produktionsleitung — Harry Nap, Annie Nap-Oléon; Co-Producteurs — TMS Films, München, Bayerischer Rundfunk, Gaumont Paris; Hergestellt in den Bavaria Ateliers München; Gefilmt ruit Arriflex; Die Musik für den film wurde aufgenommen von Erato, Paris; RegieHans Jürgen Syberberg

SYNOPSIS: To an opera already rife with symbolism Syberberg adds layers and layers of more symbolism. It starts as the opening credits roll over photos of bombed European cities and a fallen Statue of Liberty.

During the prelude Syberberg injects an opening scene that does not exist in Wagner's original work. In silence a young Parsifal plays with a bow and arrow as his mother (wearing a gown that sports Stars of David) looks on

Video cassette art of Hans-Jürgen Syberberg's film of Wagner's *Parsifal* **(courtesy Kultur Video).**

Amfortas taking on the Grail, then being wounded by Klingsor. Then the puppets also show a youth shooting a swan.

The camera pans and scenes merge. Parsifal's mother lies (dying?) holding an open book which reveals an illustration of King Arthur and the Knights of the Round Table. An older Parsifal moves across a rock-strewn set where little puppets of Wagner himself stand about doing different things — one hammers a nail into a large disembodied ear, one waves a conductor's baton.

Twenty minutes into the tape, act 1 begins. The basics of Wagner's *Parsifal* are all here with unending adaptations by Syberberg. Amfortas, king of the Grail Castle, is the son of Titurel, who was given the holy relics of the Spear and the Grail by angels. Titurel built the castle to house them and formed the knighthood to protect them.

Amfortas took over the duties of his aging father but one of the knights, Klingsor, committed some sin and was thrown out of the brotherhood. Klingsor learned sorcery, built his own castle and seeks to destroy the Grail knights by possessing the Relics.

Through Klingsor's evil magic Amfortas was bewitched by a beautiful woman and dropped the Spear. Klingsor stole it and stabbed Amfortas with it. The wound will not heal even years later.

Amfortas is brought to the lake for his

lovingly. She holds a real bow and arrow which the boy takes from her when three armored people appear, two boys and one girl. The mother weeps as the boy wanders off.

He observes a puppet show which depicts

bath. Kundry arrives and it is discovered that Gawain has departed without permission. A swan is shot by Parsifal on the grounds of the sacred forest and when brought before Gurnemanz and Amfortas he admits to the deed.

Kundry, the strange wild woman, seems to know more about the boy than he knows about himself. She tells them that Parsifal's father was killed in battle and that his mother is now dead as well. Parsifal attacks her but is stopped by Gurnemanz.

Amfortas returns from his bath and Gurnemanz takes Parsifal to the Grail Castle. They enter through a hall of flags, the first of which is a Nazi swastika. Other banners include a white crucifix, a black iron cross and a white dove.

Inside the castle reality is bent further. A large model of a swan with an arrow in it is there. Wagner's death mask is an ever-present image. Images are projected onto the sequined dress of one of the acolytes. A polygon is carried in. Girls carry the wound itself, an independent piece of flesh with a bleeding gash in it.

Parsifal (1998)

Not viewed; Copyright 1998, Unitel

CAST: Poul Elming (Parsifal); Hans Sotin (Gurnemanz); Matthias Hölle (Titurel); Falk Struckmann (Amfortas); Ekkehard Wlaschiha (Klingsor); Linda Watson (Kundry)

CREDITS: Staged and Directed by — Wolfgang Wagner; Musical Director — Giuseppe Sinopoli; Video Production Director — Horant H. Hohlfield; Orchestra of the Bayreuth Festspielhaus; Conductor — Giuseppe Sinopoli

SYNOPSIS: As of this writing the latest Bayreuth Festspielhaus production of *Parsifal* had been filmed but was not yet available on video tape.

According to a write-up on the Unitel website, however, this newest interpretation of the opera is unique. For the first time the female character Kundry is portrayed as actively participating in the Grail ceremony. Instead of dying at the end of the final act, she is the one who unveils the Holy Grail. This is revolutionary stuff in Wagnerian interpretation.

Parsifal (1998)

Title on tape, *Parsifal: The Search for the Holy Grail*; 90 minutes; Color; Documentary/Opera; Copyright 1998, RM Arts; Kutur video #1850

CAST: Placido Domingo (Parsifal); Violeta Urmana (Kundry); Matti Salminen (Gurnemanz); Nikolai Putilin (Klingsor); Feodor Mojhaev (Amfortas); Olga Frifonova, Anna Netrebko, Tatiana Pavlovskaya, Irina Djioeva, Tatiana Kravzova, Lia Shevtsova (Flower Maidens); Maria Gotsevskaya, Galina Sydorenko, Leonid Zahojhaev, Vladimir Zhivopistsev (Pages); Alexandra Iosifidi, Tatiana Zhukova (Principal Dancers)

CREDITS: Director — Tony Palmer; Music Conducted by — Valery Gergiev; With the Kirov Orchestra and Choir at Mariinsky Theatre, St. Petersburg; Chorus Master — Valery Borisov; Choreographer (Alexei Miroshnicenko; Designed by — Yevgeny Lysyk; Lighting — Vladimir Lukasewicz; Costumes — John Hibbs, Nadezhda Pavlova; Makeup — Svetlana Nepeivoda, Kim Burns; Photographed by — Simon Bray, Dave Marsh, Kate Robinson, David Swan; Online Editor — John Mayes; Dubbing Editor — Howard Halsall; Sound Records — Doug Hopkins, Alan Cridford; Sound Mixer — Alex Marcon; Sound Dubbing — Lance England; Graphics — Terry Griffiths; Facilities — Edit Video, Gemini Audio, Film & Photo, Ltd., TVI, EMI, Abbey Road; Special thanks to — Oswald Bauer, Dennis Kalashnikov, Sergei Beck, Marina Mishuk, Paramount Pictures, Ingmar Bergman, Bayreuth Festspiele, BBC Television, Transit Films, British Pathe, PLC, Ente Provinciale di Tourismo di Salemo for providing the Villa Rufolo, Ravello, Ente Provinciale di Tourismo di Amalfi for providing the Grotta della Smeraldo; Executive Producers — Reiner E. Moritz, Ettore F. Volontieri, Jane Seymour, Barbara Bellini; Ravello Festival Concert arranged by AMP Artists Management and Productions; Concert Associate Producer — Fiorenza Scholey; Special Assistant to the Director — Katya Novikova; Producer — Mike Bluett; The scenes from the Parsifal concert were filmed at the Ravello Wagner Festival organized by the Salerno Provincial Tourist Board under the aegis of the Campania regional authority (Italy); Co-producers — RM Arts, Thirteen — WNET, WDR, BR, ABC, Australia, RTE, SVT, Canal 22, Mexico; With the collaboration of the Province of

Salerno (Italy) in conjunction with RAI Radiotelevisione Italiana; Distributed worldwide by RM Associates and RAI Trade; Credited within the film — Karen Armstrong (Biblical Scholar); Wolfgang Wagner (Wagner's Grandson); Robert Gutman (Wagner Biographer)

SYNOPSIS: Part documentary and part performance, *Parsifal* is a narrated look at Wagner's final opera. Excerpts from the opera itself are performed alternately outdoors and on stages as Domingo explains the story. Scenes from other films are used as well, among them *Monty Python and the Holy Grail*, *Wagner* (the epic), *Indiana Jones and the Last Crusade* (see those entries). Other film clips include several from Ingmar Bergman's *The Seventh Seal* and various newsreels ranging from World War II–era Nazi rallies to modern-day combat helicopters launching rockets.

Domingo's narration opens with the statement, "The legend of Parsifal is one of the central stories of the last 2,000 years, the search for the Grail." He goes on to explain that the Grail is thought to be the cup used by Jesus at the Last Supper and by Joseph of Arimathaea to collect Christ's blood at the Cross.

Biblical scholar Karen Armstrong points out that only perfunctory mention of the cup is made in the New Testament. She states that it wasn't until the thirteenth century that interest in the Grail burgeoned. She attributes that rising interest to the fact that Western Europeans felt disconnected from the Holy Land and that any relic, particularly those associated with Christ, were seen as ways to bridge that gap.

Domingo's narration goes on, briefly touching on the Crusades when he says "...in fact, their [the Crusaders] achievement was the virtual destruction of an Arab civilization far more sophisticated than their own. The consequences of that we are still living with today." As these words are spoken, the helicopter gun-ships are viewed.

From the Crusades, the commentary moves directly to Adolf Hitler. The results, it is stated, of Hitler's beliefs that only the pure blood of the Aryan race could preserve the sanctity of the Grail were the deaths of "seven million Jews and at least 30 million others."

Next the Bayreuth Festspielehaus is shown and a brief history of the opera itself given. First performed at Bayreuth in 1882, Parsifal took Wanger more than 30 years to write. It was his biggest, most mature work, including a 100-piece orchestra, six choirs and four-and-a-half hours of music. Wagner was nearly bankrupt after having produced the Ring cycle and hit on the idea of selling subscriptions to his as yet unfinished *Parsifal* to help finance the building and the opera itself.

Wagner's grandson Wolfgang is interviewed and he points out some of the unique features of the Bayreuth opera house which Wagner himself designed. Described are the wooden stage, under which the orchestra was hidden as well as the ceiling (actually made of canvas), both of which are hollow for acoustical effect.

At this point excerpts from the opera itself begin, with Domingo giving an outline of what is going on and the background. He also recounts that Wagner first conceived the idea for the opera in the 1840s, but during the Revolution in Dresden, he was accused of setting fire to his own opera house and wound up in exile.

Many of the outdoor scenes are acted by performers other than those on stage. A much younger Parsifal for instance shoots the swan in the sacred woods. A truly demonic Klingsor appears in an actual oceanside cave. He calls up Kundry and his Flower Maidens from the depths of the waters and a bevy of naked swimmers respond.

Wagner biographer Robert Gutman next discusses the non–Christian aspects of Wagner's opera and the composer's anti–Semitism. Gutman states that *Parsifal* has nothing at all to do with Christianity, but is about racial purity. He says that the opera is the ultimate expression of Wagner's theories of how the besieged German race can extricate itself from its problems. Gutman posits that Wagner in fact performs a Black Mass on stage. Amfortas's pure Aryan blood has been contaminated by intercourse with the impure Kundry. According to Gutman, Wagner presents Christ as an Aryan and only the purely Aryan blood of Christ can heal Amfortas.

In the wrap up, Armstrong tells us that religion is not about dogma or whether or not to have female priests but rather it is about feelings for others. She says that if we forget that elements of the Divine are within each of us, the purpose of religion is defeated. Domingo then presents the facts that since World War II there have been 86 wars in which 100 million people have died. But as something of a saving grace for Wagner, Domingo asks us to remember that it was Wagner who wrote "Through suffering, understanding. Through understanding, compassion. Through compassion, love."

Parzival (1980)

Not viewed; Copyright 1980, West Deutsche Rundkunk, West Germany

CAST: Wolfram Kinkel; Eva Schuchardt
CREDITS: Director — Richard Blank

SYNOPSIS: Unique television production that uses puppets to perform Wolfram Von Eschenbach's twelfth century epic.

The Passing of Arthur (1974)

Not viewed; Filmstrip; Color; 35mm; Part 1: 51 frames, 19-minute record included; Part 2: 48 frames, 20-minute record included; Copyright 1974, Imperial Film Company; Released by Educational Development Corporation, Learning Resources Division; Library of Congress Call #PR5559.P3; Library of Congress Catalogue #74733460/F (Part 1) and #74733461/F (Part 2); Dewey Decimal #821

SYNOPSIS: The story of King Arthur's death from Tennyson's Idylls of the King.

The Passing of King Arthur (1969)

Not viewed; Filmstrip; 52 frames; Color; 35mm with captions; Copyright 1969, Brunswick Productions; Released by Educational Record Sales; Library of Congress Call #PR5559.P2; Library of Congress Catalogue #72736471/F; Dewey Decimal #821; From the series Our Heritage from Victorian England

Peabody's Improbable History: "King Arthur" (1961)

Not viewed; 4½ minutes; Cartoon; Copyright 1961, Associates of Television Production

CAST: Bill Scott (Mr. Peabody); Walter Tetley (Sherman); Paul Frees (Historical Characters); June Foray (Female Characters); Dorothy Scott (Female Characters)
CREDITS: Producers — Jay Ward, Bill Scott, Peter Peach, Bud Gourley; Executive Producer — Ponsonby Britt; Writers — Chris Hayward, Lloyd Turner, Chris Jenkins, George Atkins, Al Burns; Animation — Gamma Productions

SYNOPSIS: One of the regular segments of the Bullwinkle and Rocky the Flying Squirrel cartoon shows was "Peabody's Improbable History." Mr. Peabody was a genius dog and Sherman was his pet boy. Peabody built a time travel device called the Way Back Machine which the duo used to visit various moments in history. There were 91 of the four-and-a-half minute Peabody adventures. Their visit to King Arthur was episode 5.

Pendragon (1991/1996?)

Not viewed; Musical Comedy/Live Action; Copyright 1991, John Griffiths and Minerva Vision; Copyright 1996, Adrian Williams (musical score)

CHARACTERS: Granny-O; Arthur Jones; Olwen; Cul Jones; Mr. Yamamoto; Miss Tsezuki; Dai Hatsu; Bill McLaren
CREDITS: Concept, Story, Text, Lyrics — John Griffiths; Music — Adrian Williams

SYNOPSIS: A perhaps incorrect assumption is being made here. Though Pendragon was a finalist in the International Musical of the Year Competition in Copenhagen in 1996, it is not confirmed whether an actual film was presented for the competition or just a script.

Made for television as a musical comedy of two acts, the story involves a Welsh mining town named Pendragon, the town's championship rugby team led by Arthur Jones, a Japanese karaoke machine manufacturer,

Arthur's crippled brother, Cul (who is translating the *Mabinogion*), and Cul's love for a young lady named Olwen. Conflicts and confusion arise when the Japanese firm tries to acquire more land for expansion, threatening the existence of the town's rugby pitch. More problems develop when Olwen declines Cul's proposal of marriage, stating she'll only marry the man who puts Pendragon on the map.

Perceval le Gallois (1978)

140 minutes; Color; Live Action; Copyright 1978, Les Films du Losange; Co-Produced with FR3 in Cooperation with ARD, SSR, RAL, Gaumont

CAST: Fabrice Luchini (Perceval); André Dussollier (Gawain); Chorus (Solange Boulanger, Catherine Schroeder [singing, "rebec"], Francisco Orozco [singing, lute], Deborah Nathan [flute], Jean-Paul Racodon [singing, "chalumeau," armed knight], Alain Serve [singing, "chalumeau," bald squire], Daniel Tarrare [singing, collier, Garin], Pascale Ogier [singing, young girl, woman], Nicolai Arutene [singing, valet, knight], Marie Rivière [young girl, woman, daughter of Garin], Pascale Gervais De La Fond [young girl, woman, daughter of Garin]); Pascale de Boysson (The Widow); Clémentine Amouroux (The Aunt's Young Girl); Jacques le Carpentier (Proud Knight of the Heath); Antoine Baud (The Red Knight); Jocelyn Boisseau (The Laughing Girl); Marc Eyraud (King Arthur); Gérard Falconetti (Kay the Seneschal); Raoul Billerey (Gornemant of Goort); Arielle Dombasle (Blanchefleur); Sylvain Levignae (Auguingueron); Guy Delorme (Clamadieu of the Isles); Michel Etchevery (The Fisher King); Coco Ducados (The Hideous Damsel); Gilles Raab (Sagremor); Marie-Christine Barrault (Queen Guenevere); Jean Boissery (Guingambresil); Claude Jaeger (Thiébaut of Tintagel); Frédérique Cerbonnet (Thiébaut's Older Daughter); Anne-Laure Meury (The Girl with Small Sleeves); Frédéric Norbert (The King of Escavalon); Christine Lietot (The Sister of the King); Hubert Gignoux (The Hermit)

CREDITS: Director — Eric Rohmer; Writer — Eric Rohmer; Cinematography — Néstor Almendros; 12th- and 13th-century Music — Guy Robert; Production Design — Jean-Pierre Kohut-Svelko; Costume Design — Jacques Schmidt; Film Editing — Cécil Decugis; Producers — Margaret Ménégoz, Barbet Schroeder; Cameramen — Jean-Claude Rivière, Florient Bazin; Production Assistant — Alan Best; Swords — Claude Carliez; Setting — Guy Chalaud; Machinery — Georges Chrétien; Lighting — Jean-Claude Gasché; Sound Assistants — Jacques Pibarot, Louis Gimel; Sound Mixer — Dominique Hennequin; Sound Effects — Jonathan Liebling; Horsemanship — François Nadal; Still Photographer — Bernard Prim; Assistant Editor — Jill Reix; Sound — Jean-Pierre Ruh; Laboratory — Laboratoires Eclair, Paris, France; Cinematographic Process — Panavision; Animation and Titles — Atelier A.A.A.; Filmed at — Studios Eclair

SYNOPSIS: *Perceval le Gallois* is a film like no other among Arthurian movies. It is a synthesis of play, movie and opera which also blends surrealistic sets with accurate-looking medieval costuming. Taken from the unfinished twelfth century romance *The Story of the Grail* by Chrétien de Troyes, *Perceval le Gallois* is unparalleled for its creative approach to presenting a relatively accurate version of the original.

A group of medieval singers and instrumentalists forms a Greek chorus which not only narrates portions of the story but also participates in it intermittently. Members of the chorus occasionally make remarks directly to the audience, once pointing out, for instance, that certain repetitions "would be a bore." The main characters speak in a narrational style, as if reading from the text itself, even including the phrases "he said" and "she said."

The stage sets are stark but colorful. Forests are represented by a few artistically sculpted metallic-looking columns with four huge "leaves" forming a spherical, hollow top. Castles and towns are small constructions, accurate in architectural look, but barely taller than a man mounted on a horse. Back-lighting and blankness beyond the horizon of the scene give an otherworldly impression.

The son of a widow, Perceval one day mounts his horse and, carrying three spears, sets out into the forest. Five knights approach and from the noise they make he thinks they must be devils. When they come into view, he mistakes them for angels. One of the knights repeatedly asks Perceval if he has seen five knights and three damsels pass by, but the boy is too distracted with his own questions to pay attention. He wonders at the purpose of the knight's shield, his lance, his sword and his chainmail.

Amused by the incredible ignorance of the boy the knights give up and move on. When Perceval's mother learns who her son has met she becomes distraught. Perceval's two brothers both died the very day they'd been knighted and their father died shortly after of a broken heart. She had sought to keep Perceval from all knowledge of chivalry and war, but to no avail.

Perceval decides to find King Arthur and three days later he leaves. His mother's parting advice is: always help ladies in distress, never force yourself on a lady, never do more than kiss a lady, you may accept a good lady's ring, always ask a man's name, seek out worthy men and go to church often to pray. Perceval asks his mother, "What is a church?" His mother describes it as a beautiful place in which to worship God.

Finally Perceval departs and in time he comes across a tent. Thinking it so beautiful it must be a church, he goes inside to worship but instead finds a sleeping damsel. Waking her, he kisses her against her will seven times, takes her ring forcibly, eats her food and drinks the wine that is there. In spite of her pleas not to steal the ring, Perceval leaves the girl. Her friend, the Proud Knight of the Heath, returns and is angered mostly by the fact that she's been kissed, suspecting her of worse.

Next Perceval meets a collier. Perceval asks where he might find King Arthur and the collier points to a castle, but warns that Arthur is both happy and sad. He's happy because he's just beaten King Rion of the Isles, but sad because his knights have all returned to their own lands and he doesn't know how they are.

Perceval approaches the castle and meets the Red Knight outside. The Red Knight is angry because he's lost an argument with Arthur over land; he has stolen one of Arthur's gold goblets. Perceval rides his horse right into Arthur's hall. He finds the king deep in thought. Arthur explains how the Red Knight grabbed the cup right out of his hand, spilling wine on the queen. Now she is upset and has shut herself in her chambers. Perceval demands to be knighted, but refuses to dismount to receive the honor. He next states that he wants the arms and armor of the Red Knight. Kay laughingly tells the boy to go ahead and take them.

One of the singing girls addresses Perceval, saying if he survives the encounter he will be the greatest knight alive, then she smiles and laughs. It is explained by the minstrels that this girl had not so much as smiled in six long years. Kay becomes enraged and slaps the girl, then hurls one of the other singers onto the fire.

Perceval goes back outside and tells the Red Knight to lay down his arms. The knight laughs and Perceval kills him, throwing one of his spears through the knight's eye. A fellow named Yvonet comes along. He helps Perceval remove the Red Knight's chainmail and then helps Perceval put it on. Now fully armed, Perceval sends Yvonet into the castle to tell the laughing girl who Kay had slapped that before he dies, he will avenge her.

In his travels Perceval comes to another castle where he meets Gornemant. The knight takes the boy under his wing, teaches him the proper techniques of fighting with shield and lance and invites Perceval to stay for as long as he'd like. Perceval declines, stating that he must find out if his mother is all right. Gornemant's parting advice is: always spare an unarmed opponent, never talk too much, aid those in distress, go to church and stop telling everyone your mother taught you everything.

Perceval comes to a nearly deserted town where the beautiful Blanchefleur welcomes him, in spite of her poverty. She recounts how Auguingueron, seneschal to Clamadieu, has killed or imprisoned almost all the knights of the castle. They are to surrender the next day and Blanchefleur says she will kill herself rather than be taken by Clamadieu. Perceval takes her to bed with him, reassuring her that tomorrow will bring a different fate. They sleep "mouth to mouth."

Auguingueron is defeated handily and Perceval sends him to King Arthur with the message for the laughing girl that Perceval will avenge her. Clamadieu himself comes to challenge Perceval and is beaten as well. He too is sent to King Arthur with the same message for the laughing girl.

Much as he wants to stay with Blanchefleur, Perceval leaves to find his mother, promising to return. Perceval's next encounter is with a man seated in a boat, who informs him that there is no crossing point for 20 leagues in either direction. He invites Perceval to spend the night at his home and points the way. Perceval looks for the place but finds nothing then, suddenly, a castle appears.

Perceval joins the fellow from the boat, who is now seated at a table in the castle. Soon a youth enters the room carrying a lance from the tip of which drips blood. Taking Gornemant's advice that talking too much might be rude, Perceval asks nothing about this strange occurrence. Two more youths parade by, each carrying a candelabra of lighted candles. They are followed by a damsel carrying a Grail, which begins to glow brightly. Dinner is set and the whole procession passes by again. Through it all Perceval remarks on nothing. After the meal, Perceval's host is carried to bed by attendants.

Waking to an empty castle in the morning, Perceval dons his armor and leaves. When he looks back, the castle has disappeared. A wild woman on a horse rides out of nowhere and in an eerie voice interviews Perceval as to what went on in the castle. When she hears his story, she rails at Perceval that by saying and asking nothing he has done wrong. His questioning would have cured the king, she says, and now Perceval is cursed to lose his way and ultimately find his mother dead.

Crushed, Perceval wanders on. He meets a damsel riding a horse, her clothing so ragged and full of holes that it's barely enough to cover one part of her at a time. She begs him to leave, but the Proud Knight of the Heath

comes along. This is the poor girl who Perceval had kissed seven times. Perceval fights the Knight of the Heath and defeats him. He orders the lord to tend to his lady properly, then to bring her to King Arthur and tell the whole court the story. He also orders the lord to give the laughing girl his usual message, that he will avenge her.

This last is too much and Arthur decides to go looking for Perceval. Perceval happens to be riding along through the snow when a goose falls from the sky, wounded by a hawk. It leaves three drops of blood on the snow which remind Perceval of the white face and red lips and cheeks of Blanchefleur. Falling into a reverie, he sits on his horse, lost in thought. Arthur in the meantime has set up camp nearby. His men spot the statuelike knight and decide to investigate.

Sagremor goes first and when the knight seems to insultingly ignore him, he charges. As if in a shrug of afterthought Perceval raises his own lance and unhorses Sagremor. Back at camp the wise-cracking Kay ridicules Sagremor. Arthur sends Kay to try his luck. In similar fashion, Kay charges and Perceval offhandedly unseats the seneschal as well. Kay is heavily but not mortally wounded. Finally Gawain goes to Perceval and, speaking with him, convinces the knight to see Arthur.

After a brief conversation Perceval learns that he has indeed avenged Kay's slapping of the laughing girl. Perceval takes his leave, going to seek the meaning of the Grail.

Here the action switches to Gawain, who is accused by Guingambresil of having killed his lord without a challenge. A combat of honor is arranged for 40 days hence before the king of Escavalon. In the meantime Gawain becomes embroiled in the dickering of the two daughters of Thiébaut of Tintagel. He winds up championing the younger of the two and becoming her hero. Gawain next unwittingly winds up at Escavalon, where he has an affair with the daughter of the man he's been accused of killing. That too ends well, however, and the story returns to Perceval.

Having wandered aimlessly for five years and having entirely forgotten to worship God, Perceval meets a band of pilgrims. They direct him to a hermit to whom Perceval confesses his sins. The hermit, it turns out, is the brother of the man served from the Grail. Perceval's mother was their sister. The Fisher King, whom Perceval met but asked no questions of, is the son of the old king, who was served from the Grail. The old king has lived for 12 years fed by nothing except a single host from the Grail each day.

Perceval then takes part in a passion play. The film ends with Perceval departing once more, the singers stating, "The knight rode on through the forest."

Placido: A Year in the Life of Placido Domingo (1984)

105 minutes; Color; Documentary; Copyright 1984, TAF; A Transatlantic Film in Co-Production with Channel 4 and Group W; KULTUR Opera Profile; KULTUR Video #1119; KULTUR International Films, Ltd.

CREDITS: Sound—John Lundsten, Simon Okin, Terry Isted, Keith Hyde; Electrician—Tom Brown; Assistant Cameramen—Aled Morgan, David Bevan; Lighting Cameramen—Les Young, Steve Haskett, Richard Gibb; Production Assistant—Veronica Gadsby; Production Coordinator—Henrietta Brunt; *Tosca* Sequences Directed by—Jolyon Wimhurst; Videotape Editor—Peter Spink; Dubbing Mixer—Rod Guest; Editor—Graham Gilding; Associate Producer—Jane Gilmore; Produced and Directed by—Revel Guest

SYNOPSIS: An unremarkable tape unless you are a die-hard fan of Placido Domingo. At 1:27:33 into the film there is a brief segment in which Domingo describes a little of his technique for practice and memorization in his preparations for his role in *Lohengrin.*

The film is a superficially biographical look at a year of Domingo's existence on tour with short glimpses of his personal life. The bulk of the music he performs comes from Puccini and Verdi.

Placido Domingo: A Musical Life (1995)

90 minutes; Color; Documentary; Copyright 1995, Saragossa NV; An Antelope Production for Meridian; 13/WNET, Europool, KULTUR; KULTUR Video #1402; KULTUR International Films, Ltd.

CREDITS: Dedicated to—Plácido Domingo Senior, 1907–1987, and Pepita Embilde Domingo, 1918–1994; With Thanks to—Royal Opera House, Auvidis Iberica, Jan Martin, Conservatorio Nacional de Musica, Mexico, Performance Archive, Covent Garden Pioneer, Reiner Moritz Associates, Wiener Staatsoper, Shabtai Benaroyo, Ealing Studios, MCA, MGM, NVC, RAI, Sony Classical, Teldec, Unitel; Footage from Operalia 94 Courtesy—Televisa; Other Archive Material—Archive Films, British Pathé News, Universidad Nacional de Mexico; Photographs—Beth Bergman, Beto, Israel; Rostrum Camera—Simon Bedford; Film Research—Elly Beintema; Production Secretary—Milica Budimir; Production Accountant—Dee Owen; Subtitles—Jonathan Burton; Cameramen—Mike Fox, Michael Miles, Phil Gries, Jeremy Stavenhagen; Sound Recordists—Bob Withey, Bob Blauvelt, Ian Sands, Mike Sampey; On-Line Editor—Jason Farrow; Dubbing Mixer—Richard Lambert; Co–Executive Producer—Sir John Tooley; Co–Executive Producer and Writer—Michael Walsh; Executive Producer for American Masters—Susan Lacy; Executive Producer—Annie Stogdale; Production Manager—Justin Johnson; Editor—Alan Mackay; Produced and Directed by—Mick Csáky

SYNOPSIS: Though a little shorter than the other KULTUR tape on Domingo *(see Placido: A Year in the Life of Placido Domingo),* this one actually presents more complete biographical information.

At 50 minutes into the tape conductor Levine discusses Domingo's performances in Wagner's operas. There is an excerpt from *Lohengrin* with Domingo in the title role. The clip is from act 3 when Lohengrin describes the mystery of the Grail knights and reveals his identity.

Poppa Beaver's Story Time (1993)

Color; Illustrated Animation; Copyright 1993, Le Productions Cinar, Inc./GMT Productions/Typhoon Productions/France 3/Canal J

CREDITS: Producers — Ronald A. Weinberg, Jacques Pepiot, Thierry Fontaine; With the Participation of — Dominique Bourgois; Supervising Producer — Cassandra Schafhausen; Studio Typhoon Production — Jean-Pierre Dejou, Yves Fercoq, Catherine Griffaton, Jean Christophe Herbeth, Yvan Lemaire, Patricia Mavromatis, Richard Poulan, Arnand Sourgues, Franck Bonnet, Antoine Dartige, Ludovic Maire, Catherine Odet, Gilles Dayez, Sarah Francois, Vincent Guerin, Bernard Legall, Antonin Martineau, Philippe Mignon, Mireille Sarault, Anne Bonnefoy, Bruno Couette, Lionel Gasperi, Eric Mortain; Backgrounds: Philippe Dentz, Josette Mimran, Anne Cecile de Rumine, Annick Biaudet, Alexandre Duval, Michel Larzillieres, Stéphane Poumeyrol, Alain Richard, Gwenaelle Deredec, Annie Peltier, Christophe Vachier, Olivier Cheres, Isabelle Genty, Benoit Lermuzeaux, Pascale Mansano; Checking and Verification: Laurent Alchorn, Mary Ayaull, Brigitte Colesse, Pascale Jacquemont, Bruno Le Flo'ch, Myriam Rambach, Isabelle Aubert, Bertrand Bonnin, Cedric Hansen, Volande le Bec, Elizabeth Morcellet, Brigitte Simonne; Programming — Mirielle Chalvon; Title Producer — Lesley Harris; Story Boards: Meinert Hansen, Carl Linton, Robert Clark, Louis Piché, François Brinnon, Richard T. Morrison, Craig Wilson, Luc Savoie; Character Design — Marcos Da Silva, Pablo Villamayor, Sylvie LaFrance, Drew Mandigo; Graphic Research — Gabor Csakany, Mark Lague; Layouts/Key Animation: Marcos Da Silva, Meinert Hansen, Pierre Jarry, Luc Savoie, Pablo Villamayor, Steven Majaury, Craig Wilson, Nadja Cozic; Background Designers — Mark Lague, Gabor Csakany, Pablo Villamayor; Color Key Artists — Lucie Bélec, Jacynthe Lemay; Timing Directors — Louis Piché, Craig Bailey, Luc Savoie, Adja Cozic; Production Coordinator — Denyse Ouellette; Production Manager — Steven G. Blanchard; Assistant Production Manager — Thomas Lapierre; Lip Sync — Denys Tetreault; Production Assistants — Enguan Xu, James Mongomery; Sound by — Les Studios Cinar; Technical Director — François Deschamps; Sound Supervisor — John Stafford; Engineers — Pierre L'Abbé, Alan Roy, John Nestorowich; Sound Effects Editors — Mario Rodrique, Steve Wener; Rerecording — Pierre L'Abbé; Assistant Engineers — Pierre Bourcer, Vincent Regaudie; Foley Artists — Lise Wedlock, Karla Baumgardner; Editing and Titles — Joey Vekters; Post Production Coordinator — Julie Pelletier; Legal Advisor — Marie-Josée Corbel; Administrators — Don Teichroeb, Hasanain Panju, Louise Marach; English Adaptation — Jane Woods; Voice Director — Richard Dumont; A Canada/France Co-production in Association with La Société Radio-Canada, France 3 and Canal J.; With the Financial Participation of Telefilm Canada, Centre National de la Cinématographie; English version with the Participation of Telefilm Canada.

SYNOPSIS: Another children's film with an indirect reference to Arthurian legend through the character of Merlin. In this one a father beaver tells his children the story of Johnny and his family.

Disguising himself as a magpie, Merlin visits Johnny, striking a deal with the man. If Johnny will promise to visit and wish Merlin a happy New Year each year, he will tell him where the treasure of a Visigoth king is hidden. Johnny agrees and finds that the treasure is buried under his own fireplace.

In time Johnny and his wife begin abusing their wealth, though Merlin has warned them not to forget to help the poor. Johnny becomes cruel and greedy and takes a job as a tax collector. He asks Merlin to make him a baron, to make his son an abbot and to arrange for his daughter to marry a duke.

One year Johnny tells Merlin that he's too busy to come anymore. His daughter promptly dies, his son is kicked out of the abbey and Johnny loses his job. A tough lesson.

Pound Puppies: "The Legend of Big Paw" (1988)

Cartoon; Copyright 1988, Family Home Entertainment/Tonka; No further information available.

Prince Christopher **see under** *King Arthur and the Knights of the Round Table*

The Prince of Limerick **see under** *The Adventures of Sir Lancelot*

Prince of the Sun: The Great Adventure of Horus **see** *Little Norse Prince Valiant*

Prince Valiant (1954)

100 minutes; Color; Live Action; Copyright 1954, 1982, 20th Century–Fox; Copyright 1991, Fox Video; Fox Video #1326

CAST: James Mason (Sir Brack); Janet Leigh (Princess Aleta); Robert Wagner (Prince Valiant); Debra Paget (Ilene); Sterling Hayden (Sir Gawain); Victor McLaglen (Bolfar); Donald Crisp (King Aguar); Brian Aherne (King Arthur); Barry Jones (King Luke); Mary Philips; Howard Wendell; Tom Conway (Sir Kay)

CREDITS: Screenplay by — Dudley Nichols; Based on King Features Syndicates "Prince Valiant" by Harold Foster; Color by — Technicolor; Music — Franz Waxman; Director of Photography — Lucien Ballard, A.S.C.; Art Direction — Lyle Wheeler, Mark-Lee Kitic; Set Decorations — Walter M. Scott, Stuart Reiss; Special Photographic Effects — Ray Kellogg; Film Editor — Robert Simpson; Wardrobe Direction — Charles LeMaire; Orchestration — Edward B. Powell; Makeup Artist — Ben Nye; Sound — Alfred Bramlin, Roger Herman; Assistant Director — Stanley Hough; Technicolor Consultant — Leonard Doss; Cinemascope Lenses by — Bausch & Lomb; Produced by — Robert L. Jacks; Directed by — Henry Hathaway

SYNOPSIS: Harold Foster's comic strip "Prince Valiant" first appeared in newspapers in 1937. John Cullen Murphy, his associate of many years, took over the strip in 1979 and it continues today. This film was released in 1954.

The opening narration of the film states that the Christian King Aguar of Scandia has been overthrown by the traitor Sligon. The Viking king, his wife, the queen, and their young son, Prince Valiant, escape to a sanctuary provided by their friend King Arthur. Living in a secluded monastery on the northern coast of Britain, the king hopes for a time when his son can win back the throne of Scandia.

Aguar decides that the best way to prepare the boy for retaking their homeland is to send him to King Arthur's court at Camelot. There Valiant can train to become a knight.

Valiant's adventures begin on his journey to Camelot. Along the coast, he witnesses a Black Knight meeting with some Vikings.

Stumbling into their midst, he barely escapes. Next he meets up with Sir Gawain, who brings him to Camelot.

Gawain takes Val on as his squire and begins training the prince in the ways of knighthood and battle. When one of the other Knights of the Round Table, Sir Brack, rides off to find the rebel Black Knight, Valiant sneaks after him. The boy is waylaid by a band of foot soldiers and shot in the back with an arrow as he makes his escape. Riding some distance in spite of the wound, he finally collapses.

Valiant is found by the daughters of the king of Ord. Aleta and Ilene bring him home to their castle where he is tended as he heals. Val and Aleta fall in love and we learn that Ilene is in love with Sir Gawain. Then Brack shows up. They all travel together to Camelot for a big tournament. It is at this tournament that the king of Ord plans to find a marriage match for Aleta.

By this time Valiant is suspicious that Brack might be the Black Knight. After all, it is well known that Brack is an illegitimately born relative of King Arthur's and would have had the crown of Britain had Arthur not been born.

On arriving back at Camelot, Val finds Gawain in bed, badly wounded. He apparently went looking for Valiant and was ambushed by a band of foot soldiers. The blustery but good-hearted Gawain misunderstands something Val tries to tell him, causing a big love mix-up among himself, Val and the two damsels.

At the tournament Val dons Gawain's armor but is easily defeated by Brack. Just when it looks like Brack will win Aleta's hand an anonymous knight shows up and defeats Brack. The knight collapses after the joust and is revealed to be Gawain. Gawain at least partly saved the day by winning Aleta.

Val is arrested and imprisoned for impersonating a Knight of the Round Table. Brack receives word that his men have captured King Aguar and the queen. He has Val tricked into escaping prison, then the rebel Vikings capture

Robert Wagner surrenders in Henry Hathaway's *Prince Valiant* (1953).

both Val and Aleta and take them to Sligon in Scandia.

There Val manages to escape again and with the help of the other Christian Vikings he retakes the throne of Scandia. Carrying the Singing Sword of his father, Val returns to Arthur's court, exposes Brack and declares him a traitor. Brack insists on an immediate trial by combat and after a mighty sword fight, Prince Valiant kills Sir Brack.

Valiant is dubbed a Knight of the Round Table, the love confusion is cleared up and both Britain and Scandia are saved.

Though there isn't too much in the film, Foster's comic strip was known for a fair amount of historical accuracy despite the fanciful stories. The film even ignores many Arthurian details and characters. For instance no mention is made of either Gwenevere or Merlin, though Lancelot, Tristan and Galahad are present.

For a film based on a comic strip which is in turn based on a legend, *Prince Valiant* is as amusing as might be expected.

Prince Valiant (Prinz Eisenherz) (1997)

92 minutes; Color; Live Action; Copyright 1997, Constantin Film; Copyright 1998, 20th Century–Fox Home Entertainment and Constantin Film; 20th Century–Fox Home Entertainment #0470

CAST: Stephen Moyer (Prince Valiant); Katherine Heigl (Princess Ilene); Thomas Kretschmann (Thagnar); Edward Fox (King Arthur); Udo Kier (Sligon); Warwick Davis (Pechet); Gavan O'Herlihy; Ben Pullen (Prince Arn); Walter Gotell; Zach Galligan (Sir Kay); Hamish Campbell-Robertson; Marcus Schenkenberg (Tiny); Chesney Hawkes; Joanna Lumley (Morgan Le Fay); Ron Perlman (Boltar); Anthony Hickox (Prince Gawain); Jody Kidd (Lady of the Lake)

CREDITS: Director—Anthony Hickox; Screenplay—Michael Frost Beckner, Anthony

Hickox, Carsten H. W. Lorenz; Executive Producers — Bernd Eichinger, Jim Gorman; Co–Executive Producer — Robert Kulzer; Casting — Lee Ann Groff; Visual Effects Supervisor — Bob Keen; Music Composed by — David Bergeaud; Costume Designer — Lindy Hemming; Production Designer — Chrispian Sallis; Director of Photography — Roger Lanser; Production Executive — Gabriela Bacher; Associate Producer — Reinhard Klooss; Produced by — Carsten Lorenz; Film Editor — Martin Hunter; Production Assistant — Paul Martin; Camera Operator — Chris Plevin; Based on the comic strip created by Harold R. Foster; Story by — Michael Frost Beckner; A German-British-Irish Co-production Company, produced by Legacy Films Productions, Ltd., and Celtridge, Ltd. in collaboration with Babelsberg Film, in association with Hearst Entertainment, Inc.

SYNOPSIS: Harold R. Foster's comic strip is the source for this *Prince Valiant*. First appearing in 1937, the strip was taken over in 1979 by John Cullen Murphy and is still running today.

One of the unique features of this film is the use of the comic strip illustrations. A brief portion of the opening, a number of scene breaks and the closing morph interestingly into animated illustrations that look like they are right out of the Sunday paper. Though they are not credited, these illustrations appear to be Murphy's work or, at the very least, excellent imitations of it.

In this rendition, Arthur's sister, Morgan, has been banished to the cold northern land of Thule. As the film opens, she and some men are standing on a windy crag. The men dig up the grave of Merlin. Clutched in the dead wizard's hands is his book of incantations. Morgan takes the tome and, holding it aloft, declares that now she can get Excalibur.

Some time later in Camelot a tournament is in progress. Sir Gawain is hurt in a joust and his squire, Valiant, puts on the knight's armor to take his place in the lists. Valiant defeats his (or Gawain's) opponent, Prince Arn. Prince Arn, by the way, is to marry Princess Ilene, but Gawain has caught the girl's eye.

While these things are going on, Vikings sneak into the throne room and steal Excal-ibur. An unidentified knight tries to stop them but is killed. His scream alerts Arthur and the rest of the court, but they arrive too late. The thieves leave behind a scrap of tartan cloth, making Arthur believe the culprits to be Scottish. War plans are made.

In the meantime Ilene makes overtures to the fellow she thinks is Gawain. To complicate Valiant's position even more, Arthur has Valiant maintain the charade of being Gawain and orders him to escort Ilene home to Wales before the war with Scotland starts.

Back in Thule, Excalibur has been delivered to Sligon, the usurper. This Sligon is thoroughly evil, but is also a bumbler whom Morgan is using for her own purposes. Though he has taken the throne of Thule from its rightful heir — Valiant — the real leader behind the Viking forces is Thagnar, Sligon's even-more-evil second in command.

Sligon tries to wield Excalibur, but the magic sword begins to glow and plants itself in the stones of the floor. No one can pull it out. Morgan studies her magic mirror and sees Gawain accompanying Ilene's party on the road. She believes Gawain will be the only person who can remove the sword from the floor, so she sends her Vikings to get him.

Ilene's entourage approaches Wargrave Forest where, Valiant is warned, dwells the Jabberwocky, England's fiercest dragon. Ilene is kidnapped and in searching for her, Valiant finds the dragon's cave. No dragon is present but instead there is an exotic mechanism that throws fireballs out the mouth of the cave. A lone man has Ilene captive in the cave. Valiant fights with him, but the fellow leaves when he sees the Red Stallion medallion that Valiant wears.

The trip to Wales continues and Ilene and Valiant are falling in love. They must part at the border but fate would have it otherwise. Morgan's Vikings have set a trap and a battle begins. Gawain shows up in time to help but is captured. Valiant only escapes by falling into a river. Ilene dives in after him and the two are washed downstream to safety.

Through the rest of the film we learn that the Red Stallion is the emblem of the royal family of Thule, that Valiant is the son of King Aguar and that the man in the cave had been sent to find Val by friendly royalists back in Thule. The protagonists are joined by a dwarf named Pechet, who winds up financing their trip to Thule.

In a series of fights, captures and escapes, the action continues. Arn, Gawain, Sligon, Morgan and even Ilene are all killed. Happily, though, Ilene is resurrected by the power of Excalibur.

Also unique to this film are some really comical moments and special effects. The scene of Valiant walking along the bottom of the river in a full suit of armor is one. The topper, though, is in the castle at Thule. One of the many perils there is a flotilla of armor-plated alligators. During the final confrontation one of the beasts literally erupts out of the water, landing on the chamber floor. The editing did not succeed in eliminating all of the jiggling of the patently rubbery creature.

Apropos these same creatures, Pechet stumbles across one of Morgan's potions and uses it to put the alligators to sleep. Surprised and delighted at finding the bottle, Pechet declares, "Ah, Qualudium!"

Not to belabor the ridiculous, one final scene is worth mentioning. In order to help when Val and Ilene have been captured once again, Pechet has himself shot into the castle by a catapult. One is reminded of the scene where the "Frenchmen" of *Monty Python and the Holy Grail* catapult a cow out of their castle at King Arthur.

Prinz Eisenherz see *Prince Valiant (1997)*

Princess Gwenevere and the Jewel Riders (1995)

44 minutes each volume; Color; Cartoon; Copyright 1995, New Frontier Entertainment and Enchanted Camelot Productions, Inc.; Worldwide Distribution by Bohbot Entertain-

ment, Inc.; Family Home Entertainment #27639, #27640, #27641, #27661

CREDITS: Created and Directed by — Robert Mandell; Produced by — Winnie Chaffee, Eleanor Kearney; Starring the Voices of— Corinne Orr, Keri Butler, Debra Allison, Bob Kaliban, Henry Mandell, John Beach, Laura Dean; Recording Director — Peter Fernandez; Music Supervisor — Ken Kushnick; Songs Written and Produced by — Jeff Pescetto; Music Composed by — Louis Fagenson; Executive Story Editor — Shelly Shapiro; Executive Consultants — Perry W. Drosos, Diedre Barrett England, Murray Froikin; Associate Producer — Raissa Roque; Production Coordinators — Peter Mosen, Barbara Jean Kearney; Art Director for Studio B — Billy Keats; Production Manager for Studio B — Micka West; Production Assistant for Studio B — Jamie Turner; Storyboard Artists — Nicholas Filippi, Oliver Thomas, Lance Taylor, Tom Nesbitt, Glen Lovett; Storyboard Slugging — Brad Neave, Eduardo Soriano; Storyboard Revision — Colleen Holub; Timing — Ron Crown, Eduardo Soriano; Lip Assignment — Cathy Luker; Senior Design Director — Gregory J. Antore; Character Design — Kathlene Estes, Brenda Hardin, Mardon Deane, Michael Kiley, Rob Davies; Color Design — Bonnie Reid, Kellie de Vries; Prop and Background Design — Chris Labonte, Gord McBride, Trevor Bentley, Chris Roberts, Tina Louise Akland, Curt Spurging, Mike Valiquette, Ping Chang, Olaf Miller; Background Styling — Greg Gibbons, Danuta Rogula; Pre-Production Sound — Roger Jakubiec, Lynn Gillis, Debbie Warren; Post Production Supervisors — Peter Roos, Craig Seti; Video Post Production — Magno Sound and Video, Inc.; Video Editors — Larry Rubinstein, Robert Artell; Colorists — Martin Zeichner, Jack Baierlein; Audio Post Production — Pharaoh Editorial, Inc., Richard Fairbanks, Chad Collins, Peter Roos; Computer Graphic Imaging — Christopher Laskey, Idan Tetrault; Main Title Animation Director — James G. Petropoulos; Main Title Animation Assistants — Daniel Pagan, Mathew Oldfield; Main Title Sequence Design — Sam Edwards Editing Group, Inc.; Overseas Animation — Hong Ying Animation Company, Ltd.; Overseas Animation Supervisor — Christopher Labonte; Animation Director — James Tang; Bohbot Entertainment, Inc.; Executive VP/Worldwide Program Sales — Rick Levy; Senior VP/Domestic Consumer Products — Ellen Echelman; Senior VP/Managing Director — Nadia Nardonnet; Senior VP/Domestic Distribution — Chris Rovtar; Group VP/Dir. Domestic Distribution — John Hess; Group VP/Dir. International Consumer Products — Veronique Angelino; Group VP/Dir. Legal and Business Affairs — Tami Morachnick; VP/Sales Administration — Christine Muhlback; VP/Director International Sales — Leslie Nelson; Executive Producers — Allen J. Bohbot, Robert Mandell, Joseph A. Cohen, Ralph J. Sorrentino

SYNOPSIS: A made-for-television-with-simultaneous-toy-release production. *Princess Gwenevere and the Jewel Riders* combines all the worst elements of minimalist cartooning, modern commercialism and vacuous storytelling with a tiny portion of Arthurian legend. See also *King Arthur and the Knights of Justice*, the version of this genre aimed at boys.

Each tape opens with advertisements for toys representing characters from the show and for the sale of the tapes themselves. The only connections to Arthurian legend are vague ones. Gwenevere's parents are not the sovereigns of Cameliard but of Avalon. They live in a city called New Camelot. Merlin is a main character along with Archimedes, the owl (a carry-over from T. H. White's book *The Once and Future King*). There all resemblance to any literature ends.

The first tape is a single title divided into parts 1 and 2. The remaining three tapes each include two separately titled episodes. All credits for each tape are the same as above except for the writers, who are listed with each of the titles.

VOLUME 1: "JEWEL QUEST" (Written by Robert Mandell)

The evil Princess Kale steals a power jewel and wakes the Travel Trees. This threat can't go unanswered so Merlin gathers Gwenevere and her friends, the other Jewel Riders to teach them about the wild magic of Avalon, the Sunstone and the Friendship Ring.

King Jarod calls for the help of the Wolf Riders as well and the two teams of youngsters become a mighty force for good. Drake obviously likes Gwen, but Gwen is full of self-doubt and angst. Fallon and Tamara seem to be very cool about everything.

The Jewel Riders' mounts, of course, are unicorns. These creatures speak and when they do their horns flash on and off. The Travel Trees talk as well and provide a means of travel through space and time for anyone who seems to be worthy or who controls various power jewels.

Kale shows up again, captures Merlin and Sunstar, the winged unicorn, then steals the seven crown power jewels. Merlin manages to scatter the seven jewels so that Kale won't get them and Sunstar goes home. The stage is set for high adventure.

VOLUME 2, EPISODE 1: "WIZARD'S PEAK" (Written by James Luceno and Robin Young)

Drake and Gwen enter Wizard's Peak, a mountain full of peril. They tussle with the Guardian of the Hall of Wizards and manage to recover the Jewel of Burning Ice.

VOLUME 2, EPISODE 2: "TRAVEL TREES CAN'T DANCE" (Written by Christopher Rowley and Robin Young)

The Travel Trees drop Gwen in the wrong place, the Northwoods, because something is wrong with the wild magic. After some weird dancing and a battle of sorts, the Jewel Riders wrest the Jewel of the Northwoods from Kale.

VOLUME 3, EPISODE 1: "FOR WHOM THE BELL TROLLS" (Written by Marianne Meyer and Robin Young)

A troll turns the Pack Riders (these guys were the Wolf Riders in the first tape) into frogs. Two of them, Josh and Storm, get away to find help. Best line of all four tapes: "It's not easy being green" (a direct steal from Kermit the Frog of the Muppets and *Sesame Street*). Simultaneously Castle River Mist is missing and Lord Delfonse is now a swan. All ends well and another jewel is recovered.

VOLUME 3, EPISODE 2: "THE FAERY PRINCESS" (Written by Linda Shayne and Robin Young)

Faery Princess (and shepherd) Whisp is

bored and wants out of Faeryland. One of the crown jewels falls down a rainbow into Faeryland, turning three of her sheep — Fluffy, Stuffy and Muffy — bad to the bone (they become motorized biker sheep). In this tape we learn that the Crystal Palace is in the city of New Camelot. The girls salvage the Desert Stone.

Volume 4, Episode 1: "Revenge of the Dark Stone" (Written by Robin Young and Christopher Rowley)

The revelations in this episode are that Gwen's mom is Queen Anya and that six of the jewels have been saved. A map is found which reveals the location of the lair of the ancient banished wizard, Morgana. Kale disguises herself as Anya, gets into the palace and takes over with antimagic.

Volume 4, Episode 2: "Full Circle" (Written by Robin Young and Christopher Rowley)

In desperation the Jewel Riders go to the Friendship Circle where they get their powers back and a new friend named Kit the fox. Riding on magic, they find Merlin in Cloud Land. Merlin pulls Kale in with him and holds her there. Kale gets Merlin's staff and some other jewel, but she is destroyed.

Quest for Camelot (1998)

86 minutes; Color; Cartoon; Motion Picture Copyright 1998, Warner Bros.; Screenplay Copyright 1998, Warner Bros.; Original Score Copyright 1998, WB Music Corp.; Original Songs Copyright 1998, Warner-Tamerlane Publishing Corp.; Distributed by Warner Bros., A Time Warner Entertainment Company; Warner Bros. Family Entertainment #16607

Cast: Jessalyn Gilsig (Kayley); Andrea Corr (Kayley [singing]); Gary Ewes (Garrett); Bryan White (Garrett [singing]); Gary Oldman (Ruber); Eric Idle (Devon); Don Rickles (Cornwall); Jane Seymour (Juliana); Celine Dion (Juliana [singing]); Pierce Brosnan (King Arthur); Steve Perry (King Arthur [singing]); Bronson Pinchot (Griffin); Jaleel White (Blade Beak); Gabriel Byrne (Lionel); Sir

John Gielgud (Merlin); Frank Welker (Ayden); Sarah Rayne (Young Kayley)

Credits: Score Composed by — Patrick Doyle; Original Songs by — David Foster, Carole Bayer Sager; Based on the novel *The King's Damsel* by Vera Chapman; Screenplay — Kirk De Micco, William Schifrin, Jacqueline Feather, David Feather; Producer — DaLisa Cooper Cohen; Director — Frederik Du Chau; Production Designer — Steve Pilcher; Editor — Stanford C. Allen; Associate Producer — Zahra Dowlatabadi; Lead Animator, Kayley — Nassos Vakalis; Lead Animator, Garrett — Chrystal S. Klabunde; Lead Animator, Ruber — Alexander Williams; Lead Animator, Devon and Cornwall — Dan Wagner; Lead Animator, Juliana — Cynthia L. Overman; Lead Animator, Blade Beak and Minions — Stephen A. Franck; Lead Animator, Ayden — Mike Nguyen; Supervising Animator — Russell Hall; Animation Consultant — Stan Green; Lead Animators — Lennie K. Graves, Alyson Hamilton; Art Directors — Carol Kieffer Police, J. Michael Spooner; Creative Consultant — Mike Ockrent; Music Production Supervisor — Daniel Carlin; Choreographer — Kenny Ortega; Casting — Julie Hughes, Barry Moss, C.S.A.; Associate Producer — Andre Clavel; Production Managers — Igor Khait, Patrick J. Love; Production Manager, U.K. — Ian Cook; Story Department: Head of Story — Bruce M. Morris; Viki Anderson, Mark Andrews, Ken W. Bruce, Fred Cline, Jun Falkenstein, Stephan A. Franck, Daan J. Jippes, Brian T. Kindregan, Piel Kroon, Stephen G. Lumley, Wilbert Plynaar, Fergal Reilly, Harry A. Sabin, David S. Smith, Moroni Taylor, Christine F. Blum, Louis S. Scarborough, Cynthia Wells; Animation: United States Animators — Claire D. Armstrong, Dale Baer, Richard Baneham, David B. Boudreau, Adam Burke, Jennifer Cardon, Michael A. Chavez, Yarrow T. Cheney, Jesse M. Cosio, Alain Costa, Richard Curtis, Bob Davies, James A. Davis, Jeffrey P. Etter, Lauren J. Faust, Ralph L. Fernan, Steve Garcia, Heidi Guedel Garofalo, Kent Hammerstrom, Adam Henry, Ben Jones, Leon G. Joosen, Ernest Keen, Ken Keys, Juliana Koreborn, Jacques Muller, Randal L. Myers, Melma Sydney Padua, Scott T. Peterson, Anna Saunders, Sean Springer, Derek L. Thompson, Jim W. Van Der Thompson, Roger L. Vizard, Mark A. Williams, John D. Williamson, Dan N. Boulos, Larry D. Whitaker; Rough Inbetweeners: Joanne Coughlan, Ruth E. Daly, Phil E. Langone, Bowden Lee, Lane Lueras, Greg E. Ramsey; United Kingdom Animators: Cinzia Angelini, Laurent Benhamp, Alberto Campos, Luc Chamberland, Murry Debus, Sean Leaning, Paul Lee, Quentin Miles,

Stephen Perry, Thierry Schiel, Michael Schingmann, Sharon Smith, Gerben Steenks, Paul Stone, Mike Swindall, Vladimir Todorov, Jan Van Buyten, Duncan Varley, Pete Western, Gabriele Zucchelli; Rough Inbetweeners: Claire Bramwell-Pearson, Dave Coogan, Paul McKeown, Joe Mulligan; Visual Development: Key Stylist — Tony Pulham; Lighting Design — Anthony B. Christov, Laura L. Coresiglia, Joseph Ekers, Peter A. Gullerud, August N. Hall, Caroline Hu, Alan Kerswell, Dominique R. Louis, Philip Mendez, Uli Meyer, Frank Pé, Louis M. Police, Christopher J. Ure, Simon V. Varela, Claire Wendling; Sculpture — Carla Fallbeg; Maquette Casting and Sculpting — McKinnon & Saunders; Layout Department: Head of Layout and Workbook — William H. Frake III; Head of Layout — Jeff Purves; Layout Supervisor, U.K. — Brendan Houghton; Bluesketch Supervisor — Mercedes J. Sichon; United States: Layout Artists — Karen Hamrock, Arlan Jewell, Conor W. Kavangh, Davy C. Liu, Emil Miter, Gary Mouri, Robert J. St. Pierre, Audrey Stedman, Pamela B. Stefan, Craig Voight, Todd Winter, Brian Woods, Jennifer C. L. Yuan; Layout Assistants — Bryan D. Andrews, Norman R. Cabral, Louis E. Gonzales, Kory S. Heinzen, Ben Metcalf, Simon Rodgers, Lisa Souza, Bill Thyen; Bluesketch — Irma Goosby; United Kingdom: Layout Artists — Andrea Blasich, Sven Hoffer, Herve Leblen, Chris Scully; Background: Head of Background — Brian Sebern; Background Supervisor, U.K. — Ray Rankine; Background Supervisor, U.S. — Jeff Richards; United States: Background Artists — Manny Bennett, Ruben Chavez, Hye Coh, William J. Dely, Jr., Dennis Durrell, James D. Finn, Greg Gibbons, Annie Gunther, Andrew R. Philipson, Craig D. Robertson, Jonathan C. Salt, Kim Spink, Nadia H. Vurbenova, Scott Wills; Digital Background Painters — Craig R. Kelly, Briar Lee Mitchell; Background Assistants — Christopher E. Brock, Eugene Fedorov, Wendy Lynn, Joel Parod, Wei M. Zhao; United Kingdom: Background Painters — John Gosler, Natasha Gross, Rachael Stedman, Gary Sycamore, Sue Tong; Clean-up Animation: Head of Clean-up — Marty Korth; Associate Head of Clean-up — Sheldon Borentem; Clean-up Supervisor — Julia Bracegirdle; Clean-up Consultant — Dori Littell Herrick; Clean-up Leads: Kayley — Lureline Kohler; Garrett — Eric J. Abjornson; Ruber — Don Pagmele; Devon and Cornwall — Scott R. Bern; Juliana and Arthur — Doris A. Plough; Griffin — Robert Tyler; Blade Beak and Minions — Karenia S. Kaminski; Ayden — June Myung Nam; Kayley, U.K. — Nathalie Gavet; Garrett, U.K. — Jose Antonio Gerro; United States: Key

Assistant Animators — Paul A. Bauman, David Bombardier, Shelia Rac Brown, Kimie Calvert, John Eddings, Ruth Elliott, Anne Heeney, Ilona M. Kaba, Wantana Martinelli, Soonyin Mooney, Celeste Moren, Sung Noh, Bob Quinn, Domingo C. Rivera, Jr., Joe Roman, Kyung S. Shin, Maureen Trueblood, Michael A. Venturni, Tgan M. Vu, Mitchell Walker, Robin White; Assistant Animators — Beverly J. Adams, Andrew M. Beall, Gordon R. Bellamy, Wanda L. Brown, Yebbi Cho, Jeffrey D. Clark, Heidi D. Daven, Greg Flemming, Trine Frank, Ken H. Kim, Karen Marjoribanks, Vanessa J. Martin, James Mcardle, Viviane (Kamye) K. Miessen William Mims, Tao Nguyen, Doug E. Ninneman, Nicole Pascal, Andrew Ramos, Ivan Canilli Rivera, Jason S. Sallin, Mathew Scholfield, Jennifer M. Stilwell, Yevgenya Suzdaltsev, Helen T. Tse, Terry Walsh, Miri Yvon; Breakdown Artists — Steve Agular, Peter Paul R. Bautistiia, James A. Burks, Patrick T. Dailey, Miriam L. Goodman, Cathlin G. Hidalgo, Jennifer L. Jarmel, Diane Kim, Patrice Leech, Christine T. Mallouf, Robert G. Nigoghossian, Francisco Rosales, Rudy Rosales, John Rosen, Allison E. Sgroi, Stephen R. Steinbach, Henry Kim; Inbetweeners — Brian Boylan, Greg Checketts, Catherine M. Choi, Cesar S. DeVera, Guy Donovan, Yelena Geodakyan, Barrett Glenn, Jr., Danny Raül Gonzalez, Janeane K. Harwell-Camp, Guadalupe Hernandez, Suzanne F. Hirota, Joan Y. Kang, Kevin W. Koch, Kari Pearson Lancaster, Daisy Lee, Ho Young Lee, Rudi S. Liden, Shanon C. O'Connor, Chrissie Schweiger, Angela M. Sugurdson, Jennifer Sigurdson, Viorel Wronca, Elyse M. Whittaker-Pleck, Gina Russell Williams, Helen H. Yoan; United Kingdom: Key Assistant Animators — Marcus Arnull, Franck Bonay, Tony Cope, Helga Egilson, Bernard Georges, Victoria Goldner, Natalie Higgs, Helen Kincaid, Claudia Sturli, Dave Webster; Assistant Animators — Alexandra Boiger, Chris Clarke, Chris Drew, Deborah Dryland, Gerry Gallego, Fiona Gomez, Hilary Gough, Helena Grant, Andrew Griffiths, Nick Hellman, Stathis Karabateas, Darren Kordich, Nick Large, Sophie Law, Cath Lowdell, Simon Laxton, Peter Mays, Hae Sook Park, Eugenios Plakus, Antonella Russo, Christian Ryltenius, Steve Smith, Una Woods; Inbetweeners — Ramsus Andreesen, Simon W. E. Clarke, Camilla C. Fougner, Carla Hamer, Marianne Rasmussen, Dirk Keters, Richard Lowdell, Steve Martin, James Dean O'Shea, John Pickup, Maiken Riv, Jensen Bryan Rogers, Alex Stewart, Leona Nordstrom Valentin; Assistant Clean-up — Monica Brufton, Michael Cole, Carol Davies, Nigel Davies, Angeline DeSilva, Annie Elvin, Peter Gambier, Joanne Gooding, Nicholas

Harrop, Janette Hynes, Dominic Kynaston, Michael A. Lerman, Brian Malone-West, Samantha Malone-West, Nicola Marlborough, Lala Meredith-Vula, Karen Narramore, Tom Newman, Brent Odell, Theresa Smythe, Debbie Spafford, Ronan Spelman, Theresa J. Whatley, Deborah Womack, Sue Woodward; Effects Animation: Head of Effects — Michael Gagné; Effects Supervisor, U.K. — Mike Smith; United States: Effects Animators — Hamed Lactarus, Jaksas Michael Camarillo, John M. Dillon, Rich Echevarria, Marc Ellis, Earl A. Hibbert, John M. Huey, Debora Kupczyk, John J. MacFarlaine, Bob Simmons, Gary Sole, Ryan Woodward, Lynette C. Charters, Jane M. Smethurst; Assistant Effects Animators — Esmerelda C. Acosta, Mark Asai, Susan B. Keane, Bob Miller, Richard E. Olson, Young Kyurhim, Robert Rios, Mary J. Sheridan, Ryan J. Simmons; Effects Breakdown Artist — Von J. Williams; Effects Inbetweeners — Kennard F. Betts, Yan Budeen, Greg N. Bumatay, Chris G. Darroga, Robert Ism DeToscano, Noe Garcia, Daniel Killen, Matthew L. Maners, Rodd D. Miller, Jorge Hiram Ramos, Jaclyn S. Seymour, Laurie D. Sigueido, Norland M. Tellez, Jeffrey C. Tse; United Kingdom: Effects Animators — Jon Brooks, Volker Pajatsch, Antonio Pafermo, David Pritchard, Paul Smith, Tim Walton, Martin Wansborough; Assistant Effects Animators — Tracy Agate, Janet Cable, Michelle L. S. Dabbs, Carl Keeler, Terence Rikester, Lilas Leblan, Roger Lougher, Giulia Mazz, Jemshaid Mirza, Rhian Wyn Rushton, David Ruffnell; Additional Assistant Effects Animation — Dino Demostenous, Shaun McGlinchey, Ron McMinn, Albert Price, James Pyott, Barnaby Russel, Torraine Ward; Digital Effects Animation: Head of Digital Effects — Allen C. Foster; Digital Effects Artists — Mae Kim Ausbrooks, James Bentley, Andrew D. Brownlow, Steve Burch, Lee Crowe, Craig Littell-Herrick, Kevin Oakeley, Maryam Sharifi; CGI Animation: Heads of CGI — Tad Gielow, Katherine S. Percy; CGI Animators — Grace Blanco, Brad Booker, Adam Dotson, Bruce Edwards, Cory Hels, Time Keon, Darren D. Kiner, Sébastien Linage, Susan L. Olsin, Brian Schindler, Teddy T. Yang; Technical Directors — Brett Achorn, Stéphane Cros, Babak Forutanpour, Brian R. Gardner; Editorial: Associate Editors — Richard L. McCullough, Darren T. Holmes; Assistant Editors — John Currin, Rich Dietl, Sheri Galloway, Gregory Plotts, Jennifer Dolce, Evan Fisher, Barbara Gerety, Ken Solomon; Track Readers — Armetta Jackson-Hamlett, Brian Master; Assistant Production Managers — United States: Producer — Mary Alice Drumm; Director — Gary Biren; Sweatbox — Michelle O'Hara; Anima-tion — Lizbeth A. Velasco, Jackie Blaisdell; Story and Editorial — Marcia Gwendolyn Jones; Layout — J. C. Alvarez; Background — Leonard Vasquez; Clean-up Animation — Michelle Perstow, Virginie Foucoult, Susan K. Lee; Effects — Richmond Horme; Digital Effects — Gregory L. DeCamp; CGI — Timothy E. Jones; Scene Planning and Scanning — Maria R. Guierra; Animation Check — April M. Henry; Acme — Aaron Parry; Satellite Studios — Laura Leganza Reynolds; Art Director — Jill Ruzicka Leighton; Production Tracking — Joan Peter; United Kingdom: Animation and Clean-up — Steve Hollowell; Effects Scene Planning and Checking — John Phelan; Scene Planning: Head of Scene Planning — Steven Witzbach; Scene Planning Supervisor, U.K. — Kolja Erman, Silvia Barbier, Gina Bradley, Karen L. Hansen, James Keefer, George (Bingo) Ferguson, Katja Schumann; Animation Check: Head of Animation Check — Myoung Smith; Animation Check Supervisor, U.K. — Corona Mather-Esterhazy, Kathy Barrows-Fulmer, Susan Burke, Daryl Garstensen, Charlotte Clark-Pitts, Katherine Gray, Brendan Harris, Frances Jacob, Lowe C. Jhocson, Pam Kleyman, Madel J. Manhit, Helen P. O'Brien, Penelope Sevier, Debbie Skinner, Caroll Li-Chuan Yao, Nick Yates; Acme: Manager of Acme — Rhonda L. Hicks; Acme Supervisors: Color Styling — Tania M. Burton; Scanning — Irene M. Gringeri; Ink and Paint — Sarah-Jane King; Final Check — Kim Patterson; Final Scene Planning — James Williams; Color Styling — Marianne C. Cheng, Anthony C. Cianciolo, Jr., Sylvia M. Filcak, Leslie C. Hinton, Eric Jon Kurland, Annette L. Leavitt, Catherine P. O'Leary, Cathy Wainess-Walters; Scanning — David E. Bonnell, Craig Colligan, Geoff Darwin, Darrin M. Drew, Karl Dunne, Terri Eddings, Simon Edwards, Stephen Parkinson, Eric D. Schneider, Edwin S. Shortess, Dean T. Stanley; Color Model Mark-up — Constance R. Allen, Melody J. Hughes, Dawn Knight, Tanya Moreau-Smith, Helga Beatrix Vandenberg; Registration — Stevan A. King, Janet M. Zoll, Devon P. Oddone; Paint Mark-up — Renee L. Alcazar, Staci Gleed, Gina Evans Howard, Gale A. Raleigh; Ink and Paint Assistant Supervisor — Olga Tarin Duff; Digital Cel Painters — Diane R. Albracht, Amy Azzar, Tina Bastien-Antenorcruz, Kathy A. Baur, Nancy Bihary-Fiske, Martine Clavel, Elena Marie Cox, Damon Crowe, Dayle Dodge, Nika Dunne, Nance Finley, Ivis Freeman, Dawn A. Gates, Patricia L. Gold, Leonor Gonzales-Wood, Steve Kindernay, Diana D. McIntosh, David M. Nimitz, Fabio Novais, Kristian Roberts, Sheryl Anne Smith, Susan Lee So, Alice M. Solis, Dirk Von Besser, Susan

Witeman; Final Check — Dennis M. Bonnell, Thomas J. Jackson, Marisha Noroski, Randy O. Roberg, Freddie Vaziri; Final Scene Planning — Daniel Bunn, Dan C. Larsen; Production Accounting: Production Accountant — Trevor Pawtik; 1st Assistant Accountant — Michael Buchan; Music: Songs Produced by — David Foster, Carole Bayer Sager; Songs Arranged by — David Foster; Additional Song Orchestral Arrangements — Patrick Doyle, William Ross; Supervising Music Editor — Caoimhin D. Crlochám; Songs Orchestrated by — William Ros, James Sherman, Lawrence Ashmore, John Bell; Songs Recorded by — Felipe Elgueta, John Richards, Al Schmitt, Humberto Gatica, David Reitzas; Songs Mixed by — Joseph Magee; Assistant Music Consultant — Glen Kelly; Score Produced by — Maggie Rodford, Patrick Doyle; Score Music Editor — Roy Prendergast; Score Orchestrated by — Lawrence Ashmore, James Sheaman; Score Engineered and Mixed by — John Richards; 1st Assistant Engineers — John Rodd, Jimmy Hoyson; Conductor — Mark Watters; Assistant Music Editor — Kim Strand; Assistant Synthesizer Programming — Simon Franglen; Assistants to Mr. Foster — Lynne Malone, Lilly Pollard; Assistant to Ms. Bayer Sager — Laurie Gonlag; Instrumental Soloists: Penny Whistle — Jon Clarke; Penny Whistle — Andrea Corr; Irish Fiddle — Eileen Ivers, Sharon Corr; Accordion — Eilish Egan; EVI — Judd Miller; Ullean Pipe — Eric Rigler; Choir Leaders — Edie Lehmann Boddicker, Paul Slamunovitch; Concert Master — Burce Dukov; Technology; Technology Management — Lem Davis, Emmanuel C. Francisco, William Charles Perkins, David F. Wolf; Technology Engineers — George Aluzzi, Stewart Anderson, Steve Chen, Bruce Hatakeyama, Keith Kobata, Jose F. Lopez, Margaret Myers, Steven Myers, Arjun Ramamurthy, Leonard J. Reder, Alan L. Stephenson, Aaron L. Thompson, Cheng-Jiu Yu, Zizi Zhao; Acme Digital Specialists — Mark Aldridge, Will Bilton, Chris Gavin, James B. Hathcock, Dave Hogan; Technical Operations — Lori A. Arntzen, Paul Hernando, Kevin D. Howard, Alexis C. Pierre, Usha Ramcharitar, Paul Skidmore, Gene Takahashi, Alvin S. Tenpo; Production Assistants: United States — Leslie Barker, David A. Bemis, André Bivins, E. Tavares Black, Keith Brennan, Jode Craig, Laura M. Diaz, Monte Gagnier, Cirilo R. Gonzales, Jr., Scott Grieder, Jean M. Klaneky, Dao Le, Michael Leach, Sam Mendlestein, Louis Moulinet, Roubina Movsessian, Corrine Mulder, Loanne Hizo Ostlie, Ria Rueda, Thomas Shalin, Elaine Siders, Greg T. Smith, Staci Stonerook, Kathy Tajbakhish, Charlene Tinsley, Sunny Ye, Kathleen Zuelch; United Kingdom — Craig Colligan, Tim Denin, David Klein, Catrin Lloyd-Hughes, Anna Ford, Tiffany Maberley, Jason Palmer, Nick Roberts, Sarah Townrow; Assistant to Mr. Du Chau — Jennifer Vanderbliek; Assistant to Ms. Cooper Cohen — Cynthia A. Garcia; Production Management Assistant — Glenda V. Winfield; Production Support — Patrick Fitch, Madeline Fry, Joe Hernandez; Casting Associate — Jessica Gilburne; Post Production: Post Production Supervisor — Jeannine Berger; Camera Supervisor — Mark Dinicola; Supervising Sound Editors — Alan Robert Murray, Dave Horton, Sr.; Sound Designers — Chris Boyes, Tom Myers; Sound Effects Editors — Bub Asman, Adam Johnston, Andy Kopetzky, Bill Manger; Background Effects Editors — Stu Bernstein, Gregory M. Gerlich, Bruce Richardson; Re-recording Mixers — David Campbell, John Reitz, Gregg Rudloff; Assistant Editors — Todd Harris, Darrin Martin, David Werntz, J. Katz, Michael Ruiz, Rob Wilson; Assistant Sound Designer — David Hughes; ADR Supervisor — Curt Schulkey; ADR Mixer — Doc Kane; Foley Supervisor — Dave Horton, Jr.; Foley Walkers — John Roesch, David Lee Fein; Foley Mixer — Mary Jo Lange; Foley Editors — Scott Jackson, Neil Burrow, Scott Burrow, Scott Tinsley; Negative Cutter — Mo Henry; 1st Camera Operator — Christine Beck; Camera Operator — Richard Wolff; Projectionist — Preston Oliver; Color Timer — Terry Claborine; Principal Dialogue by — Troy Porter, Bill Higley, Bob Baron, Steve Hellaby; Principal Dialogue — Vince Caro; Additional Production Services — A-Film; Head of Production — Anders Mastrup; Animation Supervisor — Jesper Møller; Production Managers — Helle Hansen, Kristel Toldsepp; Layout and Background Supervisor — Matthias Lechner; Clean-up Supervisor — Bjørn Pedersen; Clean-up Supervisor (Estonia) — Tine Karrebaek; Technical Support — Hans Perk; Line Test Operator — Susanne Gloerfelt-Tarp; Assistant Production Manager — Irene Sparre; Animators: Meelis Arulepp, Svetlana Bezdomnikova, Padraig Collins, Luca Fattore, Stefan Deldmark, Michael Helmuth Hansen, Silvia Hoefnagels, Anne Holmer, Christian Kuntz, Jørgen Lerdan, Anders Madsen, Martin Madsen, Fernando Moro, Janus Sorgenfrey Pedersen, Ando Tammik; Layout Artists — Marcus Hoogvelt, John Koch, Jens Møller; Background Painters — Thomas Dryer, Bjarne Hansen, Peter Kielland; Bluesketch — Steen Dyrved, Kristina Martinson, Charlotte Worsaae; Clean-up Key Assistant Animators — Uffe Danielsen, Thomas Fenger, Hope Devlin Kristiansen, Rigmor Tokerød; Clean-up Assistant Animators — Ahto Aaremae, Morten Bramsen, Margo

Busch, Elizabeth Dankjer, Kristina Didrik, Mette Fenger, Henrik Hansen, Jørgen Hansen, Karin Hjorth, Søren Jakobsen, Tinna Jespersen, Herle Kühl, Riina Kütt, Malene Laugessen, Aavi Levin, Tom Lock, Malle Maenurm, Lars Nielsen, Merike Peil, Gunihild Rød, Lus Roden, Chai Sanul, Jesper Ezme Sørensen, Evelin Temmin, Raivo Tihanov, Krista Vanamölder; Yowsa; Head of Production — Claude Chiasson; Production Manager — Pierre Chiasson; Clean-up Animators: Vittoria Bologna, Denise Bradshaw, Ron Chevarei, Mike Demur, James McCrimmon, Ron Migliore, Paul Mota, Royston Robinson; Inbetweeners — Elsie Chen, Dave Cortesi, Rowena Cruz, Gloria Hsu, Karen Kewell, Oleh Prys; Heart of Texas Productions, Inc.: Head of Production — R. Don Smith; Production Managers — Susan E. Clark, Michele Vitale; Production Accountant — Shelley McAffe; Clean-up Supervisor — Jeff Foucart; Assistant Clean-up Supervisors — Bonnie Brantley, Manuel Garrasco; Pencil Tester — Josh Hanton; Animators — Frank Gabriel, Tom King, Alan T. Pickett, Kez Wilson; Clean-up Key Assistant Animators — Deborah Abbott, Dan Abraham, Jim Battaglia, Jr., Doug Beck, David Koppenhaver, Erica Missey, Jeannette Moreno, Lance Myers, Jimmy Tovar, Gabriel Valles; Inbetweeners — Richard Bartholmew, Lisa Bozzetto, Eddy Carrasco, Cynthia Crowell, Walt Holcombe, Inez Hunicken, John Keen, Aaron Long, John Overmyer, Erik Zumwalt; Additional Voices — Al Roker, Jess Harnell, Jack Angel, Joe Baker, Robert Bergen, Rodger Bumpass, Phillip Clarke, Sheelagh Cullen, Ken Danziger, Jennifer Darling, Fiona Dwyer, Paul Eiding, Fionnula Flanagan, Jean Gilpin, Sherry Lynn, Danny Mann, Mickie T. McGowan; Choreography/Live Action Reference; Editor — Robert H. Gordon; Assistant Dance Choreographer — Peggy Holmes; Choreography Casting — Gregg Smith; Assistant Production Manager — Shannyn Whitaker Gardiner; Dancers — Tina Marie Abas, Paul Ainsley, Michelle Elkin, Thomas Guzman-Sanchez, Michael McClure, Andrea Paige Wilson, Zahariades; Fight Choreographer — Randy Kovitz; Fighters — Bubba Carr ,John "Havic" Gregory, George Hubela, Kimo Keoke, Regan Patno; Vision Impairment Consultant and Martial Arts Expert — Lynn Manning; Braille Institute Consultant — Carmen Apelgren; Falcon Handler — Jerry Thompson; Production Associates — Carolyn Cassidy, Eva Friedberg, Henri Oganesyan, Sara Richardson, David Tong; Soundtrack Album: CURB Records/Warner Sunset Records/Atlantic Recording Corp.; "United We Stand": Written by — Carole Bayer Sager, David Foster; Produced by — David Foster, Carole Bayer Sager; Performed by —

Steve Perry; Courtesy of Columbia Records; "On My Father's Wings": Written by — Carole Bayer Sager, David Foster; Produced by — David Foster, Carole Bayer Sager; Performed by — The Corrs; Courtesy of Lava Records/143 Records/Atlantic Recording Corp.; "Ruber": Written by — Carole Bayer Sager, David Foster; Produced by — David Foster, Carole Bayer Sager; Performed by — Gary Oldman; "The Prayer": Written by — Carole Bayer Sager, David Foster; Produced by — David Foster, Carole Bayer Sager; Performed by — Celine Dion; Courtesy of Sony Music Entertainment (Canada), Inc.; "I Stand All Alone": Written by — Carole Bayer Sager, David Foster; Produced by — David Foster, Carole Bayer Sager; Performed by — Bryan White; Courtesy of Asylum Records/Elektra Entertainment Group; "The Bunny Hop": Written by — Ray Anthony, Leonard Auletti; "If I Didn't Have You": Written by — Carole Bayer Sager, David Foster; Produced by — David Foster, Carole Bayer Sager; Performed by — Eric Idle, Don Rickles; "Looking through Your Eyes": Written by — Carole Bayer Sager, David Foster; Produced by — David Foster, Carole Bayer Sager; Performed by — The Corrs, Bryan White; The Corrs appear courtesy of Lava Records/143 Records/Atlantic Recording Group; Bryan White appears courtesy of Asylum Records /Elektra Entertainment Group; "I Stand All Alone" (Reprise): Written by — Carole Bayer Sager, David Foster; Produced by — David Foster, Carole Bayer Sager; Performed by — Bryan White; Courtesy of Asylum Records/Elektra Entertainment Group; "Superman Theme": Written by — John Williams; "Looking through Your Eyes" (Reprise): Written by — Carole Bayer Sager, David Foster; Produced by — Wilbur Rimes; Performed by — Leann Rimes; Courtesy of CURB Records, Inc.; "I Stand Alone": Written by — Carole Bayer Sager, David Foster, Steve Perry; Produced by — David Foster, Carole Bayer Sager; Performed by Steve Perry — Courtesy of Columbia Records; "The Prayer": Written by — Carole Bayer Sager, David Foster; Produced by — David Foster, Carole Bayer Sager; Co-Produced by — Tony Renis; Recorded and Mixed by — Humberto Gatica; Performed by — Andrea Bocelli; Courtesy of Insieme SRL/SUGAR, Italy; Caterers — Alligator Pear Catering, Bobby Weisman Catering; Special Thanks to — The Braille Institute, The National Federation for the Blind, Raptor Rehabilitation and Release Program, UNICEF; Additional Animation and Technology Services Provided by Artscans and Cambridge Animation Systems, Inc.; Titles by — Pacific Title/Mirage; Filmed with Celco Cameras and Lenses; Paints and Color by Technicolor; Kodak Motion Picture Products

The two-headed dragon Devon and Cornwall accompanies Kayley on her adventures in *Quest for Camelot* (1998).

SYNOPSIS: With *Quest for Camelot*, Warner Bros. finally weighed in with its answer to Disney's 1963 cartoon movie *The Sword in the Stone*. That the "other" cartoon giant did so is no surprise. That it took 35 years perhaps is.

Comparisons between the two feature-length animated films are inevitable though they utilize the legends of King Arthur in entirely different ways. The main similarity they share is that both movies are taken from modern books based on Arthurian themes: *Quest for Camelot* from *The King's Damsel* by Vera Chapman and *The Sword in the Stone* from *The Once and Future King* by T. H. White.

Major direct similarities end there. *Quest for Camelot* is the story of a young girl, Kayley, who as a child dreams of becoming a knight like her father, Sir Lionel. This is no problem for her father, but her mother, Lady Juliana, has other plans for the girl. Called to a special meeting of the Knights of the Round Table, Lionel leaves home for Camelot.

Also in attendance at the gathering is the sinister Ruber. He demands more lands from Arthur and becomes enraged when Arthur re-

fuses. Leaping onto the Round Table, the villain attacks Arthur. Sir Lionel is killed defending his king. Arthur himself returns the good knight's body to his home for burial.

Crushed by her father's death and her hopes for knighthood dashed, Kayley grows up under the thumb of a kind but femininely oriented mother. Until, that is, events come crashing in to give Kayley the opportunity to pursue her dream.

Ten years after Sir Lionel's death Ruber has formulated plans for taking over the whole kingdom. He sends a giant griffin to Camelot to steal Excalibur. The beast succeeds in grabbing the sword, wounding Arthur in the process, and escapes. Merlin, however, sends a falcon after the griffin and the bird manages to force the griffin to drop Excalibur. The sword disappears into the Forbidden Forest.

The news that Excalibur has been stolen spreads through the land quickly. Excited, Kayley wants to go looking for it but her mother won't hear of it.

In the meantime Ruber has been executing the rest of his plot. Showing up at their farm, he imprisons Lady Juliana, threatening

Kayley and Garrett share a quiet moment in *Quest for Camelot* (1998).

to harm Kayley if she doesn't cooperate. His plan is to use Juliana as she leads her carts and wagons into Camelot. His men will be hiding inside them and once within the walls of Arthur's castle, they'll attack and Ruber will become the ruler of the land.

Ruber has acquired a magical fluid which makes instantaneous combinations of animate and inanimate objects. Throwing a chicken, an ax and a drop of the liquid into a hole, Blade Beak emerges. Ruber creates a small army of similar creatures in this manner — menlike things with maces and morningstars for arms and so forth.

While this is going on Juliana tells Kayley to warn King Arthur. The girl escapes, but Ruber's minions are hot on her trail. She is finally forced to enter the Forbidden Forest, where she falls into a pool of water. As two of Ruber's creatures are about to seize her, Garrett shows up to defend her.

Garrett, it turns out, is blind and the falcon Ayden acts as his eyes. Injured in an accident at Camelot, he describes to Kayley how her father had helped him when he was young. The news of the theft of Excalibur spurs Garrett to try to find it. Kayley follows him deeper into the forest.

The two have a number of run-ins including some with dragons. In dragon country they find a new friend, the deformed, two-headed dragon, Devon and Cornwall. Teaming up, the three (or four) travel on, chased all the while by Ruber. Finally discovering the ogre who has been using Excalibur for a toothpick, they manage to retrieve the sword and escape the Forbidden Forest.

Garrett refuses to accompany Kayley to Camelot, feeling he doesn't belong there. In spite of the fact that they're falling in love, the two go their separate ways. Ruber captures Kayley and using his transformation fluid, makes Excalibur an integral part of his right arm. He and his wagon train continue to Camelot, but Devon and Cornwall race back to the Forbidden Forest to get Garrett.

With Lady Juliana in the driver's seat, this otherworldly Trojan Horse is allowed in the gates of Camelot. Ruber and his minions erupt from their hiding places and in a pitched battle it seems Camelot will be lost.

Just as Ruber is about to deliver the death stroke to the weakened Arthur, Kayley swings into action, smashing the villain through a giant window. They tumble together into the circle of Stonehenge as Garrett shows up to help. Quickly overwhelmed, however, Garrett and Kayley cling to each other as Ruber sets himself for another killing blow. He lunges with the sword, they step aside just in time and Ruber inadvertently plunges Excalibur into the very stone from which Arthur had pulled it so many years ago. The magic of the sword and Stonehenge activates, destroying Ruber and setting everything in Camelot back to rights.

In a huge ceremony Kayley and Garrett are made members of the Round Table. They ride off together on a horse from which is hung a sign reading, "Just Knighted."

Quest for Camelot is a bonanza of proper (read "politically correct," to use an over-worked buzz-phrase) characters for the social and political atmosphere of the 1980s and 1990s. As is common currently, the main character is a girl. However, *Quest for Camelot* goes far beyond feminism in bringing formerly ignored groups to the fore.

The secondary protagonist, Garrett, is "vision impaired," blinded by an accident in a stable. Blade Beak and the other slaves of Ruber are monstrous freaks created by Ruber's evil magic/science, though at least Blade Beak is able to overcome the strangeness of his form and join the forces of Good. There are nods to genetic and birth defects and even to homo-sexuality in the dual personality of Devon and Cornwall, who interestingly enough choose to remain together in one body when the healing powers of the sword separate them momentarily.

The film is filled with songs of self-fulfillment, independence and love. It also includes a number of quick and humorous references to other movies (like *Taxi Driver*) and modern situations (like airline attendants' instructions to passengers). All in all, a very modern interpretation.

Quest for Courage see under *King Arthur and the Knights of Justice*

The Quest for Olwen (1990)

22 minutes; Color; Animated Still Illustrations; Copyright 1990, S4C; Copyright 1993, Films for the Humanities and Sciences; Films for the Humanities and Sciences #4062

CREDITS: Animators—Valeri Ugarov, Colin White, Yuri Kulakov, Neville Astley, Andreco Smirnov, Alexander Markelov; Designers—Lev Evzovitch, Margaret Jones; Assistant Designers—Sarah Wilkie, Eugenia Tsaneva, Julia Baranova, Natalia Toorygina; Script Writer—Gwyn Thomas; Script Editors—John Idris Owen, Wynne Jones, Elena Nikitkina; Cameraman—Michael Sutton; Sound Engineers—Eugeni Neckrasov, Vladimir Kutuzov; Dubbing Mixer—Lawrence Ahearne; Assembly Editor—Margarita Miheyeva; Assistant Editor—Richard Urbanski; Artistic Director—Igor Oleinikov; Manager—Nina Suchkova; Composer—Martinov Vladimir; Musician—Igor Nazaruk; Voices—J. O. Roberts, Robert David, Dafydd Emyr, Nia Chiswell; Voice Director—Pat Griffiths; Production Assistant—Bill Roberts; Film Editor—Richard Bradley; Production Manager—Michael Sutton; Assistant Director—Irina Litovskaya; Executive Producers—Christopher Grace, John Watkin, Eliza Babachina; Film Director—Valeri Ugarov; Producer—Louise Jones; Produced by METTA (Llangollen) and Soyuzmultfilm (Moscow) for S4C and HTV, Cymru/Wales

SYNOPSIS: *The Quest for Olwen* is a beautifully done cartoon (animated illustrations) of one of the tales, "Culhwch and Olwen," from *The Mabinogion*. Though many details of the original story are missing from the film, the simplification in no way hurts one's understanding of the gist of the tale. If anything the highlights presented in the movie make "Culhwch and Olwen" more enjoyable, particularly for younger folks.

The Mabinogion itself is a collection of 11 very old Celtic stories. *Mabinogion* is the title given to the collection by the translator, Lady Charlotte Guest, in the late 1830s. The earliest surviving manuscript recording them is the *White Book of Rhydderch* dated between 1300 and 1325 A.D. The stories themselves, however, are much older, taking on their present form perhaps as early as the eleventh century. "Culhwch and Olwen" may date back a further hundred years and the traditions it and the other tales are based on are certainly even older.

As told in this film, Culhwch's mother gave birth to him in the woods, surrounded by wild boars. She died when Culhwch was very young and some years later his father remarried. Culhwch's stepmother put a curse of love on the boy; he would love no other than the beautiful Olwen, daughter of the giant Ysbaddaden.

Ysbaddaden himself has been cursed to die on the day of his daughter's wedding, so he has no desire for her to find a lover. He kills anyone who attempts to woo the poor girl.

Smitten as he is, none of this can stop Culhwch. He goes to his cousin King Arthur for assistance. Arthur assigns Cei and Bedwyr to go with Culhwch and the three set out to find Olwen. They travel for years until finally they come upon a "valley of timeless age." There they meet a giant herdsman who informs them that Olwen comes every day to a nearby brook to wash her hair and to gather flowers.

Olwen shows up as predicted and Culhwch declares his love. She warns him that her father will set many impossible tasks before consenting to her marriage. Culhwch promises to accomplish them.

Culhwch confronts Ysbaddaden, a horrible-looking giant indeed. His huge contorted face and fiery eyes are nearly hidden by long unruly hair.

Though enraged by the young man's temerity, Ysbaddaden tells Culhwch that the boy can only marry his daughter if he accomplishes a series of labors. Culhwch must regather nine vessels of flax seeds which never grew, then replant them so that a veil can be made from the flax for Olwen's wedding dress. Next he must retrieve Ysbaddaden's comb and scissors from a wild boar so that Ysbaddaden can trim his hair for the wedding day. The problem with that is that only the great hunter Mabon is capable of running the boar down and Mabon disappeared many years ago. Finally, so that Ysbaddaden can properly soften his beard in order to shave, Culhwch must bring him the warm blood of the Black Witch who lives in the Valley of Death.

Culhwch and his companions return to Arthur's court and describe Ysbaddaden's demands. Arthur sends a number of his knights to help Culhwch.

First Gwythyr comes across a huge anthill that is on fire. He puts the fire out with his sword. The ants are so grateful that they offer to help him in any way they can and thus they are set about the task of gathering the flax seeds. That done, the seeds are planted, the flax grows and a beautiful veil is made for Olwen. Ysbaddaden is not pleased.

Next Culhwch and three of Arthur's men search for the oldest of animals, who might know the whereabouts of Mabon. A giant eagle on a mountaintop directs them to the salmon of Llyn Llyw. The salmon takes them to the castle Caer Loyw where he'd heard much lamentation coming from within the walls. Sure enough, it's Mabon trapped inside. They free the hunter and go after the wild boar that has Ysbaddaden's comb and scissors.

Finding the huge beast, Arthur's men, Mabon and Culhwch battle with it. It kills many of them and then manages to back Culhwch up to a cliff edge. It charges, but Culhwch steps aside in the nick of time. The boar falls into the ocean and begins to swim away, but one of Arthur's men rides off the cliff and into the ocean after it, retrieving the comb and scissors.

Finally, they go to the Valley of Death and defeat the Black Witch, gathering a cup of her blood. Returning to Ysbaddaden, they set up ladders to reach his head and trim his hair and shave him. The curse on the giant holds true, for after the tonsorial ministrations are complete, he takes one look at himself in a mirror and dies. Her evil father gone, Olwen is free to marry Culhwch.

The text of "Culhwch and Olwen" includes a much longer list of tasks which Culhwch must perform. However the written tale skips over any lengthy enumeration of how the several dozen labors are achieved and this film actually portrays the most salient of them.

Quest for the Holy Lance

A&E Documentary; No further information available.

The Questing Beast see Lost in Space: "The Questing Beast"

Raggio di Sole (1912)

British release title: Sunbeam; Not viewed; 1 reel, 863 feet; Black and White; Silent; Copyright 1912, Ambrosio, Italy; Library of Congress Call #FEA6315 (reference print); #FPA3899 (duplicate negative); Library of Congress Catalogue #91785058/MP

CREDITS: Writer—Arrigo Frusta; Camera—Giovanni Vitrotti

Il Re Artu e i Cavalieri della Tavola Rotunda (1910)

Not viewed; Copyright 1910, Milano Films, Italy; Great Britain Distributor: New Agency Films

CREDITS: Director—Giuseppe de Liguoro

Read On, Cover to Cover: "The Knights of the Kitchen Table" (1994)

15 minutes; Color; Book promotion; Copyright 1994, The Greater Washington Educational Telecommunications Association, Inc.; PBS Video #ROCC-1077

CREDITS: Hosted by—John Robbins; Producer—John Robbins; Director—Joseph Camp; Illustrators—Dick Cronin, John Robbins; Narrator—Paul Lally; Original Music—Todd Hahn; Production Manager—Monika Konrad; Editor—Fran Ely; Camera—Donald Brawner, Charles Ide; Audio—Lynn Allison, Eileen Griffin; WETA Executive in Charge—Cheryl Head; Advisors—Marie Aldridge, Supervising Director, Library Services, Wilkinson Annex, Washington, D.C., Rod Baer, Teacher, Randolph Elementary, Arlington, Virginia, Kathie Bentson, Reading Specialist, Fairfax County, Virginia, Ayo Dayo, Children's Service Supervisor, Chinn Park Library, Prince William County, Virginia, Susan Helper, Children's Literature Specialist, Alexandria, Virginia, Elizabeth G.

Hoke, Children's Literature Consultant, Montgomery County, Maryland, Sybille Jagusch, Chief, Children's Literature Center, Library of Congress, Washington, D.C., Maria Salvadore, Coordinator of Children's Services, Martin Luther King Library, Washington, D.C.; Permission to read from *The Not So Jolly Roger* and *The Knights of the Kitchen Table* by Jon Scieszka Courtesy Viking Penguin, a Division of Penguin Books USA, Inc.; Dedicated to the memory of Mary Jane Phillips

SYNOPSIS: This video is intended as a spur for youngsters to read, but it seems to be nothing so much as a promotion for Jon Scieszka's *Time Warp Trio* kids' book series.

The books themselves are about three boys, Sam, Joe and Fred, who evidently are able to travel through time at will. On this tape, the first episode is from *The Not So Jolly Roger*. As an excerpt from the book is read, John Robbins sketches and colors an illustration to the story about Black Beard the pirate.

The second portion of the tape presents illustrations from the book *The Knights of the Kitchen Table* as a small portion of that story is read. In it, the three boys have gone to King Arthur's time and pretend to be magicians. A 20-foot-tall giant with horrific body smells is assaulting Camelot.

As an incentive to read the stories, both portions of the tape only give snippets of the tales, leaving off at critical junctures in the action.

Return to Camelot: King Arthur and the Knights of Justice (1997)

70 minutes; Color; Cartoon; Copyright 1997, UAV Corporation; UAV Entertainment #1339

SYNOPSIS: *Return to Camelot* is a tape reissuing three episodes from the 1992 television cartoon series *King Arthur and the Knights of Justice*. Included on the tape are "Opening Kickoff," "Even Knights Have to Eat" and "The Way Back" (for cast, credits and synopses of the series and the first two episodes, see entry for *King Arthur and the Knights of Justice*). The episode "The Way Back" was not included in the original 1995 video issued by Family Time Video.

Another tape, *King Arthur's Camelot* (see that entry) includes three more episodes, one of which, "Warlord Knight," is also a new release from the TV series.

The episode "The Way Back" on *Return to Camelot* focuses on one of the Knights of Justice, Tony, and a vision he has. Seeing his mother in a hospital bed, he goes to Merlin and learns that Merlin has seen the same vision. They find a way for Tony to return to the present to visit his mom for one hour. The sound of his voice puts her back on the road to recovery and despite attempted interference from Viper and the warlords, all ends well.

Return of the Jedi see Star Wars: Return of the Jedi

Revenge of the Dark Stone see under Princess Gwenevere and the Jewel Riders

The Revolution on Broadway see Broadway! A Musical History

Richard Wagner (1997)

35 minutes; Color; Documentary; Copyright 1997, Academy Media; KULTUR Video # 1838

CREDITS: The Producers gratefully acknowledge the help of— The Wagner Museum, Bayreuth, The Wagner Museum, Tribschen Luzern; Music Performed by — The Elysium Ensemble; Violin — Robert Gibbs; Violin — Mark Denman; Viola — John Rogers; Cello — Ferenc Szucs; Production Assistant — Nissa Buacharoon; Written, Produced and Directed by — Malcolm Hossick

SYNOPSIS: A biography of the checkered life and career of Richard Wagner, which starts with his birth, childhood influences, and earliest musical involvements and productions and carries through his extramarital affairs, political activities, mature works and financial struggles. This tape gives a good thumbnail sketch of one of the world's most famous com-

posers who, among other things, wrote three Arthurian operas: *Lohengrin, Parsifal* and *Tristan und Isolde.*

The last five minutes of the tape is an enumeration of all of Wagner's works, including songs, chamber music, piano music and the operas.

The Ruby of Radnor see under The Adventures of Sir Lancelot

Sabrina the Teenage Witch: "Oh What a Tangled Spell She Weaves" (1996)

60 minutes; Not viewed; Color; Television series episode; Copyright 1996, 1997; Distributed by Hallmark

CAST: Bobcat Goldthwait (Merlin); Bob Vila (Himself); Melissa Joan Hart (Sabrina); Caroline Rhea (Aunt Hilda); Beth Broderick (Aunt Zelda); Nate Richert (Harvey Kinkle); Jenna Leigh Green (Libby Chessler); Lindsay Sloane (Valerie); Nick Bakay (Voice of Salem); Alimi Ballard (The Quizmaster); Martin Mull (Willard Kraft)
CREDITS: Director — Tibor Takacs

SYNOPSIS: Sabrina accidentally sends her aunts and their cat to Merlin's castle, where they are held captive.

Santa Claus (1959)

97 minutes; Color; Live Action; Spanish with no subtitles; Copyright 1959, Cinematiografica Calderón, S.A.; Copyright 1987, Condor Video; Distributed by VID-Dimension, Inc.

CAST: José Luis Aguirre (Trosky) (El Diablo); Armando Arriola (Arriolita) (El Mago Merlin); "La Niña Poere" presentation of Lupita Adenás — Nora Veryán, Manolo Calvo, Jesús Brook, Enriqueta Lavat, GMO Bravo Sosa Rosa, Maria Aguilar, Leopoldo Ortin, Jr., J. Carlos Mendez, Rub Ramirez-G, Angel D'Stefani, Grachela Lara
CREDITS: Augumentory Adaptatión . de — Adolfo Torres Portillo, René Cardona; Canciones: "Noche de Paz"— Dominio Púelico; "Jingle Bells"— Dominio Púelico; "Fasinacion"— Marchetti; "El Zopilote Mojado"— Miguel Macias F.; Canciones Populares de Nicos de Todo el Mundo Coros del Maestros Armando Torres; Coreografia de — Ricardo Luna; "Ballet de las Muecas" de — Antonio

Diaz Conde; "Danza del Infierno" de — Antonio Diaz Conde; Partitura y Direccion Musical de — Antonio Diaz Conde; Orquesta de la Seccion de Filarmanios del S.T.P.C. de la R.M.; Director de Fotografia — Raúl Martinez Solares; Alumbrador — Gabriel Castro; Operator — Cirilo Rodriguez; Esenografia de — Marcos Chillet; Gerente de Produccion — Rene Cardona, Jr.; Jife de Produccion — Guillermo Alcayee; Sef Jife de Produccion — Federico Serrano; Assistente del Director — Felipe Palamino; Edicita — Jorge Bustos; Agudante de Edicita — José Li-Ho; Utileria Especial — Gordillo Y Martinez; Vestuario — B. Mendora López; Magrillage — Concepcion Zamora; Peinados y Pestijos — Fernando Zamarripa; Estudios y Laboratorios — Churubusco-Azteca; Grebacion de Dialogues — Nicolas de la Rosa; Edicita de Souido — Reynaldo Portillo; Unidad Tecnica — "Mexico"; Mexiscope; Color par — Eastmancolor; Una Pelicula de — Guillermo Calderón Stell; Dirigida par — René Cardona

SYNOPSIS: In one of the strangest pairings of legendary characters, this Mexican film teams Merlin the magician with Santa Claus. Unfortunately this author does not speak Spanish and the film has no subtitles. However, as far as can be garnered, no mention seemed to be made of Arthur, Camelot or any of the other more typical associations for Merlin.

The film opens at Santa's magical kingdom which floats in space somewhere in the local solar system. There are lots of children, laughter, singing and dancing throughout the whole movie. Santa watches over things on Earth with a peculiar living computer, telescope and radio system that enables him to look right into individuals' lives from space.

In the meantime the Devil hatches a plot to interfere with some of the children on Earth. He sends one of his demons to try to influence several kids into doing wrong things. Santa sees some of the nefarious goings-on and decides he'd better do something about it. Christmas Eve is approaching, so what better time?

As part of his preparations for departure, Santa goes to his friend Merlin (who lives somewhere in Santa's astral castle) for some last-minute accoutrements. The comically doddery Merlin is hard of hearing, forgetful and walks in an exhaustingly slow hip-hop fashion.

Merlin gives Santa some kind of powder and a special flower. Whenever Santa smells the flower he becomes invisible. Next Santa visits the blacksmith, Ivan, who gives him a magic key which opens any door it touches. Santa is too fat this year to fit down any chimneys.

One of the historically interesting points of the film is that during Santa's final preparations around his sleigh, there is some talk about the planets and Sputnik, the first satellite that was launched from Earth by the Russians.

The story focuses on two children. One is a little poor girl who wishes with all her heart for a doll to play with. The other is a little rich boy who dreams of nothing more than having his parents stay home with him for Christmas for a change instead of going out all the time.

In spite of the harassments of the Devil's demon and with a little further help from Merlin, Santa is able to grant the wishes of these two kids and to deliver all the other toys in time for Christmas.

Sarkany es Papucs (Dragon and Slipper) (1989)

Not viewed; Color; Cartoon; Copyright 1989, Hungary

CREDITS: Director — Tibor Hernádi; Writer — Attila Dargay, József Nepp; Camera — Árpád Losonezy, László Rodocsay; Music — Pastoral Együttes, István Mikó

SYNOPSIS: This Hungarian film blends the Tristan and Isolde legend with Arthur himself. A mix-up with a love potion causes the problematic love triangle between Lancelot, Guinevere and Arthur.

Scooby-Doo: "Excalibur Scooby" (1984)

Cartoon; Copyright 1984, Hanna-Barbera; No further information available.

Scooby-Doo: "Scared a Lot in Camelot" (1976)

Cartoon; Copyright 1976, Hanna-Barbera; No further information available.

Scooby-Doo: "The Curse of Camelot"

Cartoon; Hanna-Barbera; No further information available.

Scouts! (1984)

Subtitle: The Rise of the World Scouting Movement; 60 minutes; Color, Black and White; Documentary; Copyright 1984, Clear Horizons Films; Released Worldwide by CineVisa International Movie Distributors, Toronto, Canada

CREDITS: Narrated by — John Neville; Written by — David Rain, Michael O. Murphey; Editing — Alan Gibb; Music — Tom Borshuk; Camera — Ted Lindsay, Colin Allison, Trevor Haws; Sound — George Tarrant, Kevin Ward; Associate Producers — James Linton, Calvin Moore; Research — David Rain, Kevin Bondy, Jackie Forty, David Horton, Kevin Greene; Documentary Film and Video, Washington, D.C.; Film Research and Production Services, London, England; Archival Services: The British Film Institute, The National Film Archive, Washington, D.C., The Library of Congress Film Archive, Washington, D.C., The National Film, Television and Sound Archive, Ottawa, Canada, Emi-Pathe, British Movie Tone, Visnews, Transit Film GMBK, The Bettman Archive, The BBC Hulton Picture Library, The Mausell Collection, The National Army Museum, The Dallas Historical Society, Mr. George Pearce, Mrs. Barber Seton, Mr. William Hillcourt; Associate Director — Daniel Murphy; Production Assistant — Tim Harlford; Best Boy — Wilf Hanevich; Art Director — Barry Lavender; Main Title Design — Let 'Er Ring! Graphics; Title Animation — Nelvana Animated Commercials; Photo Reprints — Henry Yee Studio Laboratories; Rostrum Photography — Andrew Ruhl, MetaMedia; Post Production — Wendy Lotem, Film Images, Inc.; Re-recording — Mike Hodgenboom; Opticals — Film Effects; Sound Editing — Kevin Ward, Fiona Paterson, Trudy Alexander; Executive Producers — Michael D. Murphy, James Linton, Calvin Moore; Produced with the Cooperation of— Mr. & Mrs. Gervas Clay, The Scout Association, The Boy Scouts of America, The Boy Scouts of Canada, The World Organization of the Scouting Movement and the Lord and Lady Baden-Powell; Produced and Directed by — Michael Dana Murphy

SYNOPSIS: *Scouts!* is primarily about the history of the Boy Scouts movement but a couple of silent film clips are included in the documentary. One of them is from the 1917 Edison film company production called *Knights of the Square Table* (see that entry).

That clip shows a fight between a Boy Scout troop and a gang called the Wharfrats Motherless Knights Erring of the Square Table. The leader of the gang had been inspired by the story of the Holy Grail in naming his outfit. Eventually the delinquents are turned onto the right path.

Victorian England saw a huge resurgence of interest in the Arthurian tales. One of the many results of this phenomenon was the founding of a number of boys' (and eventually girls') organizations that were based on the principles of chivalry and reverence promulgated in works by the likes of Tennyson and Pyle.

The most lasting of these was the Boy Scouts founded by Lord Baden-Powell. To this day it is traditional that Cub Scouts learn and do projects about King Arthur and the Knights of the Round Table.

Scouts! is a very well put together documentary with excellent biographical material on Baden-Powell.

The Search for Guinevere see under King Arthur and the Knights of Justice

Seaview Knights (1994)

100 minutes; Color; Comedy/Live Action; Copyright 1994, Seaview Knights PLC; Guerilla Films

CAST: James Bolan (Merlin); Clive Darby (Arthur); Anita Dobson (Concierge); Sarah Alexander (Jackie); Hildegard Neil (Psychiatrist); William Brook (Walter); Steve Osborne (Danny); Bob Flag (Fraser); Leon Herbert (Stan); Duggie Chapman (Chubby); Andrew Durant (The Sheikh); Gary Bryan (Mower); Mark Knight (Senior Policeman); Paul Molloy (PC); Richard Van Stone (DC and H Bogart); Jeremy O'Toole (DC and H Cagney); Joe Ansted (Musical Arab); Viv Fongenlo (2nd Arab);

Micky Silver (3rd Arab); Coleen Sanders (Arab Dancer); Abigail Canton (Ms. Whiplashes); Megan Jones (Old Lady); James Alexander Hamilton (Traffic Warden); Simon Desborough (Milky Bar Kid); Phil Barthrop (TV and Radio Voice Artist); Adrian Lacey (TV and Radio Voice Artist); Andy Peebles (TV and Radio Voice Artist); Vicky Osborne (Voice Artist)

CREDITS: Director of Photography — Ivan Bartos; Steadicam Operator — Andreii Austin; Focus Pullers — Peter Wignall, James Moss, Lorraine Luke; Camera Assistant — Sam Osborne; Clapper Loaders — Dominic Driscoll, Sue Quammie, Dork Russel, Ray Coates; Key Grip — Terry Williams; Grip — Colin Parker; Production Designer — Mike Grant; Art Directors — James Ridpath, Moving Jim; Costume Design — Louise Johnson; Makeup Design — Joe Allen; Set Dresser — Cathy Roddick; Prop Buyer — Rebecca Pilkington; Wardrobe Assistant — Babs Chin; Hair Stylist — Mark English; Scenic Artist — Humphrey Banghan; Production Manager — Simon Willis; Unit Manager — Ken Holt; 1st Assistant Directors — Allison Begg, Richard Bird, Will Goss; Assistant Producer — Leigh Poole; 2nd Assistant Director — Mick Pantaleo; 3rd Assistant Directors — Jeremy Engler, Tim Keates; Script Supervisor — Linda Gibson; Production Accountant — John Roddison; Production Coordinator — Bini Adams; Production Buyer — Wendy Edgar-Jones; Locations — Jon Hardy, Steve Turney; Gaffer — Gary Cross; Electrician — Andy Leo; Best Boy — Graham Newton; Publicist — Ceris Price; Stills Photographer — Andy Shannon; Video Camera Operator — Matthew Gamage; Producer's Assistant — Dominic Waters; Driver — Mark Meopham; Runners — Vee Mortimer, Will Pagett, Jason Edwards, Andi Lees, Natalie Wilson; Editor — Timothy Gio; Assistant Editor — Daniel Blundell; Sound Director — Andy Pane; Music Composed by — Oliver Davis; Music Produced by — Guy Davis; Recordists — Ian Leiper, Mike Johnstone; Boom Operators — Tony Milton, Peter Hales; Dubbing Mixer — Robin O'Donoghue; Assistant Dubbing Mixer — Dominic Lester; Assistant Sound Editing — Nick Lowe; Music Recording Advisor — Dave Hill; Lightworks Consultant — Sadeeq Mohammed; Post Production Liaison — Nick Ridley; Digital Numbers Synchronization — Cathy Houlihan; Additional Music — G. C. Edwards, C. Durney, N. Mathews; Performed by — The Prophet; Director — Richard Kurti; Original Script — Richard Kurti, Bev Doyle; Associate Producer — Julia Bracewell; Executive Producers — Christopher Parkinson, Clifford Davis; Production Associate — Bev Doyle; Producer — Lois A. Wolffe; Catering — Kennedy's, Eat to the Beat; Legal Services — Gouldens, Solicitors; Insured by — Sampson and Allan; Negative Cutter — Mike Fraser; Digital Editing Systems — Lightworks; TitlesMichael Olley; Moviecam Superamerica Camera and Canon Lenses Supplied by Sammy's; Colour by Metrocolor; Post Production Completed at Twickenham Film Studios, London; Digital Editing Facilities on Twickenham Sound Station; A huge big Seaview Knights thanks to: Pradipkumar Amin, Dean Armstrong, Tim Ashworth, Tom Auber, Jo Barnes, William Boden, John Calms, Nigel Capper, Grace Carley, John S. Carline, Mike Chadwick, Victor Christie, Simon Clayton, Richard J. Coles, Elisabeth Cooper, Mike J. Cockshall, Andrew Crank, Mark Dalgliesh, Quentin Des Clayes, David Dudeney, Jo Dyos, Ronald Eastwood, Yvonne Fairbrother, L. E. Fenton, J. C. Ford, Richard French, The Friend Family, Chris Gadd, Sue Garden, Bill Gillespie, Kate Greenwood, Elliot Grove, Brian G. Haines, Michael Hall, John Handscombe, Valerie Hawthorn, D. J. Haywood, Jane and Julian Hill, Susan D. Hodgkinson, Cathleen James, Maureen Johnson, Helen Jones, David Kut, Lloyd Lambell, William Larkins, Ken Livingston, M.P. , Steve Locking, Ken Long, Paul Lucas, Gordon McSweeney, Richard J. T. Marker, Prue Menmuir, Stewart Mitchel, Jack Murdoch, Bill Nicol, Graham Nicholas, Dan and Ron Mussey, Jain and Eddie Ockwell, Sophie Parkinson, David Pearson, Ingrid Penny, Diane and Steve Poole, Chris Potts, Arif Qureshi, John Rendal, William E. Rimmington, Ben and Sam Roberts, Liz Saxton, Kathy Searles, Bruce Sharman, Edward Shaxted, Peter Sinyard, Andrea Shaxted, N. A. Slater, Brian Strugnell, Stuart Swift, E. J. Thatcher, Irene Turpin, Craig Walsh, Brian Ward, William J. Wood, Uri and Yael Zarfaty; And further thanks to — Accord, AFM, Allied Breweries, Ltd. , Andrews Sykes, Ltd., Arena, Barr Soft Drinks, Blackpool Council, Blackpool Evening Gazette, J. W. Bollom, Bosch Power Tools, British Broadcasting Company, British Home Stores, Chapter One, Clinique, Commercial Kitchen Services, Daily Mirror, Department of National Heritage, DC Domestics, Dr. Hartens, Dunlop Stazenger, Eassons Ice Cream, Electroalgas, Express Gifts, Fleetwood Glass, Grip House, Ghost, Gretsch (U.K.) Ltd. , HSS Hire, Joe Bloggs, Lambeth Palace, The Langham Hilton Hotel, Lee Lighting, Lever Brothers, Ltd., Lynbrook Reprographic, Marytebone Printers, John McCs, Metropolitan Police, Murphy Richards, Motorola, W. H. Newson, Normid Superstor, Ogee, Penfolds, Philips Telecom, Phoenix Mike, Radio Lancashire,

Red or Dead, The Savoy Hotel, Blackpool, She an' He, STV Hire, The Telephone and Alarm Co., Transformer, Thwaites Brewery, Victorino's, Whites Hotel, William Harris Agency; This film is dedicated to Mike's Citroen, RIP

SYNOPSIS: Set in Blackpool, England, in the present, this light British comedy is a great example of the high quality a film can achieve in spite of a low budget. What it lacks in special effects and glitzy stars it more than makes up for with good storytelling, humor, intriguing filming and a terrific soundtrack.

Seaview Knights opens in the seedy hotel room of a lone bank robber just after he has successfully made away with £1 million. Apparently lacking a sophisticated getaway plan he is simply lying low. To pass the time he solves Rubik's cube puzzles, tossing them into a pile on the floor as he completes each one.

Above the head of the bed on which he is sprawled hangs a copy of the *Mona Lisa* in a huge rococo frame. This rundown hotel, its "blind" concierge and her fixation on *Mona Lisa* decor all become characters in and of themselves. The amorous efforts of a couple in the next room are not only noisy but shake the picture on the wall as well. Disgusted, the robber turns out his light to try to get some sleep. In the dark the picture falls, hitting him on the head.

The robber wakes up thinking that he is King Arthur reborn in a strange and disjointed England. He spends a day discovering the wonders of the hotel room, then ventures out to experience the lights and madness of the modern world. Watching television, he absorbs the images of an England apparently gone insane and determines that his mission is to save the country from itself.

The first person "Arthur" enlists in his cause is a cab driver/petty con artist whom Arthur is convinced is Merlin. The cabby quickly figures out who this fellow really is and determines to play along with the madman in order to get to the money.

In a wonderful series of comic coincidences Arthur puts together his fellowship of the Round Table once again. A young lady who works as a parks department lake patrol officer becomes his Lady of the Lake. She turns out to be the cabby's daughter, Jackie, and she and Arthur actually wind up falling in love. A group of ne'er-do-wells recruited by the cabby become the Knights of the Round Table and a British cricket hero becomes Lancelot.

The cabby's cadre of miscreants are of course only in it for the money too, and when the money comes up missing and Lancelot fails to show up for a party thrown in his honor, the Round Table fraternity disbands. Ultimately Arthur decides it is the Gray Knight himself who must be challenged in order to put the country to rights. This personage happens to be the prime minister of England and Arthur heads for London.

On his way the guileless Arthur is waylaid by a group of Middle Eastern terrorists who intend to bomb Parliament. They give Arthur a car with their bomb planted in it and send him on his way. In the meantime Jackie has abandoned the wild goose chase hunt for the money and talks her father into helping her try to save Arthur from getting into further trouble.

Though rescued from arrest in the nick of time Arthur is once again struck in the head, this time by shrapnel from the exploding car. He wakes up as Hamlet. The film ends with a scene of the concierge, her ruse of blindness abandoned, floating happily in the warm waters of Tahiti.

Seeing and Doing: The Legends of King Arthur
Educational, THA; No further information available.

7 Faces of Dr. Lao (1963)
101 minutes; Color; Live Action; Copyright 1963, Metro-Goldwyn-Mayer; Galaxy Productions, Inc., and Scarus, Inc.; A George Pal Production; MGM/UA Home Video #M600667

CAST: Tony Randall (Dr. Lao, The Abominable Snowman, Merlin the Magician, Apollonius of Tyana, Pan, The Giant Serpent, and Medusa); Barbara Eden (Angela Benedict); Arthur O'Connell (Clint Stark); John Ericson (Ed Cunningham); Noah Beery, Jr. (Tim Mitchell); Minerva Urecal (Kat Lindquist); Frank Kreig (Peter Ramsey); Lee Patrick (Mrs. Howard Cassin); John Qualen (Luther Lindquist); Peggy Rea (Mrs. Peter Ramsey); Codie Little Sky; Royal Dano (Cary); John Doucette (Lucas); Frank Cady (Mayor James Sargent); Argentina Brunetti (Sarah Benedict); Dal McKennon (Thin Cowboy); Chubby Johnson (Fat Cowboy); Douglas Fowley (Toothless Cowboy); Kevin Tate (Mike Benedict)

CREDITS: Music by — Leigh Harline; Director of Photography — Robert Bronner, A.S.C.; Art Direction — George W. Davis, Gabriel Scogaamille; Set Decoration — Harry Grace, Hugh East; Assistant Director — Al Shenberg; Advisor of Magic — George L. Boston; Special Makeup Created by — William Tuttle; Special Visual Effects — Paul B. Byrd, Wah Chang, Jim Danforth, Ralph Rodine, Robert R. Hoag, A.S.C.; Film Editor — George Tomassini; Assistant to the Producer — Gar Griffith; Recording Supervisor — Franklin Milton; Hair Styles by — Sydney Guilarell; Screenplay by — Charles Beaumont; Based on the Novel *The Circus of Dr. Lao* by Charles G. Finney; Directed by — George Pal

SYNOPSIS: A strange tour de force performance by Tony Randall who plays Dr. Lao and six other characters in the film. The Chinese Lao arrives in the western town of Abalone where things aren't going well for the townspeople. Clint Stark is buying up everyone's property and the local newspaper editor is the only one who seems to be fighting him. Lao becomes involved with a number of the folks, helping them out with his various alter egos, who give advice and examples of how to live and act better.

Merlin in this is a sadly doddering old magician who can't remember how to do most of his tricks. He produces hokey paper flowers like a bad Vegas act but a little boy believes in him anyway. With a British accent that sounds a lot like Nigel Bruce (Dr. Watson to Basil Rathbone's Sherlock Holmes), Merlin can't even recall if he was born in 1204 or 412. On the other hand, Dr. Lao tells the little boy that he was born 7,322 years ago.

The film is a stilted morality play reminiscent of the old television show *The Twilight Zone*. The Merlin character is gratuitous, making no reference to any Arthurian matters.

Siege of the Saxons (1963)

85 minutes; Color; Live Action; Copyright 1963, Columbia Pictures Corp./Ameran Film Ltd./Jud Kinberg.; A Charles H. Schneer Production

CAST: Ronald Lewis (Robert); Janette Scott (Katherine); Ronald Howard (Edmund); Mark Dignam (King Arthur); John Laurie (Merlin); Jerome Willis (The Limping Man); Francis DeWolff (The Blacksmith); Richard Clarke (The Saxon); John Gabriel (Earl of Chatham); Charles Lloyd Pack; Peter Mason

CREDITS: Photographed by — Wilkie Cooper; Technicolor — Jack Mills; Music — Laurie Johnson; Production Manager — Ted Wallis; Assistant Director — George Peblard; Continuity — Pauline Wise; Art Director — Constable; Editor — Maurice Roots; Sound Recordists — Ken Rawkins, Ken Cameron; Written by — John Kohn, Jud Kinberg; Produced by — Jud Kinberg; Directed by — Nathan Juran; Made at Bray Studios, England

SYNOPSIS: Edmund of Cornwall, the champion of England, defeats the Saxon champion in a joust at Camelot in the opening of *Siege of the Saxons*. An elderly King Arthur seems to suffer a mild heart attack as he crowns the winner of the competition. Edmund and Arthur's daughter, Katherine, escort Arthur inside where the king asks for Merlin rather than the doctor.

Merlin, however, left Camelot three years prior to this and no one knows where he is. Not wanting to let the Saxons learn that he is ailing, Arthur decides to fake a hunting trip to Banok, Edmund's father's place. In private he confides to Edmund that he feels sure that with Excalibur and Edmund at her side, Katherine is assured the throne should anything happen to him.

Sad to say Edmund isn't worthy of Arthur's trust, for he's plotting with the Saxon leader to take over Camelot. The Saxon is never named in the film. Neither is his henchman, the strange, black leather–clad limping man, who looks as much like a motorcycle gang member as anything else.

Arthur's entourage makes its way to Banok, but they are stopped by a highwayman. This dashing rogue is also costumed all in leather, but his outfit is entirely brown. He acts very much like Robin Hood but his name is Robert Marshal.

The reasons for these particular names, Edmund of Cornwall and Robert Marshal are vague at best. King Mark is most often associated with Arthurian Cornwall. The only "Marshal" who comes to mind when thinking of chivalry is William Marshal, a real knight of the twelfth century (see entry for *Knights and Armor*).

In any case this happy bowman's winning ways attract Arthur's attention and they become friendly. Marshal gets himself into a bit of trouble though when he accuses Edmund of cruelty to his subjects. Marshal is sent ahead to make sure all is ready at Banok.

Marshal finds the castle at Banok deserted, except for the limping man, who renders his opponent unconscious. The Saxon sympathizer takes Marshal's bow and as Arthur approaches, he shoots the king in the chest. Arthur, tough old goat that he is, survives this with barely a wince. Marshal of course is blamed and he's forced to escape. A true patriot though, he hangs around and overhears Edmund and the limping man plotting. Making his way back into the castle he warns Arthur to take Katherine and get out, but he's too late. Viking helmeted warriors attack.

This is the first of several sections of the film which will look very familiar to anyone who's also seen *The Black Knight*. The Viking outfits, particularly the pie plate–sized shields, are identical to those used in the 1954 Alan Ladd film.

In the middle of the carnage Arthur yells to Marshal to take Katherine to Merlin. Arthur is killed and Excalibur taken. Marshal manages to carry Katherine off against her will — she still thinks he's a traitor — and get her to relative safety.

On their way to finding Merlin the two stumble through a couple of adventures as Katherine is forced to realize that Marshal is one of the good guys. They come across a band of Edmund's men and discover Saxon disguises (the Viking helmets) in the men's kits. At a monastery they finally learn of Merlin's whereabouts. Marshal leaves Katherine with the monks and rides off to get the wizard.

While he's gone the Saxons/Vikings attack the monastery. They execute a group of monks and kidnap Katherine. This is the second scene right out of *The Black Knight*. The same monks line up against the same wall and the same firing squad of archers executes them.

With Arthur dead and Excalibur in his possession Edmund is able to take over all of Britain. He offers Katherine marriage but when she refuses he orders her killed. Marshal saves her from that fate and the two run off to free Merlin from the clutches of the earl of Chatham. A blacksmith gives Marshal a suit of armor (which looks remarkably like that worn by, yes, the Black Knight) and the blacksmith and his friends help Marshal and Katherine retrieve Merlin and capture the earl.

Arriving at Camelot in time to interrupt Edmund's coronation, Katherine makes her claim to the throne. No one believes her until Edmund is unable to pull Excalibur from its scabbard while Katherine succeeds. Katherine rallies the troops, the limping man kills Edmund and the Saxons attack.

The huge battle at Camelot is also a repeat of the scenes in the film *The Black Knight*. In *Siege of the Saxons,* however, the battle goes on for a longer period of time, with many individual clashes repeated several times. The same poor archer falls off the wall at least three times. The same knight spears the same enemy off his horse no fewer than four times.

Despite all that Marshal kills the limping man, the Saxons are defeated and Katherine becomes the queen. Finally, she makes Marshal a baron so that they can marry.

Other comparisons between *Siege of the Saxons* and *The Black Knight* are unavoidable.

The stories are essentially identical. The repeated themes include a common man falling in love with a nobly born daughter, his elevation to proper marriageable rank as reward for service to his country and foreigners infiltrating Camelot in collusion with locals.

Sing Along Quest for Camelot (1998)

26 minutes; Color; Cartoon; Copyright 1998, Warner Home Video; Warner Bros. Family Entertainment #16011

CREDITS: Produced and Directed by — Peter Fitzgerald; Looney Tunes Classic Animation Directed by — Friz Freleng, Chuck Jones, Robert McKimson; *Quest for Camelot* Original Animation Directed by — Frederik Du Chau; Traditional Music Arranged by — Gordon Goodwin; Edited by — Michael Thibault; Voice Characterizations — Mel Blanc; New Voice Characterizations — Joe Alaskey, Bob Bergen, Maurice Lamarche, Billy West; Dialogue Mixer — Christina Tucker; Voice Recordist — Evelyn Nickle; Voices Recorded at — Directors Sound; On-Line Editors — Michael Menczer, William J. Missett, Tim Clark, Terry Climer; Infinit Artist — Kim Gunn; Videotape Technicians — Lydia Breckenridge, Jack Heiken, Brian Homer, Rico Mejta, Ronn Seidenglanz; Electronic Laboratory — Laserpacific Media; Visual Effects — John Van Barneveld, Brian Ross; Film Restoration — Film Technologies Inc.; Graphic Designers — J. Scott Demonaco, Steve Andrews; New Music Supervisor — Dan Savant; Temp Music — Sally Conninger, Keith Johnson; Audio Mixer — Stephen J. Quinn; Dialogue and Effects Editors — Michael Porter, Bobby Mapula; Audio Post Production — Chace Productions; Avid Equipment Provided by — Digital Cut Post Inc.; Assistants to Mr. Fitzgerald — Katie Walker, Tom Bliss; Character Administrator — Cheryl Wilkinson; Music Clearances — Angela Longo; Production Accountant — Elizabeth Yanoska; Payroll Services — Axium Payroll Services; Production Insurance — Disc Insurance Services; The producers would like to acknowledge the contributions of the gifted composers, lyricists, arrangers and performers whose talents brought us the following songs:; "On My Father's Wings": Written by — Carole Bayer Sager, David Foster; Produced by — David Foster, Carole Bayer Sager; Performed by — The Corrs; Courtesy of Lava Records/143 Records/Atlantic Recording Corp.; "This Old Knight": Lyrics by — Roy Leake, Jr.; Performed by — Billy West, The Celestial Singers; Traditional Song Arranged by — Gordon Goodwin; "If I Didn't Have You": Written by —

Carole Bayer Sager, David Foster; Produced by — David Foster, Carole Bayer Sager; Performed by — Eric Idle, Don Rickles, Jess Harnell; "London Bridge Is Falling Down": A traditional English children's song performed by Mel Blanc; "Come Lads and Lasses": A traditional English folk song performed by Mel Blanc; "Look at Me I'm Robin Hood": Lyrics by — Roy Leake, Jr.; Performed by — Joe Alaskey, Bob Bergen; Traditional Song Arranged by — Gordon Goodwin; "I Stand Alone": Written by — Carole Bayer Sager, David Foster; Produced by — David Foster, Carole Bayer Sager; Performed by — Jess Harnell; "No No No You Don't": Lyrics by — Roy Leake, Jr.; Performed by — Billy West, Joe Alaskey; Traditional Song Arranged by — Gordon Goodwin; "Are You Sleeping": Lyrics by — Roy Leake, Jr.; Performed by — Joe Alaskey; Traditional Song Arranged by — Gordon Goodwin; "Jimmy Crack Corn": A traditional American folk song performed by Mel Blanc and The Celestial Singers; "We're Off to See the Wizard": Written by — Harold Arlen, E. Y. Harburg; Performed by — Judy Garland, Ray Bolger, Buddy Ebsen, Bert Lahr, The Munchkins; Special thanks to — Brian Arnet, Jerry Beck, Lorri Bond, Irene Borck, Dan Capone, Robert Carrasco, Honore Clough, Mark De Vitre, Michael Dixon, George Feltenstein, Rick Gehr, Art Geozian, Art Guillen, Kathleen Helppie, Bob Heiber, Marcus Irvin, Spencer Knox, Jackson Knox, Mary Koetting, Michael Lennox, Clare Lukasik, Liz Maffei, Lisa Margolis, Richard P. May, Roger L. Mayer, Brian Moreno, David Nichols, Ned Price, Kay Salz, Liz Tucker, Turner Entertainment Co., Joan Vento; ; A Fitzfilm Production; Made in Hollywood, USA; Looney Tunes and Quest for Camelot characters, names and related indicia, TM and ©1998, Warner Bros.; Animation, stories, backgrounds, layouts and artwork by members of the Motion Picture Screen Cartoonists Local 839; Trailer from the video *The Mighty Kong,* song *The Dolly of Pa Pali Ali Isle,* Warner Bros. Family Entertainment

SYNOPSIS: This tape is essentially an advertising prerelease for the Warner Bros. cartoon movie *Quest for Camelot* as well as several other Warner products. It contains three clips from *Quest for Camelot* as well as most of the classic Bugs Bunny cartoon "Knighty Knight Bugs" (see entry in *Friz Freleng's Looney Looney Looney Bugs Bunny Movie).* The words to all the songs in the film are printed at the bottom of the screen so that children who can read can sing along with the tape.

The video opens with ads for *Quest for Camelot,* the soundtrack album for that film, the Warner Bros. sing-along tapes, the cartoon movie *The Mighty Kong,* the cartoon movie *Scooby-Doo on Zombie Island* and the *Quest for Camelot* Audio Action Adventure compact disc and audio cassette.

In the main portion of the tape three song clips from *Quest for Camelot* are interspersed with segments from a number of old Warner Bros. cartoons. The songs from *Quest for Camelot* are; "On My Father's Wings," "If I Didn't Have You" and "I Stand Alone." The first is Kaylee singing about her future, the second is the two-headed dragon making their complaints about one another and the third is Garrett trying to discourage Kaylee from following him.

The portions of old cartoons used throughout the movie include "Knighty Knight Bugs," one of Bugs Bunny's Arthurian adventures, and Daffy Duck's version of the Robin Hood story. Voice overs have changed some of the details for this tape. For instance, King Arthur's Singing Sword in "Knighty Knight Bugs" becomes here the Sing Along Sword.

Sir Count a Lot and His Round Table

Color; Puppets and Live Action

SYNOPSIS: In this episode of *Sesame Street* the count reads the story of Sir Count a Lot to the puppet gang. In the tale no one knew how many knights were in the kingdom, other than Sir Chaser of Dragons and Sir Arguer of Chickens. Sir Count a Lot counts five knights sitting at the Round Table and there is much happy-ever-aftering.

The gang wishes that Sir Count a Lot would come to Sesame Street, so the Count sneaks off and dresses up in a suit of armor to appear as Sir Count a Lot. He renames the ecstatic Sesame Streeters Sir Telly of Triangles, Sir Baby Bear of Porridge and Zoe of Piano. They all march around the neighborhood in

their armor and decide to have lunch at a restaurant at a round table. Unfortunately there is only a square table, so they become the Knights of the Square Table.

A little girl comes along saying she's found a very sad dragon. The gang go to the rescue, finding that the dragon is really a princess who's been cursed by an evil wizard to remain a dragon until she counts to 40—but she can't count that high. The gang helps her count to 40, she transforms back into a princess and, to the melody tune from the musical *Camelot,* they sing, "For one brief shining playtime we counted with Sir Count a Lot."

Sir Gyro de Gearloose see Duck to the Future: "Sir Gyro de Gearloose"

Sir Lancelot see Treasure Island, Kids Klassics: "Sir Lancelot"

The Smurfs: "Smurfs of the Round Table" (1990)

Cartoon; Copyright 1990, Hanna-Barbera; No further information available.

Square Heads of the Round Table (1958)

Title on Tape: *The Three Stooges: I'm a Monkey's Uncle*; 55 minutes; Black and White; Live Action; Copyright 1958, Columbia Pictures Corporation; Copyright 1993, Columbia Pictures Industries, Inc.; A Screen Gems Film Presentation; Columbia Tristar Home Video

CAST: Shemp; Larry; Moe; Christine McIntyre; Phil Van Zandt; Jacques O'Mahoney; Vernon Dent

CREDITS: Produced by—Hugh McCollum; Written and Directed by—Edward Berrids; Director of Photography—Allen Siegler, A.S.C.; Film Editor—Henry DeMond; Art Director—Harold MacArthur

SYNOPSIS: "In days of old when knights were bold and suits were made of iron." So begins *Square Heads of the Round Table.* If Bugs Bunny can go to Camelot, why not the Three Stooges?

The Stooges appear as three troubadours on their way to Camelot. Since Shemp is stuck in his armor, they stop at a blacksmith's shop for help. They become embroiled in the Black Prince's plot to kill King Arthur and marry the fair Elaine. Elaine however loves Cedric, the blacksmith, and our three slapstick heroes take the side of true love.

An obese King Arthur sets a trap and captures the Stooges. Elaine sends them a cake full of tools to help them escape from prison. They create a diversion for the hero by turning on a radio and doing a dance number — in armor of course. The plot is foiled.

Star Wars: A New Hope (1977)

124 minutes; Color; Live Action; Copyright 1977, 20th Century–Fox Film Corporation; Copyright 1995, Lucasfilm Ltd.; Digitally THX Mastered; A Lucasfilm Ltd. Production

CAST: Mark Hamill (Luke Skywalker); Harrison Ford (Han Solo); Carrie Fisher (Princess Leia Organa); Peter Cushing (Grand Moff Tarkin); Alec Guinness (Ben [Obi Wan] Kanobi); Anthony Daniels (See Threepio [C3PO]); Kenny Baker (Artoo-Detoo [R2D2]); Peter Mayhew (Chewbacca); David Prowse (Lord Darth Vader); Phil Brown (Uncle Owen); Shelagh Fraser (Aunt Beru); Alex McCrindle (General Dodonna); Eddie Byrne (General Willard); Drewe Hemley (Red Leader); Dennis Lawson (Red Two); Garrick Hagon (Red Three); Jack Klaff (Red Four); William Hootkins (Red Five); Angus McInnis (Gold Leader); Jeremy Sinden (Gold Two); Graham Ashley (Gold Five); Don Henderson (General Taggi); Richard Le Parmentier (General Motti); Leslie Scholfield (Commander #1); Jack Purvis (Chief Jawa)

CREDITS: Written and Directed by — George Lucas; Produced by — Gary Kurtz; Production Designer — John Barry; Director of Photography — Gilbert Taylor, B.S.C.; Music by — John Williams; Performed by the London Symphony Orchestra; Original Music Copyright 1977, Fox Fanfare Music, Inc.; Special Photographic Effects Supervisor — John Dykstra; Special Production and Mechanical Effects — John Stears; Film Editors — Paul Hirsch, Marcia Lucas, Richard Chew; Production Supervisor — Robert Watts; Production Illustrator — Ralph McQuarrie; Costume Designer — John Mollo; Art Directors — Norman Reynolds, Leslie Dilley; Makeup Supervisor — Stuart Freeborn; Production Sound Mixer — Derek Ball; Casting — Irene Lamb, Diane Crittenden, Vic Ramos; Supervising Sound Editor — Sam Shaw; Special Dialogue and Sound Effects — Ben Burtt; Sound Editors — Robert R. Rutledge, Gordon Davidson, Gene Corso; Supervising Music Editor — Kenneth Wannberg; Recording Mixers — Don MacDougall, Ray West, Mike Winkler, Richard Forvan, Bob Winkler, Robert Litt, Lester Fresholtz; Dolby Sound Consultant — Stephen Katz; Orchestrations — Herbert W. Spencer; Music Scoring Mixer — Eric Tomlinson; Assistant Film Editors — Todd Edekelheide, Jay Markle, Colin Kitchens, Bonnie Koehler; Camera Operators — Ronnie Taylor, Geoff Glover; Set Decorator — Roger Christian; Production Manager — Bruce Sharvan; Assistant Directors — Tony Waye, Gerry Gangan, Terry Madden; Location Manager — Arnold Ross; Assistant Producer — Bunn Alsup; Assistant Director — Lucy Autrey Wilson; Production Assistants — Pat Carr, Miki Hervan; Gaffer — Ron Tabera; Property Master — Frank Bruton; Wardrobe Supervisor — Ron Beck; Stunt Coordinator — Peter Diamond; Continuity — Ann Skinner; Titles — Dan Perri; 2nd Unit Photography — Carroll Baillard, Rick Clemente, Robert Dalva, Tak Fujikoto; 2nd Unit Art Directors — Leon Erickson, Al Locatelli; 2nd Unit Production Managers — David Lester, Peter Herald, Pepi Lenzi; 2nd Unit Makeup — Rick Baker, Douglas Beswick; Assistant Sound Editors — Roxanne Jones, Karen Sharp; Production Controller — Brian Gibbs; Location Auditor — Ralph M. Leo; Assistant Auditors — Steve Cullup, Penny McCarthy, Kim Falkinburg; Advertising Publicity Supervisor — Charles Lippincott; Unit Publicist — Brian Doyle; Still Photographer — John Jay; Miniature and Optical Effects Unit; 1st Cameraman — Richard Edlund; 2nd Cameraman — Dennis Muren; Assistant Cameramen — Douglas Smith, Kenneth Ralston, David Robman; 2nd Unit Photography — Bruce Logan; Composite Optical Photography — Robert Blalack; Optical Photography Coordinator — Paul Roth; Optical Printer Operators — David Berry, David McCue, Richard Feodrella, Eldon Ridman, Jim Van Trees, Jr.; Optical Camera Assistants — Caleb Aschkinazo, Bruce Nicholson, Bert Terreri, Jim Wells, John C. Moulos, Gary Smith, Donna Tracy, Vicky Witt; Production Supervisor — George E. Mather; Matte Artist — P. S. Ellenshaw; Planet and Satellite Artist — Ralph McQuarrie; Effects Illustrator and Designer — Joseph Johnston; Additional Spacecraft Design — Colin Cantwell; Chief Model Maker — Grant McCune; Model Builders — David Beasley, Lorne Peterson, Paul Huston, Jon Erland, Steve Gamley, David Jones; Animation and Rotoscope Designer — Adam Beckett; Animators — Michael

Han Solo (Harrison Ford), Chewbacca and Luke Skywalker (Mark Hamill) walk triumphantly across the throne room before the mighty Rebel forces in *Star Wars*.

Ross, Jonathan Sean, Lynn Gerry, Peter Curan, Chris Casady, Diana Wilson; Stop Motion Animation — Jon Berg, Philip Tippett; Miniature Explosions — Joe Viskodil, Greg Auer; Computer Animation and Graphic Design — Dan O'Bannon, Larry Cuba, John Walsh, Jay Teitzell, Image West; Film Control Coordinator — Mary M. Lind; Film Librarians — Cindy Isman, Connie McCrum, Pamela Malouf; Electronics Design — Alvah J. Miller; Special Components — James Shourt; Assistants — Masaaki Norihord, Eleanor Porter; Camera and Mechanical Designs — Don Trumbull, Richard Alexander, William Shourt; Special Mechanical Equipment — Jerry Greenwood, Douglas Barnett, Stuart Ziff, David Scott; Production Managers — Bob Shepherd, Lon Tinney; Production Staff — Patricia Rose Duignan, Mark Kline, Rhonda Feck, Ron Nathan; Assistant Editor (Opticals) — Bruce Michael Green; Additional Optical Effects — Van Der Veer Photo Effects, Ray Mercer & Company, Modern Film Effects, Master Film Effects, De Patie–Freleng Enterprises, Inc.; Panavision; Technicolor; Prints by Deluxe; Photographed in Tunisia, Guatemala, Death Valley National Monument, California, and at EMI-Elstree Studios, Borehamwood, England; Music recorded at Anvil Recording Studios, Denham, England; Re-recording at Samuel Goldwyn Studios, Los Angeles, California. The producers wish to thank the government of Tunisia, the Institute of Anthropology and History of Guatemala and the National Parks Service, U.S. Department of the Interior, for their cooperation.

SYNOPSIS: Just as Boorman's *Excalibur* has become a classic Arthurian film, so too has Lucas's *Star Wars* trilogy become a classic science fiction production. Happily, there is an Arthurian connection. In a number of interviews George Lucas has made it explicitly clear that his *Star Wars* story is indeed based on Arthurian themes. For a further discussion, see the end of the synopsis of episode 6, *The Return of the Jedi*.

Lucas wrote the screenplays for these three movies as episodes 4, 5 and 6 of a planned sextet of films. As of this writing, episode 1, *The Phantom Menace*, has been released, episodes 2 and 3 to follow.

Episode 4, *A New Hope,* is the story of a group of rebels battling the evil Galactic Empire. Rebel spies have stolen the blueprints for the empire's ultimate weapon, the Death Star. This gigantic ship is capable of destroying entire planets. Princess Leia of the planet Alderon has the plans and is trying to get them to her father, who can use them to destroy the Death Star.

Leia's ship is captured by the sinister Darth Vader, but she manages to load the plans into a little robot named R2D2. R2D2 and his companion android, C3P0, escape, but Leia is taken hostage. The two robots wind up being sold to a farmer named Owen. While cleaning R2D2, Owen's nephew, Luke Skywalker, hits a wrong button and the android automatically projects part of a holographic message. The image is of Leia saying, "Help me, Obi Wan Kanobi, you're my only hope."

Luke, it turns out, is an orphan being raised by his Uncle Owen and Aunt Beru. He wants to go to the academy to become a pilot, but his uncle wants him to stay to help on the farm one more year. Dire circumstances propel him into the service more quickly than even Luke could wish for.

R2D2 sneaks off that night. Early in the morning Luke goes looking for him. He is attacked by sand people, but Obi Wan Kanobi shows up to chase them off. Taking Luke and the androids to his home, Kanobi informs Luke that he was once a Jedi Knight like Luke's father. He gives Luke his father's light saber and explains that Darth Vader had been a Jedi Knight as well, but had gone bad and killed Luke's father.

Jedi Knights are practitioners of an ancient religion that involves the Force — a universal power that ties all life together. Vader has been seduced by the dark side of the Force and works for the empire.

Kanobi accesses Leia's complete message and determines he must get the android to

Alderon. He tries to convince Luke to come along, but Luke declines. In the meantime, Imperial stormtroopers have been on the trail of the androids. They've killed Uncle Owen and Aunt Beru and destroyed the farm. When Luke discovers this, having nothing left, he goes with Kanobi. At a spaceport bar Kanobi contracts with the freelancers Han Solo and Chewbacca to take them to Alderon. The group barely escapes the relentless stormtroopers.

During the trip to Alderon, Kanobi begins training Luke in the use of the Force. These Zenlike powers are innate but need to be developed.

Back on the Death Star, Darth Vader's mind-probing attempts on Leia have failed. The decision is made to destroy Alderon. Han, Luke and the rest arrive in the quadrant as the rubble of the exploded planet scatters into space. Han's ship is captured in a tractor beam and pulled aboard the Death Star, but the crew manages to escape and goes to search for Leia. Kanobi goes off on his own to shut down the tractor beam.

After a number of running battles with the Imperial troops, Luke, Han and Chewbacca get Leia out of captivity and bring her back to their ship. Simultaneously, Kanobi has been successful at his task, but he is discovered by Darth Vader. The two Jedis, one good, one evil, face off in a fight to the death. When Kanobi sees that Leia and the rest are boarding the ship, he simply stops fighting, allowing Vader to strike him down. Kanobi's body vaporizes and his robes fall empty to the deck. His spirit has been released to become part of the Force and from there he continues to speak to Luke.

The team takes off, fighting its way clear of the Death Star and its fleet, and gets the plans to the rebels. After some study, it is discovered that a thermal vent pipe is the Death Star's weak spot and Luke and several other pilots are sent to drop bombs down the vent. Only Luke makes it and through his use of the Force manages to evade the chasing Darth

Vader and accurately drop the bomb. In a near crash, Vader's fighter ship is knocked clear just before the Death Star explodes.

In a ceremony much like receiving knighthood, Leia places awards around the necks of Luke, Han and Chewbacca. An appreciative crowd cheers the heroes.

Star Wars: The Empire Strikes Back (1980)

128 minutes; Color; Live Action; Copyright 1980, Lucasfilm Ltd.; Copyright 1995, Lucasfilm Ltd.; Copyright 1995, 20th Century–Fox Home Entertainment, Inc.; Copyright 1995, CBS/Fox Company; Digitally TX Mastered; A Lucasfilm Ltd. Production

CAST: Mark Hamill (Luke Skywalker); Harrison Ford (Han Solo); Carrie Fisher (Princess Leia); Billy Dee Williams (Lando Calrissian); Anthony Daniels (C3P0); David Prowse (Darth Vader); Peter Mayhew (Chewbacca); Kenny Baker (R2D2); Frank Oz (Performing Yoda); Alec Guinness (Ben [Obi Wan] Kanobi); Jeremy Bulloch (Boba Fett); John Hollis (Lando's Aide); Jack Purvis (Chief Ugnaught); Des Webb (Snow Creature); Kathryn Mullen (Performing Assistant for Yoda); Clive Revill (Voice of Emperor); Imperial Forces: Kenneth Colley (Admiral Piett); Julian Glover (General Veers); Michael Sheard (Admiral Ozzel); Michael Culver (Captain Needa); John Dicks (Officer); Milton John (Officer); Mark Jones (Officer); Oliver Mcguire (Officer); Robin Scobey (Officer); Rebel Forces: Bruce Boa (Gurl Rieeban); Christopher Malcom (Zev [Rogue 2]); Dennis Lawson (Wedge [Rogue 3]); Richard Oldfield (Hobbie [Rogue 4]); John Morton (Dak [Luke's Gunner]); Ian Liston (Janson [Wedge's Gunner]); John Ratzenberger (Major Derlin); Jack McKenzie (Deck Lieutenant); Jerry Harte (Head Controller); Norman Chancer (Officer); Norwich Duff (Officer); Ray Hassett (Officer); Brigitte Kahn (Officer); Burnell Tucker (Officer)

CREDITS: Director—Irvin Kershner; Producer—Gary Kurtz; Screenplay—Leigh Brackett, Lawrence Kasdan; Story—George Lucas; Executive Producer—George Lucas; Production Designer—Norman Reynolds; Director of Photography—Peter Suschitzky, B.S.C.; Editor—Paul Hirsch, A.C.E.; Special Visual Effects—Brian Johnson, Richard Edlund; Music—John Williams; Performed by the London Symphony Orchestra; Original Music Copyright 1980, Fox Fanfare Music, Inc./Bantha Music; Associate Producers—

Robert Watts, James Bloom; Design Consultant and Conceptual Artist—Ralph McQuarrie; Art Directors—Leslie Dilley, Harry Lange, Alan Tomkins; Set Decorator—Michael Ford; Construction Manager—Bill Welch; Assistant Art Directors—Michael Lamont, Fred Hole; Sketch Artist—Ivor Beddoes; Draftsmen—Ted Ambrose, Michael Boone, Reg Bream, Steve Cooper, Richard Danning; Modelers—Fred Evans, Allan Moss, Jan Stevens; Chief Buyer—Edmund Rodrigo; Construction Storeman—Dave Middleton; Operating Cameramen—Kelvin Pike, David Garfath; Assistant Cameramen—Maurice Arnold, Chris Tanner; Second Assistant Cameramen—Peter Robinson, Madelin Most; Dolly Grips—Dennis Lewis, Brian Osborn; Matte Photography Consultant—Stanley Sayer, B.S.C.; Gaffer—Laurie Shane; Rigging Gaffer—John Clark; Lighting Equipment and Crew from—Lee Electric; Makeup and Special Creature Design—Stuart Freeborn; Makeup Artists—Kay Freeborn, Nick Malley; Chief Hairdresser—Barbara Ritchie; Yoda Fabrication—Wendy Widener; Costume Designer—John Mollo; Wardrobe Supervisor—Tiny Nicholls; Wardrobe Mistress—Eileen Sullivan; Property Master—Frank Bruton; Property Supervisor—Charles Torbett; Property Dressing Supervisor—Joe Dipple; Head Carpenter—George Gunning; Head Plasterer—Bert Rodwell; Head Rigger—Red Lawrence; Sound Design and Supervising Sound Effects Editor—Ben Burtt; Sound Editors—Richard Burrow, Teresa Eckton, Bonnie Koehler; Production Sound—Peter Sutton; Sound Boom Operator—Don Wortham; Production Maintenance—Ron Butcher; Re-recording—Bill Varney, Steve Maslow, Gregg Landaker; Music Recording—Eric Tomlinson; Orchestrations—Herbert W. Spencer; Supervising Music Editor—Kenneth Wannberg; Assistant Film Editors—Duwayne Dunham, Phil Sanderson, Barbara Ellis, Steve Starkey, Paul Tomlinson; Dialogue Editors—Curt Schulkey, Leslie Shatz, Joanne D'Antonio; Optical Coordinator—Roberta Friedman; Assistant Sound Editors—John Benson, Ken Fischer, Nancy Jencks, Joanna Cappuccilli, Craig Jaeger, Laurel Ladevich; Foley Editors—Robert Rutledge, Scott Hecker; Foley Assistants—Edward M. Steidele, John Roesh; Sound Effects Recording—Randy Thom; Recording Technicians—Gary Summers, Howie, Kevin O'Connell; Production Supervisor—Bruce Sharman; Assistant Production Manager—Patricia Carr; Production Coordinator—Miki Herman; First Assistant Director—David Tomblin; Second Assistant Directors—Steve Lanning, Roy Button; Location Manager—Philip Kohler; Continuity—

Kay Rawlings, Pamela Mann; Casting — Irene Lamb, Terry Liebling, Bob Edmiston; Assistant to Producer — Bunny Alsup; Assistant to Director — Debbie Shaw; Assistant to Executive Producer — Jane Bay; Production Assistants — Barbara Harley, Nick Laws, Charles Wessler; Stunt Coordinator — Peter Diamond; Stunt Doubles — Bob Anderson, Collin Shearing; Production Accountant — Ron Phipps; Assistant Accountant — Michael Larkins; Set Cost Controller — Ken Gordon; Location Accountant — Ron Cook; Still Photographer — George Whitear; Unit Publicist — Alan Arnold; Assistant Publicist — Kirsten Wing; Studio Second Unit: Directors — Harley Corliss, John Barry; Director of Photography — Chris Menges; Assistant Director — Dominic Pulford; Second Assistant Director — Andrew Montgomery; Location Second Unit: Director — Peter MacDonald; Director of Photography — Geoff Glover; Operating Cameraman — Bob Smith; Assistant Cameramen — John Campbell, Mike Brewster; Second Assistant Cameramen — John Keen, Greg Dupre; Dolly Grip — Frank Batt; Production Manager — Sven Johansen; Assistant Directors — Bill Westley, Ola Solum; Production and Mechanical Effects Unit: Mechanical Effects Supervision — Nick Allder; Location Unit Supervisor — Allan Bryce; Senior Effects Technicians — Neil Swan, Dave Watkins; Robot Fabrication and Supervision — Andrew Kelly, Ron Howe; Effects Technicians — Phil Knowles, Martin Gant, Guy Hudson, Barry Whitrod, Brian Eke, Dennis Lowe; Effects Engineering — Roger Nicholls, Steve Lloyd; Electrical Engineering — John Hatt; Electronics Consultant — Rob Dickinson; Model Construction — John Pakenham; Effects Assistants — Alan Poole, Digby Milner, Robert Mclaren; Effects Secretary — Gill Case; Miniature and Optical Effects Unit: Effects Cameramen — Ken Ralston, Jim Veilleux; Camera Operators — Don Dow, Bill Neil; Assistant Cameramen — Selwyn Eddy, Rick Fitcher, Michael McAlister, Richard Fish, Jody Westheimer, Clint Palmer, Paul Huston, Chris Anderson; Optical Photography Supervisor — Bruce Nicholson; Optical Printer Operators — David Berry, Kenneth Smith, Donald Clark; Optical Lineup — Warren Franklin, Mark Vargo, Peter Amundson, James Lim, Loring Doyle, Thomas Rosseter, Tam Pillsbury; Optical Coordinator — Laurie Vermont; Laboratory Technicians — Tim Geideman, Duncan Myers, Ed Jones; Art Director, Visual Effects — Joe Johnston; Assistant Art Director — Nilo Rodis-Janero; Stop Motion Animation — Jon Berg, Phil Tippett; Stop Motion Technicians — Tom St. Amand, Doug Beswick; Matte Painting Supervisor — Harrison Ellenshaw; Matte Artists — Ralph McQuarrie, Michael Pangrazio; Matte Photography — Neil Kreppela; Additional Photography — Michael Lawler; Matte Photography Assistants — Craig Barron, Robert Elsmit; Chief Model Maker — Lorne Peterson; Model Shop Foreman — Steve Ganley; Model Makers — Paul Huston, Michael Fulmer, Charles Bailey, Scott Marshall, Wesley Seeds, Rob Gemmel, Tom Rudduck, Samuel Zolltheis, Ease Owyeung, Marc Thorpe, Dave Carson, Pat McClung; Animation and Rotoscope Supervisor — Peter Kuran; Animators — Samuel Comstock, John Van Vliet, Kim Knowlton, Nina Saxon, Gary Maller, Rick Taylor, Chris Casady, Diana Wilson; Visual Effects Editorial Supervisor — Conrad Buff; Effects Editor — Michael Kelly; Assistant Effects Editors — Arthur Repola, Howard Stein; Apprentice Editor — Jon Thaler; Production Administrator — Dick Gallegly; Production Secretary — Patricia Blau; Production Assistant — Thomas Brown; Production Accountant — Ray Scalice; Assistant Accountants — Glenn Phillips, Pam Traas, Laura Crockett; Production Assistant — Jenny Oznowicz; Transportation — Robert Martin; Still Photography — Terry Chostner; Lab Assistant — Roberto McGrath; Electronics Systems Designer — Jerry Jeffress; Systems Programming — Kris Brown; Electronic Engineering — L. Harry Meyer, Mike MacKenzie, Gary Leo; Special Project Coordinator — Stuart Ziff; Equipment Engineering Supervisor — Gene Whiteman; Design Engineer — Mike Bolles; Machinists — Udo Pampel, Greg Beaumonte; Draftsman — Ed Tennler; Special Projects — Gary Platek; Supervising Stage Technician — T. E. Moehnke; Stage Technicians — William Beck, Leo Loverro, Dick Dova, Bobby Finley, Edward Hirsch, Ed Breed; Miniature Pyrotechnics — Joseph Viskodil, Dave Pier, Thaine Norris; Optical Printer Component Manufacturer — George Randle Co.; Camera and Movement Design — Jim Beaumonte; Special Optics Designer — David Grafton; Special Optics Fabrication — J. L. Wood Optical Systems; Optical Printer Component Engineering — Fries Engineering; High Speed Camera Movements — Mitchell Camera Corp.; Ultra High Speed Camera — Bruce Hill Productions; Color Timer — Ed Lemke; Negative Cutting — Robert Hart, Darrell Hikson; Dolby Consultant — Don Digiroland; Additional Digital Effects — Van Der Veer Photo Effects, Modern Film Effects, Ray Mercer & Co., Westheime Company, Lookout Mountain Films; Aerial Camera System by — Wesscam Camera Systems (Europe); Aerial Cameraman — Ron Goodman; Assistant — Margaret Herron; Helicopter Supplied by — Dollar Air Services United; Pilot — Mark

Wolfe; Cloud plates photographed with Astrovision by Continental Camera Systems, Inc.; Snow vehicles supplied by Altier Fischer; R2 bodies fabricated by White Horse Try Company; Special assistance from Giltspur Engineering and Compair; Photographed on the Hardangerjøkulen Glacier, Finse, Norway and at EMI-Elstree Studios, Borehamwood, England; Music recorded at Anvil Studios, Denham, England; Re-recorded at Samuel Goldwyn Studios, Los Angeles, California; Special visual effects produced at Industrial Light and Magic, Marin County, California; Filmed in Panavision; Recorded in Dolby Stereo; Color by Rank Film Laboratories; Prints by Deluxe; A Lucasfilm Ltd. Production; A 20th Century–Fox Release; Original soundtrack on RSO Records; Novelization from Ballantine Books

SYNOPSIS: In this sequel to *Star Wars: A New Hope,* Luke Skywalker and the rebels have established a new base of operations on the ice world Hoth. Darth Vader has survived and pledged to find Luke at all costs. He has deployed thousands of search probes throughout the galaxy.

On Hoth, Luke and Han Solo have been planting protective sensors around the base area. About to return, Luke spots something fall through the sky and goes to investigate as Han heads back to the operations center. Luke is attacked by an ice creature and taken to its cave. He manages to escape but collapses in the snow. Just before Luke loses consciousness, Obi Wan Kanobi appears to him like a vision and tells him he will go to the Jedi master Yoda to learn to use his skills with the Force.

Han finds Luke and gets him back to safety. He also spots one of Vader's probes and destroys it but not before the drone has transmitted its position to Vader. Vader and the fleet head for Hoth.

With the Imperial fleet attacking, the base is evacuated. Han and Chewbacca take Princess Leia and C3PO aboard the *Millennium Falcon* and find safety in a tunnel on an asteroid. There they begin repairs to the light-drive system of the ship. Luke and R2D2 head for Yoda's home world.

Finding Yoda, Luke begins his training. Yoda is dissatisfied with Luke's impatience but

Kanobi convinces the 800-year-old master to take on the task.

Still hounded by Vader, Han and the rest are forced to flee the asteroid. They manage to escape the fleet, but a bounty hunter working for Jabba the Hutt (who wants Han Solo) is hired by Vader to follow them. Han makes his way to the cloud city of an old friend, Lando Calrissian. Unfortunately Vader and the bounty hunter get there first and force Calrissian to help in trapping them.

Luke senses that his friends are in danger and against the advice of both Kanobi and Yoda he decides to leave to help them. Vader's capture of Han and Leia was nothing more than a way to trap Luke and the lure works perfectly. In anticipation of capturing Luke, Vader experimentally has Han entombed alive in a block of carbonite and hands him over to the bounty hunter.

Lando is not really a bad guy, so he arranges an escape and the *Millennium Falcon* gets away. Luke, however, confronts Vader and, with light sabers flashing, the two battle. As they fight, Vader reveals that he is actually Luke's father. He continues to try to convince Luke to join the Dark Side, but Luke resists. Vader slices off his son's sword hand.

Cornered, Luke allows himself to fall down a tunnel and winds up hanging precariously from the underside of the cloud city. Hearing Luke's telepathic cry for help, Leia gets Lando to turn around and they retrieve the young Jedi.

The crew makes its way to the safety of a space station where Luke is fitted with a new mechanical hand and the *Falcon* receives much-needed repairs. Luke and Leia stay behind as Lando and Chewbacca leave to find Han.

Star Wars: The Return of the Jedi (1983)

134 minutes; Color; Live Action; Copyright 1983, Lucasfilm Ltd.; Copyright 1995, Lucasfilm Ltd.; Copyright 1995, 20th Century–Fox Home Entertainment, Inc.; Copy-

right 1995, CBS/Fox Company; Fox Video #147831

CAST: Mark Hamill (Luke Skywalker); Harrison Ford (Han Solo); Carrie Fisher (Princess Leia); Billy Dee Williams (Lando Calrissian); Anthony Daniels (C3P0); Peter Mayhew (Chewbacca); Sebastian Shaw (Anakin Skywalker); Ian McDiarmid (The Emperor); Frank Oz (Performing Yoda); James Earl Jones (Voice of Darth Vader); David Prowse (Darth Vader); Alec Guinness (Ben [Obi Wan] Kanobi); Kenny Baker (R2D2); Michael Pennington (Moff Jerferrod); Kenneth Colley (Admiral Piett); Michael Carter (Bib Fortuna); Dennis Lawson (Wedge); Tim Rose (Admiral Ackbar); Dermot Crowley (General Madine); Caroline Blakiston (Mon Mothma); Warwick Davis (Wicket); Kenny Baker (Paploo); Jeremy Bulloch (Boba Fett); Femi Taylor (Oola); Annie Arbogast (Sy Snootles); Claire Davenport (Fat Dancer); Jack Purvis (Teebo); Mike Edwards (Logray); Jane Busby (Chief Chirpa); Malcom Dixon (Ewok Warrior); Mike Cotrell (Ewok Warrior); Nicki Reade (Nicki); Adam Barehan (Stardestroyer Controller #1); Jonathan Oliver (Stardestroyer Controller #2); Pip Miller (Stardestroyer Captain #1); Tom Mannion (Stardestroyer Captain #2); Toby Philpott, Mike Edmonds, David Barclay (Jabba Puppeteers); Michael McCormick, Simon Williamson, Swim Lee, Richard Robinson, Deep Roy, Hugh Spirit, Michael Quinn (Puppeteers); Margo Apostocos, Ray Armstrong, Eileen Baker, Michael H. Balham, Bobbie Bell, Patty Bell, Alan Bennett, Sarah Bennett, Pamela Betts, Dan Blackner, Linda Bowley, Peter Burroughs, Debbie Carrington, Maureen Charlton, William Coppen, Tony Cox, John Cumming, Jean D'Agostino, Luis De Jesus, Debbie Dixon, Margarita Fernandez, Phil Fondacaro, Sal Fondacaro, Tony Friel, Dan Frishman, John Gavam, Michael Gilden, Paul Grant Lydia Green, Lars Green, Pam Grizz, Andrew Herd, J. J. Jackson, Richard Jones, Trevor Jones, Glynn Jones, Karen Lay, John Lummiss, Nancy Maclean, Peter Mandell, Carole Morris, Stacy Nichols, Chris Nunn, Barbara O'Laughlin, Brian Orenstein, Harrell Parker, Jr. , John Pedrick, April Perkins, Ronnie Phillips, Katie Purvis, Carol Read, Nicholas Read, Diana Reynolds, Daniel Rogers, Chris Romano, Dean Shackenford, Kiran Shah, Felix Silla, Linda Spriggs, Gerald Staddon, Kevin Thompson, Kendra Wall, Brian Wheeler, Butch Wilhelm (Ewoks); Franki Anderson, Alisa Berk, Sean Crawford, Andy Cunningham, Tim Dry, Graeme Hattrick, Phil Herbert, Gerald Home, Paul Springer (Mime Artists)

CREDITS: Director — Richard Marquand; Screenplay — Lawrence Kasdan, George Lucas; Story — George Lucas; Producer — Howard Kazanjian; Executive Producer — George Lucas; Co-Producers — Robert Watts, Jim Bloom; Production Designer — Norman Reynolds; Director of Photography — Alan Hume, B.S.C.; Editors — Sean Barton, Marcia Lucas, Duwayne Dunham; Visual Effects — Richard Edlund, A.S.C., Dennis Muren, Ken Ralston; Costume Designers — Aggie Guerard, Nilo Rodis-Jamero; Mechanical Effects Supervision — Kit West; Makeup and Creature Design — Phil Tippett, Stuart Freeborn; Sound Design — Ben Burtt; Music — John Williams; 1st Assistant Director/Second Unit Director — David Tomblin; Casting — Mary Selway Buckley; Location Director of Photography — Jim Glennon; Additional Photography — Jack Lowin; Production Sound — Tony Dawe, Randy Thom; Supervising Music Editor — Kenneth Wannberg; Music Recording — Eric Tomlinson; Orchestrations — Herbert W. Spencer; Chief Articulation Engineer — Stuart Ziff; Production Supervisor — Douglas Twiddy; Production Executive — Robert Latham Brown; Unit Production Manager — Miki Herman; Assistant Production Manager — Patricia Carr; Associate Producer — Louis G. Friedman; Conceptual Artist — Ralph McQuarrie; Art Directors — Fred Hole, James Schoppe; Set Decorators — Michael Ford, Harry Lange; Property Master — Peter Hancock; Chief Hairdresser — Patricia McDermott; Stunt Coordinator — Glenn Randall; Stunt Arranger — Peter Diamond; Stunt Performers — Bob Anderson, Dirk Yohan Beer, Marc Boyle, Mike Cassidy, Tracy Eddon, Sandra Gross, Ted Grossman, Frank Henson, Larry Holt, Bill Horrigan, Alf Joint, Julius Leflore, Colin Skeaping, Malcom Weaver, Paul Weston, Bob Yerkes, Dan Zormeier; Production Controller — Arthur Carroll; Production Accountant — Margaret Mitchel; Production Assistant — Ian Bryce; Production Coordinator — Lata Ryan; Second Assistant Directors — Roy Button, Michael Steele, Chris Newman, Russell Lodge; Assistants — Sunni Herman, Gail Samuelson; Script Supervisor — Pamela Mann Francis; Location Script Supervisor — Bob Forest; Location Casting — Dave Eman, Bill Little; Assistant to Mr. Kazanjian — Kathleen Hartney Ross; Assistant to Mr. Bloom — John Syrjamaki; Assistant to Mr. Lucas — Jane Bay; Assistant Art Directors — Michael Lamont, John Fenner, Richard Deryoung; Set Dresser — Doug Von Moss; Construction Manager — Bill Welch; Assistant Construction Manager — Alan Booth; Construction Supervisor — Roger Irvin; General Foremen —

Greg Callas, Cliff Clause, Doug Elliott, Stan Wakashige; Print Foreman — Gary Clark; Sketch Artist — Roy Carnon; Scenic Artist — Ted Mitchell; Decor and Lettering Artist — Bob Walker; Set Draftsman — Reg Bream, Mark Billerman, Chris Campbell; Production Buyer — David Lusby; Production Storeman — David Middleton; Operating Cameramen — Alec Mills, Tom Laughridge, Mike Benson; Focus Pullers — Michael Prust, Chris Tanner; Assistant Cameramen — Leo Napolitano, Bob La Bonge; Second Assistant Cameramen — Simon Hume, Steve Tate, Martin Renzie, Michael Glennon; Gaffers — Mike Pantages, Bob Brenner; Aerial Photography — Ron Goodman, Margaret Herron; Helicopter Pilot — Mark Wolfe; Key Grip — Dick Dova Spah; Best Boy — Joe Crowley; Dolly Grip — Chunky Huse, Reg Hall; Matte Photography Consultant — Stanley Bayer, B.S.C.; Rigging Gaffers — Clark Garland, Tommy Brown; Chief Makeup Artists — Tom Smith, Graham Freeborn; Makeup Artists — Peter Robb-King, Dickie Mills, Kay Freeborn, Nick Dudman; Hairdressers — Mike Lockley, Paul Le Blanc; Assistant Articulation Engineer — Eben Stromquist; Armature Designer — Peter Ronzani; Plastic Designer — Richard Davis; Sculptural Designers — Chuck Wiley, James Howard; Key Sculptors — Dave Carson, Tony McVey, Dave Sosalla, Judy Elkins, Derek Howarth; Chief Moldmaker — Wesley Seeds, Ron Young; Creature Technicians — Randy Dutra, Dan Howard, Brian Turner, Richard Epah, Jr., Kirk Thatcher, James Isaac, Jeanne Lauren, Ethan Wiley; Creature Consultants — John Berg, Chris Wallas; Production/Creature Coordinator — Patty Blau; Latex Foam Lab Supervisor — Tom McLaughlin; Animatronics Engineer — John Coppinger; Wardrobe Supervisor — Ron Beck; Costume Supervisor — Mary Elizabeth Stal; Wardrobe Mistress — Janet Tebrooke; Shop Manager — Jenny Green; Jeweler — Richard Miller; Creature Costumes — Barbara Kassal, Edwina Pellicca, Anne Polland, Elyra Angelinetta; Assistant Property Master — Charles Torbett; Property Supervisors — Dan Coangelo, Brian Lofthouse; Property — Holly Walker, Colm Van Perre; Propmakers — Bill Hargreaves, Richard Peters; Master Carpenter — Bert Long; Master Plasterer — Kenny Clarke; Master Painter — Erik Shirtcuffe; Supervising Rigger — Red Lawrence; Supervising Stagehand — Eddie Burke; Set Coordinators — Bill Kreysler, Warwick Tompkins; Set Engineering — George Bolis, Peggy Kashuba; Assistant Film Editors — Steve Starkey, Phil Sanderson, Deborah McDermott, Conrad Bute, Nick Hosker, Clive Hartley; Sound Effects Editors —

Richard Burrow, Teresa Eckton, Ken Fischer; Dialogue Editors — Laurel Ladevich, Curt Schuute, Bonnie Koehler, Vicki Rose Sampson; Assistant Sound Editors — Chris Weir, Gloria Borders, Kathy Ryan, Mary Helen Leasman, Bill Mann, Suzanne Fox, Nancy Jencas; Re-recording Mixers — Gary Summers, Roger Savage, Ben Burtt, Rand Thom; Re-recording Engineer — Tomlinson Holman; Boom Operators — David Batchelor, David Parker; Sound Assistants — Shep Dane, Jim Manson; Audio Engineers — T. M. Christopher, Kris Handwerk, Howie, Tom Johnson, James Kessler, Robert Marte, Dennie Thorpe, Catherine Coombs, W. G. Hooenfield, Brian Kelly, Susan Leahy, Scott Robinson, John Watson; English Lyrics — Joseph Williams; Huttese Lyrics — Anne Arbogast; Ewokee Lyrics — Ben Burtt; Special Effects Supervisor — Roy Arbogast; Special Effects Foreman — William David Lee; Special Effects Floor Controller — Ian Wingrove; Senior Effects Technician — Peter Dawson; Chief Electronics Technician — Ron Hone; Wire Specialist — Bob Harman; Location Special Effects — Kevin Pike, Mike Wood; Choreographer — Gilliam Gregory; Location Choreographer — Wendy Rogers; Production Accountant — Colin Hurren; Assistant Accountants — Sheala Daniell, Barbara Harley; Location Accountant — Diane Dantrardt, Pano Ragan; Transportation Coordinator — Gene Schwartz; Transportation Captains — John Fenblatt, H. Lee Nobutt; Studio Transportation Managers — Vic Minley, Mark La Bonge; Location Contact — Leanne Fike; Still Photographers — Albert Clarke, Ralph Nelson, Jr.; Unit Publicist — Gorden Arnell; Assistant Publicist — June Fine; Miniature and Optical Effects Unit: Industrial Light and Magic; Art Director, Visual Effects — Joe Johnston; Optical Photography Supervisor — Bruce Nicholson; General Manager, ILM — Tom Smith; Production Supervisor — Patricia Rose Duignan; Matte Painting Supervisor — Michael Pangrazio; Model Shop Supervisors — Lorne Peterson, Steve Gawley; Animation Supervisors — James Keefer; Supervising Visual Effects Editor — Arthur Repola; Effects Cameramen — Don Doil, Bill Neil, Selwyn Eddyal, Robert Elsmit, Stewart Barbee, David Hardburger, Michael J. McAllister, Scott Farrar, Michael Owens, Rick Fighter, Mark Gredell; Assistant Cameramen — Pat Sweeney, Robert Hill, Randy Johnson, Peter Daulton, Maryan Evans, David Fincher, Kim Marks, Kay Gilberte, Patrick McArdle, Bessie Wiley, Toby Hendel, Peter Romano; Production Coordinators — Warren Franklin, Laurie Vermont; Optical Printer Operators — John Ellis, Kenneth Smith, Mark Vargo,

David Berry, Donald Clark, James Lim; Optical Line-up — Tom Rosseter, Ed L. Jones, Ralph Gordon, Philip Barberio; Lab Technicians — Tim Glideman, Duncan Myers, Michael S. Moore; Production Illustrator — George Jensen; Matte Painting Artists — Chris Evans, Frank Ordaz; Matte Photography — Neil Kreppela, Craig Barron; Stop Motion Animator — Tom St. Amand; Chief Model Makers — William George, Scott Marshall, Larry Tan, Jeff Mann, Bill Beck, Barbara Alfonso, Marghi McMahon, Marc Thorpe, Sean Casey, Barbara Gallucci, Ira Wheeler, Mike Cochrane, Bill Buttfield, Randy Ottenberg; Head Effects Animators — Garry Waller, Kimberly Knowlton; Effects Animators — Terry Windell, Mike Lessa, Rob LaDuca, S. Stern, Renee Holt, Samuel Comstock, Annoch Thessien, Margot Pipion; Visual Effects Editors — Howard Stein, Peter Amundson, Bill Kimberlin; Assistant Visual Effects Editors — Robert Chrisolilis, Michael Cleason, Jay Ignaszewski, Joe Glass; Supervising Stage Technician — Ted Moehnke; Stage Technicians — Patrick Fitzsimmons, Ed Hirsch, Peter Stolz, Harold Cole, Joe Fulmer, Bob Finley, John McLeod, Dave Hilders, Merlin Chim, Lance Brackett; Pyrotechnicians — Thane Morris, Clive Pier; Supervisor, Still Photography — Terry Chostner; Still Photographers — Roberto McGrath, Kerry Nordquist; Electronic System Designers — Jerry Jeffresa, Kris Brown; Electronic Engineers — Mike McKenzie, Marty Brennds; Computer Graphics — William Reeves, Tom Duff; Equipment Engineering Supervisor — Gene Whiteman; Machinists — Udo Pampel, Conrad Bonderson; Apprentice Machinists — David Hanks, Chris Rand; Design Engineer — Mike Bolles; Equipment Support Staff — Wade Childress, Michael J. Smith, Cristi McCarthy, Ed Tennler; Administrative Staff — Chrissie England, Paula Karsh, Sonja Paulsen, Laura Krysen, Karen Rivers, Karen Dubé; Production Assistants — Susan Fritz-Monahan, Kathy Shine; Steadicam Plate Photography — Garrett Brown; Ultra High Speed Photography — Bruce Hill Productions; Color Timers — Jim Schurmann, Bob Hagans; Negative Cutter — Sunrise Film, Inc.; Additional Optical Effects — Lookout Mountain Film, Monaco Film Labs, Visual Concepts Engineering, Van Der Veer Photo Effects, Pacific Title, California Film, Movie Magic; Thanks to the U.S. Department of Interior, Bureau of Land Management and National Parks Service; Photographed in Buttercup Valley, Death Valley and Smith River, California and EMI-Elstree Studios, Borehamwood, England; Cameras and lenses by Joe Dunton Cameras, Ltd.; Aerial camera systems by Wesscam Camera Systems (Europe); Lighting equipment and crew from Lea Electric, Ltd.; Production vehicles courtesy of GMC Truck and Oldsmobile; Location service by Oldsmobile; Air transportation by Pan Am; Music recording at Anvil–Abbey Road Studios; Special visual effects produced at Industrial Light and Magic, Marin County, California; Color by Rank Film Laboratories; Prints by Deluxe; Sound by Dolby Stereo; A Lucasfilm Ltd. Production; A 20th Century–Fox Release; Music performed by the London Symphony Orchestra; Original soundtrack on RSO Records and Tapes; Novelization from Ballantine Books

SYNOPSIS: *The Return of the Jedi* is the final film of the original *Star Wars* trilogy. In it, Luke Skywalker has returned to the planet Tatooine to rescue Han Solo. Chewbacca, Princess Leia, C3P0, R2D2 and Lando Calrissian all participate in the attempt to get their friend from the clutches of Jabba the Hutt. After extended debates, feints and fights, Jabba is killed, Han is freed and the *Millennium Falcon* heads for home. Luke and R2D2 leave to visit Yoda, the old Jedi master.

The empire in the meantime has begun construction of another Death Star. The evil emperor orders Darth Vader to wait for Luke to approach them. He surmises that Luke is so strongly with the Force that only together can they defeat him.

Luke finds Yoda old and ailing. Yoda tells Luke he will only fully become a Jedi Knight when he confronts his father, Darth Vader. He warns Luke not to underestimate the emperor's power and his dying words are that there is another Skywalker.

The spirit of the Jedi Knight Ben Kanobi shows up. He explains to Luke that Anakin Skywalker, Luke's father, had been a good friend and a fine pilot, but Kanobi had trained Anakin instead of allowing Yoda to do so. Anakin had succumbed to the temptations of the Dark Side. During their conversation Luke figures out that Princess Leia is actually his sister.

The final battle is met when the Death Star is placed into orbit around the planet

Endor. It taps into the planet's power supplies to maintain its protective shields. The rebels determine that the only way to defeat the emperor and the Death Star is to deactivate the power generators on Endor. While Lando flies the *Falcon* in the battle in space, Han leads the attack on the planet's surface and Luke confronts both Vader and the emperor on the Death Star.

Sensing good yet in Vader, Luke ultimately refuses to fight his father. When the emperor attacks Luke, Vader finally breaks the hold of the Dark Side and hurls the emperor to his death. Mortally wounded himself, however, he dies in Luke's arms.

On the planet, with the help of the Ewoks, Han and the rest defeat the Imperial troops and destroy the power generators. With the disabling of the Death Star, the evil empire is finished.

There are numerous ties to Arthurian themes within the *Star Wars* story. Luke is the young King Arthur figure. Leia is a sort of Guinevere/Morgan combination; neither identification is perfect, of course, but she is the princess of the story and also has latent magical powers. Han Solo appears to be the Lancelot of the tale, Kanobi and Yoda are dual Merlins. Yoda's planet can be seen as Avalon. The Jedi Knights can be variously interpreted as the Knights Templar or the Knights of the Round Table.

Luke receives his father's light saber from Yoda, as Arthur's connection to at least one sword was through Merlin. Vader's red light saber and Luke's white one can be viewed as the battle of the red and white dragons prophesied by Merlin to Vortigern. Indeed, a case might be made for identifying Vader with Vortigern. As Vortigern was in legend supposed to have caused the near downfall of Britain because he allowed Saxons to enter the land and even fight for him, so Vader sided with the emperor, allowing the incursion of evil into the galaxy.

Later Luke constructs a light saber himself, the blade of which is green. This comes when Luke has become strong with the Force, the magic of the stories. Green is the color of magic.

Other interpretations are also possible. Some have suggested more of a connection to the story of Robin Hood: Luke Skywalker/Robin, Han Solo/Will Scarlet, Chewbacca/Little John, Obi Wan Kanobi/Friar Tuck, Princess Leia/Marion, Darth Vader/Sheriff of Nottingham, Emperor/Prince John. In any event, the archetypes are there and the specifics of who represents what are certainly entertaining to debate.

Starchaser: The Legend of Orin (1985)

107 minutes; Color; Cartoon; Copyright 1985, Young Sung International; Copyright 1985, Atlantic Releasing Corporation; Junior Home Video; KVC Home Video #JR13793; Canadian Video Factory

STARRING THE VOICES OF: Joe Calligan (Orin); Carmen Argenziano (Dagg); Noelle North (Elan/Aviana); Anthony Delongis (Zygon); Tyke Caravelli (Silica); Les Tremayne (Arthur); Ken Sanson (Magreb); John Mischitta, Jr. (Auctioneer/Z. Gork); Mona Marshall (Kallie); Mickey Morton (Minemaster); Herb Virgan (Pung/Hopps); Dennis Alwood (Shooter); Tina Romanus (Aunt Bella); Ryan MacDonald; John Garwood; Joseph Dellasorte; Philip Clarke; Michael Winslow; Thomas A. Watkins; Daryl T. Bartley

CREDITS: Music—Andrew Belling; Editor—Donald W. Ernst, A.C.E.; Associate Director—John Sparey; Associate Producers—Daniel Pia, Christine Danzo; Executive Producers—Thomas Coleman, Michael Rosenblatt; Writer—Jeffrey Scott; Animation Directors—Mitch Rochon, Jang Gil Kim; Character Design and Casting—Louise Zingarelli; Hardware Designer—Thomas Warkentin; Background Designers—Tim Callahan, Roy Allen Smith; Storyboard Artists—Boyd Kirkland, Mario Piluso, Paul Gruwell, Ronald Harris, Dick Sebast; Layout Supervisor—Roy Allen Smith; Layout Artists—Edward Haney, Frank Paur, Gary Graham, Boyd Kirkland, Rex Barron, David Hoover, Mario Piluso, Richard Graham, John Howley, Neil Galloway, Paul Gruwell, Robert DeWitt, John Koch, Robert A. Smith, Russell Heath, James Fletcher; Scene Planners—John Sparey, Mike Svayko, Robert Revell, Dotti Foell, James P. Finch, Ron Myrick; Technical Director—Mike Svayko;

Key Animators — Yoon Young Sang, Jung Yul Song, Bill Kroyer; Character Models — Darrell Rooney, Deborah Hayes; Animators — John Norton, Bill Kroyer, Steve Gordon, Gary Payn, Thomas Sito, Lenord Robinson, James Stribling, Marlene Robinson May; Assistant Animation Supervisor — Renee Holt; Assistant Animators — Daniel Jeup, Fred Warter, Craig Clark, Christopher Bailey, Christopher Rutkowski, Brian Ray, David Teague; Animation Inbetweeners — David Woodman, Stephen Moore, Eric Pigors, Greg Manwaring, Carlos Baeza, Anthony Zierhut, Alan Wright, James Fuji; Animation Checkers — Narelle Nixon, Dotti Foell, Robert Revell, Kim Young Mee, Don Lander; Background Supervisors — Carol Police, Kim Young Ku; Key Background Painters — Barry Jackson, John Calmette, Patricia Doktor, Edwin Hirth; Key Background Painter — Jim Schlenker; Special Visual Effects — John Van Vliet, Allen Blyth, Robert LaDuca, Michael Wolf, Michael Lessa; Effects Assistants — Kim Bae Geun, Geri Rochon; Computer Animation Planning — John Sparey, Bill Kroyer, Christopher Bailey, Craig Clark; Computer Animation Graphics — Patricia Capozzi, Edith Fandrey; Computer Assistants — Dave Woodman, Kane Anderson, Laura Capozzi Kelly, Charles Hefner; Color Key Designer — Janet Cummings; Color Key Assistants — No Soon Nyeo, Geri Rochon; Ink and Paint Assistants — Laura Craig, Madlyn O'Neill, Robin Police, Mi Kyung Kwon; Xerox — Pak Kyung Hee, Edgar Gutierrez, Judi Cassell; Production Final Checkers — Narrell Nixon, Patricia Capozzi, Sandra Kumashiro, James P. Finch, Kim Young Mee, Craig Littel-Herrick; Production Supervisors — Young Chul Choi, Kim Soon Min, David J. Corbett; Production Assistants — Thomas Watkins, Hwang Nami, Cho Myung Hee; Production Secretaries — Ronnie Clooman, Cathy Rowley; Camera Supervisor — Charles Flekal; Camera Operators — Young Boo Im, Thomas Ling Yen, Hyung Hee Kim, Bemiller Camera, R & B EFX and Animation, Paul B. Mikolyski, Yim Chul Kyn, David J. Corbett, Craig Littel-Herrick; Editorial Staff — Tony Mizgalski, Douglas Lloyd Nickel, Jonathan Pink; Sound Designer — Don Ernst; Sound Editors — Denise Horta, M.P.S.E., Eileen Horta, M.P.S.E., Dave J. West, M.P.S.E., Gary Krivacek, Kevin Spears, Rick Crampton, Robert Canton, Ted Johnston; Synthesized Sound Effects — Stan Levine; Mixers — John Reitz, C.A.S., David Campbell, C.A.S., Greg Rudloff, C.A.S.; Mixing Facility — Compact Sound Services; Synthesizer Performed by — Andrew Belling, Michael Beddicker; Music Supervisor — David Kratz; Music Performed by — The New World Philharmonic; Assistant Music Editor — Timothy Borquez; Music Recorded at — CBS Studios, London, Bodifications, Inc., L.A.; Music Coordinator — Nancy Gaelen; Production Facilities — Hanho Heung-UpCo., Ltd., Seoul; Computer Animation Software — Scott Reynolds; Computer Hardware Consultant — Harvard Pennington; Computer Processors — LNW Research Corp.; Graphic Plotters Courtesy of Western Graphics, Inc.; Titles and Opticals — Kaleidoscope Film Effects; Negative Cutting — Jack Hooper, Tim Hooper, Gary Buritt, Chuck George; Featured Voices — Ken Sanson, Daryl T. Bartley, Herb Vigran, Tina Romanus, Thomas H. Watkins, Mona Marshall, Philip Clark, John Moschitta, Jr., John Garwood, Mike Winslow, Joseph Dellasorte, Mickey Morton, Ryan MacDonald, Dennis Alwood; Background Voice Casting — Barbara Harris; Incidental and Background Voices — Rosanna Huffman, Marilyn Schieffler, Judi Durand, Greg Finley, Daamen Krall, Doris Hess, Cathy Cavadini, Susan Silo, David McCharen, Jan Rabson; Color by Deluxe Laboratories

SYNOPSIS: *Starchaser: The Legend of Orin* is a fairly sophisticated cartoon movie which throws together a lot of ideas. Among them are Arthurian elements, intelligent robots trying to defeat mankind, but most noticeably, the Star Wars scenario.

In the Vortigon star system, the humans of the planet Trinia have for centuries been subjugated by a being calling himself Zygon, whom they believe to be a god. The planet is rich in the crystalline mineral rubidimite which the humans mine as slaves in underground caverns. One day a young fellow in the mines uncovers an ancient sword. He pulls it out of some rubble and grasps it momentarily, but it flies from his hands and stabs itself into the rock floor of the cavern.

A ghostly Merlin-like figure appears who tells Orin that there is a world and universe above the mines. He continues, "He who has the sword has the power of truth. Find the blade and you will find your freedom." The image disappears and so does the blade of the sword. The hilt clatters to the ground. Orin picks up the hilt and puts it in his belt. He and his girlfriend Elan decide to try to find the upper world. They sneak off to find a safe spot to start digging upwards but Orin's blind younger brother, Kallie, follows them.

Delayed by convincing Kallie to stay behind, Orin and Elan are spotted and pursued by the robot overseers of the mines. They manage to find their way into the crystal processing plant itself, only to be captured by Zygon himself. Zygon kills Elan and Orin escapes, but Zygon wants the legendary "sword with no blade."

Orin does finally dig his way through to the surface of the planet. It isn't long, however, before he is pursued by a gang of "mandroids," bizarre mechanical beings who kill humans and graft body parts onto themselves. In fighting them off, Orin discovers that an invisible blade seems to exist when he swings his hilt at evil things. There are too many of the mandroids for one boy to defeat and they chase Orin into the swamps.

A cigar-chomping crystal smuggler named Dagg rescues Orin, taking the boy aboard his ship, the *Starchaser*. If a magical sword in a stone isn't enough, the computer that controls *Starchaser* is named Arthur.

Dagg has a load of crystals which he intends to sell on the black market. He flies to one of the huge shipping complexes but Zygon is there to stop them. Dagg and Orin battle their way out of his clutches, in the melee adding to their ranks a "fembot" named Silica. Seeing Orin wielding the magic hilt, Zygon realizes that "the Ka Khan has returned." Dagg reprograms Silica so that she becomes devoted to him, then the three head for Toga Togo, a thieves' colony where Dagg thinks he may have an easier time selling his goods.

Dagg finally manages to sell his crystals, but the *Starchaser* is shot out of the sky by one of Zygon's patrols. Orin is thrown from the wreck and found unconscious by Aviana, the daughter of the supreme governor of the Vortigon system. She takes him to the family palace where she takes care of him until he's better. Learning that Orin is not just a smuggler, and seeing the odd behavior of the sword

hilt, Aviana remembers and tells Orin of an old legend. Twelve hundred years ago, a fellow wielded that same sword against some evil assault on mankind. Six hundred years later, another person did so again, that time against Nexus, an intelligent robot who was trying to conquer mankind.

As more captures and escapes occur, they learn that Zygon is Nexus. Worse than that, Zygon has assembled a huge fleet of robot piloted warships around Vortigon and he is ready to make the final attack. In a huge battle, Dagg, Orin, Aviana and Silica destroy Zygon's fleet. In a final showdown in the caverns, Orin kills Zygon, slicing the evil robot in half with a sword he conjures up from his mind alone. Orin is now able to lead his people out of the caverns to the surface and freedom. The wizard reappears, stating that since Orin is now ready, he may leave his material form. Orin, however, chooses to stay with Aviana whom he has fallen in love with.

The Arthurian influences on this film are obvious. A young charismatic warrior, wielding a magic sword from a stone leading his people to freedom with the advice and assistance of a wizard. Even more obvious though is how much this movie borrowed from George Lucas's *Star Wars* films (see entries for *Star Wars*).

The comparisons are almost precise: Orin is Luke Skywalker, Dagg is Han Solo, Aviana is Princess Leia, the *Starchaser* is the *Millennium Falcon*, Arthur's comical meanderings resemble C3PO, Zygon is Darth Vader/Evil Emperor, the ghostly wizard is Obi Wan Kanobe, and it goes on. Orin's ability finally, to conjure up a sword is just like Luke's advancement in mastering the Force. The robot guards are too much like Vader's troopers to ignore the similarity, as are other mechanical weapons, including some which are almost identical to the "Imperial Walkers" from *Star Wars*.

One scene in *Starchaser* reverses this comparison, however. Just as Orin sliced Zygon in half, so is Darth Maul's torso separated from his legs in *Star Wars, Episode 1, the Phantom*

Menace. Additionally, both evil characters' bodies fall into a seemingly bottomless abyss of one sort or another. One wonders if Lucas may have been aware of *Starchaser* and its near replication of his *Star Wars* story and was returning the favor with this one borrowing.

Sticks in Stones see Field Trip: "Sticks in Stones"

Stonehenge (1997) see Legends of the Isles: "Stonehenge"

Stonehenge: If Only Stones Could Speak see Stonehenge: The Human Factor with Sue Jay

Stonehenge: The Human Factor with Sue Jay (1984)

Alternate title: *Stonehenge — If Only the Stones Could Speak*; 28 minutes; Color; Documentary; Copyright 1984, Television South; Copyright 1987/1988, Films for the Humanities and Sciences, Inc.; Films for the Humanities and Sciences #ASL1361

CREDITS: Narrator — Sue Jay; Graphics — Alan Scragg; Production Assistant — Pauline Taplin; Research — David Wallace; Film Research — Steve Bergson; Film Editor — Philip Witcher; Film Dubbing — Tony Cunningham; Film Cameramen — Stan Brehant, John Jackson, John Brennan; Film Sound — Maurice Hillier, John Bird; Director — Bill Thomson; Editor — Peter Williams

SYNOPSIS: An entertaining but remarkably superficial tape for a Films for the Humanities item. This video concentrates on the slightly more eccentric interpretations of the meaning of Stonehenge. Interesting views are presented of and by the festival types, who gather there to celebrate the summer solstice, including Druids and lay line believers. One fellow who calls himself John Pendragon expounds briefly on his conviction that Stonehenge is indeed the Round Table of Arthurian legend.

To be fair, archaeologist R. J. C. Atkinson is interviewed, giving his more rational opinions of the monument. Julian Richards, director of the Stonehenge Environs Project, speaks about the people who might have built it. Heather Cooper, president of the British Astronomical Society, does a fun job of interpreting nearby Salisbury Cathedral as if she were a researcher from the distant future. Her conclusions are that it was an enormous solar clock and seasonal calculator.

Storybook (1995)

89 minutes; Color; Live Action with Animation; Copyright 1995, Republic Entertainment, Inc.; A Unit of Spelling Entertainment Group, Inc.; A Lorenzo Doumani Film

CAST: William McNamara (Prince Arthur); Swoosie Kurtz (Queen Evilia); Robert Costanzo (Panzius); James Doohan (Uncle Monty); Brenda Epperson-Doumani (Brandon's Mother); Richard Moll (Woody); Gary Morgan (Pouch); Jack Scalia (Brandon's Father); Sean Fitzgerald (Brandon); Milton Berle (Illuzor); Vinny Argiro (Air Force Captain); Kathrin Lautner (Queen Benevolence); Billy Stamp (Young Arthur); Heather Olson (Young Katarina); Zachary Benjamin (Feral Leader); Erin Fitzgerald (Girl in Attic); Simon (Leo the Dog)

WITH THE VOICE TALENTS OF: Ed Begley, Jr. (Pouch); Lorenzo Doumani (Hiss); Robert Easton (Hoot)

CREDITS: Music by — Harry Manfredini; Costume Designer — Gayle Susan Baizer; Editor — Lawrence J. Gleason; Production Designer — Allen H. Jones; Director of Photography — Hanania Baer; Executive Producer — Edward Doumani; Written by — S san Bowen, Lorenzo Doumani; Produced and Directed by — Lorenzo Doumani; Co-Producers — Scott McAboy, George Shamieh; Associate Producers — Jon Carrasco, Rob Fitzgerald, Mary Ellen Fitzgerald; Visual Effects Supervisor — Frank H. Isaacs; Creature Puppets by — Makeup and Effects Laboratories, Inc., Allan A. Pone, Douglas J. White, John R. Fifer; Puppeteers — Guy Himber, Fred Folger, Jake Garber, Donald Coleman; Stunts — Milton Canady, Scott Leva, Kevin Grevioux, Joanna Shelmidine, Brennan Dyson, Oscar Dillon, Bufort McClerkins; 1st Assistant Director — Scott McAboy; 2nd Assistant Directors — Tommy Sullins, Cassandra Heredia, Gary Arian; Unit Production Manager — Scott Hohnbaum; Production Coordinator — Amy Sydorick; Casting Director — Adriana Michel, A.C.S.; Casting Associate — Amber Garcia; Set Director — Gil

Alan; Set Dresser — Mariko Braswell; Wardrobe Supervisor — Lisa Dyehouse; Wardrobe Assistant — Claudia Portillo; Costume Construction — Silvia DeRey; Makeup Artist — Kelcey Fry; Hairstylist/Wig Design — Debra Denson, Carrie McDonagh; 1st Assistant Camera — Chuck Baker; 2nd Assistant Camera — Dawn Laurel; Loader — Darcy Bellemore; Steadicam Operators — Rick Davidson, Steve Adelson; Chief Lighting Technician — Russell Caldwell; Best Boy Electric — Rick Summers; 1st Electrician — David Casey; 2nd Electrician — Domenic Sfreddo; Electricians — Henry Ritter, Dino Hortofilis, John Massarp, Antonio Olivas, Ernest Vazquez, Donald Anderson, Tony Gregorio, Lisa Bock, Steve Rollins, Thaddeus G. Hall, Alexander Crow; Key Grip — Scott Jansen; Best Boys — Mike McGary, John Overacker; Dolly Grip — Charles Crivier; Grips — James Sweeny, Merle Bertrand, Shona Peters, James O'Malley, Matt Jacobson, Greg Maselli, Brian Byran, Logan Leabo; Leo Provided by — Critters of the Cinema; Leo's Trainer — Jean Rose; Dobermans by — Jackie Martin; Studio Teacher — Virgil Fornas; Script Supervisor — Melisa Sanchez; Production Sound Mixer — David Waelder; Boom Operators — Walter Gunnar, Larry Kaufman; Stunt Coordinator — Red Horton; Special Effects Coordinator — Richard Cole; Special Effects Assistants — Wes Mattox, Stephen Haller,Stephen Delollis, Brian Allen, Don Power; Set Paramedic — Roy Irwin; Construction Coordinator — Chris Blocker; Art Directors — Kurt DeWitt, Chris A. Miller; Lead Carpenter — Randy Fitzgerald; Leadman — Marty McCoy; Set Dressing Assistants — Lynn Jackman, Armandina Lozano; Shopper — Carla Weber; Carpenters — John Davis, Robert Hart, Kevin Rodgers, Ron Husband, Peter Seibold, Brian Marn, Rick Sciacca, Donald Le Houx, Gary Villa, Dustin Weber, Ken Lucas, Zoltan Hargitay, Douglas Shaw, Anthony Maccaria, Wayne Springfield, Chris Pittas, David Kieran, Cordell Webb, Joseph Zaouk, Tim Rex, Tom Fitzgerald, Jon Jacobsen, Eduardo Esparza, Mark Simpson, Valantine Torres, Guy Herman, Thomas Salvitti, John Mastropaolo, Angus Hoover, Scott MacLachlan, Sean Healey; Scenic Artists — Jeff Leahy, Fanee Avon, Randy Burt, Michael Parent, Kathy Cook, Mark Evans, Heidi Luest, David Lopez; Painters — Randy Morgan, Phil Barnes, Allan Aguirre, Fasan Franqois, Darcy Kaye, Daniel Lucas, Norman Adams, Eva Gnaedinger, Jeremiah Redclay, Ryan Schossow; Swing/Striking Crew — Bill Arbogast, Timothy Ross, George Bates, Miguel Vidal, Leslie Young; Transportation Coordinator — Angelo Loffredo; Drivers — Fred Sanchez, Henry Ritter, Steve Butler, Javier Valasques, Don Verela,

Mike Gregorio, Robert Curcuru, Steve Underwood, Humberto Morales; Travel Coordinator — Michele Pepin; Office Coordinators — Rela Martine, Amir Khoury; Production Accountants — Shaker Khoury, Michael Collins, John Kelly; Still Photographer — Mark Sanderson; Catering — CWC Catering, Wayne Arnold; Extras Casting — David O'Day, Central Casting, Cenex West; Location Extras Casting — Phyllis Decker, Pat Jackson; Property Masters — Doug Randall, Patrick Douglas; Assistant Props — Daniel Fried, Doug Patsick; Assistant to the Director — Jennifer Bennett; Production Assistants — John Bruno, Larry Justice, Marco Diaz, James Hopper, Kathryn Kolstad, Brett Boydstun, Tory Haslinger, Gary Varela, Clayton Grubb, Ronald Shaw, Jr., David Smith, Joseph Zenas, Sibyl O'Malley; 2nd Unit: Director — Edward Doumani; Director of Photography — Moshe Levine; 1st Assistant Camera — Terry "Jamie" Barber; 2nd Assistant Camera — Greg Ferguson, Lance Fisher; Chief Lighting Technicians — Ken Blakey, David Bouza; Best Boy Electric — Arthur Whitehead; Post Production Coordinator — Geraint Bell; 1st Assistant Editors — Pamela Haskin, Howard Flaire; Assistant Editor — Scott Riddle; Post Production Assistant — Stuart Heiman; Digital Sound and Re-recording by — EFX Systems; Sound Effects Supervision — Russell Brower; Sound Design and Editing — Robert Hargreaves; Dialogue Editors — Jim Brookshire, M.P.S.E., Mark Keatts, Drew Padget; ADR Editors — Cathie Speakman, Robert Guastini, Terri Fikalko, Marc Fishman; ADR Engineers — Jeff Vaughn, C.A.S., Erin Hoien; Foley Artists — Greg Barbanell, Vince Nicastro; Foley Mixer — Brian Greer; Foley Assistant — Gary Sula-Goff; Re-recording Mixers — Ken Teaney, C.A.S., William Freesh; Re-recording Assistants — Mark Fishman, Tony Soreno; Sound Services Manager — Paul Rodriguez; Digital Visual Effects — Vision Art; Animators — Bethany Berndt-Shackelford, Ted Fay, Barry Safley, Doreen Haver, Pete Shinners, Rob Bredow, Carl Hooper, Rich Cook, Rodney J. McFall; Digital Tape to Film Transfer — Vision Art; Transfer Operators — Sonya Henderson, Celine Jackson; Roto Animation — Tony Alderson, Frank H. Isaacs; Titles and Opticals — Title House; Negative Cutter — Chris Webber; Color Timer — Bill Scott; Orchestrations — Bobby Muzingo, John Dickson, Arlon Ober; Music Engineer — Jerry Lambert; Music Mixed at — Almaviva Studios; "If You Believe": Music by — Harry Manfredini; Lyrics by — Harry Manfredini, Lorenzo Doumani; Performed by — Brenda Doumani; The producers wish to thank the following: TAG RAG, Surf Fetish,

Moretz Mills, Inc., Vans, City of Paso Robles, California; Processing by — Alpha Cine; Coming Soon: *Storybook: The Next Chapter*

SYNOPSIS: Here is a complete reworking of the story of King Arthur with almost no connection to any originals. The only references to familiar elements are King Arthur himself and a magical sword. The sword, however, is not named in this film.

In the opening scene, a little girl finds a magnificently bound storybook in an attic. When she opens it, strange mists rise. Fascinated, she walks into them and disappears.

Twenty years later a mother and her young son, Brandon, have packed up and moved away from an air force base. They take over a spooky-looking house that apparently the family is no longer using. Uncle Monty is there to greet them when they arrive. We learn that Brandon's father is missing after a plane crash. Monty says the house is enchanted, not haunted.

Brandon finds the same storybook in the attic and steps into another world. Trouble starts right away. Queen Evilia sends rats after the boy. His dog falls into a trap but a lumberjack named Woody saves them.

In the meantime, King Lovall has been killed in a hunting accident. The dying Queen Benevolence left the magic sword to her son, Arthur, but Arthur has been captured by Evilia. The little girl who disappeared 20 years ago is Katarina, Brandon's aunt. Katarina has managed to hide the sword to keep it out of evil hands.

While Arthur is being tortured (one day it's the "tickle-poke" torture), Brandon, Woody and the dog seek the Cave of Faith to get more information on how to recover the sword. The cave is guarded by Pouch, a boxing kangaroo who loses a bout with his own shadow. In the cave they meet Illuzor who asks three questions of Brandon. The boy answers them. The adventurous trio gets a special stone for the storybook and disappears.

They find the sword in a glowing stone and only Brandon is able to pull it out. Head-ing for Evilia's castle to free Arthur, the gang is joined by a group of other kids. They are all children who came here the same way Katarina and Brandon did but failed to retrieve either the stone for the book or the sword.

Evilia manages to capture and imprison everyone, but the dog and Hoot the owl help them escape. Arthur finally gets the sword and all is well. Arthur sends Brandon home on Christmas Eve and Brandon's father comes home safe and sound.

Stuck on You (1984)

85 minutes; Color; Comedy/Live Action; Copyright 1984, Troma Films; Troma Team Video #1078

CAST: Irwin Corey (Judge Gabriel); Virginia Penta (Carol Griffiths); Mark Mikulski (Bill Andrews); Albert Pia (Artle Poulet); Norma Pratt (Bill's Mother); Daniel Harris (Napoleon); Denise Silbert (Cavewoman); Eddie Brill (Caveman); June Martin (Eve); John Bigham (Adam); Robin Burroughs (Isabella); Carl Sturmer (Columbus); Julie Newdow (Pocahontas); Patricia Tallman (Queen Guenevere); Mr. Kent (King Arthur); Barbie Kielian (Josephine); Louis Homyak (Lance Griffiths); Ben Kellman (Indian Chief); William E. Kirksey (Narrator); Richard Rothenberg ("Nice Tits" Man); Marla Kassoff (Mona Lisa); Ed Fenton (Leonardo Da Vinci); Sherry Hoard (Angie); Charles Stanley (Used Kleenex Salesman); Don Costello (Man with Figleaf); Joe Perce (Attila); Wendy Adams (Amy); Connie Repplier (Receptionist); Charles Kaufman (Dead Body in Coffin); Fred Salador (Carol's Boss); Joe Davies (Street Bum); Karen Massettier (Mermaid); Bob Bonds (Priest); Agim Coma (Bailiff); Ed Wolfe (Bailiff); Susan Kaufman (Egg Yolk); Ellen Christiansen (Stenographer); Betty Pia (Woman in Pool); Mary Dunne (Woman in Pool); Rick Angelostro (Peeing in Pool Man); Steve Shubert (Max); Richard Duggen (Pete); Kire Godal (Cavewoman); George Kamisky (Horny Caveman); Regan Kennedy (Gay Caveman); Dick Warren (Gay Caveman); Al Kulick (Panda); Dale Furnie (Herring Salesman); Neal Fury (Columbus's Crew); Mark Damon (Columbus's Crew); Jerry Turner (Columbus's Crew); Frank (Tow Truck Operator); Ed Preston-Guess (Law Clerk with Ladder); Adam DiPetto (Law Clerk with Ladder); David Carpenter (Law Clerk with Briefs); Dr. Freedman (Law Clerk with Briefs); Brendon (Small Claims Boy); Mary Ellen David

Publicity still from 1984's *Stuck on You* (courtesy Troma, Inc.).

drew Krowetz (Judge Dork); Bill Klaber (Rabbi/Band Member); Peter Nichols (Rabbi/Band Member); Michael O'Brien (Rabbi/Band Member); Teri Smith (Rabbi/Band Member); Norman Sukkar (Rabbi/Band Member); David Allen (Rabbi/Band Member); George Betilas (Rabbi/Band Member); John Paratore (Voice of God); Special Guest Appearances by: Gary Moscowitz, Ken Von Kohorn, Mel Sachs, William Horne, Don Costello, Jody Eisemann

CREDITS: Produced by — Lloyd Kaufman, Michael Herz; Directed by — Michael Herz, Samuel Weil; Executive Producers — William E. Kirksey, Spencer A. Tandy, Joseph L. Butt, The Maverick Group, Inc.; Supervising Editor — Ralph Rosenblum; Editors — Darren Kloomok, Richard Haines; Choreography — Jacques D'Amboise; Written by — Stuart Strutin, Warren Leight, Don Perman, Darren Kloomok, Melanie Minz, Anthony Gittleson, Duffy Ceaser Magesis, Michael Herz, Lloyd Kaufman; Additional Material Written by — Jeff Delman; Director of Photography — Lloyd Kaufman; Art Director — Barry Shapiro; Associate Producer — Stuart Strutin; Costume Designers — Rosa Alfaro, Walter Steihl; Production Executive — Eileen Nad Castaldi; Location Executive — Nelson Vaughn; Post Production Coordinator — Ellen Christiansen; Production Manager/1st Assistant Director — Kate Eisemann; Production Manager/1st Assistant Director — Susan Dember; 1st Assistant Camera; 2nd Unit Director of Photography — Jim Lebovitz; Director of Lighting — Paul Gibson; Location Manager — Scott MacQueen; 2nd Assistant Director/Casting Director — Claudia Gutworth; 2nd Assistant Director — Lynne Christiansen; Sound Recordist — Richard Feist; Administrative Executives — Maris Herz, Pat Swinney; 1st Assistant Editor/Unit Manager — Michael Kewley; Assistant Editors — John Michaels, Jeanne Marcous; Assistant Art Director — Ruth Siekevitz; Transportation Captain — Roy Pontecorvo; Casting Services — Becky Arntzen; Grip — Bob Mackey, Tom Pokorney; Special Effects — Leslie Larrain, Dale Ward; Makeup Apprentice — Angie Reyes; Carpenter — Walter Taylor; Chicken Wardrobe — Bar-

(Barbarian Woman on Tree); Marshall Davies (Poulet Executive); Freanne Snyder (Rental Agent); Dale Furnie (Head Mishigoth); Ric Randig (Three Stooges/Moe); Jim Heinman (Three Stooges/Larry); Wayne Rubin (Three Stooges/Curly); Tina Stahl (Girl near Chicken); Candy Waters (Big Girl at Pool); Edith Blume (Cavewoman); Scott MacQueen (Vito); Charlie Kurnitz (Joe); Stephen Ommerle (Arthur's Squire); Mr. Dickie (Guenevere's Squire); Mr. Gary (Man Who Yells for Blood); Mr. Vincent (Joust Victim); Ray Pontecorvo (Cab Driver); Sue Dember (Woman with Carriage); Bob Mackey (Bruce); Barry Shapiro (Bruce's Girlfriend); Karen Vaccaro (Mrs. Schlemmer); Roma Mattia (Attila's Sister); Ernestine Mercer (Attila's Mother); David Aarons (Attila's Father); Kayta Coleman (Attila's Teacher); Barbara Defonzo (Clown); Judith Baertseh (Clown); Mark Wolz (Clown); Sarah Richardson (Clown); Peggy Pelletier (Clown); Barry Kloss (Clown); Tom Delahunty (Myron Lunch); Chris Liano (Lem); Sue Ellen Viscuso (Stella); Anbara Johnson; Poultry Consultant—Roger W. Kirby; Creative Consultants—Ira Kanarick, Milton Zieberg, Stanley L. Kaufman; Creative Doctor—Dr. Edwin W. Wolf; Troma Historian—Ruth Kaufman; Color by—Gaffanti Film Labs; Optical Effects by—Videart; Title Design and Animation by—John Paratore; Sound Services by—Magno Sound; Mixer—Aaron Nathanson; Production Services by—Troma, Inc.; Special Thanks to—The New York City Mayor's Office of Motion Pictures and Television, The New Jersey Film Commission, Jibb Ellis, Lee Hessel, Prospect Hospital, Bronx; Production Apprentices: Susan Alpert, Michael Arillo, Chris Burke, Martha Cinader, Whitnee M. Cobb, David Cohen, Jerry Deli, John Garcia, Lee Gordon, Adam Greissman, Alison Hoffman, Robin Katz, Philip Kay, Joshua Koerner, Mark Krasselt, Charlie Kulis, Charlie Kurnitz, Scott MacDonald, Helene Orenstein, Gladys Pizarro, Steve Palatnick, Gary Rosenblatt, Scott Salem, Traci Sampson, Scott Sniffen, Debbie Tilzer, Doug Zimmerman; "Love Will Keep Us Together": Words and Music by—Neal Sedaka, Howard Greenfield; Produced by—Buddy Pollack; Performed by—Fair Witness; "Since You've Been Gone": Lyrics and Music by—Michael Meryfine, Chris Murphy, Steve Sarabande; "The Heat Is On": Lyrics and Music by—Steve Sarabande, Randy Klein; "Lady Love": Lyrics and Music by—Melissa Bell; "The Paradise Cafe": Performed by—Alan Cove; Written and Produced by—Alan Cove, Jim Morgan; "Ghetto Rap," "Sanitation Man," "Disease": Written, Recorded and Performed by—Junk Rock; "Honey Don't Stop": Lyrics and Music by—Steve Sarabande; "Just Like You": by—Gabriel Seabrook; Produced by—John Manchester; Sung by—Gabriel Seabrook; "Tell Me I'm Right": Composed and Performed by—Ned Libea, Stuart Glasses; Produced by—Ned Libea; "Free with Me": by—John Manchester, Jamie Barnett; Sung by—Jamie Barnett; Produced by—John Manchester; Engineered by—C. Martinez; "Dreaming": Composed, performed and produced on a Fairlight CMI Computer Musical Instrument by—Ned Libea; "Stooges," "Twilight," "Lonely Horn": Composed and performed for MSP on a Fairlight CMI by—Ned Libea)

SYNOPSIS: The Troma Film company is best known for its campy, sophomoric productions of horror and comedy movies. *The Toxic Avenger* is one of their creations. *Ferocious Female Freedom Fighters* is another of their titles. *Stuck on You*, a 1984 Troma film, includes a scene involving King Arthur and Guenevere.

Set in the present, *Stuck on You* tells the story of Bill and Carol, a young couple who have lived together for three years. Their relationship is on the rocks and Carol is suing Bill for palimony. The judge, who turns out to be their guardian angel, takes them to his chambers and shows them that couples through the ages have had similar problems.

There is a caveman-cavewoman scene, another of Adam and Eve meeting at a singles bar, then one of Columbus sailing with Queen Isabella in a Ford Pinto. The Dark Ages is represented by barbarians while the Renaissance offering is King Arthur.

In the Arthurian segment, Guenevere and Arthur are so furious with each other that they are actually engaged in combat. Wielding swords and maces, they don't harm each other but manage to kill several pages on the sidelines.

After a dream-sequence trial in which they are judged by all the characters from history whom they've seen, the young couple solve their problems. The guardian angel/judge gets his wings.

Sunbeam see *Raggio di Sole*

Super Friends
Not viewed; Color; Cartoons; Copyrights—various

SYNOPSIS: Over the years (from approximately 1966 through the present) Superman and other superheroes teaming up with him have appeared in a number of cartoons involving Arthurian themes. Some of the titles are *The Demon Within* (1998, Warner Bros.), *The Ghost* (1977, Hanna-Barbera), *Merlin's Magic Marbles* (1966, Filmation), *Space Knights of Camelon* (1979, Hanna-Barbera) and *The Time Trap* (1978, Hanna-Barbera).

Swan Knight see *World Famous Fairy Tales: "Swan Knight"*

The Sword in the Stone (1963)

79 minutes; Color; Cartoon; Copyright 1963, Walt Disney Productions; Buena Vista Home Video; Walt Disney Home Video #229

WITH THE TALENTS OF: Sebastian Cabot (Sir Ector); Ricki Sorensen (Wart); Ginny Tyler (Little Girl Squirrel); Norman Alden (Kay); Karl Swenson (Merlin); Junius Mathews (Archimedes); Martha Wentworth (Madame Mim, Granny Squirrel); Alan Napier (Sir Pellinore); Richard Reitherman

CREDITS: Directing Animators—Frank Thomas, Milt Kahl, Ollie Johnston, John Lounsberry

Character Animation—Hal King, Eric Cleworth, Cliff Nordberg, Dick Lucas, Eric Larson, John Sibley, Hal Ambro; Effects Animation—Don MacManus, Jack Boyd, Jack Buckley; Character Design—Milt Kahl, Bill Peet; Layout—Don Griffith, Vance Gerry, Dale Bernhart, Basil Davidovich, Sylvia Cobb, Homer Jonas; Background—Walt Peregoy, Bill Layne, Al Dempster, Anthony Rizzo, Ralph Hulett, Fil Mottola; Production Supervisor—Ken Peterson; Sound Supervisor—Robert O. Cook; Film Editor—Donald Halliday; Music Editor—Evelyn Kennedy; Music—George Bruns; Orchestration—Franklyn Marks; Songs—Richard M. and Robert B. Sherman; Art Direction—Ken Anderson; Director—Wolfgang Reitherman

SYNOPSIS: This classic Disney cartoon film is based on White's *The Sword in the Stone.* As usual with children's films, most of White's social and political commentary has been excised and only the bare bones of his story remain.

The opening song states that the king is dead and that the people prayed for a miracle. One comes along in the form of a sword in a stone, but no one is able to pull it out to be declared the new king.

Next we find Merlin anticipating the arrival of Wart, the young Arthur. Wart is out hunting with Kay and drops in on Merlin. They have tea and Merlin decides that it's time to pack up and bring Wart to the castle to begin Wart's training. Pellinore arrives with the news that there is to be a tournament on New Year's Day and the winner will become the king.

As Wart's first lesson he and Merlin become fish to learn about using one's intellect and about being weak versus strong. Merlin's magic next turns Wart into a squirrel for a lesson on love.

Finally Wart becomes a bird and inadvertently runs into the wicked Madame Mim, a sorceress adversary of Merlin's. Merlin comes to the rescue and engages in a duel of magic with Mim. He ultimately wins by turning into a germ and making her sick.

After all the educating he's done, Merlin becomes angry that Wart still wants to be Kay's page. In a rage the old wizard rockets off to Bermuda.

While Merlin is gone the tournament takes place. Kay loses his sword and Wart retrieves the one from the stone for him. Of course he becomes King Arthur but he's depressed because he feels he can't really rule yet. Merlin returns from the twentieth century wearing Bermuda shorts, sunglasses and sneakers, just in time to help the boy out.

The Sword in the Stone (1973)

Not viewed; 2 Filmstrips; Part 1: 108 frames; Part 2: 110 frames; Color; 35mm, with teacher's guide; Sound version also available; Copyright 1973, Walt Disney Productions; Released by Walt Disney Educational Materials Company; From the book by T. H. White; Library of Congress Call #PZ7; Library of Congress Catalogue #73733401/F/r88; Dewey Decimal #398.2

SYNOPSIS: For elementary grades, these filmstrips describe Merlin's transformation of Arthur into various animals and Arthur's subsequent acquisition of the throne.

The Sword of Lancelot (1963)

115 minutes; Color; Live Action; Copyright 1963, Emblem Productions, Ltd.; Copyright 1995, 1996, MCA Home Video, Inc.; MCA/Universal Home Video #80077

CAST: Cornel Wilde (Lancelot); Jean Wallace (Gwenevere); Brian Aherne; George Baker; Archie Duncan; Adrienne Cori; Michael Meacham; Iain Gregory; Mark Dignam; Reginald Beckwith; John Barry; Richard Thorp; Joseph Tomelty; Graham Stark; Geoffrey Dunn; Walter Goyell; Peter Prowse; Christopher Rhodes

THE MOST FABLED LOVE STORY IN ALL ROMANTIC HISTORY!!!

The forbidden love that hurled army against army...the stolen love that pitted heroic Lancelot against King Arthur and the Knights of the Round Table...the secret love that set the world of Camelot aflame!

LANCELOT AND GUINEVERE

TECHNICOLOR®
PANAVISION®

CORNEL WILDE · JEAN WALLACE · BRIAN AHERNE

Ad mat for *Lancelot and Guinevere* (aka *The Sword of Lancelot*).

CREDITS: Music Composed and Conducted by — Ron Goodwin; Director of Photography — Harry Waxman; Additional Camera Work — Robert Thomson; Title Background Photographs by — Karsh; Editor — Frederick Wilson; Production Manager — David W. Orton; Art Director — Maurice Carter; Camera Operator — Robert Thomson; Assistant Director — Rene Dupont; Costume Designer — Terrence Morgan; Continuity — Connie Willis; Assistant Art Director — Jack Maysted; Sound Recordist — William Daniels; Sound Editors — Don Sharpe, Kevin Connor; Makeup Artist — George Blackler; Hairdresser — Buddy Chrystal; Screenplay by — Richard Schayer, Jefferson Pascal; Associate Producer — George Pitcher; Produced by — Cornel Wilde, Bernard Luber; Directed by — Cornel Wilde

SYNOPSIS: A classic Hollywood epic with medieval castles and costumes. Much less stilted and stiff than Robert Taylor's *Knights of the Round Table,* for instance, but full of its own oddities.

A message is delivered from Leodegrance to an aging King Arthur. Leodegrance rejects Arthur's proposal of marriage to Leodegrance's daughter, Gwenevere, until a trial by combat determines Arthur's true claim to kingship. To the joust Arthur sends his champion, Sir Lancelot; Leodegrance sends Sir Dorjack.

Interestingly there is no plate armor in the jousting — only chainmail. The fight is short but bloody. In a scene unusual for the era in which it was produced, Lancelot actually cleaves Dorjack's helmet and skull.

That established, Lancelot is sent to bring Gwenevere to Camelot. They are ambushed on the trail back, fall in love and the seeds of doom are planted.

There follows another incredible scene with a very human perspective. The wedding of Arthur and Gwenevere is of course a formal, Latin Mass affair. Lancelot is chosen to escort Gwenevere down the aisle. On the way to the altar Gwenevere pleads with Lancelot to stop the wedding.

Soon after the marriage Gwenevere and Lancelot meet in her private garden and the romance is on. It is soon interrupted though by an attack on Arthur's realm. Ulfus and Brandegors are making a play for power. Lancelot takes half of the ready force to slow their advance while Arthur gathers the allies for a full counterattack.

Lancelot manages to bottle up the barbarians in an undefendable position and while Ulfus and Brandegors escape, the enemy force is destroyed. Unfortunately a fellow named Tors, who was wearing a spare tabard of Lancelot's, was killed in the battle. When his body is returned to Camelot Gwenevere mistakes it for her lover's. When the look on her face is seen by others, the rumors about their affair begin to fly.

The situation becomes so intolerable that Sir Lamorak talks Lancelot into leaving Camelot until things cool off. He suggests going to France, where the Huns are attacking. That night Lancelot and Gwenevere consummate their love and then Lancelot is ambushed by Mordred and his men. Lamorak and Lancelot fight their way out. In the melee

Lancelot unwittingly kills the unarmed Gareth, Gawain's brother.

Mordred captures Gwenevere and Arthur is forced to condemn her to death. At this point Merlin mentions that he had urged Arthur not to marry the girl. Lancelot rides in to save her and carries her off to Joyous Gard.

Arthur chases him and lays siege to the castle. Gwenevere urges Lancelot to accept the personal challenges to combat of Arthur and Gawain. Lancelot finally fights and beats Gawain but refuses to kill his old friend. He instead sends a message to Arthur that he'll give himself up if Arthur will free everyone else. Arthur banishes Lancelot to France and Gwenevere to a convent at Glastonbury.

Years later Gawain finds Lancelot in Brittany. He's come to forgive him and to tell him that Arthur and Merlin are dead. He also tells Lancelot that Mordred has destroyed the nunnery at Glastonbury but that Gwenevere escaped to Wales. Lancelot rides for vengeance and in a huge battle kills Mordred. It's too late to save the relationship with Gwenevere, however — she's become a novice in the order.

The opening of this film seems a bit silly but as the story moves on an element of reality creeps in that many Arthurian films don't achieve. Lancelot and Gwenevere become sympathetic characters and their agony is felt more than in most films, particularly by the end of the movie. Poor Arthur never seems as real as the two younger lovers.

The biggest disparities between *The Sword of Lancelot* and most other versions are, first of all, Mordred surviving Arthur and then Lancelot killing Mordred. Within the film it makes sense, but the jump that is made to Arthur's relatively unexplained and unmemorialized death is a bit fractured.

Sword of the Valiant (1983)

Subtitle: The Legend of Sir Gawain and the Green Knight; 102 minutes; Color; Live Action; Copyright 1983, London Cannon Films, Ltd.; Copyright 1984, London, The Cannon Group, Inc.; MGM/UA Home Video #M700593; A Golan-Globus Production; A Stephen Weeks Film

CAST (in order of appearance): Thomas Heathcote (Armorer); Miles O'Keeffe (Sir Gawain); Leigh Lawson (Humphrey); Trevor Howard (The King); Sean Connery (The Green Knight); Emma Sutton (Morgan Le Fay); Douglas Wilmer (The Black Knight); Cyrielle Claire (Linet); Lila Kedrova (Lady of Lyonesse); John Seret (Priest); Brian Coburn (Friar Vosper); Mike Edwards (Tiny Man); David Rappaport (Sage); Ronald Lacy (Oswald); Peter Cushing (Seneschal); John Pierce-Jones (Sergeant); James Windsor (1st Recruit); Ric Morgan (2nd Recruit); Peter McKriel (3rd Recruit); Jerod Wells (1st Torturer); Harry Jones (2nd Torturer); John Rhys-Davies (Baron Fortinbras); John J. Carney (Messenger); Bruce Lidington (Sir Bertilak); Wilfred Brambel (Porter)

CREDITS: Screenplay by — Stephen Weeks, Howard C. Pen, Philip M. Breen; Production Designers — Maurice Fowler, Derek Nice; Editors — Richard Marden, Barry Peters; Photographed by — Freddie Young, QBE, Peter Hurst; Music by — Ron Geesin; Executive Producers — Philip M. Breen, Michael Kagan; Produced by — Menahem Golan, Yoram Globus; Directed by — Stephen Weeks; Action Sequences Director — Anthony Squire; 2nd Unit Director — Sture Rydman; Costume Designer — Shuna Harwood; Production Coordinator — Michael Hartman; Associate Producers — Sture Rydman, Basil Keys; Story Consultant — Roger Towne; Additional Dialogue — Rosemary Sutcliff, Theresa Burdon; Production Manager — Adam Kempton; Location Managers (France) — Claude Gresset, Juliette Toutain; Location Managers (Wales) — Ben Laycock; Unit Manager (France) — Basil Somner; Production Assistant — Jeanne Ferber; Production Runner — Patrick Rattray; 1st Assistant Directors — David Bracknell, Ken Tuohy, Richard Hoult; 2nd Assistant Directors — Zsuzsanna Mills, Michel Mercy, Andrew Warren (2nd Unit); 3rd Assistant Directors — Rod Lomax, Jerry Daily; Producer's Secretary — Felicity Newton; Director's Secretary — Joan McLoughlin; Production Secretaries — Frances Stephenson, Sally Pardo, Dominique LeFevre (France); 1st Unit Camera Operators — Roy Ford, Chic Anstiss; 2nd Unit Camera Operators — Trevor Coop, Kevin Pike; 1st Unit Camera Focus — Chris Pinnock, Mike Rutter; 2nd Unit Camera Focus — Ian Henderson, John Deaton; Peter Robinson; 1st Unit Clapper Loaders — David Watkins, Danny Shelmerdine; 2nd Unit Clapper Loader — Ken Groom; 1st Unit

Camera Grips — Chunky Huse, Tony Cridlin, Peter Hopkins; 2nd Unit Camera Grip — Dickie Lee; 1st Unit Continuity — Marilyn Clarke; 2nd Unit Continuity — Ceri Evans; Sound Recordists — George Stephenson, Malcolm Davies; Re-recording Mixer — Hugh Strain; Boom Operators — Colin Wood, Mike Turner; Sound Assistant — Denis Nisbett; Assistant Editors — Roy Birchley, Simon Manley; Sound Editors — Tony Message, Nick Stephenson, Ted Mason; Assistant Sound Editors — Robert Robinson, Richard Fettes; Makeup — Richard Mills, Ernie Gasser; Hairdressers — Mary Sturgiss, Norma Webb, Ramon Gow; Mr. Connery's Makeup/Hairdresser — Ilona Herman; Mr. O'Keeffe's Makeup/Hairdresser — Marcello Longhi; Miss Claire's Makeup — Regine Navarro; Wardrobe Masters — Don Mothersill, Jimmy Smith; Wardrobe Assistants — Alan Flyng, Judy Shrewsbury, Vanessa Mimms; Casting — Maude Spector; Assistant Casting — Ann Stanborough; Stills Photography — David Farrell; Production Accountants — Patrick Isherwood, Sandy Langdale; Location Cashier — Craig Barwick; Assistant Art Director — Michael Pickwoad; Set Dresser — Val Wolstenholme; Production Buyer — Brian Read; Draughtsperson — Julie Graysmark; Property Masters — Eddy Francis, Harry Newman; Dressing Propmen — Alf Smith, Eric Strange; Standby Propmen — Jack Towns, David Reilly, Dennis Simmonds, Robert Douglas, Johnny Chisholm, Bert Gadsden, Derek Creedon; Property Storeman — Ray Rose; Construction Manager — John Hedges; Stagehand — Tim Hayes; Carpenters — Denis Bovington, Gary Hedges, Les Butterfield; Printer — Danny Tuhey; Riggers — Bill Howe, John Fields, David Williams; Special Effects Supervisor — Nobby Clarke; Special Effects Technicians — Peter Davey, Geoffrey Smith, Philip Clark, John Workwell; Green Knight Head Effects — Aaron Sherman; Toad Created and Made by — Tim Rose; Special Effects Prosthetics — Daniel Parker; Visual Effects — Cliff Culley, Neil Culley; Armor Designed and Made by — Terry English; Armorers — Glyn English, Peter Corrigan; Stunt Coordinators — Peter Diamond, Tim Condren; Stuntmen — John Lees, Tim Walsh, Graeme Crowther, Brian Bowes, Dinny Powell, Gareth Milne; Horsemaster — Gerard Naprons; Electrician Gaffers — Roy Rodhouse, Tom Brown, Graham Miller; Best Boys — Reg Parsons, Ken Thoms; Electricians — David Tyler, James Smart, James Terry, Jack White, Brian Martin, Les Weighell, Russell Padwick; Generator Driver — Jack Coggins; Cameras and Anamorphic Lenses — J. Dunton Cameras, Ltd.; Lighting Equipment — Lee Electric Lighting, Ltd.; Grip Equipment — Grip House London, Ltd.; Transport. — D&D Film and Television, Location Facilities, Ltd.; Travel Agents — Lily-Value Travel Agency; Motor Homes — Location Facilities, Ltd.; Freight Forwarders — Southland Air Services, Ltd.; Costumes — Bermans and Nathans, London, National Theatre Company, London, Bristol Old Vic Company, Bristol, Aristide Boyer, Marseilles, Cornejo, Madrid; Cutting Rooms — New Central Film Service, London; Sound Re-recorded at Delta Sound Services, Ltd., Shepperton Studios; Music Score Created on — Fairlight Music Computer; Photographed on — Fujicolor from Fuji Photofilm (U.K.), Ltd.; Film Processing — Rank Film Laboratories, Denham, London; Titles — Ron Hickson for Tony Long Opticals, Ltd.; Optical Effects — Westbury Design and Optical, Ltd.; National Publicity Representation — Solters/Roskin/Friedman; The producers gratefully acknowledge the help given by: The Welsh Office for the use of Caerphilly Castle, Castell Coch, Cardiff Corporation for the use of Cardiff Castle, Caisse Nationale Des Monuments Historiques for the use of Pierrefonds Castle, Papal Palace, Avignon; Filmed entirely on location in Wales, France and England; Produced in Association with Stephen Weeks Company

SYNOPSIS: *Sword of the Valiant* is a remake of Weeks's 1973 film *Gawain and the Green Knight*. This more recent work boasts a bigger budget and a glitzier cast than the first.

The king (never identified in this movie as Arthur), stops a feast in boredom and disgust at his fat, lazy knights who haven't done anything lately. In the middle of his diatribe a mysterious Green Knight shows up, offering a "game" for the assemblage. Providing his own ax, he challenges anyone present to chop off his head with one blow but he reserves the right to return the blow.

When the challenge is met with an embarrassing silence, the king starts to accept the challenge. A squire named Gawain jumps into the breach, is knighted on the spot and performs the deed. The Green Knight's head then calls to its body, which responds, placing the head back on its shoulders.

First the Green Knight grants Gawain a year "to grow a beard" before having to face his own decapitation. Then he offers the boy salvation through a riddle, stating that if Gawain comes to understand all of it his life will be restored to him. In short, the riddle says: where life is emptiness there is gladness, where darkness there is fire, where golden there is sorrow, where lost there is wisdom. The Green Knight then rides out of the great hall, disappearing into a shimmering green light.

The king outfits Gawain with armor and assigns a squire named Humphrey. Gawain's first encounter on his adventure is with a unicorn. He chases the beast, trying to kill it, but the unicorn disappears. Next a tent appears, filled with wonderful food and drink. A damsel appears in the tent and she sends Gawain and Humphrey to Lyonesse and the Chapel of a Hundred Steps.

On the seashore hangs a huge horn. When Gawain blows it a rainbow appears, but the guardian of Lyonesse is also summoned. This Black Knight, with a Darth Vader metallic voice, fights with Gawain but is defeated. His dying request is that Gawain take him to Lyonesse.

On his arrival at Lyonesse the people try to kill Gawain. Linet enters the scene and gives him a ring of invisibility. She tells him that Lyonesse is lost in past and future dreams. Gawain and his benefactor try to escape but Linet is caught and the city disappears, leaving Gawain standing on a beach.

Morgan Le Fay turns out to be the culprit who sent Gawain to this place. The Green Knight turns her into a frog, freeing Gawain to wander some more. He next encounters a group of monks. The friar sends Gawain to the rock of wisdom where he meets a sage. The sage sends Gawain back into "the game" and Lyonesse. Gawain finds Linet frozen in time and covered by cobwebs. He places the ring on her finger, bringing her back to life.

Baron Fortinbras' son, Oswald, the Red Knight, abducts Linet. Gawain sneaks into their castle with a group of conscripts, is himself captured and put on a torture rack. Sir Bertilak arrives to try to get Fortinbras to stop his raids, Gawain and the friar battle their way out and a fire breaks out in Linet's chamber.

It seems that she's been killed and Gawain, wounded, wanders off by himself.

Eventually he comes to Bertilak's castle where he finds Linet safe and sound. He stays to heal, then leaves to face the Green Knight. Before his departure Linet gives Gawain a green scarf.

On his way Gawain runs into Oswald again, but this time he kills the Red Knight. Finally the Green Knight comes, takes Gawain to his abode and takes his agreed-upon stroke at Gawain's neck. Linet's scarf is cut but not Gawain. Gawain kills the Green Knight then watches as the creature's body magically dissolves back into the earth.

Linet returns to Lyonesse.

The Table Round see under ***Fables and Legends: English Folk Heroes***

Taiyo no oji: Horusu no Daib oken see ***Little Norse Prince Valiant***

Teen Knight (1998)

90 minutes; Color; Live Action; Copyright 1998, The Kushner-Locke Company; Copyright 1998, Canarom Productions, Inc., and Castel Films; Chesler Perlmutter Productions; Pulsepounders!; Full Moon Releasing Item #7006

CAST: Kristopher Lemche (Peter); Caterina Scorsone (Alison); Benjamin Plener (Ben); Paul Soles (Mr. Percy/Perceval); Kimberly Pullis (Claudia); Marc Robinson (Raykin); Claudiu Trandafir (Eurik); Dan Fintescu (Tommy); Eugen Cristea (Wiggins); Mihai Sandu Gruia (Phil); Mihai Verrintchi (Dungeon Master); Critian Nicolae (Gary); Juliana Ciugulea (Mom); Marius Galea (Hugo); Iona Anghel (Mrs. Sweeney); Steven Bunker (Jimmy); Dan Franculescu (Kyle); Dumitru Bogomaz (Knight); Corina Ifrim (Babe); Felix Totolici (Bus Driver); Livia Constantin (Natalie)

CREDITS: Casting—Marsha Chelseay, CDC; Costume Designer—Oana Paunescu; Composer—Trevor Morris; Production Designer—Cristian Niculescu; Editor—Mark Sanders; Director of Photographer—Gabriel Kosuth; Executive Producers—David M. Perlmutter, Lewis B. Chesler; Executive Producer—Vlad Paunescu; Executive Producers—Peter Locke, Dana Scanlan; Produced by — Cris Andrei; Written by — Antony Anderson; Director — Phil Comeau; Co-Producers — Gari Antal, Michael J. Mahoney; Production Manager — Stefan Angheluta; 1st Assistant Director — Cristian Mungiu; Script Supervisor — Cornelia Stefan; Assistant Script Supervisor — Corina Pana; Slate — Gabriella Gogoanta; Production Coordinator (Romania) — Alina David; Production Coordinator (Canada) — Brenda Torrance; Makeup — Dana Busoiu; Hairstylist — Letitia Stoenciu; Wardrobe Supervisor — Michaela David; Dressers — Hilda Canciu, Doina Raducut, Cristina Anton; Armors — Tiberiu Stanescu, Stefan Curelaru; Art Director — Viorel Ghenea; Property Master — Cristian Baluta; Props — Ghita Ion; Effects Props & Rigs — Ionel Popa; Props Studio — Mihai Alexandru; Construction Coordinator — Iona Corciova; Construction Supervisor — Szoli Szabo; Carpenters — Fratila Marin, Stan Constantin, Stelian Marin; Effects Supervisor — Lucian Iordache; Effects — Daniel Parvulescu; 1st Assistant Camera — Gigel Dumitrescu; Loader — Ilie Georgica; Key Grip — Sorin Urdea; Grips — Marcu Laurentiu, Cristi Epure; Gaffer — Colin Constantin; Electricians — Marius Bercu, Alexandru Nicolae, Marcu Ion, Radu Ion; Generator Operator — Bebe Surgiu; Location Sound — Tibi Borcoman; Boom — Dan Alexe, Nicolae Pertrianu; Video Assist — Radu Nicolae; Stills Photographer — Toni Cartu; Assistant Director Trainees — Eduard Reghintovschi, Silvia Iliuta; Casting Coordinator (Romania) — Calin Dordea; Extras Casting — Doru Bobesiu; Transportation Coordinator — Iona Danian; Cashier — Alfred Bauer; Production Accountants — Chris Elkins, Donald Palmer; Set Production Assistants — Adrian Conerti, Bogdan Constantinescu; Secretary — Cristina Mitea; Production Secretary — Oana Stanoevici; Translator — Ava Maria Radu; Post Production Supervisor — Lisa Kalushner; Post Production Coordinator — Brenda Torrance; Post Production — Eyes Post Group; Colorist — Sue Chambers; On-line Editor — Frank Biasi; Post Production Audio — Trackworks, Inc.; Supervising Sound Editor — Steve Munro; Dialogue Editor — David Drainie Taylor; ADR Editor — Tim Roberts; Effects Editor — Colin Baxter; Foley Artist — John F. Thompson; ADR/Foley Recordist — Steve Pollett; Trainee Assistant Editor — Timothy Mehlenbaacher; Re-Recording Mixers — Steve Munro, Tim Roberts; Visual Effects by — Sundog Films, Inc.; Visual Effects Supervisor — Wayne Trickett, Doug Campbell, Mario Ferreira, Kent Ing, Dave Bachelor, Steve Gordin, Cisco Ribas, May Leung, Greg Astles; Visual Effects by — Aris Studios, Iorigica Adriana, Sergin Negulici, Stefan Cios, Dana Palcu; Film Processing — The Lab in Toronto, Inc.; Insurance Provided by — B.F. Lorenzetti & Associates, Inc.; Production Financing Provided by — Equicap Financial Corporation; Financial Legal Services Provided by — Heenan Blaikie; Completion Bond — Film Finances; Special Thanks to — Robert Beattie, Elizabeth McGuinness, Harian Freedman, Annette Grot, Steve Ransohoff, The Weather Channel; Filmed on location in Romania at Castel Film Studio; A Canada-Romania Co-Production; Produced with the participation of Canada and with the participation of the Government of Ontario; The Onario Film and Television Tax Credit

SYNOPSIS: *Teen Knight* is another time travel film, this time involving teenagers at a Medieval Adventure castle. Though the main story is about an evil 14th Lord and his equally evil magician accomplice, the film skates around several Arthurian references.

The first scenes are of Prince Alfred having Lord Raykin and the magician Eurik put in chains and thrown into a cart. Raykin swears he'll get revenge and tear down King William's rule and take over the kingdom.

In jail, Raykin is furious with Eurik, calling him "pathetic, just like Perceval who trained you." Harassing Eurik into using his hypnotic powers on the jailer, the two escape and reacquire Eurik's magic gems. With them Eurik places a spell on the castle such that Raykin can summon the place forth whenever he is ready and take over the kingdom for one day in which to work his coup.

The scene switches to a group of armored men chasing one other fellow through some woods. The runner spots a sword in a stone and runs up to it. From a small pantry-like niche in a tree stump he removes a mug, then he moves a lever which is in the hilt of the sword. A carbonated beverage issues from a spigot on the sword and the man drinks. It's a television commercial for "Silver Streak Cola, the choice of champions." The narrator goes on to encourage viewers to enter the Medieval Mansion contest.

Teenager Peter has his heart set on winning and going on the trip. Later Peter helps an elderly neighbor named Mr. Percy move a large package up to his apartment. It is a painting of Prince Alfred's battle defending the very castle that the adventure is to take place in. Sharing a cola with the boy, Percy toasts, "To King Arthur and the end of my long quest for Rigu's masterpiece." Percy has the winning bottle cap, which he gives to Peter so that the boy can enjoy the Medieval weekend.

Percy appears later as Perceval, the wizard who helps Peter and the rest of the kids battle Raykin and Eurik when they show up. A dragon is involved in the story, as well as plenty of damsels in distress, but no further Arthurian elements are present in the story.

Excalibur as a soda fountain has to be a low point in Arthurian film.

Tekwar: Teklab (1994)

105 minutes; Color; Science Fiction/Live Action; Copyright 1994, Grosyenda Park LI Ltd. Partnership; Universal, an MCA Company; Atlantis Films Ltd.

CAST: Greg Evigan (Jake Cardigan); Eugene Clark (Sid Gomez); William Shatner (Walter H. Bascom); Michael York (Richard Stewart); Joel Bissonnette (Tristan/Mark Stewart); Laurie Holden (Rachel Tudor); Richard Curnock (Prince Albert); Maurice Dean Wint (Lieutenant Winger); Catherine Blythe (Centra); Liisa Repo-Martell (Galahad); Jody Racicot (Merlin); Donald Ewer (Cabbie); David Brown (Falconer); Keram Malicki-Sánchez (Mustapha); Eric Himmel (Guide); Jonathan Scarfe (Tekkid #1); Paul Brogren (Tekkid #2); Cynthia Eastman (Svetlana); Theo Brand (Uhudan); Shan Cauvery (Vishnu); Carlo Rota (Doorman); Leslie Yeo (Inspector Melville); Marion Gilsenan (Elizabeth)

CREDITS: From the Tek novels by William Shatner; Production Designer — Stephen Roloff; Director of Photography — Rodney Harters; Editor — Dave Goard; Music — David Michael Frank; Song Composed and Performed by — Warren Zevon; Supervising Producer — Seaton McLean; Producers — Jamie Paul Rock, Stephen Roloff; Screenplay — Chris Haddock; Screen Story — Westbrook Claridge; Director — Timothy Bond; Executive Producers — William Shatner, Peter Sussman; Supervising Executive for the Action Pack — Alex Beaton; Camera Operator — Gordon Ladgevin; Gaffer — Kevin Murphy; Key Grip — Mark

Silver; Location Sound Mixer — Bill McMillan; Boom Operator — Don Gaunsten; Construction Manager — Kirk Cheney; Head Carpenter — Jim Veale; Scenic Painter — Otto Fondan; Transportation Manager — Frank Mizzi; Post Production Supervisor — John Hardcourt; Post Production Coordinator — Steve D'Onufrid; Sound Effects Editor — David Evans; Dialogue Editor — Wayne Griffin; Re-recording — Allen Ormerod, Lou Solakofski; Sound Editing Services — Casablanca; Business Affairs — Kelly Lynne Ashton, Randi Hirshenbaum; Production Controller — Elaine Scott; Production Accountant — Anne Marie Cormier; Action Pack Theme by — Ray Bunch; Filmed at Cinevillage Studios, Toronto; Special thanks to: Ontario Film Development Corporation, Toronto Film Liaison Office, Silicon Graphics Canada, Inc.; Prerecorded videotape supplied by CNN; Copyright Cable News Network, Inc., 1993; Produced by Atlantis Films Ltd., in Association with W.I.C. International Communications Ltd., Lemli Productions, Inc., and Universal City Studios, Inc.

SYNOPSIS: Tekwar is a series of science fiction novels written by William Shatner. Shatner of course is most famous for his role as Captain Kirk of the original Star Trek television series of the late 1960s. To date there are nine Tekwar novels, four of which have been made into television movies. One of those, Tekwar: Teklab, involves Arthurian themes.

As a brief background to the story, Tek is an addictive and illegal virtual game of the future. A police detective named Jake Cardigan was setup by the Teklords and falsely convicted of dealing Tek. He was sentenced and placed into cryogenic suspended animation. Some time later, though, Walter H. Bascom gets Cardigan released. Bascom is a powerful and independent chief executive officer of a worldwide corporation. He puts Cardigan on his staff as a kind of super spy, or agent, in a perennial battle against the Teklords.

In Tekwar: Teklab, Cardigan and his partner, Sid, are assigned to be present at a gala being hosted by Prince Albert Stewart of Britain. With Prince Albert are his son, Prince Richard, and his secretary, Rachel Tudor. In the story, the two main political parties in Britain are the Monarchists and the Roundheads. The actual monarchy has been dormant for more than 50 years but Albert has become a popular contender in the upcoming elections, which could place a royal heir at the head of the government once more.

Back home in England there is considerable unrest over the election. Riots break out between Monarchist and Roundhead factions. In an effort to raise more financial and popular support worldwide, Albert and his entourage are displaying the Stewart family inheritance, namely the Crown Jewels of England and the sword Excalibur.

In the opening scene of the film Prince Albert wanders into the display room and examines first Excalibur, then the statues of some of the characters from Arthurian legends. Merlin, Lancelot, Galahad and Tristan are each there in full armor. The statues turn out to be real people. When Albert leaves the room, Merlin removes a device from his robes which he uses to shut down the electronic force fields protecting himself and the knights.

Released, the group tries to remove Excalibur from its high-tech display case. The code for neutralizing the field around the sword however is more complex and the alarms are set off. Security staff and our protagonists go into immediate action, but the culprits manage to escape on motorcycles with the sword.

In the confusion, two critical things happen: Prince Albert is killed and Richard recognizes Tristan, the leader of the thieves. The death of Albert immediately places Richard in line to take office. Unhesitatingly, he fills the role.

Cardigan and Sid meet with Bascom. In the face of Cardigan's cynicism about Camelot, Bascom informs the detective that Excalibur is a crucial symbol to the people of Britain and that the king cannot take the throne without it. He sends them to England to retrieve the sword.

Before leaving, Cardigan and Sid learn from Rachel that the only other possible heir to the Stewart family inheritance was a cousin, Mark. Mark, however, apparently died in a plane crash several years ago. She also informs them that the Stewarts are essentially bankrupt.

In England the two are captured by the Tekkids, an underground group led by none other than Tristan. Tekkids are the children of people who've become addicted to Tek and who've abandoned their normal lives. Tristan, who it turns out is actually Mark Stewart, is the King Arthur of a subterranean society that believes in the principles of chivalry. They go by Arthurian names and wear appropriate costumes.

A distraction enables the detectives to escape. Bascom gets in touch with them and states that Richard and the Monarchists are being funded by the Teklords. Cardigan and Sid sneak into the Stewart mansion and eavesdrop on a holographic meeting between Richard and the Teklords. They gather evidence that he is planning to build a Tek manufacturing facility for the Teklords in England in return for money.

Richard reveals that Mark is alive and is the one who stole Excalibur, but he reassures the Teklords that it won't be a problem. Richard has captured Rachel Tudor and is holding her hostage. He knows Mark loves Rachel and will do anything to ensure her safety, including returning the sword. As security alarms go off around them, they manage to grab a copy of Richard's illegal business plan and escape.

Mark challenges Richard to a duel and Richard accepts. Instead of going himself though, Richard sends an android duplicate of himself. Mark wields Excalibur against the android's electronic sword and only avoids being killed by the robot with help. In the meantime, Richard has taken Rachel to the Tower of London where he intends to behead her. Having destroyed the android, the entire group races to the Tower where Cardigan winds up with Excalibur and defeats Richard.

Obviously Arthurian themes abound in *Tekwar: Teklab* but in a confused manner, blended with lots of other things. The actual sword Excalibur exists as a British national symbol, a subculture of latchkey kids lives out a futuristic version of the Round Table, the sixteenth- and seventeenth-century royal families (Stewarts and Tudors) are brought into the fray. It's only a surprise that the Plantagenets were not included.

There are almost too many details to enumerate, but to name just a few more: Mark takes on the persona of Tristan. This recalls the Tristan legend itself but combines two of the main characters, King Mark of Cornwall and Tristan, the star-crossed lover of Isolde.

Mark is also the true King Arthur of the film, since he pulls the sword from the high-tech stone. He also hides it in a pool of water at one point, though no Lady of the Lake is involved. This King Arthur has no conflict with Lancelot over Guinevere. Rachel Tudor, Mark's Guinevere, is true and unencumbered by any distracting affair.

References to other films are also frequent. An anachronistic band of chivalric motorcycle riders is reminiscent of the movie *Knightriders*. The Tek virtual addiction looks like it was pulled directly from an episode of the television series *Star Trek: The Next Generation*. A virtual fencing match between Cardigan and Richard also smacks of the holodeck from the same television series.

Tennessee Ernie Ford Meets King Arthur (1960)

Not viewed; 2 reels, 2,160 feet; 16mm; Black and white; Comedy/Live Action; Copyright 1960, NBC Television Network; Ford Startime; A BriBuck Production; A Hubbell Robinson Productions, Inc., Presentation; NBC Inventory Box #327; Library of Congress Call #FSA3894-3895 and #FSA3896-3897; Library of Congress Catalogue #96501931/MP

CAST: Danny Arnold (Fricke); John Dehner (The Commentator); Robert Emhardt (Professor Van Brainn); Tennessee Ernie Ford (Himself); Alan Mowbry (King Arthur); Vincent Price (Sir Bors); Addison Richards (The Doctor); Alan Young (Clarence); Mary Menzes (Dancing Girl); Carl Balantine (Merlin)

CREDITS: Director — Lee J. Cobb; Writer and Producer — Roland Kibbee; Executive Producer — Clifford Stone; Music — Harry Geller; Art Director — Edward Stephenson; Choreography — Ward Ellis

SYNOPSIS: Tennessee Ernie Ford is caught in a time machine and sent to King Arthur's England. When condemned to burn at the stake, he uses the *Old Farmer's Almanac* to predict the eclipse that saves his life. Ford was a low-key comic, actor and singer known for his down-home humor.

The Theft of Excalibur see under The Adventures of Sir Lancelot

These Halls of Camelot (1972)

Not viewed; Filmstrip; 111 frames; Color; 35mm, 33⅓ 12-inch 40-minute record included; Copyright 1972, Scott Foresman and Company; Library of Congress Call #DA152.5; Library of Congress Catalogue #72737247/F/r88; Dewey Decimal #942.01

CREDITS: Script — Thomas Wettengel; Consultant — Leslie Alcock; Photographers — Leslie Alcock, Thomas Wettengel

SYNOPSIS: A look at the archaeological and literary research that has been done in trying to establish the existence of King Arthur.

Thundercats: "Excalibur" (1985)

Cartoon; Copyright 1985, Rankin-Bass; No further information available.

The Time Tunnel: "Merlin the Magician" (1966)

Television series 1966–1967; 1 hour episode from second season; Color; Copyright 1967, Kent Productions, Inc.; 20th Century–Fox Television, Inc.; Irwin Allen Productions; Distributed by the American Broadcasting Company

CAST: James Darren (Dr. Tony Newman); Robert Colbert (Dr. Douglas Phillips); Lee Meriwether (Dr. Ann MacGregor); Whit Bissell (Lt. Gen. Heywood Kirk); John Zaremba (Dr. Raymond Swain); Wesley Lan (Master Sergeant Jiggs); Sam Groom (Jerry); Christopher Carey (Merlin);

Jim McMullan (King Arthur); Vincent Beck (Wogan)

CREDITS: Story Editor—Arthur Weiss; Associate Producer—Jerry Briskin; Music Supervision—Lionel Newman; Theme—Johnny Williams; Production Supervisor—Jack Sonntag; Production Associate—Hal Herman; Unit Production Manager—Bob Anderson; Director of Photography—Winton Hoch, A.S.C.; Post Production Supervisor—George E. Swink; Director—Harry Harris; Art Directors—Jack Martin Smith, Rodger E. Mans; Set Decoration—Walter M. Scott, Norman Rockett; Assistant to the Producer—Paul Zastupnevich; Film Editor—Dick Wormell; Special Photographic Effects—L.B. Abbott, A.S.C.; Makeup Supervision—Ben Nye; Hair Styling—Margaret Donovan; Production Coordinator—Les Warner; Supervising Sound Effects Editor—Don Hall, Jr.; Sound Effects Editor—Robert Cornett; Post Production Coordinator—Robert Mintz; Color by DeLuxe; Assistant Director—Steve Bernhardt; Supervising Music Editor—Leonard A. Engel; Music Editor—Sam E. Levin; William Self in charge of production; Filmed at the Hollywood studios of 20th Century–Fox Television, Inc.; Created and produced by Irwin Allen

SYNOPSIS: *The Time Tunnel* was a television series which ran for two seasons (1966–1967). It was about a multimillion-dollar time travel research project which fell under congressional scrutiny. Worried over a potential loss of funding, one of the scientists fired up the machine to prove it could work and became trapped in time. Another of the scientists entered the vortex to try to find him. While they bounced around in time, the rest of the team continued working in the present to try to save them.

"Merlin the Magician" was an episode in which the time travelers are enlisted by Merlin to help King Arthur battle invading Vikings. Merlin it seems has a limited number of "miracles" which he can perform at any given time, so he snatches Tony and Doug because of their advanced technological knowledge compared to the people of sixth century Britain.

The lab workers pin down the time that the fellows are trapped in as A.D. 544 and they place them on the coast of Cornwall. That's about as accurate as anything in this show gets regarding Arthurian history or legend.

Guinevere's father, Lodegan of Carmellide, finally brings his army into the fight. Merlin's last miracle is to make them all look like Vikings. One wonders about the logic of this until the battle scenes begin. Footage from the 1954 movie *Prince Valiant* starring Robert Wagner is used. This also explains the incredibly bad black Dutch boy wig King Arthur wears; it matches Wagner's from the old film.

Times Medieval (1998)

Documentary for grade school; Copyright 1998, Discovery Channel; No further information available.

To Parsifal (1963)

16 minutes; Color; Copyright 1963, Canyon Cinema Co-op; Copyright 1997, Bruce Baillie; Copyright 1997, ARTHOUSE, Inc.; ARTHOUSE Videotape #46; Bruce Baillie Selected Films Volume #2

CREDITS: Director—Bruce Baillie; Canyon Cinema; Sponsored by—Audio Film Center; From the Legend and Richard Wagner's Music

SYNOPSIS: Rather than try to interpret this film in any way, perhaps a simple recounting of the scenes is in order. The opening consists of the sounds of a Coast Guard warning broadcast as a fishing boat rocks in a harbor. Cut to scenes of windblown fields and coastal surf. The fishing boat moves into the ocean. Views of birds on the water. Scene of fish being cut up, gulls and the boat. A rocky coast, boat horns, passing under the Golden Gate Bridge in fog. A railroad track crew, a forest stream and sunshine. A large freight train labors up a mountain grade, then an almost subliminal shot of long blond hair in the bushes of a field or perhaps near the tracks. Ants, naked human feet and a female leg in a stream (presumably still attached to the rest of the person). Back to the work crew, the train, then back to the naked figure in the stream. The music builds in tension. View of a woman's bare stomach, a man's hand on it. Back to the train, mountains and trees.

Tom Thumb (1991)

30 minutes; Color; Still illustrations; Copyright 1991, Gary Delfiner Productions; World-Vision Home Video, Inc.; Not affiliated with World Vision, a religious and charitable organization

CREDITS: Retold and Illustrated by — Richard Jesse Watson; Narrated by — Dom DeLuise; Produced and Directed by — Gary Delfiner; This Adventure Dedicated to — Samantha, Adam, Jacob, Alexander, Zachary; Executive Producers — Robert Sigman, Lonnie Delfiner, Gary Delfiner; Associate Producer — Stephen Decker; Editor — Stephen Rosenfeld; Camera — Stephen Decker; Original Music — Joe McSorely, Joe Parente; Visual Continuity — Stephen Star; Assistant Editors — Stephen Clarendon, Mark Negreann, Anton Rosner; Electronic Graphics — Melissa Snyder; Sound Mix — Ron Kirves; Audio Editing — Paul Michaels; Video Package Designed by — A.L.&O. Creative Consultants; This program based upon the book *Tom Thumb* retold and illustrated by Richard Jesse Watson, Harcourt Brace Jovanovich, Publishers, Copyright 1989 by Richard Jesse Watson; Special Thanks to — Susan Solomon, Mindy Delfiner, Barry Mintz, Barb Fisch, Stacey Heusel, Arthur Weisfeld; Special thanks to the very talented staff of Magno Sound & Video whose assistance with this project was invaluable; About the Illustrator: Richard Jesse Watson has worked as a farmhand, welder, carpet layer, letter carrier and graphic designer, as well as an artist. His love of art and literature began when he was a child, and he cannot remember a time when he was not drawing and writing. After studying art at Pasadena City College and the Art Center College of Design, he was an assistant art director for World Vision International and an artist for Hallmark Cards. Illustrator of *Bronwen, the Traw and the Shape Shifter* by James Dickey, which was voted a Parents' Choice Award Book for Illustration in 1986, he was named Ezra Jack Keats Fellow of 1987 by the Kerlan Collection of the University of Minnesota. Richard Watson lives with his wife, Susi, and their children in Murphys, California.

SYNOPSIS: Tom Thumb is one of many characters from the pantheon of "fairy tales" and legends which became nursery rhymes and chapbooks in the sixteenth and seventeenth centuries. Fairy tale is really a misnomer, since many of the stories involve no fairies at all.

The first reference to Tom Thumb cited in the *Oxford English Dictionary* comes from the year 1579. By 1621 Richard Johnson had written *The History of Tom Thumb*. Since then there have been dozens of permutations of the story, not all of them retaining the original connection with King Arthur and the Knights of the Round Table.

This video retelling of the story recounts the visit of a poor old man to the home of a farmer and his wife. Though poor themselves, the couple generously feed the man, who turns out to be the wizard Merlin in disguise. Taking their kindness to heart Merlin grants them their one wish, to have a child, even if, as the wife puts it, he's no bigger than her husband's thumb.

When Tom is born he matures but never gets any bigger than the size of his father's thumb. He experiences lots of problems because of his size and has a number of adventures. One of them is an encounter with a giant.

Giants are normally unruly, violent beings, the story explains, but this one had been subdued by a trick of the fairies. They tied a seashell to his ear and the soothing sound of the sea emanating from it kept his disposition in check. Inadvertently the shell is broken and the giant becomes surly. Tom winds up in the belly of a fish, which is caught by King Arthur's royal fisherman.

Tom becomes a darling of the court but, as politics often go, he falls out of favor and is unjustly imprisoned. When the giant attacks King Arthur's kingdom, Tom gets his animal friends to help him escape. Knowing the secret of pacifying the giant, Tom becomes the hero when the giant is once again quieted.

As reward, King Arthur makes Tom a knight and grants him all the gold that he can carry home to his parents in special carts built for the squirrels and rabbits to pull.

Tom Thumb in King Arthur's Court (1963)

16mm film and video cassette; 16 minutes; Color; Cartoon; Copyright 1963, Coronet Instructional Media; Coronet Films and Video; As of 2/99 rights owned by Phoenix Learning Group and available on video tape. No cast or credits listed on 16mm film

SYNOPSIS: Designed as a movie for the primary grades, *Tom Thumb in King Arthur's Court* is a charming cartoon rendition of the legend of the most diminutive of persons to achieve knighthood in Camelot. The short film is accompanied by an instructional guide with several related questions and projects for use by teachers.

In the film, Tom is born to a humble but happy couple who live in a cottage and run a small farm. Tom's miraculously small size is an amazement to them, but they make adaptations and all goes well. As Tom grows older he helps his father with the chores, but he longs for something more exciting. One day Tom decides to run away from home to become a knight "like Sir Lancelot."

Heading for Camelot, Tom meets an old rabbit who gives Tom a large leaf to use as a boat. In the boat Tom falls asleep as he floats down the river. A streetwise fellow named Limbo plucks Tom up. Limbo has his sights fixed on King Arthur's treasure and he sees in Tom a likely assistant. Introducing Tom to his pet spider Satan, Limbo scares Tom enough that the little fellow manages to escape the thief's clutches.

As he is scampering towards home, a raven snatches Tom up. Flying over his parents' cottage Tom regrets his decision to leave. Before the bird can get Tom to its destination, however, Tom slips from its grasp and falls into the river where he is swallowed by a fish. This very fish is later caught and served to King Arthur at a feast, where Tom finally gets free.

Becoming the star of the court, Tom is taught by none other than Sir Lancelot how to fight with a sword and lance and how to ride. Guinevere gives Tom a knitting needle for a lance and a gold thimble for a helmet. Galahad's belt buckle becomes Tom's shield and a mouse is his horse. He uses one of Lancelot's helmets for a bedroom.

One day while battling one of the castle's cats, Tom spots Limbo and his spider stealing jewels from Arthur's treasure. Attacking, Tom engages the spider in a sword fight and sends his mouse to get help. The guards capture Limbo and Tom defeats the spider.

For his heroism, Arthur knights Tom and grants him a boon. Tom's request is to go home. King Arthur declares that he and all the Knights of the Round Table will escort their hero home.

Tortilla Flat (1942)

100 minutes; Black and white; Drama/Live Action; Copyright 1942, Turner Entertainment Co.; Copyright 1990, MGM/UA Home Video Inc.; MGM/UA Home Video #M201126

CAST: Spencer Tracy (Pilon); Hedy Lamarr (Dolores Sweets Ramirez); John Garfield (Danny); Frank Morgan (Pirate); Akim Tamiroff (Pablo); Sheldon Leonard (Tito Ralph); John Qualen (Jose Maria Corcoran); Donald Meek (Paul D. Cummings); Connie Gilchrist (Mrs. Torrelli); Allen Jenkins (Portagee Joe); Henry O'Neill (Father Ramon); Mercedes Ruffino (Mrs. Marellis); Nina Campana (Senora Teresina); Arthur Space (Mr. Brown); Betty Wells (Cesca); Harry Burns (Torrelli)

CREDITS: Producer — Sam Zimbalist; Screenplay — John Lee Mahin, Benjamin Glazer; Based on the book by John Steinbeck; Director of Photography — Karl Freund, A.S.C.; Musical Score — Franz Waxman; Lyrics — Frank Loesser; Recording Director — Douglas Shearer; Art Director — Cedric Gibbons; Associate — Paul Groesse; Set Decorations — Edwin B. Willis; Special Effects — Warren Newcombe; Gowns by — Kalloch; Men's Costumes by — Gile Steele; Makeup Created by — Jack Dawn; Film Editor — James E. Newcom; Director — Victor Fleming

SYNOPSIS: The film *Tortilla Flat* is taken from the John Steinbeck novel of the same name. Steinbeck had a lifelong love of the legends of King Arthur and the Knights of the Round Table. Here, he applies Arthurian themes to a group of campesinos near Monterey, California.

The movie opens on a scene of two fellows sleeping under a tree in the hills on the ocean coast. Pablo wakes up hungry and rouses Pilon. Pablo states he'd like to eat a mackerel. Pilon suggests he go down to the wharves and throw rocks at the fishermen. He explains that the fishermen won't throw their nets or tools at Pablo, since they don't want to lose them. They will throw mackerel at him.

Thus is introduced Pilon's whole means of existence and philosophy of life. Always full of ideas and advice on how to get by without working, Pilon is the manipulative driving force among a small group of friends.

As they make their plans a lawyer drives up looking for Danny Alvarez. Danny unfortunately is in jail, so the three men go there and Danny is informed that his grandfather has died and left him a pocket watch and two houses in Tortilla Flat. Tito Ralph, the jail-keeper, is easily swayed into letting Danny out to go see his houses.

Pilon convinces Danny that watches are bad things and he trades the watch for three gallons of Torrelli's wine and gets Danny's guitar out of hock. The party moves to Danny's new property where Danny immediately begins to show signs of possessiveness about the place. Pilon points out that when people are poor they say they will always share with their friends, but as soon as they have property, things go downhill.

After getting Danny to cooperate more with his plans, Pilon sends Pablo out to pawn some of the pots from the cupboards. With that money they can pay the $3 fee to get the water turned on. Tito observes that Pilon has a pretty big ring in Danny's nose.

The beautiful Dolores Ramirez is one of Danny's new neighbors. Pilon warns Danny that she's Portuguese and all those girls want to do is get married. In spite of Pilon's objections, Danny falls in love with the girl.

In the meantime more derelicts are gathered into Pilon's fold. Portagee Joe is one. Another is an old hermit named Pirate. Pirate has five dogs with whom he lives in a chicken coop. He cuts wood and peddles it, collecting 25¢ each day. Pilon's larcenous side emerges when he tries to calculate how many quarters the old man must have after working so many years.

Pilon and the gang get Pirate to move in with them. They are all humbled, however, when Pirate entrusts them with his money, telling them the story of why he's collecting it. His purpose is to buy a golden candlestick for St. Francis to whom he once prayed for the health of one of his dogs. The dog was cured and Pirate vowed to buy a candlestick "of a thousand days" for the saint.

All the members of the gang tacitly agree not to touch Pirate's quarters, except Joe. He steals some and is soundly beaten by Pilon and the rest of the men. They count the money and find that there is more than Pirate needs to buy the candlestick. That accomplished, they are all present to witness the dedication of the gift to the church.

Though he's been doing good deeds, in the meantime Pilon has been trying to sabotage Danny's relationship with Dolores. Danny has become so serious about the girl that he has his eyes on a fishing boat. Pilon is successful at getting them to argue and temporarily split. Danny disappears on a five-day drunk, showing up at his own heavily occupied house to throw rocks at it.

One day Danny goes to confront Dolores at the cannery where she works. In a tussle with the foreman, some equipment falls on him and Danny is hospitalized with a punctured lung. Word gets out that he is dying.

Pilon is himself crushed by what he has done. He experiences an epiphany when he witnesses Pirate duplicating the candlestick dedication service in the woods for the benefit of his dogs, who weren't allowed in the church for the real dedication. Pilon goes to the church and promises St. Francis a second candlestick if he will only heal Danny. Pilon disappears from Tortilla Flat, having gone to work cutting shrimp on the wharves.

Five weeks later, knowing that Danny is finally on the mend, Father Ramon finds Pilon. He tells the reprobate that St. Francis doesn't want another candlestick, but a boat for Danny would be a better gift. In the end Danny recovers and he marries Dolores and Pilon and his followers go back to sleeping under the stars.

The simple and rollicking story of *Tortilla Flat* is a thinly veiled Arthurian tale. Pilon, of course, is a wayward King Arthur, leading a happy-go-lucky band of knights of a different kind of Round Table. Pablo is patently the poor abused seneschal, Sir Kay, coming out of the later medieval tradition where Kay was portrayed as a buffoon.

Danny is the favorite son-who-might-have-been, Sir Lancelot. He also incorporates elements of the Fisher King, having received a wound fatal but for the intervention of the Grail quester. King Arthur in this story has no Guinevere, so the whole imbroglio of adultery and betrayal is avoided when Danny finds his own Guinevere in Dolores.

The Galahad/Parsifal figure is old Pirate, the one who heals the Round Table and the land through his purity and achievement of the Grail. Pirate's Grail is a simple candlestick, but his motive and its symbolism are no less significant to the story than the holy vessel itself.

Pirate is perhaps the most clearly delineated Arthurian character in *Tortilla Flat*. On a superficial level, he is Galahad because he does achieve the Grail. His innocence and purity are total and unquestioned even by the rowdy Pilon gang. But he is also Parsifal. His mental simplicity gives him the "innocent" aspect of the Von Eschenbach and Wagnerian character. His total trust in Pilon's gang with his money gives him the "fool" aspect, rounding out the picture of the innocent fool that is the essence of the Parsifal figure.

Interestingly, there is even the Wagnerian anointing scene with Pirate. When Parsifal returns to the Grail Castle from his years of wandering he and his transformation are recognized by Gurnemanz and Kundry. They anoint his head and feet before he enters the Grail Castle. Pirate is similarly prepared for his appearance at the church when Pilon and Pablo lather his unruly hair and beard. They even dress him in the finest clothes available from the gang.

In turning against the court by stealing some of Pirate's money, Portagee Joe might be considered the Mordred of the story. Happily though, this is not Camelot but *Tortilla Flat,* where this Mordred is turned around and no to-the-death confrontation between him and his Arthur is necessary.

Transformers: "A Decepticon Raider in King Arthur's Court" (1985)

Cartoon; Copyright 1985, Marvel; No further information available.

Travel Trees Can't Dance see under *Princess Gwenevere and the Jewel Riders*

Treasure Island, Kids Klassics: "Sir Lancelot" (1959)

29 minutes; Color; Cartoon; Copyright 1959, New World Productions, Mel-O-Toons; Copyright 1993, Good Times Home Video

SYNOPSIS: "Sir Lancelot" is one cartoon of five on this collection of early Mel-O-Toons. A six-minute musical cartoon, it is the second on the tape.

The gist of the story is that at bedtime, a little boy is reading the book *Knights of Old*. As he reads, we see enacted the story he is reading. The song's chorus immediately starts up:

> Who's the bravest of the brave?
> Who's the strongest of the strong?
> Who's the friend of serf and slave?
> Who will fight to right a wrong?
> Who is sworn to serve his king?
> Who can make a broadsword sing?
> Lancelot,
> Sir Lancelot,
> King Arthur's bravest knight.

The next verses describe the events depicted by the cartoon: first Lancelot kills a dragon that has attacked Camelot, next Lancelot catches some highway robbers and finally he saves Queen Guinevere from her kidnapper, the Black Knight. The boy falls asleep and dreams of being Sir Lancelot. The entire song is repeated, this time with the action taking place in the boy's neighborhood.

The Mel-O-Toons cartooning style was unique for its unsophisticated, innocent look and "Sir Lancelot" is a perfect example of that. Other titles included on the tape are "Treasure Island," "Paul Bunyan," "Panchito" and "Hep Cat Symphony" (a 1946 cartoon).

Tristan et Iseult (1972)

Not viewed; Copyright 1972, Film du Soir

> CAST: Yvan Lagrange; Clair Wauthiou
> CREDITS: Director — Yvan Lagrange

Tristan et Yseult (1909)

Not viewed; Copyright 1909, Pathé Frères, S.C.A.G.L.

> CAST: Paul Capelliani; Stacia Napierkowska
> CREDITS: Director — Albert Capellani

Tristan et Yseult (1911)

Not viewed; Copyright 1911, Il Film D'Arte Italiana, S.A.P.F.

> CREDITS: Director — Ugo Falena

SYNOPSIS: Tristan and his slave Rosen go to Ireland to accompany Yseult back to Mark of Cornwall. Rosen becomes jealous when he sees the attraction Tristan and Yseult have for each other. He attempts to poison them but the potion makes them fall in love instead of killing them.

Once in Cornwall, Tristan and Yseult go off together and Rosen tells Mark what is going on. Although Mark forgives them, the two commit suicide.

Tristan et Yseut (1920)

Not viewed; Copyright 1920, Nalpas, France

> CAST: Sylvio de Pedrelli; Frank Heurs; Andr Lionel
> CREDITS: Director — Maurice Mariaud

SYNOPSIS: Ireland demands tribute of Cornwall and Tristan defeats the messenger. Severely wounded in the fight Tristan is put to sea to die. He is found along the Irish coast and nursed back to health by Yseut, daughter of the Irish king.

Tristan is sent back to Ireland to bring Yseut to marry King Mark of Cornwall. The two have fallen in love and after the marriage they sneak off together. They are caught, Yseut returns to Mark and Tristan leaves to meet Yolande of Brittany who also falls in love with him.

Yolande's lover mortally wounds Tristan and Yseut is sent for but Tristan dies before she arrives. Yseut dies of a broken heart.

Tristan und Isolde (Osaka, 1967)

203 minutes; Black and White; Opera; German with no subtitles; Live performance April 10, 1967; Copyright 1967; Legato Classics; LCV #005

> CAST: Birgit Nilsson (Isolde); Wolfgang Windgassen (Tristan); Hans Hotter (King Marke); Herthe Töpper (Brangaene); Hans Andersson (Kurvenal); Gerd Nienstedt (Melot); Georg Paskuda (Sailor); Sebastian Feiersinger (Shepherd); Gerd Nienstedt (Steersman)
> CREDITS: Orchestra and Chorus of the Osaka Festival; Conductor — Pierre Boulez

SYNOPSIS: For anyone not fluent in German this film of *Tristan und Isolde* is difficult. As it has no subtitles, one has to be very familiar with the story to follow along.

It's a shame that it was not subtitled, for it is a fine staging. The black-and-white filming lends another kind of starkness to the already grim Wagnerian version of the story. The sets are simple and use shadows heavily.

Another problem with the tape is there are no credits or identifying graphics of any kind. The above cast and credit listings are from the jacket only.

Tristan und Isolde (1975)

Not viewed; Filmstrip; 85 frames; Color; 35mm, with narrative script and background articles; Copyright 1975, Metropolitan Opera

Guild; Library of Congress Call #100.W24; Library of Congress Catalogue #74732974/F; Dewey Decimal #782.1

SYNOPSIS: Scenes from and description of the Metropolitan Opera's production of Wagner's *Tristan und Isolde*.

Tristan und Isolde (Bayreuth, 1983)

240 minutes; Color; Opera; German with English subtitles; Copyright 1983, Unitel; Copyright 1991, Philips Classics Productions

CAST: René Kollo (Tristan); Matti Salminen (King Marke); Johanna Meier (Isolde); Hermann Becht (Kurwenal); Robert Schunk (Melot); Hanna Schwarz (Brangäne); Helmut Pampuch (A Shepherd); Martin Egel (A Helmsman); Robert Schunk (Young Sailor)

CREDITS: Chorus of the Bayreuther Festspiele; Chorus Master—Norbert Balatsch; Orchestra of the Bayreuther Festspiele; Conducted by—Daniel Barenboim; Set Design, Costumes, Staging and Direction—Jean-Pierre Ponnelle; Artistic Supervision—Wolfgang Wagner; Stage Manager—Walter Huneke; Costume Realization—Heike Ammer; Lighting—Manfred Voss; Makeup—Inge Landgraf, Hans-Rudolf Müller; Musical Assistance—Helmut Weese, Taijiro Iimori, Udo Metzner, Rosemary Jarvis; Choral Assistance—Julius Asbeck; Assistant Directors—Friedemann Steiner, Jutta Gleue; Technical Supervision—Klaus Griese; Sound—Gernot R. Westhäuser, Josef Wanninger, Gudrun Maurer; Audio Producer—Christopher Raeburn; Video Engineer—Josef Renkel; Camera—Oskar Herting, Wolfgang Fritzberg, Dieter Schmidt, Harald Weber, Harry Bell, Günther Mohn, Horst Thomas; Film Editor—Charlotte Hirschhorn; Assistant Film Director—Wolfgang Schröter; Videotape Editors—Joachim Meißner, Rolf Prochnow, Anton Danzer; Executive Producer—Horant H. Hohlfeld; A production of Unitel Film und Fernsehproduktionsgesellschaft, mbH & Co., Munich

SYNOPSIS: A faithful rendering of Wagner's opera version of the legend, using strikingly simple sets. Each act is dominated by one object—a tree, a rocky crag, the deck of the ship. Strongly symbolic use of light versus darkness throughout.

There are of course dozens of versions of the "Tristan and Isolde" story from the Middle Ages. These, as is true of so many Arthurian tales, are rooted in older traditions, Celtic and Welsh most notably. Gottfried von Strassburg's *Tristan* from around 1210 is the rendition Wagner was probably most familiar with.

Wagner stripped the legend down to its bare essentials in writing *Tristan und Isolde*. Sparse even by Wagnerian standards, *Tristan und Isolde* eliminates much from the stories, making room for extensive operatic discourses on love, life, death, loyalty, revenge, friendship and betrayal. Missing from this opera are Tristan's familiar harp, his tutor and traveling companion Governal, the dragon that appears in many versions and even the second Isolde, Blanchemains.

Where Wagner's operas *Parsifal* and *Lohengrin* can be seen as social and political statements, *Tristan und Isolde* was evidently a much more personal work for the composer, centering almost exclusively on love. Wagner's affair with Mathilde Wesendonck cannot be ignored as an influence on his writing of the piece.

Act 1 opens on board the ship which is carrying Isolde to Cornwall to wed King Marke. Isolde discusses with Brangane why she does not want to go and calls upon the magic of her mother to raise the seas and the winds to stop the ship. Isolde demands to speak with Tristan, calling him a vassal. Tristan refuses, stating that Morold is dead as answer to the Irish calls for tribute.

Next Isolde recounts to Brangane how she healed a wounded knight who called himself Tantris. Tantris of course turned out to be Tristan. She details her discovery of his sword which was missing a chink matching what she had found in the skull of Morold, her betrothed. Morold had been sent to Cornwall to exact tribute from Marke, but had died at the hand of Marke's champion. On the verge of killing the wounded Tristan, Isolde found that something in his eyes stayed her hand, and she now agonizes at length at not having followed through with her revenge.

Isolde determines to poison herself and

Tristan with one of the many potions her mother has sent along with her to Cornwall. She calls on Tristan to join her in a "draught of atonement," and the two drink and collapse. Just as the ship arrives at Cornwall, however, they wake up, smitten with love for one another. The act ends as King Marke appears.

Act 2 finds Isolde and Brangane in a forest at night. Brangane describes Isolde's wedding to Marke, but Isolde expounds only on her love for Tristan and the joy it is giving her. Brangane confesses her guilt about having switched a love potion for what Isolde thought to be poison. She also tells Isolde that she believes Sir Melot is plotting against the lovers, but her warnings fall on deaf ears. As a signal to summon Tristan, Isolde puts out the torch she has been carrying (literally, not figuratively) and the hero soon arrives. Brangane discreetly disappears and Tristan and Isolde spend the night together in the forest.

Morning comes and the lovers are found out. Melot has led Marke to the site of the tryst. In the struggle that ensues, Tristan seems almost to attempt suicide as he all but hurls himself onto Melot's sword. Mortally wounded, Tristan collapses and the act ends.

Act 3 takes place on a crag near Tristan's home, Kareol. His faithful friend Kerwenal has carried him there and the dying Tristan lies on the stones overlooking the sea. A shepherd sits nearby, playing a mournful tune on a flute. Kerwenal has sent for Isolde, thinking that only she can heal this second wound Tristan suffers from.

Tristan awakes and believes he sees Isolde's ship approaching. To encourage him, the shepherd and Kerwenal play along. Tristan hallucinates that Isolde comes to him, followed by Marke and Melot. Marke states that once he learned of the love potion, he came to forgive them and to bestow Isolde on Tristan, but he is too late. Isolde does finally show up, but too late as well, and she is transfigured by her grief. The act ends with Kerwenal alone on the crag, cradling the body of Tristan.

Tristan und Isolde (1987) see *Wagner: Tristan und Isolde*

Tristan und Isolde (1995)

Not viewed; 223 minutes; Color; Opera; Copyright 1995, Unitel; Currently not available

CAST: Siegfried Jerusalem (Tristan); Waltrud Meier (Isolde); Uta Priew (Brangäne); Falk Struckmann (Kurwenal); Mattias Hölle (King Marke); Poul Elming (Melot, Young Sailor); Peter Moss (The Shepherd); Sándor Sólyom (Steersman)

CREDITS: Staged and Directed by — Heiner Müller; Orchestra — Orchestra of the Bayreuth Festspielhaus; Conductor — Daniel Barenboim; Stage Design — Erich Wonder; Costumes — Yohji Yamamoto; Television Director — Horant H. Hohlfeld

Tristana (1970)

98 minutes; Drama/Live Action; Spanish with English subtitles; Copyright 1970, the Estate of Raymond Rohauer; Janus Films; Public Media Home Vision #TRI060

CAST: Catherine Deneuve (Tristana); Franco Nero (Don Horacio); Fernando Rey (Don Lope Garrido; Lola Gaos; Antonio Casas; Jesus Fernandez; Vicente Soler; Fernando Cebrian; Antonio Ferrandis; Candida Losada; Jose Calvo; Jose Maria Caffarel; Joaquin Pamplona; Maria Paz Pondal; Juan Josè Menendez; Josè Blanch; Alfredo Santa Cruz; Serfio Mendizabal; Luis Aller; Luis Rico; Saturno Cerra; Jesus Combarro; Leo Lenoir Scavino; Vicente Roca; Ximenez Carrillo; Adriano Dominguez; Josè Riesgo; Rosa Gorostegui; Antonio Cintado; Pilar Vela; Lorenzo Rodriguez

CREDITS: Director — Luis Buñuel; Screenplay by — Luis Buñuel; With the Collaboration of — Julio Alejandro; Inspired by the novel of the same name by Benito Perez Galdos; Background Effects by — Luis Buñuel; Art Director — Enrique Alarcon; Film Editor — Pedro Del Rey; Special Effects — Julian Ruiz; Production Supervisor — Juan Estelrich; Director of Photography — Jose F. Aguaio; Cameraman — Jose F. Aguaio, Jr.; Production Managers — Manuel Torres, A.T.C., Giulio Pappagallo; Assistant Directors — Jose Pujol, Pierre Lary, Roberto Giandalia; Assistant Editor — Carmen Salas; 2nd Assistant Editor — Alvaro Lion; Production Inspectors — Esteban Gutierrez, Martin Sacristan; Production Secretaries — Gloria Fontana, Giancarla Caperna; Assistant Cameraman — Alberto Paniagua; Lighting Assistant — Josè A. Hoya;

Catherine Deneuve stars in Luis Buñuel's *Tristana* (1970) (courtesy Public Media, Inc.).

Stills — Mario Tursi, Alejandro Digez; Hairdresser — Nives Ruiz; Costumes — Rosa Carcia; Sound Engineer — Bernardino Fronzetti; Assistant Set Designer — Lois Arguello; Assistant Editor — Julio Pena; Equipment — Mengibar-Luna-Mateos; Tailor — Cornejo; Set Construction — Asensio; Electric Equipment — Kinolux; Sound Equipment — Estudios Moro S.A.; Studios — Verona S.A., Madrid; Exteriors Photographed in — Toledo; Negative by — Eastmancolor; Sound Editing — Fono Roma s.p.a., Roma-Milano; Prints by — Deluxe; An Italian, French, Spanish Co-Production; Selenia

Cinematografica s.r.l., Roma; Les Films Corona, Nanterre; Epoca Films S.A., Talia Films S.A., Madrid

SYNOPSIS: A modernization of the legend of Tristan and Isolde set in Spain in the 1920s. This film confuses the characters a bit, giving the young lady the name Tristana, but it retains the basic format of an older man in conflict with a younger man and a woman.

Don Lope Garrido is a charming old gad-about who refuses to grow out of his flirtatious ways. Now in his sixties, he manages to live without really working as he waits for his sister to die, when he will inherit the family fortune. His sole means of support of late has been refereeing duels of honor, but when that activity goes by the boards he is forced to begin selling heirlooms and furnishings from his house.

When one of the women of the city falls ill, on her deathbed she requests of Don Lope that he see after her daughter, Tristana. Don Lope takes the girl into his home, then takes advantage of her. Tristana grows to hate Don Lope and longs for escape.

A telling moment in their relationship occurs during a walk through the city one day. Strolling through a colonnaded piazza, Tristana asks Don Lope which of two columns he likes better. One is the same as another to Don Lope but Tristana points out that she can always find a preference between two things. This little theme is illustrated throughout the film when, for instance, she even picks one bean from a plate before another.

The opportunity for escape finally arrives for Tristana when she meets Horacio, a young artist. Horacio falls in love with Tristana and the two go off together. Tristana however refuses to marry Horacio — Don Lope's libertarian ways suit her purposes despite her disgust with his treatment of her.

During the two years that Horacio and Tristana are gone Don Lope's sister passes away. Finally comfortable, he buys back the things he had to sell but he morosely awaits Tristana, who he is convinced will return to him. Amazingly enough, she does.

Stricken with a cancer in her right leg Tristana demands that Horacio take her back to Don Lope. Horacio agrees and Don Lope once again takes the girl in, providing the best doctors for her. Her leg has to be amputated at the knee but Tristana adapts with grim determination. She dismisses Horacio out of hand and makes a cold decision to marry Don Lope.

Don Lope of course is delighted until he learns that there are to be no marital relations of any kind. Tristana gradually discovers the power she wields, first as an invalid, then as the lady of the house. Having chosen her course, she sticks to it and bit by bit takes her revenge.

Don Lope's health gradually fails until one winter night he has a heart attack. Calling Tristana to his side he pleads with her to phone the doctor. Tristana fakes the phone call, then opens wide the windows in Don Lope's room. With Don Lope's death Tristana is finally free.

In *Tristana*, Don Lope takes the place of King Mark from the Tristan and Isolde legend. Tristana herself can be seen as both Tristan and Isolde. She is Isolde in the sense that Don Lope vies for her favors with Horacio, but she is like Tristan in that she goes to find a mate and then winds up with two contending suitors. Tristan had involvements with two Isoldes, Tristana has the Dons Lope and Horacio.

Where Tristan was sent by Mark, however, Tristana goes out into the world herself to find someone else. Where Tristan died (and Isolde too), Tristana causes the death of her "Mark." Another mixing of the original details of the legend is Tristana becoming the invalid or disfigured person. Where a dwarf was involved in some versions of the legend and even in the film *The Eternal Return,* here it is Tristana herself who loses part of a limb.

The legend classically involves a love potion which becomes the cause of Tristan and Isolde's agonies. It might be said of *Tristana* that cancer takes the place of the love potion. The cancer is what brings Tristana and

Horacio back to Don Lope. The cancer is what utterly and completely changes life for Tristana. But as with the other reversals in this film, rather than destroying Tristana's life, the cancer ultimately gives her power over the people around her and the determination to use that power.

Whether or not the results are any happier than they were for Tristan and Isolde is debatable. Superficially at least, Tristana is able to make the decisions Tristan could not. She has no trouble choosing between the men in her life as the need arises. She winds up freeing herself from both of them but the cost is a high. At the risk of stating the obvious, Tristan, Tristana, whatever the permutation the word, seems rooted in the Latin *tristitia,* meaning sadness, gloom and harshness. All three definitions certainly apply.

The True Legend of King Arthur see The Legend of Arthur

The Ugly Duckling see under The Adventures of Sir Lancelot

Unidentified Flying Oddball (1979)

92 minutes; Color; Live Action; Copyright 1979, Walt Disney Company; Walt Disney Home Video #160

CAST: Dennis Dugan (Tom Trimble); Jim Dale (Sir Mordred); Ron Moody (Merlin); Kenneth More (King Arthur); John le Mesurier (Sir Gawain); Rodney Bewes (Clarence); Sheila White (Alisande); Robert Beatty (Senator Milberg); Cyril Shaps (Dr. Zimmerman); Kevin Brennan (Winston); Ewen Solon (Wathers); Pat Roach (Olf); Reg Lye (Prisoner)

CREDITS: Director of Photography — Paul Beeson, B.S.C.; Art Director — Albert Witherick; Costume Designer — Phyllis Dalton; Editor — Peter Boita; Production Manager — Robin Douet; Casting Director — Maude Shector; Assistant Director — Vincent Winter; Location Manager — Barrie Melros; Continuity — Georgina Hamish; Camera Operators — Malcolm Vinson, Ray Sturgess; Sound Editor — Peter Best; Special Photographic Effects — Cliff Culley; Makeup — Roy Ashton, Ernie Sasser; Hairdresser — Joyce James, Betty Sherriff; Stunt Coordinator — Vic Armstrong; Assembly Editor —

Jack Gardner; Sound Recordists — Claude Hitchcock, Ken Barker; Music Composed and Conducted by — Ron Goodwin; Assistant to the Producers — Don Tait; Associate Producer — Hugh Attwooll; Screenstory and Screenplay by — Don Tait; Based on Mark Twain's *A Connecticut Yankee in King Arthur's Court*; Produced by — Ron Miller; Directed by — Russ Mayberry

SYNOPSIS: A comically low-key, somewhat disjointed version of Twain's *A Connecticut Yankee in King Arthur's Court, Unidentified Flying Oddball* takes the tale into the future of time travel.

A nutty professor has designed a space vehicle that can travel at the speed of light and therefore through time as well as space. The only way the government will continue to fund

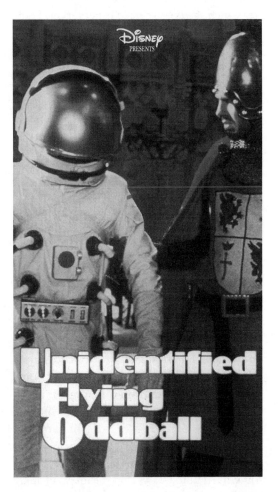

VHS cover for *Unidentified Flying Oddball* (1979).

it, however, is if no human crew is involved. The professor has his assistant, Tom, build a robot to "man" the ship.

Tom makes the robot identical to himself, including some of his emotions. Moments before the launch of the craft Hermes, the robot, decides that he is afraid to leave. Tom is sent on board to talk the robot into continuing with the mission. A bolt of lightning ignites the rocket's engines and both Tom and Hermes are fired into space.

Hermes is damaged during the lift-off so Tom takes over the command duties. Achieving time-travel speed, he lands in England in the year A.D. 508. The first person he meets is Alisande. The simple girl is on her way to Camelot to see Merlin. She is carrying a gander which she is convinced is her father. Some evil magic must have transformed him into the bird since he was home when she left to do some chores but was gone and the bird was in his place at the table when she returned.

Mordred comes along, captures this space-suited monster and brings him to Camelot. In the court Merlin is performing tricks for the gathered nobility. Displaying little puffs of flame and smoke, with pig-latin incantations he makes small creatures disappear ("at-ray, anish-vay!"). After a long hearing, Mordred suggests that Tom be burned at the stake the next day. An unexcitable Arthur agrees.

While being held in the dungeon Tom discovers that Mordred also has Alisande's father imprisoned. Mordred's plot is to swindle people out of their land and raise enough money and men to take over Camelot.

Tom's space suit saves him from the flames and he climbs down from the pyre. Merlin and Mordred are enraged at his escape but in the confusion Tom disappears into the castle. The page Clarence is sent into the castle to fetch Mordred's sword. Tom and Alisande find "King Arthur's sword" embedded in a stone. Tom pulls it out to use to defend himself. Alisande states that she knew all along that his heart was pure.

Clarence decides to help them out. He brings Mordred's sword to Tom. Tom magnetizes the blade. When Mordred attempts to kill Tom, his sword keeps gathering ironware from around the hall until it is finally too heavy and cluttered to wield. Tipping off a tower wall, Mordred and his sword fall into the moat.

Honor must still be served and Mordred demands a joust to the death. Tom resurrects Hermes the robot to joust for him while he scours the land records in the castle. Hermes holds up just long enough against Mordred for Tom to find the evidence he's after. Exposed for the scoundrel he is, Mordred departs, declaring war on Arthur.

Though Hermes lost an arm and his head in the battle he is still salvageable for the final war with Mordred. Alisande becomes even more confused about things when she learns that she's been falling in love with a being filled with "squirmy things and smoke." Tom finally convinces her of his true humanity.

Camelot prepares for war and Mordred attacks, but ultimately it's the magnetic time-travel engines on Tom's ship that save the day. When Tom turns them on, all of Mordred's armored men are clangingly smashed into the sides of the ship.

Improvising a rocket fuel from local materials Tom is ready to leave but can't risk bringing Alisande along since he doesn't know if she'll age 1,400 years on the trip. They part sadly, but 100 or so years into the future Tom finds Alisande's gander on board the ship and the bird is none the worse for the time displacement. He turns the ship around to get his girlfriend.

Unidentified Flying Oddball is essentially a complete rewriting of Twain's *Connecticut Yankee*. Almost none of the original story is left in this version; even Hollywood's favorite bits that get repeated in so many other films are gone.

The original protagonist, Hank Morgan, has been changed to Tom Trimble. The means of his travel to ancient Camelot has been switched from a blow to the head to intentional time travel. The solar eclipse which was Hank Morgan's salvation has been eliminated. Hank's becoming Sir Boss and spending years in sixth century Britain, introducing all kinds of industrial and scientific inventions, is also ignored. Even the line about Clarence looking more like a paragraph than a page does not occur here.

On the one hand such a major reworking of the story is disappointing, but on the other the film claims only to be "based" on Twain's tale. With thirteenth century costumes, the film doesn't try for any historical accuracy either. What it does achieve is a uniquely relaxed and quiet comedy.

The Very Best of the Ed Sullivan Show (Vol. 2, 1992)

97 minutes; Color, Black and White; Excerpt from a television series; Copyright 1992, SOFA Entertainment; Buena Vista Home Video #1351

CREDITS: Hosted and Narrated by—Burt Reynolds; Produced by—Susan F. Walker; Director of Photography—Ralf Bode, A.S.C.; Written by—Peter Elbling, Andrew Solt; Directed by—Andrew Solt; We appreciate the talents of the many creative people who worked on *Toast of the Town* and *The Ed Sullivan Show* during its 23 years on the air.; *The Ed Sullivan Show* originally: Produced by—Robert Precht, Marlo Lewis; Directed by—John Wray, Tim Kiley, John Moffitt, Bob Schwarz; Edited by—James Gallagher, Jr., Tim Tobin, Leslie Tong; Co-Producer—Greg Vines; Segment Producer—Peter Elbling; Additional Editing—Bruce Bailey, Susan Eisner; New Music—Andrew Belling; Original Music—Ray Bloch and His Orchestra; Talent Executive—Carole Propp; On-Line Editor—Larry Chun; Unit Production Manager/Assistant Director—Michael Gallant; 2nd Assistant Director—Susan Norton; Art Director—Val Strazovec; Main Title Design—James House; Post Production Supervisor—David Rodriguez; Assistant Editor—Debra Sanderson; On-Line Assistant—Ray Wolf; Logo Design—Norman Moore; Re-recording Mixer—Tom Davis; Legal Clearances—Melody Siroty, Media Rights, Inc.; Clearance Administrator—Kristine Cascone; Production Coordinator—Catherine DeMeis; Photo Research—Claudia Falkenburg; Researcher—Jeff Gold; Set Decorator—Maxine Shepard; Lighting—Michael LaViollette; Key Grip—Dylan Shepard; Audio Production Mixers—Bruce Bisenz, Alan Barker; Audio Consultant—Art Shine; Hair and Makeup—Brian McManus, Gloria Levisohn, Mary Resnick; Announcer—John Harlan; Assistant to Mr. Solt—Bennett Crocker; Editorial Assistants—Bruce Gruman, Les Hidregi, Brett Hurt; Graphic Artist—Lee Scott; Production Staff—Kevin Cope, Lori Kleban, Patricia Maloney, Scott Cruchley, Christine Lenihan, Jonathan Platt; Restoration Consultants—David Crosthwait, Ron Furmanek, Paul Surratt; Still Photographs—CBS Photo Archives, Irv Haberman, L. Lautenberger, Romano, Bob Stahman, Pictorial Parade, UPI/Bettmann; We Gratefully Acknowledge—Neil Aspinall, Bob Crestani, Ronald Greenberg, Jack Haley, Jr. , Tom Hansen, Gary Hovey, Ricky Jay, Allen Klein, Marcy Levine, Greg Lipstone, Prince Rupert Loewenstein, Tom McGuire, Bill Mechanic, Elizabeth Precht, Robert Precht, Joseph Rascoff, Jerry Schilling, John Solt, Steve Warner, David Wolper; Executive in Charge of Production—Steven L. Pollock; Executive Producer—Andrew Solt

SYNOPSIS: One of several tapes which includes clips of Julie Andrews and Richard Burton doing scenes from the original Broadway musical *Camelot* (see also *The Best of Broadway Musicals, Broadway! A Musical History, Julie Andrews Sings Her Favorite Songs,* and *Lerner and Loewe Special*).

On this tape Burton and Andrews perform the title song from the musical during a 1964 appearance on the *Sullivan* show. The clip of them on *The Best of Broadway Musicals* tape is from 1961.

The rest of this tape is made up of clips of literally dozens of other acts which appeared on *Sullivan*. They range from 1951 to 1970 and include athletes, singers, rock-and-roll bands, actors, circus acts, dancers and comedians.

The Video Resume Writer (1987)

Not viewed; 30 minutes; Instructional; Copyright 1987, Filmatics Career Video, Inc., Vancouver, Washington

SYNOPSIS: An instructional tape on writing resumes, set in the time of King Arthur. Merlin lectures and gives examples of proper resume composition.

A Visit with King Arthur see Great Moments in History: "A Visit with King Arthur"

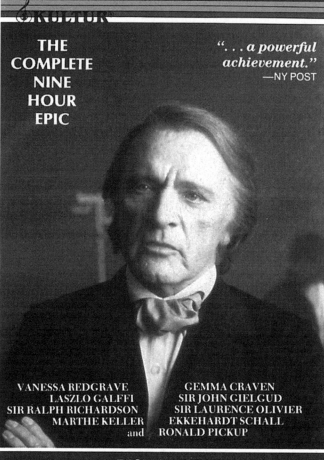

Video cassette art for *Wagner* (1982) (courtesy Kultur Video).

Wagner (1982)

9 hours; Color; Live Action; Copyright 1982, London Trust Cultural Productions, Ltd.; In Association with Hungarofilm and Magyar Televizio (Budapest); KULTUR Opera Profile; KULTUR Video #1247

CAST: Richard Burton (Wagner); Vanessa Redgrave (Cosima); Sir Laurence Olivier (Pfeuffer); Sir John Gielgud (Pfistermeister); Sir Ralph Richard-son (Pfordten); László Gálffi (Ludwig II); Marthe Keller (Mathilde Wesendonck); Ekkehardt Schall (Liszt); Ronald Pickup (Nietzsche); Gemma Craven (Minna); Bill Fraser (Mayor of Bayreuth); Jess Thomas (Niemann); Tony Palmer (Conductor); Gyorgy Gonda (Foreman); Brook Williams (Rubinstein); Manfred Jung (Unger); Stephen Oliver (Richter); Ernst Lenart (Brandt); Friedrich Schwardtmann (Violinist); Goetz Von Langheim (Fenstal); Richard Pasco (Otto Wesendonck); Claudia Solti (Isolde Von Bülow); Siegmar Schneider (Kaiser Wilhelm I); Laszlo Horvath (Hanslick); Brook Williams (Jonkowsky); Christoph Dittrich (Levi); Philipp Brammer (Siegfried); Niall Toibin (Lutz); Andrew Cruickshank (Narrator); Miguel Herz-Kestranek; John Shrapnel; Lisa Kreuzer; William Walton; Franco Nero; Arthur Lowe; Joan Plowright; Liza Goddard; Peter Woodthorpe; Peter Hofmann; Daphne Wagner; Adele Leigh; Vernon Dobtcheff; Arthur Denberg; Mark Burns; Sigfrit Steiner; Gabriel Byrne; Joan Greenwood; Stephan Paryla; Gwyneth Jones; Cyril Cusack; Jean-Luc Moreau; Yvonne Kenny; Heinz Zednik; Christopher Gable; Patrick Rollin; Jan Biczycki; Prunella Scales; Corin Redgrave; Barbara Leigh-Hunt

CREDITS: Written by—Charles Wood; Directed and Edited by—Tony Palmer; Photographed by—Vittorio Storaro; Music Conducted by—Georg Solti; Played by—The London Philharmonic, with The Budapest Symphony and The Vienna Philharmonic Orchestras; Executive Producers—Derek Brierley, Endre Flórián; Costumes Designed by—Shirley Russell; Production Designed by—Kenneth E. Carey; Produced by—Alan Wright; Additional Photography—Nic Knowland; Additional Music Conducted by—Ivan Fischer; Music Recorded by—Andrew Cornall, Stan Goodall, John Dunkerley, Collin Moorfoot; Facilities and additional recordings courtesy of the Decca Record Company, Ltd.; Sound Dubbing—Alan Dykes, Garth Marshall, Tony Gould-Davies, Tony Martin, Dean Humphreys, Jeff Roberts, Malorie Nicholls; Location Sound—Brian Saunders, Andras Horvath, Laszlo Nyiri; Musical and Historical Advisors—John Culshaw, Gordon Parry, Oswald

Georg Bauer, Tibor Erkel; Military Advisor — John Mollo; Wardrobe — Richard Pointing, Rebecca Breed, Maria Lenart, Karin Schmatz, Waltraut Freitag, Paul Vachon, Linda Burtenshaw, Ian Hickinbotham, William Pierce, Sue Honeybourne, Last Picture Frock, Cosprops, Ltd., Morris Angel & Son, Ltd., Theatre Kunst, Berlin, Kostumhaus Heiler, KG; Hairdressers — Christopher Taylor, Hannelore Uhrmacher; Wigs — Suzanne Stokes-Munton, Wig Creations; Makeup — Ron Berkeley, Craig Berkeley, Alan Folgoas; Art Direction — Terry Pritchard, Roger Cain, Dave Edwards, Phil Stokes, Antal Varga, Gyula Krasnyanski, Stephen Gorton, Peter Russell, Michael Drexler, Robyn Hamilton-Doney, Adolf Nurschinger, Andras Langmar, Eddy McMahon, Freddie Dobsack, Laszlo Makai, Peter Pasztorfi, Paul Templeman, Chris Bradley, Larry Duer, Harald Seidl, Robert Neuwirth; Rostrum Camera — Bert Walker, Zephyr Films; Camera Operator — Enrico Umetelli; Steadicam — Wolfgang Dickmann; Focus — Mauro Marchetti; Assistant — Stephen Navanson; 2nd Unit — Max Marrable; Key Grips — Alfredo Marchetti, Mario Marchetti, Antonio Marra, Sergio Ambrosi; Gaffers — Filippo Cafolla, Laszlo Richter, Mario Bafetti, Alberico Novelli, Luciano Giammei, Leo Lamoratta; Production Manager — Lorant Horvath; Supervising Editor — Graham Bunn; With — Scott Thomas, Alan Knight, Matthew Whieman, Ronnie Rothman, Amos Zuckerman, Xavier Russell; Unit Manager — William Walter Wilson III; Location Managers — Martin Bruce-Clayton, Martin Escher, Peter Koltai, Lazslo Tiszeker, Gerhard Hegele; Assistant Directors — Janos Szirtes, Paul Tivers; With — Ildiko Barnai, Lisa Bryer, Judith Goodman; Continuity — Sally Hay, Elke Luthi; Dialogue — Ossi Ragheb; Casting — Renate Arbes; Stunts — Mike Potter, Sue Crosland, Tim Condren; Production Executive — Wolfgang Odelga; Production Coordinator — Hilde Odelga; Production Accountants — Helga Ploiner, Ron Allday; Production Manager — Gerard Czepe; Production — Maureen Murray, Anne Ebbsworth, Eudes Brophy, Sonja Wengersky, Gerhard Rupp, Heribert Neumann, Margaret Schmidt, Mary Wilson, Vivien Allen, Sylvie Pateisky, Johann Patry, Brook Williams; Production facilities courtesy of WIEN-Film Ges. mbH; Film processed by Technicolor, S.P.A., Rome Marcello Gilberti, Ernesto Novelli; Sound Re-recorded by — Ladbroke Films; Optical Transfer — Thorn-EMI Elstree Studios, Ltd., Rank Film Laboratories, Ltd.; Dolby Stereo; Camera Equipment — Technovision; A record of music by Wagner conducted by Sir Georg Solti is available from the Decca Record Company, Ltd., or its licensees; Associate Producers — Simon Channing-Williams, Agnes C. S. Havas, Alan Capper, Granard Communications, Ltd.; Made on location in Hungary, Austria, Switzerland, Germany, Italy, Ireland and England.; Produced by Richard Wagner Film Ges. mbH (Wien) in association with Hungarofilm and MTV (Budapest); Assistant to the Director — Irina Pinter

SYNOPSIS: A Herculean production, this nine-hour, four-cassette epic biography of Richard Wagner concentrates heavily on his political involvements, his love affairs and his financial woes. It does not go into any detail on his thinking behind the adaptations of British legends for his three Arthurian operas, *Lohengrin, Tristan und Isolde* and *Parsifal*.

After the opening credits roll over scenes of Wagner's casket and funeral, the film starts in Dresden in 1848. There Wagner held the post of *Kapellmeister* to the king of Saxony. He is seen making speeches and agitating for republicanism versus Prussia, Hess and the monarchy. He calls on the king to declare Saxony a free state. As his audience cheers, sounds from a World War II–era Nazi rally are subtly overlaid.

When the revolution is attempted Wagner joins the crowds in the streets but the Prussians crush the effort. Branded a political criminal, Wagner flees to Zurich. His wife joins him there after some time and they move to Bordeaux, France. Wagner has an affair there, then they travel to Paris and to Switzerland.

Wagner's next affair (and ultimately the cause of his separation from Minna) is with Mathilde Wesendonck, the wife of one of his most faithful financial supporters. In the meantime Wagner has suffered a collapse and spent two months in a sanitarium. The next move is to Venice and though he is still watched for revolutionary activities, the police chief leaves him in peace.

Wagner travels again to Switzerland to dun Wesendonck for more money, then moves to Paris again, this time to stage *Tannhauser*. When opening night is disrupted by thugs hired by Wagner's enemies, the composer moves to Vienna, spends a short time in Russia and returns to Vienna.

Relentlessly faithful, Wagner's wife, Minna, succeeds in winning amnesty for him back in Dresden. However the newly enthroned 18-year-old king of Bavaria, Ludwig II, sends for Wagner. The lad is infatuated with Wagner's work and gives him free rein in Munich.

Simultaneously Wagner has been carrying on an affair with the daughter of one of his best friends, pianist Franz Liszt. Liszt warns Wagner of the dangers of a scandal, but Cosima becomes pregnant.

With Prussia threatening his kingdom, Ludwig's advisors talk him into sending Wagner away. Wagner and Cosima take a house together and Ludwig comes to live with them. Wagner talks Ludwig out of abdicating, but the king loses the war to Bismarck of Prussia.

Wagner and Cosima marry in 1870. As finances for his dream begin to gel, Bayreuth is chosen as the ideal location for Wagner's opera house, midway between king and kaiser. The construction begins in 1872 and takes five years. Wagner dies in 1883 in Venice.

It's a shame that with so much film time, so little of Wagner's life and thinking are included in this movie. Nothing is said of the early influences on Wagner, which included a father and stepfather who were both interested in the theater and several older sisters who became opera singers.

Nothing is said of his intellectualizing, his extensive readings and writings. Instead we learn of his sexual prowess, his shameless grubbing for money, his brush with homosexuality and his stupendous egotism.

Nothing is said of his theories on opera and "music drama," his socialistic ideas, his views on humanity in general. Yes, the film shows that he associated here and there with Nietzsche but any influences the two men may have had on one another are completely ignored.

There is no doubt that Wagner was a controversial figure and that in the pursuit of his own goals he did little to endear himself to other human beings on a personal level. Artistically and intellectually, however, Wagner had much to say. The fact that his music was used nearly 100 years later by Hitler's Reich should not negate closer examination of his works and their intent.

Though enticing because of its sheer length and phenomenal cast, this film is disappointingly superficial.

Wagner: Tristan und Isolde (1987)

55 minutes; Black and White; Live Performance; Copyright 1987, NBC Enterprises, Inc.; Copyright 1990, BMG Music; NBC International, Ltd.; Arturo Toscanini Collection, Volume 7; BMG Classics Video; RCA Victor Gold Seal Video #60338-3-RG

CREDITS: Executives in Charge of Production—Wayne Stuart, Sergio Getzel; Video Post Production Services—Du Art Video, a Division of Du Art Film Labs, Inc.; Audio Post Production Services—Howard Schwartz Recording, Inc.; Announcer—Martin Bookspan; Archival Materials Provided by—Library of Congress, Lincoln Center Research Library, National Broadcasting Company, Inc., RCA Records, Voice of America, Wave Hill; We thank the following individuals for their creative and technical support—Arthur Fierro, Robert Hupka, John Pfeiffer, Bob Carbone, Joe Dettmore, Roy Latham, Maria Orrico, Stas Pyka, John Rehberger, Laura Vaccaro; Special thanks to American Federation of Musicians—Donald McCormich, Glen Palmer, Mortimer Frank, Dave Koslow, Chris Burns, Robert Carneal, Michael Gray; NBC gratefully acknowledges the cooperation and assistance of the Toscanini family in the production of the television concerts.

SYNOPSIS: From March 1948 to March 1952 NBC television broadcast ten concerts of the NBC Symphony Orchestra conducted by Arturo Toscanini. This tape, volume 7 of the series, is a recording of the December 29, 1951 performance at Carnegie Hall in New York City.

Included are the Prelude to act 1 of *Lohengrin* and the Prelude to act 1 and Liebestod from act 3 of *Tristan und Isolde*.

Wagner and Venice (1982)

27 minutes; Color; Documentary; Copyright 1982, Filmarte, s.r.l.; Copyright 1987, Italtoons Corporation; Worldwide Distribution by Italtoons Corporation, New York; Waterbearer Films #WBF 8020

CREDITS: The Voice of Richard Wagner — Orson Welles; Commentary — Marla Scott; Music — Richard Wagner; Siegfried's Funeral March from the opera *Gotterdammerung* performed by the Radio Prague Symphony Orchestra; Conducted by — Antonino Polizzi; Musical Consultant — Franco Ferrara; Musical Direction — Josef Ceremuga; Directed by — Peter Ruttner; Cinematography — Ervin Sanders; Screenplay — Peter Ruttner; From an Idea by — Giuseppe Pugliese; Technical Services — Kratky Film Prague; Artistic Consultant — Luigina Bortolatto; With grateful appreciation to — La Regione Veneto, Benedetto Marcello Conservatory of Music, The Levi Foundation, The Association of Sette Mari di Venezia, Bailo Civic Museum of Greviso, Brandino Brandolini d'Adda, Alberto Geraldo, Brother Rey, Piero Verardo; English Language Version by — Sync, Ltd., Hollywood

SYNOPSIS: A brief but nicely done examination of Wagner's attachment to the city of Venice, particularly during the time he was writing the second act of *Tristan und Isolde*.

Gorgeous scenes of Venice and the Alps are accompanied by music from the opera as well as by "Siegfried's Funeral March." Excerpts from Wagner's letters, journals and other writings are read, which describe his feelings, struggles with a passage here and there and other thoughts.

Wagner Concert in Leipzig (1988)

90 minutes; Color; Live Performance; Copyright 1988, Fernsehen der DDR; KULTUR Music Series; KULTUR #1243

CREDITS: Ein Richard-Wagner-Abend aus dem Neuen Gewandhaus, Leipzig; Gewandhaus Orchester, Leipzig; Dirgent-Gewandhauskapellmeister — Kurt Masur; Solisten — Karan Armstrong, Sopran, Theo Adam, Baß; Gewandhauschor; Gewandhaus Kinderchor; Gewandhaus Jugendchor; Rundfunkchor Leipzig; Choreinstudierung — Georg Christoph Biller, Ekkehard Schreiber, Jöge Peter Weigle; Kamera — Hermann Grübler, Dietmar Hösel, Jens Kelle, Gerd Rü-

bartsch, Ingrid Jänicke, Rudolf Clauß, Rainer Kipping; Grafische Gestaltung — Georg Mohr; Technischeleitung — Volker Rosenburg; Bildtechnik — Manfred Kämmer; Bildschnitt — Rolf Wellingerhof; Tonregie — Dietlinde Kretzschmann; Tontechnik — Albrecht Krieger, Werner Stoph; Produktionsleitung — Heinz Hafemeister; Aufnahmeleitung — Erika Pakusa; Regieassistenz — Martina Haberecht; Redaktion — Manfred Nitschke, Ute Fendal; Regie — Gabriele Mohr

SYNOPSIS: At 40 minutes into the tape the overture from *Tristan und Isolde* is played. At 52 minutes into the tape Karan Armstrong sings Liebestod from *Tristan und Isolde*.

Wagner in Bayreuth (1992)

69 minutes; Color; Documentary; Copyright 1992, Unitel (Opera excerpts); Copyright 1992, Philips Classics Productions; Philips Video Classics #070 258-3

CREDITS: Special thanks to — The management and staff of the Bayreuth Festspiele, Unitel Film und Fernsehproduktionsgesellschaft, mbH & Co., Munich, The management and staff of the Richard Wagner Foundation, Bayreuth, Dr. Manfred Eger; Consultant — Peter Emmerich; Editorial Coordination — Barbara Gessler; Sound — Martin Dubbeldam; Assistant Producer — Colette Melsen; Video Editor — Harry Van Loo, PG Editing International; Producer — Job Maarse; Executive Producer — Paul Schwendener; Director/Camera — Dick Kool; With excerpts from the Unitel films of the Bayreuth productions.

SYNOPSIS: Because of his fractious political views and his less-than-exemplary personal life, Richard Wagner spent many years wandering from one European country to another. He did spend a portion of his life, however, in the fulfillment of his dream of constructing the ideal opera house.

With the financial support of King Ludwig II of Bavaria, contributions from friends and even an international fundraising effort the Festspielhaus was finally built in Bayreuth. Wagner also built a home there, "Wahnfried."

In the first 22 minutes of this tape Wagner's grandson, Wolfgang Wagner, discusses a number of aspects of his grandfather's life and the Bayreuth opera house itself. Wolfgang speaks in German and subtitles are provided in English.

Wolfgang describes Wagner's move to Bayreuth and the numerous problems that cropped up in the building of the theater. With money a constant problem, the structure that stands to this day was actually intended as a temporary facility.

Wolfgang's account of the details of Wagner's design for the opera house are particularly interesting. Wagner took much from ancient Greek amphitheater design and applied what he called "democratic" principles to the floor plan. Seating was arranged so that every member of the audience had an undisturbed view of the stage.

Wagner was the first to darken the theater during performances. His curtain opened from the center like the iris of an eye. The orchestra was placed under the stage, making the music seem to come from all around the performers.

Wolfgang also conducts a tour of Wahnfried. Wagner's study is shown as is the practice room where soloists were introduced to their parts. The original manuscript of Wagner's "farewell to the world," the opera *Parsifal,* is on display there.

The remainder of the tape is a series of three- to five-minute excerpts from ten of Wagner's operas. Included are a scene from act 3 of *Lohengrin,* one from act 1 of *Tristan und Isolde* and one from act 3 of *Parsifal.* They are all sung in German with no subtitles.

Waxwork II: Lost in Time (1991)

104 minutes; Color; Live Action; Copyright 1991, Electronic Pictures, Inc.; An Anthony Hickox Film; Live Home Video #9893

CAST: Zach Galligan (Mark Loftmore); Monika Schnarre (Sarah Brightman); Martin Kemp (Baron von Frankenstein); Bruce Campbell (John Loftmore); Michael Des Barres (George); Jim Metzler (Roger); Sophie Ward (Elenore); Marina Sirtis (Gloria); Billy Kane (Nigel); Joe Baker (The Peasant); Juliet Mills (The Defense Lawyer); John Ireland (King Arthur); Patrick MacNee (Sir Wilfred); David Carradine (The Beggar); Alexander Go-

dunov (Scarabus, the Master); George "Buck" Flower (Stepfather); Jack Eisman (Cabbie); Buckley Norris (Judge); Paul Hamp (Prosecution); Stanley Sheff (Speaker for Jury); John O'Leary (Herr Vogel); Elisha Shapiro (Felix); Stefano Mitsakakis (Frankenstein's Monster); Maxwell Caulfield (Mickey); Erin Gourlay (Ghost Girl); Bryan "Travis" Smith (Peasant Boy); Steve Matteucci (Master's Guard); Guy Luthan (Master's Officer); Kate Murtagh (The Matron); Eyal Rimmon (Chief Worshipper); Shanna L. Teare (Panther Girl); Anthony Hickox (King's Officer); Piers R. C. Plowden (King's Guard); Harrison Young (James Westburne); Ivan S. Markota (Press Man); Marie Foti (Press Woman); Frank Zagarino (Zombie Killer #1); Martin C. Jones (Zombie Killer #2); Darryl Pierce (Zombie Killer #3); John Breznikar (Mark's Father); Lisa Oestreich (Mark's Mother); Brent Bolthouse (Cabbie #2); Caron K. Berstein (The Master's Girl); Gerry Lively (Lead Prisoner); Yanko Damboulev (Lead Prisoner); Jim Silverman (Lead Prisoner); Paul Madigan (Lead Prisoner); Kim Henderson (Party Babe); Treasure Little (Party Babe); Lisa Jay (Party Babe); Elizabeth Notteli (Party Babe); Achena Massey (Party Babe); Marcia Santos (Party Babe); Felicia Hernandez (Party Babe); Cristal Calderoni (Party Babe); Bob Keen (Mad Monk); Chris Breed (King's Announcer); Emile Gladstone (The Jester); Michael Viela (Dr. Jekyll); Greg Woertz (Zombie Killer); Ilona Margolis (Zombie Killer); Martin Mercer (Lead Zombie); Dorian Langdon (Romero); John Mushroom Mappin (Argento); James Hickox (Polanky); Jonathan Breznihar (Shelly); Mark Courier (Scott); Robert Kass (Hitchcock); Steve Painter (Nosferatu); Drew Barrymore (Vampire Victim); Hadria Lawner (Vampire Victim); Paul Jones (The Hand); Alex Butler (Jack the Ripper); Yolanda Jilot (Lady of the Night); Godzilla (Himself)

CREDITS: Written and Directed by — Anthony Hickox; Produced by — Nancy Paloian; Executive Producer — Mario Sotela; Executive in Charge of Production — Gregory Woertz; Director of Photography — Gerry Lively; Production Designer — Steve Hardie; Editor — Christopher Cibelli; Original Score by — Steve Schiff; Special Makeup and Effects by — Bob Keen; Costume Designer — Mark Bridges; Special Optical Effects — Robert D. Bailey; Casting — Caro Jones, C.S.A., Jack Jones; 1st Assistant Director — Paul Martin; 2nd Assistant Director — Phil Robinson; Associate Editor — James Hickox; Production Coordinator — Michelle R. Erby; Stunt Coordinator — Bobby Bragg; Stunt Players — Shanna Teare, Kane W. Hodder, Solly Marx, William Oliver, Spiro Razatos; Production

Accountant — Stephanie Rose; Production Manager — Elaine Fiona Ferguson; Camera Operator — Richard Clabaugh; 1st Assistant Camera Person — Troy Cook; 2nd Assistant Camera Person — Erin-Bruce T. Cook; Apprentice Camera Assistant — Lisa M. Jones; Gaffer — Russ Brandt; Best Boy Electricians — M. Phil Shearer, Adam Santelli; Electricians — Carlo J. Papica, Tim Day, Roger Meilink, Warren Eig, Linda Perry, Bill Tannicliffe; Key Grip — Duane Journey; Best Boy Grip — Basil Schmidt; Grips — Chris Godfrey, Anthony Roush, James D. Wickman, Jeff Journey, Eric Mayer, James Morton; Swing — Kagan Erturan; Art Director — John Chichester; Set Decorator — David Allen Koneff; Lead Person — Lisa Maria Ozanine; Set Dresser — Stephen R. Blandino; Swings — Travis Bell, Ruben Depaoli; Property Master — Peter Mark; Property Assistant — Roy R. Sifuentes; Associate Costume Designer — Sigrid Insul; Costumer — Eden E. Clark; Hair and Makeup Supervisor — Rudy Sotomayor; Makeup Artist — Beatrice Marot; Hair and Makeup Assistant — Lisa Rosenberg; Script Supervisor — Paul F. Bowers; Sound Mixer — Rick Wadell; Boom Operator — David Lester; Special Makeup Effects by — Image Animation; Special Makeup Effects Creator — Bob Keen; Special Makeup Effects Designers — Steve Painter, Martin Mercer, Paul Spateri, Paul Jones; Special Makeup Effects Technicians — Steve Norrington, Richard Darwin, Fiona Leech, Martin Parual, Bernard H. Wood, Dave Chagouri, Shaun Harrison, Ian Morse, Gary Tunnicliff; Special Makeup Effects Assistant — Mark Coulier; Contact Lenses and Special Makeup Materials Supplied by Bob May; 1st Assistant Editor — Robb Sullivan; 2nd Assistant Editor — Trudy Yee; Editor's Apprentice — Mushroom Mappin; ADR Editor — Stephen Isaacs; ADR Assistant Editor — Zac Lovas; Sound Designer — Leonard Marcel; Sound Effects Editors — Peter Carlstedt, Scott Weber; Assistant Sound Designer — Larayne Decoeur; Assistant Sound Effects Editor — Steve Christopher; "The Hand" Voice — Wayne Anderson; ADR Mixer — Alan Holly; ADR Recordist — Kelly Cabral; Foley Walkers — Elisha Birnbaum, Brian Vancho; Recording by — Dominick Tavella, Sound One Corporation, New York; Negative Cutters — Magic Film Works, Syd Cole, Arleen Goldenberg, Marie-Helene Desbiens; Post Production Delivery Coordinator — Stephen A. Isaacs; Associate Post Production Delivery Coordinator — Jason Lovas; Construction Coordinators — Frank Taylor, Benedict L. Paglia; Scenic Designer — Carla A. Pagiaro; Scenic Painter — Des Martin; Still Photographer — Abram Perlstein; Titles and Optical Effects by — Digital Visions; Optical Line-up — Phil Barberio; Special Animation Effects by — Lynda Weinman; Additional Animation by — Glenn Campbell; Special Effects Coordinator — Kevin McCarthy; Special Effects Foreman — G. Bruno Stemple; Special Effects Assistant — Casey Quinn; Location Manager — Tom Ingersoll; Transportation Coordinator — John W. Barbee; Honeywagon Driver — Robert Giosson; The Shotmaker Driver — Bill Isaacson; Keylite PSI Driver — Hector G. Gallardo; Drivers — Mike Painter, Todd Painter; Steadicam Operators — John Naler, Peter C. Jenson; Publicist — Marilynn Heston; Associate Publicist — Laurence Cohen; Animal Coordinator — Shanna Jacobs; Raven/Redtail Hawk Wranglers — Frank DiSesso, Glenn DiSesso; Panther Wrangler — Ric Glassey; Horse Wranglers — Kristin Cotner, Stacy Soules, Terri Pencek, Darlyne Terry, Dennis Flowers; Stage Maintenance — David Allen; Extras Casting — Pas Casting; Craft Service — Jil Kummer; Catering — Custom Mobile Catering; Chef — Currie Dobson; Assistant Chef — Ernesto Hernandez; Video Playback — Marc Marcum; 2nd Unit: Director — Bob Keen; Director of Photography — Russ Brandt; Production Manager — Michelle R. Erby; 1st Assistant Director — Linda Morgenstern; 2nd Assistant Director — Brian Garbellini; Electric Pictures Executives — Eyal Rimmon, David K. Brownstein, Scott Edel; 2nd 2nd Assistant Director — Joseph John Schultz; Producer's Assistant — Pamela J. Paloian; Director's Assistant — Emile Gladstone; Office Production Assistant — Yanko L. Dambouley; Production Assistants — Chris Milani, Cari Frankson, Steve Alwood, Scott Parent, Craig K. Angell, Paul Niekerk, Phil McIntyre; Orchestrations and Additional Music Score — Arthur Barrow, Robert Irving; Score Engineer — Scott Gordon; Insurance — Alber G. Rubin & Company; Completion Bond — Film Finances, Inc.; Production Financing — Banque Paribas; Payroll Services Provided by — IDC Services; Cameras and Lenses Provided by — Panavision; Production Equipment Provided by — Keylite Production Services, Inc.; Dolly and Track Provided by — J. L. Fisher; Camera Crane Provided by — Leonard/Chapman Studio Services, Inc.; Color by — Foto-Kem Lab; Editorial Facilities Provided by — Directors Sound; "Lost in Time" (title song): Written, Produced and Performed by Dwayne "Muffla" Simon and Darryl "Big Dad" Pierce of the Los Angeles Posse (appearing courtesy of Atlantic Records); ADR Stage Services Provided by — Matrix Alliance, Inc.; Music Video — I.O.U.1 Productions; Music Video Directed by — Anthony Hickox; Music Video Producers — Judi McCreary, Martin C. Jones; Special

Thanks to — Westside Pavilion, Universal Studios, Mohammed Yusef, Guy Collins, Hannah Leader, Steve Ransohoff, Michael Mendelsohn, Bruno Hoefler, Catherine Hasler, Daniel Zbojniewicz, Bill Nisselson, Dennis Spiegelman, John Breznikar, Laureen Foti, Diane Marcoff, Ken Manson, Jr., Coca Cola, USA, Stanley Sheff, Larry Michalski, Dan Donovan, City of Vernon, City of Los Angeles, Rick Johnson, Benedict L. Paglia, The Roxbury, Paul Fisher and IT Models, The Living Room, Steve Dagger, Teresa Wells, Stewart Thorndik; Filmed entirely in the 4th Dimension

SYNOPSIS: Yes, King Arthur has appeared in a horror film. Unfortunately (or perhaps fortunately), there is no real Arthurian content in the segment, including no Arthur. He is not once called Arthur by the characters around him, but he is identified as the king of Britain and is listed in the credits as King Arthur.

Waxwork II: Lost in Time is a tour de force of what might be called referential movie making. It spoofs horror and science fiction films, comically reproducing scenes from a number of classics of the genres.

As can be surmised from the title, *Waxwork II: Lost in Time* is the sequel to a film called *Waxwork*. In that first film, the twisted founder of a waxwork has in mind unleashing the forces of evil in the universe. Happily his plans are thwarted and the waxwork is destroyed but not before a lot of carnage and death.

The sequel opens with a young couple, Sarah and Mark, escaping the inferno of the burning waxwork. A bodiless hand follows Sarah home and kills her father. Sarah is accused of the crime but before she can be convicted she and Mark escape into the tunnels of time by using a Cartagrian Time Door Opener which they've inherited from their mentor in the first film.

In their third random bounce through the centuries they land in Britain at the time of King Arthur. Several knights in black armor come along and carry Sarah off by force. Mark stumbles across a beggar who informs him that the men are the minions of the wicked Scarabus, the Master.

The beggar further explains that Scarabus took his woman, Lenore, and that Mark can find the Master at the Castle Poe. He then gives Mark a sword which, as he hands it over, seems to glint with a magical light. Mark heads off to find Sarah.

This is a particularly exotic and kinky Britain. Scarabus and his men are reminiscent of heavy metal rock-and-roll band members. There are lots of half-naked women lolling around, belly dancers performing here and there and a strange cult of black magic panther worshippers lurking in the basement.

In her ancient Britain guise, Sarah is Scarabus's sister, whom he intends to marry off to the king. Arthur and his men arrive to share dinner with the weird bunch. Scarabus drugs the king, then assumes his appearance with the intent of marrying Sarah himself and taking over the throne. Mark arrives in time to expose the plot, Arthur is saved and the movie wanders off to its conclusion.

The only thing the movie includes that is even remotely related to knights and chivalry, let alone Arthurian legend, is the costumes of Arthur's men. They are in silver armor covered by white tunics with red crosses on their chests. None of the men are named. There is no Lancelot, Gawain or any of the rest, no Merlin or Guinevere.

Arthur himself is a handsome but balding elderly fellow in a red tunic. Mark's sword never turns out to be magical and, though it was hinted at, is never called Excalibur.

The Way of the Wizard see ***Deepak Chopra: "The Way of the Wizard"***

What Is a Melody? see ***Leonard Bernstein's Young People's Concerts: "What Is a Melody?"***

Where Is Parsifal? **(1983)**
Not viewed; Copyright 1983

CAST: Orson Welles (Klingsor); Donald Pleasence (MacKintosh); Tony Curtis (Parsifal Katzenellenbogen); Erik Estrada (Henry Board II);

Peter Lawford (Montague Chippendale); Berta Dominguez (Elba); Ron Moody (Beersbohm); Christopher Chaplin (Ivan); Nancy Roberts (Ruth)

CREDITS: Director — Henry Helman; Producer — Daniel Carrillo; Executive Producer — Terence Young; Writer — Berta Dominguez; Editors — Russell Lloyd, Peter Hollywood; Music — Hubert Rostaing, Ivan Jullien; Production Design — Malcolm Stone; Cinematography — Norman G. Langley; Best Boy — John Rogers; Lighting — Lee Lighting Ltd.

Willy McBean and His Magic Machine (1965)

94 minutes; Color; Puppets (Animagic); Copyright 1965/1992, Solar Home Video, a Division of Xenon Entertainment; A Magna Pix Distribution Corporation Release; A Marshall Naify Presentation; A Videocraft/Dentsu Picture

FEATURING THE TALENTS OF: Larry Mann; Billie Richards; Alfie Scopp; Paul Kligman
WITH: Claude Ray; Corrine Connely; James Doohan; Peggi Loder; Paul Soles
CREDITS: Continuity Design — Antony Peters; Additional Dialogue — Lon Korobkin; Animation Supervision — Tad Mochinaga; Choreography — Edward Brinkman; Music by — Edward Thomas; Songs by — Jim Polack, Edward Thomas, Gene Forrell; Musical Supervision by — Forrell, Thomas and Polack Associates, Inc.; Soundtrack Supervision — Bernard Cowan; Associate Director — Kizo Nagashima; Producers — Jules Bass, Larry Roemer; Written, Produced and Directed by — Arthur Rankin, Jr.

SYNOPSIS: The evil but redeemable Professor Rasputin Von Rotten plots to become the most famous person in history. Having built a time machine, he plans to personally invent fire and the wheel, build the pyramids, become the best king in the world, discover America and shoot Buffalo Bill to become the fastest gun in the West.

The heroes are Willy McBean, a science whiz kid, and the professor's escaped Mexican monkey, Pablo. Teaming up to chase Von Rotten through time, they manage to foil his dastardly schemes.

Willy McBean and His Magic Machine is a series of musical peeks (there are lots of song-and-dance numbers performed by the puppets) at five moments in history.

In the third segment of Willy's adventures he and Pablo meet King Arthur and a few of the Knights of the Round Table. Appearing are a Lancelot who sure does dance a lot, Gawain, Ivanhoe (believe it or not) and of course Merlin.

The wimpy and rotund King Arthur is worried that he won't be able to pull the famed sword from the stone. Von Rotten, figuring that it's just rusted in place, pours some rust remover on it, intending to come back later and claim the throne of England. Interestingly, Excalibur is alive as well, with a face at the cross point of the hilt and pommel.

Merlin enlists the aid of a very sexy Morgan Le Fay. Von Rotten, distracted by her wiles, is immobilized when she surreptitiously tightens the bolts on all the joints of his armor. Arthur pulls the sword and a celebration follows. Irrelevantly a dragon decides to interrupt the festivities but Excalibur flies around the room, scaring off the gate-crasher. All ends well for sixth-century England but Von Rotten escapes, headed for ancient Egypt.

For any adult stuck watching this there are a few comical moments. The best are provided by Pablo, the monkey. With his heavy Mexican accent, some of his side quips are over the heads of small children.

Witch's Brew see under The Adventures of Sir Lancelot

Wizard's Peak see under Princess Gwenevere and the Jewel Riders

The Woman Next Door (La Femme d'à Côté) (1981)

Color; 106 minutes; Drama/Live Action; French with English subtitles; Copyright 1981, Les Films du Carrosse S.A., TF1/UA; Copyright 1992, Janus Films/Films Incorporated; Janus Films; Public Media Home Vision #WOM040

CAST: Fanny Ardant (Mathilde); Michele Baumgartner (Arlette); Gerard Depardieu (Bernard);

Henri Garcin (Phillippe); Veronique Silver (Odile Jouve); Roger Van Hool; Philippe Morier-Genoud; Nicole Vauthier; Muriel Combe; Olivier Becquaert (Thomas)

CREDITS: Director—François Truffaut; Screenplay—François Truffaut, Suzanne Schiffman, Jean Aurel; Music—Georges Delerue, Editions Sidonir; Director of Photography—William Lubtchansky; New Subtitle Adaptation by—Laurent Bouzereau; Assistants—William Lubtchansky, Caroline Champetier, Barcha Bauer; D'Écors—Jean-Pierre Kohut-Svelko; Assiste de—Pierre Compertz; Accessoire—Jacques Preisach; Son—Michel Laurent, Jacques Maumont; Assistant—Michel Miellier; Bruitage—Daniel Couteau; Montage—Martine Barraqué; Assiste de—Marie-Aimée Debril, Catherine Drzymalkowski; Assistant Director—Suzanne Schiffman; Assiste de—Alain Tasma, Gilles Loutfi; Scripte—Christine Pellé; Costumes—Michèle Cerf; Assiste de—Malika Brahim; Maquillage—Thi Loan N'Guyen; Coiffure—Catherine Crassac; Régisseur Général—Roland Thénot; Assiste de—Jacques Vidal, Françoise Héberlé; Attaché de Presse—Simon Mizrahi; Photographes—Alain Venisse; Administrateur de Production—Jean-François Lentretien; Secritaires de Production—Josiane Couedel, Anny Bartanowski; Electriciens—Robert Beulens, Emmanuel Demorgon, Patrick Lemaire; Machinists—André Atellian, Michel Gentils; Directeur du Production—Armand Barbault.

SYNOPSIS: There is some debate as to whether or not *The Woman Next Door* was intended as a modernization of the Tristan and Isolde legend. Since all the basic elements of the tale are present and since the film appears in other lists of Arthurian films it will be treated here as a version of the legend (see also *The Eternal Return* and *Tristana*).

There is an older man with great responsibilities who marries a younger woman. There is a young man, married to another, who loves the older man's wife. The young people cannot resist each other and wind up dying together. There is a disfigured individual involved who, in this case, acts as narrator.

Bernard Coudray and his wife, Arlette, have lived in a suburb of Grenoble for some time. Bernard trains and tests tanker-ship pilots at a nearby facility. His job is of little significance but makes an amusing connection with Tristan and Isolde. Tristan took ships a number of times in the legend, sailing from Cornwall to Ireland at least twice in the service of King Mark. Then it was a ship he awaited as he lay dying, hoping for news of Isolde.

By contrast, Bernard looks a bit comical when involved with his job. The training vessels are scale models of freighters and tankers, just big enough to stay afloat with two men in them. They sail about in a pond owned by the pilots' administrating bureau.

As the film opens Phillippe Bauchard and his new wife, Mathilde, move into the house next door to the Coudrays. Phillippe is an air traffic controller at the Grenoble airport while Mathilde wants to write and illustrate children's books. Phillippe is considerably older than Mathilde and he explains at one point to Bernard that he saw her as his last chance for happiness.

It turns out that Mathilde and Bernard had been on the verge of marriage themselves some eight years ago. In fact Mathilde had gotten pregnant by Bernard but had had an abortion.

So from the outset it is easy to tie this film to the Tristan and Isolde legend. Phillippe is the older Mark, Bernard the young Tristan and Mathilde takes the place of Isolde. Arlette might be seen as Tristan's second Isolde—the one he married in the legend, just as in this film.

Their renewed proximity is more than Bernard can stand at first. When his wife invites the Bauchards to dinner, Bernard pretends to be late at work and never shows up for the meeting. Instead he spends the evening with Mme. Jouve, the manager of the local tennis club.

Mme. Jouve is an attractive middle-aged woman with a crippled right leg. Over dinner Bernard learns that Jouve had jumped from a seventh-story window because of a lover.

Jouve seems to be the disfigured individual often associated with the Tristan and Isolde legend. It was Gottfried von Strassburg who introduced the dwarf, Melot, into the tale.

Melot spied on Tristan for King Mark. In the film *The Eternal Return* the dwarf's name is Achille. In the movie *Tristana* the deformity is placed on Tristana herself with the loss of her right leg from the knee down. In *The Woman Next Door,* a right leg is permanently injured but not lost.

Where the dwarf in Gottfried and *The Eternal Return* acts as a spy, Jouve in *The Woman Next Door* is a neutral observer and the narrator of the story. She exhibits a bemused air in her recounting of the tale.

Mathilde and Bernard are only able to avoid each other for a short time and they soon start an extramarital affair. Mathilde however has second thoughts and tries to end things with Bernard. When Phillippe announces at a garden party that he and Mathilde are leaving on a honeymoon-type vacation, it is too much for Bernard. He goes berserk, actually attacking Mathilde in his efforts to get her to stay with him.

With the accumulated shock, embarrassment and pressure of the situation, Mathilde suffers a nervous breakdown. She is held in a hospital for some time and it is only Bernard's presence that finally brings her back to some normalcy. Mathilde and Phillippe move away.

The denouement comes when one night Bernard hears an unlatched door banging in the wind at the now uninhabited house next door. He dresses, sneaks out and finds Mathilde alone in the dark of her empty former residence.

They make love but while still lying in post-conjugal bliss, Mathilde pulls a revolver from her purse and kills Bernard. She then turns the gun on herself and that is how their bodies are found. In narrating the close of the film, Mme. Jouve states that if she were asked to choose an epitaph for them it would be "Neither with you nor without you."

World Famous Fairy Tales: "Swan Knight" (1987)

Not viewed; Color; Copyright 1987, Hosca Home Video Productions, Inc.; Library of Congress Call #VAA9344 (viewing copy); Library of Congress Catalogue #87707936/MP

CREDITS: Producer — Eric Harding; Engineer — Eric Harding

The World of Joseph Campbell: Transformations of Myth Through Time (1989)

Each episode approximately 60 minutes; Color; Documentary; Copyright 1989, Mythology Limited; Public Media Video; A Public Media, Inc., Release

CREDITS: Produced by — William Free; Directed by — Roy A. Cox; Hosted by — Peter Donat; Production Supervisor — Mark Krigbaum; Edited by — Richard Sydel, Brad Sanders; Camera Operators — Brian Pratt, Alan Babbitt, Dan Goodman, Robin Mortarotti; Lighting Director — Dan Goodman; Video/Audio — Steve Calou, Dan Lutz, Kean Sakata; Photo Research — Lynne Dal Poggetto, Rosemary O'Connell; Production Services — Eclipse Productions; Post Production — Eclipse Productions, Realtime Video, BAVC, Varitel Video; Executive Producer — Stuart L. Brown; A production of William Free Productions and Mythology Ltd., in Association with Holoform Research, Inc.; Major funding for this program was provided by Laurence S. Rockefeller

SYNOPSIS: *The World of Joseph Campbell: Transformations of Myth Through Time* is a nine-tape collection consisting of 13 episodes. Each episode runs for approximately 60 minutes, covering the gamut of topics on mythology from "In the Beginning: Origins of Man and Myth" to the final episode, "In Search of the Holy Grail: The Parzival Legend."

Perhaps best known for his huge four-volume work, *The Masks of God* (1959–1967), Campbell was a long-time member of the literature faculty of Sarah Lawrence College. His research and prolific writings on comparative mythology are known worldwide.

The *Transformations of Myth Through Time* videos are presented in lecture format with Campbell expounding before a live audience of students. In a marvelously rambling style, Campbell draws together history, archaeology, mythology, sociology, psychology, linguistics and other subjects in examining the sweep and connectedness of mankind's myths, legends and religions. The final three episodes of the series deal with the Arthurian legends, the prime myth of Western civilization.

EPISODE 11: "WHERE THERE WAS NO PATH: ARTHURIAN LEGENDS AND THE WESTERN WAY"

Campbell's main point in this segment of the series is that the Arthurian legends represent the absorption of the communal thought of Christianity by the more individualistically minded Europeans. His prime example and demonstration of this thesis comes from a poem written by an anonymous Cistercian monk, "The Quest for the Holy Grail." In this story, which Malory later incorporated into his work, the Grail appears in King Arthur's court during a feast. When it vanishes Gawain proposes the quest to find the Grail. All the knights agree but Campbell points out that they also state it would be a disgrace for them to go in a group.

So each knight goes his separate way, entering the forest of adventure "at his own chosen point where there was no path," Campbell says. Anytime in the myth that a knight follows someone else's path, Campbell continues, he goes astray.

Campbell says this theme exists at the very heart of Western thought. His recurring statement is that the individual, though bound by societal forms and limitations, must "find his own joy," in other words, his own path through life.

Campbell cites the 100 years from 1150 to 1250 A.D. as the Arthurian romance period and as the counterpart to the Homeric period of the Greco-Roman world. In describing what led to the sudden flowering of medieval writings about Arthur's knights, Campbell gives a sweeping if somewhat disjointed history of Europe, Rome, the Celts and a few other odds and ends.

In discussing Bronze Age influences it is noted that burial mounds in Mycenae are remarkably similar to those from the same period found in Ireland. Stonehenge is shown to have its counterparts in other parts of Europe. Of Iron Age developments Campbell describes the migrations first of Hallstatt Celts, then later the LaTène peoples. While he calls the Hallstatts stolid "ox-cart" sorts, the LaTène are characterized as charioteers and warriors. The next cultural overlay in Europe comes from Rome.

Finally Campbell delves into a historical interpretation of King Arthur himself. The one piece of physical evidence Campbell cites is a monument discovered in St. Pé, a town near Lourdes. This stone, dating from the first century A.D. bears an inscription which reads, "Lexeia, daughter of Odan has gained merit through her vows to Artehe." The name of this god, Artehe, Campbell says, is related to the names of gods and goddesses like Artemis, the star Arcturus and others. "Arthur," he says, is a version of this name and so one can see the association possible between an individual named Arthur and the old gods.

According to Campbell a military man trained originally by the Romans gained fame for his prowess in battle. When Rome pulled out of Britain this *dux bellorum,* named Arthur, assisted the native kings in their battles against the invading Angles and Saxons. As the legends of his exploits grew this Arthur became more closely tied to ideal and mystical things. For instance the twelve great victories attributed to Arthur may be nothing more than a mixing of his stories with the signs of the zodiac.

Escaping the foreign attacks, many people emigrated from southern Britain to Brittany. The hopeful legend of Arthur's return grew among these people, who came to be called Bretons. The sleeping warlord would restore them to their native land.

EPISODE 12: "A NOBLE HEART: THE COURTLY LOVE OF TRISTAN AND ISOLDE"

By the twelfth century, Campbell notes, Europe was not so much interested in Arthur as in all the characters who swirled around him. By that time the legends had been turned into something very different from their original form. The Celtic heroes who had fought with Arthur had been transformed into "armor-clad Christian knights," as Campbell puts it.

Geoffrey of Monmouth was the first to call Arthur a king but Chrétien de Troyes was the first to put the legends in their medieval form in writing. Arthurian legend was completely taken over by the idea of courtly love.

The first half of this episode is a discussion of courtly love and its influences. Since among the upper classes marriages were arranged, love was something known almost exclusively outside of marriage. This was not only accepted but expected. Campbell speaks of courts of love in which women sat in judgment of cases. One case he uses as an example concluded with the court deciding that marriage and love are contradictory terms.

In this system of male-female relationships the woman was expected to go through a lockstep series of appraisals of a suitor. Any man seeking the heart of a lady was at her mercy as she assigned him any task or trial that she thought might show his character. Her main goal would be to determine whether or not the man had a gentle heart. Once assured that this was not just a lusty adventurer the woman was expected to grant *merci,* that is, some physical yielding to him. If she did not then she was termed *sauvage.*

In the second half of the lecture Campbell describes at some length six of Chrétien's tales. Though Chrétien's first story, *Tristan,* is lost, it is known that it was not as well received as his later works. The tale as told by Chrétien evidently did not meet the peculiar proprieties of courtly love, and according to Campbell, it was rejected by the ladies of the time.

There is nothing remarkable in Campbell's outline of *Erec and Enide* or *Cliges,* but his sense of humor is at its most obvious in his discussion of Chrétien's Lancelot story, *The Knight of the Cart.* Campbell is particularly

amusing in his recounting of "the trial of the perilous bed." This formulaic trial involves a knight entering a bedroom, lying down and being attacked by unseen enemies. Spears, arrows, even lions may suddenly enter the chamber and try to kill him. The bed itself rushes crazily around the room. Campbell's interpretation is that this is "the masculine experience of the feminine temperament. It doesn't make sense, just endure it and the boon of womanhood is yours."

The last portion of episode 12 deals with the Tristan legend. The most important version of *Tristan and Isolde,* Campbell states, was by Gottfried von Strassburg. In his review of Gottfried's work, Campbell's most salient point relating to his discussions of courtly love is that the love potion introduced into the story absolves the two of sin.

The conflict between honor and love created by courtly love is a difficult one to resolve. In order that these activities occur, a husband and marriage vows must be betrayed, Christian principles stretched and broken. A love potion is an easy but perfect solution. Tristan and Isolde are innocent since they literally cannot help themselves.

EPISODE 13: "IN SEARCH OF THE HOLY GRAIL: THE PARZIVAL LEGEND"

In this, the final episode of the series, Campbell tells the Parsifal, or Parzival, story of Wolfram Von Eschenbach. In the opening he reiterates the fact that, as the Arthurian legends were taken up by Europeans on the Continent — particularly the French — interest was focused primarily on Arthur's knights, not on Arthur. The French had their Charlemagne. They didn't need King Arthur.

Each of the knights, Campbell says, came to represent something specific in human nature. Lancelot became the man consumed by love. Galahad was the monkish knight. Parzival, especially in Wolfram's work, represented the victory of spontaneous, natural action as opposed to the soul-crushing indoctrinations of the church and societal expectations.

Campbell gives credit to Chrétien's as the earliest version of the Grail story put into verse. Though unfinished, *The Story of the Grail* is Chrétien's longest work. As many medieval authors did, Chrétien claimed his poem to be based on a mysterious but now lost ancient text. Wolfram too made a similar claim but with a difference. His source, Campbell points out, was one Kyot from Spain, who in turn is supposed to have gotten the tale from a Moorish alchemist.

This theme of the acceptance of things not Christian runs throughout Wolfram's work. Campbell discusses the fact that Wolfram's Grail is of stone, like the Muslim stone from heaven which resides at Mecca. In Wolfram it is neutral angels who bring the Grail to Earth, angels who did not take sides in the war in Heaven when Lucifer would not bow before man. The very name "Parzival," Campbell says, means piercing the veil — the veil of opposites. The veil that Wolfram's Parzival pierces is that which separates the natural goodness that can be the result of the spontaneous acts of a noble heart from the wasteland of the old ways of life: courtly love and arranged marriages, the oppression of the church and so on.

Wolfram's Parzival marries for love, not convenience or politics. And no priest presides over the marriage ceremony. Parzival asks permission of his wife to search for his mother. Parzival comes upon the Grail king, who has been castrated in a joust with a pagan. Campbell says that this is Wolfram's way of saying that all of Europe has been castrated by the church. Parzival's failure to ask the right question of the Grail king is a temporary perpetuation of the wasteland, Campbell says, and the knight spends five years finding his way back to the Grail Castle, to the goodness of spontaneous action taken by a noble heart.

The World's Most Mysterious Places
PBS Documentary; No further information available.

Xena, Warrior Princess
Television series episode; No further information available

Ymadawiad Arthur (Arthur's Departure) (1994)
97 minutes; Black and White; Live Action; Copyright 1994, S4C; Cynhyrchiadau'r Bae Ar Gyfer S4C; Welsh with no dubbing or subtitles

CAST: Moriajs Thomas, Gillian Eusa, Toni Carrol, Nia Samuel, Yland Williams, Janet Aethwy, Ioan Evans, Rhian Grundy, Aiun Horan, Dytan Roberts, Phil Reed, Maldwyn John, Llyr Ifans, Morgan Hopkin, Eluned Jones, Wyn Bowen Harries, Tracy Spottiswoode, Jeuan Thomas, Gert Ellyot-Davis, Emyr Evans, Eiur Jones, Dafydd Wyn Roberts, Huw Lloyd Morris, Aled Samuel, Tony Jones, Gareth Potter, Mark Lugg, Jenny Ogwen, Brinley Jenkins

CREDITS: Sgript — Marc Evans, Aled Samuel; Cynhyrchydd — Geraint Jones; Cyfarwyddwr — Marc Evans; Jonathan Cecil, Joanne Phillips, Zoe Moore, Joe Price, Chris Keny, Alan Henry, Mark Turner, Tony Mabey, John Munro, Vicki Page, Dic Roberts, Michael Snell, Gavin Walter, Dai Hopkins, Conor Connolly, Mike Turner, John Downer, Derek Lloyd, Michas Koc, Tony Llewelyn, Simon Morris, Betty Chivers, Dan Beak, Dave Feeney, Keith Maxwell, Linda Morgan, Alan Taylor, Charlotte's Kitchen, Chris Redman, Susan Jeffries, Lee Williams, Paul Daley, Mike Davey, Jamie Bat, Jon Everett, Sarah Morton, Tim Ricketts, Edwina Williams-Jones, Richard Meyrikk; BBC Enterprises, British Pathe News, British Movietone News, Hughe Green, Archbuld Ltd., Michael Samuelson Goleuadan Cymru, Rank Film Laboratories; Cyfansoddwy — John Hardy; Cynllunwyr — Eryl Ellis, Phil Rawsthorne; Galygydd Ffilm — Trevor Keates; Ffotograffioeth — Nina Kellgren

SYNOPSIS: *Ymadawiad Arthur* or *Arthur's Departure* is entirely in Welsh, with no subtitles. As I was unable to acquire a translation, it was all but impossible to determine the storyline of the film. What little can be garnered from a cursory viewing, however, is as follows.

The film opens with a scene of what looks like King Arthur sleeping atop a stone tomb. A narrator, speaking in Welsh, gives an introduction.

Moving on to the action, the Cardiff,

Wales, rugby team is playing a championship game against a British team. The star player of the team is a young fellow named David Arthur. Because of his prowess on the field, the fans have dubbed him "King Arthur."

As preliminary events go on at the stadium, his family, wanting to watch the broadcast of the game, struggles with the reception on a seemingly defective television. They get the picture cleared up in time to see the queen meet the team members and then the opening kickoff.

The game proceeds and the scene switches to what looks like the laboratory of a group of aliens. Their devices seem to be the cause of the television interference and power surges in the area. They place one of their number in what may be a transporter device. He disappears. Just as David Arthur makes a scoring dive in the rugby game, the picture disappears from his family's TV. His dive is completed onto a table in the aliens' lab.

The complications and activities that follow are impossible to follow without being able to understand the conversation.

A brief description of the film by Tristan Williams of S4C calls *Ymadawiad Arthur* "a dark, satirical and surreal fantasy." The movie won the Spirit of the Festival Award at the Celtic Film Festival in 1995. It also won several BAFTA awards, including Best Single Drama.

Yogi Bear: "Merlin's Lost Book of Magic" (1985)

Copyright 1985, Hanna-Barbera; No further information available.

A Young Connecticut Yankee in King Arthur's Court (1996)

95 minutes; Color; Live Action; Copyright 1996, Cabin Fever Entertainment, Inc.; Timeless Adventures; Filmline International; Images Television International; Screen Partners; Item #CF153

CAST: Michael York (Merlin); Theresa Russell (Morgan Le Fay); Nick Mancuso (King Arthur); Philippe Ross (Hank); Polly Shannon (Alisande/Alexandra); Jack Langedijk (Ulrich); Paul Hopkins (Sir Galahad); Ian Falconer (Sir Lancelot); David Schaeffer (Clarence); Michael Nelson (Herman); Romualdo Weber (Sir Charles); Robert Russell (Farmer); Lisa Flores (Guinevere); Chase Stewart (Herald); Christopher Clarke (Jimmy); Jiri Patocka (Flute Maker); Jeremy Willis (Guard Captain); Anne Taber (Linnet's Mother); Katherine Lindsey (Linnet); Olivia Millard (Sara); Petr Du Bois (Scribe); Janet Lazare (Teacher); Richard Toth (Gaoler); Gavin Stewart (Guard #1); Damon McGee (Guard #2); Eouin Dubsky (Squire);

CREDITS: Director of Photography—John Berrie; Production Designer—Ronald Fauteux; Art Director—Jiri Matolin; Casting—Elite Productions; Costume Designer—Jan Ruzicka; Edited by—Yves Langlois; Music Composed by—Alan Reeves; Line Producer—Vivienne Leebosh; Co-Producers—Simone H. Hsarrari, Kent Walwin; Screenplay by—Frank Encarnacao, R. L. Thomas; Produced by—Nicolas Clermont; Directed by—R. L. Thomas; Production Supervisor—Rolande Zuratas; First Assistant Directors—Michael Williams, Miroslav Lux; Production Manager—Vaclav Eisenhauer; Production Controller—Christian Fluet; Producer's Assistant—Renee Hebert; Unit Manager—Zoenek Flidr; Production Coordinator—Dominique Miller; Location Manager—Martin Kuk; Production Accountant—Aranka Valova; Production Cashier—Ivanka Fialova; Assistant Location Manager—Lada Viesnerova; Production Secretary—Pavlina Prikavlova; Production Translator—Vera Frantikova; Set Translator—Katarina Slampova; Second Assistant Directors—Barbora Bucharova, Martin Rus, Jan Zeman; Art Department Coordinator—Magda Fournier; Camera Operator—Jiri Maxa; First Assistant Camera—Ivan Jiranek; Loader—Jindrich Cipera; Steadicam Operator—Jiri Pechar; Still Photographer—Jaroslav Trousil; Wardrobe Mistress—Hana Kucerova; Wardrobe Assistants—Sarka Zvolenska, Maria Hubackova; Head Makeup Artist—Michele Dion; Makeup Assistants—Eva Malikova, Radek Petr; Hair Stylist—Jiri Farkas; Sound Engineer—Alain Curvelier; Boom Operator—Rene Mikan; Gaffer—Lubos Simecek; Electricians—Jiri Svenha, Jiri Vrana, Petr Sulc, Pavel Stark; Key Grip—Ivan Chalupa; Best Boy Grip—Jaroslav Ungr; Grip—Bedrich Hermanek; Property Master—Bohumil Kadlec; Assistant Property Master—Rudolf Kinsky; Assistant Props—Milan Sebo, Martin Oberlender, Petr Kazoa, Stanislav Luksan; Casting: Czech Republic—Petr Brodsky; Stunt Coordinators—Ladislav Lahoda, Petr Drozda; Wrangler—Pasvel Holik; Sword Master—Vaclav Luks; Stuntmen — Leos Stransky, Martin Hub, Rudolf Bok, Jaroslav Sanda, Dusan Hyska, Jaroslav Peterks, Jaroslav Psenicka, Zdenek Dvoracek, Jiri Kraus, Jaroslav Bezdek, Vaclav Pacal, Miroslav Hulhavy, Filip Kadlec, Victor Cerrenka, Frantisek Stupka, Karel Vavrovec, Martin Navratil, Pavel Kratky, Dimo Lipitkovsky, Jindrich Klaus, Petr Sekanina, Zdenek Krumpl, Jsan Holicek; Riders — Pavel Holik, Pavel Vokoun, Vaclav Svitil, Petr Brousek; Catering — Beni Trans; Drivers — Tomas Modry, Libor Spachman, Miloslav Svestka, Jiri Marek, Frantisek Volf, Bretislav Vinkler, Stanislav Huser, Jan Lojda, Vaclav Kochman, Tomas Sterba, Richard Vondruska, Lasdislav Koutek, Jiri Ubl; Mazda Camera — Zoenek Mrkvicka; Ford Lights — Petr Kurtz; Avia Lights — Peter Juran; Avia Grip — Milan Dvornik; Avia Prop — Jan Sykora; Avia Tent — Mojmir Vaclavek, Roman Proschek; Makeup Bus — Vilem Malik; Wardrobe Bus — Milan Novak; Motor Homes — Viteslav Lucky, Jan Janega, Jiri Kavorik, Tomas Rod; Generators — Anton Kollar, Vaclav Hola; Post Production Supervisor — Georges Jardon; Assistant Editor — Isabelle Levesque; Sound Supervisor — Michel B. Bordeleau; Sound Editors — Natalie Fleurant, Isabelle Massicotte; Assistant Sound Editors — Mireille Morin, Natacha Dufaux, Sylvain Richard; ADR Supervisor — Jacques Plant; ADR Editor — Diane Boucher; ADR Recording Engineers — Gavin Fernandes, Andre Turcot; Foley Artist — Syd Lieberman; Assistant Foley Artist — Amy Buddin; Foley Recording Engineers — Gavin Fernandes, Andre Turcot; Re-recording Engineers — Michel Descombes, Luc Bondrias; Visual Effects Supervisor — Francois Aubry; Assistant Supervisor — Ed Ackerman; Animator — Bertrand Langlois; Optical Camera — Ian Elliott; Layout — Gunther Bush; Titles — Francois Aubry; Sound Studio Coordinators — Paul Gagnon, Monique Brodeur; Laboratory Coordinator — Serge Nadeau; Timing — Michel Proulx; Negative Cutting — Negbec; Lenses and Panaflex Camera by — Panavision; Filmstock by — Eastman Kodak; Laboratory — Astraltech; Re-recording Studio — Sonolab; Optical Effects — Images Infinies, Film Opticals of Canada; Edited on — Lightworks Editing System; Music Administration — S.M.C.L. Productions, Inc.; Newton is a registered trademark of Apple Computer, Inc., used with permission.; Filmed on location in the Czech Republic in cooperation with Balzar International Films, Ltd., Prague.; A Filmline International, Images Television International, Screen Partners, Official Canada/France/U.K. Co-Production.; With the participation of ASTRAL Programming Enterprises, Inc., a division of ASTRAL Communications, Inc.; In association with World International Network (WIN) and Weintraub/Kuhn Productions.

SYNOPSIS: This version of Mark Twain's novel has by far the most regal — and medieval — look of all of them. The costuming and armor are extensive, the European castle is huge. For a change King Arthur is not as moronic as he is often portrayed in these *Connecticut Yankee* films.

The twist given to the story this time is that Hank Morgan is sent off to dream of Camelot by a jolt of current from an electric guitar amplifier. Like a recent Disney version, *A Kid in King Arthur's Court,* the Hank Morgan of *A Young Connecticut Yankee in King Arthur's Court* is a teenager.

Hank is 17 and the keyboardist of a high school rock-and-roll band. During a practice session in the school gym, the lead guitar player dons a suit of armor which he found in a wardrobe room. As he attempts to play his guitar with the armor on, the metal causes a short and the guitar is damaged.

Hank is something of a computer whiz and all-around electrical engineer type. He looks the part with an old-fashioned haircut and glasses. A new girl in school catches his eye, but he's too shy to approach her.

Hank takes the guitar home to fix and it's in his garage that the accident occurs, knocking him to the floor, unconscious. He "wakes up" near a real-looking medieval village, amplifier and tool box in hand.

From here the film follows the usual essentials of the story, with minor changes thrown in for our modern times. The armored person who takes Hank to Camelot turns out to be the beautiful Alisande (who looks just like that new girl in school). We learn later that Alisande wants to be a knight. At court Merlin, Morgan Le Fay and the obnoxious Ulrich make much of the strangeness of the boy in spite of Alisande's defense of him.

Among myriad things in Hank's toolbox there happens to be an instant camera. Hank's doom is sealed when he takes a photo of Ulrich which Merlin interprets as having captured Ulrich's soul on parchment. Arthur has Hank thrown in the dungeon, then decides to burn him at the stake at noon the next day.

To try to help, Alisande recovers Hank's notepad computer and gets it to him. It is from that little gadget that Hank learns of the total eclipse that will take place at the same time as his burning and of course he plays that for all it's worth.

At the stake Hank calls upon the Gods of Rock and mostly on the king of them all, Elvis, to grant him the power to darken the sky. It seems to work and Merlin is particularly enthralled by this Elvis whom he has never heard of. In fact, he goes off for a time in search of Elvis.

As payment for allowing the sun to shine again, Hank gets a workshop and helpers and is made a knight. King Arthur actually uses Excalibur to dub Hank "Sir Dude."

Hank's plan is to build a generator so that he can power the amplifier to duplicate the accident that sent him traveling through time. Hank and Alisande fall in love but she is betrothed against her will to Galahad. In the meantime, Morgan and Ulrich are plotting to turn the people of the kingdom against Arthur and then kill Lancelot, clearing the way for Ulrich to take the throne.

To further her scheming Morgan shows Galahad that the youngsters are in love despite his claim on Alisande. Galahad challenges Hank to a joust. Lancelot tries to train the boy but it's hopeless. Even the generator experiment fails. Hank builds a big capacitor which he hides in an umbrella and zaps Galahad with

the discharge from it. Galahad is so terrified of Hank's powers that he decides to go in search of the Holy Grail, which may, it is said, take a couple of years.

Hank resigns himself to staying at Camelot and tells Arthur about Ulrich's extra taxation on the people. Arthur can't believe it so he, Hank and Clarence go off disguised as peasants to see how things are in the kingdom. Morgan and Ulrich get wind of the jaunt from their spy and they have the three captured.

Merlin returns from his search for Elvis knowing that the king is in trouble. Lancelot, Alisande and some men rescue the king and Hank while Merlin takes care of Morgan once and for all.

Just as things are looking like they'll settle down happily, Hank is returned to his own time. He's been unconscious on the garage floor for three minutes. Deciding he won't hesitate about things any more, he rushes back to school and finds the new girl rehearsing for a play. Presenting himself boldly, he meets Alexandra, who is not from Camelot but Kansas.

As with all film versions of Twain's *A Connecticut Yankee in King Arthur's Court*, this one cuts large sections out of the story and mixes up many details. The habit of drastically simplifying the tale is continued by *A Young Connecticut Yankee in King Arthur's Court*. The many fights, the major battles and the extent of Hank's influence on Camelot and all of Britain are either greatly diminished or completely ignored. Twain's diatribes and social commentaries are nonexistent in this film, just as in the others based on the book.

APPENDIX I:
CHRONOLOGICAL
LISTING OF FILMS AND
TELEVISION PROGRAMS

1904	Parsifal
1907	Lohengrin
1909	Lancelot and Elaine
	Tristan et Yseult
1910	Il Re Artu e i Cavalieri della Tavola Rotunda
1911	Tristan et Yseult
1912	Parsifal
	Raggio di Sole
1917	Knights of the Square Table
1919	The Adventures of Sir Galahad
1920	Tristan et Yseut
1921	A Connecticut Yankee in King Arthur's Court (Fox)
1922	The Light of Faith
1931	A Connecticut Yankee (Rogers)
1933	Don Quixote
1936	Lohengrin
1942	King Arthur Was a Gentleman
	Tortilla Flat
1943	The Eternal Return
1944	Knights of the Round Table
1947	Lohengrin
1948	A Connecticut Yankee in King Arthur's Court (Crosby)
1949	The Adventures of Sir Galahad
	Knights Must Fall
1950	Bugs Bunny's Easter Funnies: "Knighty Knight Bugs"
	Lauritz Melchior in Opera and Song
1951	The Adventures of Sir Lancelot
	Parsifal
1952	A Connecticut Yankee in King Arthur's Court (Karloff)
1953	Knights of the Round Table
	Parsifal

1954	The Black Knight
	A Connecticut Yankee (Bergen)
	Prince Valiant
1955	Bugs Bunny's Hare Raising Tales: "Knight Mare Hare"
	A Connecticut Yankee (Albert, Karloff)
1956	King Arthur and the Magic Sword
1958	Square Heads of the Round Table
1959	Santa Claus
	Treasure Island, Kids Klassics: "Sir Lancelot"
1960	Leonard Bernstein's Young People's Concerts: "What Is a Melody?"
	Tennessee Ernie Ford Meets King Arthur
1961	Alakazam the Great
	Fractured Fairy Tales
	Peabody's Improbable History: "King Arthur"
1962	Jack the Giant Killer
1963	La Espada en la Piedra
	I Was a Teenage Thumb
	7 Faces of Dr. Lao
	Siege of the Saxons
	The Sword in the Stone
	The Sword of Lancelot
	To Parsifal
	Tom Thumb in King Arthur's Court
1964	All These Women
	Mr. Magoo's Literary Classics: "King Arthur"
1965	Willy McBean and His Magic Machine
1966	Gumby: The Movie
1967	Camelot (Musical)
	Good King Arthur
	Lost in Space: "The Questing Beast"

The Time Tunnel: "Merlin the Magician"
Gumby's Supporting Cast
Tristan und Isolde (Osaka)
1968   Little Norse Prince Valiant
1969   A Connecticut Yankee in King Arthur's
        Court
        The Passing of King Arthur
1970   A Connecticut Yankee in King Arthur's
        Court (cartoon)
        Lancelot and Elaine
        Tristana
1971   King Arthur and William Tell
        King Arthur: From Romance to
        Archaeology
1972   Bugs Bunny in King Arthur's Court
        These Halls of Camelot
        Tristan et Iseult
1973   The Ballad of King Arthur
        The Coming of Arthur
        Gawain and the Green Knight
        The Sword in the Stone
1974   Lancelot du Lac
        Lancelot of the Lake
        Monty Python and the Holy Grail
        The Passing of Arthur
1975   The Changes
        A Choice of Weapons
        Dying
        King Arthur, the Young Warlord
        Tristan und Isolde
1976   Merlin el Encantador
1977   Merlin's Magic Cave
        Star Wars: A New Hope
1978   A Connecticut Yankee in King Arthur's
        Court (Basehart)
        The Moon Stallion
        Perceval le Gallois
1979   Lovespell
        Merlin's Magic of Learning
        Unidentified Flying Oddball
1980   Parzival
        Star Wars: The Empire Strikes Back
1981   Excalibur
        Friz Freleng's Looney Looney Looney Bugs
        Bunny Movie: "Knighty Knight Bugs"
        King Arthur and the Knights of the Round
        Table
        Knightriders
        Mr. Merlin
        The Woman Next Door
1982   Camelot (HBO)
        A Disney Christmas Gift
        Disney's Halloween Treat
        Excalibur: The Raising of the Sword
        Fire and Sword
        Into the Labyrinth: "Excalibur"
        Lohengrin (Bayreuth)
        Parsifal (Syberberg)
        Wagner
        Wagner and Venice

1983   Great Moments in History: "A Visit with
        King Arthur"
        King Arthur
        King Arthur and the Legends of
        Glastonbury
        Merlin and the Sword
        Star Wars: The Return of the Jedi
        Sword of the Valiant
        Tristan und Isolde (Bayreuth)
        Where Is Parsifal?
1984   Arthur and the Square Knights of the
        Round Table
        Beowulf and the Old English Tradition
        Hanya, Portrait of a Pioneer
        Highway to Heaven: "A Divine Madness"
        King Arthur and His Country
        The Natural
        Parsifal (Bayreuth)
        Placido
        Scouts!
        Stonehenge
        Stuck on You
1985   Geoffrey Chaucer and Middle English
        Literature
        The Legend of Arthur
        Starchaser: The Legend of Orin
1986   Best of the Fests, 1988: "Cerridwen's Gift"
        Fables and Legends: English Folk Heroes
        The Lady of the Lake
        Lohengrin (The Met)
        The New Twilight Zone: "The Last
        Defender of Camelot"
1987   Duck to the Future: "Sir Gyro Gearloose"
        New Adventures of a Connecticut Yankee in
        King Arthur's Court
        The Video Resume Writer
        Wagner: Tristan und Isolde
        World Famous Fairy Tales: "Swan Knight"
1988   Broadway: A Musical History, Vol. 1
        Broadway: A Musical History, Vol. 4
        In the Shadow of the Raven
        The Live Short Films of Larry Jordan
        Wagner Concert in Leipzig
1989   A Connecticut Yankee in King Arthur's
        Court (Pulliam)
        Connemara
        Doctor Who: "Battlefield"
        Indiana Jones and the Last Crusade
        Isolde
        The Jousters
        Julie Andrews Sings Her Favorite Songs
        MacGyver: "Legend of the Holy Rose"
        Sarkany Es Papucs
        The World of Joseph Campbell
1990   Chevalier de la Table Ronde
        Lohengrin (Bayreuth)
        Lohengrin (Vienna State Opera)
        Merlin and the Dragons
        The Quest for Olwen
1991   Exploring the Celtic Lands

The Fisher King
Gawain and the Green Knight
King Arthur: The Legend and the Land
Land of the Lost: "Day for Knight"
The Legend of Prince Valiant
MacGyver: "Good Knight MacGyver"
Merlin of the Crystal Cave
Pendragon
Tom Thumb
Waxwork II: Lost in Time

1992 All the Great Operas in 10 Minutes
Army of Darkness
Ginevra
Great Castles of Europe: "The British Isles"
King Arthur and the Knights of Justice
Merlin
Northern Exposure: "Wake Up Call"
The Very Best of the Ed Sullivan Show
Wagner in Bayreuth

1993 Babylon 5: "Grail"
The Best of Broadway Musicals
The Legend of Percival
Le Morte D'Arthur
Parsifal (Berlin)
Parsifal (The Met)
Poppa Beaver's Story Time

1994 The Adventures of Timmy the Tooth
Animaniacs Stew
Gargoyles
Goodknights
Guinevere
Knights and Armor
Read on, Cover to Cover: "The Knights of the Kitchen Table"
Seaview Knights
Tekwar: Teklab
Ymadawiad Arthur

1995 Artus, Merlin a Prchlici
Babylon 5: "A Late Delivery from Avalon"
Camelot (Documentary)
Camelot (Musical, 30th Anniversary Edition)
Deepak Chopra: "The Way of the Wizard"
Dragonheart
First Knight
Four Diamonds
Frank and Ollie
John Steinbeck
A Kid in King Arthur's Court
Kids of the Round Table

King Arthur: His Life and Legends
The Last Enchantment
Merlin's Shop of Mystical Wonders
Mysterious Places of England
Placido Domingo
Princess Gwenevere and the Jewel Riders
Storybook
Tristan und Isolde

1996 Deepak Chopra: The Art of Spiritual Transformation
The Holy Quest
Johnny Mysto, Boy Wizard
Lerner and Loewe Special
Sabrina the Teenage Witch: "Oh What a Tangled Spell"
A Young Connecticut Yankee in King Arthur's Cour

1997 Camelot (Enchanted Tales)
Camelot (Fairy Tale Classics)
In Search of History: "The Holy Lance"
In Search of History: "The Knights of Camelot"
King Arthur's Camelot
Lancelot: Guardian of Time
Legends of the Isles: "King Arthur"
Legends of the Isles: "Merlin the Wizard"
Legends of the Isles: "Stonehenge"
Legends of the Isles: "The Holy Grail"
Merlin: The Magic Begins
The Mighty
Prince Valiant
Return to Camelot
Richard Wagner

1998 The Angry Beavers: "Alley Oops"
Arthur's Quest
Babylon 5: "A Call to Arms"
Camelot: The Legend
The Excalibur Kid
Field Trip: "Sticks in Stones"
A Knight in Camelot
Merlin
Merlin, Arthur and the Holy Grail
Parsifal
Parsifal: The Search for the Grail
The Quest for Camelot
Sing Along Quest for Camelot
Teen Knight

1999 Crusade
Hercules: The Legendary Journeys: "Once Upon a Future King"

APPENDIX II:
FILMS AND TELEVISION PROGRAMS WITH POSSIBLE ARTHURIAN CONTENT

The Affairs of Martha (aka *Once Upon a Thursday*), 1942, MGM, comedy, B&W, a character named Guinevere in cast.

An Ambition Reduced to Ashes, 1995, Cambodia.

The Armorer, filmstrip, 40 frames, 35mm, by John Gregory, from the series The Appreciation of Metalwork, no. 6, on the development of weapons and armor.

Arthur Takes Over, 1948, 20th Century–Fox.

Arthur's Deep Resolve, 1916, Universal Pictures/Victor, B&W, silent.

The Birth of Europe (A.D. 410–1084), 1978, 16mm, CRM Films.

The Black Knight, 1977, U.K., television, color.

Blake's 7: "Project Avalon" (season 1, episode 9), 1977, BBC, female character named Avalon starts cells of resistance to the evil Federation.

Bosko's Knight-mare, 1933, cartoon Looney Tunes, Warner Bros. #3316.

Chaos Queen, Die, 1997, Germany, television, color, characters named Arthur and Ortud in cast.

The Connecticut Yankee, 1910, B&W, silent, starring William V. Mong.

Crazy Knights, 1944, Monogram Pictures, Three Stooges.

Crusader Rabbit, 1949, cartoon, Jerry Fairbanks/Creston Studios, early TV series.

The Dark Ages and After, 1977, filmstrip, 35mm, Visual Publication, NY, color.

Dragonhunt, 1987, Canada.

Earliest Times to 1066, 1954, Coronet/MTI Film and Video, from English History series.

Entre Ces Mains-Là, 1995, television, character named Perceval.

The Flying Dragon, 1978, Sweden.

Ginevra Degli Almieri, 1936, Italy, B&W.

The Grail, 1923, B&W, silent.

The Great Age of Chivalry, filmstrip, 35mm, color.

The Great Merlini.

Gumby: "The Black Knight," 1966, 16mm, color.

The Huckleberry Hound Show: "Huck's Hound Table," 1958–1961, cartoon, Hanna-Barbera.

In the Days of Chivalry, 1911, Edison Co., B&W, silent.

King Leonardo and His Short Subjects: "Knight of the Square Table," 1960–1963, cartoon, Total Television.

Kings and Queens of England: The Anglo Saxons to Elizabeth I, Films for the Humanities and Sciences, color.

Knights and Ladies, 1913, B&W, silent.

Knights Before Christmas, 1930, Standard Cinema Corp., comedy, B&W.

Knights for a Day, 1936.

Knights of the Earth, 1944, Castle Films, Abbott and Costello.

Knights Out, 1929.

Knutzy Knights, 1954, Three Stooges.

Lady of Shalott, 1915, Vitagraph, comedy, B&W, silent.

Legend of a Girl, Chivalry, 1986, IAVC, Inc.

Like Knights of Old, 1912, B&W, silent.

Magic, 1978, 20th Century–Fox, color, character named Merlin.

Medieval Knights, 1974, filmstrip, 35mm, Stockmyer Educational Materials, color.

Merlin, 1976.

Merlin, 1991, Spain.

Merlin and Myself, The Big Mouth Bass, 1993, American Television Network.

Merlin the Magician, Jr., 1970?, Rankin-Bass.

The Mothers-in-Law: "On Again, Off Again, Lohengrin," 1967, television series episode.

New Nations Arise: The Dark Ages, 1953, filmstrip, 35mm.

No. 1: Licensed to Love and Kill, 1979, U.K., character named Merlin.

A Pendragon Legenda, 1974, Hungary.

Prince Violent (aka "Prince Varmint"), 1961, cartoon, Warner Bros. #6114, Bugs Bunny and Yosemite Sam.

Puppe, Die, 1919, Germany, B&W, silent, character named Lancelot.

The Quest for the Mighty Sword, 1990, Italy, sacred sword of Graal.

Regine, 1934, Germany, character named Merlin.

The St. Tamany Miracle, 1994, character named Coach Merlin.

Sangraal: La Spada Di Fuoco (Holy Grail: The Sword of Fire), 1982, Italy, Visione Cinematografica, color.

Silent Knight, 1985, 20th Century–Fox.

Son of Dracula, 1974, U.K., Ringo Starr (drummer of the famous British rock-and-roll group the Beatles) plays Merlin.

Space Cases: "The Impossible Dream," 1996, television series episode, questing knight after a monster.

Space Rangers: "Planet Avalon," television series episode.

Spellbinder: Land of the Dragonlord, 1997, Film Australia Southern Star, television series.

The Super Globetrotters vs. Merlo the Magician, 1979, cartoon, Hanna-Barbera.

Super Mario Brothers: "King Mario of Camelot," 1989, cartoon, episode 3, TV?

Towser and the Black Knight, 1982, Journal Films.

2019: Dopo la Caduta di New York, 1983, Italy, character named Parsifal.

When Knights Were Bold, 1908, Biograph, B&W, silent.

When Knights Were Bold, 1916, U.K., B&W, silent.

When Knights Were Bold, 1936, U.K., character named Rowena.

Wizard and the Brigands, 1911, U.K., silent.

Wotta Knight, 1947, cartoon, Paramount/Famous Studios, Popeye.

BIBLIOGRAPHY

Ashe, Geoffrey, editor. *The Quest for Arthur's Britain*. Chicago: Academy Chicago Publishers, 1994.

Bede. *Ecclesiastical History of the English People*. Translated by Leo Sherley-Price, London: Penguin Books, 1990.

Brewer, Dr. Ebenezer Cobham. *Brewer's Dictionary of Phrase and Fable*. Centenary Edition. Revised by Ivor H. Evans, New York: Harper & Row, 1981.

Cahall, Gary, Joseph McLaughlin, and Irv Slifkin, editors. *The Movies Unlimited Video Catalog, 1997*. Movies Unlimited, 3015 Darnell Road, Philadelphia, PA 19154, 1-800-466-8437. movies@moviesunlimited.com.

Coghlan, Ronan. *The Illustrated Encyclopaedia of Arthurian Legends*. New York: Barnes & Noble Books, 1995.

Compact Edition of the Oxford English Dictionary. Glasgow: Oxford University Press, 1971.

Connors, Martin, and James Craddock, editors. *VideoHound's Golden Movie Retriever 1997*. Detriot: Video Ink Press, 1997.

Cross, Milton. *Milton Cross's Complete Stories of the Great Operas*. New York: Doubleday, 1952.

Day, David. *The Search for King Arthur*. De Agostini Editions Ltd., New York: Facts on File, 1995.

Delrio, Martin. *Prince Valiant*. New York: Avon Books, 1998.

Detsicas, Alec. *Peoples of Britain: The Cantiaci*. Gloucester: Alan Sutton Publishing Ltd., 1987.

Eschenbach, Wolfram Von. *Parzival*. Translated by Helen M. Mustard and Charles E. Passage, New York: Vintage Books, 1961.

Foley, Catherine, and Milos Stehlik, editors. *Facets Complete Video Catalog No. 14*. Chicago: Academy Chicago Publishers, 1996. Facets Video, 1517 W. Fullerton Ave., Chicago, IL 60614. 1-800-331-6197, sales@facets.org.

Ford, Boris, editor. *The Cambridge Cultural History of Britain*. Volume 1, Early Britain. Cambridge: Cambridge University Press, 1992.

Gildas. *De Excidio Britannia*. Translated by J. A. Giles. Willets, California: British American Books, 1986.

Godwin, Malcolm. *The Holy Grail: Its Secrets and Meaning Revealed*. New York: Viking Studio Books, 1994.

Halmi, Robert (foreword). *Merlin: The Shooting Script*. New York: Newmarket Press, 1998.

Harty, Kevin J. *Cinema Arthuriana: Essays on Arthurian Film*. New York: Garland Publishing, 1991.

Jacobs, Joseph, editor. *Celtic Fairy Tales*. London: Senate Studio Editions Ltd., 1995.

Jiménez, Ramon L. *Caesar Against the Celts*. New York: Sarpedon, 1996.

Jones, Gwyn, and Thomas Jones, translators. *The Mabinogion*. London and Rutland, Vermont: Everyman Library, 1996.

Jullien, Adolphe. *Richard Wagner: His Life and Works*. Translated by Florence Percival Hall, Neptune, N.J.: Paganiniana Publications, 1981.

Lacy, Norris J., and Geoffrey Ashe, with Debra N. Mancoff. *The Arthurian Handbook*, Second Edition. New York and London: Garland Publishing, 1997.

Lacy, Norris J., editor. *The New Arthurian Encyclopedia*. Garland Reference Library of the Humanities, New York and London: Garland Publishing, 1996.

LaGravanese, Richard. *The Fisher King: The Book of the Film*. New York: Applause Theatre Book Publishers, 1991.

Malory, Sir Thomas. *Le Morte D'Arthur*. Volumes 1 and 2, Edited by Janet Cowen. New York: Penguin Books, 1969.

Malory, Sir Thomas. *Works*. Second Edition, Edited by Eugène Vinaver. Oxford: Oxford University Press, 1971.

Maltin, Leonard, editor. *Leonard Maltin's Movie and Video Guide, 1996 Edition.* New York: Signet, 1996.

Mancoff, Debra N. *The Return of King Arthur: The Legend through Victorian Eyes.* New York: Harry N. Abrams, 1995.

Matthews, John. *King Arthur and the Grail Quest.* London: Blandford, 1994.

Monmouth, Geoffrey of. *The History of the Kings of Britain.* Translated by Lewis Thorpe. London: Penguin Books, 1996.

Nennius. *Historia Brittonum.* Translated by J. A. Giles. Willets, California: British American Books, 1986.

Rolleston, T. W. *Celtic Myths and Legends.* London: Senate Studio Editions Ltd., 1994.

Salway, Peter. *The Oxford Illustrated History of Roman Britain.* New York: Oxford University Press, 1993.

Savage, Anne, translator and collator. *The Anglo-Saxon Chronicles.* New York: Crescent Books, 1995.

Steinbeck, John. *The Acts of King Arthur and His Noble Knights.* Edited by Chase Horton. New York: Del Rey/Ballantine Books, 1976.

Steinbeck, John. *The Short Novels of John Steinbeck: Tortilla Flat.* New York: Viking Press, 1953.

Stone, Brian, translator. *King Arthur's Death, Morte Arthure, Le Morte Arthur.* London: Penguin Books, 1988.

Tennyson, Alfred Lord. *Idylls of the King.* New York: Bantam Pathfinder, 1965.

Tolkien, J. R. R., translator. *Sir Gawain and the Green Knight, Pearl, Sir Orfeo.* London: George Allen & Unwin Ltd., 1975; New York: Ballantine Books, 1992.

Troyes, Chrétien de. *The Complete Romances of Chrétien de Troyes.* Translated by David Staines. Bloomington & Indianapolis: Indiana University Press, 1990; First Midland Book Edition, 1993.

Twain, Mark. *A Connecticut Yankee in King Arthur's Court.* New York: Tor, 1991.

Umland, Rebecca A., and Samuel J. Umland. *The Use of Arthurian Legend in Hollywood Film.* Westport, Connecticut: Greenwood Press, 1996.

Video Yesteryear Video Cassette Catalogue #15, Box C, Sandy Hook, CT 06482. 1-800-243-0987, video@yesteryear.com.

White, T. H., *The Once and Future King,* New York: Berkeley Books, 1982.

Websites

Below are listed the websites I found most useful for the listings in this book. In all cases the site's home page is specified.

Commerical Sites

These provide better-than-average inventories of films and carry a larger-than-average number of Arthurian films. There are hundreds of good online video stores and I make no claim to having visited anything but a small percentage of them. For those unfamiliar with online ordering, "secure" ordering means that data is encrypted before being transmitted to or from the site. The claim is that encrypted online ordering is safer than handing your credit card to a stranger behind a store counter.

Big Star
http://www1.bigstar.com/index.ff
Based in Texas, excellent service, good selection, online secure purchasing.

Facets Multimedia
http://www.facets.org/catalog/secure_main.html
Security for entire site rather than just ordering, excellent inventory and very strong in lesser known and art films.

Movies2Go
http://movies2go.com/
Somewhat awkward search and ordering system, but online ordering is secure and any minor inconvenience is more than offset by an outstanding inventory.

Reel.com
>   http://www.reel.com/cgi-bin/nph-reel.exe?OBJECT=welcome.html
>
>> Huge inventory, excellent features and service, secure ordering. Probably the most heavily advertised movie site on the web.

Video Online Express
>   http://www.videoexpress.com/bin/nph-main/Td4flR5CumhO.b
>
>> Plenty of selection, secure ordering, excellent service.

Videoflicks.com
>   http://www.videoflicks.com/index.htm
>
>> Toronto based, excellent inventory and service, secure ordering.

VideoServe.com
>   http://speedserve.com/videoserve/videoserve.html
>
>> Excellent inventory and service, secure ordering.

Noncommercial Sites

These are resources for information on Arthurian films and/or the history or legends of King Arthur. There are literally hundreds more websites devoted to the subject and this short list by no means implies that any of those not mentioned are less worthy.

ARGE: Archaeological Resource Guide for Europe: United Kingdom
>   http://odur.let.rug.nl/~arge/Countries/uk.html

Arthuriana
>   http://dc.smu.edu/arthuriana/
>
>> This is the website of *Arthuriana,* the scholarly journal devoted to the study of King Arthur.

Camelot Project at the University of Rochester
>   http://www.ub.rug.nl/camelot/
>
>> "Arthurian texts, images, bibliographies and basic information." This outstanding site was designed by Alan Lupack, curator of the Robbins Library of the Rush Rhees Library at the University of Rochester, and Barbara Tepa Lupack.

CBA: Council for British Archaeology
>   http://www.britarch.ac.uk/

Early British Kingdoms
>   http://freespace.virgin.net/david.ford2/Early%20 British%Kingdoms.html

Internet Medieval Source Book
>   http://www.fordham.edu/halsall/sbook.html
>
>> An awe-inspiring reference site providing links to original texts, manuscripts, historical materials, course curricula, etc.

Internet Movie Database
>   http://www.imdb.com
>
>> Though technically a commercial site, the only way to purchase films here is through the site's links to Reel.com (see above). The real goal of the Internet Movie Database is to provide information on films from around the world. With dozens of search possibilities (by title, cast or crew name, crew function, etc.), plot summaries, reviews, lists and many other features, the IMDB is a massive and very useful repository of movie information.

Library of Congress Catalogues
>   http://lcweb.loc.gov/catalog/online.html#ess

Mystical World Wide Web
>   http://www.mystical-www.co.uk/arthuriana2z/index.htm
>
>> A database of thumbnail sketches of names, terms and places from Arthurian legend.

Odin's Castle of Dreams and Legends
>   http://www.odinscastle.org/index.html
>
>> This magnificently organized and enormous collection of links to sites on world history includes a special section of Arthurian links.

Saxon Shore
http://www.geocities.com/~gkingdom/saxonshore/dubris.html

An outstandingly researched site specializing in the historicity of King Arthur. Includes full texts and excerpts from a number of the earliest Arthurian writings, maps and much more.

UCLA Film and Television Archive
http://www.cinema.ucla.edu:80/

University of Missouri Academic Support Center
http://med.asc.missouri.edu/htbin/wwform/145/wwk770

Special thanks to these folks for allowing this unaffiliated individual to rent a number of their films which I was unable to find elsewhere.

INDEX

Boldface numbers indicate photographs.